The Lie That Sounded Nice:

How I Learned the Difference Between Truth and Control

Garrick David Pattenden

To: _____

Best Wishes,

Garrick David Pattenden

Copyright © 2025 Garrick David Pattenden

All rights reserved.

ISBN: 978-1-83417-010-7

DEDICATION

For the ones still finding their voice.

This book is for the children who sit quietly in crowded classrooms and wonder why their truth doesn't sound loud enough to be believed. It's for the ones who shrink in hallways not because they're weak, but because no one ever told them they were allowed to take up space. You are not invisible. Your story counts, even when no one claps for it. This book is for the ones who learned to smile on command. Who've been told to "get over it," "calm down," "stop overreacting," or "toughen up." For the ones who were blamed for things that never made sense, punished for speaking honestly, or ignored when they spoke at all. This is for you. You are not too sensitive. You are paying attention.

This book is for the kids who got called names behind the teacher's back. The ones who got excluded by the cool crowd and then blamed for standing alone. The ones who eat lunch at the edge of the schoolyard because being alone feels safer than guessing wrong again. You are not the problem. You are learning to protect yourself. This book is for the ones who tried to explain, only to be told they misunderstood. Who questioned themselves so many times they started to believe the lie. For the ones who whispered, "Maybe I'm just being dramatic," even though their gut told them something wasn't right. You were right to wonder. You were right to doubt the doubt.

This book is for the child who was told that "sticks and stones" hurt worse than words. That "it's just teasing" or "they're only joking." It's for the one who still hears those "jokes" at night and wonders why they still sting. Words can wound deeper than bruises. And silence can scar. This book is your proof that feelings are real—even if no one else sees them. This book is for every child who apologized too many times for things they didn't do. Who said sorry just to make it stop. Who learned to keep peace by disappearing. Who stopped raising their hand, stopped speaking their mind, stopped trusting their own thoughts. You were never supposed to disappear. You were meant to be seen.

This book is for the children who had to grow up too fast. The ones who translated moods before they understood words. Who read faces like weather maps and learned to tiptoe around the storms. You were not born to be a mirror for someone else's pain. You deserve to be known for who you are—not who they made you pretend to be. This book is for the ones who carry their homes like questions. Who wonder what's waiting for them after the bell rings. Who wish someone would ask where they go at night or what they eat for dinner. You don't have to answer here. But know this: there are people who will care enough to ask again—and mean it.

This book is for the children who saw through the smiles. Who knew that kindness can be a weapon. That compliments sometimes come with strings. That praise can feel like pressure. If you've ever felt loved and controlled at the same time, if you've ever flinched from a soft voice or doubted a gentle hand, you're not crazy. You've just been trained too well. And now, you're unlearning. This book is for the ones who fought back by being kind. Who held the door open even when it was never held for them. Who sat beside the lonely kid, stood up for the one no one liked, or gave a smile to someone too tired to return it. You're not naive. You're brave. Kindness isn't weakness. It's rebellion in a world that tries to train it out of us.

This book is for the children who know what it's like to lose a friend to someone meaner, louder, or more charming. Who watch from the edges while the manipulator gets applause. Who know the pattern too well: the charm, the lie, the cruelty, the cover-up. You are not alone in seeing it. You are not wrong to walk away. This book is for the children who've heard "You're just jealous" or "You're being dramatic" one too many times. For the ones who cried behind their bedroom doors, afraid to be too much, or not enough. For the ones who got labelled "trouble" just for telling the truth. Your truth matters, even when it isn't convenient.

This book is for the kids who want to ask, "Is this normal?" but never do. For the ones who stare at the ceiling at night, replaying everything, trying to figure out if they're the broken one. You're not. The brokenness is in the way you've been treated, not in who you are. And asking questions is how truth begins. This book is for the child who needed this book five years ago—and for the child who won't need it for five more. For the ones in Grade 3 or Grade 9, still figuring out how the world works and how to stay soft without being fooled. You will get there. You already are.

This book is for the quiet ones. The loud ones. The ones who haven't spoken yet. It's for the one reading this while hugging their knees or sitting on the bus, pretending to be fine. It's for the brave and the scared and the not-sure-which-they-are. All of you belong here. All of you deserve to be heard. This book is for you. Whoever you are. Wherever you are. You are not alone anymore.

FOREWARD

There are books that whisper comfort. Others that shout answers. And then there are books like this—ones that hold up a mirror not just to a child's face, but to the bruises no one sees. The Lie That Sounded Nice is not a fantasy, nor a fable, nor a tale meant to tuck a child in at night. It is something deeper. This is a guide for children living in the fog of confusion, for those trying to make sense of manipulation disguised as love, and for those brave enough to wonder, "Is it me… or is something wrong here?"

We often teach children to be kind, but rarely do we teach them how to recognize kindness that comes with a leash. We tell them to trust adults, but we do not always tell them what to do when those adults twist the truth. We celebrate obedience, but seldom do we praise the child who says, "This doesn't feel right." This book changes that. It gives permission to question. To pause. To breathe before apologizing. And to recognize the quiet power of walking away from someone who needs to control you.

At the heart of this story is a boy who once behaved like the villain, only to learn he was repeating what had been done to him. Around him are friends who don't offer empty forgiveness but instead show him something rarer—redemption through honesty, support through action, and love without performance. There are no saints here, no perfect children or flawless rescues. What you'll find instead is what the real world offers: complexity, mistakes, regret, and the tender art of repair.

You will not find magic in this story. But you will find something stronger: emotional intelligence taught through children's voices. You'll see gaslighting laid bare. Narcissism confronted without fear. You'll witness the difference between true kindness and manipulation, between control and care, between silence and peace. These lessons are tucked within conversations at lockers, glances across classrooms, the soft press of a hand on a shoulder. This is the kind of learning schools rarely teach—but every child needs.

This book was written for the child who's already gone through it, and the child who hasn't—but might. For the one being blamed, and the one doing the blaming. For the teacher who doesn't yet recognize the signs, and the one who does but doesn't know what to do. For the parent searching for words, and the one who refuses to listen. For every adult reading this now: let the children lead. They see more than you think. They always have.

This story was never meant to be a fairy tale. It was meant to be a flashlight. A tool. A shield. A quiet companion that sits on a nightstand and says, "You were right to feel what you felt." Because the most dangerous part of gaslighting is not just the lie—it's the erosion of memory. It's the slow disbelief in one's own perception. This book does what so few are willing to do: it gives that belief back.

It's not easy to speak of narcissism in a language children understand. But this book does just that. It reframes cruelty as fear, domination as insecurity, and shows how power, when used selfishly, always leaves a residue behind. And yet, it never glorifies the bully. Nor does it shame the one who used to be one. Instead, it pulls apart the wiring, piece by piece, and offers something tender in its place: the chance to begin again.

Every chapter is built on something real. There are no caricatures here—only children. With all their mistakes, hesitations, and small triumphs. Children who learn to say no when it matters. Children who hold each other accountable without cruelty. Children who notice when someone is sitting alone at recess. Children who don't need to be perfect to be powerful. That's what makes this book sacred—it respects them.

We live in a world that often punishes sensitivity and rewards performance. A world where telling the truth sometimes costs more than telling a lie. This book doesn't pretend otherwise. It prepares children for the world they're already living in, while giving them tools to thrive within it. It speaks in their language. Not from above, but beside. As a peer. As a protector.

It shows how manipulation hides in compliments. How a joke can be a knife. How being "nice" isn't the same as being safe. And most importantly, it shows how love—real love—doesn't require changing who you are to be worthy of it. Real love doesn't punish honesty. It celebrates it. That is the message behind every page.

To the reader: If you're a child, this book is your permission slip. You're allowed to think. You're allowed to feel. You're allowed to say no. You're allowed to stop playing a game that hurts people. You're allowed to tell someone what's going on—even if it's hard. You are not alone anymore.

To the adult reading alongside them: Let this book teach you. Let it remind you how confusing childhood can be, and how courageous it is just to survive it with your heart intact. Every chapter invites you to see what children feel but cannot always articulate. Listen with your eyes, not just your ears. They've been trying to tell you. This book simply translated it. The words you're about to read are not entertainment. They're education. They are survival. They are hope. And if you let them, they might change the way you speak to a child forever. Because truth doesn't bruise—but lies do. And finally, someone wrote that down.

PREFACE

This book, The Lie That Sounded Nice: How I Learned the Difference Between Truth and Control (Children's Edition), is not just a story—it's a quiet revolution in how we teach children about psychological survival. It doesn't shout. It doesn't preach. It walks beside the reader, hand in hand, showing them how to spot the difference between real love and manipulative control, between truth and tactics, between a friend who sees you and a bully who rewrites your memory to keep power.

At its core, this book is about emotional literacy—specifically how children can learn to protect themselves from narcissistic behaviours and gaslighting, even when the adults around them fail to notice or intervene. It invites readers into the lived experiences of children who learn, through each other, what happens when kindness is used as a weapon, when apologies are counterfeit, and when silence can be strength instead of surrender.

This is a story written by the hands of survivors, held in the voices of children who dare to speak clearly about what happened to them. It tells the truth—fully and without shrinking. For the child who's been confused by compliments that feel like traps. For the one who's been told they were the problem when all they did was ask questions. For the one who is gaslit, day after day, until they no longer trust what they saw, what they heard, or what they remember. This is for you.

You will not find fantasy here. There are no dragons to slay, no wands to lift, no secret portals to other worlds. What you will find is something much harder to face and far more powerful to overcome: psychological manipulation, as it happens in the real world, through the smiles of classmates, the words of friends, the silence of teachers, and sometimes, the cruelty of parents. This book pulls no punches—but it also holds no grudges.

The children in these pages do not always get it right. They do not always speak at the right time, or notice every red flag, or respond with perfect wisdom. They are learning as they go, just as real children do. But they do learn. And in the learning, they uncover tools that most adults never had. They name the behaviours. They see the patterns. They ask the questions adults were too frightened—or too wounded—to face. And they stand beside each other while doing it.

This story centres around Leo, a child once shaped by abuse, gaslighting, and control, who believed for far too long that cruelty was strength. But it also centres the children who did not turn away. Ty, who asks without fear. Jasmin, who listens without apology. Ella, who forgives without forgetting. Jeremy, who hugs without needing a reason. Each child in this story reflects a different part of what it means to heal: through truth, through community, and through choice.

You will also meet Alex. And with him comes a truth few wish to admit: sometimes the bully is hurting most of all. Sometimes the one who lashes out is the one who needs holding. This book never excuses abuse. But it does examine its origin. It opens the door to redemption for those brave enough to walk through it. And for those too scared to walk alone, it offers a hand.

What makes this book different is not that it's written for children. It's that it's written as children. The language, the pacing, the truth—it all flows through the way children speak to one another when no adults are watching. That is the power. That is the point. These aren't lessons handed down from authority. These are lived truths passed between peers. That's how children learn best—when they're heard, not handled.

Every school hallway in this story exists. Every insult was said somewhere. Every apology held in trembling silence has happened. And every act of courage, however small, reflects a real possibility in a child's life. Whether they're eight, eleven, or fourteen, the reader will see themselves in these pages. Not always in the hero. Sometimes in the confused one. Sometimes in the hurting one. And sometimes in the one who stayed silent. All are welcome here.

This book is also a warning. It warns adults not to look away when a child says they feel invisible. It warns teachers not to dismiss the quiet ones. It warns peers not to laugh when someone is called "too sensitive." But more than that, it is an invitation. An invitation to see. To name. To speak. To mend. It calls children into their own strength—not through defiance, but through truth. And that kind of truth is armour no manipulator can break.

It's important to say this plainly: gaslighting is not just a word for adults. Children experience it every day. From home, from school, from peers, from systems. It twists their sense of self and shapes their future unless someone tells them, "You are not wrong. What you felt was real." This book is that someone. To every child who has ever felt they were the problem when they were simply being honest, this book says: You are not the villain. You are not too much. You are not crazy. And you are not alone.

To every adult reading this: Read it again. Then read it out loud. Then ask the child beside you what they think it means. They'll understand more than you expect. They always have. Because somewhere in every classroom, every gymnasium, every lunch table, and every lonely walk home, there is a child who needs this book. Not next year. Not when they're older. Right now. Before the lie sounds nice again. And this time, they'll know the difference.

PROLOGUE – THE LIE THAT SOUNDED NICE

It didn't sound cruel. It didn't shout or threaten. It sounded like kindness. It said, "I'm just trying to help." It said, "You're overreacting." It smiled when it said, "You're too sensitive." The words were gentle. Soft. Careful. Like honey on a spoon. But it didn't feel nice, not inside the body. Not when the heart skipped, or the stomach curled, or the hands clenched beneath the desk. That's the thing about lies—they're not always loud. Some of them are quiet enough to convince you they're true.

At first, it felt like friendship. The jokes didn't seem so bad. The compliments sounded a little strange, but no one else seemed bothered. Everyone laughed, so you did too. Everyone looked away, so you learned to blink at the right time. It was easier to stay quiet. Easier to say, "It's fine." That's how it always starts. Not with a punch. Not with a bruise. But with a sentence that changes shape depending on who's watching.

The lie sounded nice. It promised safety. It offered love, but only if you played along. It smiled in public but whispered in private. And when you tried to speak, it said, "You misunderstood." So you stopped speaking. You stopped asking. You started apologizing for things you didn't do, for feelings you weren't supposed to have, for memories you were told weren't real. That's how it works. That's how it wins.

But even then, somewhere deep, you knew. You knew something wasn't right. You didn't have the words for it yet—manipulation, gaslighting, narcissism. You only had the feeling. The twist in your chest. The heat behind your eyes. The way your voice shrank just to keep the peace. That's where this story begins—not in a classroom, but in that feeling. The one no one else seemed to notice. The one you thought you had to ignore.

This book is for the moment before the truth. The moment before the rescue. The moment a child thinks, Maybe I deserve this. Because that's the most dangerous lie of all. It doesn't come with warning signs. It doesn't wear a villain's face. Sometimes, it walks through the school doors with a grin and a charm that makes teachers proud. Sometimes it's a friend. Sometimes it's a parent. Sometimes it's the voice inside your own head.

Every chapter you are about to read began with a moment like that. A lie that felt like a hug. A rule that kept changing. A compliment that came with claws. The children in this story were not handed the truth. They found it piece by piece, in each other's questions, in each other's pain, in the stillness of a hug that didn't ask anything in return. They were not taught by adults who knew better. They were taught by pain—and by one another.

Some children will read this and feel seen for the first time. Others may not yet know what it means to be controlled with kindness. Some will remember the day someone made them doubt their own eyes, their own words, their own memory. Some will cry. Some will stay quiet. All of that is okay. Because silence is not weakness. Silence, when chosen, is a kind of power. And asking questions is a kind of light.

This book doesn't offer magic spells. It doesn't promise happy endings. It doesn't tell you what to do. It tells you what happened. What happens still. What happens when children are expected to be polite while someone rewrites the truth in front of their face. What happens when no one stops the lie. And what it looks like when someone finally does.

Leo didn't change because he was punished. He changed because someone saw him. Ty didn't speak because he wanted to be a hero. He spoke because the silence was too heavy. Jeremy didn't hug because someone told him to. He hugged because it hurt not to. These are children. Real ones. With real eyes and real questions and real scars that don't show up on the outside. You will know them. Maybe you already do.

Some parts of this book may feel too close. That's not an accident. The pain is real because the truth is real. But so is the healing. So is the laughter. So is the power that comes when one person stops playing the game and says, "No more." This is not a story of victims. This is a story of children who refused to be rewritten. Who stood still long enough to feel the full truth rise inside them—and then shared it.

So if the lie ever sounded nice to you, this story is yours. If you've ever wondered if maybe you imagined it, this story is yours. If you've ever needed someone to hold your truth when no one else would, this story is yours. And if you've never needed it—yet—you now have it, just in case. Because before the truth can set you free, you have to know it was taken from you. And now, page by page, we take it back.

💡 WHAT THE BOOK IS REALLY ABOUT:

1. The Hidden Damage of Gaslighting in Childhood

Children who are gaslit begin to doubt their feelings, their memories, even their right to feel hurt. This book makes gaslighting visible in a way that children can understand. Through Leo's transformation—from manipulator to protector—and through characters like Ty, Ella, Jasmin, and Jeremy, young readers learn to trust their instincts again. They learn that confusion is not proof that they're wrong—it's often a sign that someone is twisting their truth.

2. Narcissistic Behaviour—Learned, Not Born

Rather than painting "bad kids" with a villain's brush, this book shows that narcissistic behaviours often come from places of deep wounding and imitation. Alex's story, especially, proves that children absorb the emotional habits of the adults who raise them. When no one teaches empathy, children learn control. When no one offers real safety, children learn to survive by manipulation. But that story doesn't have to end there.

3. Real Love Doesn't Keep Score

Children learn that true love doesn't trap. It doesn't use guilt, pity, or favours as currency. Through the moments where hugs are offered without request, apologies are written in pen, and rooms fall silent in reverence of truth, young readers discover that real love listens, protects, and lets go of control.

4. The Lie That Sounded Nice

The title itself is genius. Children are often told comforting lies: "He's just teasing you." "You're too sensitive." "You're overreacting." This book challenges those mantras head-on. It teaches children to name the lies that make abuse invisible—and to speak the truth, even when their voice shakes.

5. Emotional Self-Defence Without Turning Cold

Unlike books that teach children to "toughen up" or build walls, this story teaches the Shadow Warrior's Way—a metaphorical lens that honours emotional depth, strategic awareness, and quiet courage. Children learn to walk through schoolyards like protectors, not victims. They learn that gentleness is not weakness, and that being quiet does not mean being blind.

CONTENTS

	Acknowledgments	i
1	Nico's Truth	1
2	The Smile That Wasn't Real	25
3	The Rules Always Change	44
4	How Love Bombs Work	68
5	What a Gaslight Feels Like	92
6	Words Can Hurt	116
7	When No One Else Sees It	142
8	The Shadow Warrior's Way	170
9	The Day I Learned to Say No	198
10	What If They Say It's Your Fault?	225
11	The One Who Always Had to Win	254
12	Summer Time Fun & Lessons	281
13	What Jeremy Learned That Summer	306
14	When Kindness Is a Weapon	333
15	What I Would Tell My Younger Self	361
16	True Happiness Vs. False Happiness	387
17	When the Villain Was Once the Victim	409
18	You're Not Alone Anymore	437

CHAPTER 1: NICO'S TRUTH

It started like a splinter—not pain, exactly, just something that didn't belong. Nico felt it most after the bell rang and the hallway emptied out too fast. There'd be noise and lockers slamming and kids shouting whose turn it was to bring the basketball, but underneath all that was the feeling. It didn't yell or pull. It just sat there. Low in his chest, like someone knocking but never opening the door. He tried to ignore it. Everyone else seemed fine. Everyone else laughed at Leo's jokes. So, Nico smiled, too. That's what you do, right? You smile and pretend nothing weird is happening. But the feeling stayed.

Sometimes it showed up during lunch when Leo would nudge him too hard on the shoulder and say something like, "Don't look so serious, Nico, you're scaring the sandwiches." Everyone laughed, but not because it was funny. They laughed because Leo always expected them to. Then he'd look around like he was checking who passed the test. Nico always laughed a little too late. It never reached his eyes. Jasmin didn't seem to notice. She just popped open her thermos and talked about her dog's vet appointment like everything was normal. But Nico wasn't so sure anymore. The sandwich wasn't the problem.

The library felt safer, and that's where he started going when the noise in the cafeteria was too sharp. The librarian didn't care if you actually read. She just liked the quiet. That's where Nico first saw Ty—noticed is a better word, because Ty didn't really ask to be seen. He sat with his back to the window, always reading something with no dragons or explosions. Psychology books, Nico found out later. Ty called them his "how-people-work" books. Nico called them strange. But somehow, that made sense. Ty never stared. Never asked why Nico was there every day. Just gave a little nod like he already knew.

That week, Leo started asking weird questions. Little things, but sharp. "Why don't you eat with us anymore?" "Too good for the table now?" "You always get so quiet, it's creepy." None of it sounded mean at first, not if you said it in the right tone. But Leo said it like bait. Like he wanted Nico to react. And if Nico didn't, the next line came sharper. "Lighten up." "It's a joke." "You're too sensitive." Those three words—too sensitive—landed harder than Leo's shoulder bump ever did. Nico didn't know why they stung, but they did. And that quiet feeling in his chest? It twitched.

He didn't talk about it. Not to Jasmin, not to his parents. They'd say it was normal. "That's just how kids joke," or "Ignore it, he's probably jealous." But jealous of what? Nico didn't make the basketball team. He wasn't top of the class. He just existed, quietly. Maybe that was the threat. Maybe Leo couldn't stand quiet. Or maybe Nico was just imagining things. That was the scariest part—not what Leo did, but the way Nico started doubting his own eyes. Had he made it up? Was he actually being weird? The feeling in his chest didn't answer. It just stayed.

One afternoon, Ty glanced up from his book and asked, "You ever feel like something's off, but everyone acts like it's fine?" Nico blinked. He didn't answer. Not right away. Then he nodded. Just once. That was all it took. Ty didn't explain what he meant, and Nico didn't ask.

But the next day, there was a seat saved beside Ty at the table by the window. No one else noticed. But Nico did. And that small nod between them felt heavier than any conversation he'd had that week.

At home that night, Nico tried to think of examples. Things Leo said. Things he did. Nothing felt big enough to explain. It wasn't like Leo hit him. It wasn't name-calling. It was... smaller. Like taking the air out of a room, slowly. Like laughing one second too long. Like saying sorry in a way that made you feel guilty. Nico stared at the ceiling, wondering if maybe he was too soft. Too serious. Too... something. Then he remembered Ty's nod. That tiny yes without words. Maybe Nico wasn't the only one who felt it.

The next day, Leo gave him a high five in front of the math teacher and said, "There's my guy!" Like they were best friends. Like nothing weird had ever happened. Nico flinched, just barely. The math teacher smiled. Nico didn't. That was when he knew—Leo wasn't just being nice. He was being watched. When adults were around, Leo was syrup and sunshine. When they weren't, he turned the volume down and the tension up. Nico walked faster toward the library that day, like the bookshelves might shield him.

When he sat down across from Ty, he didn't say hello. Ty just looked up and pushed a thick book across the table. "Page ninety-two," he said. "Don't read the whole thing. Just the bold part." Nico opened it slowly. It was a definition. A word he didn't know. Narcissist. He read it twice. Then looked at Ty. "You think that's what he is?" Ty shrugged. "You tell me." Nico didn't answer. But for the first time all week, the tightness in his chest didn't grow. It stayed still.

That night, Nico sat at his desk and wrote the word in pencil on a scrap of paper. He folded it once. Slid it into his sock drawer. He didn't know what he'd do with it yet. But now he had a name. The feeling hadn't gone away. But at least it had a face. And tomorrow, he'd sit beside Ty again.

Leo never shouted. He didn't slam lockers or throw things or make scenes. He was the kind of kid teachers liked—the "good influence" type with clean shoes, good posture, and a grin ready to flash at roll call. He always had gum but never got caught. Always helped pick up pencils when someone dropped them. Said "yes ma'am" and "no sir" with just the right tone to earn nods from adults who never saw what came after. He said "buddy" a lot. Too much. Always with that sideways smile like he knew something Nico didn't. And when teachers turned their backs, Leo's grip would tighten just slightly—on Nico's arm, his shoulder, the back of his neck. Never hard enough to leave a mark. Just enough to remind you that the smile was only half the story.

There was a day Nico still thought about, even though it wasn't loud or dramatic. Just weird. He'd walked past Leo's desk without noticing something had fallen—Leo's pen, or maybe a flashcard—and Leo whispered, "You gonna pretend you didn't see that?" His voice was low, flat, calm. Nico blinked, bent down, handed it back. "Thanks, buddy," Leo said. But the "buddy" was sharp now, like it had edges. Jasmin didn't notice.

She was laughing about something on her phone. But Nico's stomach clenched anyway, the way it did when someone looked at you too long in a hallway. It wasn't what Leo said. It was the way he said it—like Nico owed him something now. For nothing.

After that, Nico started hearing the "nice" things differently. When Leo said "We should hang out," it didn't sound friendly—it sounded like a test. When he said, "Man, you're smart," it landed like bait, like Leo was waiting to yank it back if Nico dared to believe it. There was one afternoon Leo held open a door and said, "After you, sir." It was supposed to be funny. Everyone laughed. But Leo's hand stayed on the door just a second too long, blocking the frame until Nico smiled back. Then he let it go. That was the moment Nico realized something: Leo wasn't being nice. He was playing nice. And it was a game Nico didn't want to win.

Nico didn't tell anyone. Who could he tell? That someone was too polite? That his jokes weren't funny enough to count as jokes? It didn't sound like bullying. Not the kind they warned you about during assemblies. No fists. No name-calling. Just... pressure. Constant, low pressure. Like walking through fog and pretending it's not there. And when Nico tried to act normal, the fog got thicker. Leo noticed everything—when Nico answered too quietly, when he didn't laugh, when he looked away during a story. "Don't be weird, man," Leo would whisper with a chuckle, slapping Nico's arm just hard enough to sting. Then the teacher would say, "So great to see you two getting along." And Nico would nod, too fast.

Once, Nico made the mistake of standing too far from Leo during a group project. Leo's hand shot out and grabbed the back of Nico's hoodie. "Come on, buddy, you're not scared of me, are you?" His voice was sugar, but the pull was sharp. Nico stepped closer. Everyone laughed. "He's so jumpy," someone said. Nico laughed too. He always did. But that night he sat on his bed and stared at the ceiling, wondering why nice things felt so heavy. Why "buddy" felt like a leash. Why he didn't feel like himself anymore, just someone trying not to upset a lion wearing a party hat.

It was Ty who helped put it into words—not all at once, but slowly, in pieces. One afternoon in the library, Nico said, "Leo's not mean. He's just..." and trailed off. Ty looked up from his book. "Nice doesn't mean safe," he said, and turned the page. That stuck with Nico. The idea that someone could act nice, say all the right things, smile wide enough to blind a room—and still be dangerous. Not in the obvious way. Not with bruises or insults. But with expectation. With pretend kindness. With invisible strings.

There was another day Nico remembered too clearly. Leo offered him half a cookie. A big one. Chocolate chip. "You've been off lately," Leo said, his voice syrup-thick. "You good, buddy?" Nico hesitated. Took the cookie. Said thanks. "See?" Leo grinned. "Told you I was your favourite friend." The whole class laughed. Nico's face burned. He hadn't said that. Not ever. But now it was a joke, so he had to smile. Had to take the cookie. Had to pretend this was normal. And that's when the fog pressed down again—soft but unrelenting.

It wasn't until he walked past Ty that something clicked. Ty didn't say anything. Just raised one eyebrow. Nico stopped. "You ever get offered something nice... but it feels more like a trap?" he asked quietly. Ty nodded without looking up. "Yeah," he said. "Happens a lot." And just like that, Nico didn't feel crazy anymore. He still didn't know what to call it. But now he knew someone else had felt it too.

That night, Nico sat at his desk again. He didn't write anything. Just opened the drawer where he'd hidden the paper with that new word—narcissist. He hadn't looked at it since the day Ty gave him the book. Now he unfolded it slowly, traced the letters with one finger. Leo wasn't just being annoying. He wasn't awkward or just joking. He was doing something else. Something bigger. Nico still didn't have all the pieces, but he was starting to see the picture.

Tomorrow, he'd keep quiet. Listen harder. Watch more closely. And maybe, when the next "buddy" landed with that heavy, fake sweetness, he'd finally hear it for what it really was. Not kindness. Not friendship. Just another string.

It started with a pencil. Nico dropped it—by accident, just a slip of the fingers—and Leo laughed. Not a chuckle. Not a small smirk. He laughed the way people laugh at movies with explosions and pratfalls, loud and sharp and a little too long. "Nico's got butterfingers!" he shouted. "Better not let him near the science table—he might drop the beaker and flood the room!" Everyone turned. Some smiled. One kid snorted. Nico bent to pick up the pencil and kept his eyes on the floor. It wasn't a big deal, right? Just a joke. Except it didn't feel like a joke. It felt like a target being painted without his permission.

Leo had this way of saying things that sounded like teasing but landed like something else. He made sure the room heard. Always loud enough. Always with a smile. And the weirdest part was that no one ever stopped him. Teachers never caught it. Friends just shrugged. "Leo's always like that," they'd say. "Don't take it so seriously." But Nico didn't remember anyone else being laughed at for picking up a pencil, or dropping a paperclip, or asking to borrow a ruler. Just him. And Leo always led the laugh.

One morning, Nico tied his shoes too fast and left one slightly loose. He bent to retie it after the bell rang, just outside the classroom door. Leo walked by and said, "You tying those again? What, did your mom forget to teach you how to do bunny ears?" He said it quietly, but he grinned as he passed. Nico's ears burned. When he walked into the room a minute later, Leo was already mimicking him—bent over, fake-tying a shoe, wobbling like a duck. A few kids laughed. Jasmin told him to stop, but she was laughing too. Nico smiled, but it cracked halfway through. The joke wasn't funny. It wasn't even a joke. But it worked.

Nico started noticing the pattern. It wasn't just about being mean—it was about timing. Leo chose moments when Nico looked unsure. When his backpack strap slipped. When he answered too softly in class. When he paused before speaking.

That's when Leo struck, saying something just weird enough to be a joke and just pointed enough to hurt. It was like Leo had a radar for vulnerability, like he could smell discomfort and knew exactly how to make it worse without looking like a bully. And somehow, people kept laughing.

One time in gym, Nico tripped over a cone during warmups. He caught himself—barely—and got back in line. But Leo had seen. "We've got a natural disaster on aisle three," he called out. "You okay, Butterboots?" The teacher was busy adjusting the scoreboard. Leo grinned wide. Jasmin looked over and made a face, but no one said anything. Nico wiped his palms on his shorts and kept jogging. But inside, something coiled up tight. Leo didn't yell. He didn't curse. But his words still cut. Not because they were clever, but because they made Nico feel like the punchline to a joke he didn't tell.

The worst part wasn't the joke itself—it was the moment afterward. That flicker where Nico scanned the room to see who laughed. Who looked away. Who pretended not to hear. It made him feel small. Made him wonder if maybe he was being weird. Maybe he did walk funny. Maybe he talked too quietly. Maybe he deserved to be laughed at. That's the thing about these jokes—they sneak into your skin and make you think you planted the seeds yourself.

Ty didn't laugh. That meant something. He didn't frown or roll his eyes either. He just kept reading, maybe listening, maybe not. But Nico noticed that Ty always looked straight at him when Leo spoke. Not at Leo. At Nico. Like he was watching to see how deep it went. One day, Nico asked, "Do you think he's just joking?" Ty paused. "Do you think it's funny?" Nico shook his head. Ty said, "Then it's not a joke." Just like that. Simple. True.

Nico didn't want to believe Leo was cruel. Cruel sounded too big, too harsh. Leo never hurt anyone's body. He didn't throw things or steal or shout. But the laughing? The jokes that weren't really jokes? They chipped at things no one else could see. Like tapping at glass until it cracked. And when Nico thought about it, he realized something else—Leo never made fun of people stronger than him. Only quieter ones. Only the kids who wouldn't push back. And somehow, that made it worse.

That evening, Nico wrote in his notebook—not a journal, just a page at the back where he sometimes doodled. He wrote: Not all jokes are funny. Not all smiles are kind. Then he drew a mask. Half happy. Half blank. The mask looked a lot like Leo. He stared at it until the lines blurred. Then he closed the book and hid it under his bed. Tomorrow, he wouldn't laugh. Not even a little. Not at Leo's jokes. Not when other people did. He didn't know what that would change—but it felt like a start.

Jasmin meant well. She always did. Her laugh was the kind that filled a room, bright and round and easy to trust. She was the kind of friend who brought two granola bars just in case someone forgot lunch, and who always had extra pencils.

Jasmin didn't like drama, not because she was scared of it, but because she believed everything could be solved by talking it out. So when Nico finally said something—quiet, half-broken, nothing big—about Leo's jokes feeling different lately, she didn't get mad. She just smiled, waved it off, and said, "He's like that with everyone."

Nico nodded like he agreed. But inside, something dropped. That was the moment he realized Jasmin hadn't noticed. Or maybe she had, but not in the same way. Maybe she heard the jokes and thought they were funny. Maybe she saw the shoulder pats and thought they were friendly. Maybe she didn't feel that twist in her chest when Leo leaned in too close or said "buddy" with his hand gripping too tight. And if she didn't feel it, how could he explain it? You can't make someone hear the echo if they weren't in the hallway when it bounced.

They sat together at lunch like always. Jasmin told him about her dog throwing up grass and her little brother calling her "Captain Bossypants." Nico laughed in all the right places. He didn't want to ruin the moment. He didn't want to say, "Hey, remember when Leo called me Butterboots? That wasn't funny." He wanted her to see it for herself. But she didn't. Or wouldn't. Either way, she still laughed when Leo made a joke. And every time she did, Nico's stomach folded in tighter.

After school, they walked the same route for two blocks before she turned left toward her street. On the corner, she bumped him with her elbow and said, "You know Leo's just teasing, right? He likes you. He doesn't do that with people he doesn't like." Nico wanted to say, That's the problem. But instead, he just smiled. Because the truth was heavier than his backpack, and Jasmin didn't ask to carry it. So he kept it.

The thing is, Jasmin didn't defend Leo like some kids would. She wasn't cruel. She didn't say Nico was too sensitive or tell him to toughen up. She just didn't see it. And Nico realized then that maybe most people didn't. Maybe that's what made it work so well. Leo didn't make a mess in the open. He dripped it quietly under tables and behind backs, one drop at a time, until the whole room smelled wrong—but no one knew where the rot started.

Ty was the only one who didn't flinch. Nico thought about asking him what to do about Jasmin, but the words felt wrong. What could he say? My friend is kind, but she doesn't believe me? That didn't feel fair to her. Jasmin hadn't done anything wrong. She just didn't feel the shift. The one that came when Leo's jokes moved from silly to sharp. The one that made Nico smile with his mouth and not his eyes.

Later that week, during math, Leo leaned over and said something just loud enough: "Careful with your answers, genius. We wouldn't want another Butterboots incident." Jasmin giggled from two seats away. Not mean. Not mocking. Just easy. Nico didn't even look at her. He stared at the worksheet, fingers tightening around his pencil, and said nothing. That laugh, soft as it was, stayed with him all day. It wasn't betrayal. Not really. But it scraped.

That night, Nico sat on the edge of his bed, socks curled under his toes, staring at the crack near his closet door. He whispered the words once, not to anyone—just to himself. She doesn't see it yet. He didn't mean it as an excuse or an accusation. Just a fact. Like gravity or sunrise. Like the way some people can only see shadows when the lights go out. Jasmin still thought the lights were on.

He didn't give up on her. But he stopped waiting for her to notice. That was the difference. Before, he'd looked to her to confirm he wasn't imagining it. Now, he'd seen enough to believe himself without her nod. Ty had taught him that. Your feelings don't need witnesses to be real. They just need truth.

The next day at lunch, Jasmin offered him a granola bar and asked if he was okay. He said yes. Not because he was. But because she needed to hear it. And maybe, just maybe, she'd start to feel the flicker one day. That little crack behind Leo's smile. And when she did, maybe she'd remember this moment. The pause. The weight. And realize Nico had been telling the truth all along—even when he didn't say it out loud.

The cafeteria was loud. Not just with voices, but with elbows, tray clatter, and laughter that cracked too close to his ears. Nico used to sit with Jasmin and the others near the middle table—three down from the vending machines, two across from the janitor's closet. But lately, the noise stuck to his skin. The sound of Leo's voice, too casual to be kind, always slipped between sentences like it belonged there. So one day, Nico didn't follow the crowd. He ducked into the hallway, turned left at the science wing, and slipped through the double doors of the library like a fish sliding under ice. He told himself it was just for today.

Ty was already there. He usually was. He didn't sit at the front where the computers hummed or near the windows where the sun drew lines across the tables. He liked the back—near the reference shelves and the beanbags nobody used because they squeaked when you moved. Ty didn't look up when Nico entered. He kept reading something thick with a green cover and a cracked spine. Nico wandered to the opposite wall, pretending to scan titles, but he felt Ty's presence like a second thought. Not loud. Just there.

At first, Nico didn't sit. He stood for long minutes flipping through pages without reading a word. But the next day, he came back. Sat a little closer. Third day, he brought a book of his own—one he'd already read, so he wouldn't have to concentrate. Ty glanced at it. "That one's good," he said, just once. Then nothing more. Nico nodded. That was enough. No questions, no greetings, no "why aren't you at lunch?" Just shared space, quiet and clean. It became a kind of truce.

By the end of the week, Nico found himself heading there automatically. He didn't explain it to Jasmin. She didn't ask. Leo hadn't noticed yet, or if he had, he didn't say anything. Maybe that was the best part—being invisible for a bit.

The library had rules. No shouting. No pushing. No sudden jokes disguised as kindness. Just books, whispers, and Ty's silent company. Nico began to breathe differently there, slower. He didn't realize how fast his chest moved in the cafeteria until it stopped racing between shelves.

Ty didn't smile much, but he listened. Nico could tell. He turned pages like he meant it, but every now and then, when a door creaked or a voice rose, Ty's eyes flicked in that direction. He noticed things. Noticed the way kids flinched, the way teachers paused before answering questions, the way someone's footsteps slowed when they passed a certain group. Nico watched Ty more than he watched the books. There was something about the stillness in him—like a candle that stayed lit no matter how drafty the room.

One afternoon, Ty moved his bag over without being asked. Nico sat beside him without comment. They read for twenty minutes. Then Ty said, "You don't like loud rooms." Nico shrugged. "Too much echo," he mumbled. Ty nodded, eyes still on his book. "Same." That was it. But for Nico, it was the first time he felt understood in weeks. Like someone had looked inside his chest and named the ache without asking for a diagram. He didn't need Ty to say more. The quiet was already doing the talking.

Another day, Ty closed his book and asked, "You know how to disappear without hiding?" Nico blinked. "No." Ty tapped the table. "You change the game. You stop reacting. Narcissists hate that." Nico didn't answer. He didn't even know what a narcissist was. But the word dropped like a stone into a still pond. He folded it into his brain, just in case.

That week, Leo passed him in the hall and said, "Still skipping lunch, ghost boy?" Nico just kept walking. Didn't smile. Didn't frown. Didn't offer any explanation. Leo paused for a second, like he wasn't used to silence. Then he walked off, louder than before. Nico's stomach still knotted, but it didn't twist as hard. Maybe Ty was right. Maybe not reacting was a kind of defence.

Nico started sitting closer to Ty during library time. Never too close. Just near enough. They didn't talk every day. Sometimes Ty just handed him a book and said, "This one's about patterns. People have them." Nico read it slowly, like the words were bricks he could build walls with. Each chapter gave him tools. Each sentence said, You're not imagining this. That kind of truth felt different. It didn't scream. It hummed.

On Friday, Nico stayed late after the bell. Ty packed up but left one book behind. Nico picked it up and flipped to the marked page. In bold letters, it read: Manipulation is most dangerous when it wears a smile. He closed it gently. Then he wrote the sentence in the corner of his math notebook. Just small enough that only he would see it. Because sometimes the library wasn't just an escape. It was a beginning.

Ty didn't carry the kind of books other kids did. No wizards, no battles, no space invaders or time machines. His books didn't have shiny covers or blurbs that screamed epic adventure inside!

They were thick, quiet books with creased spines and folded corners—books that looked like they'd been read for answers, not escape. Nico noticed that the titles always had words like behaviour, patterns, mind, and control. The kind of books adults kept high on shelves. Ty kept them on his lap, page open, eyes still.

One afternoon, Ty caught Nico glancing at a chapter heading—Emotional Triggers and Response Loops. It sounded like something from a robot manual. "Boring, right?" Ty said, not looking up. Nico shrugged. "Maybe a little." Ty smiled—not the kind Leo gave, but a real one, a sideways smirk that didn't ask for anything back. "It's about people," he said. "How they work. What makes them tick." That word—tick—sat in Nico's ear like a drumbeat. Not snap, not break, not explode. Just tick. Like a machine. Like a clock. Like a warning.

Nico asked, "Why do you read that stuff?" Ty didn't blink. "Because some people are puzzles, and if you don't figure them out, they mess with your pieces." He turned the page slowly. "Also because I used to think I was the broken one." That line settled hard in Nico's chest. He didn't ask what Ty meant. He didn't have to. That sentence explained more than anything else had in weeks.

Over the next few days, Nico caught glimpses of titles—The Mask of Manipulation, Silent Control: Identifying Psychological Traps, Children Who Gaslight. They didn't sound like kid books. They didn't pretend. They just told the truth, flat and sharp and still. Ty never read out loud. But when Nico asked questions, he answered in pieces. Like dropping breadcrumbs on a trail that only led forward. "People use kindness to trap you," he said once. "They say sorry to keep you quiet." Another time, he murmured, "If you always feel like the bad guy, maybe someone's rewriting the story."

Nico started scribbling notes in the margins of his own homework—not school notes, but thoughts. Words Ty used. Manipulate. Devalue. Idealize. Shame. At first they were just sounds, foreign and strange. But then he started matching them to moments. Things Leo had said. Things Jasmin had brushed off. Things Nico had felt but couldn't name. Now he had names. Not adult words. Not teacher words. Just keys. And with each one, another door creaked open inside his head.

They didn't talk every day. Sometimes Ty just slid a book over, open to a chapter, and said nothing. Nico learned to read fast, eyes scanning until something stuck. He underlined things in his mind. The louder the charm, the deeper the hook. A narcissist creates confusion so they can stay the hero of your story. If you feel like you're walking on eggshells around someone, it's not your feet that are wrong. That last one made Nico breathe differently for the rest of the afternoon.

One day, Ty asked, "Ever felt like someone was watching you even when they smiled?" Nico nodded slowly. "And then when you didn't react the way they wanted, they acted hurt?" Nico nodded again.

Ty closed his book and said, "That's not friendship. That's surveillance with frosting." Nico laughed—really laughed—for the first time in days. It was sharp, short, and honest. Ty smiled again, then went back to reading. No further comment. But that sentence stayed with Nico all the way home.

At dinner, Nico watched his parents talk across the table. Nothing strange. No yelling. But he noticed things now—the way his dad's jaw tightened when his mum interrupted, the way his mum apologized for something she didn't even do. He didn't say anything. He just watched. The books weren't about Leo anymore. They were about everything. Patterns. Traps. Loops. People. And how the wrong kind of "love" could feel like chains made of compliments.

By Friday, Nico started bringing his own books. Not the heavy ones. Just fiction. But he read differently now. He looked at characters sideways, like they might be hiding something. He noticed which ones twisted their words, which ones called people crazy, which ones were nice until they didn't get their way. Ty noticed too. He didn't say it, but Nico could feel the nod before it even happened.

At night, Nico wrote one sentence over and over in the back of his notebook: If I can understand it, maybe I can stop it. It wasn't a promise. Just a step. And every step mattered. Because now, when Leo smiled, Nico saw the clockwork behind it. Tick. Tick. Tick.

Ty said it like it was no big deal. Just another vocabulary word, like "photosynthesis" or "hemisphere." But it didn't sound like those words. It hit different. "Narcissist," he said again, slower this time, his thumb sliding down the page of a dictionary thick enough to stop a soccer ball. Nico blinked. He'd never heard the word before. It sounded sharp, with too many teeth for something so quiet. "What is it?" he asked, already feeling like he should've known. Ty didn't look smug. He just pointed.

The dictionary definition was simple: a person who has an inflated sense of their own importance and a deep need for attention and admiration, often with a lack of empathy for others. Nico read it twice. Then a third time. The words tasted dry. But something in his stomach twisted. Not in fear—but in recognition. He didn't say anything right away. Instead, he let the silence press down between them like a heavy coat.

Ty closed the book gently. "It means they want everything to be about them. Always. And if it's not, they get mean, or they sulk, or they twist stuff around to make you feel guilty for not clapping for them." He didn't say Leo's name. He didn't have to. Nico looked down at his shoes. They were scuffed near the toes. He couldn't remember when that happened, but it felt like it mattered now. Like little marks showed what had been walked through. What had been survived.

"I thought it was just teasing," Nico said after a while. "Like, annoying stuff. But it's more than that, huh?" Ty nodded. "Teasing ends when you ask it to. Narcissists don't stop. They just find new ways to make it your fault."

Nico stared at the far wall of the library. It was lined with encyclopedias no one touched anymore. All those facts, all those pages, and no one had ever taught him this.

Ty leaned back in his chair. "You ever feel like someone's using your feelings like puzzle pieces, but they don't care what the picture is? They just want the control?" Nico nodded slowly. "Yeah. And like... if you don't laugh at their joke, they act like you hurt them." Ty cracked a small grin. "Exactly. That's the move. They mess with your head until you say sorry for their words." Nico blinked. It was like someone had taken the fog out of his brain and replaced it with a window.

"Why doesn't anyone talk about this?" Nico asked. "I mean, if people like that are real." Ty shrugged. "Because they look normal. They smile. They get good grades. Grown-ups like them. And if you say something, they act like you're the crazy one." The truth slid into place like the last piece of a jigsaw puzzle. Nico had always felt it—something was off. Now he had a name for it. A label to hang on the shadow that kept whispering in his ear that maybe he was the problem.

Ty reached into his bag and pulled out a smaller book, one with dog-eared pages and a pencil tucked in the spine. "This one's better," he said. "It's written for teens, but it's clear. Talks about how to spot the signs and what to do." He slid it across the table. "You don't have to read it. Just… maybe knowing helps." Nico ran his hand across the cover. It felt like armour. Soft, worn armour, but still something to carry.

Later that day, Nico tried saying the word to himself, quietly. "Narcissist." It still felt weird in his mouth. But he liked knowing it. Like knowing the name of a storm. You couldn't stop it from coming, but you could prepare. You could say, This isn't random. This is real. And sometimes, that's all the difference in the world.

That night, he wrote the word in the back of his school planner. Then underneath, in tiny letters, he added: If it's always about them, it can never be safe for you. It wasn't something a teacher had told him. It wasn't on a worksheet. But it felt like one of the most important lessons he'd ever learned.

The next morning, Nico arrived at the library five minutes earlier than usual. Ty was already there, same seat, same calm. The book with the pencil still sat on the edge of the table like it was waiting to be read again. Nico picked it up and opened to the glossary in the back. His finger paused on a word he now knew how to pronounce without hesitating. Narcissist. There it was in print, bold and plain. Someone who uses others to feed their need for control, admiration, or validation. Often plays the victim, twists blame, and lacks true empathy. Nico read it once. Then again. Then pointed to the line that made his throat close. Acts like the victim when they're not. Ty didn't say anything. He just nodded.

In his head, Nico heard Leo's voice: "Why are you always so quiet? I was just kidding. You're too sensitive. You should really work on that." He remembered the time Leo shoved his chair out from under him and laughed like it was a game, then told Miss Kara he was "trying to help Nico loosen up." He remembered how Leo would glare when Jasmin chose to sit beside Nico, only to smile wide and whisper something that made her frown five minutes later. Leo didn't hit. Leo didn't shout. But Leo left bruises in places no one saw—like behind the ribs, between thoughts, under trust.

They read the page together in silence. It felt heavier than it should've. Like the truth weighed more than the book. "Does it have to be a grown-up?" Nico asked, still staring at the page. Ty shook his head. "Nope. Kids can be narcissists too. Especially the smart ones. The ones who figure out how to play people early. They learn to wear masks. Make teachers love them. Make friends feel special. Then suddenly make those same friends feel... small."

Nico thought about the way Leo gave compliments that came with strings. The way he always had to be the loudest laugh, the first to finish a test, the one who told the jokes even if someone else had already made them. How he interrupted stories to tell his own, always one-upping like a competition no one else knew they were in. And how when Nico finally pushed back, Leo clutched his chest like he'd been shot and told everyone Nico had "changed." Like it was a crime.

"I think I've been gaslit," Nico said quietly. The word tasted like gravel. "A lot." Ty looked at him, serious now. "You have." Just that. No sugar-coating. No soft landing. But the honesty was gentle in its own way. Nico didn't feel attacked. He felt confirmed. The way you feel when a song names the feeling you didn't know how to explain. The dictionary didn't use words like mean or bully. It used manipulate, distort, deceive. Big words, but the meaning was clear enough now. Leo was in the dictionary. Not in name. But in shape.

"Is it my fault?" Nico asked. It came out before he could stuff it down. Ty's answer was fast. "No. But if you stay in it, it can become your damage." He paused, then added, "The earlier you name it, the faster you can leave it behind." Nico didn't nod. He didn't need to. He just sat still, the air around him thick but finally breathable.

That afternoon, Leo caught up to him in the hallway. "Heard you've been hiding in the library with that weirdo," he said, still smiling. "You know you don't have to do that, right? I'm not mad." Nico stared at him. He could see it now—the performance. The innocence worn like a coat. Leo even tilted his head like he cared. Like he wasn't the reason Nico had stopped eating in the cafeteria. "You okay?" Leo added, all concern. All lie. Nico didn't respond. He walked past him without flinching. And for the first time, he didn't feel rude. He felt free.

Ty was right. Understanding wasn't just power. It was armour. It didn't stop the arrows from flying, but it made them easier to dodge. Nico still had questions. Still had fear. But he had a word now. And inside that word was a flashlight. It lit up the dark in ways that made it impossible to unsee.

Back in the library, Nico wrote in the margin of Ty's book—tiny, just a note for later. I see him now. And I think he knows I do. He closed the book and pushed it back across the table. "Thanks," he said. Ty didn't answer with words. Just gave him a look that meant, You're learning to read the truth.

It came back to him on the walk home, like a scene playing in his head without asking first. Leo had texted three times in a row, all in caps, asking where Nico was. The last message had said, "Wow. So you're ignoring me now?" Nico had been at dinner with his gran. He hadn't seen the phone light up on the counter. By the time he'd texted back, Leo had replied, "Forget it. I don't need this drama." But the next morning, Leo had smiled like nothing had happened. Gave him a playful punch on the arm. Said, "Sensitive much?" with a laugh loud enough for Jasmin to hear. She'd rolled her eyes, like boys are always like this. But Nico remembered feeling like he'd been slammed against a wall—except nobody saw the bruise.

He told Ty the story at lunch, low and careful like it might crack if spoken too fast. Ty didn't blink. He just nodded. "That's textbook," he said, flipping to a dog-eared page in the smaller book. "That's how they test your obedience. Narcissists don't want friends—they want mirrors. You didn't reflect him when he wanted it, so he cracked you. Then laughed when you flinched." The words stung, but they rang true. Nico sat back, the cafeteria noise buzzing in the distance. It wasn't just about the text. It was what came after. The guilt. The confusion. The feeling that maybe he'd really done something wrong.

"I didn't even know I was allowed to be mad about it," Nico admitted. "Like, I thought it was just how friendships worked sometimes." Ty scratched at the edge of the table with a pencil. "That's what they want. They make bad things feel normal. They stretch your rules until your heart doesn't know where the line is anymore." Nico nodded slowly, the ache in his chest finally making sense. "He always makes me feel like I broke something I didn't touch."

Ty didn't rush to fix it. He just let the silence sit there, honest and thick. Then, gently, he said, "When someone yells at you for not doing what they expect—and then laughs and calls you sensitive when you react—that's not a friend. That's a controller." Nico took that in like a breath he didn't know he'd been holding. He leaned back and looked at the ceiling, blinking hard. "That's what he did to me," he whispered, almost like it wasn't real until now.

The cafeteria clattered around them. A tray dropped somewhere near the milk fridge. Someone shouted for extra ketchup. But at their table, the world narrowed down to truth. Nico looked at Ty. "So why do people like Leo get away with it?" Ty shrugged. "Because they know how to perform. They pick victims who won't scream. They act nice just enough. They build a wall of charm, then shove you behind it where no one hears you."

Nico ran his fingers along the crack in the table where someone had etched a name last year. "I didn't want to believe it. I thought if I was just nicer, he'd stop." Ty shook his head slowly. "Narcissists don't stop when you're nicer. They stop when you disappear—or when you shine so much truth at them that their shadows run." It didn't sound like magic. It sounded like armour. And Nico liked the weight of it.

He glanced down at the book again, rereading the part Ty had shown him. They alternate between praise and punishment, making their victims question reality. That was it. The text message, then the silence, then the joke. The light, the dark, the trap. Nico didn't want to fall for it again. "He said I was boring when I didn't laugh," Nico added quietly. "Said I was no fun anymore." Ty nodded. "Fun's not real when it comes with strings."

After school, Nico didn't go straight home. He sat on the edge of the swings behind the library, hands gripping the chains. His phone buzzed once. Leo. "You good? Seemed off today." Nico stared at it, then slid the phone back into his pocket without answering. He wasn't off. He was waking up. That was different.

That night, in his notebook, he wrote down the word Narcissist again. Underneath, he wrote: If they yell, then laugh, then blame you for feeling bad—that's not love. That's a trick. He underlined trick three times. Not because he needed to remember. But because someone else might read it one day. And maybe that would be the page that saved them.

He'd said it in front of everyone. "I'm sorry you feel that way," Leo had muttered just loud enough for the class to hear, after making a joke about Nico's handwriting and holding up his worksheet for laughs. Miss Kara had raised an eyebrow, but she didn't intervene. She'd assumed the boys were sorting it out themselves. Nico had stood frozen, cheeks burning, hands damp. Leo had smiled wide—more to the room than to him—like he was being gracious. Like he'd given a gift. That night, Nico had told Ty about it, expecting maybe a new word, a bigger term. But Ty just shrugged. "That's not an apology. That's control with a smile."

Now they sat under the old oak at the edge of the field, just after school. Jasmin was pulling grass and braiding the stems into tight knots like she always did when nervous. Nico hesitated, then said it. "I think Leo might be... one of those people Ty talks about. A narcissist." Jasmin looked up, her brow folding. "Because of that worksheet thing?" she asked, unsure. "I mean, yeah, that was dumb. But he said sorry, right?"

Nico exhaled through his nose, slow. "Not really. He said he was sorry I felt that way. That's not the same as being sorry for doing it." Jasmin blinked. "Isn't it kind of the same?" she asked. "Like, maybe he just didn't know how to say it right." Nico shook his head. "It's not the words. It's what he meant. It was like he was saying the problem was mine. Like my feelings were wrong."

Jasmin didn't answer right away. She picked another blade of grass and twisted it tighter than the last. "He's just awkward sometimes," she said finally. "You know how he is. He doesn't mean it." Nico sat back against the trunk. It wasn't anger he felt. It was that quiet sadness that crawls up when someone you trust doesn't see what you see. "I didn't think he meant it," Nico said. "I think he meant to sound like he meant it."

They sat in that pause, the one where two people used to be close and suddenly find the air a little colder between them. Jasmin pulled her knees in. "He helped me with my science project last week," she said. "Stayed after school and everything." Nico nodded slowly. "That's the thing. He's nice, when he wants to be. But it's not kindness. It's control. It's like... giving you candy with a hook inside."

Jasmin winced. "That's harsh." "So is pretending someone cares when they're making you feel crazy," Nico answered. It wasn't a snap. It was tired truth. She looked at him again, eyes softer now. "You really think he's doing it on purpose?" Nico nodded. "Yeah. I don't think he's confused. I think he just wants to win."

There was a silence after that, but not the cold kind. The thoughtful kind. Jasmin looked past the field, toward the bikes parked at the far fence. "I didn't see it," she said. "I mean... I saw the jokes. But I didn't feel them the way you did." Nico didn't say it's okay. It wasn't. But it wasn't her fault either. He just said, "Now you know."

She looked back at him, unsure. "Does this mean we have to hate him?" Nico thought about it. "No," he said. "It means we don't have to believe him." Jasmin nodded, slow like a learner tracing new letters. "Okay," she said. "I can start there."

That night, Nico didn't dream of arguments or fake smiles. He dreamed of mirrors breaking—softly, like sand cracking under bare feet—and of a voice, not Leo's, saying, That wasn't your fault. That wasn't kindness. That wasn't real. And when he woke up, he felt just a little lighter.

On Monday, Leo handed Nico half his sandwich at lunch. "You didn't bring yours, right?" he said, smiling like it was no big deal. Tuesday, Leo didn't speak at all. Wednesday, he glared at Nico for laughing at someone else's joke. "Thought we were tight," he muttered, loud enough to sting. Nico never knew which version of Leo would show up. Some days he felt pulled close, like a prize. Other days he felt dropped, like garbage. There was no map. Only landmines.

Nico had once believed friends stayed the same. Maybe they argued, maybe they changed over time—but they didn't shift shapes overnight. Leo made him question that. Made him rewrite his expectations daily. Sometimes hourly. A joke that was fine yesterday became disrespect today. A silence that was peaceful once became suspicious later. Nico started keeping notes. Not to accuse, not to prove anything, just to see if the madness had a pattern. In the back of his planner, he scribbled a single line: Leo said I was his only real friend today. Last week, he said I was needy.

Ty had told him that manipulators never follow rules—they make them. Then they change them just before you think you understand. "It's like playing tag," Ty explained, "but they're the only ones who know when you're 'it.'" Nico had laughed when Ty said it, but later, in bed, it didn't feel funny. It felt like a trap disguised as friendship. Like a maze that grew new walls while you slept.

That Thursday, Leo ignored him during math, then waited by the lockers with an arm slung over Jasmin's shoulder. "You good, man?" he asked. Nico nodded, too startled to lie, too scared to answer. Later, he wrote: Leo only calls me "man" when other people are watching. He calls me "idiot" when they're not. The page was messy. His handwriting crooked from the nerves. But it was there now. It existed. And somehow, that felt like a shield.

By the end of the week, the journal had five entries. Short ones. Just fragments. "Leo gave me a gift. Told me not to lose it. Then got mad when I left it in my desk." "He said Jasmin was confused. That she didn't understand him. Asked me if I understood." "He said I was too sensitive for not laughing when he joked about my shoes." These weren't feelings. They were facts. And when facts were written down, they didn't change shape.

The idea of "truth" had become slippery. Adults talked about it like it was obvious. Black-and-white. But when Nico looked at Leo, he saw something else—truth used like a knife. Pointed at whoever was in reach. Some days it was Jasmin. Some days it was Ty. Usually, it was Nico. That night, he wrote something bold in the journal's corner: The rules are always changing. That means they're not rules. They're traps.

At school, Nico started watching—not just Leo, but everyone. He saw who flinched when Leo raised his voice. Who laughed just a little too quickly at his jokes. Who avoided eye contact after being teased. He noticed that Leo smiled more when teachers passed, but his smile didn't reach his eyes. And he saw something else: Ty didn't flinch. Ty watched too. Not like prey. Like someone who'd seen it before.

He didn't feel brave yet. But he felt like he was becoming something. Someone. Like the version of himself who was no longer confused by sudden silence, or fooled by sudden gifts. Like a scout in unfamiliar woods, drawing his own map before anyone else dared admit they were lost. Truth wasn't loud. It was quiet, and it sat in the back pages of his planner, written in pencil, waiting to become permanent.

That afternoon, he showed Ty one line. Just one. "Leo only says sorry when people are listening." Ty nodded once. No praise. No wow. Just that quiet knowing. "Then write that," he said. "The truth doesn't shout. It stacks." Nico smiled, just a little.

The next morning, he flipped open his planner and wrote a new title above the entries: Shadow Notes. Not a diary. Not a rant. Something better. Something that watched when no one else dared. He didn't need to be seen. He needed to see. And that, he realized, was enough to make him dangerous—in the best way.

Ty didn't use big words when he explained things. He just used the right ones. The kind that made you stop and feel like your insides were turning a page you weren't ready to read. "They don't want love," he said, flipping a pencil between his fingers as they sat under the stairs during a rainy lunch. "They want control." Nico blinked. "Then why do they act like they care?" Ty's answer was quiet: "Because pretending you matter is how they get you to stay."

That sat in Nico's mind like a stone dropped in water. He thought about the time Leo had brought him a doughnut just because. Said it was because Nico "looked like he needed one." That same day, Leo had snapped at him for not laughing fast enough at something Jasmin said. Then apologized—kind of—then handed him the doughnut. At the time, Nico had smiled and said thanks. Now he saw it for what it was. Bait. "So they only act nice when they want something?" he asked. Ty shrugged. "Sometimes. Sometimes they do it just to keep you confused."

Nico's Shadow Notes were growing. He'd written things like "Leo got mad, then gave me gum." And "Said I was lucky he still liked me." It wasn't just that Leo wanted to be liked. He wanted Nico to feel small, and then rescued—by Leo. It was like watching someone tie a knot around your wrists, then offer to cut it if you smiled nicely. It was never really about friendship. It was about power that felt like kindness until you looked too closely.

"They need you to need them," Ty said. "That way, when they hurt you, you'll still feel like you have to stay. Because they're also the one who fixes it." Nico felt that sentence wrap around him like smoke. "But it's fake fixing," he muttered. Ty nodded. "Yep. It's like stepping on your foot and then offering you an ice pack. You're supposed to forget who hurt you."

That night, Nico wrote something new: Leo doesn't love. He performs love. The words felt harsh. But when he said them aloud to himself, they sounded... fair. Like they belonged. He wasn't trying to be mean. He was trying to understand. And Ty was helping him see that understanding wasn't mean—it was survival.

"Why do they want control so bad?" Nico asked the next day. Ty looked up from his book, something about emotional patterns in early development. "Because if they're in control," he said slowly, "they never have to feel small." Nico thought about that. Maybe Leo had once felt small. Maybe someone had made him feel invisible. Maybe this was his way of making sure no one ever ignored him again. But that didn't make it right. Hurt people hurting people still hurt.

"So what do we do?" Nico asked. "You notice," Ty said. "That's the first thing. You stop pretending it's love. You stop making excuses. And then…" He paused. "Then you figure out if you need to step back." Nico knew what that meant. Stop showing up. Stop feeding the game. Stop giving your peace to someone who only gave back pieces.

Later that week, Jasmin walked up to Nico at recess. "You ever feel like Leo's nice... until he's not?" she asked, half-laughing. Nico didn't laugh. He just nodded. "He's nice when he's in charge," he said. Jasmin went quiet. "Yeah," she whispered. "Exactly that."

It wasn't just him anymore. The noticing was spreading. And that, more than anything, felt like truth cracking through the lies like sun through cloud. Nico added it to his notes that night. Just one line: Others are starting to see. That's how the power fades.

Ty told him not to make it a movie moment. "No speech," he said. "No final scene. Just a door." Nico blinked. "A door?" Ty nodded. "Yeah. Open it. Walk out. That's it." It sounded too simple. But Nico was learning that simple didn't mean easy. He had wanted Leo to understand. He had wanted him to care. To change. But that was a trap too. One that started with the idea that you could teach someone to be kind by bleeding in front of them. Ty was right. There was no speech. Only space.

He tried it once in the hallway. Leo was waiting, bouncing a ball off his locker. "Hey, you got your math book?" Nico kept walking. "I'm busy." It wasn't loud. It wasn't cruel. But it was new. Leo stared, then laughed too loud, like Nico had told a joke. "Busy?" he echoed. "You're always free, dude." Nico didn't answer. He just turned the corner. His heart thudded in his chest like footsteps that didn't want to stop, but he didn't run. He just kept walking.

That night, he wrote it down. I don't owe my presence to someone who uses it to hurt me. The words felt big. Almost too big for a kid to write. But Nico didn't feel like a kid anymore. Not in the way he used to. He felt like someone who'd stepped behind the curtain and seen the strings pulling the puppet. Leo didn't want friendship. He wanted an audience. And Nico was done clapping.

"You don't need to explain why," Ty had said. "People who need a reason are usually the reason." Nico had nodded. "What if they don't take the hint?" Ty shrugged. "That's their problem. Not yours. Keep your words short. Clear. Not mean. Just solid." Nico wrote some of them on a sticky note inside his locker. I need space. I don't want to talk. I'm busy. Three lines. Not a battle cry. A boundary.

Jasmin noticed the shift before Nico said a word. She watched him turn away from Leo in class. Watched him sit beside Ty at lunch instead of pretending Leo's circle was safe. One day, she sat with them too. "Leo's been weird lately," she said, poking at her sandwich. "Like... he gets mad when I don't text back right away." Ty didn't look up. "That's not weird," he said. "That's control."

Nico let Jasmin sit in the silence. He didn't push her. He didn't say I told you so. That wasn't the point. Truth didn't need a billboard. It just needed space to be seen. Eventually, she whispered, "He called me dramatic. For saying I didn't like being teased in front of people." Ty raised an eyebrow. "Let me guess. He said sorry later?" Jasmin blinked. "He did. How did you know?" Nico and Ty didn't answer. They just nodded, and that was enough.

Walking away wasn't one giant step. It was a hundred small ones. Choosing the other hallway. Sitting beside someone else. Not laughing when the joke felt sharp. Not replying just because you felt guilty. It was like teaching your body not to flinch when someone said your name. Not out of fear, but out of freedom. Nico felt it slowly. The weight on his chest hadn't vanished, but it had shifted. It didn't own him.

Leo tried again the next week. "You good?" he asked in passing, too casual to mean nothing. Nico didn't stop. "I'm busy," he said. No anger. No sadness. Just space. Leo didn't follow. And that was all Nico needed to know.

Later, he wrote a single sentence in his Shadow Notes: Silence isn't weakness when it's your way out. It was the first time the page didn't feel heavy. It felt like armour.

Nico stared at his sandwich and didn't take a bite. The bread was dry. He couldn't remember what was in it. Ty was halfway through a page in his behaviour book when Nico finally said it. "What if he gets mad?" His voice was small, like the question didn't want to be heard. But Ty closed the book anyway. "He might," he said plainly. "That's what they do when they lose control." The words weren't cruel. Just honest. That made them heavier somehow.

"What if he calls me a liar?" Nico asked. His fingers twisted the corner of his lunch bag until it tore. "He might do that too," Ty replied. "That's how it works. They flip it on you. Make it sound like you're the problem." Jasmin sat across from them, not talking yet. But she was listening harder than ever. Nico could feel it. Her quiet was different now—quieter like a decision, not like denial.

Nico's stomach turned at the memory. Leo in the hallway, voice too loud, too bright: "Why would I be mean to you, dude? You're just sensitive. Chill." And kids had looked. Some laughed. One had nudged another like it was funny. Nico had gone red. He hadn't said a word. He had walked away. But the shame stayed like gum on a shoe. Now, just thinking about it made his ribs ache.

"I don't want to deal with that again," he whispered. Ty leaned forward, elbows on the table. "Then don't deal with it alone," he said. "That's the trick. They win when you go quiet. But you've got people now. Me. Jasmin. Even teachers—if you pick the right one." Nico looked up. "But what if no one believes me?" Ty nodded slowly. "Then you show them what you wrote. You explain how it made you feel. And if they still don't listen? You find someone who will."

It wasn't perfect. Nico knew that. Some teachers didn't get it. Some adults liked to say, "Just ignore him." Like that ever worked. But Ty wasn't offering a magic solution. He was offering backup. A witness. That meant something. It meant the weight wasn't all on Nico anymore. Jasmin finally spoke. "I thought maybe it was just me," she said. "Like maybe I was making too big a deal of it." She looked at Nico. "But I wasn't. Was I?" He shook his head. "No. You saw it."

She nodded once, sharp. "Then I'll say something too. If it happens again." It was quiet, but firm. Like a rope tied to something solid. Nico felt it wrap around him, not like a trap—but like safety.

After school, Nico walked past Leo by the bike racks. Leo didn't smile. Just gave him a look like ice on a puddle—shiny and breakable. Nico didn't flinch. He just kept walking. Leo muttered something under his breath, but Nico didn't hear the words. He didn't need to. He didn't stop.

That night, Nico wrote in his Shadow Notes: Truth doesn't need permission to exist. He stared at it a while. Then added: But it grows faster when you're not alone. The page didn't feel heavy this time. It felt strong. Jasmin had his back. Ty had his back. And if Leo got mad again—Nico had a plan. He'd tell someone. He'd show the notes. He'd keep walking.

Because staying quiet to keep peace had never really brought peace. Just silence. And silence is only safe when it's chosen—not when it's forced.

Ty leaned back against the bookshelf like it was a throne only he knew how to sit in. The library was half-empty, soft afternoon light dripping between the dusty blinds. Nico felt something shift in the air—like a string pulled tight was about to snap. Ty didn't raise his voice. He never did. "You're a Shadow Warrior now," he said, flat as paper. Nico blinked. "What's that?" Ty smirked like he'd been waiting for the question. "Someone who sees what others pretend not to. And keeps going anyway."

Nico looked down at the book in his lap. He hadn't even noticed what title Ty handed him this time. Something about survival, or systems. Didn't matter. What mattered was the word—warrior. It didn't feel like him. "I'm not brave," he mumbled. "I just got tired." Ty nodded. "That's how it starts. You don't swing swords. You sit still. You don't fight with fists. You remember everything."

He tapped his temple with one finger. "Shadow Warriors don't chase attention. They don't shout. They blend in. They gather truth. And when they need to, they act—quick, quiet, clean." Nico thought of all the times he'd swallowed his words. All the things he'd wanted to say and didn't. How heavy that silence had felt. "So staying quiet... wasn't weakness?" he asked. Ty shook his head. "It was training."

Jasmin sat across from them, listening now with a strange look on her face. "I didn't notice things like you did," she said. "Does that mean I can't be one too?" Ty turned to her. "Shadow Warriors don't all start the same. Some learn fast. Some learn slow. What matters is that you learn. And that you see." Jasmin crossed her arms. "Well, I'm seeing now. And I don't like what I saw." Nico smiled. It was the first time she'd sounded angry for the right reason.

Ty pulled a folded paper from his notebook. "There's a test," he said. "Not like in school. Just a list. Things you've done, or felt, or realized." He handed it over. Nico read silently:

1. You noticed when something felt wrong—even if no one else did.

2. You questioned a person who said "I'm nice" but made you feel small.

3. You kept your truth inside until you knew who to trust.

4. You chose peace over revenge.

5. You watched, listened, remembered.

6. You walked away without explaining yourself.

7. You believed your feelings mattered.

8. You helped someone else see it too.

Nico finished the list and passed it to Jasmin. She stared at it for a long time. "I did number eight today," she said. "Finally." Ty shrugged. "That's one of the hardest ones." Nico traced his finger over number one. "I felt it in my chest. Like something was wrong. Weeks ago. That counts?" Ty's voice was soft. "That's how all of us start. With a feeling."

They sat there, quiet for a while. The library clock ticked like a heartbeat. Outside, footsteps echoed down the hall. A bell rang faintly in the distance. Nico breathed in and out, slow. "So... what now?" he asked. Ty stood. "Now you keep watching. Keep writing. Keep walking away from the ones who treat you like furniture. And when someone new says, 'Something feels wrong,' you help them name it."

Jasmin folded the paper and tucked it into her pocket. "Then I guess we've got more warriors to find." Nico stood up, not taller, but steadier. He didn't need a sword. He had memory. He had truth. And he had allies.

That night, in his Shadow Notes, he wrote: The test isn't to win. The test is to see clearly. The real test is not flinching when the truth finally has a name.

Jasmin didn't ask to sit with them. She just pulled out a chair at their library table and unwrapped her snack like it had always been her spot. Ty looked up once, gave a short nod, and went back to his book. Nico offered her a pencil from the centre pile, even though she hadn't asked. Jasmin didn't smile, not yet. But she was there. That was the part that counted.

"Leo told Devon he was selfish," she said after a while, not looking up. "Just because Devon didn't want to trade seats in class." Her voice didn't sound shocked, just annoyed—like she was starting to get tired of surprises that weren't surprising anymore. Nico looked up from his journal, then glanced at Ty. Ty stayed quiet, but he closed his book gently, marking the page with a red ribbon.

"I used to think he was just teasing," she said. "Like, you know, joking. But now I can't unhear it. Every time he says 'relax,' it feels like a trap." Nico nodded, heart thudding. It was strange to hear her say it. Strange in a good way. Like watching someone else open the same door you'd been staring at for weeks. "That's how I felt," he said. "But I didn't have words for it."

Jasmin tapped her fingers on the table. "It's like... like he's playing a game that only he knows the rules to. And when you don't play right, he acts like you're the one who broke something." She didn't look at either of them. "I saw it again this morning. He told Emily she was being dramatic because she said she didn't like being yelled at. He even laughed. And everyone else just sat there."

Ty waited until she finished before speaking. "That's a guilt trick," he said calmly. "It's when they make you feel bad for having a normal reaction to their bad behaviour." Jasmin finally looked up. "So it's not just me?" "Nope," Ty said. "It's a pattern. You're just seeing it now. Like when your eyes finally adjust to the dark."

Nico leaned in. "You didn't say anything to him?" Jasmin shook her head. "I froze. I thought about saying something, but... it's like my brain got fuzzy. Like I was afraid to make it worse." "That's normal," Ty said. "That's part of the trap. They make you feel like silence is safer." He pulled out a folded sheet of notebook paper and slid it over to her. The list. The Shadow Warrior test.

Jasmin didn't smile, but her jaw set like someone finding a missing puzzle piece. She didn't need to ask what it was. She started reading. After a moment, she said, "Number three. That's me. Keeping it in until I knew it was safe." Nico felt something warm spark in his chest. That used to feel lonely. Now it felt like a club.

She finished the list and nodded slowly. "Okay. I still don't want to call him a narcissist. That word's too big. Too sharp." Ty shrugged. "You don't have to. Call him what you see." Jasmin hesitated. Then said, "I think he wants power. And he uses people to get it. And I think he hates when anyone sees that." Ty smiled slightly. "That's more accurate than the dictionary."

The library bell rang, warning them of the end of lunch. Jasmin packed her things in silence, but just before she zipped her bag, she spoke. "Next time he does it, I'm not freezing. I'll say something. Even if it's small." Nico slid her a folded sticky note. On it was written: I'm not confused—I'm being confused. Jasmin read it once. Then folded it again and put it in her pencil case. They walked out together. Not as three strangers anymore. Not as three scared kids. But something else. Something forming. Something steady.

It was just after last bell, the kind of moment where footsteps blur and doors swing and teachers shout reminders no one hears. Nico had taken the long hallway near the lockers, the one he used when he wanted time to think. That's when Leo showed up. Not loud, not cruel—just there. Like a shadow curling at the edges of the light. "Hey," Leo said, like nothing had happened. "You've been weird lately."

Nico's stomach tightened. He didn't answer. He wanted to walk past, but Leo leaned casually against the lockers like they were old friends waiting on a bus. "Look, I get it," Leo said, running a hand through his hair. "You're sensitive. That's fine. Just don't go telling people I'm some bad guy, okay?" His voice dropped lower. "That's not cool. Especially when I've always been there for you."

Nico stared at him. The words hit like soft punches. No fists. No shouting. But each one carried weight, the kind you couldn't explain to anyone who wasn't listening. Then Leo leaned in slightly. "Remember what I told you before?" he asked, almost a whisper. "Everyone leaves you. I'm the only one who stays." Nico remembered. Not just the words, but the day—the weather, the sound of his own breath, the way his heart dropped like a stone. It hadn't felt comforting. It had felt like a trap disguised as care.

Before he could reply, Jasmin stepped around the corner. Her eyes swept from Nico to Leo, then back again. "Hey," she said calmly. "You ready to go, Nico?" Leo blinked. "I was just talking to him." Jasmin didn't flinch. "Yeah. I heard." She didn't raise her voice. She didn't accuse. But her tone had changed. Like steel wrapped in velvet. "And he doesn't need that kind of talk."

Leo scoffed, brushing invisible dust from his jacket. "I'm trying to help him. That's what friends do." Jasmin tilted her head. "Friends don't say 'everyone leaves you.' Friends say 'I'm here if you need me.'" Nico's throat tightened. Jasmin kept her gaze steady. "I used to think you were just sarcastic," she said. "But now I hear the twist in your words."

Leo's smile cracked. Only slightly, but it was enough. "Whatever," he muttered. "You guys are so dramatic." He stepped back from the lockers, already shifting into a grin as two younger kids walked by. "See you around." Then he was gone. Just like that. But the pressure in Nico's chest stayed for a few more seconds.

Jasmin waited. Then she said, "That thing he said to you—about being the only one who stays. That's not loyalty. That's a chain." Nico nodded. "I know. I just... didn't know how to say it until now." "Now you don't have to say it alone," she replied.

They walked out together, feet falling into step without a plan. Behind them, the hallway emptied. The echoes faded. But that memory? It still stung. Not because it had power anymore—but because it had once. That night, Nico wrote in his Shadow Notes: Some truths don't scream. They whisper for years. But the moment someone else hears it too, the whisper becomes a sword.

The next day came quiet, like the world was holding its breath. Nico didn't expect much. He packed his bag slowly, folded his math notes neatly, tucked them behind a novel in his backpack. He already knew Leo would ask. Leo always asked. Not with politeness, but with a shrug, like Nico owed it—like friendship was measured in what could be taken, not shared.

He found Leo waiting near the classroom door, one sneaker up against the wall, arms folded like someone who didn't care about the answer but still expected yes. "Hey," Leo said, not bothering with a smile. "You bring the notes?" The pause between the question and the answer stretched like a held breath. Nico kept his eyes soft, casual. "I didn't bring them."

It wasn't true. But it felt truer than anything he'd said to Leo before. And Leo, for once, had no reply. His lips parted like he might push—but Nico turned and walked down the hall before he could. Every step felt weirdly light. Like air returning to lungs that had forgotten how to breathe. Like silence that finally belonged to him.

Ty was at the usual table in the library, legs curled under the bench, head buried in a book about body language. Nico slid in beside him, opened his bag, and let the notes sit there—untouched. "I didn't give them to him," Nico said, without looking up. Ty didn't ask who. He already knew. "How'd it feel?" "Strange," Nico admitted. "But... good strange."

Ty smiled and flipped a page. "That was the first rule of boundaries," he said. "Saying no—even when you're scared the yes would be easier." Nico nodded. Then leaned in slightly. "But what if the person who acts like Leo isn't a kid?" Ty blinked, then closed his book halfway. "You mean... grown-ups?"

Nico hesitated. "Yeah. Like, what if it's your uncle, or a teacher, or your mom's friend... and they use that same guilt voice? Like you're the problem if you don't do what they want?" Ty looked down for a moment, then said, "Same rules still count. Doesn't matter how old they are. You still get to protect yourself." He pulled out a folded card from his pocket. It was handwritten. "I made this," he said. "For myself. I call it the Shadow Code."

Nico took the card. On it were four sentences:
1. I trust what I feel, even if they say I shouldn't.
2. I don't owe access to people who scare me.
3. I can leave without explaining everything.
4. If I'm confused, it might not be my fault.

Nico read it twice. Then put it in the front pocket of his backpack. "What about when you have to see them?" he asked. "Like, family stuff?" Ty looked serious for a second. "Then you act like a Shadow Warrior. Quiet, smart, alert. You don't fight. You don't freeze. You observe. You prepare. You talk to someone safe after."

The bell rang, echoing like a call to arms. But Nico wasn't nervous. Not this time. "I said no," he said under his breath, almost to himself. "And I didn't explain it. And the sky didn't fall." Ty stood, slinging his bag over one shoulder. "It never does." As they stepped out of the library, Jasmin waved from down the hall. She smiled—not the fake kind, not the practiced kind. The real kind. The kind you save for people who get it. Nico smiled back. One small no. One big win. And the beginning of something better.

CHAPTER 2: THE SMILE THAT WASN'T REAL

Leo's voice had a way of wrapping itself around people's ears. It didn't shout. It didn't argue. It slipped in smooth, like warm butter over bread, especially when teachers were close enough to nod in approval. "Jasmin's the smartest girl in class," he said, chin tilted like he meant it. But it came after she slid her math sheet across the desk to him when Mr. Rafferty wasn't looking. After her pencil rolled toward his hand on purpose. After the answer to question seven—the tricky one—found its way into Leo's margins without ever being spoken. And when he said it, that compliment, it felt heavy. Like she owed him now.

Jasmin didn't smile the way she usually did when someone praised her. Normally, her face lit up like someone turned on a switch behind her eyes. This time, she blinked slow, then bit the inside of her cheek. It wasn't that she didn't like being called smart. She did. But something about the way Leo said it made it sound less like a gift and more like a deal. A trade. You give me what I want, and I'll say the right thing in front of the right people. It didn't feel like praise. It felt like pressure dressed up in sugar.

Nico saw her face twist for a second. Not big. Just a flicker. The kind you miss if you're not already watching. He noticed because he used to do that too—back when Leo first started calling him "buddy" every day after lunch, then asking for his snacks when no one else brought extra. It always started with kindness. That's how Leo did it.

Ty said people like Leo "prime the pump." That meant they say what you want to hear so you'll forget what you just did for them. So you'll do it again. Nico didn't know what pump they were talking about, but he understood the part where your stomach gets tight even though the words sound nice. That's what happened to Jasmin now. Tight smile. Chewed cheek. Pencil gripped just a little too hard.

"Thanks," Jasmin said finally, her voice a half-step slower than usual. Leo was already looking away, cracking a joke with someone else. She turned to Nico and raised one eyebrow, like she wanted to ask something without saying it. But the words didn't come. Not yet. Later, after math, Nico asked, "Did that feel weird?" Jasmin paused like she hadn't thought about it that way. "Kinda," she said. "But it was still nice, wasn't it?"

"I guess," Nico said. "Just... the timing." He didn't want to sound like he was making drama. But the way Leo's words came right after he got what he wanted—that timing was like a thread. Jasmin nodded slowly. They sat together at lunch, not saying much at first. Ty was already flipping through his notebook, the one he never let anyone read. But today he looked up and said, "That's how it starts, by the way."

Jasmin tilted her head. "What starts?" "Love bombing," Ty said. "It doesn't always look like hearts and flowers. Sometimes it looks like fake compliments. Stuff you can't say no to without sounding mean." Jasmin looked back down at her sandwich. "He does that a lot, huh?" Nico didn't answer. He didn't need to. The way Jasmin stayed quiet said she was rewinding her memory, playing back every nice thing Leo had ever said—and wondering what it had cost her.

"I only helped him because he said he didn't get it," Jasmin whispered. "I didn't think it was... cheating." Ty didn't judge. "They don't always tell you it's wrong. They just make it feel easier to say yes than no." And there it was again. That tug. That invisible string Jasmin hadn't seen until it pulled. Mr. Rafferty walked by and clapped Leo on the back. "You've been improving, kid. Keep it up." Leo just smiled and nodded like he'd earned every mark himself.

Jasmin stared at the floor. Her hands were still. "I think he used me," she said. "You think?" Ty asked gently. "I know," she replied, and her voice didn't shake. Nico watched her pick up her tray without a word. But before she walked away, she turned to them and said, "Don't let him do that to me again." That was the beginning. Not of something loud or angry—but of Jasmin finally noticing the strings tied around her wrists. And for the first time, she reached for a pair of scissors.

Ella didn't even get to sit down before Leo was at her side. New backpack still zipped. Name tag still half-curled at the edges. She hadn't said more than four words before he smiled that too-big smile and slid his water bottle out of her way like it was an honour to make space. "Hey, new girl," he said, not even pretending to ask her name first. "You want gum?" She blinked, nodded, and took the piece like maybe it was just a friendly welcome. But it wasn't just gum. It was the beginning of the trick.

By recess, he'd carried her books, stood up so she could have the better seat near the front, and declared that they had the same favourite music—though no one asked either of them. Ella smiled shyly at first, like she wasn't used to being noticed so quickly. But Leo's attention was louder than her comfort. He leaned in when he talked to her, always watching her face like it was a mirror. He laughed at things she hadn't said. Agreed with things she hadn't finished. She barely had time to breathe between being introduced to his friends and being pulled into his jokes.

Nico saw it from across the room. The pace of it. How Leo moved like a charm spell—pressing in with just enough kindness to trap. Ella didn't see it yet. How could she? She was new. New meant vulnerable. And Leo knew how to spot that from across a hallway. His compliments were like falling dominoes. Too smooth. Too quick. Too tidy. The way he said, "You're gonna be the most popular girl here by Friday," made it sound like a promise—but it felt like a bet.

Ty leaned close to Nico during science and said, "Watch how fast he moves. He doesn't leave room for doubt." Nico nodded. That was the thing. Leo didn't give you time to think. Just praise after praise, favour after favour, until saying 'no' would feel rude. Or worse—ungrateful.

At lunch, Leo gave Ella half his fries before she'd even opened her tray. She looked surprised, touched. But she also looked like she wasn't sure what she was agreeing to. "Thanks," she said, voice soft. "You don't have to." Leo smiled. "I want to." That kind of want is heavy. It has a hidden weight that no one notices until it's too late.

Jasmin watched too, fork paused in midair. "He didn't even ask her name until after he gave her gum," she whispered. Nico didn't reply. The pattern was clear now, repeating like a script. Jasmin shook her head. "It's too much." She didn't mean the gum. She meant the speed. The full-throttle friendliness that didn't give Ella time to understand what kind of story she'd just been pulled into.

Ella laughed a little too loud at something Leo said during lunch. Not a full laugh. A nervous one. The kind that asks for safety. Leo leaned in and said something none of them heard, but Ella's shoulders stiffened. Then she nodded. Nico's eyes narrowed. That nod looked rehearsed.

Ty's pencil moved across his notebook. He wrote something, showed it to Nico and Jasmin under the table: love bombing 101. Jasmin exhaled slowly, like it made more sense now, even if it still felt wrong. "Why does he do this every time?" she asked. "Because it works," Ty said, eyes on Ella. "He overloads them. Fast kindness is hard to run from."

By the end of the day, Leo had walked Ella to the bus line, held her backpack for her, and promised to show her all the secret tricks to surviving elementory school. She laughed again, softer this time, but her eyes darted to the side—just once. Like she wasn't sure if she should still be smiling. Like the spell was starting to itch.

Jasmin muttered, "Too fast. It's like he's trying to win a race no one else signed up for." Nico nodded. "It's not a friendship. It's a takeover." They all knew it. But Ella didn't yet. She was still floating on the compliments, still picking up the pieces of every nice thing Leo had handed her. And no one wants to throw away a gift, even when it's poisoned. Ty tapped his pen against the table, then said something that made Jasmin blink: "The faster it starts, the harder it crashes." They all looked toward Ella, her smile still half-lit, her laugh still trying to sound easy. She wasn't falling yet. But she was already leaning.

And Leo? Leo looked pleased. Not happy—pleased. Like a magician who knows his trick landed. Like someone who'd been here before and would be again. He was already choosing the next line. Already writing the next compliment. Already setting the stage for the moment when Ella wouldn't be smiling anymore.

At first, it looked like Ella had landed on the best square of the board game. She was glowing. Not sparkly, attention-seeking glowing—but that new-kid joy, when someone's actually nice to you and you feel like maybe, just maybe, elementory school won't be terrible. She sat straighter in class. She smiled without flinching. She waved at people she didn't know, because Leo already knew them, and he waved back, so why wouldn't they? For a few days, her whole face stayed bright. Until something shifted.

It started small. Leo didn't take the seat next to hers anymore. He moved one desk over. Still close enough to smile. Far enough to send a message. When Ella asked if he was saving the spot, he shrugged and said, "Nah. Needed a new view." It was said with a grin, the kind of grin people assume is harmless. But Ella's smile cracked a little. Just a flick.

Later, he ignored her when she waved at lunch. Jasmin noticed first, elbowing Nico as Leo passed Ella without a glance. Ella lowered her hand slowly, then tugged her sleeve down like she was cold. "He didn't see her," Jasmin whispered. "He saw her," Nico replied. "He's teaching her something." Jasmin looked confused, but Ty, a few feet away, nodded once without turning around.

That afternoon, in art, Leo complimented another girl's sketch right in front of Ella. Loudly. "You've got actual talent," he said. "Not like some people who just trace stuff." He didn't look at Ella when he said it, but he didn't need to. The silence that followed made it obvious who the "some people" were. Ella coloured carefully after that, barely lifting her head.

At recess, he laughed with his friends, throwing glances in Ella's direction but never inviting her over. Nico watched her sitting alone, tying and untying her shoes. That glow she'd had was flickering now. Dimmer. Not out yet—but tired. Like someone trying to pretend the light was still on when it wasn't.

"Why is he doing that?" Jasmin asked quietly. Nico didn't answer right away. Ty spoke instead. "It's the second phase." He didn't look up from his notebook. "Idealize, devalue, discard." Jasmin squinted. "In English?" Ty sighed. "First he makes her feel like gold. Then he makes her feel cheap. Then he leaves." He flipped a page. "It's a pattern. Narcissists do it without thinking."

Ella asked Leo a question during group work. He replied with a smirk and didn't answer. Then turned and asked someone else the exact same question, like it never happened. Ella blinked twice, lips parted as if she forgot how to close them. Nico felt it in his chest. That was the moment. The one where confusion takes root.

At the lockers, Ella finally asked, "Did I do something wrong?" Leo laughed. "Why would you think that?" His voice was all smooth edges again. "Don't be dramatic." She opened her locker with trembling hands. She didn't speak the rest of the day.

By the next morning, her usual wave was gone. Her smile was thin. She ate lunch with her head down, pushing carrot sticks around her tray. And when Leo walked by without stopping, she didn't even flinch. That was the part that hurt Nico the most—the part where Ella pretended it didn't hurt at all.

Jasmin leaned in during study hall. "I feel like we're watching her sink." Nico nodded slowly. "And she doesn't know she's underwater yet." Ty joined them a few minutes later, silent. He placed a folded paper on the table between them: "Don't fall for the light. Check the heat." Jasmin frowned. "What does that mean?" Ty replied, "Some things glow because they're fire. Not because they're safe."

That afternoon, Ella apologized to Leo for "being weird lately." He patted her on the head like a puppy and said, "It's fine, just don't be so clingy." Then walked off. No hug. No smile. Just instructions. And she thanked him.

Jasmin covered her mouth with her hand. "Did she just—?" Nico's jaw tightened. "Yeah. She thanked him." Ella didn't even realize that her glow had dimmed because he took the switch with him. She was still trying to light the room with the memory of what he gave her at the start. Leo never looked back. But that's what made it worse. He didn't have to. He knew she was following. Or at least waiting. And that was enough. By the end of the day, Ella wasn't glowing. She was surviving.

Ty didn't rush when he explained things. He waited until Nico and Jasmin were both sitting still, books closed, no distractions except the slow ticking of the library clock and the weight of what they'd just watched happen to Ella. She'd left the lunch table early again, barely speaking. Leo had said nothing cruel—but he didn't need to. He'd said nothing at all. That was the trick. The sudden quiet from someone who'd once filled your ears with sugar. It echoed worse than words.

"She's getting love-bombed," Ty said finally. His voice wasn't dramatic or sharp. Just level. Like he was pointing to a diagram in a textbook. "He did it to Nico before. He tried it on Jasmin. Now Ella." Jasmin furrowed her brow. "Love bombed?" The phrase sounded fake. Too silly for what they'd seen. But Ty nodded. "It's when someone throws compliments like confetti," he said, "but only so you'll clap louder. And when you stop clapping, they get cold. Fast."

Nico felt the truth settle in his ribs like bricks. He remembered how Leo used to call him "my guy" and share snacks he didn't even like. Until the day Nico didn't laugh at one of his jokes. After that, everything changed. "Love bombing's not about love," Ty continued. "It's about control. It feels good at first because it's fast and bright and full of nice things. But it's not real. It's a setup."

Jasmin looked down at her hands. "So, all those things he said to Ella—how she's funny, cool, awesome... that wasn't real?" Ty shrugged slightly. "Some of it might've been. But it wasn't safe. Real love doesn't punish you for slowing down. Leo's version does. And that makes it fake." They were quiet for a minute. The table felt heavier than before. Like the truth had weight they hadn't planned for.

"And the guilt?" Nico asked. "Where does that come in?" Ty opened his notebook, flipping to a page titled Guilt Mines. Beneath it were sketches of cartoon landmines with words written on them: "I thought you liked me." "You're too sensitive." "I did all this for you." "After everything I've done…" "He lays them like traps," Ty said. "Makes you feel bad for not being grateful. For needing space. For saying no."

Jasmin whispered, "So even the nice stuff is a trick?" Her voice was careful, not angry. She didn't want to believe it—but she was starting to. "It's not always a trick," Ty said. "But if it's tied to obedience? Then yeah—it's a leash." They all stared at the page. Leo had been praised for being polite. For helping Ella fit in. No one had seen the strings. Just the bows tied at the top. "Ella's stuck between the bomb and the guilt," Nico murmured. "If she says something, she looks ungrateful. If she doesn't, she keeps getting hurt."

"Exactly," Ty said. "And that's why it works. Because it feels kind. Until it doesn't." Later that afternoon, Ella was at her locker. Nico passed by and heard Leo telling her, "I guess I just care more than you do." His voice was soft. Hurt, even. Ella blinked fast and said, "That's not true." Leo sighed. "Then act like it." Nico turned the corner, pulse racing. It was the same tone Leo had used with him once. Back when Nico didn't answer fast enough. Back when he didn't say thank you for something he hadn't asked for.

"Guilt mines," Nico whispered to himself. "Right on schedule." In study hall, Jasmin passed Nico a note. Why doesn't anyone else see it? He stared at the paper for a full minute before writing back: Because love bombs are shiny. And people don't notice until the light burns. They didn't know if Ella would notice in time. But they knew the pattern now. They knew the way it began, the speed it moved, the silence it left behind. And they knew the next part would hurt more than anything so far. Because guilt makes you stay. Even when you want to run.

Jasmin had always liked being good at things. She didn't say it out loud, but she knew her answers were usually right. She got picked for class monitors, small reading groups, science partnerships. And at first, Leo's compliments felt like simple echoes of what teachers had already said. "You're sharp." "You always catch stuff." "Wish I could think that fast." But over time, those words stopped sounding like admiration and started sounding like instructions.

Leo smiled when she helped. That was the pattern. If she corrected his grammar before a presentation, he'd grin and say, "See? Told you she's a genius." If she handed him the right answer before he asked, he'd whisper, "My favourite brain." But when she didn't offer—when she paused, hesitated, or asked him for something—that smile didn't just disappear. It flipped.

It wasn't a frown with eyebrows. It was tighter than that. A pulled-lip half-grin that felt more like a dare. Like, Really? You're going to make me do this on my own? She caught it once during a group project when she said, "Maybe we should split the work evenly." He chuckled, loud enough for others to hear, and replied, "Didn't think you'd suddenly go lazy on me." Laughter followed. Not hers. Not really anyone's. But it was enough to keep her quiet.

Nico noticed it first during art. Jasmin had drawn something personal—bright watercolours shaped like questions. Leo leaned in and said, "That's cool... not really your usual thing though." It sounded neutral, maybe even honest. But Jasmin stiffened like someone had touched a bruise she didn't want anyone to see.

Ty called it praise-to-pressure. "It's when compliments get locked to performance," he told them. "Like, you're only special if you do what they like. If you mess with the formula, they get mean." Jasmin hadn't used those words yet. But she knew the feeling. It was the way Leo leaned closer when she nodded along, and leaned back the second she disagreed.

At lunch, Leo passed her a cookie. "For being awesome." She smiled, touched. Then, as a joke—though not really—he added, "But I might take it back if you keep disagreeing with me about the science lab." Her hand froze halfway to her tray. He laughed like it was funny. Everyone else laughed too. Jasmin bit into the cookie without tasting it.

Later, Nico asked her directly, "Do you feel like he's only nice when you're useful?" Jasmin hesitated. "I feel like I can't relax," she said. "Like if I don't say the right thing, everything will change." Ty nodded. "That's not friendship. That's a transaction." Jasmin's face tightened. "Then what was it before?"

They didn't answer right away. The library was quiet, and the weight of that question didn't deserve a rushed reply. When Jasmin told Leo she didn't want to work together on the next assignment, his smile vanished for a split second. Blink-and-miss-it. But she caught it. And so did Nico. Then came the pivot. Leo smiled wider. "Cool. I'll ask Ella. She's way more chill anyway."

Jasmin nodded, pretending it didn't sting. But it did. Not because she cared who he picked—but because the smile came with a consequence. He wasn't praising her now. He was punishing her. Politely. Quietly. Like someone flipping a light switch off and blaming the bulb for going dark. "I think he only sees value," she whispered to Ty later. "Not people." Ty looked up from his notes. "That's the cleanest way I've ever heard it," he said. "And the scariest."

That night, Jasmin lay awake thinking about all the moments Leo had been kind, generous, thoughtful. Then rewound them. And saw what they cost. Compliments followed by expectations. Smiles followed by silence. Praise that came with homework, and favours that left her feeling empty. She realized she hadn't felt comfortable around Leo for a long time. She'd just been surviving. Smiling back. Saying thank you for being boxed in. And once you notice the trap, pretending you're free feels worse than being caught.

It started as something small—barely noticeable, if you weren't looking for it. At first, it seemed like Leo was just being friendly, maybe even a little playful. But then Nico caught him doing it twice in the same day.

Once in history class, when Nico answered a question using the word "assume" in a very specific tone. Leo copied it half an hour later, voice pitched just the same, with a smirk that didn't reach his eyes. Later, Nico watched him flip his pen across his knuckles during lunch the exact way Jasmin did when she was bored. He didn't look at her when he did it—but he knew she'd see.

It wasn't mimicry like a joke. It wasn't teasing. It was deliberate. Smooth. Like he'd filed the edges off and was wearing someone else's habits like a coat. Nico felt a chill crawl up his arms. He didn't like it. He didn't like how his own phrases were coming back to him from Leo's mouth like borrowed breath.

Ty was the one who named it. They were in the library again—always the quiet places where truth got its voice back—and Nico leaned in and said, "I think Leo's... copying us." Ty didn't flinch. He just nodded once and said, "He's echoing." Nico waited. Ty kept writing for a few seconds, then finally looked up. "It's a way of pretending to be you, so you trust him faster. If someone moves like you, talks like you, laughs like you—you think they get you. You think they're safe."

Jasmin frowned. "But why?" Her voice was too sharp for the space they were in. She caught herself and softened. "Why bother copying someone just to be liked?" "Because it works," Ty said simply. "It's part of the performance. If you don't trust him fast enough, the act takes longer. He wants shortcuts."

Nico thought about it for a long moment. "Is that why I liked him in the beginning?" he asked. "Because he seemed like... familiar?" Ty nodded. "That's the trick." At recess, Leo complimented Nico's shoes. Then told someone else he was "totally into quiet thinkers, like Nico." Jasmin raised an eyebrow. "He's never said that before," she muttered. "Not until after Nico started getting attention from Miss Kara."

In science, Leo told Jasmin he liked how she gestured with her hands when she explained things. "It's like you're painting while you talk," he said, warm as sunlight. But Jasmin saw his fingers mimic hers a few minutes later—same rhythm, same movement, even the same way she paused. Her stomach turned. Ty whispered again. "Echoing is a kind of flattery. It's not about liking you. It's about learning your moves so he can use them."

That night, Nico looked through old photos, remembering how he used to smile at Leo like they were actually friends. The truth felt heavy now—he hadn't been liked for who he was. He'd been scanned. Imitated. Reflected back until he believed it. Jasmin spoke quietly the next morning. "He doesn't have a real version of himself, does he?" Ty nodded again. "He's whatever you want him to be. Until you want him to stop."

In art, Leo copied Ella's brushstroke pattern and said, "You're rubbing off on me." She laughed weakly. Jasmin narrowed her eyes. "He's building versions of us," she said under her breath. "And then blaming us for the blueprints."

Later, when Leo stood beside Nico and used the exact phrase Nico had used days earlier—"Let's not assume things yet"—Nico didn't reply. He turned away, jaw clenched. The echo no longer sounded like flattery. It sounded like theft. Because when someone copies who you are just to use it later, it's not admiration. It's invasion. And the worst part was—no one else noticed the sound of their own voice until it was too late.

It started with a question that wasn't really a question. "You'll finish the worksheet for both of us, right?" Leo said, eyes lazy with certainty, not concern. He said it the way people say "pass the salt"—with full expectation, like the answer was already decided. Jasmin looked down at her page. She had two lines left. His page was blank. The pencil in his hand hadn't moved in twenty minutes. She didn't answer right away.

He tilted his head. "You're the smart one," he added with that grin, the one shaped like a compliment but sharpened underneath. "C'mon. You're always done first anyway." She didn't look up. "I don't feel like it today." Leo blinked. The pause was longer than usual. He chuckled, a breath too short. "You okay?" he asked, like the problem was her tone, not his request.

Jasmin forced a shrug. "Just tired," she said softly, pretending to erase something. She didn't say it again, but it was there. A quiet no, written between the graphite. For the next ten minutes, Leo barely moved. Then he scooted his chair toward Ella instead. "You're good at this stuff, right?" he asked her, bright and airy. "Wanna be awesome and help a guy out?"

Ella nodded too fast. Jasmin saw it. Her stomach twisted. The praise had shifted direction. She'd felt it leave, like a flashlight beam turning away. Later, at lunch, Leo told a joke he'd told before. He looked straight at Jasmin when he said the punchline. She didn't laugh this time. She just blinked and sipped her juice. He didn't tell another one.

Nico saw the tension even before it broke the surface. "Did you just... tell him no?" he asked as they sat under the tree by the fence. He sounded more impressed than surprised. "Sort of," Jasmin said. "I didn't say the word. But I didn't say yes." "That counts," Ty nodded from behind his book. "He noticed. He won't say it, but he noticed." That night, Jasmin replayed it all in her head. The shrug. The lack of eye contact. The quiet refusal tucked between syllables. She didn't feel powerful. She felt small. But in that small space, something had changed. She'd bent a line that had never bent before.

In class the next day, Leo didn't sit next to her. He chose Ella again. Jasmin told herself it was fine. That it was even better this way. But part of her still missed the fake sun he used to shine on her. That was the part she didn't want to admit. Ty caught her staring and said, "It always hurts a little when you stop playing their game. Even if it was fake." Jasmin nodded slowly. "He didn't get mad, though."

"Not yet," Ty said. "First comes the test. Then comes the switch." Jasmin didn't understand what that meant—not fully—but she tucked it away like a note inside her shoe. Something she'd remember when the air changed again. At recess, Leo walked past her without saying a word.

His hand brushed Ella's backpack as he passed. He didn't smile. Neither did Jasmin. But her silence this time wasn't confusion. It was choice. Because saying no—even a small no—had done something. Not to him. To her. It reminded her that the space inside her belonged to her alone. And Leo? He'd just learned it wasn't his anymore.

Ella was late to the lunch table. Her steps were slower than usual, her tray wobbling in her hands. She sat down across from Jasmin, trying to smile like nothing happened, like she wasn't holding something in her throat that wanted to come out as a sound but couldn't. The others were already eating. Ty glanced up from his notebook. Nico paused mid-chew. Jasmin just waited. She always waited better than anyone else.

"I asked Leo why he didn't text me back," Ella said suddenly, too loud for how quiet she'd entered. "He said I was clingy." Her voice dropped like a rock thrown in water. The surface rippled, but not enough to make a splash. No one laughed. Not even her. But she smiled anyway. That strange kind of smile that looked like a sticker—there, but not stuck.

Ty tilted his head. "What did you say back?" Ella played with her spoon, swirling her peas in slow circles. "Nothing. He was with his friends. They laughed after. I think… I think he meant for me to hear it." Nico narrowed his eyes. "You think?" "I know," she whispered. The table stayed quiet, but it wasn't empty. Jasmin reached across slowly and nudged Ella's tray closer. "Eat," she said gently. "Don't let him make you starve."

Ella gave another smile. This one cracked at the corners. Her eyes shimmered, and for a moment, she blinked hard. Then looked up fast, like she could outrun it. Ty saw it—the tiny shift, the quick wipe with her sleeve, the way her head tilted just enough to hide the evidence. He didn't say anything out loud. But Nico caught his glance, the same way soldiers nod before they move.

Later, outside by the monkey bars, Ella stood with her back against the post, arms crossed, eyes scanning for someone who wouldn't come. Leo was laughing on the far side of the yard, loud enough to sound happy. Maybe even proud. Jasmin watched him, then turned back to Ella. "He's not a nice person," Jasmin said quietly. "Even when he acts like one." Ella shrugged. "He was nice at first."

"They always are," Ty said, appearing from behind the swing set. "That's how they work. They love-bomb you so hard, you forget what real love looks like." Ella sniffed, pretending it was from the wind. "But I didn't even ask for much. I just wanted him to talk like he used to." "Exactly," Ty said. "And now he's punishing you for remembering." Nico sat on the sand beside them, letting the silence hang. Then he pulled something from his pocket. A folded paper star—one of those origami ones he made when his hands needed a job. He handed it to Ella. "He doesn't get to take your sparkle away."

Ella stared at it. For a second, her lip wobbled. Then she breathed deep, and nodded once. She didn't cry—not really—but something inside her shifted. That night, Jasmin wrote in her journal. She didn't mention Leo by name. Just "someone." Someone who made you feel like you were lucky to be noticed. Until you noticed they'd stopped noticing you. Then made it your fault.

Ty stayed up too, rereading his psychology flash cards. He didn't do it for school. He did it for Ella. For Jasmin. For the ones who still smiled when it hurt. And Nico? He sat at his window, watching the streetlight buzz. He didn't write. He didn't speak. He just thought about the way Ella's tear almost didn't fall. Almost. But he saw it. And now it wouldn't be forgotten.

Jasmin sat on the edge of the blue bench near the schoolyard fence, her fingers fidgeting with the zipper of her jacket. The sun was too warm for October, but the breeze still whispered cold things across her neck. Across the blacktop, Leo stood in a circle of kids, his voice louder than anyone else's, laughing like a movie star. The kind of laugh that made people lean in, even when they didn't know the joke.

Beside her, Keira—a girl from their reading group—broke the silence. "I don't get it," she said, not looking up from her bag of apple slices. "Leo's never mean to me. He gave me one of his pens last week. The cool kind with the clicky top." Jasmin's zipper paused mid-track. She glanced sideways, watching Keira's calm expression, then returned her gaze to Leo. "Yeah. He can be like that."

"He's always smiling," Keira added. "Like, always. Maybe he's just joking when he says weird stuff. Some people don't know how to be funny the normal way." The words settled uneasily in Jasmin's stomach, like a bowl of soup gone cold. She didn't answer right away. Instead, she followed Leo's movements with her eyes—the way he clapped Max on the back, the way he looked at Ella when he thought no one else was watching. The smile was still there. But it didn't reach his eyes.

"I mean," Keira continued, crunching an apple slice, "some kids just take things the wrong way. My cousin gets teased all the time, but he's super sensitive. Maybe Ella's like that too." Jasmin folded her hands in her lap, her fingers gripping her thumbs. She wanted to say something. Wanted to explain. But the words curled like paper against heat. "Maybe," she mumbled, not because she believed it, but because she didn't want to argue.

But the knot in her stomach tightened. It always did when something didn't sit right. Back in class, Leo held the door open for three kids, bowed like a gentleman, and winked at Ms. Kara when she complimented his manners. Jasmin watched it all from her seat. Watched how Ella hesitated in the hallway, then slipped past quickly, avoiding his eyes.

When Ty sat beside her and unpacked his pencil case, he didn't look up. "Did Keira say it too?" he asked quietly. Jasmin nodded. He sighed. "They always do. Until it's their turn." Jasmin's mouth opened, but the words didn't come out.

Instead, she looked down at her math book, trying to focus on the numbers. But every digit looked like a question mark. At recess, Leo asked Keira if she wanted to share his cookies. She lit up like a firework. Jasmin watched the scene from the library window, arms crossed tight. It was like watching a play she'd already seen—the same lines, the same act, only with a different face.

"Do you think I'm overthinking it?" she asked Nico later. He didn't answer right away. He just took a sip from his water bottle, then said, "You ever smell something that seems fine until it lingers too long?" Jasmin frowned. "Like what?" "Like sour milk. You don't always know right away. But when it clings to your nose, you just… know." She thought about that all evening. About milk and smiles and the way kindness, when twisted, smelled off even when it looked clean. That night, she dreamt Leo was handing out cookies to everyone in class. Smiling big. And when it was her turn, the cookie crumbled in her hand. Hollow. Dry. Empty inside. She woke up with her heart racing. And the knot still there.

Ty sat with his back against the rough brick wall beside the gym doors, legs stretched out, one sneaker tapping the edge of the faded hopscotch grid. His voice wasn't loud, but Jasmin could hear every word, like the air itself leaned in to catch them. Nico sat cross-legged nearby, his arms draped over his knees, watching the way Ty picked at a frayed thread in his hoodie sleeve without ever looking up.

"It's not about being kind," Ty said finally, "it's about being in charge." Jasmin blinked, squinting toward the soccer field where Leo shouted instructions like he was the coach. "But he's not in charge," she whispered, almost to herself. Ty smiled, but it wasn't the happy kind. "He is if everyone acts like he is."

The words hit hard. Jasmin shifted her weight and hugged her knees. She remembered when Leo gave her that glitter pen last month—just because, he said. But when she forgot to bring it one day, he made a joke in front of three kids about how "some people can't keep track of anything special." She'd laughed with them, back then. But it hadn't felt like a joke. Not really. "Fake kind of nice," Nico added, quietly. "The kind that feels heavy."

"Yeah," Ty nodded. "The kind that makes you say thank you even when you didn't want what they gave you." Jasmin opened her mouth, then shut it again. It made too much sense. Leo had a way of making you feel like you owed him something. Even smiles. Especially smiles. "Real kindness," Ty said, now pulling the string harder, "doesn't expect a payment."

Jasmin's fingers gripped the hem of her shirt. She thought about all the times Leo held the door and waited just a beat too long for a thank you. Or offered snacks only when the teachers were watching. Or helped with homework, then bragged about it the next day like it was a medal.

"It's a power thing," Ty said. "Smiles don't always mean safe." The gym bell rang in the distance, but none of them moved. Jasmin stared at the sky. Clouds passed like secrets. The kind people didn't want to say out loud but knew were there. "He smiled at Ella when he told her she was 'too sensitive,'" Jasmin said. "Like... like it made her the problem."

Ty nodded. "That's the mask part. You push someone just enough, then when they push back, you make it seem like they're the ones being mean." "And if they don't push back?" Nico asked. "They disappear inside themselves," Ty answered. "Like Ella." The silence after that wasn't empty. It was full of every moment they hadn't noticed before. Every time they'd laughed too quick, agreed too easily, walked away too silently. "He ever smile at you like that?" Jasmin asked Ty.

"Once," Ty said. "When I got picked for art club and he didn't. Said I 'must've known the teacher's secret favourite colour.'" His voice didn't change, but something in his eyes did. "It wasn't a compliment." Jasmin's mouth was dry. The breeze tickled her ankles, but she didn't move. She remembered how Ella looked the other day when she sat down at lunch and Leo got up. No words. Just a shrug and that tight, empty grin. And Ella's face? Like she'd been unplugged.

"We see it now," Nico said. "Yeah," Jasmin whispered. "But how do we show the others?" Ty stood, brushing the dust from his jeans. "We don't. Not all at once. We just stop giving him what he wants." "Which is?" Jasmin asked. "Control," Ty said. "Even when he wraps it in a smile." Jasmin stood beside him. Nico followed. The three of them didn't speak as they walked back to class, but something had shifted. A string had snapped. A door had creaked open. And behind that smile Leo wore like a badge, they'd seen the handle he was turning all along.

It sparkled when she moved her wrist. Soft lilac beads woven between thin silver threads, the kind of bracelet that looked like it came from a grown-up store, not one of those vending machines near the school canteen. Ella had worn it every day since Leo gave it to her. At first, everyone said it looked beautiful. So did she—smiling, almost blushing, like the bracelet made her lighter. But that didn't last.

Jasmin noticed it first during science. Ella kept tugging her sleeve down to hide the bracelet. Not because it was cold. Just... something else. Nico saw it, too. Ella used to swing her wrist so it would catch the light. Now she sat stiff. Still. Like her wrist didn't belong to her anymore. Leo sat behind her, whispering. "You'd better wear it tomorrow," he said once, loud enough that Nico could hear. Ella didn't answer. Her pencil snapped in half.

In the hallway, Leo bragged. "She's wearing my bracelet," he told Owen. "That means she's mine." He laughed like it was a joke. But even Owen didn't laugh back. Not really. Ty explained it to Jasmin later, sitting on the library floor with their backs against the atlas shelf. "Gifts that come with chains," he said. "They're not gifts. They're traps." "But she didn't ask for it," Jasmin said. "It was a surprise."

Ty shrugged. "So was the leash." Nico sat nearby, thumbing through an old dictionary. He didn't like Leo's tone lately. It was changing—less playful, more proud. Like he'd built something. Like he owned something. The bracelet wasn't just jewellery anymore. It became a map of Ella's silence. Leo started talking louder when she was near. Called her "his girl." Winked at her when she was reading. Once, when she didn't answer a question in class, he whispered, "Guess the bracelet didn't make you smart." Jasmin flinched. Ella didn't even blink.

"You ever try to give it back?" Ty asked her gently one day, behind the bleachers. Ella looked at him like he'd spoken another language. "He said I'd embarrass him," she whispered. Jasmin stared at her. "That's not a gift," she said. "That's a collar." Ella's lip trembled, but she didn't cry. She lifted her wrist and slowly turned it, watching the way the beads caught the sun. "I used to like it," she said. "Now it just feels like something I have to wear."

Later that week, during art, Leo passed a note to Ella. She didn't read it. She just pushed it aside. Jasmin watched. So did Nico. Leo's smile faltered for a second. Just a second. But it was enough. In the locker room, Ty said something Jasmin couldn't forget. "If a gift costs your voice," he said, "then it's not a gift. It's a price tag." Ella didn't wear the bracelet the next day.

Leo noticed. He didn't say anything in class. But during lunch, he knocked her tray onto the floor. "Oops," he said, smirking. "Should've watched where you were going." Ella knelt to pick up the pieces. Jasmin knelt too. So did Nico. Ty didn't. He stood up and stared straight at Leo. "You dropped something," Ty said. Leo narrowed his eyes. "What?" Ty didn't answer. Just picked up the bracelet from the floor—where Ella had let it fall—and set it on the edge of the table. It glinted for a moment in the light. Then it was gone.

The library smelled like warm paper and dust. That smell you could almost see, like floating breadcrumbs in the air. Jasmin liked it better than the playground lately. Books didn't whisper behind your back or make you feel small when you were quiet. Books stayed where they were put and never changed their faces when no one else was watching. Nico sat curled up in the corner chair with his knees drawn up, a thick book on emotional survival opened across his thighs. Ty was lying on his back beneath the window, chewing the cord of his hoodie like he always did when he was thinking hard.

Jasmin stood in the aisle between them, pretending to scan a shelf of biographies she'd never read. She wasn't really reading anything. She was trying to line up the words in her mouth the way they made sense in her head. But they wouldn't go straight. They kept curling and twisting, like the feeling in her stomach every time Leo's voice got soft.

"He's not just teasing," she said. The words felt heavy. Not big. Not smart. Just heavy. Ty looked up first. Nico didn't move. Jasmin bit the inside of her cheek and looked down at her shoes. "I think…" she started, then stopped. Her throat itched. "I think he's… twisting things. Not just playing around." Ty blinked slowly. Then sat up. "I know teasing," Jasmin said, her voice steadier now. "My brother does it. He hides my socks. He pulls my braid and runs. But Leo… Leo gives you something just so he can take it back."

Nico didn't speak, but his fingers tightened around the pages in his lap. "He says things that sound nice," she continued, "but they don't feel nice. They feel like… like glue." Her hands made a shape in the air. "You smile when he says them. But then you realize you're stuck." Ty nodded once. He didn't say anything yet, just gave her space to say more. That was something he always did right—he didn't jump in too soon. "And when you stop smiling," Jasmin whispered, "he punishes you."

Nico finally looked up. "How?" Jasmin sat down cross-legged on the carpet. "He calls you moody. Says you're being weird. Then he tells everyone you're overreacting." Her voice cracked. "And maybe I believed him." "Maybe?" Ty asked. Jasmin shook her head. "No. I don't anymore." The three of them sat in that triangle of sunlight. No adults. No noise. Just the soft hum of the school's air system and the crackling of courage as it warmed up inside Jasmin's chest.

"It's like he wants everyone around him to feel small so he can feel big," she said. "That's not teasing," Ty murmured. "That's control." "I hate that word," Jasmin said. "Control?" Nico asked. "No," she said. "Teasing. Because that's what they always say it is. Like it's harmless. Like we're just being sensitive." "Well," Ty said carefully, "maybe being sensitive is how we survive." That made Jasmin blink. "What do you mean?"

"If you can feel it," Ty said, "you can name it. If you can name it, you can stop it." Nico shifted in his seat. "Or at least not let it shape you." They sat in silence again. Not the uncomfortable kind. The kind that made room. "You were brave to say it out loud," Ty told her. "I didn't feel brave," Jasmin said. "I felt like I was going to throw up." "That's how most bravery feels," Nico muttered, turning a page.

The bell rang, far away like an echo through walls. They didn't move right away. Jasmin watched the dust dance in the light, and for the first time in weeks, she didn't feel like it was her fault. She wasn't confused anymore. Just angry. And awake. "I think I need to write it down," she said. "Everything he's said. Everything that didn't sit right." Ty nodded. "That's how we keep the story straight." "I'll help," Nico said softly. Jasmin smiled. It wasn't a big smile. But it was real. And that made it bigger than it looked.

The note slid across the desk like a feather on the edge of a storm. Jasmin barely saw it until it bumped her pencil case. Ella's handwriting was small and shaky, the kind that tried not to take up space. It was folded twice, crisp but careful, not crumpled or panicked. That made it worse somehow. Like she'd had time to think about the words before writing them down. Like she had planned the sadness in advance.

Jasmin looked over without moving her head. Ella was staring straight at the board, not at her. Her hands were in her lap, fidgeting with the hem of her sleeve. There was no smile on her face, but there wasn't a frown either. Just that in-between expression kids wear when they're trying to look invisible.

Slowly, Jasmin opened the note. He said I ruin things. But I don't even know what I did. Just that. Thirteen words. Each one tiny and sharp like a splinter. Jasmin blinked. Her throat tightened. She folded the paper back the exact way she found it—corner to corner, edge to edge. But her hands were shaking.

The teacher's voice at the front of the room became a blur. Something about fractions or field trips. It didn't matter. There was only the note now. Jasmin kept it under her palm like it might fly away or scream if she let it go. She didn't look at Ella again. Not yet. It was the kind of message that stayed under your skin.

She remembered what Ty had said—that when someone gives you something beautiful and then punishes you for it, it's not love. It's leverage. She remembered the library. The air thick with dust and truth. She remembered Nico's quiet eyes and the word control. And now, here it was. In a ten-word confession scribbled in pencil, passed in silence. A cry without volume.

At recess, she didn't run to the swings like usual. She waited near the water fountain until Ella came out. The younger kids dashed around them like bees, all elbows and lunch crumbs. Jasmin stepped in beside her, not too close. Just near enough to make sure Leo didn't walk up first.

"You okay?" she asked without looking. Ella shrugged. "I'm fine." That answer again. The one that kids give when they mean I'm tired of explaining. "I read it," Jasmin said. Ella flinched like she'd been caught. "You didn't do anything wrong," Jasmin whispered. Ella's eyes flicked sideways. "Then why do I feel like I did?"

Because he made it feel that way. That's what Jasmin wanted to say. But it was hard to put into words without sounding like an adult. Instead, she said something else. Something that felt more like a friend talking. "He says stuff that feels true even when it isn't." Ella didn't answer, but her eyes blinked slow, like she was chewing on that.

"I can't prove it," Jasmin went on, "but I think he does it on purpose." Ella looked down. "What if it's not just him?" Jasmin frowned. "What do you mean?" Ella's voice dropped low. "What if everyone ends up being like that? Smiles that lie. Gifts with traps. Nice words that turn mean later." The thought settled between them like a shadow with no shape. "They don't," Jasmin said finally. "Ty's not. Nico's not. I'm not."

"But how do you know?" Ella asked. "Because we're here," Jasmin said. "Listening. And scared too. And that means something." Ella breathed out, like a balloon with a slow leak. Then she reached into her pocket and handed Jasmin the note again. "Keep it," she said. "I don't want to look at it anymore." Jasmin took it. She didn't ask why. Some truths weren't meant to be carried by one person alone.

The bell rang with its usual sharpness, and the hallway spilled over with backpacks, sneakers, and noise. Nico kept close to the lockers, eyes moving, ears tuned not to the shouts and slams, but to the quiet spaces between them. He'd started doing that lately—watching where no one else looked, listening for the truths buried under laughter and footsteps. That's when he saw it happen.

Ella was coming out of science, arms full of books that didn't fit in her bag. She moved carefully, chin tucked, one foot dodging the river of kids coming the other way. Leo wasn't looking. Or maybe he was. He turned just enough to meet her shoulder with his. Her books dropped like dominoes across the linoleum. The hallway didn't slow down. Nobody cared.

"Sorry," Ella mumbled, bending to gather her books. Leo didn't bend. He didn't even pause. He rolled his eyes so wide that three kids nearby saw it and smirked. "Maybe watch where you're going next time," he said flatly. It wasn't the words. Nico had heard worse. It was how he said them—like Ella wasn't even worth getting annoyed about. Just an interruption. Just a bump in the hallway.

Then came the smile. It was quick. Just one side of Leo's mouth tilted up. Not friendly. Not warm. It was the kind of smile that didn't touch the eyes. The kind that dared anyone to say it was mean, because technically it wasn't. It was invisible cruelty, worn like a badge. Nico stood a few lockers away. He didn't move. Didn't flinch. He just watched.

Ella gathered her books like someone repacking shame. She didn't say another word. She didn't cry either. She just walked away, slower than before, but without looking back. Her steps were careful now, like she didn't trust the ground. Leo turned toward the water fountain. Someone clapped him on the shoulder, laughing about something else. He laughed too, the smile gone, like it never existed. But Nico had seen it. And that was enough.

That moment stayed with him. It wasn't the first time Leo had smiled like that, and it wouldn't be the last. But it was the first time Nico saw it land. Saw the bruise it left, even if no one else did. Some wounds weren't purple. They were quiet. At lunch, Nico didn't bring it up. Neither did Ella. But Jasmin glanced from one to the other and said, "I heard what he said." "He didn't yell," Ella replied, "so I guess it's not bullying." "It doesn't have to be loud to hurt," Nico said.

Ella looked at him. Her eyes were tired, but her voice held curiosity. "Then how do you know when it's real?" "You just... feel it," he said. "Like a tug in your chest. Or like something inside you shrinks when they talk." Ty, who had been silent, added quietly, "And the real kind of nice doesn't leave bruises, even the invisible kind." Nobody said anything after that. But something shifted between them. A small pact, unspoken. Nico knew they were beginning to understand that not all meanness roared—and not every hallway fight left a mark you could see.

The schoolyard felt colder than usual, though the sun was out and the sky held no clouds. Jasmin sat on the far edge of the wooden bench near the fence, knees pulled in close, chin resting on them.

Her fingers traced lazy shapes in the dirt with a broken twig she'd found on the way to recess. She hadn't spoken much since morning, not even when Ella gave her half a cookie at snack time, not even when Nico tried to tell a joke about spelling tests and pigeons. The smile wouldn't come.

Ty saw her first. He didn't call out, didn't wave like most kids would. He just walked past her once, silent. Then again. On the third pass, he slowed. His hand brushed the fence post beside her. He tapped it twice, then once. Tap-tap. Pause. Tap. Nothing fancy. Not a big show. Just sound.

Jasmin lifted her head. She blinked. Her eyes followed the rhythm. Tap-tap. Pause. Tap. She didn't know what it meant, not really. But it felt like something old. Like the way kids nod when they understand each other without talking. Like how shadows touch but don't speak. Ty sat at the end of the bench, not beside her, not too close. He didn't look directly at her. Just kept his eyes on the yard, on Leo, who was laughing with a group near the tetherball pole. "That's the code," Ty said, soft and steady. "Shadow Warrior signal. It means, 'I see it too.'"

Jasmin didn't answer right away. Her twig stopped moving. "You made that up just now?" He shrugged. "Maybe. Maybe not." She looked down at her knees. "I feel like I'm losing my mind. Like, maybe I'm just sensitive. Like it's not even that big of a deal." "It is," Ty said. "You're not imagining it. They make you feel like it's small so they can stay big."

She nodded, but slowly, like her head was tired of moving. "But if I say something…" "They say you're dramatic." "If I don't say something…" "They win." Silence fell again, thick but not empty. Kids shouted in the distance. A ball bounced. A whistle blew. The world kept going. But on that bench, something had paused. Ty leaned closer, not touching her, just letting his voice drop into the small space between them. "There are people who see everything, Jasmin. Who know what lies look like when they're dressed as smiles. They don't need to fight in loud ways. They just make truth heavier. So it doesn't float away."

She stared ahead. "You mean like… secret good guys?" "I mean like us." Her throat tightened. "But we're just kids." "Exactly. Nobody expects us. That's the best part." She finally looked at him, really looked. "So what now?" He smiled—but not Leo's smile. Ty's smile was quiet, sideways, honest. He tapped the fence again. Tap-tap. Pause. Tap. "You learn the signs. You don't tell everyone what you know. You watch, you wait. And when someone's falling… you give the signal."

Jasmin's fingers returned to the twig, drawing a circle. Then another. Her shoulders eased a little. "I thought I was alone." "You were," Ty said. "Until now." The bell rang. Children scattered like marbles. Jasmin stood up slowly, brushing off her jeans. As they walked back together, neither of them said the word gaslighting. They didn't need to. That wasn't the Shadow Warrior way. The truth didn't always have to shout. Sometimes, it only had to nod.

The last period of the day moved like syrup. Not sweet syrup—slow, sticky, and hard to get through. The kind that clings even when you're trying to wash it off. Jasmin stared at the clock, its second hand clicking in perfect rhythm, while her pencil rested untouched on the corner of her desk. She wasn't thinking about numbers or maps. She was thinking about the look in Ella's eyes during lunch. And the absence of Leo beside her.

When the bell finally rang, the room burst open like it always did. Kids flew into the hallway, backpacks swinging, voices rising in waves. Jasmin moved slower. She packed her things carefully, not out of neatness but because her hands weren't sure what they wanted to do next.

By the time she stepped into the corridor, the hallway had thinned. She expected to walk alone, to find her way out in silence. But Ella was there—just outside the door, leaning against the wall, arms crossed but not tightly. She wasn't looking around. She was waiting. Their eyes met. Neither of them smiled. Jasmin didn't say anything. She didn't need to. She just shifted her bag to her left shoulder, leaving space on her right.

Ella stepped forward and fell into step beside her. Not behind. Not ahead. Just beside. They walked together down the stairs, shoes scuffing lightly against the concrete. At the front doors, Leo stood near the bench, cracking jokes with two other boys. He laughed like nothing had changed, like Ella hadn't vanished from his orbit. She didn't glance at him. She didn't wave. She didn't wince. And she didn't smile.

Instead, Ella kept walking. Quietly. Like a ghost who'd come back not to haunt, but to reclaim her name. Outside, the sky had turned soft with evening light. The playground shimmered with leftover warmth, the shadows stretching longer now. Nico waved from the swings. Ty sat under the tree with a notebook open, sketching something small and careful. Jasmin and Ella crossed the field without speaking. Then Jasmin pointed to the tree. Ella nodded.

They joined Ty in the shade. Nico dropped from the swing and came running, sneakers kicking up dust. Nobody asked why Ella had switched sides. Nobody asked what Leo said last. None of them needed to. Because sometimes, the truth is what doesn't happen. Ella didn't flinch when someone called her name. She didn't fold her arms when the others laughed. She didn't pretend to be okay. She just sat. And that was the bravest thing any of them had seen all week.

Ty passed her a leaf he'd been pressing between notebook pages. She held it like it might break. Jasmin offered her a piece of gum from her pocket—chewed through the wrapper from being carried too long. Ella took it anyway. Nico sat cross-legged and whispered, "He's not the story anymore." Ella looked at him, unsure. "You are," Jasmin said. "If you want to be." And Ella didn't smile. But she nodded. And that—finally—was enough.

CHAPTER 3: THE RULES ALWAYS CHANGE

It always started the same way—with a smile. Not the kind that spreads gently like sunlight, but the flash of something controlled, something sharpened. Leo's smile changed depending on who was watching. When it was Nico, last week, he smiled like he'd discovered treasure. Called him "brainiac" in front of everyone, laughed at his jokes before they were even funny. Sat beside him in class, copied his math answers, shared gum during art. Then Monday came. That smile didn't just fade. It vanished. Replaced by a shrug and a new name—one he gave to Ty this time. Just like that, Nico wasn't special anymore. He was extra. Forgotten. A bookmark left in the wrong chapter.

At recess, it was the same. Leo had a way of walking that told everyone where the attention should go. His eyes scanned like a spotlight. If you got caught in it, you mattered. For a while. Ty was in it now. Nico watched from the edge of the basketball court as Leo leaned close to Ty, whispering something that made him grin. But it wasn't the grin that worried Nico—it was the pause afterward. The pause where Leo glanced backward, directly at him, and then turned his body just slightly away. Enough to send a message. You're not in this.

Jasmin didn't say anything until lunch. She'd seen it too, but she let Nico bring it up first. He didn't. Instead, he chewed slowly, one bite at a time, eyes low. Every now and then, he looked toward Leo, who now sat beside Ella and Ty, telling some story with wide hands and perfect timing. The kind of story that made the table lean in. Nico had told stories like that last week. He hadn't changed. But the rules had. "Did you notice?" Jasmin asked finally, her voice soft so only he could hear.

Nico nodded once, just enough. "Yeah." "He didn't even say hi this morning." "I know." "And yesterday, he called you his best friend." Nico's throat tightened. He took a sip of his juice, hoping it would wash away the feeling. It didn't. "I guess I got replaced." "That's not how friends work," she said.

He wished she was right. But she hadn't been Leo's favourite yet. She didn't know how fast it happened. Or how fast it ended. Being Leo's favourite wasn't about who you were. It was about how easy you made him look good. The moment you stopped making him shine, you stopped being worth his light.

In gym, it happened again. They were picking teams. Leo was team captain. His eyes passed right over Nico like he wasn't even standing there. Picked Ty first. Then Ella. Then two kids he barely spoke to. Nico stood until the only two left were him and Max—the kid who still forgot which shoe went on which foot. Leo glanced at the teacher, then said, "I'll take Max." Just loud enough. Just cruel enough. And when Nico joined the other team by default, Leo didn't even smirk. He just turned away.

It wasn't that Nico needed to be picked first. It wasn't about winning. It was about knowing that everything could shift without warning, and you'd never be told why. That you could wake up one day and be invisible, and it wouldn't even be called punishment. It would be called normal.

After class, Ty walked with him partway down the hall. He didn't say sorry. He didn't pretend it hadn't happened. He just bumped Nico's shoulder lightly and said, "It's your turn out. Mine was last month. You'll be back in rotation soon." "That's not comforting," Nico said. "It's not meant to be. It's just true."

Nico didn't want that kind of truth. The kind that made your stomach feel like it was chewing itself. He wanted the kind of truth that stayed still, that didn't flip like a card in a rigged game. But he knew better now. Leo's game had rules that only he could rewrite. Everyone else was just a piece.

At home that night, Nico didn't do his homework right away. He sat on the floor of his bedroom, staring at his backpack like it had the answers tucked inside. But nothing came out of it but silence. He thought about the way Leo laughed at Ty's joke during math. The same joke Nico had told last week. Word for word. Back then, Leo had yawned. Today, he'd nearly fallen off his chair laughing. "You didn't do anything wrong," Nico whispered out loud, like saying it could make it stick. But even as the words left his lips, they floated back at him like ghosts. He wasn't sure if he believed it.

He wrote it down instead. One sentence. Over and over. "I didn't do anything wrong." It looked better on paper than it sounded in his head. Stronger. Less wobbly. Later that night, his phone buzzed. It was a message from Jasmin. Just two words. Still here. He stared at the screen a long time. Then typed back. Thanks. Sometimes, the difference between breaking and bending is knowing someone's still looking at you when everyone else turns away. Leo might play favourites. But favourites fade. Real friends don't.

Jasmin didn't know when it began. That was the strange part. One minute, Leo was asking her to sit next to him at lunch, helping her sharpen her pencil in the library, waving her into his group projects like she belonged there. Then, like the snap of a twig in a quiet forest, it stopped. There was no fight. No words. No dramatic turn. Just a gap. A silence. The kind you don't hear until it's sitting next to you at your desk, pretending it was always there.

It wasn't the kind of silence that meant peace. It was the kind that made her wonder if she had said something wrong, laughed at the wrong time, worn the wrong hair clip. The worst part was that Leo never looked angry. He just looked past her. Like her name had been erased from his chalkboard and he didn't even notice it was missing. That stung more than any insult could've. An insult would mean she still mattered. This meant she didn't.

She watched the switch happen in real time during music class. Leo used to pass her the tambourine with a grin, like she was in on the joke. Today, he gave it to Ella without blinking. Jasmin hadn't even finished raising her hand. And Ella, wide-eyed and surprised, didn't say no. Of course she didn't. Why would she? Leo was smiling at her now. The same smile Jasmin used to get when he wanted something. It always meant something was coming.

Jasmin sat down without a sound. She held her breath without realizing she was doing it, as if that might hold in the sharp feeling rising behind her ribs. Ty was watching. She saw him across the room, fidgeting with a rubber band wrapped around his fingers, eyes flicking between Leo and her. He didn't smile. He didn't look away either.

That afternoon, Jasmin walked home slower than usual. She didn't tell Nico what happened. Not yet. It wasn't big enough, she told herself. Just a weird day. A nothing day. But the thoughts kept knotting in her chest—tight, tight, tighter. Why was it always Leo who got to decide when people mattered and when they didn't? Why did it feel like her name had become a password she forgot?

At dinner, her mum asked how school was. Jasmin said "fine." She pushed her rice around the plate and listened to the clock tick. It didn't feel fine. It felt like sitting in a room with the heat turned off, knowing no one else noticed. Her mum smiled and changed the subject. Jasmin didn't bring it up again.

The next day, the silence followed her in. It walked behind her like a ghost in bright daylight. In the hallway, Leo laughed at something Ella said. He didn't even glance at Jasmin. When she sat at her usual spot during lunch, the conversation moved around her like water around a rock. Not unkind. Just... not there. Not for her. That was worse somehow. She wasn't being bullied. She was being skipped.

She told herself to say something. But to who? To Leo? He'd just blink. Say, "What are you talking about?" Maybe he'd laugh. Maybe he'd call her sensitive. That was the trick of it. When the rules change silently, you can't point to them. There's no evidence. Just feelings. And feelings, Leo always said, were "drama."

Jasmin sat on the library floor beside the non-fiction shelf and opened a book she didn't care about. Nico slid in next to her a minute later. He didn't ask. He didn't talk. He just pulled a second book from the shelf and sat. That helped more than anything else could have. Because silence has two shapes. One is cold. One is kind. Nico's was kind.

"I think I got rotated out," Jasmin whispered. "Yeah. Me too. Last week." She nodded, her throat thick. "Does it stop?" "No," Nico said, honest. "But you stop caring as much." "How?" "You find people who don't rotate." That night, Jasmin took out her notebook and wrote the word "invisible" at the top. Then she crossed it out. Wrote "silent." Crossed it out too. Finally, she wrote: Not wrong. Just ignored.

It sat on the page like a weight. Heavy. Real. But hers. She tucked the notebook under her pillow and laid down. The silence didn't go away. But now it had a name. And sometimes, naming something is the first way to beat it.

The first time Leo made the joke, it sounded harmless. It came with a smirk and a sideways glance, loud enough to get a chuckle from the boys near the lockers, soft enough to blur the edge of what he actually said. "Ella's got enough questions to power a windmill," he joked, as she bent over her notebook, asking Nico something about the assignment. Everyone laughed—everyone except Ella, who gave a small smile that didn't reach her eyes and closed her book quietly.

Later, Leo said he was just kidding. "You take everything so serious," he muttered when Nico caught up to him in the hallway. He said it like a sigh, like he was the one burdened by everyone else's inability to laugh. It wasn't the words that hit hardest—it was the shrug. The way he brushed it off like a leaf on his shoulder, as though Ella's face hadn't changed at all, hadn't flushed and tightened when she heard it. Like none of it had happened.

By the third time, the jokes got sharper. "Careful," he said during group work. "Ella might cry if you don't agree with her." Another chuckle, another round of eyes avoiding hers. Jasmin frowned, but didn't speak. Ella's hands froze mid-pencil stroke. Leo noticed and leaned back in his chair, grinning like he was proud of something. When Nico looked at Jasmin, he could tell she was watching too. She felt it now, the sting she'd once brushed aside. It was real this time. Too real to ignore.

During lunch, Nico brought it up. Quietly, carefully, with the kind of voice that didn't want to scare anyone away. "Do you think Leo's jokes are kind of... not really jokes?" he asked, folding and unfolding the corner of his napkin. Ella didn't respond at first. Jasmin blinked slowly, then said, "They're jokes. But they don't feel funny." Ella nodded, just once.

"He hides behind them," Nico said. "That way, if you say it hurt, he says you're overreacting. And if you laugh, he thinks you're fine with it. Either way, he gets to keep doing it."

Ella looked down at her tray. Her lunch hadn't been touched. "It's like I'm part of the joke," she said. "But not on purpose."

That afternoon in the library, Nico stayed behind after the bell. The librarian, Mr. Clarke, was straightening the returned books cart and humming something old and slow. "Excuse me?" Nico asked, soft but steady. Mr. Clarke looked up, one brow raised. "Could I tell you something?" Nico asked. "It's not about a book."

He told him everything. Not every detail—just enough. Enough for Mr. Clarke to understand that Leo had a way of turning jokes into thorns. That Ella wasn't laughing. That Jasmin wasn't either. That maybe Leo wasn't teasing—maybe he was testing. And failing wasn't funny.

Mr. Clarke didn't laugh or wave it off. He didn't call it drama or say kids will be kids. He listened. When Nico finished, he nodded once. "Thank you for telling me," he said. "I'll keep an eye on it." Then he looked Nico in the eye. "You were right to say something."

The next morning, Ms. Henley, their homeroom teacher, asked Nico to stay after class. "I just wanted you to know," she said gently, "Mr. Clarke spoke with me. About Leo. I'll keep an eye too." She didn't ask Nico to repeat the story. She didn't make it a scene. Just a promise. "Thank you," she said. "It helps."

It didn't fix everything. Leo still joked. Still smiled. Still called Ella "Princess Questions" in front of the others. But now, when it happened, Mr. Clarke's eyes would flick from the checkout desk. Ms. Henley would pause just slightly when walking past. They were watching. That mattered more than anyone expected.

Nico told Jasmin later, after school. She looked surprised. "They believed you?" "They didn't brush it off," Nico said. "That's close enough." Jasmin exhaled slowly, like she'd been holding her breath without realizing it. "I didn't think they would," she admitted. "I thought they'd say we're just being sensitive." "Maybe they would've," Nico said. "If I'd gone alone. But we all saw it."

That night, Ella wrote something in her planner and left the page open when Jasmin sat beside her. In tiny, careful letters, she'd written: It's not my job to laugh when it hurts. Jasmin didn't say anything. She just underlined it twice and closed the planner gently. The next time Leo made a joke, Ella didn't laugh. She didn't frown either. She just looked at him like he was a riddle missing half the pieces. Jasmin caught Nico's eye. No one said a word. But the air felt different. Not clean yet. But not poisoned either.

It was during spelling review when Ty first said it out loud. Nico had asked what "shifting standards" meant, since it came up in their assigned reading. Most of the kids had just shrugged, but Ty turned in his seat with a quiet click of understanding in his eyes. "That's when the rules change all the time," he said. "Like when someone says you did great, then the next day they say it wasn't good enough after all." Jasmin looked up from her notes. She didn't say anything, but the way she froze made Nico look at her instead of Ty.

"You mean like Leo?" Nico asked. Ty nodded just once, like he hadn't expected anyone to catch that. "Yeah," he said. "With Leo, the goalposts move. First, he says you're smart when you help him. Then he says you're bossy when you have your own ideas. It's not about what you do. It's about what makes him feel bigger."

They'd heard adults say it differently—phrases like "inconsistent expectations" or "emotional manipulation"—but those words never really landed. This did. This felt like something Nico could hold in his hands. Jasmin finally spoke. "He told Ella she asked good questions. Then said she talks too much." She blinked hard. "He said I was strong for standing up for myself. Then told me I was dramatic when I disagreed with him."

Ty nodded again. "That's how they make you chase it," he said. "The 'right way' is always just a little bit different every day. So you keep trying to guess it. And while you're guessing, they're winning."

Nico felt that land in his stomach. Not like a punch—more like a stone quietly added to the ones already sitting there. Heavy. Familiar. "That's why I feel tired around him," he said. "Even when he's not doing anything mean. It's like I'm bracing for it." "You're trying to stay ahead of it," Ty said. "But you can't. That's the trap."

At recess, Jasmin watched from the swings as Leo talked with Ella by the fence. Yesterday, he'd said she was brave for standing up to him when he ignored her. Today, he told her she was overreacting. "You're too sensitive," he said just loud enough to carry. "You always think someone's being mean. Maybe you're just guilty about something." Ella had looked down at her shoes. Nico had seen it from across the yard. That frozen, hunted look.

Jasmin whispered to herself, "Goalposts." It made the pieces click. "He makes you feel like you're always behind." Later in the hallway, Ty handed Nico a small slip of paper folded three times. "Wrote it down," he said, as if explaining himself. Nico opened it and read:

Goalpost Game – Warning Signs

Praise that doesn't last

Rules that only apply sometimes

You always feel like you're wrong

They act like it's your fault you don't understand

You never know where you stand

Nico tucked the paper in his planner, right next to his math test schedule. "I want to give this to Ella," he said. Ty shrugged. "Sure. But maybe wait until she sees it too. People don't always believe it when they're still in it."

That afternoon, Leo asked Jasmin if she was mad at him. "You've been quiet," he said. "We're still cool, right?" Jasmin hesitated. She didn't know what to say. If she said yes, she'd feel fake. If she said no, he'd say she was being dramatic again. So she just shrugged. Leo laughed. "See? Girls are so confusing."

She smiled politely. That tiny, hollow smile Nico was starting to recognize. The one that says, I see you, but I'm not ready to fight you. Yet. At the back of the class, Ty tapped Nico's elbow and whispered, "See how he changed the question? It's not about what he did. It's about how you feel. And if you feel weird, now you're the problem." Nico shivered. Not from cold. From clarity.

That night, Nico opened his dictionary and looked up "manipulate." The second meaning said: To control or influence someone cleverly, unfairly, or unscrupulously. He underlined unfairly. Then he wrote in the margins: "When the game keeps changing, you're not losing—you're being played."

Miss Kara had a soft spot for Leo. She always had. "He's just got energy," she used to say with a warm chuckle, as if energy made everything else invisible. She said it again that morning when Leo volunteered to carry the lunch baskets for her without being asked. "See that?" she said aloud in front of the class. "That's leadership. That's initiative." Jasmin didn't speak, but she turned to Nico and gave a look that wasn't confusion—it was disbelief.

Leo smiled politely, as if the compliment barely mattered. But his eyes flicked to Jasmin, then to Ty, then to Nico—quick, quiet measurements behind the grin. Nico had seen that look before. It was the same one Leo gave right before saying something mean enough to sting but smart enough not to get in trouble. Miss Kara didn't notice. She clapped her hands once and said, "Let's get to morning reading!"

Ty whispered just loud enough for only Nico to hear. "When adults like a kid, they miss a lot." Nico nodded. He was starting to see that pattern everywhere. Not just with Miss Kara. It happened with parents too, and lunchroom aides, and even the librarian, Mrs. Haller. The grown-ups didn't live in the same world the kids did. Not really. They saw smiles and thought that meant kindness. They saw loud confidence and mistook it for good leadership. But kids didn't see the show—they saw the dress rehearsal.

That week, Leo told Ella she needed to lighten up when she didn't laugh at his joke. "You're such a downer," he said with a grin, loud enough for three kids to hear. Ella flushed pink and mumbled an apology. Nico watched from the other table, his fingers tightening around the edge of his milk carton. Miss Kara had walked by only a minute before. She hadn't seen anything. She only heard Leo's laugh. That was enough for her.

Later, during cleanup, Mr. Clarke walked by their row and frowned. "Leo," he said in that flat, grown-up way that meant he'd had enough. "Quit being a jerk. You're not funny." Leo blinked. For once, he didn't grin. He said nothing at all. Nico stared, surprised. It was rare to hear an adult say the truth straight. Jasmin nudged Nico with her elbow. "One adult sees it," she whispered. Nico held onto that like it was a prize.

But Miss Kara pulled Leo aside afterward. She bent down, talking softly, her hand on his shoulder. Nico couldn't hear her words, but he saw Leo's body shift. The droop of his shoulders, the small shake of his head, the dramatic sigh. When he returned to his seat, he whispered to Jasmin, "Guess I'm just always the bad guy now." Then louder: "People always believe what they want." He looked directly at Nico when he said it.

Ty later said, "That's the trick. Make the adults feel sorry for you. Act like the victim. Flip the whole thing around." Nico replied, "But it works." And it did. Miss Kara gave Leo a second chance during group work, saying, "I know you meant well." Jasmin rolled her eyes. "He didn't mean anything well. He just knows what words to use."

The hardest part was the pretending. Not Leo's pretending—but everyone else's. Pretending not to notice. Pretending it wasn't a pattern. Pretending it would just get better on its own. Kids weren't stupid. They saw the small things. The whispered jabs. The compliments that boxed people in. The rules that only worked one way.

Nico found himself writing things down in the corner of his planner. Truth they don't see: 1. Compliments as control. 2. Silence as pressure. 3. Jokes as cover. 4. Charm is camouflage. He circled the last one twice. Miss Kara saw charm. Mr. Clarke saw patterns. But only the kids lived inside the maze of it.

That afternoon in the library, Nico checked out a book about mazes. Not for class. Not even to read. He just wanted to look at the diagrams. The twists. The dead ends. The places you think lead out but don't. He slid a pencil across the page and whispered, "Feels like this."

Ella was quieter than usual that day. Jasmin sat beside her at lunch and passed her a cookie without a word. Sometimes kindness wasn't loud. Sometimes it was just presence. Miss Kara smiled at the table. "Such good friends," she said. "Such harmony." Nico didn't correct her. Harmony wasn't real. Just silence in the wrong places.

As they left the cafeteria, Leo tossed his tray and said to no one in particular, "Some people can't take a joke. Or a compliment." Ty answered without turning around. "Some compliments are traps." Miss Kara called after them to play nice. Leo laughed. Nico didn't. That night, Nico wrote in his notebook. "They don't always see it. But we do. And we don't have to wait for them to believe us. We already know." Then he underlined the word know. Not believe. Not wonder. Not guess. Know.

Leo handed Jasmin a plastic charm bracelet during second recess. "For the smartest girl I know," he said, voice sweet like it was dipped in syrup. Jasmin took it because saying no felt like breaking a rule she didn't know she was under. But her fingers tightened around the plastic beads, already feeling the weight of a chain instead of a gift. "Thanks," she muttered, unsure if that was the right word. Leo smiled, but it wasn't a warm one. It was the kind that measured things. Scored them. Filed away who owed what.

She didn't wear it the next day.

That was enough.

"You didn't like it?" Leo asked by the lockers, just loud enough for Ella and two other kids to hear. Jasmin shrugged. "I left it at home." He raised an eyebrow. "Guess that's what I get for being nice." Then came the grin—the grin that covered his jab like wrapping paper over a broken toy. "Some people don't know how to take a compliment," he said. The others chuckled, unsure whether to join in or disappear. Jasmin didn't answer. But the knot in her chest tightened, wound like string around something delicate that might snap.

Ty found her under the art wing stairs, sketchbook open but empty. "You okay?" he asked, crouching down beside her. She blinked. "Do gifts have to mean something?" she asked. "Only if they come with strings," he said, not even pretending to smile. She closed the book. "He makes it feel like if you don't say thanks the right way, you're rude." Ty nodded. "That's control. Wrapped in a bow."

Nico overheard part of the exchange when they rejoined class. He tried not to stare, but his thoughts ran ahead of him. That night, while drying dishes beside his mum, he finally said, "Mum? What if someone gives you something nice, but it doesn't feel nice?" She paused, still holding a damp plate. "What do you mean, sweetheart?" He hesitated. "Like... someone gave Jasmin a gift, but it made her feel stuck. Like she had to act happy. Even if she didn't want to."

His mother frowned. "Are you saying someone forced her?" "No," he said quickly. "It's not like that. It's just... Leo gave it to her. But when she didn't wear it, he made a scene. Kind of like she was ungrateful." His mum's mouth tightened. "That boy again?" she asked. "You've mentioned him before." Nico nodded. "Yeah. But now it's worse."

She wiped her hands and said gently, "Maybe Jasmin can talk to her own parents about it." Nico looked down. "She doesn't want to make trouble. She thinks no one will believe it's a big deal." His mum tilted her head. "And do you think it is?" He didn't even pause. "Yes. Because it's not about the gift. It's the way he makes people feel bad for not clapping when he wants them to."

She leaned back against the counter. "Do other kids feel this way?" "Ty does," he said. "And Jasmin. They see it. But it's hard to explain." His mum sighed. "Sometimes adults forget what that feels like." Nico nodded. "You don't have to yell to be mean."

The next evening, Ty and Jasmin came over for homework club. They barely touched their worksheets. Instead, Jasmin looked Nico's mum in the eye and said, "It's like he rewrites the rules all the time. You do what he wants, he smiles. You say no, and he says you're being ungrateful. Or dramatic. Or mean." Ty added, "It's not teasing. He's nice on purpose. Until he's not."

Nico's dad overheard from the hallway and stepped in quietly. "Who's this?" Nico explained, and the room felt heavy with unspoken things. "It's not bullying the way teachers look for," Ty said. "It's not name-calling or pushing. It's smarter than that." Jasmin nodded. "He makes you feel wrong. Just for saying no." Nico's dad nodded slowly. "That's harder to see," he said. "But not less real."

They didn't call Leo a narcissist. Not yet. But the word hung in the air like a coat nobody wanted to wear but everyone knew fit. Nico's mum didn't brush them off. She asked questions. She listened. That was enough—for now.

The next morning, Jasmin brought the bracelet in her pocket. She didn't wear it. At lunch, when Leo asked about it, she looked him in the eye and said, "I didn't want to." He smirked. "Wow. You're welcome, I guess." Jasmin answered, "You don't get to decide what I owe you." Leo blinked, and for the first time, he didn't have a comeback.

Nico watched the moment like it was history. Something shifted. Something fell out of place. Or maybe back into place. Later, Ty leaned over and whispered, "Not every gift is kind." Nico wrote it down in the back of his planner. Then he added: Not every smile is real. Not every 'thank you' is safe. Some strings are tied too tight to see.

Ella sat at the end of the lunch bench where the sun didn't reach. The tray in front of her still held most of her sandwich, untouched. She picked at the crust with her fingernail and stared past the playground doors like she was waiting for something to change on the other side. Jasmin noticed first. The way her shoulders folded in. The way her hair covered half her face. She didn't speak, not yet. Just moved her tray a little closer, enough to make space between them smaller. Ty followed, sliding in across the bench like it was the most ordinary thing in the world. Nico arrived last, slower than the others, but not uncertain. They all saw it. The way Leo had looked at her this morning—like she'd taken up too much space by simply saying hello.

"I think I messed up," Ella whispered after a long time. Her fingers kept tracing the edge of her lunch tray. "I don't know what I did, but I must've done something." Ty looked at her, quiet but firm. "What makes you think that?" She shrugged, eyes not lifting. "He used to wait for me after science. Now he walks with Jenna. He told me I ask too many questions." Jasmin reached over, not to interrupt but to anchor. "You don't ask too many questions. You ask good ones. I listen to them." Ella blinked, as if hearing that cost her something.

"But he laughed at me," she added, voice flat as notebook paper. "Said I was overthinking everything. Said no wonder my last friends stopped talking to me." She didn't cry, not the kind you'd notice. It was the sort that stayed behind the eyes, weighing the lashes down. Nico leaned forward, hands clasped. "He says things like that to all of us, just in different ways." Ella's lip trembled. "Maybe he's right. Maybe I do ruin things." And there it was—the sharpest lie, carved into the softest place.

"No," Ty said, not loud but low, steady. "No, he's not." Jasmin nodded. "You didn't ruin anything. You trusted someone who made it feel safe. That's not a mistake. That's not your fault." Ella looked up, eyes glassy but not broken. "Then why do I feel like the bad one?" Nico tilted his head. "Because that's what he wants. If you feel bad, he doesn't have to." The sentence hung in the air, cold and too true.

They didn't argue about it. They didn't explain too much. Instead, Jasmin reached across the table and took Ella's hand in both of hers. Ty moved closer and pressed a hand to Ella's shoulder. Nico didn't say anything else—he just wrapped his arms around both of them. They stayed like that longer than the lunch bell allowed. No one told them to hurry. No one asked questions. They didn't need to. The hug wasn't to fix her. It wasn't to make the pain disappear. It was to prove she wasn't carrying it alone.

Ella let out a breath she didn't know she'd been holding. Not a sob. Not even a sigh. Just air, as if her lungs remembered they could still work. She whispered, "Thanks," but they shook their heads. "You don't owe us," Jasmin said. "Friends don't keep score." Ty added, "And the good ones don't disappear when you stop clapping." Nico smiled softly. "We see you, Ella. Not the version he's trying to make you be."

They didn't use the word "narcissist." That would come later, when the patterns became undeniable. When the wounds started spelling the same names in every chapter. For now, they used truth like a flashlight. Small. Quiet. But enough to change the shape of shadows. Ella leaned into them just slightly, and the silence between them grew warmer instead of colder.

She didn't finish her sandwich. But she didn't throw it away either. She packed it carefully in her lunch box like it mattered again. When they left the table, she walked in the centre of the group instead of trailing behind. Not because she was fixed. Not because it was over. But because something had shifted. The spell of blame had started to crack. That night, Nico wrote in his notebook: "The first lie a hurt person believes is that they caused the hurt." Then underneath it: "Truth is louder when it stands beside you, not above you."

The next day, Ella sat beside Jasmin in homeroom without asking. Jasmin didn't move over. She made space. Ty nodded at her from across the room, and Nico raised one finger to his temple in salute. Just enough to say, We're still here. We still see you. And Leo? He watched from two rows back. Still smiling. But no longer in control of the story.

The rain had started just before lunch, soft at first, then steady enough to keep everyone indoors. The noise in the multipurpose room bounced off the walls like rubber balls. Most of the kids were huddled in their usual cliques, eyes half-on their sandwiches, half-on the clock. But in the corner—beneath the coats hanging in uneven rows—Ty, Nico, Jasmin, and Ella sat cross-legged on the rubber mats. They weren't playing a game. They weren't even really talking. Until Ty broke the silence with a story. Not loud. Not dramatic. Just a soft drop of truth falling into the space between them.

"There was this man," Ty began, his fingers plucking at the seam of his jeans. "He lived across from my aunt. Everyone said he was the nicest guy on the street. Always helped carry groceries. Mowed lawns when people were sick. Even handed out candy that wasn't the cheap kind at Halloween." He paused. "But my cousin told me something once—said when the door closed behind him, he turned into someone else. Someone who yelled at his wife for breathing wrong. Who told his kid he was garbage if he didn't win at something. But outside, all smiles."

Ella swallowed. "Like Leo," she whispered. "But grown-up." Ty nodded. "Worse. Because grown-ups don't get grounded. They don't get sent to the principal's office. They know how to hide it better."

Jasmin frowned, her knees drawn up. "Did anyone do anything?" Ty shook his head. "No one believed the kid. Not until way too late. Adults said, 'He's always so helpful.' Just like Miss Kara says about Leo." Nico stared at the floor. "That's the worst part. When the person hurting you is the same one they praise the loudest."

Ty's voice didn't shake. It didn't try to sound brave. It just was. "That's when I started looking at people differently. Not by how they acted in crowds, but how they treated someone who couldn't give them anything." He turned to Ella. "That's how you know. If someone's only kind when others are watching, they're not kind. They're performing."

The room was too loud to notice that something important was happening in the corner. A kind of unpeeling. A quiet shift. Ella leaned back against the wall and stared at the ceiling. "I used to think grown-ups knew everything. But now I think they just pretend better." Jasmin added, "Not all of them. But the bad ones? They act like their age makes them right."

Nico nodded slowly. "Some kids grow up and carry the same tricks. They don't change. They just get better at pretending." Ty gave a half-smile. "Yeah. Some people sharpen their masks more than their hearts."

They didn't laugh. They didn't cry. But they stayed close, each word adding a weight to the floor beneath them—real and unmoving. Ty stretched out his legs. "The thing about that man was... his kid still tried to make him happy. Still tried to win his approval. Even after everything." Nico whispered, "Why?" Ty looked right at him. "Because when someone breaks you slow enough, you think the pieces are your fault."

That made Jasmin press her hand to her chest like the wind had been knocked from her. Ella whispered, "That's exactly what it feels like. Like I owe Leo something. Even though I don't know what." Ty nodded again. "They teach you to feel guilty for walking away. That's how they keep you close." Nico looked up. "But you can walk away?" "Yeah," Ty said. "You just have to believe the pain isn't proof you did something wrong. It's proof they did."

They all sat in silence again, but it wasn't empty. It was filled with understanding that hadn't been there ten minutes ago. Ella reached out and touched Ty's wrist. "Thank you," she said quietly. He just nodded. "You're welcome. I didn't say it to be thanked." Outside, the rain softened. Inside, the air between them cleared. A kind of clarity that only came from truth—the hard kind. The kind that leaves a mark. And though no one said it out loud, every single one of them was thinking the same thing: if adults can do this... we really need to know what to look for. And we really need to tell each other. Before someone else thinks they're the one who's broken.

It started with pencils. Leo walked past the row of desks like a judge at a talent show, holding up someone's pencil and saying, "Now this is sharp. Not like yours, Jasmin." The class laughed, but not because it was funny. It was because laughing made you safe. Laughing made Leo walk past you. Nico watched it happen all week—small things, mean things, packaged like compliments. He'd tell Ty, who nodded. Jasmin pretended it didn't sting. But Ella? Ella was starting to sink under it.

That Thursday, Leo handed Ella a note during group work. "At least you're better than Nico at spelling," it read. Nico caught a glimpse before she folded it shut. "Don't listen," he whispered. Ella didn't reply. Later, Leo leaned toward Nico and added, "She's improving, thanks to me." Nico looked him straight in the eye and didn't blink. "She was always good. You just never noticed."

In the lunchroom, Leo praised one kid's project and trashed another's in the same breath. "Your colours are amazing," he told Hannah. Then turned to Thomas. "Yours look like you gave up." Ty muttered, "It's bait. He praises just enough to turn people against each other." Nico said nothing. But the decision was already forming in his chest like thunder. He wasn't going to let this slide again.

After school, Nico stood outside the vice-principal's office and waited until he was called in. Mr. Arnett listened quietly as Nico explained everything—the jokes, the gifts, the compliments that hurt. Mr. Arnett nodded slowly. "I've noticed some behaviour issues," he admitted. "But I'll need to speak with Leo directly." That wasn't enough. So Nico asked for a meeting with the principal. And to his surprise, they didn't say no.

The next morning, Leo was pulled into the office. No one knew what was said, but when he returned, he wasn't smiling. He sat quietly for the first half of the day. But by the afternoon, he was back to his tricks. He whispered to Nico, "You really think they can stop me?" Nico didn't answer. He didn't need to. The answer would come soon.

Just before lunch, the hallway buzzed with noise. Lockers slamming. Backpacks thudding to the floor. And right there, near the water fountain, Leo made another jab—loud enough for everyone to hear.

"At least Jasmin's not crying today. That's progress." The hallway hushed. Teachers were nearby. Leo didn't care. But neither did Nico. He stepped forward. "That's enough." His voice was calm, not loud, but it echoed more than yelling would have. Leo blinked. "Excuse me?" Ty walked up beside Nico. Jasmin joined them. Then Ella. Four kids. One truth.

"You twist people," Jasmin said. "You make us feel small so you can feel big." Ella held her ground. "You gave me things and made me feel like I owed you. That's not kindness. That's control." Ty added, "We talked to the principal. You've been warned. But here's ours: You don't get to do this anymore."

Students were watching. A few teachers had turned. Mr. Clarke stepped closer, arms crossed. Miss Kara stood behind him, eyes wide but not surprised. Leo laughed, but it cracked halfway through. "You're just sensitive," he tried. "That's what you always say," said Nico. "But that doesn't make it true."

The silence afterward was heavy. Not scared. Not confused. Just still. The kind of still that comes before a storm changes direction. Leo looked around, but no one came to his defence. Not this time. The students near the lockers stepped back. A teacher nodded—just slightly—and walked toward the front office. Leo's face shifted. Not angry. Not sad. Just... unsure. He hadn't expected it. He hadn't expected them to stand. To speak. To be believed.

After Leo walked away, Jasmin whispered, "That was loud without yelling." Nico said, "It needed to be." Ty added, "You don't fight darkness by hiding. You fight it by stepping into the hallway and turning on the lights." They didn't feel powerful. They felt... right. Like the truth had been bottled too long, and now it was finally breathing again. Ella touched her wrist where she'd worn that bracelet. It was gone now. "You think he'll stop?" she asked. "No," Nico said. "But he'll think twice." And sometimes, that's enough to begin.

The moment came at recess. Jasmin hadn't planned it. She wasn't the type to start fights, not even quiet ones. But there it was, curling at the back of her throat—something unsaid, something that had festered. Leo had just finished telling a group of kids that Jasmin "couldn't take a joke." The others laughed nervously. She didn't. She watched him. His grin didn't reach his eyes anymore. It rarely did. And something in her—something old and tired—stood up.

"Leo," she said, her voice steady. "That wasn't a joke. You knew it would hurt." He turned, eyes narrowing just a little. Enough for her to see it. "Wow," he said. "I thought we were friends." His tone shifted. Softer. Almost gentle. But Jasmin had heard this tone before. It wasn't kindness. It was a trap dressed up like concern. And suddenly she felt the heat of it—how many times she'd swallowed his comments, brushed off his digs, told herself it was just Leo being Leo.

"You don't treat friends like that," she said. "You laugh at me in front of people. You give me things, then bring them up like I owe you. You don't listen when I say stop. That's not what friends do." Her hands were shaking, but she didn't look away. Not this time.

Leo blinked slowly. "You're making a big deal out of nothing." He said it with that same smirk. The one that always made people second-guess themselves. But it didn't work this time. Jasmin's voice didn't crack. Her eyes didn't shift. The air around her didn't fold.

Nico stood by the monkey bars, frozen. He'd heard it all. Ty leaned on the fence with his arms crossed, watching. Ella sat on the bench, eyes wide, as though trying to memorize the moment so she wouldn't forget how it looked when someone finally spoke.

Leo's voice dipped low. "You're turning people against me." Jasmin laughed, not meanly, just softly, like someone waking up from a dream. "You did that all by yourself." The words landed like truth always does—quiet, unshakable, final.

He stepped forward. "Careful, Jasmin," he whispered. "People will think you're dramatic." The threat was gentle, almost sweet. That was his power. Sweet threats. Sugar-covered control. But she didn't flinch. "No," she replied. "People will think I'm done being tricked."

He walked away after that, muttering something under his breath. It didn't matter. He didn't matter—not like he used to. Something had cracked in the air. Not broken, but opened. Jasmin felt taller somehow. Not because she won anything. But because she had stopped pretending.

Nico came over slowly. "You okay?" he asked. She nodded, then shook her head, then shrugged. "I don't know," she admitted. "But I'm glad I said it." Ty joined them and said, "That's how they lose control. The moment you stop apologizing for noticing."

Jasmin looked at the grass, her feet shifting in the dirt. "I thought we were friends," she repeated quietly. "But I think I was the only one who thought that." Ella stepped forward. "You weren't," she said. "I thought so too."

They stood there, the four of them, in a kind of silence that wasn't empty. It was full of understanding, of tired hearts finally stretching their limbs. Jasmin didn't cry. But her hands were still trembling. Nico saw it, and without a word, passed her a small stone he'd found earlier. "For grounding," he said. "It helps sometimes." She held it, cool and smooth, and nodded.

Across the playground, Leo leaned against the wall alone. For the first time, no one laughed with him. No one chased after him. And though he'd never admit it, he noticed.

Jasmin sat beside Ella on the bench. "I hate that it took me this long to say something," she whispered. Ella said, "I'm glad you did. It gave me words too." Ty looked at them both. "That's how it works," he said. "Truth is contagious when someone's brave enough to speak it first." Nico looked at his friends—not perfect, not fearless, but growing stronger together. "Let's keep telling it," he said. "Even when they say we're wrong." Jasmin gave the smallest smile. "Especially then." And for the first time, her smile didn't hide a bruise. It lit the air.

Mr. Rafferty blew his whistle like always, short and sharp, calling kids off the field with a flick of his clipboard and that usual, tired line: "Boys will be boys. Girls, don't start drama." He didn't shout it. He didn't even frown. That's what made it worse. He said it like it was the weather. Like it couldn't be changed. Ty stood still on the cracked pavement, arms crossed, staring at the patch of grass where Leo had just mocked a kid for crying after being shoved. "You saw that, right?" Ty asked him, voice flat. "He pushed Jordan on purpose." Rafferty didn't even look up. "They'll work it out."

Ty didn't say anything at first. Just nodded, slowly, like someone placing a file into a locked drawer. Then he turned to Jasmin. "That's the kind of adult who doesn't want to see it. The kind that thinks pain just works itself out if you ignore it long enough." Jasmin didn't disagree. She'd heard the same from teachers, neighbours, even relatives. "It's just teasing." "He's just being friendly." "Don't be so sensitive." Every excuse felt like a stone tossed on the back of a kid trying to stand tall. But not all grown-ups were blind. Mr. Clarke proved that.

He wasn't flashy. He didn't carry a whistle or bark orders. He wore simple slacks, tucked-in shirts, and always carried a faded canvas notebook. Most of the students didn't know if he was a guidance counsellor or a vice-principal or something else entirely. But they noticed he paid attention. And he remembered things. Names. Schedules. Faces. One day after lunch, he tapped Ty's shoulder gently and said, "I saw that." Ty blinked. "Saw what?" Clarke didn't smile. "The way Leo stared you down after you helped Ella pick up her books." There was no question in his tone—only confirmation.

Ty followed him into his office, quiet but not afraid. Clarke sat with both feet flat, notebook unopened on the desk. "You don't have to explain everything," he said. "But I know patterns when I see them." Ty's eyes narrowed. "You believe me?" Clarke nodded. "I've been a kid longer than I've been an adult. I remember how quiet things get when power's being abused. Especially when the person doing it knows how to smile in public."

It was the first time Ty had heard an adult describe it so clearly. Not like a lecture, but like someone naming the shape of something you'd only felt in the dark. "Why don't more grown-ups see it?" he asked. Clarke leaned back. "Some don't want to. Because once you see it, you have to act. And acting means change. It means being uncomfortable."

That hit Ty harder than he expected. He thought of Rafferty, of Miss Kara brushing off Leo's charm as leadership. He thought of Nico's parents finally listening only after two other kids backed up the story. "So what do we do?" he asked. Clarke tapped the desk. "You keep telling the truth. Quietly. Calmly. Often. And we'll do the same on this side of the hallway." When Ty returned to the playground, Nico asked what happened. "He gets it," Ty said. That was all. And it was enough. Jasmin, nearby, whispered, "One adult's enough to start tipping the scales."

Later that week, Mr. Clarke sat beside Miss Kara in the staff room and slid over a folded note. It was simple. Bullet points. Specific behaviours. Names. Kara frowned at first, but as she read, her face changed. She glanced up at Clarke. "You sure?" He didn't blink. "I've watched long enough." She looked again. "Alright. I'll keep my eyes open." That's how it started. Meanwhile, Rafferty kept blowing his whistle.

At recess, Leo pulled another stunt—sarcastic praise, loud enough for others to hear, designed to make Ella shrink into herself. Nico stepped forward, not with fists, not with anger, but with a sentence sharp as a pin. "That's not funny," he said. "You're not being nice. You're being mean and pretending it's kindness." Leo rolled his eyes. "You're so dramatic." Ty stepped beside Nico. "No. We just don't lie anymore."

Jasmin smiled quietly, watching from a bench. It wasn't that the adults had stopped the problem. It was that the kids weren't waiting for permission to name it. And now at least one adult stood behind them. That evening, Clarke wrote in his notebook, not for a file, not for a report—but to remember. "They're not just brave," he wrote. "They're training each other. And they'll teach the rest of us, if we let them." Some adults never see it. Others were once shadow warriors themselves. And those ones never forget.

Ella hadn't done anything wrong. Not that day, not the day before, not any time that week. But when the project group handed in their work—three pages stapled, neat, with everyone's name on the cover—Leo stood up and said in front of the class, "It would've been better if Ella hadn't messed up the spelling." The teacher, distracted by a phone ringing in the staff cupboard, barely glanced up. Just nodded. Moved on. But Ella turned red. She hadn't touched the spelling. That had been Leo. She remembered it exactly because she'd wanted to change it, and he'd insisted he was "pretty much a grammar god."

After class, he cornered her by the coat hooks. "You should say sorry. That looked bad on all of us." She blinked. "For what?" Her voice wasn't even a whisper—just a breath with shape. Leo crossed his arms. "For embarrassing me." Then he smirked. "Unless you want the others to think it was your idea to mess it up." His tone slid down her spine like melting ice. She bit her lip, fingers twisting around the zipper of her coat.

Nico and Jasmin watched from the hallway. Ty stood slightly behind them. "Same trick, different day," he muttered. Jasmin nodded. "Blame and frame." They'd seen it before. Leo would accuse, then step back, hands clean, while the other person panicked, unsure of what was real. It was his game. His shuffle. A lie danced around with just enough truth to confuse.

Ella almost apologized. Almost. She looked at Leo's face, at the curve of satisfaction on his lips. She knew what it would sound like: "I'm sorry, Leo." And how he'd answer: "It's okay. Just don't do it again." That's how it always ended—her shrinking, him shining. But this time, something changed.

"Mr. Clarke wants to talk to you," Nico said aloud, just loud enough for Leo to hear. The hallway went still. Leo blinked. "Why?" His voice had lost a bit of its polish. Nico shrugged. "He said it's about the group project." Ella watched Leo stiffen. Ty added, "I think he wants to hear from all of us."

They went together—Ella, Nico, Ty, Jasmin, and Leo, who walked with just a little less swagger. Mr. Clarke sat with the window open behind him, breeze tugging the edge of his tie. "Thanks for coming," he said. "Take a seat."

He looked at Leo first. "You blamed Ella for a mistake that was yours." His tone was not accusing, but certain. Leo opened his mouth. Clarke held up a hand. "I've already checked the draft files. The edit history's clear. You typed the sentence. You changed the spelling. And then you said something untrue in front of the whole class."

Leo tried again. "I didn't mean it like that." Clarke didn't flinch. "You meant it exactly like that. That's the problem." Ella's chest rose and fell in quiet, steady breaths. Jasmin sat beside her, back straight. Ty didn't say a word, but his hand sat flat on the table, fingers spread, like an anchor.

Mr. Clarke leaned forward, elbows on the desk. "Do you know what accountability means, Leo?" Leo gave a shrug so faint it barely moved his shoulders. Clarke continued, "It means taking ownership. Not spinning it. Not handing it off. Not turning it into a performance. It means saying, 'I did this,' and meaning it."

Leo didn't speak. Clarke turned to Ella. "You have nothing to apologize for." Then to the others, "And you three did the right thing by bringing this forward. Not every mistake is malicious. But when a pattern appears, we name it." Leo's jaw clenched. "So I'm the villain now?" Clarke shook his head. "No. You're a student. But students can choose the kind of person they're becoming."

That hit harder than any lecture. Afterward, the hallway felt colder, but clearer. Ella turned to Nico. "Did he just... call it out?" Nico nodded. "Word for word." Jasmin smiled, small but real. "Mr. Clarke doesn't play games." They walked to the lunchroom together. Ty said nothing at first, then murmured, "Truth sounds louder when it's not just kids saying it."

Ella stopped near the vending machine. "Do you think he'll change?" Jasmin answered, "I don't know. But I think we did." Leo stood alone by the lockers, watching the group pass without him. He didn't speak. Didn't smile. For once, the blame had no one to land on. The shuffle had stalled. The music had stopped. And the silence? It told the truth.

Nico had spent most of the week second-guessing every sentence that came out of his mouth. Whether it was asking to borrow a pencil, correcting a mistake in the science lab, or even saying someone's name the wrong way by accident, the first thing that always jumped from his throat was, "Sorry." Sometimes it came before anyone reacted. Sometimes it came even when he wasn't the one who did anything wrong. It was a habit. One he didn't like. One that came from trying to keep peace in rooms where the air changed too quickly.

He knew where it came from—years of being told he was "too much," "too quiet," "too sensitive," or "not trying hard enough." Adults rarely said it to be cruel. Sometimes they smiled when they said it. That made it worse. Because then you learned to smile back, even while your stomach twisted in knots. And after a while, sorry just became a way of surviving. A way of not being seen too clearly. Or blamed too loudly.

Leo thrived on that. He picked up on it early. Used it like a lever. Made Nico feel like every decision was a misstep unless Leo approved. If Nico made a joke that didn't land, Leo smirked and said, "Try again next time." If Nico got a higher mark, Leo muttered, "Teacher's pet." If Nico said nothing, Leo would ask, "You mad at me or just being weird again?"

This time, it happened in the hallway near the art room. Leo had been whispering something to Ella about Nico—something that made her shoulders slump and her hand clutch the strap of her backpack tighter. When Nico walked up, Leo looked at him like he was interrupting a show. "Oh look," Leo said. "It's Nico the Not-Quite-Genius." Then he laughed and added, "I'm kidding, relax." Nico opened his mouth. The word "sorry" almost escaped. But he caught it. Bit it back. Closed his lips, breathed through his nose, and stared at Leo.

"I'm not sorry," Nico said. The words weren't loud, but they didn't need to be. They just needed to exist. Leo blinked. "What?" Nico didn't move. "I didn't do anything wrong. So I'm not saying sorry." There was a strange silence after that. Not awkward. Not empty. But heavy. Like the moment before a fire alarm, when something deep in your chest tells you to brace.

Leo stepped forward, fast. "You've got an attitude now?" he said, voice sharp. "Is that what this is?" His finger pointed, almost touching Nico's chest. "You think you're better than everyone now? That you're above saying sorry?"

Nico stood still. He didn't flinch. His hands stayed at his sides. Behind him, Jasmin and Ty had just turned the corner. Ella hovered near the lockers, watching with wide eyes. Leo's voice rose. "Say it. Say sorry for talking back. Say it, or—" "Leo," said a voice behind him. Deep. Calm. Firm.

Leo turned slowly, like someone who already knew what he was about to see. Mr. Arnett stood just behind him, arms folded. She wasn't smiling. "I heard everything," she said. Leo opened his mouth. No words came out. Imani stepped forward. "Follow me. Now." Her tone had no room for negotiation.

Leo's face burned red as he turned and walked down the hall behind her. For the first time, there was no smirk. No last word. Just footsteps echoing down the corridor. Ella ran to Nico first. "Are you okay?" she asked. Nico nodded, still staring at the empty space where Leo had stood. "You didn't flinch," Jasmin said, like she couldn't quite believe it. "You really didn't flinch."

Ty put a hand on Nico's shoulder. "That was a Shadow Warrior move." Nico let out a shaky breath. "I was so close to apologizing," he admitted. "But you didn't," Ty said. "And that's the point." In that moment, Nico realized something he hadn't before. Not apologizing didn't make him rude. It didn't make him arrogant. It made him honest. And honesty didn't have to shrink. They walked to class in silence, but it wasn't the same kind of silence as before. It was the kind that followed a small, quiet victory. The kind that left room for breathing. And somewhere down that hallway, Leo was finally the one explaining himself.

It happened the next day, like it always did. As though none of it had ever happened. No warning. No explanation. Leo walked into class with a grin wider than usual and a pack of fruit snacks in his hand. He tossed one onto Nico's desk, another at Ella's elbow, and one landed squarely in front of Jasmin. "Morning, legends," he beamed, like he hadn't just tried to tear them down the day before. "Feeling fresh?"

Jasmin blinked. The fruit snacks stayed untouched. Ella looked at Nico, who didn't even glance at the wrapper. Ty, already reading near the windowsill, didn't move at all. His stillness was louder than a shout.

Leo sat like nothing was strange. He tapped his pencil, hummed to himself, even complimented Mr. Clarke on his tie. "Sharp look today, sir," he said, all sugar. Clarke didn't respond. He marked a paper slowly, deliberately. Jasmin watched the way his hand paused on the page. Not frozen—but waiting.

The strangest part wasn't Leo's smile. It was how empty the classroom felt with it in it.

Jasmin stared at her fruit snacks. They were her favourite kind—cherry and grape—and that made it worse. It felt like a trap disguised as a treat. Her hand didn't reach for it. Her fingers curled around the edge of her desk instead.

"I thought things were better now," Leo said at recess, voice full of pretend confusion. "Didn't we all clear things up? I even said I was sorry to the principal." He looked at Nico as if expecting him to nod in agreement. Nico said nothing. He had already learned that silence was sometimes stronger than debate.

Leo turned to Jasmin, his voice softer now. "You know, I missed talking to you. It's not the same when you're all mad." She opened her mouth, not to speak, but to breathe—to buy herself a second to stay grounded. Then she said what she hadn't dared to before. "I'm not mad," she said. "I just don't believe you."

The air around the bench shifted. Leo's eyes narrowed, just a flicker, but enough to expose the crack in the performance. "You think I'm faking it?" he asked. But he didn't sound hurt. He sounded tested. Jasmin shrugged. "You were mean yesterday. You're nice today. That's not kindness. That's confusion." Ella nodded slowly beside her. "You don't get to reset like nothing happened."

Leo's smile returned, but it didn't reach his eyes. "You girls are intense," he said. "Too serious all the time." He walked away like he hadn't heard anything at all.

Inside, Mr. Clarke stood by the window. He had watched the entire interaction. The way Leo's posture changed. The way Jasmin's hands stayed in her lap. The way Ella leaned closer to Nico without realizing it. He tapped his finger against the sill, then turned toward the classroom. "Miss Jasmin," he said calmly, "a word?"

She stepped inside, unsure if she was in trouble or not. But Clarke didn't close the door. He just leaned on his desk, eyes steady. "That was well said out there," he began. "It's hard not to flinch when someone who hurt you pretends they didn't." Jasmin didn't answer. She just nodded, eyes steady, throat tight.

"People like that," Clarke went on, "they don't always understand what kindness means. To them, it's something to give when they want something. Not when someone needs it." Jasmin looked down. "He makes me feel like I'm the one being too serious. Like I should just laugh and move on."

"You're not too serious," Clarke said. "You're just awake." She met his eyes. "But if I say that, I sound like I'm accusing." "You're not accusing," Clarke said. "You're observing. There's a difference." When she walked back to the group, Ty gave her a slow nod. Nico looked over, wordless, but proud. Ella touched her wrist—just once, gently—as if to say thank you without needing to say it. Leo sat on the far side of the field. Alone. Still smiling. Still pretending he had done nothing at all. But the others didn't pretend anymore. They didn't touch the fruit snacks. They didn't laugh at the jokes. And they didn't apologize for walking away.

They sat on the low stone wall near the edge of the schoolyard, just out of view from the swings but close enough to the sandbox that the wind still carried laughter. Ty passed Ella a juice box without looking at her. He didn't speak at first, not because he was unsure, but because he was choosing the shape of the words. When he finally spoke, his voice was calm, softer than usual, like it had been measured before it left his throat.

"When someone's rules keep changing," he said, tapping the side of the juice box with one finger, "it's not because they're confused. It's because they don't want you to win." Ella stared at her hands. The plastic straw squeaked faintly as she twisted it against the foil top. "He acts like he's being nice now." Ty nodded. "I know."

"But yesterday he said I talk too much. And the day before that, he said I was the only one who really gets him." "That's the game," Ty said, eyes still on the grass. "Make you guess which version you'll get today. If you guess wrong, it's your fault. If you guess right, he says you're finally learning."

Ella sighed. "It feels like... if I do the wrong thing, he'll just stop being nice again. And I don't want to start the fight back up." Ty finally looked at her. "Then don't fight him." She blinked. "What?" "Don't fight him," he repeated. "Flip the game." Ella narrowed her eyes. "What do you mean?"

Ty smiled, but it wasn't a mischievous one. It was knowing, older somehow than his age allowed. "You don't have to yell. You don't even have to call him out in front of everyone. Just stop reacting the way he wants. Smile back. Say thank you. Be polite. Be kind—but don't give him anything that matters."

Ella looked uncertain. "Isn't that fake?" Ty shook his head slowly. "It's not fake. It's controlled. It's what Shadow Warriors do. They know how to walk through traps without setting them off. They give nothing away, but they don't cause noise either. Just quiet moves." Ella looked at him, searching. "And that works?" Ty leaned back, let the breeze brush across his face. "It doesn't fix him. But it protects you."

She didn't respond right away. She sat in the quiet with him, watching the leaves above them shiver. Her heart still felt heavy, but something about Ty's calm gave her spine a little more steel. At lunch, Leo approached her with a grin. "Hey," he said, cheerful as ever, "you didn't sit with us this morning. I missed our talks."

Ella smiled—gently, warmly. "Oh, sorry," she said, with no weight behind it. "I was just talking to Ty." Leo's eyebrows lifted. "Ty? What's he got to say that's so interesting?" "He told me something smart," Ella replied, her voice pleasant. "That people who change the rules don't actually want anyone to win." Leo's grin faltered just slightly. "He say that about me?" Ella blinked, smile unmoved. "No. He didn't say any names."

Leo laughed a little too loud. "Well, sounds like he's talking nonsense as usual." Ella nodded. "Maybe. I just liked the way he said it." Leo stood there, suddenly unsure. For the first time in a long while, he couldn't read her. She wasn't angry. She wasn't nervous. She was... calm. Not defensive. Not flinching. Just still. And in that stillness, he found no place to plant his next move. He gave a half-shrug and walked off, unsure if he'd won or lost. That was the point.

From across the room, Ty gave Ella a nod—barely noticeable, just a twitch of the chin. She returned it without a word. Jasmin glanced between them, reading the moment in silence. Nico, sitting nearby, caught her eye and smiled. There was no war. No yelling. No show. Just a warning. Delivered with kindness. And silence that Leo didn't know how to break.

It didn't end with a scream or a slammed locker. It didn't need to. The real ending came in whispers and choices, in the slow pulling back of chairs from a lunch table that used to matter. That Monday, Leo sat where he always did—centre seat, water bottle perfectly placed, backpack opened just enough to flash a bag of candy he'd hand out in twos. But this time, no one reached for it.

Nico slid into a seat three tables away, unfolding his sandwich slowly, one eye on Jasmin. She gave him a nod and joined him without a word. Ty was already there, elbows on the table, chewing like nothing had changed. But everything had.

Ella walked in last. Her steps were slower than usual, but her gaze didn't dart anymore. She knew Leo was watching. She didn't turn to meet it. She sat beside Jasmin and opened her notebook instead of her lunch. The notebook had two folded notes tucked into its back cover—both from Leo. She didn't take them out.

Leo glanced over once, then again. The third time, he stood up. His footsteps were confident, his shoulders loose. But there was a tightness around his eyes that didn't match the swagger. "Hey," he said casually, as if strolling past on accident. "You're all quiet today."

Jasmin didn't look up. Nico did. "We're just tired," he said. "Right," Leo said, dragging the word. "Tired of what?" Ella looked up then. Her eyes were steady. "Tired of guessing what you're going to be today." Leo's face didn't change. But something flickered just under the surface. "I don't know what you're talking about," he said lightly. "I've been the same."

"That's the problem," Ty said, not bothering to lift his head. "You've been the same." Leo took a step back, the air around him suddenly heavier. "You're all acting like I've done something wrong." "No," Jasmin said, finally closing her book. "We're acting like we've finally noticed." The words weren't sharp. They weren't cruel. But they didn't leave room for argument. They didn't need to.

Leo stared for a long moment, then shrugged. "Suit yourselves. It's not like I need you." He turned and walked off. The sound of his footsteps felt smaller than before. No one watched him leave. There was no celebration at the table. No victorious grins or secret winks. Just four kids finishing lunch, together, without fear of which version of their friend would show up next. "Do you think he'll try again?" Ella asked after a long silence.

Nico shrugged. "Probably." "But it doesn't matter," Jasmin added. "We don't have to play." Ella nodded, more to herself than anyone else. That night, Nico sat on the edge of his bed, scribbling thoughts into a worn notebook. He wasn't sure if it was a diary or a blueprint, but it felt important. At the top of the page, he wrote:

"If the rules keep changing, maybe it's time to leave the game." He stared at the sentence, then underlined it twice. Once for himself. Once for the friends who sat beside him when it counted. Leo would still be at school tomorrow. He'd still smile too wide. Still charm the teachers. Still act like the storm never came. But now, Nico and the others had found their umbrella. Not a shield. Just the decision not to get soaked on purpose. And that was enough.

CHAPTER 4: HOW LOVE BOMBS WORK

The first time Sophie stepped into the school yard, her shoes were too clean, her backpack too new, and her voice too soft to be from around here. She didn't say much that morning. Just nodded when the office helper showed her where her locker was. But by recess, Leo was already standing beside her, his hands in his pockets and that practiced half-smile curled across his face like he owned the air between them. "Hey," he said, not loud, not quiet, just perfectly placed. "You're not like the others. You're... quieter. I like that."

Sophie blinked once, then tucked a strand of hair behind her ear. Her thank you came out as a whisper, but it reached him. That was all he needed. Leo didn't offer to introduce her to a group. He didn't mention where the gym was, or the library, or who sat with who at lunch. He just pointed at himself with a thumb and said, "Stick with me. I'll show you who's worth talking to." Sophie gave a small nod, unsure if it was agreement or habit.

Ty saw it from across the pavement, by the edge of the monkey bars, arms crossed and eyes narrowed like a scout watching storm clouds roll in. He nudged Jasmin with his elbow and tilted his chin toward the scene. Jasmin followed his gaze, then frowned when she saw the way Leo leaned close to Sophie, too close for a first day. "Already?" she muttered. Ty didn't answer. He knew the pattern. He knew what came next.

By second recess, Leo was telling Sophie which teacher was "cool," which kids were "weird," and which ones to avoid. Every sentence dripped with charm, like honey on the edge of a blade. Sophie laughed once. A tiny breathy laugh. It sounded honest, but Jasmin winced when she heard it. The same laugh she had once made. A laugh that didn't belong to her but to someone else's approval.

In the classroom, Leo pulled out the chair beside his desk and patted it. Sophie hesitated for half a second before sitting. Their teacher, Miss Kara, gave a small smile and said, "Glad to see you making friends already, Sophie." Leo grinned wider, like he'd just been crowned king of kindness. Sophie nodded and whispered, "Yeah... he's really nice." Nico looked over his shoulder, catching just enough of her expression to know she didn't believe the words yet.

At lunch, Leo opened his lunchbox and handed Sophie a cookie without asking if she wanted it. "Just take it," he said. "You're probably too shy to ask for anything anyway." Sophie took it, cheeks warming. "Thanks," she said softly. "You're the only one who's talked to me today." Leo leaned back, arms behind his head like he'd just won something. "That's because I see things other people don't."

Ty nearly choked on his apple slice. "Here we go," he whispered under his breath. Jasmin just shook her head and closed her eyes for a moment. "It's starting," she said. "Again." Nico said nothing. He was counting. Counting how many compliments Leo gave in one hour. Fourteen. All too good. All too early.

By the end of the day, Leo had offered to walk Sophie halfway to her bus, told her he liked her hair, said her handwriting looked "like art," and asked if she wanted to sit with him tomorrow too. Sophie said yes before she realized it. There was no pause between the offer and her answer. Like it had been written into her already.

The next morning, Leo was waiting by the front door. Not just standing—waiting. When Sophie stepped onto the school grounds, he held out a hair tie. "Thought you might need one. You wore pink yesterday." Sophie took it with a smile that didn't quite reach her eyes. "Thanks," she said. Her voice was steadier now, like she wanted to sound sure.

Nico and Ty exchanged glances. Jasmin whispered, "That's five gifts in two days." Ty whispered back, "She'll owe him by Friday." Jasmin didn't answer. She just watched Sophie walk beside Leo, not behind, but not ahead either. Somewhere in the middle. Just where Leo liked people to be. Close enough to praise. Close enough to control.

Later that day, during reading time, Leo slid a note onto Sophie's desk. It was folded twice, with her name spelled perfectly in block letters. Inside was a drawing of her—kind of. More like a cartoon. Big eyes, long hair, hearts floating above. The words underneath said, "You're the only girl I talk to." Sophie looked over at Leo, who winked. Jasmin saw it from the other desk and felt her stomach knot. "Same play," she muttered. Nico nodded slowly. "Different name."

At recess, Sophie held the drawing close to her chest, unsure whether to fold it or show it. Ella wandered over, curious. "That from Leo?" she asked. Sophie nodded. "He's sweet," she said, but her tone climbed like a question. Ella didn't say much. She just patted Sophie on the shoulder and walked away. She had held that same drawing once, though hers had said, "You make this school better."

Ty stood near the soccer field, hands in his hoodie pockets. "He moves fast," he said to no one in particular. "Like a fire that only wants dry wood." Nico joined him. "She doesn't know yet." Ty replied, "She will."

The hallway before last bell was crowded. Leo brushed past Sophie and whispered something. No one heard it but her. Whatever it was, she froze for a second, then smiled. A practiced smile. The kind that hides questions. The kind that waits for permission.

And Leo, as always, walked away before she could ask what he meant.

The hallway was loud that morning—lockers clanging open, shoes squeaking on tile, voices bouncing in uneven rhythm. Sophie walked slower than usual, holding the straps of her backpack tighter than they needed to be. Leo had already taken her seat for her. He always got there first. This time, though, he stood just outside their classroom, leaning on the wall like he was waiting for a bus that only he could see. When he spotted her, his grin widened into something rehearsed. He stepped forward, blocking her path with his shoulder like a dance move that didn't belong in the hallway.

"Morning, sunshine," Leo said, low enough that only she could hear. Before Sophie could answer—before her breath could catch or her thoughts could line up—he leaned in and kissed her cheek. Not hard. Not loud. But deliberate. Quick. Measured. Like he knew the exact timing to make it look like nothing but feel like something. Sophie stood still, mouth parted, her blush rising like a slow spill. Leo winked. "You looked like you needed it."

She didn't answer. Not because she was upset—but because she hadn't yet decided how she felt. It was her first week. First kiss. First hallway moment. Her face burned, but her lips curled. She didn't know whether to smile or ask why. Leo didn't wait. He turned his back like it hadn't even happened, stepping through the classroom door without so much as a backward glance. Jasmin saw the whole thing.

Across the hallway, Jasmin's jaw tensed like it was clenching secrets. She didn't say anything. She didn't need to. Her silence hit the tile floor harder than any locker door. She looked at Ty, who had frozen mid-step. Nico stood near the trophy case, watching through the reflection in the glass. He didn't blink. Not once. He watched Sophie's hands. They didn't move. He watched her shoulders. They dipped.

Sophie entered the classroom like someone trying not to wake a sleeping idea. She sat down without speaking, not quite meeting Leo's eyes. Leo, of course, acted like he'd done nothing. He tapped his pencil against his desk. Click-click. Click-click. No rhythm. Just noise. Jasmin passed Sophie a sharpened pencil. Their hands didn't touch.

By the second period, the whispers had started. Someone had seen. Someone had told. "He kissed her," a voice giggled behind a math book. "Right on the cheek!" another one squeaked. Sophie heard it. Leo pretended not to. He drummed on the desk harder, now a full rhythm that mimicked a heartbeat trying to escape. Sophie shifted in her seat.

Ty finally spoke, quiet and close. "He made it look like nothing." Jasmin's eyes narrowed. "But it was something." Nico nodded. "That's the trick. If she complains, it's 'just a kiss.' If she smiles, he owns it." Jasmin's nails dug into the desk. "It's not fair." Ty replied, "It's never fair. That's how he plays."

Lunch came. Leo tossed a bag of chips onto Sophie's tray. "Extra snack," he said. "For my favourite girl." The words were sweet. The tone was sugar-dipped steel. Sophie smiled, but it trembled. "Thanks," she said. Her voice had grown softer again. Too soft. Jasmin leaned over. "You don't have to take everything he gives you." Sophie's eyes dropped to her tray. "I know," she said. "But sometimes it's easier."

By afternoon, Sophie hadn't laughed once. She smiled on command. She nodded at all the right times. But the glow from day one had faded. She wasn't the shiny new girl anymore. She was the girl he had kissed. The girl who owed him a laugh, a thank you, maybe something more. Leo dropped a note on her desk. It said, "You looked cuter yesterday."

Jasmin saw it and stood up. "That's not okay," she said aloud, but the teacher hadn't noticed. Leo shrugged. "It's a joke." Sophie forced a laugh, barely a breath. Ty caught her eye. "You don't have to laugh if it's not funny." Sophie looked down. "I don't want to make things weird."

The final bell rang like an alarm clock you didn't set. Students filed out. Sophie stayed behind for a moment, packing slower than usual. Leo leaned toward her one more time. "You tell anyone?" he asked, voice low. "About this morning?" She shook her head. "Good," he said. "Wouldn't want people thinking we're... complicated." He winked and left.

Ty stepped beside her. "You alright?" She nodded. "Just tired." Jasmin joined. "He doesn't get to do that, you know." Sophie whispered, "I know. But it's hard to explain. It happened so fast."

Nico waited outside the classroom, watching shadows stretch across the tile. He didn't say anything, just held the door open as Sophie walked out between Jasmin and Ty. That was the thing about Leo. He always made it feel like your idea. Even the blush. Even the silence.

Sophie found the bracelet in her locker on Thursday. It was soft purple with gold thread woven through, tied in a loop that looked handmade. No card. No name. But she knew. It smelled faintly of peppermint gum—Leo's favourite. There was also a folded piece of paper tucked inside a plastic sandwich bag, protected like treasure. When she opened it, she found a pencil sketch of her laughing, half-finished, smudged at the corners, but unmistakably her. She traced the outline of her own hair with the tip of her finger, not sure whether to smile or frown.

She wore the bracelet all day. The first class, Leo didn't say anything. Second class, he tapped her shoulder and nodded at it. "Looks good on you," he whispered. Sophie smiled, but her lips pressed too tight. He slid into the seat next to her like it had been reserved. Between periods, he passed her a crumpled note. "You looked lonely. I fixed that," it said in blocky letters. She folded it three times and slipped it into her math book.

That afternoon, he messaged her a playlist titled Only for Sophie. Songs with lyrics about angels, missing someone, saving someone. One had her name in it, almost. She listened to it twice. Her head tilted with the rhythm. Her fingers traced the bracelet again. Jasmin leaned across the table. "You alright?" Sophie nodded. "He's just... nice. Really nice." Jasmin didn't blink. "Too nice too fast is a clue."

By Friday, the pattern had a pulse. A box of gum on her desk. A second drawing. Another note that said, "When you don't talk, I miss you." Nico watched her open that one. "You know," he said quietly, "missing someone shouldn't feel like homework." Sophie looked away. "I don't want to be rude." Nico shook his head. "It's not rude if you never asked for it."

Then came Saturday. She didn't reply to his message right away. She was helping her mum grocery shop and left her phone in the car. When she returned home, she had five unread texts. The last one just said, "Fine." She answered: "Sorry, I didn't see them." He didn't write back.

Monday morning arrived with cold air and heavier steps. Sophie found her bracelet in the bottom of the trash can near the library doors. The purple thread was frayed, the knot loose. A piece of gum was pressed to it like a stamp. The paper with her sketch was gone. Jasmin found her staring. "You okay?" Sophie didn't answer right away. "He threw it out," she said finally. "Like it didn't matter."

"He wanted it to matter," Jasmin replied. "Only if you thanked him right." Ty joined them. "Gifts like that aren't free. They come with rules." Sophie's eyes narrowed. "He said I was special." Ty shrugged. "He says that a lot. Doesn't mean it's true every time."

Later that day, Leo didn't look at her. He high-fived other girls. Called another one "sunshine." Sophie sat by herself at lunch. Jasmin brought her an extra juice box. "You don't owe him anything," she said gently. "Not your replies. Not your thanks. Not your guilt."

Sophie bit the inside of her cheek. "I didn't do anything wrong," she whispered. Nico sat beside her. "That's how you know it's real. When it hurts, and you didn't do anything wrong." Sophie blinked fast. Her eyes stung. She didn't cry. Not yet.

After school, Leo passed her in the hall. "Guess you didn't like the playlist," he muttered, just loud enough for her to hear. Sophie stopped. "I did," she said. "But I don't owe you for that either." Leo looked over his shoulder, smirked, and kept walking.

Ty caught up with her before she reached the buses. "That was brave," he said. Sophie gave him a sideways smile. "It didn't feel brave. It just felt like... enough." Jasmin nodded. "That's how it starts."

Nico stood behind them, watching the sunset hit the school windows. "He gives like a prince," he murmured. "But takes like a thief." Sophie looked down at her wrist, now bare. "I'd rather wear nothing," she said, "than wear something that hurts." And she meant it.

The day started quietly. Sophie didn't rush to meet Leo before first bell. Instead, she walked with Jasmin and Ella, her backpack bouncing lightly against her shoulder. Jasmin was telling a story about a squirrel that stole her sandwich on a camping trip. Ella kept giggling, nudging Sophie like they'd known each other forever. Sophie laughed for real—not the polite laugh she gave Leo. Not the careful kind. This one bubbled up naturally, like sunlight through a window no one noticed had been closed.

Leo saw them during recess. He stood near the edge of the playfield, one hand in his pocket, the other resting on the fence like he owned it. His eyes followed her across the yard. When she didn't break away from the girls to come over, his face twitched. Jasmin noticed. "He's watching," she said. Sophie shrugged. "Let him."

Later, when she stopped by her locker, Leo appeared from nowhere. His voice was casual, but the edges were sharp. "You're acting weird now." Sophie blinked. "What?" He leaned against the locker beside hers. "I mean, you used to talk to me all the time. Now you're off with... them."

Sophie didn't answer at first. Then she tilted her head. "I'm just talking to friends." Leo laughed—flat and humourless. "Sure. Friends." He tapped his fingers against the metal. "You know, it's just funny how quick people change." That word—"change"—stuck in her chest like a nail. "I didn't change," she said. "I just didn't see everything before."

Leo's jaw shifted. "You think I'm bad now?" His tone was still playful, but something behind it felt like a warning. Sophie took a step back. "I didn't say that." Leo stepped forward. "But you're acting like it." His smile tried to stretch across his face, but it broke before it got to his eyes. She stared at him. "You're being a jerk," she said. She didn't raise her voice. She didn't flinch. But it felt like shouting.

The hallway behind them stayed quiet. No one laughed. No one moved. Leo blinked slowly, like he wasn't used to hearing that word pointed at him. "Wow," he said. "That's harsh."

Sophie folded her arms. "No, Leo. What you said was harsh. I didn't do anything wrong." He scoffed. "Right. Because you're perfect now." She frowned. "I didn't say that either."

Jasmin appeared a few steps away. She didn't interrupt. She just stood close enough to be seen. Leo glanced at her, then back at Sophie. "Whatever," he muttered. "Have fun with your new crew." He walked off like he didn't care, but his shoulders were too stiff, and his pace too quick.

Sophie exhaled. Jasmin came over. "You alright?" Sophie nodded. "I think so." Jasmin leaned closer. "He's used to people chasing him after he throws a tantrum. You didn't." Sophie smirked faintly. "That was a tantrum?" Jasmin grinned. "A narcissist's version. All pout, no tears."

Later in science class, Leo didn't look her way. He laughed too loud with the boys beside him. Told a story that ended in a punchline she'd heard before—one he told her two weeks ago when she laughed politely. Now it sounded stale. Now it sounded desperate.

Ty passed her a sticky note during group work. It said: "You don't owe him softness." She smiled, tucked it into her pocket, and went back to her worksheet.

By the end of the day, the school felt different. Not heavier. Just clearer. Sophie wasn't floating in Leo's attention anymore, but she also wasn't sinking in his silence. She stood. On her own. Beside friends who didn't expect her to perform, didn't score her kindness like points in a game.

As they packed up to leave, Ella squeezed her hand. "You didn't do anything wrong," she whispered. Sophie nodded. "I know. That's why it hurt. Because he made it feel like I did." Jasmin touched her shoulder. "He's counting on that." Sophie looked up. "Then maybe it's time he loses count." And so he would.

Lunch was quieter than usual. The air didn't carry the same noise, the usual clatter of trays and shoes bouncing across the floor. Sophie sat between Jasmin and Nico, her fork pushing peas around like they were chess pieces she hadn't agreed to move. She hadn't said much since the hallway. But she hadn't flinched either. That said enough. Ty slid into the seat across from them, arms crossed, jaw locked like he'd already written the next chapter in his mind. "Alright," he said, voice low but steady. "It's time we called this what it is."

Jasmin raised her brow. Nico leaned forward, chin on his hands. Sophie didn't look up, but her fingers stopped fidgeting. Ty opened his lunchbox, stared at the sandwich he wasn't going to eat, and then looked each of them in the eye. "It's called love bombing," he said. "It's not a real kind of love. It's a setup. A trap made of compliments and attention that feels so good you don't realize it's fake."

Sophie blinked. "Love... what?" He nodded. "Love bombing. When someone wraps you in words that feel like hugs. When they text you every five minutes, say you're perfect, bring you little gifts. And you think, 'Wow, I've never been this liked before.' But it's not about liking you. It's about controlling you." Jasmin frowned. "That sounds awful." Ty nodded. "It is."

He shifted forward, lowering his voice so the hum of the lunchroom drowned out their corner. "It's a manipulation trick. Like playing a game where only one person knows the rules, and they change them whenever they want to win. They love you loud, so you forget what quiet feels like. And when you stop clapping for them—when you don't reply fast enough or you sit with someone else—they flip. That's when the compliments vanish. That's when the guilt comes in."

Sophie finally looked up. "But it felt real." Her voice cracked. Just a little. "I mean, I thought..." Ty softened his tone. "Of course it felt real. That's what makes it work. It's not fake because you're stupid. It's fake because they're planning it." He reached into his backpack and pulled out a folded page from a dictionary. "Look." He passed it to Sophie. She opened it. The word was there in bold.

Love bombing: A manipulation tactic characterized by excessive attention, affection, and gifts early in a relationship, often used to quickly create an intense bond and control the other person. It can manifest as constant communication, lavish gifts, and an overwhelming show of love that feels too intense or fast-paced.

She read it twice. "So... that's what this was?" Ty nodded. "Every single thing. The notes. The cheek kiss. The bracelet. All of it. Too much, too fast."

Nico tapped the table. "And then when she stopped replying right away, he snapped." Jasmin chimed in, "And blamed her. Made her feel like she did something wrong. Like she owed him something." Ty let out a slow breath. "Exactly. That's the hook. The gifts come with invisible strings."

Sophie looked at the paper again, her voice quieter than before. "But I liked the bracelet." Ty nodded. "Of course you did. That doesn't make you wrong. That makes you human. They give you things you'd like. That's part of it." Nico added, "It's not about the stuff. It's about what they expect in return."

The cafeteria buzzed on, kids laughing and tossing napkins, but at their table, it felt like a different world. One where truth had started uncoiling, slowly but with purpose. Ty reached into his bag again. This time, it was a pen and a new piece of paper. "Let's list the signs," he said. "So we don't forget. So we help the next person who walks into it."

Jasmin nodded. "Like a Shadow Warrior's field notes." Ty smiled, but only a little. "Exactly that." He wrote as he spoke. "Sign one: Everything feels too good, too fast. Sign two: You're always the centre of their attention... until you're not. Sign three: The gifts and words feel heavy, like you have to pay them back."

"Sign four," Nico said, "They get upset when you do anything that isn't about them." Sophie touched the edge of the page. "Sign five... They blame you for changing when all you did was breathe." Ty looked at her. "That's the hardest one. Because you think the air you need to survive is the same air they gave you. But it's not. It's yours."

Sophie folded the dictionary sheet again and tucked it into her pocket. "I want to keep this." Ty nodded. "It's yours now. You earned it." Jasmin smiled softly. "We all did." And in the corner of the cafeteria, four kids wrote down the blueprint for surviving the sweetest poison ever poured. And from that day forward, they'd never forget how to taste the truth behind the sugar.

Sophie sat on the edge of the bench near the east courtyard, the one with ivy running halfway up the bricks. Her lunchbox stayed unopened beside her. She hadn't touched it all day. Jasmin sat close, knees nearly touching, not to invade her space but to make sure she wasn't alone in it. The sky above had gone a little grey, and it matched Sophie's face. Her cheeks were flushed, but it wasn't from laughter or warmth. "I thought he was sweet," she said softly, turning her bracelet round and round on her wrist like she didn't know what it was anymore.

Jasmin didn't answer right away. She let the words settle. Sophie's voice was still shaky, like it hadn't decided if it wanted to cry or vanish. "I thought maybe," Sophie went on, "he just gets sensitive too easy. Like, maybe he has a rough time at home or something. Maybe he's just bad at showing feelings."

Her mouth tried to curve into a smile at that, but the smile didn't make it past her lips. It collapsed under the weight of doubt. Her eyes flicked toward Leo near the far wall, where he was joking loudly with two other boys. Sophie watched him like he was a storm cloud that hadn't finished.

"He gets mad fast," she added. "Like, one second he's laughing, and the next—he's ice." Jasmin nodded. "I've seen it." Sophie's hand tensed around the strap of her backpack. "But he said I was special. On the second day. He said he never met anyone who got him like I did. That's not... bad, right?" Jasmin took a breath. "No. It's not bad to want to be seen. It's not bad to hope someone means it. But it's not your job to guess when the bombs go off."

Sophie laughed a little, but it came out flat. "Bombs. Ty said that too. Love bombs. He said it's not about love at all. It's about power." Her eyes flicked again. Leo was pretending to dance now. Loud. Harmless-looking. But Sophie kept glancing like she was bracing for him to turn around. "He hasn't texted me since yesterday. And then at recess, he told Noah I was getting clingy. I never even texted first."

Jasmin rested her hand over Sophie's, gently. No squeeze. No rush. Just enough pressure to say, I'm here. "That's what they do," Jasmin said. "They push and pull. When you're close, they shove. When you're far, they reel you back." Sophie's fingers trembled under hers. "I just... I liked the way he looked at me. Like I mattered." Jasmin's voice didn't waver. "You do matter. But if someone only shows it when it benefits them, it isn't real. That's not love. That's a trick."

The bracelet shimmered faintly in Sophie's hand. A light purple band, now fraying at the ends. "He gave me this. Said he made it himself. But when I sat with you and Ella, he stopped talking to me." Her voice dropped to a whisper. "And when I asked what I did wrong, he told me I always make it about me. I didn't say anything else after that." Jasmin clenched her jaw. "That's how they keep you quiet."

Sophie's gaze drifted. Her eyes were sharp with confusion, a mess of wanting to understand and not knowing where to place the blame. "What if it's just me?" she whispered. "What if I expect too much?" Jasmin shook her head, slow and sure. "You expected kindness. That's not too much. That's the bare minimum." Sophie didn't cry, but her throat bobbed like she was holding back something deeper. "He was so nice at first."

"They always are," Jasmin murmured. "That's the hook." Sophie ran her hand over her jeans, wiping off sweat that wasn't there. "I feel stupid." Jasmin leaned closer. "You're not stupid. You were kind. That's not the same thing." The sky shifted, a breeze rustling through the ivy. It felt like the earth was trying to comfort them too.

"Do you think... do you think he ever really meant any of it?" Sophie asked, not looking up. Jasmin stared at Leo, then back at Sophie. "I think he meant to be the person you'd trust. That's what he meant." Sophie shook her head. "That's so messed up." Jasmin nodded. "Yeah. But now you know. And once you know, it doesn't work the same."

Sophie looked down at her bracelet again. She didn't take it off. She didn't throw it away. But she didn't stroke it anymore either. "Maybe I'll keep it," she said. "To remember not to fall for fake things." Jasmin smiled, small but warm. "Then it becomes your armour, not his gift." Sophie blinked, once. No tears. But her smile—the real one—cracked through like a sunbeam.

"He's looking over here," Sophie muttered. Jasmin didn't flinch. "Let him look. You're not who you were last week. And that scares him more than anything." Sophie nodded slowly. "Okay. Then maybe I won't smile next time." Jasmin said nothing. She just grinned. "Or maybe," Sophie added, "I'll smile because I want to. Not because he expects it." And for the first time all week, Sophie didn't check where Leo was standing. She just sat with her friends. And ate her lunch. Like peace didn't have to be earned—it just had to be reclaimed.

Sophie sat at the back of the classroom near the windows, her phone hidden beneath her math workbook. The lesson on decimals blurred in the background as another message popped up from Leo: "Why are you ignoring me now?" She hadn't replied to the last three. Not because she was angry—she wasn't even sure if she was allowed to be angry. Just tired. Confused. Every time she tried to step away, he buzzed her back with a joke, a memory, or worse, a compliment that made her heart twist.

She looked up. Across the room, Leo was laughing with two boys over something drawn in a notebook. He didn't even glance her way. No frown. No wave. No sign that they had spoken all morning. Sophie checked her phone again. Two more messages now. "I miss how you used to talk to me." And then: "You're not like other girls." That one was old. It had worked last week. She locked the screen and stared at the number line on the board, but her mind couldn't hold numbers today.

It had become a pattern—affection over text, silence in person. Or sometimes the reverse. Sometimes he was all over her in public, joking loud, leaning close, brushing his hand against hers like it was by accident. Then her phone would stay silent for days. Jasmin called it "the see-saw." Ty called it "breadcrumbing." But Sophie didn't want metaphors anymore. She wanted answers. Real ones. She needed to know what made people act this way—what made someone so warm one second and so cold the next.

During recess, while the others circled the field in lazy laps, Sophie sat near the tetherball post with her tablet. She typed carefully: "Why does someone act super nice and then ignore you for no reason?" Dozens of articles popped up. She clicked one titled Signs of Narcissistic Behaviour in Relationships. At first, the words felt too big. But she read slowly. Carefully. Until they stopped being big and just became true.

The part that stuck with her read: "Narcissistic behaviour is when someone needs constant admiration, uses others to feel powerful, and can't feel what you feel." Her lips pressed together. She thought about the bracelet. The playlist. The cheek kiss. The jokes. The silence. The stare-downs when she spoke to other people. The compliments that had teeth inside them. She copied the sentence into her notes app, under a heading she called "Why I'm Not Crazy."

Back inside, her phone buzzed again. "So you're just done now?" She read it three times before typing back: "You only talk to me when it makes you look good. That's not friendship. That's not anything." Her finger hovered over the send button. Then she pressed it. Her hand shook a little, but it felt like her spine got straighter the second it went through.

Leo didn't reply. Not right away. When she looked up, he wasn't in his seat anymore. Probably the washroom. Maybe the office. Maybe looking for someone easier. The absence didn't comfort her—it pressed against her chest like a reminder of all the times she thought being noticed meant being valued. But now she knew better. Sometimes silence wasn't punishment. Sometimes it was just what came after you took your power back.

At lunch, she told Nico what she'd found. He didn't laugh. He didn't say "that's heavy." He nodded like he'd known it already but was waiting for her to name it herself. "Words have power," he said. "Especially when they're true. Now you can't unsee it." Sophie bit her lip. "What if I made it worse?" Nico shrugged. "It was already bad. Now it's just seen."

Later that day, during art period, Leo stood behind her chair and dropped a paper crane onto her sketchbook. It had her name written in looping marker across the wings. No note. No smile. Just that smug quiet he always wore when he thought he was being clever. She didn't touch it. She pushed the crane to the edge of her table and kept shading her drawing like it didn't matter. Because now, it didn't.

After class, Jasmin caught up with her. "He's still playing games," she said. Sophie nodded. "But I'm not." The words came out flatter than she intended, but they felt honest. Real. Like a small boundary had been drawn with a thick, black marker. "I know what he's doing now. He makes you feel like the best person in the world, and then vanishes. Or throws guilt at you when you stop clapping for him."

Ty added later, "That's how they win—by making you forget how strong you are. But you didn't forget." Sophie shook her head. "No. Not this time." She scrolled through her texts one more time, then deleted them all. Every message, every heart emoji, every half-apology he'd ever sent. Gone. "I don't need proof anymore," she said. "I've got clarity."

In the hallway before the final bell, Leo finally stopped her. "Hey," he said, voice soft. "That text earlier—was that about me?" Sophie blinked slowly. "You know it was." He smirked. "You're sensitive." She smiled. Not fake. Not mean. Just sad. "No," she said. "I'm just finally aware." He didn't reply. He didn't need to. She turned and walked away.

It was just one hour. Maybe less. Sophie had left her phone in her desk tray during P.E., along with her jacket and the sketch she hadn't finished colouring in. By the time she got back to it, Leo had already typed out the sentence: "some people are just fake." It didn't tag anyone. It didn't need to. His followers—mostly kids from their class—clicked the little heart, one after another, like it meant something clever. Someone reposted it with laughing emojis. Another added, "Fr for real tho."

Sophie read the post three times before the sweat even cooled on her skin. She knew it was about her. Jasmin knew it too. Even Nico, who never checked school drama feeds, looked up from his science book and muttered, "He's starting again." Sophie felt her stomach sink, but not with guilt. It was confusion—deep and hard, like a lump in her chest. She had done nothing. Just one hour without a reply. And suddenly she was "fake."

She didn't even open his last message. She couldn't. Not now. Not after what he had posted. The words weren't angry, not on the surface. They were slick, sideways, shaped like a smile but meant to sting. She kept asking herself if she'd done something wrong. Should she have messaged back during lunch? Was she cold? Distant? Had she missed some rule that Leo had set but never said aloud? That's what scared her. The rules were invisible. And they moved.

Jasmin sat beside her in the library and spoke softly. "If someone treats you like an egg and waits for you to crack just so they can say they were right about you, that's not kindness. That's control." Sophie didn't answer. Not right away. Her hands stayed folded on the table, thumbs pressing into one another until the knuckles blanched white. "But I didn't even do anything," she whispered. "I was just... being normal."

"That's enough," Ty said from across the table. "That's what makes them mad. When you're not clapping. When you're not texting back the second they need their ego fixed." Sophie shook her head. "It's like he wants me scared of silence." Ty nodded once. "Exactly."

It should've ended there. A whisper in the library. A brush-off post on Leo's feed. But when Sophie got to her next class, she noticed that two girls she'd worked on a project with last week weren't talking to her anymore. They weren't rude. Just different. Like a line had been drawn with an invisible marker. Like whatever Leo wrote had turned her into something suspicious.

The sting didn't last long. It turned into something else—something sharper. Anger wasn't usually her friend. She avoided it most of the time. But today it burned steady in her chest. So when she opened her phone again, this time she didn't scroll or shake. She took a screenshot of Leo's post. She walked up to Mr. Clarke's desk during the quiet reading period and asked, quietly, if she could see the principal.

Mr. Clarke didn't ask for details. He nodded. Wrote her a hall pass. "Be brave," he said. It wasn't patronizing. It was clear. Simple. Real.

In the office, Sophie showed the vice principal the screenshot, along with the texts Leo had sent the day before. The tone. The timing. The pattern. She didn't cry. She didn't shake. She just told the truth. That she'd been love bombed, then ignored, then cornered again. And now he was using posts to make her look like a liar. "He doesn't say my name," she said. "But he doesn't have to."

The vice principal didn't dismiss her. She listened. She wrote things down. She asked if Sophie wanted to go home. Sophie said no. She wanted to stay. To finish her day. To not let Leo take up that kind of space in her world anymore. By the time the bell rang for dismissal, Leo had been called to the office. His friends were watching the hallway like hawks, whispering questions no one could answer. Leo didn't return to class that day. Sophie didn't ask why.

Outside, waiting for her ride, Jasmin stood beside her, arms crossed, eyes on the gravel. "That was bold," she said. "It wasn't brave," Sophie said. "It was just necessary." "Same thing," Jasmin replied. "Sometimes necessary is the bravest thing you'll do all day." Ty joined them before the bus pulled in. "You okay?" Sophie nodded. "For now." She wasn't smiling. Not the fake kind. Not the unsure kind either. Just still. Still and honest. And finally free of pretending she didn't know what this was anymore. The truth was out now. And the game had changed.

Jasmin didn't ask permission. She saw the open seat beside Sophie and took it, sliding her lunch tray onto the table without saying a word. Her body moved like she already knew the answer to a question no one had asked yet. She didn't look at the other kids in the cafeteria or even pretend to laugh at the joke Nico was trying to tell across the aisle. Instead, she angled her chair closer to Sophie's and let the silence stretch until it softened. "He did the same thing to Ella," she said, barely above a whisper.

Sophie blinked. Her spoon stopped halfway to her mouth. She'd been picking at the noodles, swirling them around, pretending she had an appetite. But Jasmin's voice cut through the fuzz in her head. Not like a knife—more like the end of a storm when you realize the thunder is finally moving on. Sophie didn't know what to say. Her jaw tightened. Her eyes stayed down. "But it felt so real," she whispered. "It really felt real."

Jasmin nodded. No hesitation. No coddling. Just truth. "That's why it worked," she said. She didn't smile. She didn't blink. "He makes it feel real. He has to. That's the only way it sticks." Sophie swallowed. It wasn't tears this time. It was the lump of betrayal that still sat in her throat, unchewed, like something she couldn't quite digest. "I didn't even want him to like me at first. I just thought he was being nice. Then he gave me all this attention, and... I guess I got used to it."

"He makes you feel special," Jasmin said. "So that when he takes it away, it hurts even more." She slid her sandwich across the table and offered half without ceremony. Sophie shook her head, but the gesture made something ache a little less. "Did Ella ever talk about it?" she asked, still looking at the noodles. Jasmin nodded again. "Only once. After he ghosted her. She said it felt like she disappeared, like she was never even real to him. And I think that's the worst part."

Sophie finally looked up. The cafeteria didn't look the same today. It was louder, messier, and yet she felt more alone inside it than she ever had in the library, even on the quiet days. "Why didn't anyone say anything?" she asked. Jasmin leaned forward. "Because he never broke a rule you could see. Because grown-ups don't hear fake kindness. They only notice when you scream."

At that exact moment, a tall figure moved through the cafeteria doors. Mr. Arnett—the principal—walked across the floor without speaking. The lunch monitors noticed. Even a few students stopped mid-chew. His eyes didn't scan the room like a hawk. He already knew where he was headed. When he reached the far end, he leaned down and whispered something to Leo, who sat alone for the first time that week. Leo's shoulders tensed. He didn't say anything. Just stood and followed.

Sophie's breath hitched. "Is this because I told them?" Jasmin shook her head. "No. It's because we all did." Sophie blinked. "You too?" Jasmin smiled faintly, but it didn't reach her eyes. "I asked Ty to talk to Mr. Clarke after your screenshot. Nico backed him up. Then I went myself this morning before class started." Sophie couldn't believe it. She hadn't even known they were watching, let alone standing with her. Jasmin leaned her elbows on the table. "You're not alone. You never were. That's just how Leo wants you to feel."

A few students glanced their way. Rumours spread fast, but Jasmin didn't flinch. Her voice stayed calm. "It's not about revenge. It's not about being mean back. It's about ending the trick." Sophie nodded slowly. Her eyes found the exit where Leo had just disappeared. "He's going to be furious," she said. Jasmin shrugged. "Let him be. He's not our weather. We don't have to let him rain on us."

For the first time that week, Sophie exhaled fully. Not because the problem was solved—but because someone else had carried a piece of it with her. She hadn't been imagining it. She hadn't overreacted. Jasmin saw it. Jasmin named it. And now the adults were hearing it too.

In the corner of the cafeteria, Nico gave her a subtle nod, eyes steady and expression unreadable. Ty raised his juice box in her direction like a silent toast. None of them made a big show out of it. No clapping, no cheer. Just presence. Just truth.

Sophie didn't cry. She didn't want to. She just sat a little taller in her chair. The bracelet Leo had given her was gone, tossed away yesterday. But her friends were still here. Still showing up. Still saying the thing that mattered most, without ever needing to say it out loud. "You matter," Jasmin said softly. "Even if he acts like you don't." And Sophie believed her.

The classroom was half-empty during last period, a quiet slot meant for free reading or extra assignments. Most students used it to draw in the margins of their notebooks or sneak glances at the clock. Sophie sat by the window with her math open, though the numbers hadn't moved in her mind for ten minutes. Nico sat one desk over, elbows on his knees, eyes on the floor, saying nothing. He waited, not for the right words, but for her to be ready to hear them.

She spoke first. "You knew what he was doing, didn't you?" Her voice wasn't angry. Just tired. Nico nodded slowly. "Yeah. I knew." He didn't look up at first. "Leo's been doing this kind of thing since last year. First it was jokes. Then favours. Then if you didn't laugh loud enough or do what he wanted fast enough, he'd go quiet. Or mean."

Sophie shifted in her chair. "You too?" He finally looked at her. "He used to say I was the only one he trusted. Said I was 'real,' not fake like the others. Made me feel like I had to keep being that person, or else…" His voice trailed off. "Or else he'd take it away."

She knew what that "it" was now. The warmth. The praise. The way Leo made you feel like you were the most important person in the room—until you weren't. "I thought I did something wrong," she said. "I thought maybe I said the wrong thing or didn't say thank you enough."

Nico shook his head. "That's the trap. He gives you just enough to make you feel lucky. Then takes it away to make you feel scared." The words hung between them like smoke. No bell rang. No teacher interrupted. It was just them in the corner, wrapped in the invisible web Leo had spun around both of them at different times.

"Did you tell anyone?" Sophie asked. Nico shrugged. "I tried. People said I was being dramatic. Said Leo was just friendly. That I was reading too much into it. But then Ty said something once that stuck with me."

Sophie leaned in. "What did he say?" Nico breathed in. "He said, 'If someone's kindness feels like a trick, it probably is.'" That was when he started noticing the patterns. How Leo's compliments were always followed by favours. How silence became punishment. How one smile could hide a thousand tiny threats.

Just then, the classroom door opened. Mr. Arnett, the principal, stepped in. He didn't raise his voice. "Everyone, eyes up for a minute. I'd like to say something important." A hush settled as chairs squeaked and heads turned. He didn't go to the front. He stood by the middle of the room and spoke as if the floor itself needed to hear.

"There are people," he began, "who use nice words to control others. They don't always yell. They don't always push. Sometimes, they smile while they hurt you. That's called manipulation. And it's just as serious as any loud kind of bullying."

Several students froze. Sophie felt the air shift. She didn't dare blink.

"I want you to understand something," Mr. Arnett continued. "Being kind is not about what someone says when they want something from you. It's about how they treat you when they don't need anything at all." He looked around the room. "If someone only likes you when you do what they want, that's not kindness. That's control."

Nico met Sophie's eyes across the desk. Her shoulders, so tense for days, seemed to loosen slightly. Mr. Arnett wasn't done. "You are not in trouble for speaking up. You are not weak for saying something feels wrong, even if no one else sees it at first. If someone makes you feel small, confused, or afraid—tell someone. Tell me. Tell any adult you trust."

The room remained silent, but Sophie's pulse started to slow. For the first time, she felt seen—not as the girl who'd been "too sensitive" or "too needy," but as someone whose confusion had a name, and whose voice had a place. After the principal left, Nico turned back toward her. "I didn't know what to call it before," he said quietly. "But I know now. It's not you. It's him." Sophie nodded. "It feels weird, hearing an adult say it out loud." "It means we're not the only ones who see it anymore," Nico replied. "That matters."

She turned her math notebook toward him and tore out a blank page. "Write it down," she said. "What he did. Everything. So we don't forget. So we can show someone next time." He took the paper and began scribbling, not because he needed proof for himself anymore, but because others might. And because truth, once spoken, has to be kept alive in words.

The bell finally rang, but neither of them moved right away. In that corner of the classroom, they had reclaimed a piece of something—dignity, maybe, or just the right to be heard without having to yell. As they stood to leave, Sophie whispered, "Thank you." Nico smiled, but not the kind of smile Leo used. It was quiet. Unearned. Real.

The library was colder than the rest of the school. The windows were tall, the shadows long, and every chair made a sound when you shifted. Ty sat cross-legged in the beanbag corner, arms folded, his brow low over a book. Jasmin leaned over the table, chewing the edge of her pencil, and Ella twisted her necklace between her fingers so hard it left an imprint. Sophie hadn't said anything since first period. Nico was the one who brought them here—not to study, not even to talk. Just to look.

There was an old beige dictionary, thick as a brick, sitting crookedly on the bottom shelf of the reference stack. Nico pulled it out like it was sacred. "Let's look up the word," he said. "The one Ty told us." The one that made Sophie shiver when she heard it the first time. The one Ella had scribbled in her notebook in blocky capitals and circled three times. Love bombing.

He placed the book on the table and flipped to the 'L' section. The pages were tissue-thin, the kind that made you afraid to turn too fast. "Here," he said, jabbing a finger to the tiny print. "Love bombing. A form of manipulation in which excessive affection, gifts, and attention are used to gain control over another person."

Sophie's eyes didn't blink. Jasmin reached for the page like she might touch the word and feel it hum beneath her fingers. "This," she said, "this is what happened to me. And to Ella. And now Sophie." "And to you," Ella added gently, turning toward Nico. "You were the first. You just didn't have a name for it."

Nico nodded. His chest felt tight, but not the bad kind. It was the feeling of something clicking into place. The relief of not being the only one who noticed the smoke before the fire. "I thought maybe it was me," he said. "That I was the one twisting things in my head. That I was making stuff up." "That's how it works," Ty said. "They make you question yourself so you won't question them."

Silence fell again. Not the scared kind. The sacred kind. The kind that comes just before truth drops its final weight. Sophie whispered the words aloud, like they might change shape if she owned them too fast. "Love bombing." She didn't cry. She didn't flinch. She just stared at the word like it had betrayed her and saved her all at once. Nico closed the dictionary. The soft thud echoed louder than expected. "This isn't love," he said. "It's a trick."

Leo had been sitting two tables away the entire time. No one had noticed him slide in. He was supposed to be at lunch detention, but he'd talked his way out of it, again. He leaned back in his chair now, arms crossed, eyes burning. "You've got it all wrong," he said, loud enough to crack the stillness. "I was just being nice."

Ty didn't move. "That's not what nice looks like." Leo stood up, voice rising. "You're just jealous. You all are. Because I actually know how to make people feel special." "No," Jasmin said, steady as stone. "You know how to make people need you. That's different." Leo's eyes narrowed. His hands were in fists now, knuckles white, but he didn't lash out. He just looked at them, each one of them, like he couldn't decide who had betrayed him most. "You're turning people against me," he said. "And you're going to regret it."

Sophie stood. For once, she wasn't shaking. "No, Leo. You did that to yourself." Mr. Arnett, the principal, entered the library just then. He hadn't been called. He was already on his way. Leo's voice had carried further than he realized. Mr. Arnett stood behind Leo, arms crossed, eyes sharp. "Is there a reason you're not where you're supposed to be, Mr. Cain?"

Leo's mouth opened, then closed. He turned, stammered, and the mask cracked. The charm fell off like paint in the rain. Mr. Arnett motioned toward the door. "Come with me. Now." Leo walked out, but not before giving one last glare to the group. But this time, it didn't land. No one flinched. No one looked down. No one wondered if they were wrong anymore.

Once the door closed, Ella let out a breath she'd been holding for minutes. "We said it," she whispered. "We named it." "And now we can't unsee it," Ty added. "That's the point," Nico said. "We're not supposed to unsee it. We're supposed to remember. So it doesn't happen again. Not to us. Not to anyone." They stayed in the library until the bell rang. They didn't say much more. But something had shifted. Something permanent. Now they had the word. The power. The truth. They were no longer just kids trying to make sense of confusion. They were witnesses. They were warriors. They were done being tricked.

Miss Kara was shelving books in the back of the resource room when Sophie stepped in. The afternoon sun stretched long across the carpet, leaving wide shadows where dust hung in quiet lines. Sophie stood at the door a full minute before speaking. Her fists were clenched around the fabric of her sleeves. Her shoes made no sound. But her breathing gave her away. It was shaky, low, and pulled tight from somewhere behind her ribs.

Miss Kara turned when she felt the silence grow heavier. "Sophie?" she asked, placing a novel down on the return cart. "You okay, love?" Sophie didn't nod. Didn't say yes just to be polite. Her lips trembled before her voice did. "I need to tell you something." The words felt scraped from inside her throat, but they came out clear. Not soft. Not small. Not hidden.

Miss Kara's expression shifted at once—shoulders down, eyes steady, no interruption, no urge to fill the silence. She walked over to the little round table where the kids sometimes coloured and motioned gently. "Let's sit," she said. "I'm listening." Sophie sat. Her hands stayed in her lap, clenched so tight her knuckles turned white. She didn't look up right away. But she didn't whisper either. "He tricked me," she said. "Leo. He made me feel like I was... amazing. Like I was the best thing he ever met."

Miss Kara waited. Not a sound interrupted them. Not even the copier in the hall. Sophie kept going. "He said I was the only one he really talked to. He gave me things. A bracelet. A drawing. A playlist with songs that said things I thought he meant. He kissed my cheek outside class like I mattered. But then I didn't text him back. Just once. Because I was tired. And then he posted something. It wasn't about me, not by name. But it was. Everyone knew."

Her voice cracked then, not from fear, but fury. The kind that comes when kindness was never real and you only see it when it turns sharp. Miss Kara's lips parted slightly, but she didn't speak. She waited again, her posture still, her presence gentle. "He texted me ten times that night. Then ignored me the next day. Then smiled in class like nothing happened. Then said I was acting weird. Then called me fake without saying my name. I felt like I was spinning. I thought maybe it was me."

The tears came now. Not just tears—but tight, shaking sobs, the kind that carried more than sadness. They carried betrayal. They carried the weight of wondering if you were the villain in a story someone else wrote. "I thought it was my fault. That I was ungrateful. That I should've said thank you louder or smiled harder or said something when I didn't know what to say."

Miss Kara moved her chair an inch closer, but not too close. Her voice was soft now, but not dismissive. "It wasn't your fault," she said. "None of this was your fault, Sophie." Sophie nodded, not because she believed it yet—but because she wanted to. "There's a word for what he did," she said. "Ty told me. It's called love bombing. It's when someone gives you too much too fast so you'll trust them before you know better. Then they take it back, piece by piece, and make you feel like it was you who broke it."

Miss Kara blinked slowly. Her eyes were glassy now. She'd heard stories before. She'd read the trainings, filled the reports, memorized the protocols. But this wasn't a line item on a safety checklist. This was a child in front of her who'd tasted the sweetness of manipulation and found it bitter. "I believe you," Miss Kara said, placing a hand on the table between them—not touching, just offering.

Sophie's breath hitched. "He's done it to other girls. Jasmin. Ella. He hurt Nico, too. He made them feel small when they said no. He made them feel wrong for asking why." "I believe them too," Miss Kara said. "I told Mr. Arnett," Sophie added. "I showed him the messages. I told him what Leo said when no one else could hear." "And Mr. Arnett is taking this seriously," Miss Kara said. "He's spoken with Leo. He'll be suspended. And he'll be watched, closely."

Sophie looked up, really looked, and for the first time, her shoulders weren't curled in like a paper crushed in someone's hand. "You believe me?" "I believe you, Sophie. Not just your story. You." Something uncurled inside Sophie. Not all at once. But enough. Enough to know she wouldn't sit in silence anymore. That her voice had weight. That her pain wasn't invisible. That kindness wasn't always real—but truth could be.

Miss Kara leaned forward. "Do you want to help me write a statement? Not just for the school, but for the other kids. So they know what love bombing looks like?" Sophie nodded. "Yes," she whispered. "Yes, I do." And just like that, her voice became a sword. Not to hurt— but to protect. To warn. To stand. To say what someone else might need to hear before it's too late.

It happened by the lockers, near the Grade 6 hallway where the sunlight always hit too bright in the afternoon. Sophie was just reaching for her gym shoes when Leo strolled past with two other boys—Connor and Seth—loud enough to make sure people were listening, but not loud enough to call it yelling. His voice curled in the air like smoke from a match just struck. "She's making it all up," he said. "You know how dramatic some girls get when you don't like them back."

Sophie froze. So did Nico. So did Jasmin. So did Ty. All four of them were standing nearby, and they hadn't been looking for a fight. But this wasn't a surprise. This was Leo doing what he always did when the truth backed him into a corner—turning the light away and making you question what you saw.

"I swear," Leo went on, smiling at Seth now. "She's obsessed with me. Like, actually obsessed. I said hi to her one time and now I'm her boyfriend in her head or something." "Maybe she just likes the drama," Connor added, egging it on. Leo smirked, leaning against the lockers. "Girls like attention. You just have to stop giving it and they flip out."

Sophie didn't say a word. Her hands tightened around the edge of her locker door. Her lips pressed into a line so thin it could've vanished. But her eyes—her eyes didn't water. They flared. They burned. Ty took a step toward her, but she didn't move. Then Jasmin stepped up beside Sophie and said, in a voice that didn't shake, "We all heard what you said. And it's not true."

Leo laughed. "You too? Wow. Did you guys make a group chat or something?" "Don't flatter yourself," Nico muttered, stepping beside them. Leo's smile stayed stretched like rubber, fake and thin. "I didn't even do anything. If I was such a bad guy, don't you think someone would've said something by now?" That's when Miss Kara came around the corner.

She wasn't running. She wasn't stomping. She didn't even look angry. She looked awake. Awake in a way that said she'd heard everything. Her eyes were on Leo, but not like a teacher. Like a person. Like someone who'd once believed someone like him, and regretted it. Deeply. "Leo," she said, and her voice was as soft as snowfall. "Walk with me, please." Leo blinked. "Why?"

Miss Kara didn't raise her voice. She didn't explain. She just tilted her head toward the hallway that led to the principal's office. Her silence was heavier than any shout. And Leo followed, but not before throwing a look behind him—half smirk, half scowl, full of the same rot that always lived behind his grin.

As the footsteps faded, Sophie let out a breath. "He called me obsessed," she whispered. "He said I made it up." "We know you didn't," said Nico. "We were there." "He always turns things around like that," Jasmin said. "Like it's your fault for having feelings." Sophie blinked twice. Her breath was still uneven, but she was standing straight. "Do you think Miss Kara believed him?" Ty shook his head. "No. She believed you. That's why she took him straight to the office."

Meanwhile, in the principal's office, Miss Kara didn't sit in the usual chair across the desk. She stood by the window, arms crossed, her voice sharp but steady. "This isn't just teasing," she said to Mr. Arnett. "This is emotional manipulation. This is calculated cruelty. I've taught for twelve years. I've seen boys try to be funny. This isn't that. This is dangerous."

Mr. Arnett didn't interrupt. He just nodded slowly. "We've had... several reports now. From different students. From staff. Today will be his last warning." "No," Miss Kara said. "Today has to be his consequence." And that was how the gaslight storm began. With laughter in the hallway, with truth in the silence, and with one teacher finally saying, enough. Not as a staff member, but as someone who remembered what it felt like to be manipulated and not believed. Leo wouldn't be laughing by the end of the day. Because when the light comes back on, the shadows don't just vanish. They get seen. They get named. And finally, they get stopped.

It happened at lunch, in the middle of the cafeteria, with trays still clattering and the scent of warm buns lingering in the air. Sophie didn't plan it. She hadn't told Jasmin or Ty or even Nico. But something inside her cracked open like a shell underfoot. And when she stood, when she looked across the room and saw Leo laughing with his mouth too wide, his voice just loud enough to dominate every table nearby, she didn't flinch. She rose slowly, holding the edge of her tray like it might steady the storm building in her chest.

Leo noticed. His smile faltered. One eyebrow lifted.

Sophie stepped forward. Not fast. Not timid. She didn't stomp, didn't shout. But every child within hearing range fell quiet. Even the lunch monitors paused. And when she stopped beside Leo's table, her voice came out like stone pulled from deep water—quiet, yes, but heavy with truth. "You kissed me," she said, her eyes locked on his. "You gave me gifts. You told me I was the only girl you talked to. And then you called me obsessed. You told people I was making it all up."

A fork hit a plate somewhere. No one moved. Sophie's voice trembled, but not from fear. From the force of holding in so many torn-up words for too long. "You made me feel special. And then you made me feel small. You were kind so I'd trust you, and cruel so I'd stay confused. That's not love. That's control." Leo started to laugh. "You're seriously doing this? Right here?"

Miss Kara stepped out from the side of the cafeteria line. She hadn't sat down since entering. Mr. Clarke followed, folding his arms across his chest. They'd both heard enough already, but now they had the words from Sophie herself. And they were letting them land. Sophie kept going. "You texted me twenty times in a day. And when I didn't answer once, you said I was fake. You made me think I'd done something wrong. But I didn't. I just wanted a moment. That's not being fake. That's being human."

Leo looked around like someone searching for backup. But even Connor shifted in his seat. "I believed you when you said I was special," Sophie said, her voice smaller now, but still clear. "And then I thought I'd ruined it. That I was too clingy. That it was my fault." Mr. Clarke took a step forward. "It wasn't." Leo rolled his eyes. "She's making this more dramatic than it is. I mean—"

Miss Kara interrupted, and her tone cut through his sentence like scissors through ribbon. "Leo," she said, firmly. "No. We've seen this before. Many of us. And what you've done—this pattern of false affection followed by guilt and gaslighting—it's not only manipulative. It's abusive."

Every head turned. The word abusive landed like thunder. Jasmin stood now. "He did the same to Ella. Then tried it with me." Ty nodded. "He echoes what you say to earn trust. Then uses it against you." Nico folded his arms. "He tells teachers what they want to hear. But it's not real. It never is." Leo's smile vanished entirely. He looked at Mr. Clarke, but there was no safety there. Then he looked at Miss Kara, but her jaw was set. The truth had finally outrun him.

The principal entered not long after—called by text from Miss Kara. He didn't ask questions. He listened. And he heard from Sophie, from Jasmin, from every child who had held something in too long. He heard about the praise that turned into punishment, the gifts that came with guilt, the jokes that felt like jabs.

Sophie's tray still rested on the lunch table, untouched. Her hands shook a little now, the way they might after holding something too heavy. But she didn't regret it. Not once. Because the silence was over. Because the gaslight had been snuffed out, and the truth burned brighter than Leo's charm ever could.

Mr. Clarke placed a hand gently on her shoulder, just before she returned to her seat. "You did the hardest thing," he said. "You told the truth when it cost you." She nodded. "He can't take it back now." And he couldn't. The silence had broken. And the room had changed.

The hallway that morning felt different. It was quieter than usual. Even the tile under their feet seemed softer. Ty, Nico, Jasmin, and Ella waited just outside the principal's office door, where they'd been told Leo would pass through. Sophie stood with them, shoulders squared— not because she felt brave, but because she had to. Each of them recalled the way he'd made them laugh, then question themselves. But now, the hall felt lined with something new: the hush of truth taking hold.

Mr. Clarke emerged first, clipboard in hand. His face was steady but firm. Miss Kara followed, her posture steady, as though she was bracing for wind. Then Leo came—alone, shoulders slumped, eyes scanning the hallway like he was searching for a safety he no longer believed in. He saw them, paused. Then kept walking, slow but certain. It was the first time none of them flinched under his gaze.

Mr. Clarke spoke, quietly but clearly. "Leo is suspended for one week, effective immediately." The words landed like a statement of fact, not punishment, but reality. Everyone heard. What had felt secret was now public. The consequences had come, and not because of anger—but because someone finally cared enough to stop ignoring the darkness.

Sophie felt the tension loosen in her chest. Not because she wanted Leo to be punished. But because the permission to be safe, to be heard, had finally come. They watched Leo's back recede down the hall, his feet lighter than the weight of his actions had ever been. No bravado. No laughter. Just footsteps.

"I feel... weird," Ella whispered, voice low. She hooked her finger on her backpack strap, some invisible anchor to steady herself. Jasmin let out a breath. "It's okay," she said. "We did it." Nico nodded. "Consequences don't mean we hate him. They mean we stopped pretending it was okay." Ty's eyes tracked the hallway door until it snapped shut. "It means we're safe now," he said. Sophie closed her eyes and let the real words land in her heart. Safe.

Miss Kara handed Sophie a sheet of paper — a note she could read privately later — reminding her she could always talk again, anytime. Sophie folded it carefully, sealing it in her pocket like a promise. "I never thought I'd think about him and nothing would ache," she said, almost to herself. Mr. Clarke turned to the group and spoke softly. "When someone hurts others with hidden tactics, it's not enough to say 'stop.' There must be real consequences." He nodded at them. "You were brave. You spoke truth. That matters."

As the group walked to their next class, they noticed how the hallway seemed less crowded, but more real. Faces passed them. Some avoided eyes. Others offered small nods. Nothing was the same anymore — and that was okay. Later that day, Sophie sat under her favourite tree outside, journal open. She wrote: "When the mirror breaks, the truth shows us our own face." She looked at the words and let them settle. It didn't feel like victory. It felt like the world righting itself just a little.

She thought about what it meant to deal with someone like Leo—not with fury, but with boundaries. She remembered reading that being around someone who acts entitled, who needs constant attention, often comes from things they carry—hurt, confusion, fear. And that to keep yourself safe, you must set clear lines—and live by them.

She thought of the advice adults sometimes whispered: "Set boundaries, speak truth, protect your heart." That's what they'd just done. Not with violence, but with clarity and courage. The afternoon sun dropped behind the leaves, and Sophie felt the quiet promise of tomorrow climbing in her chest. She was learning not just to survive the darkness—not just to shine, but to grow roots. To be a tree that stands, firm against storm winds.

And somewhere in her, a new story began: one where truth didn't have to hide. Where love didn't coagulate into control. Where boundaries weren't walling in—but protecting the gardens inside. She closed her journal and stood. The day wasn't over yet. And this new story had many chapters left to live.

The afternoon air felt different—cooler, calmer, and edged with that strange quiet that only settles after something real has been said. The playground was half-empty now, the buses already gone, the echoes of recess replaced by the rustle of leaves and the hush of ending things. On the back bench near the tree line, Jasmin sat with Ty, Nico, Ella, and Sophie. No one was crying. But no one was pretending to be okay, either.

Sophie looked down at her hands. The red thread bracelet Leo had once given her was gone now. Not tossed out in anger, not burned in revenge—just quietly removed, slipped into a desk drawer like a chapter she wasn't going to reread. She picked at the crease in her jeans and finally said aloud, "We're not mean for noticing." Her voice wasn't strong, but it wasn't shaking either. "We're not bad for walking away."

Jasmin looked up, nodded once, and didn't offer a smile. Not because she was upset. But because some moments don't need smiles—they need truth. "He made us think we were being dramatic," she said. "He made us think noticing was wrong." Nico leaned forward, arms on knees. "It was like... the nicer he got, the more confused we became. Like he used kindness like a fishing line. Pulling us in just enough. Then letting go when we stopped clapping." He didn't sound angry anymore. Just tired. And maybe older than he had been two weeks ago.

Ty ran his finger through the dirt near his sneaker. "Smiles can lie," he said. "Words too. But the feeling in your stomach—that one doesn't lie." Ella nodded, tight and slow. She still hadn't said much since Leo's suspension was announced, but her silence was no longer small. It was the kind of quiet that holds knowledge, not fear.

Miss Kara had spoken to each of them privately. So had Mr. Clarke. But the moment that stayed with them most was the final one, when Mr. Clarke stood before their whole sixth-grade class and told the truth plainly. "Leo won't be coming back to this classroom," he said. "He's been strongly informed that if this happens again—at this school or any other school in Ontario—he will be expelled completely." There had been no applause. Just stillness. The kind that means something's been understood.

Sophie looked over at the bench's edge where Leo used to sit, tossing his bag down like he owned the ground. "I believed it all," she said. "The way he talked to me. The way he made it feel like a movie." She blinked hard. "I didn't know that movies could lie, too."

Ty handed her a folded slip of paper. On it, one word had been written in careful block letters: enough. She held it for a long time before folding it smaller, smaller, smaller—until it fit neatly in her palm. "I keep thinking," said Ella, finally speaking, "about how he made me say sorry. Even when I didn't know what I'd done wrong." She looked up, voice clear. "I'm not saying sorry for that anymore."

"No one should," Jasmin said. "Not when you're being controlled. Not when someone flips the rules just to stay on top." The wind picked up then, rustling the leaves above them. Nico looked up at the sky, not to escape, but to feel the air on his face. It was the kind of sky that held stories—the kind where truth could land and take root. "Leo made his choice," Ty said quietly. "And now we've made ours."

They stood, one by one, stretching limbs made heavy by truth but stronger for having carried it. No one said goodbye. They didn't need to. They understood each other now in a way no argument, no explanation, no teacher's note ever could. As they walked home, footsteps soft against the sidewalk, they didn't speak much. But Sophie kept turning one sentence over in her head. Not all smiles are safe. And that was okay. Because she didn't need every smile. Just the ones that meant what they said.

Behind her, the school stood tall and still. Somewhere inside, Mr. Clarke sat writing a report, Miss Kara sipped tea with her thoughts, and Leo's locker was already being reassigned. Life kept moving. But not in circles anymore. In the notebook Sophie kept tucked inside her desk, she added one more sentence under the others: Truth is what love looks like when it's not afraid anymore. She closed the book, zipped her backpack, and kept walking.

CHAPTER 5: WHAT A GASLIGHT FEELS LIKE

Leo wasn't in his seat. That was the first thing Jasmin noticed when she stepped into the classroom. His desk, always a bit askew with his jacket hanging from the back like a warning flag, sat perfectly straight. Nobody dared claim it. Nobody touched it. The room had a strange hush, like it hadn't figured out whether it was relieved or holding its breath. Miss Kara didn't mention him. She moved on with morning announcements like there wasn't a boy suspended for psychological manipulation. But every chair had eyes that flicked toward his empty spot at least once. And Jasmin couldn't stop herself from doing it, too. Even with him gone, she still heard his voice, soft and sharp. "You're too sensitive." Like a breeze through her ribs. That's what gaslighting did. It didn't yell. It whispered.

Ty sat next to her, folding a paper airplane. Not to fly it—just to fold. He wasn't even looking at it. He looked at her. "He's not here," he whispered. Jasmin didn't nod. She didn't blink. She didn't have to. "I know," she said softly, like saying it too loud might summon him back. That's what it felt like. Like saying his name three times would bring him around the corner. Nico came in last. He slid into his chair without his usual backpack thud. No jokes, no scribbles on his notebook. Just that same unsettled quiet. "Static," he said suddenly. Jasmin turned. "What?" Nico looked up. "That's what it feels like. Like there's still... static in the air."

At recess, the four of them sat near the bench under the maple tree, where the shade pooled like a lake. Ty had brought a dictionary from the library. He didn't open it. He just rested his hand on the cover. "It doesn't matter that he's gone," he said, more to the wind than to them. "The stuff he said is still stuck in our heads." Ella rubbed her arms. "I keep thinking I made everything up." She looked down. "Like maybe it wasn't that bad." Nico leaned forward. "But it was." His voice didn't waver. "It was that bad. You're not making it up. That's what he wanted you to think." The four of them sat there for a long time. No games. No running. Just trying to scrape his shadow off their skin.

Back in class, Jasmin found herself checking her own answers three times before handing in her math sheet. She knew how to divide fractions. She wasn't even bad at it. But something in her kept whispering she'd done it wrong. That voice didn't belong to her. It belonged to Leo. "That's not how Miss Kara taught it. Don't you ever listen?" But he hadn't said that today. He wasn't even there. Still, she hesitated before handing it in. Miss Kara smiled at her. Not the fake kind. The real kind. But Jasmin still turned away fast, just in case she imagined it.

Ty finally opened the dictionary in the library, after school. "Gaslight," he read, "To manipulate someone by psychological means into questioning their own sanity." Jasmin swallowed. "That sounds like a horror movie." Ty nodded. "It is. Except the monster makes you the monster." Ella sat next to him, twisting a string from her hoodie. "Can someone do that without even yelling?" Nico answered this time. "Yeah. It's worse when they don't yell." He paused. "Then nobody believes you."

Miss Kara handed Jasmin her test with a small gold star on top. Jasmin looked at it like it was a trap. She didn't trust it. She didn't feel smart. She didn't feel anything. Just fog. That's what it was. Not a storm. Not a fire. Just a thick, creeping fog. The kind that makes you forget what the sky looked like before. Leo had covered everything in fog, and even gone, the fog didn't lift. It lingered in desks and pencils and the way your own name sounded in your head.

Ty told them it had a name—residue. "That's what's left after someone like Leo messes with your thoughts." Jasmin tilted her head. "Like... smoke after a fire?" "Exactly," Ty said. "Except you breathe it in, and it stays." Nico added, "That's why we're going to name it. If you name it, it can't hide."

Ella hadn't said much until they reached the bikes. Then she said, "I didn't lie, did I?" They all stopped. She looked at each of them. Her face said she needed an answer, not comfort. "No," Nico said. "He did. And he convinced you it was the other way around." Ty put a hand on her shoulder. "Gaslighting makes you think your memories are broken. They're not." Ella nodded slowly. But her fingers trembled as she unlocked her helmet.

That night, Nico sat in his room writing in the notebook Ty gave him. He started the page with one sentence: Leo told me I lied about the hallway, but I didn't. He stared at it for a long time. Then he wrote it again. And again. Until the page was full. Until it didn't feel like maybe anymore. Until it felt like truth.

Jasmin stood in the mirror brushing her hair. She said aloud, "I'm not too sensitive." She didn't say it loud. But she said it like she meant it. Her voice sounded small, but it belonged to her. She wasn't quoting Leo anymore.

The next morning, Miss Kara gave an assignment. "Write something true that no one can argue with." Jasmin's pencil hovered above the page. She wrote, I remember how it felt. That's enough.

Leo's fog didn't vanish. But it started to lift—inch by inch, thought by thought. The four of them weren't trying to fight him anymore. They were trying to find themselves again. That was harder. But it was theirs.

And even though no one said it, they all noticed that Ty started sitting a little straighter. Ella laughed twice at lunch. Jasmin held eye contact with Miss Kara for six full seconds. And Nico didn't erase anything on his quiz, not even once. Some fog leaves on its own. This kind, the kind Leo left, had to be pushed. Slowly. Gently. Together.

Ella stood at the foot of her bed, gripping the hem of her hoodie so tightly the fabric creased into her palms. The hallway wouldn't let her go. She had bumped into Leo. Or maybe he bumped into her. She couldn't tell anymore. It had happened so quickly—just one of those swerves between classes, arms full of textbooks, a blur of elbows and footsteps.

She had said sorry. She remembered that part. She thought she did. But the moment kept looping in her mind, rewinding and skipping forward like an old tape that someone had stepped on. His voice had been cold. "Maybe watch where you're going next time." She hadn't answered. She hadn't even blinked. She just smiled, because smiling was safer than speaking.

The more she thought about it, the less certain she felt. Had she smiled too much? Did her silence make her guilty? Maybe he hadn't meant it the way it sounded. Maybe she had misheard him. That's what gaslighting does. It's not about yelling. It's about erasing. And Ella was starting to feel like her memory had been scribbled over with someone else's pen. She whispered the words under her breath again: "I'm sorry." Her voice sounded strange in the quiet of her room, like it didn't belong to her. She tried again, slower: "I said sorry." But the more she repeated it, the more hollow it felt.

She walked in circles. Her socks dragged softly over the carpet. It wasn't the bump. It wasn't the words. It was the echo that followed—the guilt that didn't have a shape. She didn't know why she was the one who felt ashamed. She hadn't pushed him. She hadn't said anything cruel. And still, it gnawed at her like she had done something deeply wrong, something she couldn't name. That's the part no one talks about. The way gaslighting doesn't scream—it whispers inside you, quietly enough that you think it's your own voice.

At school the next day, Ella avoided the corner of the hallway where it had happened. Her eyes flicked away from the spot like it burned. She walked with her arms tighter to her sides. Her backpack straps dug into her shoulders as if to remind her to stay small. Nico noticed it. He didn't say anything at first. He just walked a step behind her, close enough to feel like a shield. At lunch, he nudged her gently with his elbow. "You've been quiet." She didn't answer. He gave her a second. Then he said, "You didn't do anything wrong."

Ella looked up. Her mouth opened, then shut. She wasn't sure how to argue, but her stomach didn't agree. "I don't know," she mumbled. "It's all fuzzy." Nico didn't push. He just nodded. "That's what happens. He fogged it up on purpose." He passed her a cookie from his tray. "Eat something. You need to anchor." That word—anchor—stuck with her. Maybe her mind was floating, unhooked, drifting between what happened and what Leo wanted her to believe happened. Maybe that's why she couldn't stop spinning the scene in her head.

Ty joined them later and brought a folded note. "For when it gets blurry," he said, sliding it across the table to Ella. She opened it when no one was looking. In Ty's handwriting, it read: If you said sorry, that means you cared. If he made you doubt it, that means he didn't. That sentence hit her chest like a bell. Not loud, not painful—but deep. She folded the note slowly, as if it might fall apart if rushed. For the first time since the bump, she breathed without wincing.

Jasmin met her at the lockers before last bell. She handed Ella a small pink eraser shaped like a heart. "It doesn't actually erase anything," Jasmin said, "but I like holding it when I feel erased." Ella clutched the eraser in her palm, pressing it until her fingers tingled. It wasn't the hallway she kept replaying—it was the moment after. The second Leo looked at her like she was dirt, and the second she wondered if maybe she was.

Gaslighting wraps around a person like clingfilm. It doesn't scream. It doesn't even tighten all at once. It just makes breathing a little harder, day by day. Ella began writing down everything she remembered about that moment. Not because she thought it would prove something. But because she needed a place where her version of the story lived, untouched.

In her notebook, she drew two columns: "What I felt" and "What he made me feel." On the left side, she wrote, Startled, but polite. Caught off guard. Sorry. On the right side: Clumsy. Guilty. Wrong. It wasn't easy to write, but it made the fog sit still for a minute. She looked at the words like they were a map out of the maze.

By the end of the week, Leo still hadn't returned, but Ella's memory of the moment didn't feel any clearer. What changed was her relationship to the doubt. It still sat in her chest, but she wasn't feeding it anymore. She was watching it, questioning it, pulling back its covers to see what lay underneath. That's what awareness does. It doesn't fix the damage. It names it.

At lunch on Thursday, she leaned against the fence with Jasmin. "I remember saying sorry," she said quietly. Jasmin nodded. "Then that's what happened." Ella's eyes stung, not from tears—but from the relief of being believed. It was a strange kind of victory, quiet and heavy. But it was hers.

Gaslighting doesn't always need to be called out to be defeated. Sometimes it just needs to be seen. And slowly, Ella was starting to see what Leo had tried to blur. She remembered her own softness. She remembered that bumping into someone didn't make her a villain. She remembered that truth isn't always loud. Sometimes it's just still.

Nico sat on the lowest bench by the far wall, one sneaker half-on, heel folded beneath, the other swinging like it had something to say but wouldn't. The gym buzzed from afterschool kids chasing rubber balls and shrieking with leftover energy, but his thoughts were quieter than usual. Too quiet. That kind of quiet that feels like walking through fog barefoot. He had been thinking about what Leo said to him before the suspension. Or after. Or maybe it was both. Or maybe he imagined it. That part wasn't sitting still. He clenched his jaw, not because he was angry, but because the confusion felt like pressure, like something heavy trying to move through him.

He tried again, pressing the memory like a leaf between pages, hoping it would flatten into truth. It was in the hallway, right before the bell, wasn't it? Leo had looked at him—maybe not directly—but kind of through him. "Why do you always make things worse?"

That's what Nico thought he heard. But maybe it was, "You're always in the way." He chewed the inside of his lip, tasted copper. Or maybe Leo didn't say anything. Maybe Nico just imagined it because he expected it. It was hard to know. When someone messes with your thoughts often enough, you start to help them do it. That's the worst part.

Ty sat down next to him, back to the wall, knees up like a pair of tents. He didn't speak for a while. That was something Ty was good at—holding space like it was a shield. Nico didn't look at him, just whispered, "You ever forget something on purpose?" Ty didn't answer right away. His eyes were on the floor, where a bit of lint rolled between their shoes like a tiny tumbleweed. "I think sometimes I forget so I don't have to admit it was real," he said. "But this isn't that."

Nico swallowed hard. "I don't know if he said it. Maybe he didn't. Maybe I made it worse." That part—maybe I made it worse—had become his loop. It curled around his ribs every time he breathed. Ty turned his head slowly. "You didn't," he said. Just that. No list. No story. No examples. Just the words. Nico wanted to believe him. He really did. But when your memory starts swimming, even a lifeboat can feel like it's drifting.

"Did he push me that day?" Nico asked, eyes narrowed like he was trying to catch the truth in midair. "I remember bumping into him, but... was it on purpose? Did I bump him? Or did he bump me? Was I in the way? I don't remember saying anything." Ty blinked. "He stepped into your path. I saw it. You didn't do anything wrong. He did." Nico blinked back, unsure whether his eyes stung from disbelief or relief.

"But why can't I hold onto it?" Nico said, voice shaking now. "Why does it feel like the more I try to remember, the less I'm sure?" Ty leaned his head back against the wall. "Because gaslighting isn't about making you forget," he said slowly. "It's about making you not trust your remembering. They break your brain's compass. They don't hide the truth. They blur it."

A dodgeball bounced by and hit the wall near them, but neither flinched. Nico hugged his knees, forehead pressing into denim. "I wish I could replay it. Like rewind a tape and just see what happened." Ty tapped his notebook. "That's why I write stuff down. When I don't, it gets fuzzy. Like dreams when you wake up. You think you'll remember, but you don't." Nico nodded slowly, then looked up. "Even if I wrote it, who'd believe it? He's not even here anymore, and I still feel like I have to prove I'm not lying."

Ty's face tightened. "You don't have to prove anything to people who already believe you. The only one you need to remind is you." That part hit deeper than expected. Nico wiped his palms on his jeans, the sweat cold even though the gym was warm. "Okay," he whispered. "Okay, yeah." But it still felt like his memory had holes in it, like a net instead of a blanket.

"I think I'll start writing it down," Nico said after a long pause. "Everything. Not just the big stuff. Even the stuff I'm not sure about." Ty nodded. "That's how you see patterns. That's how you make fog into lines again." Nico almost smiled. Not quite. But almost. It was enough to make the room feel a little less tilted.

From across the gym, Jasmin waved. She'd been with Ella in the library earlier, and now both girls were walking toward them, backpacks half-zipped, looking tired but steady. Nico waved back, hand slow, unsure. "You think they feel like this too?" he asked. "Like they're losing parts of what happened?" Ty stood. "They do. But they don't have to lose them alone."

They walked toward the others without saying more. But Nico felt the knot inside him shift. Not untie—but loosen. It was still there, but now it had air. That was something. He didn't know exactly what Leo had said or hadn't. But he knew what it had done. And maybe that was enough to write down. And so he would. Even if the page stayed half-blank for now, Nico would fill it with something true. One word at a time. Even if the memories were blurry, his voice didn't have to be.

Jasmin didn't remember walking toward the bathroom. Her feet had moved on their own, like dream-legs in one of those chase scenes where everything's slow and foggy. Her head ached in two places—the front, where the thoughts were piling too fast, and the back, where something deeper and colder was whispering things she couldn't answer. The echo of Leo's words clung to her like syrup. Not his loud ones—the soft ones. The praise that slid in under the skin. The way he used to call her "so smart" and "cooler than the rest." It all felt like a trick now. But what if it wasn't? What if she was reading too much into it?

She pressed her fingers against the cold tiles near the sink, her stomach twisting hard. Her reflection blinked back at her from the mirror, but she couldn't tell if her eyes looked angry or guilty. Or both. She looked like someone she didn't quite recognize anymore. Her smile—had it been too much? Had she made him think she liked him that way? Did she give him the wrong message when she laughed at that joke, even though she hated it? The questions spun like leaves in a storm, each one sharper than the last. She could barely hear her own thoughts over the gust of them all.

Somewhere in her gut, something gave way. Her body moved before her brain could catch up. She lurched sideways toward the wall, one hand clutching the paper towel dispenser like it might hold her upright. Her stomach turned inside out. She barely made it to the floor drain just beside the girls' bathroom door. The vomit came fast—hot, bitter, and sudden. It hit the floor with a splash she couldn't unhear. For a second, she just stayed there, breathing through her nose, the taste in her throat almost secondary to the shame that followed.

She wiped her mouth with the sleeve of her cardigan, trembling. Not because she was sick-sick. She knew that kind. This was worse. This was the kind that didn't come from germs but from thoughts. From that gnawing feeling that maybe she was the bad guy. That maybe she had caused all this. That maybe everything happening to Ella, to Nico, even to Ty, had something to do with her somehow being… too much. Too talkative. Too friendly. Too everything.

The bathroom door creaked open behind her, but Jasmin didn't move. A gentle voice—Ella's—whispered, "Are you okay?" Jasmin shook her head once, barely. She didn't want to cry. Crying would mean she needed comfort, and right now, she didn't think she deserved it. Ella crouched beside her and didn't say anything else. Just sat there, legs crossed, shoulder touching Jasmin's. That part—the not-talking—felt like the only thing keeping Jasmin's shame from spilling over.

"I think I messed everything up," Jasmin said after a long silence. Her voice was scratchy and small. "I laughed when I shouldn't have. I told him he was funny. I sat next to him on the field trip. Maybe he thought… I don't know." Ella didn't interrupt. She just reached into her pocket, pulled out a half-used tissue, and handed it over without a word. Jasmin took it with shaking fingers. "What if I made him think I liked him?" she whispered.

Ella finally spoke. "What if he made you think that?" The question landed like a hand on Jasmin's shoulder—not heavy, but grounding. Jasmin didn't know how to answer it. Because now, looking back, everything felt edited. Like the story had been rewritten after she already turned the page. And somehow, the edits made her the villain.

She thought about the lunch table, how Leo used to save her a seat, and how proud she'd been the first time he said she was cool. How it felt like being chosen. But now, those memories felt like traps wearing party hats. They weren't gifts. They were setups. And she had thanked him for each one like a fool. That's what stung the most.

Ty's voice echoed in her mind, something he said the day before: "Gaslighting doesn't start with the lie. It starts with the charm." She hadn't understood it then. She did now. Charm gets through the door. Lies come after. And once they're inside, they redecorate your whole head until you don't know what's real anymore.

Jasmin wiped her face again, harder this time. She stood slowly, legs stiff, heart still pounding like a warning bell. Ella stood with her. Neither of them looked at the puddle on the floor. It would get cleaned up. But Jasmin wasn't sure how long it would take to clean up what was happening inside her. She wasn't even sure if that kind of mess had a mop.

As they walked back toward the classroom, Jasmin spoke again, voice steadier now. "If he ever comes back and tries to make me feel like that again… I think I'll know better." Ella nodded. "I think we all will." There was no celebration in that. Just a quiet agreement. Like soldiers after a small battle. A promise not to forget.

Nico met them halfway down the hallway, Ty just behind him, both of them slowing when they saw Jasmin's face. She didn't smile. But she didn't flinch either. And for now, that was enough.

Ty didn't usually like writing on the whiteboard unless the teacher asked him to. It made him feel like a try-hard. But today he did it on purpose. It was after math class, during inside lunch because it had rained all morning and the playground was still soaked. He waited until Mr. Rafferty had gone to the staffroom and the other kids were clustered around their snacks. Then he uncapped a red marker and wrote the word big across the top: Gaslighting. The marker squeaked a little at the curve of the G, and Nico looked up right away.

At the front table, Jasmin raised her eyebrows and tilted her head. She didn't speak. Neither did Ella, but she moved a little closer, her half-eaten granola bar forgotten in her hand. Ty stood beside the board like a substitute teacher with something he couldn't keep inside anymore. "I didn't make this word up," he began, turning around. "It's real. It's in dictionaries. But it's not about fire or gas or anything like that. It's about what people do when they want you to feel confused on purpose."

He underlined the word once, neatly, and looked back at them. "Gaslighting," he continued, "is what happens when someone tricks your feelings into lying to you. They do it so you stop trusting yourself. And when you stop trusting yourself, you start trusting them instead." Jasmin's fingers closed around the edge of her desk, white-knuckled. Nico didn't blink. Ella nodded slowly, eyes locked on the red letters like they were still burning.

Ty walked back toward them, keeping his voice low so the other kids wouldn't hear. "They make you doubt stuff you know happened. They say things like, 'That never happened,' or 'You're too sensitive,' or 'You're remembering it wrong.'" He paused to let the weight of those phrases sink in. "You know how it feels? Like your brain is being picked apart by someone with a toothpick. One poke at a time."

Ella whispered, "Leo used to say that all the time." Her voice barely reached across the table. "He said I was being dramatic… even when I was just asking a question." Jasmin nodded. "He said I was overthinking things. That I was making him look bad when I didn't agree with him." Nico stared at the board like it held answers to every confusing thing he'd felt in the last three weeks.

"Gaslighting," Ty said again, quieter this time, "isn't loud. It's slow. It's the kind of thing that makes you say sorry when you didn't do anything. It makes you think maybe you're the problem. That maybe you're the one being mean, or silly, or difficult." He sat down finally, folding his hands in his lap. "But you're not. It's them. They just want you to question yourself, because then they're the only one who seems sure of anything."

Jasmin's face was unreadable, but the way she kept looking at the word made it clear that something was unfolding inside her. Nico reached into his desk and pulled out a sticky note. "Can you write it again?" he asked. "I want to put it in my binder. Just so I don't forget." Ty nodded and jotted it down, then handed it over. Nico peeled the paper off and stuck it right beside his timetable, right next to the multiplication table he never needed anymore.

"I didn't know it had a name," Ella said quietly. "I thought it was just… me." Ty leaned forward, elbows on the desk. "That's how it works. It makes you feel alone. Like you're the only one who can't think straight. But it's not you. It's what they want you to think. That you're broken. But you're not." He paused. "If someone really cares about you, they don't try to confuse you. They try to understand you."

They sat in silence for a few moments, the kind that wasn't awkward, just full. The room buzzed with quiet wrappers and soft lunch talk in the background, but the four of them were wrapped in something else entirely. Something warmer. Something stronger than confusion.

Jasmin finally broke the silence. "So what do you do when it happens?" Ty didn't answer right away. He turned the marker in his fingers like a puzzle piece. "You talk to someone who sees it too. Like us. And if someone makes you feel like your brain's lying to you… you write down what really happened. You keep your truth somewhere safe. So they can't take it away."

Nico nodded like a judge agreeing with a verdict. "And if they still try to mess with your head?" Ty looked straight at him. "You walk away. Even if it's scary. Even if they say you're overreacting. Because your peace is worth more than their pretend kindness."

Ella leaned back in her chair, eyes still on the red ink. "Gaslighting," she repeated softly. "It sounds like lighting a match and blowing smoke in someone's eyes." Ty smiled just a little. "That's not far off," he said. "But now we've got goggles." They didn't laugh. They didn't need to. The truth had landed. And it stayed.

Ella didn't say it right away. She held the words in her hands like marbles—cold, slippery, and maybe a little broken. They were sitting outside the art room, the four of them, waiting for the rain to stop. Nico was sketching. Ty was flipping through a wrinkled book of samurai stories. Jasmin was quietly tearing the edges off her juice box straw. It was Ella who finally spoke, her voice small but steady: "I think I'm just confused."

No one jumped in. No one rushed to fix it. That's why she kept going. "It's like, I remember what he said… but then I think about it again and it feels different. Like maybe I heard it wrong. Or maybe I'm the one who made it weird." Her shoulders were rounded forward like a question mark. Nico didn't look up from his paper. "Or maybe," he said gently, "he made you feel that way on purpose."

Ella blinked. "You think?" Ty didn't even glance away from his book. "I know." That was enough to open the window inside her mind. Ella took a deep breath and looked over at Miss Kara, who had just walked past with a basket of watercolours and brushes. She paused when she caught the group's eyes on her. "Everything alright, crew?" she asked, warm but alert. Jasmin nodded, but something in Ella's face must've said more. Miss Kara knelt beside her, set the basket down, and said, "You don't have to tell me. But I can sit here if you want."

Ella hesitated. Then she said, "I think I got… turned around by someone. Like, I thought we were friends. And then… I didn't know what we were. Or what I was." Miss Kara's face didn't flinch. She nodded once, slowly. "Sixth grade," she said softly, like a secret that had been hidden in her throat. "That was the year someone did that to me, too." All four kids went still.

Miss Kara didn't smile. She looked down at her knees, then back up. "He'd say I was pretty when I helped him. Said I was needy when I wanted help. I remember feeling like I had to keep guessing what version of me would make him be nice again. And no matter what I did, he always changed the rules."

Ella's eyes were wide. "You remember that?" Miss Kara nodded again. "I didn't have words for it back then. But now I do. Gaslighting. It's when someone makes you question your memories or feelings, just so they can stay in charge. So they don't have to admit they're being unkind." Nico exhaled through his nose. Jasmin stopped shredding her straw. Ty finally closed his book.

"You think I'm being dramatic?" Ella asked, her voice barely audible. Miss Kara shook her head. "No. I think you're being clear." She paused. "And I think you're braver than I was. I didn't tell anyone when it happened to me. I didn't even tell myself the truth until I was much older." Jasmin scooted closer to Ella and placed her hand beside hers without touching. "I feel like… it's like you're in a fog. And the fog smells like compliments, but it still stings your eyes."

Miss Kara smiled at that. "Yes. Fog with perfume." Ty added, "And it gets in your throat so you can't speak right." Nico nodded. "And when it finally clears, you're standing in a different place than where you started. But you don't remember how you got there."

Ella finally let herself lean into Jasmin's side. "I hate that I still think about it." Miss Kara shook her head. "That's not weakness. That's your mind trying to make sense of something unfair." She picked up her basket, then looked over her shoulder. "Come find me later if you want to talk more."

The moment she was gone, Nico whispered, "I like her more now." Jasmin smiled. "She was always nice. But now she's… real." Ty tapped the edge of his book against his knee. "Even adults get gaslighted." Ella said, "I didn't know they remembered being kids." Nico said, "Some of them never forget." They all sat a little straighter after that. Not because they had answers—but because the questions didn't scare them as much.

It happened three times before Jasmin noticed. The first was in the hallway after recess, when she didn't say much and someone asked if she was okay. "Sorry," she mumbled. "I'm just quiet today." The second was in the group chat when she didn't reply to Nico's message about a new art set. An hour passed, and then she typed, Sorry, I was doing homework, even though no one had said a word about her delay. The third was in the library, when a tear slid down her cheek as she listened to Ella talk about feeling invisible. "Sorry," Jasmin whispered, brushing her face quickly. "I don't even know why I'm crying."

That was the moment Ty closed his book. He didn't speak, not at first. He just tilted his head slightly like he was watching a bird balance on a wire. Nico looked up from his drawing and blinked slow. Ella didn't ask what was wrong. Instead, she scooted closer to Jasmin on the carpet, so their knees were touching. Jasmin kept her eyes down, trying to swallow whatever feeling had caught in her throat. The feeling wouldn't move.

"Why am I sorry?" she asked, the words barely louder than the humming of the overhead lights. It wasn't a question thrown into the air—it was a question aimed at the centre of herself, as though she'd found a knot in her soul that had been tightening for months without her noticing. "I didn't do anything wrong."

"You didn't," Nico said simply. Ty nodded. "People like Leo make you feel like everything's your fault. So you start saying sorry for existing." Ella added, "It's like your brain tries to protect you by shrinking. Like maybe if you're small enough, they won't aim at you anymore." Jasmin took a breath, but it came out shaky. "I used to say sorry all the time to my cousin, even when she made fun of my clothes. She'd tell me I looked weird, and I'd say sorry like I had broken something." Ty said, "You didn't break anything. She did."

Jasmin's lip trembled. Her hands were still folded tightly in her lap, fingers digging into her sweater sleeves. "I keep thinking if I'm quiet, if I'm polite, if I say sorry enough times, I'll be safe. But it never works. I still get hurt." "That's because kindness doesn't work on people who use kindness as a trap," Nico said, with his pencil resting across his palm like a sword sheathed in thought. "They don't want you to be kind. They want you to be obedient."

Ella reached out and gently touched Jasmin's wrist. "You don't have to apologise to us. You don't even have to explain." The tears were back, but this time Jasmin didn't brush them away. She let them fall slowly, each one a little lighter than the last. When she finally looked up, all three of them were watching her—not with pity, but with presence. They didn't look away. They didn't interrupt.

"Can I…" Jasmin started, then paused. "Can I just sit with you for a while?" "We were already sitting with you," Nico said. That's when Ty leaned forward and wrapped his arms around her without asking. Ella followed, then Nico, one arm around each of them like a bridge. Jasmin was caught in the middle—not trapped, but held. And in that moment, she realized she didn't feel small. She felt seen.

"I don't want to keep being sorry," she whispered into Ty's hoodie. "Then don't," he said gently. "Not with us." They stayed that way for a long time, until the clock buzzed and the hallways stirred again. But the warmth didn't leave. It stayed tucked under Jasmin's ribs like a handprint that said, You're allowed to take up space. You always were.

Nico stood in the boys' washroom, one foot angled against the door like it might swing open without warning. The mirror was foggy from someone's hot water hand rinse, but he didn't wipe it clean. His eyes were already staring back at him through the smear, like they didn't trust the glass to give him anything true. "Was it really that bad?" he whispered, not expecting an answer. But his stomach twisted the moment he asked it, curling like something wounded trying to protect itself from further bruising.

He'd been fine all day—on the outside. He'd laughed when Ty cracked a joke in math class. He'd handed out two glue sticks during art. He'd even told Miss Kara he liked her new hairband, which she said made her feel "ten years younger." But inside, there was static. Not the loud, wild kind, but the itchy, low buzz that sits in the corners of your thoughts and waits for quiet. That static grew the moment he stepped into the washroom and saw himself.

The worst part wasn't the memory of what Leo had said. It was that he couldn't quite remember how Leo had said it. Had it been sarcastic? Mean? Was he smiling when he said it? Or frowning? Had it been said in front of the others? Or privately, with that casual cruelty he saved just for one-on-one moments? Nico tried to pin it down, but the memory kept shifting like water in cupped hands—always slipping before he could name the shape.

He remembered feeling small. That part was clear. He remembered feeling like his spine wanted to fold inward, like shrinking might make the words bounce off instead of pierce. But when he tried to explain it later, even to Ty, the edges of the event softened. "Maybe I'm exaggerating," he'd said. Ty didn't agree. But Nico hadn't been able to stop thinking that.

He leaned closer to the mirror, forehead nearly pressing the surface. "Was it really that bad?" he asked again. His reflection didn't answer. But his gut did—a slow lurch like a wave gathering beneath his ribs. He clutched the sink edge. Cold porcelain. Smooth. Real. Solid. Something to hold onto when his thoughts weren't.

"I don't even know anymore," he muttered. His voice sounded strange in the tile space—echoey, almost like someone else had said it. The door didn't open. No one came in. He was alone with it, which almost made it worse. When Leo had said the thing—whatever it was—it had felt sharp. But now? Now it just felt like Nico was the problem for remembering it wrong.

He bent over the sink and breathed slowly through his nose. One, two, three...like Ty taught him to do when anxiety started to rise. His stomach flipped again, and for a second, he thought he might throw up. His hands gripped the sink tighter. His legs trembled beneath him. "This isn't normal," he said to the wall, to the faucet, to the silence. The bell rang faintly in the distance. He didn't move. The nausea didn't, either.

Jasmin had said something yesterday—about how Leo's words stuck like gum under your shoe. They didn't leave, even after you scraped them off. Nico was beginning to think it was worse than that. Leo's words didn't stick. They rewrote. They edited memories, rearranged feelings, made you doubt things you knew had happened. Nico had been there. He knew. And yet here he was, trying to convince his reflection he hadn't imagined it.

He finally turned on the tap and splashed water on his face. The cold helped. A little. Enough to slow the spinning. He didn't want to look back up—but he did. The mirror hadn't changed. But the boy in it had. His shoulders were tighter. His eyes were shinier. Not quite tears. Just the weight of almost. "You're not crazy," he said aloud. It felt weird to say it, but it helped. "You didn't make it up." The stomach ache eased just a little. Not gone. But acknowledged.

He thought about what Ty had said after class. "When someone lies to you enough times, you start lying to yourself. That's how gaslighting works." Nico hadn't fully understood it until now—not until he stood in front of the mirror and realized he didn't trust his own memory anymore. That scared him more than Leo ever had.

He stepped back, dried his hands, and stared once more into his own eyes. "Remember what you felt," he said softly. "Not what he told you to feel." When he finally left the bathroom, the air in the hallway felt thinner. Lighter. Like maybe truth didn't fix everything. But at least it didn't make him sick.

Ty didn't say anything right away. He just watched them—Jasmin, Ella, even Nico—from across the table in the library. His pencil stayed still on the lined paper, the eraser pressing softly against the margin like it had a thought of its own. Jasmin had just winced when a chair scraped behind her. Ella had ducked her shoulders when someone burst out laughing near the photocopier. Nico noticed both. Ty had seen more. "You're not scared of people," he said at last. "You're scared of reactions."

Jasmin blinked at him. Ella didn't speak. Nico's fingers curled on the edge of the table. The fluorescent lights hummed above them—normal, safe, bright. But the way everyone sat, backs slightly bowed, shoulders near their ears, said nothing felt safe right now. Nico rubbed his hand against the table's edge. "I feel like I'm going to say the wrong thing every time I talk," he muttered. "Like, even if I try to say something nice, it'll get twisted."

"That's the part people don't see," Ty said. He leaned forward, his voice softer now. "Gaslighting doesn't just mess with your memory. It messes with your body." He tapped his chest. "Right here. It teaches you to flinch before you even know what you're afraid of." His eyes moved to Jasmin. "Like how you flinched when Liam laughed too loud just now. Or how you looked over your shoulder twice before you sat down."

"I didn't realize I was doing that," Jasmin whispered. "You don't, at first," Ty replied. "That's what makes it so powerful. It makes you react to things without asking permission." Ella picked at the edge of her notebook. The corner had started to curl up. Her voice was small when it came out. "I feel like... I don't know what's real anymore." Her fingers froze. "Like maybe I'm just sensitive. Or dramatic. Or maybe I deserved some of it."

Ty shook his head, calm but firm. "You didn't deserve any of it." He looked her straight in the eyes. "That's what gaslighting wants you to think. That you're the problem. That your feelings are too big. That your memories are too messy. So you stop trusting yourself." Nico nodded slowly. "It's like you're afraid all the time. But you can't explain why. Like there's this... fog in your brain." "Exactly," Ty said. "And the worst part? You start shrinking. Not just in what you say—but in who you are."

Jasmin crossed her arms. "I used to speak up more. I used to say what I thought." Her voice cracked a little. "Now I keep second-guessing. Like, if I tell the truth, maybe someone'll say I made it up. Or that I'm too much." "Or not enough," Ella added, without lifting her eyes. There was a long pause. The kind where no one fills the space because the silence itself feels heavier than words. Nico broke it with a breath. "Leo's not even here, and I still feel like I'm walking on eggshells."

Ty pressed his palms against the table. "That's how you know it was real. If it was just a bad moment, it would've passed. But this isn't just a moment. It's a pattern." Ella looked up at him. "So... how do we stop it?" Ty didn't answer right away. He looked out the library window toward the far fence of the schoolyard. "We don't fix it all at once," he said. "We start by listening to ourselves. By believing what we remember. By trusting what our bodies are telling us."

"And what if someone says we're wrong?" Nico asked. "Then we say, 'Maybe to you. But not to me,'" Ty replied. "And we keep walking. Even if it's still on eggshells. At least we're walking forward." Jasmin rubbed her arms and nodded. "I want to stop shrinking." "You already have," Ty said. "You're talking about it. That's huge." Ella's lip trembled. "I didn't know I was allowed to." "You are," Nico said gently. "You always were." And for the first time that day, no one flinched.

Leo's version of what happened hit the school like a whisper with a megaphone. It wasn't loud at first—just a few kids in the stairwell saying, "He didn't even do anything that bad. It was a misunderstanding." Then a few more repeated it beside the water fountain, then again at lunch. According to Leo, he'd been suspended because Nico had "twisted the story" and made a big deal out of "a joke." He said Jasmin and Ty had ganged up on him, turned the class against him. "People just want to feel special," he'd added, tossing his hair like some movie star wrongly accused. But it wasn't true. And the part that scared Nico the most was how easy it sounded like it could be.

Ty heard it first from one of the Grade Fives on the swing set. "Leo said your group lied about everything," the boy whispered. "He said you were jealous." Nico didn't respond at first. He just chewed his sandwich and stared at the ants crawling around the concrete beneath the picnic table. Jasmin was quieter that day. Her hands were clenched under the table, thumb digging hard into the palm of her other hand. Ella wasn't at school. The story had gotten to her too.

In the girls' bathroom, someone had scrawled on the wall with pink marker: "Drama Queen. Crybaby." No names, but the circle knew. Jasmin had scrubbed it with paper towels and water from the sink until the paint smeared like bruises across the tile. Then she dried her eyes and went back to math class. She didn't tell the teacher.

Leo's story was clever—not because it was detailed, but because it wasn't. He kept it vague. "They misunderstood me." "I was joking." "They're overreacting." He knew how to plant doubt without watering it too much. Just enough to make people think maybe he wasn't all bad. Maybe he'd just been unlucky.

But kids remember what it felt like. They remember the cold shoulder. The laugh that hurt. The joke that stayed too long. Even if Leo's words were slippery, the memories stuck like burrs under skin. Nico didn't need to yell or post signs or chase people down. He just watched. And what he saw was change.

First, the kids who used to orbit Leo stopped laughing at his stories. Then they stopped sitting next to his empty seat in music class. Ty said it was like watching someone drop a rock into a pond—and instead of ripples spreading out, the water went still. Quietly. Firmly.

By Wednesday, nearly ninety percent of the class knew that Leo wasn't coming back until Monday. And nearly all of them knew why—not from gossip, but from how they felt when he was around. Some had stayed quiet during his tricks. Some had laughed along. But now, the fog had lifted. And no one wanted it back.

That's when Mr. Arnett the Principal stepped into Miss Kara's class with a folded sheet of paper and a voice that didn't waver. He didn't say Leo's name—but he didn't have to. "Students," he said, "we've heard a lot of stories going around about why one of your classmates isn't here this week. I'd like to clear that up." Every head in the room turned. Some hands dropped from pencil cases. Even the window blinds stopped fluttering.

"The student in question was suspended for behaviour that violated our code of conduct. This included emotional harassment, targeted psychological manipulation of peers, and repeated incidents of verbal intimidation. These actions were observed, documented, and confirmed by staff and students alike. He was not suspended because of any single person's story. He was suspended because of his own repeated choices."

Jasmin's mouth opened slightly. Nico's shoulders relaxed for the first time in days. Ty glanced at the window, then at the door, like a soldier checking exits. "Furthermore," Principal Hardy continued, "the student has been formally warned that if this behaviour continues, he will face expulsion. That is final. The well-being of every student in this school is our priority. No one has the right to make you feel unsafe, unheard, or unworthy. If that ever happens again, you come to us."

And then he folded the paper and left. The silence that followed was different than before. It wasn't afraid or confused. It was the kind that holds its breath so it can listen. Jasmin glanced at Nico. He gave her the smallest nod. She didn't smile. But she didn't flinch. Leo's story had failed. And this time, the truth had its own voice. No shouting. No drama. Just the sound of lies crumbling under their own weight. And the calm that came next felt like sunlight finally reaching the floor after months of fog.

The letter was folded neatly into four parts. No stickers, no emojis, no coloured paper—just the plain white kind from a printer tray, with Ty's name typed in small, neat black font at the top. He gave one to Nico first. Then Jasmin. Then Ella. Each folded square slipped quietly into a locker slot during the morning bell, and no one said a word about it until lunch.

Nico opened his during quiet reading. His hands were a little sweaty. He thought maybe it was a joke. Ty wasn't usually the kind of friend who handed out letters. He liked books and puzzles, not handwritten speeches. But the moment Nico read the first line, he knew it wasn't for show. It wasn't even for comfort. It was for truth. Not the kind you tell when someone's crying, but the kind you tell because it's real. Because if you don't tell it, it gets stolen from you.

The letter began simply: "When you think you're confused, write what you know happened. That way no one can take it from you." Nico read it again. Then a third time. Each word felt heavier than it looked. "If you ever wondered why I remember everything I read and why I read weird stuff, here's the truth. I'm Autistic. I don't talk about it much. I don't always look like what people expect. But I see patterns. And I see people. I remember the way things are said. I remember what wasn't said too."

Nico blinked. The cafeteria felt louder than usual, but somehow the paper quieted it. The next line made his throat feel like it had something stuck in it: "Most times, I don't let things like Leo get to me. I see through people like that. But this time, he didn't come through me. He came through all of you. That's how he got to me."

Jasmin read hers behind her library book. Her eyes didn't blink for two pages, and her nose twitched in that way it always did when she was about to cry but refused to let the tears fall. She folded the letter gently, lined the edges up, and tucked it in the back of her math binder behind her quiz scores and her pencil case. She didn't say anything right away. But something in her shoulders settled.

Ella's hands shook when she read hers. She held it close, like a note passed in class that she couldn't risk anyone else seeing. When she finished it, she didn't fold it. She pressed it flat against the lunch table and ran her fingers over the final line. "You're all my best friends. And I want you to know that I will always be there for every one of you."

It wasn't a big deal, but it was. No one stood up to clap. No one made a scene. But one by one, all four found Ty sitting under the reading tree after lunch, alone, eating pretzels and staring into space like he didn't know he'd dropped emotional dynamite into their day. Sophie and Jasmin sat beside him first. Nico followed. Ella came last. She brought the letter with her, unfolded.

They didn't say anything for a few minutes. Just sat there in a crooked little row, like ducks in a line who'd all survived the same storm. Ty didn't move. He just looked over at them once, raised an eyebrow like he didn't know why they were acting so weird. "Did you really mean that?" Ella asked, tapping the paper on her lap. Ty shrugged. "I don't lie."

Jasmin leaned forward, hands between her knees. "Why now?" "Because I didn't want Leo to take anything else from us," he said, voice flat but not cold. "Not even our memories. Not even who I am." Nico handed him back the letter, but Ty waved it away. "Keep it. If anything ever gets confusing again, read it." They stayed there, beneath the leaves. The sunlight came in through branches in slow waves, and the pages of the letter fluttered in the breeze. Ty didn't smile, not exactly. But something in his face softened.

And then, in the simplest, most ordinary line any friend could write, the final words on the bottom of the page spoke louder than anything else that day:

Love always, your friend,
Ty.

It wasn't fancy. It wasn't loud. But it was clear. Truth doesn't need volume. It only needs to be spoken once—and kept.

It had been weeks since the first time Leo called her "too emotional." She remembered the way he said it—casual, like he was pointing out the weather. As if naming her feelings made them inconvenient. As if emotion was a burden that belonged in someone else's hands, not his. Back then, she didn't know what to say. So she laughed, nervously. And he laughed too, louder, like her discomfort made it funnier.

The second time came two days later. She had asked a question—just one. "Why didn't you sit with me?" He raised his eyebrows and said it again. "You're too emotional." But this time, it wasn't playful. It was sharp. The kind of sharp that made her feel like asking was a mistake. That maybe wondering things out loud was annoying. That maybe being herself was somehow... too much.

The third time she'd forgotten. Not because it didn't matter—but because it got buried under other things. The ignored texts. The way he stopped waiting for her at recess. The whispered jokes she couldn't hear but could feel in her chest. But the fourth time—oh, the fourth—was different. Because by then, she had heard the word gaslighting. Because by then, Ty had written the letter. Because by then, Jasmin had stopped saying sorry for crying. And Nico had stopped folding into himself like a question mark.

So when Leo called her "too emotional" again—this time from across the hallway, loud enough for two other kids to hear—it didn't slide in quietly. It landed. And it didn't sink. It echoed.

Ella sat in the library that day, her hands resting on an open novel she couldn't read. The words blurred together, not from tears, but from clarity. Clarity, it turned out, didn't always feel good. It felt like cold water down the back of your neck. It felt like a mirror you weren't ready to look into. It felt like silence that made more sense than noise.

She hadn't realized how often she had gone quiet. How often she bit her tongue just before asking a question. How many times she had checked a text before sending it—Will this sound weird? Will he think I'm needy? Will he say it again? Those little pauses. Those tiny hesitations. They weren't habits. They were warnings. Her own instincts waving red flags that she'd been taught to ignore.

Ella traced the corner of her book with her finger, not reading. Just sitting. Remembering.

The first time Leo had smiled at her, she had thought it meant something. Not because she liked him—but because being noticed felt like being safe. That was the trick. That was always the trick. They make you feel like being chosen means you're protected. But it doesn't. It means you're being watched. Judged. Measured.

She blinked and the words from the letter came back—Ty's letter. Write what you know happened. That way no one can take it from you. Ella reached into her pencil case and pulled out a folded scrap of notebook paper. She hadn't planned to write anything. She wasn't poetic like Jasmin. Not sharp like Nico. Not steady like Ty. But today, she needed to anchor herself.

She scribbled, He said I was too emotional. But it was always after I said something true. And now I know what that means.

The page felt light. Her chest felt less so. She folded it and slid it into the back pocket of her backpack. Not to show anyone. Not yet. But to have it. To remember it. Because memory, once doubted, becomes soft clay in the hands of people like Leo. She wasn't going to let that happen again.

Later, Jasmin joined her at the library table, no words exchanged. Just a knowing look. Ella didn't need to explain what she was thinking. Jasmin had already lived the same moment with different lines. They sat in the kind of quiet that didn't feel empty. It felt safe. Honest. Like a hallway without traps.

Ty passed by with two books under his arm. He gave them both a little nod—barely a movement—but it was enough. A signal. They weren't crazy. They weren't broken. They weren't alone. And when Ella looked back down at the book she couldn't read earlier, she didn't try to force the words. She just let them sit. Because now she knew—gaslighting wasn't just a bad feeling. It was a thief. Of voice. Of memory. Of permission to feel. But now she was starting to see it. And that was the beginning of getting it back.

The red crayon broke before Jasmin finished her first stroke. It didn't snap loud. Just a soft click in the stillness of the Art room. Still, it echoed in her fingers. She stared at the broken stub in her hand, then reached for another, same shade—blood red, the kind she used to avoid. Not because she didn't like it, but because it said things too loudly. Today, she needed that volume. No more whispers.

Miss Kara had told the class to draw something that made them feel brave. Not happy. Not proud. Just brave. Jasmin stared at the blank page a long time before she moved. She didn't draw a superhero or a sunset. No lions or castles or bright yellow suns. She drew a line.

Straight across the middle of the paper. Not jagged. Not curved. Just one bold red line that stopped at each edge of the page like it knew its place. Jasmin sat back in her chair and stared at it. She hadn't planned on saying anything. She didn't want to explain. But the words formed anyway. "This is where I stop pretending I'm okay."

Nico was seated beside her. He had been sketching a compass, a crooked one, where all the directions pointed somewhere else. He looked over, his pencil pausing mid-turn. Ty, one row behind, closed his sketchbook without finishing the final corner of his maze. Neither of them spoke. But they heard her.

No one laughed. No one teased. And that silence—different from the kind Leo used to spread—felt like sunlight on a cold floor. It filled the space between their desks with something real.

Miss Kara didn't interrupt. She looked up from her chair in the corner and nodded once. Not a big smile. Just enough. Enough to say, I heard that too. Jasmin kept drawing. She added a second line beneath the first, then a third. A red fence. A border. A boundary. Her boundary.

For weeks, she'd been painting herself smaller. Shrinking her feelings. Rewriting her expressions to match someone else's expectations. And even when Leo was suspended, the echo of his rules still rattled inside her. Don't cry. Don't question. Don't make it about you. Be funny. Be quiet. Be easy to like.

But this line—this simple, stubborn line—was a refusal. She was done shaping herself into shapes that made other people feel more powerful. Ella shuffled over from her table, holding her page close to her chest. She didn't say anything either. She didn't have to. Her eyes held their own message. Something like: Thank you for saying it first.

Ty leaned forward. "Nice line," he said. "Yeah?" Jasmin asked, her voice steadier than she expected. "Strong," Nico added. "Real strong." That was the moment. Not a battle. Not a scream. Just a red crayon line and the truth behind it. No one had ever taught her that courage could look like a single stroke across a white page. Leo had taken many things from her—her peace, her certainty, her way of walking without fear. But he hadn't taken her voice. She had buried it. Hidden it under jokes and apologies and nervous glances. But it was there.

She pressed the crayon harder, deepening the red, letting it bleed just slightly into the page's fibres. No one could erase this. Later, after the bell, she left the drawing on Miss Kara's desk. Not signed. Not explained. Just placed there like a quiet flag. Ty gave her a look that meant well done. Nico, walking beside her toward the hallway, asked if she wanted to sit outside for lunch. "Not inside today," he said. "Outside's better." Jasmin nodded. She didn't need noise. She didn't need praise. She just needed her line. And now, she had it.

Miss Kara had paused mid-roll call. Her eyes, usually fixed on the list, had caught Jasmin dabbing the sleeve of her cardigan just beneath her eye. It wasn't a sneeze. Not allergies. Just a single tear, trying hard to stay invisible. But Miss Kara saw it. And this time, she didn't glance away.

She knelt down beside Jasmin's desk and lowered her voice—not soft with pity, but steady, like a rope dropped from above. "Was someone making you doubt yourself?" she asked.

Jasmin didn't nod. She didn't shake her head either. She blinked and bit her lip, the way someone does when they're not sure if crying will make things better or worse. Ty, two desks away, leaned in slightly. Nico looked up from his math book. The room had gone quiet, even though no one had asked it to. The question Miss Kara asked didn't have Leo's name in it. But the answer did.

By the time second period began, something strange had happened. Teachers—more than one—started moving a little differently. Mr. Clarke didn't joke when Leo's name was mentioned in the staff room. Miss Hathaway, who usually smiled through everything, didn't when she overheard students whispering about "Leo's version" of his suspension. Mr. Rafferty, who had once dismissed it all as "kids being kids," stood outside Room 6C during recess. Just watching.

There were six sixth-grade classrooms. All with windows. All with doors. But now the doors stayed open. The windows weren't just for sunlight anymore—they were for seeing in. Jasmin didn't feel watched. She felt... noticed. There's a difference.

The moment that changed everything came during music period. Mr. Ellis, old school and known for never skipping announcements, tapped the side of his music stand with his baton and addressed the class—not just Jasmin's, but all the sixth-grade groups combined for an assembly rehearsal. "There are times when a student may make others feel small, confused, or wrong," he said. "And sometimes that student will smile while doing it. That is not leadership. That is not clever. That is not tolerated."

You could've heard a pencil drop. Jasmin swallowed hard. Nico shifted in his chair. Ty's fingers locked behind his neck like he was steadying his thoughts. It wasn't Leo's name. But it was Leo's game. And it had just been called. After the rehearsal, three teachers gathered quietly near the art room. Miss Kara. Mr. Clarke. And Miss Jean from 6B. They weren't whispering because it was gossip. They were discussing how to handle support. Not punishment. Not reports. Just real support.

Jasmin, for the first time in weeks, felt like the adults weren't behind the curve anymore. They were walking beside her. Behind her. And ahead, clearing the way. The staff posted a notice—student-led peer support groups could meet in the library during lunch under quiet supervision. No grades. No reports. Just space. That was Miss Kara's idea. Ella was the first to go. Not to talk. Just to sit.

Mr. Clarke started checking in daily. Never long chats. Just a "How's today?" to Nico, or a silent thumbs-up to Ty in the hallway. No drama. Just presence. The truth is, gaslighting doesn't always stop with the words. It keeps echoing long after the liar is gone. But belief—the moment someone finally believes you—is louder. It cuts through the fog.

Jasmin didn't need Leo to say sorry. She needed someone to see what he did. And they did. All of them. Mr. Rafferty even pulled her aside one day and said, "I got it wrong. You were right. And I'll do better."

It wasn't dramatic. No assembly. No banner in the gym. Just that rare thing every child silently waits for: an adult who admits when they've been too late, and chooses not to be again. That night, Jasmin folded her crayon drawing from earlier and placed it beside her bed. The red line didn't bleed anymore. It held. Strong. Steady. Just like her.

Nico didn't talk much about the notebook. Not even to Ty or Jasmin. It wasn't a secret, not exactly. Just something he kept folded inside his backpack, tucked between a math test he hadn't handed in and the loose-leaf drawing Ty made of their friend group the day Leo got suspended. The notebook wasn't flashy. Just plain grey, with a red elastic strap, and the words Things I Know written in his blocky printing across the first page.

The rule came to him after the hallway moment—when Leo smirked and claimed he hadn't said what Nico clearly remembered him saying. Not once. Not twice. But over and over, with the same rhythm, like a bad song stuck in his brain. "You're too sensitive." "I was joking." "Stop acting like a baby." But when Nico repeated those words to the teacher, Leo's grin cracked sideways: "That never happened."

That was the moment Nico created the rule. The Shadow Warrior Rule. Not for everyone else. For himself. "If someone says something that hurts," he wrote, "and then says it didn't happen—write it down. Even if no one believes you yet, you do."

That single line became a ritual. Every time something didn't sit right—when Jasmin flinched, when Ella stared too long at her lunch tray, when Ty got too quiet—Nico would jot down the pieces. Not in full sentences. Just pieces. "Red bracelet." "Too emotional." "Cheating test praise." "Didn't happen." He didn't show anyone. But he carried the notebook like armour.

At lunch, Ty noticed it once. "You keeping track?" he asked, softly. Nico nodded. Ty didn't ask more. Jasmin only found out by accident. They were studying together at the library, and his notebook slipped out of his binder. She caught the red strap before it hit the floor. Her eyes scanned the title. "You call it 'Things I Know'?" she whispered.

"Because people keep trying to tell me I don't," he said, without smiling. Jasmin passed it back. She didn't read the rest. She didn't have to. Her own mind was starting to rebuild itself too. Piece by piece. The notebook never left his side. Even at home, Nico kept it under his bed, beside the flashlight and the folder of old birthday cards from his grandparents. His mum once asked what it was. He just said, "It's how I remember real stuff." She nodded. Didn't press. But something in her posture changed after that.

The next day, she came home from the pharmacy with a second notebook. This one blue. She slid it toward him during dinner. "Backup," she said, without explaining further. Nico smiled for the first time that week.

He shared the rule with Ella on Wednesday. She'd just been told—again—by someone in class that Leo's story was probably true. She looked down, unsure. Nico tapped his notebook and said, "You don't have to argue with them. Just write your part." Ella didn't speak. She just nodded and pulled a pink sticky note from her pencil case. She wrote: "He said I was too much. Then he said he never said it."

That sticky note went into her pocket. Then into a notebook of her own. By Friday, even Ty had added something to his. "Autism doesn't mean I forget. It means I remember too much," he wrote. "That's why gaslighting doesn't work on me for long." Jasmin drew her red line across the inside cover of her agenda and wrote: Start Here. None of them said the words "shadow warrior" aloud. But Nico had told them once—quietly, during a cloudy walk home—that real ones don't fight with swords. They fight with what's written. What's witnessed. What's remembered.

Leo had taken their confidence and tried to erase the chalk lines of memory. But Nico had the chalk in his hand now. And he was carving a path where the truth couldn't be edited. If it happened, it's written. If it's written, it's real. And if it's real—you don't have to ask permission to believe it.

Monday came like thunder after a long fog. Not loud, but undeniable. In the corner of the school yard, under a line of maple trees just beginning to turn, the kids whispered and waited. No one said his name aloud. But everyone knew what day it was. Leo was coming back. One week after the suspension. One week after the lie. One week after the hallway cleared out, after silence grew teeth, after truth stopped hiding.

Ty sat on the bench by the basketball court, hands folded, gaze calm. Nico paced the gravel path near the lunch tables, notebook tucked under one arm like a shield. Jasmin walked beside Ella, not in front of her, not behind—beside. Their shoulders bumped, and for once, Ella didn't flinch. Even Sophie, the newest to understand what Leo had done, had already told three other kids: "No, he's not just mean. He's manipulative."

Inside the school, the fog hadn't fully cleared. Not yet. But it was thinner now. You could see through it if you squinted. Miss Kara nodded to Jasmin with something soft in her eyes, like, I see it now. Mr. Clarke met Nico's eyes in the hallway and gave the smallest tilt of the head. They weren't blind anymore. Not all of them. Then Leo walked in.

It was almost ordinary. He wore the same hoodie. Same smirk. Same bouncing step like nothing happened. But the school wasn't the same. His footsteps echoed louder. No one ran up to greet him. No one offered him gum. The group he used to lead—three boys from his class, two from Grade 7, and one tall kid from Grade 8—all scattered like they'd never known him.

Even in Grade 8, the whispers had spread. "He lies," someone muttered near the lockers. "Gaslights people," another said. "Manipulates friends." Leo tried. He approached a group by the water fountain. They turned away. He swung his bag onto a desk beside someone from science class. They moved to another seat. No one yelled at him. No one insulted him. But no one looked him in the eye. Ella sat at her desk without shrinking. Jasmin kept writing. Sophie spoke clearly in class. Nico opened his notebook as if nothing had happened. Ty watched like a quiet guard. He didn't need to say anything. He was ready, and Leo knew it.

At recess, Leo circled the yard twice. No one followed. No one invited him into a game. The silence wasn't cruel—it was just final. A wall had gone up, not of hatred, but of truth. And truth doesn't entertain tricks twice. By lunch, Leo had stopped trying. He slumped in his chair. Headphones in. But no music played. He kept looking around like someone might offer him a way back in. But they didn't. Not because they were cold. Because they remembered. They wrote it down. They told each other. They believed one another.

Ella smiled softly when Jasmin passed her a note with a tiny doodle of a flashlight. "Truth doesn't disappear," it said. "It just waits for the fog to lift." Nico didn't cross anything out in his notebook. He only added. He returned. But not to power. Not to control. Just to silence. And this time, it was ours.

Ty wrote a new sentence on the chalkboard at the back of the class during free period. He didn't explain it. He just wrote: If someone lies enough, their truth stops working. Then he put the chalk down and walked away. At dismissal, Leo stood near the school gates. Alone. No one told him to leave. But no one followed him home. And for the first time, the fog didn't follow either.

CHAPTER 6: WORDS CAN HURT

Leo walked into the classroom like nothing had happened. His sneakers squeaked against the linoleum as he stepped through the doorway, and for the first time, no one looked up. The room didn't fall silent because it had never been noisy to begin with. There were whispers at first, murmured between groups of two or three, quiet enough to be respectful but loud enough to sting if Leo was paying attention. Which he was. His usual smirk was gone. His walk slowed. And when he reached his desk—third row from the front, beside the window where he always liked to sit—he noticed that the seat beside it was the only one still empty. Every other student had found their spot. Just not that one.

The teacher, Miss Kara, offered him a gentle nod as he walked by her desk. She didn't say his name. She didn't announce that he was back. She didn't need to. Everyone already knew. She simply said, "Let's begin," and turned to the board. The letters from last week's spelling list had been erased, replaced by a quote written in tidy, curling chalk: 'Words are seeds. Be careful what you plant.' Nico had seen it first. Ty had read it twice. Jasmin hadn't looked up once from her notebook. But Ella… Ella was watching Leo. Not out of fear. Not out of kindness. She was studying him the way someone studies the weather—trying to decide if it's going to storm again.

Leo slouched into his chair, the legs of the desk creaking under his weight like they didn't want to hold him. He unpacked his binder slowly, letting the zipper sound longer than necessary. No one told him to stop. But no one turned around either. In fact, even the younger kids—Grade 3s and 4s who had once looked up to him like he was a character from a show—stared straight ahead. That was the first bruise Leo felt that morning, though no one could see it. Not even him.

At recess, he didn't race out like before. No one followed. No one trailed behind him hoping for gum or a nickname or the chance to be picked first for soccer. Instead, the air had changed. There was no orbit around him now. No small sun that made kids bend toward his attention. Even the kids who didn't understand all the stories—like the Grade 1s and 2s—still avoided him on instinct. They had overheard enough. They'd seen the older ones stepping away. And in school, survival often means following the quiet rules, not just the ones written on the posters.

Ty stood near the monkey bars, arms crossed, watching. Not glaring. Just making sure. Jasmin was sitting on the bench near the trees, brushing an eraser crumb off her jeans. Nico leaned against the wall by the basketball court, not playing. Just thinking. All of them saw Leo wander across the yard, looking for somewhere to land. Somewhere to prove he still had pull. But there was nowhere left.

Ella had her headphones on. Not plugged in. Just resting around her ears like armour. Leo walked past her twice. Each time slower. Each time hoping for a glance. She didn't give him one. The third time, he kicked a pebble near her shoe. She shifted slightly, enough to make it clear: I saw that. And I'm not moving.

In the lunchroom, the noise of trays and footsteps and zipped lunch kits couldn't cover the silence surrounding Leo. He sat by himself. Not in the corner—he didn't want to look like he was hiding. But also not in the middle. That would have looked desperate. He chose a table two spots from the centre, the kind of spot where you expect someone to join you. But no one did. Even those who might've once sided with him—kids who used to laugh at his jokes or mimic his bravado—chose other tables. Not because they suddenly grew a conscience, but because they saw the social tides had turned. And no one wanted to be pulled under with him.

Miss Kara sat with the other teachers, sipping lukewarm coffee from a paper cup. She looked over at Leo twice. The second time, she made a small note in her planner. Nico noticed. He wondered if it was a sympathy note or a cautionary one. Either way, it didn't matter. Leo wasn't just dealing with the teachers now. He was facing something bigger. Something scarier. A classroom that no longer bent around him.

Jasmin passed Nico a folded slip of paper during art class. He didn't open it right away. He waited until the teacher turned around and the crayons were all passed out. The note read, "Do you think he knows?" Nico didn't answer with words. He just looked over at Leo, hunched over his sketchpad, colouring something too hard. His pencil lead broke. He shook the sharpener three times, then once more for drama. No one asked what he was drawing.

Ty whispered later, "It's like he forgot how to be alone." And that was true. Leo had always been surrounded—by noise, by followers, by laughter, fake or not. Now he was surrounded by silence, and it echoed louder than applause. Even Mr. Clarke, passing by during class change, nodded to Leo and said nothing else. Just a nod. Professional. Flat. That was when Leo flinched. Not much. But enough.

In the boys' washroom, someone had scrawled "Words still count" above the mirror in dry-erase marker. Nico didn't write it. Neither did Ty. But both of them smiled when they saw it. Jasmin might've. Or Ella. Or someone who'd once been called a name they still remembered in bed at night. Whoever it was, the message held.

That night, Leo walked home alone. No detours. No bragging. No gum wrappers flicked at fences. He didn't know yet that this wasn't punishment. It was reflection. The kind you don't get to run from. The kind that happens when the crowd disappears and you're stuck listening to the echoes of your own voice. All those words he thought were clever. All those jokes that weren't jokes. All those smiles that hid claws. And still, there was no bruise on him. No scrape. No scratch. Just silence. And silence, unlike names, doesn't scab over.

The morning bell rang like it always did, but the classroom didn't move the way it used to. Leo stepped in right after the second chime, the one that usually meant, now you're late enough to be noticed. But this time, no one looked. Not really. Jasmin didn't glance up from her binder. Nico had his hoodie half-zipped and was focused on tracing a pencil's shadow across the grain of his desk.

Ty sat two rows from the front, tapping his eraser against the corner of a novel—not looking behind him. And Ella's backpack was at her feet, not across the aisle like before, not close enough to be asked to move it for Leo to sit down. Even Miss Kara barely lifted her head from the attendance sheet. There were no jokes, no loud greetings. Just the sound of sneakers on tile and one boy pretending it didn't matter that the air had changed.

Leo walked past his old seat slowly. The chair beside it was still tucked in, pristine. It hadn't been used since he left. Not once. No one had wanted it. Not even for a day. It was funny, he thought. The room was crowded—twenty-six kids in desks meant for twenty-four—but somehow that seat had stayed empty. The spot beside him had become a ghost town. Like it had been fenced off by something no one said aloud, but everyone obeyed.

He slid into the chair with too much ease, almost like he wanted it to look like muscle memory. Like he hadn't noticed the chill in the space next to him. But his eyes betrayed him. They darted to the hallway twice. First when Nico passed by the open door with a crumpled worksheet in hand. Then again when Ella's voice echoed faintly from the coat hooks outside. His ears were sharper now—trained for sounds that didn't arrive. For footsteps that might stop beside him. But none did.

The seat beside him stayed empty all through homeroom. And for someone like Leo, who once measured power by who sat near him, that emptiness was not just awkward. It was loud. Every second, it seemed to speak, and what it said was simple: You're not welcome here anymore.

Miss Kara handed out worksheets without eye contact. She called out names, handed papers left, right, centre, but not a single glance rested on Leo longer than necessary. He got his sheet like everyone else. No smile. No frown. Just the basics. Just procedure. That should've made things easier. Less attention, less pressure. But instead it felt like a slow freeze. Like being put in a jar and labelled Do Not Touch.

Ty leaned over once to whisper something to Jasmin. Leo noticed. Not what was said—just that something was. And it hadn't been shared with him. For once, the whisper wasn't his to control. He drummed his fingers on his desk once. Then again. A third time. No one flinched.

By mid-morning, he started tapping his pen cap. Subtle. Annoying. Not enough to be a rule break, just enough to draw eyes. Except none came. Even the new kid, who didn't know the full story, didn't glance at him. Leo didn't know his name yet. And that, too, was strange. Leo used to know everyone's names. On purpose.

Recess came, and Leo stood up slower than usual. He looked around like he might stretch or pretend to tie his shoe—anything to not be the first one out. But the others were already halfway to the door. Nico had his hoodie up again. Jasmin was helping a younger student zip their coat.

Ella laughed at something Ty said, loud enough to be real. Leo stared at the back of the room. At the window that had once caught sunlight just the way he liked. Today it was cloudy. Even the weather had moved on.

He walked into the yard and sat at the far end of the picnic bench. It was the same spot he used to claim like a king—arm draped, foot up, making room for whoever was lucky enough to earn a place beside him. Now there was no one. The bench stretched long and flat, and Leo sat on the very edge, like he didn't want to seem like he was waiting. But his body gave him away. His back was straight. Too straight. His hand hovered over his pocket like it might buzz with a message. It didn't.

A group of Grade 5s walked past him. One of them pointed. Another shook his head. They kept walking. Leo didn't move.

In the lunchroom, the empty seat followed him again. This time, even louder. Someone had left their juice box on the table beside him. He pushed it away and hoped the owner would come back. They didn't. Instead, Jasmin took a seat two rows behind him. Nico joined. Ella came soon after. Ty stood for a bit before sitting too. None of them faced Leo. But none of them were hiding. That was the part that burned. They weren't scared of him anymore. Just finished.

Miss Kara passed by his table, picked up the abandoned juice box, and walked away. She didn't say anything. Didn't comment on the way Leo sat in the middle of three empty chairs, like a planet that had lost all its moons. There was no lesson in it. No scolding. Just space. Cold, quiet space.

Later, in art class, the substitute teacher asked Leo if he had a partner. His answer came too quickly. "I'm good." He said it like it meant I chose this. Like it meant I don't need anyone. But his hands shook when he sharpened his pencil. Just slightly. Enough to leave marks on the table.

At the final bell, he was the last one out of his row. Nico saw it. So did Ella. No one waited. No one slowed down. And the seat beside him? Still empty. Still unclaimed. Still telling the truth no one had to say out loud.

It wasn't a loud moment. Most of Leo's worst ones never were. They crept in like shadows between words, woven into the way he smiled when he said something sharp, then laughed just loud enough to make you feel silly for being hurt. Jasmin could still remember the first time he'd said it. She had asked him, gently, to stop teasing Ty about his handwriting. "It's not funny to him," she had said. Her voice had trembled, just a little. She wasn't trying to cause a scene. She just wanted him to be kind. Leo had leaned back in his chair and grinned. "You're too sensitive," he said. And just like that, she became the problem.

The words had stayed with her. Not just the sentence itself, but how it felt. Like being told your feelings were wrong. Like being told that the hurt wasn't real unless he said it was. Jasmin had replayed that moment so many times in her head. She had wondered if maybe she was too sensitive. Maybe she needed to "toughen up," like people said. Maybe kindness was weakness. Maybe silence was smarter.

It wasn't until much later—after Leo's suspension, after the hallway stared at his back instead of his face—that Ty finally gave that moment a name. They were walking home after school, the four of them: Nico, Jasmin, Ty, and Ella. The wind was sharp but dry, carrying little leaves along the sidewalk. They weren't talking about Leo at first. They were talking about phrases—things people said when they didn't want to take the blame.

"That one," Ty said, "the 'you're too sensitive' thing. That's not an opinion. That's a trap." Jasmin blinked. "What do you mean?" He stopped walking. "It's blame, dressed up as advice. It makes you think you're the one who did something wrong, just for saying it hurt." Nico nodded. Ella looked down. But Jasmin looked straight at Ty, and something unknotted in her chest.

That night, Jasmin wrote it down. In her planner, under the homework column. "You're too sensitive = not true." She circled it twice. Then underlined it. She stared at it for a long time before closing the book. Not because she wanted to forget. But because she didn't need to look at it again to remember it.

At school the next day, Leo said it again. Not to her. This time, to a boy named Dev who had flinched when Leo mimicked his stutter. Dev had said, quietly, "That's not funny." And Leo had chuckled, leaned back, arms behind his head like a king in a comedy club, and said it again. "You're too sensitive." But something was different this time.

Dev didn't look small. He didn't shrink. He looked confused—but not ashamed. He looked toward Jasmin's table. Toward Ty. Toward Ella. And for a moment, his eyes locked with Nico's. And Nico, without saying a word, just gave a small nod. Not loud. But enough.

Jasmin's hand rose slowly. "Miss Kara?" The teacher turned. "Yes?" "Leo just made fun of someone again." She didn't stutter. She didn't mumble. She said it the way you'd say the answer to a math problem. Like it was just fact. Because it was.

Miss Kara's eyes narrowed. Leo started to explain, same routine—arms wide, eyebrows raised, "I was joking! He's being too—" "Don't," Ty said. Just loud enough. "Don't say it again."

Leo's mouth stayed open half a second longer than it needed to. Then it closed. No one laughed. No one jumped to defend him. Even the two boys at the back—the ones who used to repeat his jokes—stayed quiet. The classroom hummed with pencils and paper again, but it wasn't the same hum.

Later, in the hallway, Ella whispered, "It's weird. He used to say that to me too. When I cried, even a little, he'd smile and say it like it was a spell that made him right and me wrong." Jasmin nodded. "It always felt like it froze my feelings in place. Like I wasn't allowed to feel them anymore." Nico added, "That's the point. He doesn't want to be mean without getting caught. So he makes you feel guilty instead."

It wasn't just Leo. The phrase echoed beyond him. They heard it from other kids. From adults. From commercials. From the world. "You're too sensitive" had been used to keep kids quiet for generations. But now, they knew. Now they had names for things. Now they had each other.

At the end of the day, as Jasmin packed her bag, she looked at the empty chair Leo had once claimed beside her. It stayed empty. But this time, it didn't haunt her. It didn't whisper guilt or second-guessing. It just sat there, quiet and irrelevant.

On her way out the door, she caught Miss Kara's eye. The teacher gave a small smile. Jasmin didn't return it—not out of rudeness, but out of quiet strength. She didn't need to smile back to feel seen.

Words could hurt. But they could also heal. They could build bridges between kids who had once felt isolated by shame. They could call out lies. They could label the trap, name the twist, and undo the knot. Jasmin had her words now. And no one could take them away by calling her too sensitive.

The note was folded the way kids fold secrets—into triangles with flaps tucked tight. Ella found it wedged inside her math textbook, in the corner of her desk. It wasn't new. The edges were worn, a little grey from fingers or maybe time, like it had been passed around before it landed where it wasn't meant to. She didn't open it right away. She just stared at the crease where it folded, like it was a wound stitched shut with tape. Then her fingers peeled it back. The ink was blue, sloppy, rushed. A nickname scrawled in the middle: "Crybaby Cupcake." Then a doodle of a cupcake with tears drawn on the icing, like some twisted cartoon. No signature. But she knew the handwriting.

She didn't cry. She didn't ball it up or rip it into a storm of paper. She just held it. One hand flat beneath, the other barely touching the corner, as if gripping it tighter would let it crawl inside her. Her face didn't change, but her breath did. Quieter. Shallower. Like her chest didn't want to be part of the room anymore.

Jasmin leaned in first. She didn't ask what it said. She just saw Ella's hands and her silence and knew. Nico followed after, then Ty. No one said Leo's name aloud. They didn't need to. It was in the ink. In the shape of the letters. In the way Ella's shoulders curved in, like she wanted to hide her ribs from the air.

"Is it bad?" Nico asked gently. Ella nodded. "Just dumb." She tried to hand it to Jasmin, but her fingers held on too long, like they weren't quite ready to let go. Jasmin read it. Didn't react. Just passed it to Ty. Ty barely looked. Then Nico took it, read it once, and slid it back onto Ella's desk like it was evidence in a case that had already been solved.

"If it made you feel small," Nico said quietly, "it wasn't a joke." Ella didn't respond right away. Her lips opened slightly, then closed. Then, finally, she breathed out one word. "Thanks."

Later, they sat in the library, not talking much. Just being near each other. Ella had the note in her hand again. She hadn't crumpled it or ripped it. She had folded it neatly, placed it on the table like a question. "Why do people laugh at this stuff?" she asked. Not angrily. Just tired. Jasmin shrugged. "Because it's easier than feeling bad." Ty added, "Or maybe they're scared to be the next one."

Nico nodded. "Leo was never funny. He was mean with rhythm. That's all jokes are sometimes. Just meanness that rhymes or rhymes with a smirk." Ella blinked hard, but no tears came. "It didn't feel like a joke. Not when I found it." Jasmin reached across the table. Not to hold her hand, but just to let hers rest nearby, like a presence. Like proof that no one sat alone today.

In the hallway that afternoon, Leo stood near the lockers, trying to make another kid laugh with something whispered. The kid didn't. He just looked at Leo, then at Ella walking by. Then back at Leo. And the laugh never came.

Ella didn't say a word. She walked right past Leo, note still folded in her pocket, but her spine straight. Not stiff. Not afraid. Just straight. And Leo looked at her like she'd changed shape. Like she wasn't the girl he thought he could fold like paper anymore.

At home that evening, she unfolded the note once more. She laid it flat on her desk. She picked up a black pen and wrote across it: This isn't funny. This is how cowards speak. Then she folded it back up, walked to the kitchen, and dropped it into the recycling bin without a word.

That night, she told her mum the truth. Not everything—just enough. That a boy used to say things that made her want to disappear. That he used to joke, but it didn't feel like laughing. Her mum didn't interrupt. Didn't ask for names. Just said, "Thank you for telling me." And hugged her like Ella hadn't been hugged in a long time—tightly, quietly, with no questions.

In the mirror, Ella brushed her hair and stared at her reflection longer than usual. Her cheeks were still pink from the hug. But her eyes held something steadier. Not proud, exactly. But sure. Words could slice. Words could rot. But they could also be broken down and thrown away. They could be rewritten. They could be answered with silence, with friendship, with truth. By the next morning, the seat beside Ella was never empty again.

Ty didn't like repeating himself, but this time, he had to. "It's not what they said. It's how they used it." He let that sit in the air between them. Nico looked puzzled. Jasmin kept one eyebrow raised. Ella, still shaken from the cupcake note, folded her arms across her desk like she was trying to keep her thoughts from falling out. Ty leaned closer, elbows planted, voice low but firm. "When someone wants to trick you," he said, "they don't have to lie. They just twist the words."

Nico scrunched his face. "Like how?" Ty held up his fingers, ticking them off. "One: they give a compliment that sounds sweet—but it's only sweet if you do something for them first. Two: they ask you questions that aren't really questions. They're traps." Ella blinked. "Like what kind of questions?" Ty turned to her. "Like, 'Don't you trust me?' That's not a real question. It's a trick. If you say yes, they get away with stuff. If you say no, they make you feel guilty." Jasmin exhaled slowly. "Like a lose-lose." "Exactly," Ty said.

They were sitting outside on the back steps behind the library, where the custodian's mop bucket always sat like a guard. The bell had already rung, but Mrs. Locke had given them ten more minutes to cool off before math. "Word traps are sneaky," Ty continued. "They're not mean on the outside. They're mean on the inside. Like chocolate that's actually soap." Nico made a face. "Ew." Ty cracked a half-smile. "Yeah. And you don't know it's soap until it's already in your mouth."

Ella shivered, not from cold. "He used to say, 'Wow, you look so good when you smile.' But only when I smiled at him." Jasmin's hands curled on her lap. "That's not a compliment. That's ownership." Nico nodded. "Like he's saying your smile belongs to him." Ty pointed at them both. "That's how it works. They take something nice, and they twist it until it becomes a chain."

Nico frowned. "But how do we explain that to someone who doesn't see it?" Ty tilted his head. "You don't. Not always. Sometimes you can't. You just have to know it yourself. And walk away from it." Jasmin glanced toward the school. "Is that why Leo always says, 'Don't be dramatic'? Like it's your fault for reacting?" Ty's expression darkened. "That's another trap. It's like saying, 'You're not allowed to feel how you feel.' That way, they stay the good guy, and you start to feel like the problem."

Ella wiped at the corner of her eye. "I used to think I was overreacting." Her voice dropped. "Now I think I was underreacting." Nico picked at a scuff on his sneaker. "Leo once said, 'I didn't mean it like that.' After calling me pathetic in gym." Jasmin's voice sharpened. "That's not an apology. That's a dodge." Ty added, "Real apologies don't come with excuses. They come with change."

For a while, the four of them just sat in the quiet. The breeze swept through a plastic bag in the field like a ghost. Somewhere inside, a door slammed shut. It echoed across the bricks. "He said sorry a lot," Ella whispered. "But never when it mattered." Nico nodded. "That's because he wasn't really sorry. He just didn't like being caught."

Ty reached into his pocket and pulled out a crumpled Post-it. He wrote something with his blue pen and handed it to Ella. "Keep this," he said. She unfolded it. In uneven block letters, it read: If the apology still hurts, it wasn't one. She smiled, barely. Not big. Not for anyone else. Just enough for herself.

"Words can help or hurt," Jasmin said finally. "But when people use them like a net, we don't have to get caught in it." Nico nodded. "We can cut our way out." Ella glanced at Ty. "And warn others?" He gave her a look like she already knew the answer. "That's what Shadow Warriors do." When the bell rang again, they stood. Their backs were straight, their books were heavy, but their feet felt light. No more traps. Not today.

Ella's thumb hovered over the message for a long time. The screen lit her face with that cold blue glow, making her eyes look more tired than they were. Why aren't you answering? Leo had texted her again. Three times since lunch. One of them said just say something, and another said are you mad or just being weird again. But the third one was the worst. I didn't even do anything wrong. She stared at it without blinking, letting the letters burn into her skull. And then she hit block. The phone gave no confetti, no cheer. Just a silent goodbye.

Ty was sitting across from her on the carpet in the reading nook, his fingers lazily flipping through a book on insects. Jasmin was beside him, tracing the word deceive in the dictionary with a pencil eraser. Nico sat cross-legged, phone turned off, not just on silent—off. It was the only way he felt free. He looked up at Ella. "Did you block him?" he asked gently. Ella gave a single nod. "All of them," she whispered. "Even the nice ones."

Jasmin didn't flinch. "The nice ones are just bait," she said. "If you answer one, it pulls you into the next." Ty looked up. "It's like clicking the wrong ad. You think it's nothing, but now they know you're still looking." Nico reached into his pocket, pulled out his own phone, and showed them the blank screen. "I deleted the whole thread. All his texts. I don't want to reread poison."

Ella looked startled. "You deleted them?" He nodded. "They're not memories. They're traps."

For a while, no one said anything. The sound of a chair scraping echoed from down the hall, and the clock above the whiteboard ticked louder than usual. Jasmin finally spoke. "You know what's weird? Silence used to make me nervous. But now... I think it's safer." Ty nodded, closing his book. "When you stop replying, you stop giving them the script. It's like taking back the pen."

Ella hugged her knees. "What if he shows people my old replies? Like, stuff I said when I still liked him?" Jasmin leaned in. "Let him. That's old footage. People change channels." Nico added, "And the people who know the truth won't care what you said back then. They'll care what you did now." Ty nodded. "And the ones who don't care? They were never your people."

It wasn't revenge. It wasn't payback. It was something deeper. More powerful. Like a drawbridge quietly lifted while the enemy's still outside shouting. Ella smiled—not the kind that stretches the mouth but the kind that settles in the heart. "I'm tired of explaining myself to someone who never listens."

Nico leaned back. "Silence isn't weakness. It's choice." Ty said, "It's a full sentence." Jasmin added, "And sometimes, it's the smartest one."

That night, Nico wrote something in his sketchbook. Just one page, at the top: You don't have to reply to noise. He drew a quiet forest below it. Trees tall and soft. A path without footprints. No phones in sight.

Ella didn't cry. She didn't brag either. She just moved forward like a swimmer breaking the surface after holding breath too long. The next morning, she walked into class, passed Leo without looking at him. His hand twitched toward his phone. But nothing came. Not a smile. Not a glare. Not a sound. Just Ella, walking on her own side of the hallway like it belonged to her now.

Leo looked confused. He muttered something under his breath, but no one laughed. No one looked. Ty sat straighter. Jasmin cracked her knuckles. Nico tilted his head and smiled just slightly, as if to say: Now you know.

That was the moment the four of them understood something most adults still hadn't: that silence wasn't the absence of a voice—it was the presence of a boundary. And sometimes, the loudest truth comes in the space where no one's speaking.

Mr. Rafferty stood by the coat hooks, sorting through a box of forgotten mittens and hats when Nico approached. He wasn't nervous, not really. Just tired. Tired of feeling like only bleeding counted. "Sir?" he said quietly. Mr. Rafferty turned, polite but distracted. "Yes, Nico?" The boy didn't blink. "Leo never hit anyone. But that doesn't mean he didn't hurt us." The words sat in the air for a second. Just sat there. Uncomfortable. Bare.

Rafferty raised a brow, amused in the way adults sometimes are when a child speaks seriously. "Well, I'm glad no one was harmed," he said, turning back to the mittens. Nico didn't move. "But we were," he said, firmer. "Just not in a way you can see." That made the teacher pause. One mitten slipped from his hand, quiet against the carpet. He turned fully now, arms crossed.

"I understand he was unkind," Mr. Rafferty said slowly, like the words were instructions. "But Nico, sometimes people get their feelings hurt and don't mean to. It's—" "It's not just feelings," Nico cut in. "It's patterns. It's on purpose. Like traps." Rafferty blinked. "Traps?"

Nico nodded. "He gives compliments to make you trust him. Then when you mess up—when you stop being useful—he pulls them back and acts like you're the one who changed. He jokes and waits until people laugh. If you don't, he calls you 'too sensitive.' If you cry, he says 'I didn't mean it like that.'" Nico's voice wasn't angry. It was exhausted. Tired of rewriting pain to make it more palatable for adults.

Mr. Rafferty hesitated. He knelt down, not because Nico was small, but because the weight of what he said brought the conversation lower. "Is that how it felt to you?" Nico shook his head. "It's not just me. Ask Jasmin. Ask Ty. Ask Ella. We're all walking around with invisible bruises."

The teacher opened his mouth, then closed it. Nico's eyes didn't flinch. "Do you remember that rhyme?" Nico asked. "The one everyone says—'sticks and stones may break my bones, but names will never hurt me'?" Rafferty nodded slowly. "Yes, it's... meant to help kids be strong."

Nico didn't smile. "It's a lie." Silence stretched between them. "Broken bones heal," he continued. "But words… they echo. They stay. They crawl into your brain and whisper when you're trying to sleep. Leo never pushed me. But he made me afraid to speak in class. Afraid I'd say something dumb and he'd repeat it to everyone."

Across the room, Ella sat at her desk, fingers tracing over the spine of her notebook. She hadn't smiled in days. Jasmin, quiet but sharp, scribbled something in the margins of a textbook. Ty was watching from the corner, not interrupting, not interfering. Just guarding. Nico looked back to his teacher. "We bled on the inside. We still are."

Rafferty finally exhaled, the kind of breath teachers don't learn how to take during training. "Why didn't anyone say anything sooner?" he asked softly. Nico looked away. "Because every time we did, people said 'but he's so nice.' And we started to wonder if maybe we were the mean ones." His voice dropped. "That's how it works. That's the bruise."

The teacher stood slowly, rubbing the back of his neck. "I didn't know," he said. Nico didn't respond. The statement didn't fix anything. Awareness didn't erase damage. But it was a beginning. A shaky one, but real.

After Nico walked away, Rafferty didn't return to the mittens. He sat down instead, pen in hand, and wrote the words invisible bruise on a yellow sticky note. It wasn't much, but it was a start. Nico saw it later, stuck to the side of Mr. Rafferty's computer screen. He didn't mention it. Just nodded once, privately.

That day, Leo made another joke at lunch. No one laughed. One of the sixth graders told him it wasn't funny. Another said, "You should stop talking." Leo looked around, confused. "You all need to lighten up," he muttered. But there was no audience anymore.

Ella wrote something that night in her journal. Just because I'm not crying doesn't mean I'm not cracked. She underlined it twice, then closed the book. Outside, the stars had no idea what had happened. But inside that classroom, bruises had started healing the moment someone believed they were real.

It wasn't the first time Leo had been called to the office, but it was the first time he'd been called in alone, without a teacher escorting him or classmates whispering down the hallway. The door clicked shut behind him with a sound quieter than usual, but it still echoed inside his chest. Principal Clarke didn't stand when Leo entered. He didn't motion for him to sit either. He just looked up from his desk, pen still in hand, the note in front of him folded once, then twice, then flattened out again. Leo stayed near the door.

The office was too quiet. The buzzing from the old ceiling light made his shoulder twitch. Mr. Clarke didn't raise his voice. That was the worst part. It would've been easier if he'd yelled. Instead, he gestured to the seat opposite his desk. Leo sat slowly, the leather of the chair creaking under his weight like it didn't want to hold him. "You know why you're here," Clarke said, not as a question, but as a fact.

Leo shrugged. "Not really."

Clarke looked up from the paper, his eyebrows narrowing by just a degree. "I find that hard to believe." His voice wasn't angry, just exhausted. Like someone who'd explained the same rule too many times and had run out of patience without running out of breath. Leo didn't answer. His eyes moved to the window, then to the corner of the desk where a stack of sticky notes sat unused.

There was a pause, long and square-edged. Then Mr. Clarke placed the folded paper in front of him and tapped it once with his index finger. "This is your last warning." The sentence was soft, but it hit like pavement. Leo shifted in his chair, but the cushion didn't make it easier. "I'm not suspending you again," Clarke continued. "Next time, it won't be a warning. It'll be a removal. Permanent."

Leo frowned. "I didn't even do anything this time."

Clarke didn't flinch. "Exactly." He leaned back in his chair. "You didn't push anyone. You didn't throw anything. But you've used words like knives, Leo. And even dull ones leave scars." He let the silence return. "You've lost the room. And I don't just mean the classroom. I mean the entire hallway. From first grade to eighth. I've had students who barely know you walk up to me and ask if you're going to hurt anyone else. That's not nothing."

Leo swallowed, but it was dry. He glanced at the corner of the office where the clock ticked slowly. Clarke didn't move. "You're lucky they haven't given up on you," he said, voice low. "You're lucky some of them still hope you'll figure it out." He leaned forward then, just slightly, elbows on the desk. "But I need to ask you something. Not as your principal, but as someone who's seen kids crash hard. Do you even want to fix it?"

Leo looked at the floor. His sneakers scuffed against the tile. He didn't answer.

Clarke didn't press him. "You don't have to say anything. Just think about it." He slid the folded paper across the desk. "This is your written notice. It's not going home. Not yet. But it will if this happens again." Leo didn't reach for it. Clarke placed a pen on top of it anyway. "You can read it later. But it's written in plain words. Words that matter. Unlike the ones you've been tossing around like confetti."

Outside, the hallway was alive again. Lunch break had started, and the clatter of shoes and distant chatter filtered faintly through the door. But inside that room, the quiet held.

"People forget this part," Clarke added. "They forget that silence can be louder than yelling. When no one laughs at your jokes anymore. When no one saves you a seat. When no one tells you why they stopped trusting you." Leo shifted again, but his fingers stayed in his lap, fiddling with the hem of his sleeve. He still didn't speak.

Clarke stood and walked to the window. He didn't turn back when he said, "You used to smile a lot more. Before you learned how to twist it." Leo blinked. For a second, just one second, the room felt tilted. He didn't even realize he was holding his breath.

The note stayed on the desk. Clarke didn't tell him to take it. He didn't say goodbye. He just said, "Door's unlocked," like a sentence from a different book. Leo stood, hesitated, then walked out. The hallway was louder now. Kids were laughing, shuffling books, talking in circles. None of them looked at him. None of them waited.

The paper remained folded where it had been left. Mr. Clarke didn't pick it up. He just returned to his chair and wrote one more sentence on the bottom corner of it in careful, patient handwriting: If this doesn't change, nothing will.

Jasmin was the kind of person who heard everything even when she wasn't trying. She didn't mean to eavesdrop. But sometimes, the hallway spoke before people saw her walking by. That's how she heard it. Leo's voice, just around the corner near the lockers outside the music room. "It was just a game," he said. "They're overreacting. They always do." Jasmin paused. She could feel her stomach dip, like when a swing stops mid-air before it swings back too hard. The tone in Leo's voice wasn't sorry. It wasn't even curious. It was bored.

Across the hall, Ty stood near the vending machine, arms crossed. He'd heard it too. His eyes locked with Jasmin's for just a second before they both walked past the corner together, quiet like shadows. But Leo saw them. He didn't flinch. He just laughed. "See? Drama team's back at it." And then, softer, to the person next to him—probably a sixth grader with no idea what had really happened—he added, "They're always looking for something to cry about."

Ty stopped walking. Jasmin did too. It was one of those moments where everything slowed, but not enough to fix itself. Not enough to rewind. The air between them thickened. Ty turned. Just once. Just enough to speak.

"If it was just a game," Ty said without raising his voice, "then why are we the only ones crying?"

The hallway didn't hush, but it folded. The kids who were laughing kept laughing, but a few turned to look. Leo scoffed, but his reply didn't come quick like it usually did. He hesitated—just a breath too long. It cracked the confidence he wore like a sweater, one thread loosened at the collar.

Ella was farther down the hall, standing beside Sophie and Nico. She hadn't heard what Leo said. But she saw Ty's face. She saw Jasmin standing still, fists balled in her sleeves. And without asking what happened, she walked up, placed a hand on Jasmin's arm, and waited. Leo finally spoke, but his voice was too light, too fake. "You all take stuff way too seriously."

Ty didn't answer. He just kept walking. But Jasmin stayed. Her voice shook when she finally spoke, and that made her more brave than anything else. "If it was a game," she said, her eyes sharp, "you should've stopped when we said it wasn't fun." Leo rolled his eyes. "No one ever said that." "I did," Jasmin said. "So did Ella. Nico, too. And you laughed when we did."

He shrugged. "You're twisting stuff again." "That's what you do," she said. "You say something, then pretend it meant something else." The person standing next to Leo shifted their weight. They looked unsure now, the kind of unsure that turns into doubt. Leo didn't like that. You could see it in how fast his smile disappeared.

Across the hall, Nico finally walked up. He said nothing. Just stood beside Ty. There was nothing performative about it. No pose, no speech. Just presence. Real and patient and heavier than all the noise. Mr. Clarke didn't show up this time. Neither did Mr. Rafferty. No teachers needed to. This wasn't about discipline anymore. This was about truth. Leo tried one more thing. "You all really love acting like victims."

And this time, it was Ella who spoke. Her voice was soft, steady, but it cracked through everything. "It's not acting if it's real." Leo blinked. He wasn't expecting that. He wasn't expecting to lose the room without shouting, without a big scene. But the hallway kept moving. The bell rang, and kids shuffled off to class, but no one looked back at him. Not even the sixth grader who had laughed at his joke minutes earlier.

Jasmin exhaled. It wasn't triumph. It wasn't revenge. It was something else—something slower, sadder, maybe even more honest. She wasn't proud. She was just done. Done making excuses for someone who never made any for her. Nico touched her shoulder. "Let's go." Ty nodded once. "Yeah." And together, they walked down the hallway. The swing had stopped mid-air. But this time, it didn't swing back. It just hung there—still, balanced, and done pretending it wasn't heavy.

Recess used to be Leo's favourite time. It was where he could be the loudest, the fastest, the funniest. Or at least, where he thought he was. He always picked the joke, picked the person, picked the moment. And most days, people went along with it because they didn't want to be next. But not today. Today was different, and Leo felt it before he even stepped onto the pavement. He tried to shake it off—the weird silence in class, the way the desks beside him had stayed empty all morning. He figured a good laugh would break the ice. Or maybe break them. That was his usual trick.

He spotted Nolan first—a shorter boy in Grade 5 with thick glasses and scabby knees, standing near the basketball court, watching the others play without asking to join in. An easy target, Leo thought. No backup, no noise. Just a kid in the corner with a name easy to rhyme. Leo didn't even wait. He raised his voice just loud enough, made his grin wide enough to draw attention, and called out across the playground, "Hey Nolan! You run like a baby giraffe on skates!"

He expected laughter. Not because it was clever—it wasn't—but because he was used to getting it. Laughter used to come easy. But today, it didn't come at all. Nolan's face didn't change. He just looked at Leo and blinked. No flinch. No retreat. He turned back to watch the basketball again. But it wasn't Nolan's silence that got to Leo. It was everyone else's.

Jasmin and Ella were sitting on the wooden bench beneath the shade tree. Neither of them looked at Leo. Sophie, playing foursquare nearby, paused her serve but didn't comment. Ty was watching from near the bike racks, arms folded, head tilted like he was waiting to see what Leo would do next. And then there was the worst part—no one laughed. Not even the Grade 3s. Not even the younger kids who used to giggle when Leo said anything, even when it didn't make sense.

Leo's face twitched. He tried again. "What, no one got that one? Come on, that was gold!" But his voice cracked a little. Just enough for Nico, standing near the far fence, to hear it. Nico didn't say anything. He just kept tossing a tennis ball up and down like nothing had happened. The silence stuck to Leo like syrup.

And that's when it happened. A tall Grade 8 kid named Ronan stepped out from the side of the court. He wasn't one of Leo's usual targets, and he wasn't part of the crowd that hung around Leo. But today, Ronan walked straight up to him. Not fast. Not slow. Just straight. He didn't say anything either. He just stopped right in front of Leo and looked him in the eye. "What?" Leo said, trying to smile. "You gonna say I'm not funny too?"

Ronan didn't smile. He didn't blink. He just lifted one arm, pulled back, and punched Leo in the nose. One quick, solid thump. Leo stumbled back a step, clutching his face, and the world slowed. The kind of slow that feels thick with heat and breath and the smell of blood. Everyone froze. Even the soccer ball rolled to a stop nearby.

Leo let out a sound—not a scream, not quite a cry. More like a shocked animal whimper. He held his nose, red running down his upper lip, and looked around wildly, expecting someone to run to his side. But no one did. Not even the teachers. Because Mr. Arnett had seen it. The principal had been watching from the portable steps the whole time, coffee in one hand, clipboard in the other. He didn't move. Didn't shout. He just stood there, arms folded now, like someone who had finally seen a math problem solve itself.

Ronan turned, walked away without a word, and nobody stopped him. Leo stood there alone, sniffing blood, staring around like someone who had forgotten how the rules worked. He glanced toward Mr. Arnett, expecting a lecture, an escort to the office, maybe even an ambulance. But the principal just said, loud enough for Leo to hear, "You'll have detention after school."

Leo's mouth dropped open. "But he hit me!" Mr. Arnett nodded. "And he walked away. You're still talking." The playground noise resumed like someone pressed play on a remote. Kids returned to games, the sound of bouncing balls and shouting picked up again, but Leo stood frozen. He wasn't the centre anymore. He wasn't the ringmaster. The audience had walked out.

Nico walked past him, didn't stop, didn't stare. Just said two words over his shoulder, calm and low: "Spotlight's gone." Jasmin gave Leo a look. Not cruel. Not smug. Just honest. The kind of look people give when they stop hoping you'll change. Ty and Ella followed behind her, both quiet. No nods, no laughs, no reaction. Leo sat down near the tetherball pole, tissue pressed to his nose, and for the first time, really saw what silence looked like when it wasn't used to hide—but to hold the truth steady.

Nico sat at the farthest end of the library table, same spot as always—back corner, third chair from the window, where the sunlight hit just right but never blared. His journal lay open in front of him, the same one he'd been writing in since the first week of school. The blue ribbon bookmark hung loose, and his pencil tapped the corner of the page like a heartbeat. It wasn't that he didn't know what to write. It was that he remembered too much. And sometimes, putting memories into words made them real again.

He wrote slow. One sentence at a time. Bruises heal. Names don't. He stopped, stared at the words, then underlined them. Not once. Twice. Not because he thought it looked cool—but because the truth deserved extra space. A bruise fades. A scratch scabs. Even a bump on the head eventually turns soft again. But the thing Leo called him that day by the bike racks—that stayed. That still echoed in his ears like it had been whispered just now, not shouted two months ago.

He hadn't even told anyone what the word was. Not even Ty. Not even Jasmin. It wasn't a swear. Wasn't even long. But it made him feel like the world had turned sideways and dumped him out. It had wrapped itself around his chest like one of those weighted blankets people said were supposed to help with anxiety, only heavier. More like chains. Leo had said it with a grin, of course. That grin that always showed teeth but never warmth.

The worst part was that it had worked. Nico didn't correct him. Didn't fight back. He just blinked and smiled, because sometimes you laugh when it hurts more than you want anyone to know. And then he spent two weeks avoiding mirrors and wishing he could unzip his skin. Not literally. Just... wanting to step out of himself, just for a little bit. Maybe enough to feel like he could breathe again.

He flipped the page. Mr. Rafferty said words don't leave scars. He's wrong. I still have the scar. Nico didn't blame him. Adults liked to say that stuff. They thought they were helping. They thought if they reminded you how strong you were, you'd stop hurting. But strength wasn't the issue. Nico was strong. He just didn't want to carry it alone anymore.

He glanced across the library where Jasmin and Ella were working on a project together, leaning in over a paper filled with colour-coded headings. Ty sat near the window, sketching something in his notebook, earphones dangling but not plugged in. The quiet felt safe now. Like maybe this was one of those rare days where you could breathe deep and not worry that someone would mock the way you exhaled.

His pencil moved again. Leo said it like it was a joke. But the word stuck like gum on the bottom of my shoe. I scrape it, but it's still there. That part felt gross. But it was true. It stayed. Even when you didn't want it to. Even when you pretended it didn't. Some kids wore their pain on their faces. Nico wore his in the way he chewed the inside of his lip during math class.

He had started to keep a list. Not of names. Of words. Not all bad. Just the ones that clung. "Weird." "Needy." "Crybaby." "Annoying." "Teacher's pet." "Too quiet." "Fake." "Try-hard." And the ones that weren't even insults—but somehow hurt worse. "Fine." "Whatever." "Chill." "Relax." They were the kind of words people used like a sponge to soak up your feelings and throw them away without looking.

Sometimes, the words weren't even spoken. They were mouthed across the room. Typed in a message that vanished the next day. Passed on through other kids like secret poison. Leo knew how to do that best. He didn't need to scream to hurt you. He could just talk soft and smile sharp. That was his power. He could burn you with compliments, and no one else would smell the smoke.

Nico didn't want revenge. Not really. He didn't want Leo to get punched again. He didn't want Leo to cry in the hallway or get sent away. He just wanted him to stop acting like words were weightless. Because they weren't. They landed. They built up. They stacked until the floor creaked beneath your feet and no one understood why your shoulders stayed hunched all the time.

He drew a small box in the margin. Inside it, he wrote: "It's not what he said—it's that he said it like he meant it." That was the part that haunted him most. Not just the insult. But the tone. The pause. The way Leo had stared straight through him like Nico's insides were a glass window and there was nothing worth saving behind it.

The librarian passed by and offered a kind nod. Nico smiled, tight but real. He tucked his pencil beneath the binding and closed the journal slowly. His hand stayed on the cover for a second longer than it needed to. The blue fabric was fraying at the corners, and the spine had started to bend. But it still held everything. It held him, even when he didn't know what he was holding himself together for.

He looked over to Jasmin again. She met his eyes and gave a small nod, the kind that said, I see you. I remember too. And maybe that was all Nico needed just then. Not for the memory to vanish. But for someone else to admit it mattered. Not everything needed to be said out loud. But the things that were said—the words that bruised without fists—those needed to be written. Because someone else might read them one day and say, me too. And that might be enough to help them feel less invisible.

Nico slid the journal into his backpack, zipped it slowly, and stood up without making a sound. But in his chest, something heavy had shifted. Not disappeared. Just... shifted. And sometimes, that's where healing starts.

The chairs were pulled into a circle that afternoon. Not by teachers. Not for a lesson. Just kids. Ty was the one who asked for the library space, and the librarian, Mr. Lewis, simply nodded and unlocked the back room. No one needed to explain why. The lights weren't harsh, the blinds were open to let in the soft end-of-day glow, and by four-thirty, every seat was filled. Grade ones sat cross-legged on cushions. Grade eights slouched like statues trying not to show emotion. Everyone else filled the middle, like puzzle pieces trying to make something whole.

Ty stood. Not in the centre. Just next to the book cart. His voice didn't rise like a speech, and he didn't pace like a teacher. He looked nervous. Then calm. Then brave. "If you want to say something," he said, "this is where you can. If you don't, that's okay. But no one's here to fix it. Just to say it. That's enough." And that was it. He sat back down next to Nico, who hadn't blinked once since the first grader sat down across from him and whispered, "Is it really okay to talk?"

Jasmin was the first to speak. Her voice cracked a little. "Leo said I act like a know-it-all." She paused. Nico saw her knuckles whiten as her fingers curled into her sleeves. "But I believe I'm smart. And I like asking questions. That's not a bad thing." A murmur of agreement moved around the circle like a hush turned into strength. No one clapped. No one made it loud. It just rippled—a silent kind of support.

Next was Ella. Her eyes didn't rise until she started. "He told me I talk too much. That I talk just to hear my voice." Her head turned slightly toward the shelves. "I believe my voice matters. Even if it shakes. Even if it's small. I get to talk." A first grader beside her leaned over and squeezed her hand. Ella didn't flinch.

Nico thought about staying quiet. Thought maybe he'd just listen. But when Ty's eyes caught his, something in him unfolded. So he stood. Slowly. Carefully. "Leo called me fake," Nico said, his mouth dry. "Said I just act nice so people will like me. But I'm kind because I choose to be. Not because I want something back." He didn't sit down right away. He waited. Just a breath. And when he did sit, he noticed his hands weren't trembling anymore.

The room was so still it almost felt like the air held its breath too. Then a seventh grader—Gabe, the quiet one who always walked the long way to class—spoke. "He told me my drawings were babyish. That I should grow up." Gabe pulled a folded sheet from his pocket. It was worn, the lines faded. He unfolded it carefully and held it up. "This is what I drew the day he said that. I didn't stop. And I won't." Someone whispered, "It's awesome," but Gabe didn't look for who said it. He already knew.

One by one, the voices filled the circle. A fifth grader who said Leo mocked his stutter. A second grader who said Leo called her weird for collecting rocks. An eighth-grade girl who shared, in a voice sharper than the rest, that Leo said she'd never get friends if she stayed "so serious all the time." She met every gaze in the circle and said, "I believe I'm enough. I don't need to smile to make people comfortable."

And then, Ty again. "He told me boys aren't supposed to cry." Ty looked down. "I cried last night. I'm not ashamed of it. I believe feelings don't make you weak. They just mean you care." His voice didn't rise. His hands didn't shake. But there was something in his posture that held the room still. As if the truth had made the walls pause.

The circle continued. Not everyone spoke. Some nodded. Some doodled in notebooks as they listened. Some just kept their eyes fixed on their shoes like they were afraid to look up and find tears waiting. But no one laughed. No one rolled their eyes. No one made it a joke. The air didn't allow it. It had become sacred—without anyone calling it that.

In the doorway, Mr. Clarke watched with folded arms and no words. He didn't step in. Didn't comment. Just stood guard like someone who knew this moment wasn't his to lead. When a first grader whispered something about Leo saying her name wrong on purpose every day, Jasmin gently leaned in and helped her find the right words. "Say what you believe now," she said. The little girl blinked, then whispered, "I believe I matter. Even if he didn't say my name right."

Some of the eighth graders shared stories about times they laughed with Leo just to stay on his good side. One admitted he once repeated Leo's words just to avoid being the next target. "I don't believe in being mean just to survive anymore," he said. "I believe it's braver to stand up."

By the time the last voice fell quiet, the sun outside had dropped behind the far wing of the school. Shadows stretched long across the carpet, and the circle sat in the dim warmth of the room like something ancient. No one moved at first. It wasn't silence from awkwardness. It was silence from knowing something real had just happened—and not wanting to be the first to make it end.

Ty stood again. "Thanks," he said. Just that. Nothing more. Then the kids began to stand. Slowly. Like waking from something deep. They didn't hug. They didn't high-five. But their eyes held something that hadn't been there before. A knowing. A quiet kind of shield.

And when they left the library that day, the circle stayed. The chairs weren't moved back. Mr. Clarke didn't rearrange them. He just walked in, switched off the overhead lights, and left the room exactly as it was. Because some things shouldn't be cleaned up. Some things need to stay where they happened. Even healing.

Leo said it at the lockers. Not in front of a teacher. Not in the library. Not even face-to-face, really. He mumbled it like a line from a play he didn't audition for. "Sorry about before," he said, eyes darting toward the hallway clock as if his own words bored him. Ella didn't respond. Not because she hadn't heard. But because what he said wasn't shaped like a real apology. It didn't land. It didn't ask to.

Nico and Ty were near enough to hear it. Jasmin too. She raised an eyebrow—not in disbelief, but in that way people do when they've already prepared themselves for something that disappoints. Leo waited two seconds longer than he probably wanted to. Then he turned and adjusted his hoodie like he'd just scratched an itch. That was it. A confession with no cost.

Ella's hands stayed tucked into the sleeves of her red sweater. She didn't turn toward him. She didn't flinch. But her voice, when it came, was quieter than before. "That's not an apology," she said. "That's just words with no feeling in them." And still, she didn't look at him. She spoke into the air. Like a statement meant more for herself than for him.

Ty glanced at Nico, and Nico gave the smallest nod. They didn't need to say it aloud: they'd seen this kind of moment before. A script. A performance. An illusion of remorse without its heart. It was the kind of apology meant to fix a problem without owning it. The kind that moves on without staying still.

Leo's face didn't change. Not in the way they expected. No anger. No sarcasm. Just a blankness. A flicker of something unreadable behind his eyes. But instead of answering, he walked away. No eye contact. No pause. Just the steady, practiced rhythm of someone who'd done this before—used words as currency without ever paying the debt.

Jasmin sighed. "He thinks sorry is just saying the word," she whispered. "He doesn't know it's supposed to feel like something." She picked at the edge of her notebook. The hallway was beginning to fill with the lunch crowd, but their small group stayed still, anchored to the weight of what had—and hadn't—just happened.

"I've had better apologies from my little cousin," Ty muttered. "And he once said sorry for hitting me with a plastic shovel... when he meant it." That made Nico crack a smile, but it didn't erase the heaviness. Because this wasn't about shovels or jokes. This was about something deeper. A bruise that didn't show.

Ella leaned against the locker, not out of weariness, but out of purpose. "If you don't mean it," she said, "then don't say it. Don't throw 'sorry' at me like it's a magic trick to make everything go away." Her words were even. Clear. Measured. But they weren't soft. They were the kind of words that came after silence had taught someone how to stand up.

A group of younger students passed by. One of them looked at Leo, then looked away fast. Nico noticed. So did Ty. The echo of Leo's reputation still carried. But now it wasn't just fear. It was disinterest. Distance. People weren't angry anymore—they were done. "He doesn't even ask what he did," Jasmin said suddenly. "Real sorry people... they ask. They listen. They wait. They don't try to fix it with a whisper in the hallway." Her words didn't shake. She wasn't venting. She was remembering.

Nico crouched to retie his shoe, but really he just needed a second to think. "I think he thinks we want him to feel bad," he said slowly. "But we don't. We want him to understand." That, more than anything, was the missing piece. Not guilt. Not shame. Just the absence of understanding.

The bell rang overhead. Sharp, mechanical, and uncaring. The hallway scattered. Feet shuffled. Backpacks zipped. But their little circle didn't move. Not yet. Not until the last echoes of that almost-apology faded from the walls. Ella finally stood straight. "He didn't even say my name," she added. "That's how I know it wasn't real. If you hurt someone and you don't say their name when you're trying to make it right... you're just fixing your own image."

They walked to class together. Quiet. But not crushed. And as they rounded the corner, Nico said something small—something soft enough that only Ty and Jasmin caught it. "A real apology makes space," he said. "That one just took up air." And though Leo had already disappeared around the opposite hallway, it was clear he'd left something behind. Not forgiveness. Just silence.

Ella sat on the bottom step of the library stairs, her knees drawn up, hands folded across the tops of them like she was trying to hold herself together. She wasn't crying. She wasn't shaking. But she was still. And in that stillness, there was a quiet heaviness that didn't belong to an eleven-year-old. Jasmin came and sat beside her—not too close, not too far—and leaned slightly forward, elbows on her thighs, chin balanced between two small fists. The bell had already rung. Everyone else had scattered. These two stayed.

Jasmin didn't start with a joke. She didn't try to distract her. She didn't even say hello. She just watched the grey light pour in through the tall windows and said, "You didn't deserve it. Not one bit." Her voice didn't wobble. It landed flat and steady, like a stone placed gently on the ground. Ella blinked once. Slowly. But didn't speak. Jasmin didn't mind. Not all truths need answers.

Ty sat down next. No invitation was needed. He dropped his backpack to the floor with a thunk, leaned back against the wall, and crossed his arms—not like a wall, but like someone taking his turn to hold watch. "We believed him because we didn't know better," he said. "Now we do." He didn't look at Ella when he said it. He looked straight ahead, like the words were for the room, not just for her.

Nico stood nearby. He didn't sit. He leaned his shoulder into the doorway and watched the three of them with a look that had grown more serious since Leo's return. He didn't say anything yet. He'd already said what he needed to earlier that day. But his silence meant he was present. And presence, to some kids, speaks louder than anything.

Ella finally exhaled. Her fingers unfurled slowly from her sleeves. "Why did I think I had to keep trying?" she asked. Not out loud to anyone in particular. Not loud enough to demand an answer. But loud enough to hear herself admit it.

"Because we're told to be nice," Jasmin said. "Even when someone's being mean. Even when it hurts. People tell us to 'be the bigger person,' like that makes it okay to stay in the fire." She nudged Ella's shoulder lightly. "But you don't have to stay in it. Not anymore."

Ty ran a thumb over the seam of his jeans. "We didn't know there were rules," he said. "And even if we did, Leo kept changing them." Then he added with a shrug, "That's what narcissists do. Make you forget you were right. Then punish you for remembering."

Ella looked between them both. She didn't ask what a narcissist was. They'd talked about it already—too many times to count. Instead, she asked, "Do you think he knows what he's doing?" It wasn't an accusation. It was curiosity. Like trying to figure out if the storm meant to strike or if the clouds just didn't know how to hold their water.

Jasmin hesitated, then said softly, "Maybe. Maybe not. But we don't have to wait around to find out." She held her knees a little tighter. "You're allowed to leave even if you don't have proof. Even if you're not sure. Just feeling hurt is enough."

Nico finally stepped forward. He sat one stair above them and spoke without looking at anyone. "I used to think being kind meant staying. Now I think being kind means helping someone leave when it's not safe to stay." His words didn't float. They anchored.

Ella's mouth curled just slightly—not quite a smile, but not a frown either. The kind of expression that says, Maybe I'll feel better tomorrow. She tilted her head back against the wall and closed her eyes. "I think I'm done saying sorry for what wasn't my fault." Jasmin nodded once. "Good." Then she said, "Let's go to class late. Together." She stood up and reached out a hand. No pressure. Just offering. Ella took it.

Ty followed, brushing crumbs off his sweater as he stood. "No more apologising for Leo's behaviour," he said. "He's not a puppet master. We're not strings." The hallway beyond the library gleamed with that afternoon haze. The kind of light that only lasts ten minutes and somehow makes everything look older.

They walked slowly, not because they were dreading what came next, but because they weren't rushing to outrun anything anymore. What they carried wasn't shame. It was experience. And that's heavier, but it's also more honest. Ella glanced over her shoulder, just once. "Thanks," she said, not whispering. "For saying it out loud." "We always will," Jasmin answered. "That's what real friends say."

The class was quieter than usual. Not the kind of quiet that buzzed with hidden whispers or the low hum of pencils scratching paper. This quiet was different. Still. Uneasy. Mr. Clarke didn't stand behind his desk like he normally did. He walked between the rows slowly, the soft tap of his shoes the only sound for a moment. Then he spoke. "The words you speak become memories in someone else's mind," he said, stopping beside the back row. "Make sure they're memories that don't hurt."

He didn't raise his voice. He didn't lecture. He didn't even glance at Leo, though Leo was the only one who wouldn't look up. Everyone else did. Heads turned. Eyes met. Even the students who usually doodled in margins or stared at the clock looked forward. Mr. Clarke had said something that didn't just sit in the room—it echoed through it.

Jasmin gripped her pencil tighter. The quote bounced in her ears long after he said it. She remembered when Leo called her "overdramatic" for asking him not to yell at her in front of the others. That memory didn't leave. It never had. Even now, it lived in the back of her thoughts like an old bruise that throbbed whenever someone raised their voice.

Ty tapped the eraser of his pencil on the desk twice, then stopped. Mr. Clarke wasn't a perfect teacher. He didn't always say the right thing. But this time, he had. Ty nodded to himself, a small thing, but real. Words could turn into permanent echoes. And sometimes, they hit you when you least expected them.

Ella didn't move. Her eyes stayed fixed on the corner of her desk. She had stopped writing five minutes earlier, long before Mr. Clarke spoke. But now, something in her posture straightened. Her hands unclenched from around the pages of her journal. And when she blinked, it was slow, careful, like she was giving herself permission to be present again.

Nico kept his gaze forward. He didn't want to look at Leo. Didn't want Leo to think this was about revenge. It wasn't. This was about truth. And if truth hurt, it wasn't the kind that needed to be whispered away. It was the kind that needed to be named, spoken, and kept safe in daylight.

Mr. Clarke moved again, walking back to the front of the classroom. He didn't speak further. He just picked up a piece of chalk and wrote the sentence on the board. "The words you speak become memories in someone else's mind." And then he underlined it once. Slowly. Deliberately.

Leo shifted in his seat. Just once. He didn't say anything. He didn't argue. His eyes moved to the board, and for the first time in days, he looked like he was listening. Not because he wanted to. But because he had no choice but to sit in what was being said—and what he'd already said.

Sophie raised her hand. Mr. Clarke nodded. "Sometimes people think they're being funny," she said. "But the person listening doesn't feel like laughing. And you don't always get to explain it away after."

"That's exactly it," Mr. Clarke replied. "You can't erase someone else's memory of your words. You can only take responsibility for planting it there." He didn't need to elaborate. The silence did the rest.

Nico wrote the sentence in the top margin of his notebook and boxed it in with ink. He thought about how many names he'd been called. Stupid. Sensitive. Weak. Weird. Quiet. Broken. None of those words were his. But they had stayed with him like barnacles, stuck to the corners of his confidence. He wasn't letting them stay anymore.

Jasmin looked over at Ella. Ella met her eyes and gave the smallest nod. It wasn't a nod of forgiveness. Not for Leo. Not yet. Maybe not ever. It was a nod of understanding. That these memories were real. That they weren't overreacting. That this moment mattered.

Ty turned in his chair and whispered to Nico, "Imagine if we said things that stuck for good reasons." Nico didn't smile, but he agreed. That's the difference between cruelty and kindness. Both last. One just hurts more quietly.

Mr. Clarke clapped his hands once. "Let's take the next ten minutes to write," he said. "Anything you want. Just make it something honest. That's the only rule." Pencils began to move. Pages rustled softly. Even Leo picked up his pen. But for once, no one was watching him.

No one was trying to win his approval or dodge his reaction. His spotlight was gone. And it wasn't coming back. In its place stood something sturdier. Not applause. Not popularity. Just truth. Firm and echoing.

Ella wrote one line on the top of her page: "The things people say to you don't leave easily. So make sure the things you say to people can stay." She didn't know if she'd show it to anyone. But she didn't hide it either. The bell rang. Desks scraped. Backpacks zipped. But Mr. Clarke didn't erase the board. He let the sentence stay.

Nico stood at the back of the classroom with his notebook in both hands. He didn't look nervous, not this time. He had asked Mr. Clarke if he could read something, and Mr. Clarke, who usually asked for a preview, simply nodded and said, "If it's from the heart, then it's the right thing." Nico didn't clear his throat. He didn't stall. He just began to read, his voice steady and small, but sharp enough to hold every word in the room.

"If words can hurt, then they can also heal," he read aloud. "I just needed to hear them from someone who meant it." The line sat there like a truth carved into stone. No one clapped. No one whispered. They just listened. Because it wasn't a performance. It was a moment. Nico's voice didn't tremble. He didn't rush. He paused where it mattered and let each syllable land like a step taken forward.

Mr. Clarke stepped forward when Nico sat back down. He didn't take over the room. He didn't adjust his tie or pick up chalk. Instead, he turned to the whiteboard behind him and picked up a marker. He wrote slowly, each word heavy and deliberate. "Stupid. Dumb. Irresponsible. You'll never amount to anything." He didn't turn around. Not yet. Just kept writing. Below the sentence, he wrote: "Said by my father when I was your age."

Then he turned. "That was my script for a long time," he said. "I memorized it without meaning to. It followed me into every classroom I ever sat in. I thought maybe it was true. Until a teacher told me I was good at explaining things. I didn't believe her at first. But then I saw someone else nod. And someone else. And eventually—I believed them more than I believed the voice in my head."

He looked out at the students, his eyes meeting them one by one, not like a spotlight, but like a steady lantern moving from face to face. "So, I rewrote the script. And I'm still rewriting it. Every time I teach. Every time I listen. Every time I choose not to repeat what was done to me." He set the marker down with care. "That's how words can heal."

No one spoke. Even Leo didn't shift in his seat. Sophie sat in the second-to-last row, a few chairs behind Jasmin. Her hands were folded tightly on her desk, and her feet barely touched the ground. She hadn't said anything the whole period. Not one word since they walked in. Most kids forgot she was even there—she was always quiet, always folded into corners, always shrinking herself a little smaller to avoid notice.

But now, something flickered. Nico turned his head. Jasmin followed. Then Ty. Sophie's eyes stayed low, but they were glossy. She didn't cry. Not fully. Just blinked twice too fast. Mr. Clarke looked her way and said, without naming names, "Some of the hardest hurt is the kind no one sees. But it still needs to be said out loud."

Sophie swallowed hard. The room remained hushed. Then, with a voice no louder than a whisper caught in fabric, she spoke. "He kissed me." The room blinked in unison. "The second day I got here," she added. "I didn't even know his name yet." She didn't say Leo. She didn't have to.

Jasmin's hands curled. Ty looked at Leo without a word. Nico's fists were resting against his thighs, knuckles pale. Mr. Clarke didn't rush to soothe. He didn't dismiss it as confusion. He didn't tell her to calm down or lower her voice. He simply asked, "Did you want him to?"

Sophie shook her head once. "Then it was wrong," Mr. Clarke said. "And I am so sorry." She exhaled like she had been holding her breath since the moment it happened. "The other kids... they forgot it. Like I didn't even exist after. Like it didn't happen. Like I was a ghost." "You're not a ghost," Jasmin said, not loudly, but not quietly either. "You're here. We see you." Her voice cracked, but her spine stayed straight. Ty nodded. "We should have said something. We should have remembered."

Leo's head was down. His fingers moved against the edge of his desk, restless. But the room wasn't about him anymore. It hadn't been for a long time. It was about Sophie. About Nico's poem. About Mr. Clarke's script. And about every word that had been left unsaid until now.

Sophie didn't say thank you. She didn't smile. But she didn't shrink either. She leaned back in her chair, still quiet, still small—but no longer invisible. The room made space for her. For her voice. For her silence. For her truth. Mr. Clarke picked up the marker again. Under his childhood memory, he wrote another sentence. "Words can build too." Then he stepped aside and let it stay. Ella scribbled something into her notebook. Ty watched her. Jasmin folded a fresh page. Nico underlined his poem's last line three times, just to be sure it stayed. They were rewriting things now. Together. And this time, the script belonged to them.

CHAPTER 7: WHEN NO ONE ELSE SEES IT

Leo stood beside Miss Kara's desk with one hand on his chest and the other gesturing softly, as if he were defending someone else, not himself. "I was just trying to help," he said, his voice dipped in honey and hesitation. Miss Kara paused, pen in hand, and blinked as though unsure whether to scold or praise. She glanced at Nico, who stood a few steps behind Leo, silent, uncertain. There was something hollow about Leo's words. They rang polite, but not true. And Nico's gut knew it before his mind could catch up.

The moment had started earlier when the class was asked to form reading partners. Leo had waited, lingered, then slid into the seat beside Sophie with a smile and a sharp whisper. "Looks like we're partners now." Nico had seen her flinch. Just barely. She didn't answer him, didn't nod, didn't smile. But Miss Kara had already looked away by then, calling out instructions, clipboard in hand. By the time Sophie tried to shift her chair, Leo was already saying she was lucky to have someone who "reads fast."

At recess, it came to a head. Sophie told Jasmin what had happened. "He touched my wrist," she said quietly. "Not hard. But I didn't want him to." Jasmin didn't ask if it hurt. She asked, "Did you tell him to stop?" Sophie nodded. "He said it was just part of helping me with my page." Nico had walked up right then, having heard enough to know what needed to happen next. They didn't have to plan it. Jasmin stepped into Miss Kara's line of sight and raised a hand. "We need to talk to you," she said. That's how Leo ended up standing at the front of the class, spinning silk.

"I just thought she was struggling. I mean, I'm not saying she's slow," Leo said with a soft chuckle, eyes darting to Miss Kara's expression. "I just figured she'd appreciate a little support. Like, I didn't mean anything bad." There it was—"support." A safe word. A word that adults liked. A word that could be worn like a mask. Nico stared at the floor, jaw tight. His fists weren't clenched, but his breath had gone shallow. Something about the way Leo used those words made him feel invisible again.

Miss Kara tilted her head. "Sophie, is that how you saw it?" Sophie looked down. Then at Jasmin. Then at Nico. Her voice was barely above a whisper when she said, "No." It cracked halfway through. One word, small but loud. Miss Kara blinked, and for a moment, just a flicker, the look in her eyes changed. Doubt broke through. But Leo was fast. "Maybe I just misunderstood," he said, stepping back. "If she didn't want help, I get it. I'll be more careful."

That's when Nico's chest burned. The kind of burn that isn't heat but fury. Leo hadn't apologized. Not really. He had twisted the truth like clay and shaped it into something soft enough to survive. And worst of all, he'd made it sound...nice. That was the worst kind of lie, Nico thought. The ones that sound helpful. The ones adults nod along with. The ones that bury what actually happened under sugar and spin.

After the conversation ended, Miss Kara said they would "move forward" and reminded everyone about respecting personal space. She didn't say Leo's name again. She didn't say Sophie's either. Nico watched Leo walk back to his desk with that same expression he always wore after getting away with something—like someone who'd dodged raindrops and made it across the playground dry. It wasn't guilt. It was satisfaction, tucked inside a fake shrug.

Back in their seats, Nico leaned toward Jasmin and whispered, "He does this all the time." Jasmin nodded. "But it's different now. She said no. Out loud." Sophie sat between them, hugging her elbows, eyes on the window. She didn't speak, but she didn't leave either. And that felt like a kind of win. The kind of quiet win that most people wouldn't see. The kind of win that needed no applause.

After class, Ty met them near the cubbies. "What happened?" he asked. Nico told him everything. Ty didn't look surprised. He looked angry in that way only Ty could manage—tight-lipped, eyebrows drawn low, one thumb flicking against his pant seam. "That's not help," Ty said. "That's control dressed up like kindness." Nico nodded. "She knew," he said. "Even if it was late. She knew."

The rest of the day moved slowly. Nico couldn't stop replaying Leo's words in his head. "I was just trying to help." The softness of it made it worse. He'd heard adults say the same thing before. Even kids. But now he knew how false it could be. And that's what made it dangerous. Not the yelling. Not the cruelty. But the camouflage.

That night, Nico wrote it down. His new rule. He wrote: "If a lie sounds too nice to question, question it twice." He underlined it three times. Folded the paper. Put it in his desk drawer. Some truths needed to be written where they wouldn't be erased.

The next morning, Leo smiled at everyone like nothing had happened. Like words didn't leave marks. Like smiles could undo bruises. But when Sophie walked past him, she didn't look at him. When Jasmin passed, she didn't even slow down. And when Nico followed, he kept his chin up and eyes forward. He didn't need to speak. The truth was walking beside him.

Jasmin sat on the brick ledge outside the library doors, elbows resting on her knees, fingers twisting the bottom edge of her shirt in slow, nervous circles. Nico stood beside her, but it was Ty who crouched low enough to meet her eyes. She wasn't crying, not exactly. But her face looked like someone who'd been made to feel foolish for noticing things too carefully. It wasn't the first time Leo had said it, and it wouldn't be the last: "You're too suspicious, Jasmin. Not everything is some big plot." That morning, she believed him—just long enough to flinch.

It wasn't even a big moment. Leo had said something offhand to one of the younger kids, something that sounded fine on the surface, but had a barb tucked deep in the middle. Jasmin noticed. She mentioned it.

And suddenly, she was the problem. "You twist everything," Leo had said with a light laugh. "You always think someone's out to get someone. Relax." Everyone else had laughed too, not because it was funny, but because laughter's easier than tension. That laugh haunted her still, the way it pointed inward.

Ty saw it differently. "That's the trick," he said quietly. "Liars don't just lie with words. They lie with how they make you feel. They make you feel like the broken one, so you stop checking their facts." His voice didn't wobble, didn't shift. It was steady as always, like a string tied to something buried and unshakeable. Jasmin looked at him, eyes glassy. "But what if I am overthinking it?" she asked. "What if I'm just making it worse?" Ty didn't blink. "You're not."

They'd all heard Leo spin things around before. He was a master of flipping stories, reshaping the edges of memories so that the sharpest parts pointed away from him. When Nico once told him, "That wasn't okay," Leo had answered with, "You just took it the wrong way." When Ella said, "You embarrassed me," Leo had said, "No, you embarrassed yourself." Every time someone pushed back, Leo had a mirror ready—warped just enough to twist their own reflection into something ugly.

Jasmin replayed those moments in her mind now. The first time Leo called her "bossy" just because she had a better idea. The time he said, "You act like you're smarter than everyone," in front of the group. It hadn't felt like a joke. But it also hadn't felt safe to argue. She'd swallowed it, smiled through it, nodded even. And when she brought it up later, he just smirked and said, "That's not what I meant. You're reading into it."

That phrase—you're reading into it—was starting to rot her bones. Ty watched her fold her arms tight across her chest, like she was trying to hold something broken in place. He didn't touch her. Didn't offer false comfort. He just said, "My uncle used to do that. Make you think you were the one losing it. But you're not. They know what they're doing. They're just hoping you won't."

Inside the school, Leo was beginning to feel the shift. The kind of silence that doesn't echo—because it's not absence, it's withdrawal. Eyes were less quick to meet his. Conversations quieted when he walked near. He caught Ty watching him once through the window and looked away faster than he meant to. Ty didn't glare. He just watched. The way someone watches a puzzle that finally stops changing.

Back at the library ledge, Nico leaned forward. "Do you remember last year when I said Mrs. Dunlop got my name wrong on purpose?" Jasmin nodded. "Everyone thought I was making it up," Nico said. "Even I started to think I was just being whiny. But then she did it again. And again. And when someone else pointed it out, it finally mattered." He sighed. "Just because no one sees it yet doesn't mean it's not real."

Jasmin swallowed hard. "Then how do you know when to trust yourself?" Ty answered before Nico could. "If it feels off, it's off. You don't need a courtroom to believe your own gut." He stood then, brushing off his knees. "The more someone tells you you're wrong for noticing, the more likely they're hiding something." That thought hit the air like thunder. Jasmin didn't smile, but she stood too. Inside, Leo cracked a joke about Sophie again. Only this time, no one laughed. The silence that followed made him turn to see who had heard. Mr. Clarke did. And Mr. Clarke didn't blink. Just like Ty.

Ty never bragged about it, but everyone knew his dad worked in law enforcement—real law enforcement. Not just a constable. Not just a suit behind a desk. His father was a Special Investigator with the RCMP, the kind who knew how to spot lies before they were even spoken. Ty didn't talk about it much unless the moment called for it. This was one of those moments. "That's not what he said yesterday," Ty muttered to Nico, keeping his voice low as they watched Leo retell the story of what happened in gym class. A day ago, Leo claimed he helped pick up the cones. Now he said he had set them up all by himself. Nico raised a brow. Ella looked confused. Jasmin crossed her arms. Leo's story had shape-shifted again.

What Ty had learned from his dad wasn't magic. It wasn't a secret recipe. It was observation. Patterns. Micro-expressions. Things adults ignored, but Ty noticed. Like how Leo smiled too soon before the punchline, how his eyes flicked downward—not just anywhere, but down and to the left—every time he changed a detail. "People look left when they make something up," Ty had told Nico weeks ago. "It's not always true. But it's true often enough to matter." And today, Leo's eyes danced exactly that way.

Back when Ty was little, his dad used to pause the TV. Freeze-framing a witness interview on a police drama. "See that twitch under his left eye?" his father would say. "That's not nerves. That's suppression. He's hiding something." Ty had soaked it in the way kids soak in everything—quietly, deeply, like ink sinking into paper. Now, in a school hallway with the stakes set lower but no less real, Ty used the same methods on a twelve-year-old liar in a track hoodie.

"He's shifting his weight," Ty whispered again. "That means he's uncomfortable. Look at how his voice goes higher when he explains the part about the cones. That's called a vocal shift. The pitch jumps when people lie. Sometimes they can't help it. Their throat tightens. The sound comes out too high." Nico nodded but said nothing. It was like watching a magician unmask a trick while the audience still believed in it.

Ella tugged at the hem of her sweater. "I believed him," she said, barely above a whisper. "The first time. Yesterday." She didn't cry, but she looked like she'd aged a year in that second. Jasmin put a hand on her back, anchoring her like a lighthouse in fog. "It's not your fault," she said simply. "People who lie make the truth sound shiny."

What made Leo dangerous wasn't just the lies. It was how quickly he dressed them up. How he stitched them together with compliments, jokes, borrowed phrases from grown-ups. Ty had once called it "truth-dragging." It's when someone wraps a lie in just enough truth to make you hesitate. To make you second-guess what you saw with your own eyes.

Jasmin watched Leo's hands. "He always tugs at his sleeve when he's caught," she said. "Every time." Nico had never noticed that before. But she was right. The sleeve-tug happened again as Leo insisted, "I just wanted to help Coach. That's all." His voice stretched the words like gum. Too smooth. Too rehearsed.

It was the voice that cracked it. Ty leaned into Nico again. "Notice his rhythm?" he said. "He's talking slower now. But yesterday, when he told it to me, it was faster. That's vocal cadence. People slow down when they're trying not to mess up a lie. They're buying time for the next sentence." Nico scribbled it in his notebook later, under a new heading: Lie Detector Clues.

They didn't confront Leo—not yet. This wasn't about catching him in front of everyone. Not this time. This time was for collecting facts. Building the timeline. Remembering the feeling of the switch. Ella's confusion was clearing. Jasmin's patience was thinning. Ty's eyes missed nothing. Nico's hand kept writing.

"Most people think lying is just about the words," Ty's dad once said. "But it's in the face. The voice. The posture. Even the breath. Watch what doesn't match." In Leo's case, everything looked like it matched—until you looked harder. Then the cracks showed. Not big ones. Little seams. Fractures. Mismatched memories.

That's how Leo worked. He stayed just on the right side of believability. If he changed the story just enough, most kids didn't notice. But now Ty had taught the others what to look for. Now Leo's tricks weren't invisible anymore. Now the eyes that had once glanced away were sharpening.

Even Ella, gentle Ella, had begun to see the unevenness. "He keeps saying he forgot," she murmured. "But he remembers everything when it makes him look good." She didn't mean to sound brave. But she did. She was no longer at the mercy of the first version she heard. She now had the power to compare. And remember.

Leo finished his story, grinning like he'd won. But no one clapped. No one smiled back. He walked away, thinking he'd escaped suspicion. But behind him, four quiet minds were assembling a pattern. Leo didn't know it yet. But this time, his lie wouldn't stick. Ty looked at the others. "That's strike two," he said. Nico added, "He doesn't even know we're keeping score." And now, they were.

It happened by the water fountain. Just after the bell and just before the hallway cleared. Leo was zipping up his hoodie when someone—not one of the core four, just another kid from their class—asked, "Hey, where were you yesterday?" A plain question. Innocent. Casual. The sort of question you answer without thinking. Unless you've got something to hide.

Leo smiled too wide. Too slow. He scratched his head and laughed lightly. "Where was I?" he echoed, voice a little too high-pitched. He blinked as if the question had come from nowhere. "Oh, um… yeah, I was sick." His hand tugged at his sleeve, and his foot tapped, just once, before going still. It should've been nothing. But it wasn't.

Ty's eyes locked in like a hawk. "That," he muttered under his breath, "was a stall." Nico nodded, already jotting something down in his notebook. Jasmin frowned, not out of confusion but because she already knew what Ty was about to explain. Ella stood a few feet away, watching Leo the way a person watches a window that might shatter.

The pause wasn't just a beat. It was a build. A delay. A preparation for fiction. "When someone repeats a question," Ty had once said during one of their after-school debriefs, "it's usually to buy time. Especially when the answer should be instant." Leo's reply had taken five seconds longer than it should've. Five seconds too long to be truth.

Leo didn't expect anyone to notice the hesitation. But Ty did. "He's fabricating," Ty whispered. "His eyes shifted up right first, then down left. Visual recall followed by synthetic construction. Classic." He said it like a codebreaker reading Morse. Nico knew the signs now too. The silence. The false laugh. The delayed answer packed in soft words and filler noise.

Then Ty stepped forward. Not loudly. Not to make a scene. But clearly. "You weren't sick," he said. Not a question. A statement. Nico, Jasmin, and Ella didn't flinch. Mr. Arnett, walking past with a clipboard tucked under one arm, paused at the edge of the hallway and tilted his head. He didn't interrupt. He just listened.

Leo's smile twitched. He shrugged. "What do you mean?" he asked, another stall, trying to flip the spotlight. But Ty didn't blink. "You were outside the school at lunch," he said. "My friend's older brother saw you at the corner store near Ridgeway. You weren't sick. You just didn't want to be here."

For once, Leo didn't have a retort. Not one that came fast, anyway. His mouth opened, closed, then opened again. "That's not true," he managed. But his voice cracked. It cracked right down the centre, like glass under pressure. Mr. Arnett stepped a little closer now, just enough to hear without intruding. Nico made a mental note: no defence, only denial.

"Then why'd you repeat the question?" Ty asked. "Why did you need time to think if you were just sick?" Leo's feet shifted. His hands went to his pockets. A classic lock-up. When the truth dries up, the body starts to scream it instead. Jasmin leaned into Ella and whispered, "He's cornered."

Leo started to speak, but it came out jagged. "Why do you care?" he snapped. "I don't have to explain everything I do." Nico stepped forward now. "No, you don't. But when you lie to people, you lose their trust. And you've lost a lot already."

It wasn't a pile-on. It was a reckoning. Quiet. Firm. Factual. Like everything Leo had built—the charm, the jokes, the performative sweetness—was being peeled away one word at a time. Ella didn't say anything. She didn't have to. Her silence was the heaviest note of all.

Mr. Arnett cleared his throat but didn't interject. His eyes, usually unreadable, flicked to Ty with a glance of cautious approval. Leo noticed. He straightened his spine and tried to pivot. "This is stupid," he muttered. "You guys are obsessed with me." But his voice was soft now. Unsteady. The kind of voice you use when you know the room's against you.

"Then stop lying," Ty said. Again, no yelling. No accusation. Just a fact placed in the centre of the room like a chess piece on check. Leo scoffed, rolled his eyes, turned on his heel. But even that didn't come with confidence. He walked away without swagger. That pause—that crack—had been enough.

After Leo disappeared around the corner, Mr. Arnett stepped up beside Ty. He didn't speak right away. He just looked at where Leo had vanished, then at Ty, then at Nico. "That was handled calmly," he said at last. "Professionally." Ty said nothing. He just nodded. "I saw the shift too," Mr. Arnett added after a beat. "And the delay. You're not wrong." He didn't offer more. He didn't praise. But in his tone was something unspoken: understanding. A recognition that Ty wasn't imagining things. That someone did see it this time.

Back at the water fountain, Jasmin whispered, "He's not used to being called out with evidence." Nico closed his notebook. "He'd better start getting used to it," he said. "We're not playing anymore." Not one of them raised their voice. Not one insult was used. It didn't have to be. The pause had said it all. And this time, someone besides them had noticed it too.

Leo talked a lot that day. More than usual. About how he helped his little cousin with homework, how he stood up for someone on the bus last week, how he once gave his lunch to a kid who forgot theirs. He listed these things like badges. Medals. Proofs of kindness worn like armour. But the longer he spoke, the less real it felt. Like he was performing a speech no one asked for.

Jasmin sat across from him during math group. She didn't say much. Just watched. She'd heard stories from kind people before. The good ones didn't brag. They didn't list their kindness like a receipt. They just were kind. Quietly. Without needing the spotlight. But Leo didn't know quiet. He only knew how to fill silence with self-praise.

"I don't even know why people think I'm mean," he said to no one in particular. "I'm one of the nicest people here." His voice was light, but his eyes bounced too quickly from face to face. Waiting for someone to nod. Waiting for someone to agree. Nico didn't flinch. Ty barely looked up. Ella sharpened her pencil until the tip snapped.

"It's weird," Leo went on. "You try to be a good friend and suddenly you're the bad guy." Jasmin blinked slowly. The sentence wasn't just defensive—it was bait. A way to flip guilt back onto anyone who questioned him. Ty whispered, "Overcompensating. Big time."

Then came the story about the time he picked up garbage around the playground just because it "felt like the right thing to do." No one asked. No one prompted it. But Leo told it with the rhythm of a bedtime story. Smooth. Practiced. Like something he'd said before.

Jasmin tilted her head. "Why would you need to prove you're good," she asked, soft but steady, "if you already are?" Her voice didn't rise. She didn't accuse. But the words cut deeper than any insult. Leo laughed—too loudly, too suddenly. "I'm not proving anything," he said. But even he didn't sound convinced.

People who tell the truth don't rehearse it. Jasmin had heard that somewhere—maybe from Ty, maybe from her own gut. Truth doesn't come with decoration. It arrives bare. Honest. But Leo's version came glittered and wrapped with ribbon. Every word was overwrapped. Overcooked.

"Sometimes the best people get misunderstood," he tried again, this time with a shrug. "That's just how the world is." Nico scribbled something into his notebook: When someone talks too much about being kind, they're probably trying to sell it.

Ty didn't interrupt. He just leaned back and let the room breathe. It was the kind of stillness Leo didn't like. No applause. No reassurance. Just silence thick enough to feel. He tapped his pen against the desk. Once. Twice. Then stopped. "I guess some people just want to believe the worst," Leo added. Still fishing. Still hoping someone would take the bait. But Jasmin was done biting. Ella crossed her arms. Ty spun his pencil slowly, saying nothing. And Nico flipped his notebook closed with finality.

"You're very talkative today," Jasmin said. It wasn't sarcastic. Just observant. Calm. The way a weather report says, chance of rain. Leo narrowed his eyes, not because the statement hurt—but because it landed. Because it was true, and truth felt like thunder when you're not expecting it.

Mr. Clarke walked past at that exact moment. He didn't pause, but he glanced at the group. He always did when Leo talked too loud for too long. There was a note in his eyes—not judgement, not yet. Just awareness.

An invisible pencil, drawing lines. Leo cleared his throat. "Anyway, I'm just saying—I don't need to prove anything." But no one had asked him to. That was the thing. No one demanded proof. He just offered it up anyway, like someone hiding behind a wall of trophies they built themselves.

After group work ended, Jasmin and Nico walked back to their lockers. "He's selling a story," she whispered. Nico nodded. "But no one's buying it." Ella caught up to them and added, "It's like he thinks we forgot." "But we didn't," Ty said, appearing behind them. "And we won't." They didn't need him to say another word. Because in Leo's endless words that day, they found something louder. The silence between them. And what wasn't being said.

It was a small moment, so small that most wouldn't have caught it. But Nico wasn't like most. He had begun watching closely now—not because he liked it, but because he had to. Leo stood across from Ella near the coat hooks, arms folded with that too-casual look he used when pretending not to care. "Yeah," Leo said, "you're right." His voice curled around the words like smoke. But his head? His head moved the other way.

He was saying yes. But he was shaking no. The contradiction wasn't loud. It didn't come with music or a flashing light. It came in the form of a twitch—barely half an inch, a sideways shift that didn't match the sentence. Nico narrowed his eyes. That kind of nod wasn't real. It was the kind people used when their mouth was performing and their body refused to join the lie.

Ella didn't seem to catch it. Not fully. She stood with one hand on her backpack strap, eyes lowered. Maybe she was still hoping it would all smooth out—like wet paint drying into something clean. But Nico knew better. He stepped closer, like he was checking the schedule taped to the wall. "That's a no pretending to be a yes," he whispered.

Leo's eyes flicked toward him. Quick. Calculating. Not afraid, but aware. The kind of glance someone gives when they know they've been caught, but don't think you'll do anything about it. Nico didn't flinch. He just leaned back against the cubby wall, letting the moment settle like dust.

"You always think I'm lying," Leo said, casual but clipped. The words were aimed at Nico now. "You've got some kind of problem with me." But the accusation felt hollow. No real fire behind it. Just noise to cover up the click of a truth locking into place.

Jasmin walked over just in time to catch the tail end of Leo's line. "Nico's not the one nodding the wrong way," she said, folding her arms. "Maybe check your mirror." Leo's smile flickered. Not vanished—just bent, like light through a cracked window.

Body language doesn't lie. That's what Ty always said. People's words might, but their shoulders, their eyebrows, their feet—those things couldn't keep secrets forever. Ty wasn't even in the room, but his voice echoed in Nico's head: The face says yes, the body says no. Trust the body.

Leo cleared his throat and adjusted his collar. "All I said was she had a point. What's wrong with agreeing?" Nico didn't answer. He just tilted his head, mimicking Leo's fake nod—slow, sideways, and obviously wrong. Jasmin stifled a smirk.

Ella looked between them, her expression unreadable. But there was something soft in her posture now. A kind of understanding, even if she hadn't seen it herself. Nico wasn't trying to make her feel stupid. He just wanted her to see what he saw. That the truth isn't always loud— but lies? They flinch.

Mr. Arnett walked past the open hallway and gave a half-wave. None of the kids responded. They were too deep in something unspoken. The kind of silence that means more than shouting. Ella finally said, "I guess I missed it." But Nico shook his head. "You didn't miss it. You felt it. You just didn't name it yet."

Leo tried to recover, but recovery wasn't his talent. He was better at charm, at distraction. "Okay, fine," he said, voice lighter now. "Maybe I was thinking out loud." Another trick. If words don't land well, pretend they weren't meant seriously. But Nico wasn't buying it anymore.

"You know what I think?" Jasmin asked, stepping forward. "I think you nod and agree and pretend just long enough for people to stop watching. And then you do whatever you wanted anyway." Leo opened his mouth to fire back, but Nico beat him to it.

"Just don't lie with your body next time. It's bad acting." The words weren't shouted. But they might as well have been. A couple of kids from another class slowed as they walked by, hearing just enough to raise eyebrows but not enough to understand.

Leo shrugged. "Think what you want." He turned on his heel and left the conversation without waiting for a reply. That, Nico thought, was the truest thing he'd done all day. Walking away before the truth could corner him again.

Jasmin bumped her shoulder lightly against Nico's. "You've been watching." "Yeah," he said. "And I've been learning." Ella let out a breath she hadn't realised she'd been holding. "Next time I'll look harder." Nico didn't correct her. "Just listen to what doesn't match," he said. The bell rang overhead, long and sharp. Students scattered like marbles. But the three of them stayed for just a moment longer. Long enough to remember that sometimes the lie isn't in what people say. It's in what they do when they think no one's watching.

Leo had a habit of talking too much when no one asked him to. That wasn't new. But lately, it had started to itch beneath the skin. Like a sweater with the tag still on, Nico couldn't shake the irritation. Every time Leo entered a room, he opened his mouth and unloaded a story. A grand one. A complicated one. Always with moving pieces and dramatic pauses, and always without invitation.

It happened again on Wednesday, just after first bell. The class was quiet, waiting for Miss Kara, when Leo launched into a monologue. "So, I was walking home yesterday," he began, loud enough for the first three rows to hear, "and I saw a raccoon in the middle of the street. But get this—" He paused for suspense. No one had asked him anything. No one even looked up.

Nico exchanged glances with Ty, who barely blinked. "There it is again," Ty whispered. "Unasked details. It's a pattern." Jasmin leaned in from behind her notebook. "What's the pattern for?" she murmured. Ty didn't look away from Leo. "When people lie, they build castles out of words. Big ones. And then they hide inside them so you can't find the truth."

Jasmin didn't need convincing. She'd heard Leo tell three different versions of what happened during their group project. Each version painted him as the hero. Each one slightly longer, slightly more polished than the last. It was like watching a magician rehearse until the trick looked real. "So what do we do?" she asked.

"We notice," Ty said simply. "That's the first thing. We notice the shape of the castle. The way it gets bigger when no one asks for it. The way he fills silence like he's trying to keep it from saying something."

Leo's story had now wandered to a neighbour who supposedly chased the raccoon with a broom. Nico looked around. No one was laughing. No one was even pretending to care. And still, Leo talked. He wasn't storytelling. He was smoke screening. A fog machine in the middle of a test.

Later that day, in the lunchroom, it happened again. Ella sat with Ty, Jasmin, and Nico, picking at her sandwich. Leo dropped his tray across from them and began another tale. This time, about how he had "accidentally" helped a younger student clean up spilled milk and "totally didn't expect anyone to say thank you." Again, no one had asked. And again, he led the conversation off a cliff no one was walking toward.

Nico didn't interrupt, but he did lean over and scribble something in his notebook. Ella peeked at it. It read: When someone says too much without being asked, they're not giving— they're covering. Ella tapped her pen against her lip. "So... what's he covering?" she asked quietly.

Ty answered. "Doubt. Guilt. Control. Whatever he doesn't want us to see. Or whatever he doesn't want to admit happened." His voice wasn't angry. It was calm. Too calm for someone Leo had tried to tear down. But maybe that was the point. Ty wasn't playing anymore.

"Why not just stay quiet?" Jasmin asked. "Wouldn't that be safer?" Nico responded this time. "Because silence leaves space for someone else to speak. And Leo doesn't like that. He fills every silence so you don't have room to call him out."

Ella sighed. "It's exhausting." Ty nodded. "That's part of the plan, too. Wear you down with words until you stop trying to find the ones that matter." She looked down at her apple, untouched. "He talks so much that I stop listening."

"That's the other trick," Nico said, closing his notebook. "If you talk long enough, people forget what the original question was." Jasmin frowned. "Was there even a question?" They all went quiet, but it wasn't the kind of silence Leo liked to fill. It was the kind that spoke for itself.

When Miss Kara walked by and asked how they were doing, Leo perked up and launched into a description of how he'd helped clean the whiteboard during morning recess. She nodded politely, but it was clear she hadn't heard the first half. "That wasn't even true," Jasmin whispered after she left. "I was in the room. I did it."

Ty looked at her, then at Leo. "And yet he said it. Confident. Calm. Just loud enough to be believable. That's the castle again. Big, clean, and hollow inside."

Mr. Arnett entered the room, clipboard in hand. Leo stopped mid-sentence. That, too, was a pattern. Leo never built castles when real accountability walked in the room. It was only when he believed he was the tallest in the room that he added another storey.

Nico scribbled one more sentence before closing his book: Truth doesn't build castles. It just walks out the door and doesn't look back. He slid the notebook into his backpack. Ella was already standing.

"You don't have to believe him to be polite," she said, as if declaring it to herself. "And you don't have to listen when no one asked the question." They stood. Jasmin followed. Ty slung his bag over his shoulder without a word. Leo watched them walk away, words still building behind his tongue. But none of them looked back. The castle stayed behind them, unfinished.

Sophie had never spoken much in front of the group. She was the kind of quiet that didn't announce itself—more like a still pond no one dared to step into. But today, she broke that silence with a sentence that froze the table in place. "He stared the whole time he lied," she said, her voice clear but low. "Didn't blink once."

They were sitting outside near the fence by the soccer field, the part of the yard where teachers couldn't hear but could still see. The weather was warm, but the chill in her voice cut through. Jasmin lowered her juice box without drinking. Nico leaned forward, eyebrows lifting slightly. Ty, who usually led these sorts of observations, said nothing—just listened.

Sophie blinked now, slow and thoughtful, like she was trying to undo the memory. "It wasn't a regular stare," she added. "It felt like... like he was trying to glue his words onto my face. Like, if he didn't blink, I couldn't look away." Nico nodded once. "Laser-eyes," he whispered. "Yeah," Sophie said. "That."

Leo had a way of making eye contact feel like pressure, not presence. He didn't just look at people. He locked onto them. As if blinking would let the truth slip out through the cracks. Ty reached into his backpack and pulled out the printed article Mr. Clarke had given them two weeks ago. "Some liars stare more, not less," Ty read aloud. "It's a control move. They want to see your reaction and force belief through eye contact."

Jasmin furrowed her brow. "But I thought liars avoided eye contact?" Ty shook his head. "That's old thinking. Mr. Clarke said it's about what kind of liar they are. Leo's the type who doubles down. He stares not because he's honest—but because he's performing." Nico added, "Like a magician who says, 'Watch closely.' He wants you to believe it's real, even when you're watching the trick."

Sophie's face stayed still, but her eyes moved slowly from Ty to Nico. "Then why does it work?" she asked. "Why did I believe him?" No one answered for a moment. They weren't sure how to. It wasn't just that Leo lied—it was how much he made others believe they were wrong for questioning him.

Ella touched Sophie's sleeve gently. "Because we're trained to think staring means truth. It doesn't. Sometimes it just means they've practised the lie enough to stop blinking." Sophie bit her lip. "He told me I made him uncomfortable, that I was staring too much when I was just listening. But he stared at me the whole time."

"That's called projection," Ty said. "When someone accuses you of what they're doing." Jasmin let out a sigh. "He does that a lot, doesn't he? Calls people dramatic when he's the one causing drama. Says you're the problem so you won't see that it's him."

Sophie looked down at the grass. "He said I was the reason people weren't talking to him. That I 'poisoned' their minds." Nico clenched his jaw. "He wants us to question ourselves. That's part of how the lie sticks. Not just by being told—but by making you unsure of what you saw, what you felt."

They sat in silence again, the good kind. The one where you let hard truths land. Then Ty smirked a little, tapping the article. "You know what Mr. Clarke said last week? That Leo could work for a tabloid magazine. They lie for a living too." A few chuckles broke through, even from Sophie. Not loud ones, but real.

"That's what makes him dangerous," Jasmin said. "He lies like it's his first language." Sophie nodded slowly. "He even made me feel like I was lying. Like I'd imagined everything."

"You didn't," Nico said firmly. "We believe you. And you're not alone." He placed his hand flat on the bench between them—not a reach, but a reminder. Ella added, "And next time he stares, you blink on purpose. Don't let him pin you with his eyes."

Ty folded the article, then looked up at the sky. "They say the eyes are the windows to the soul. But some windows are tinted." Nico snorted. "Or cracked." Jasmin smiled. "Or just painted shut."

Sophie's shoulders eased. "I used to think I had to match his stare to prove I wasn't afraid. But now I know—I don't owe him my eyes. Or my silence." She stood up slowly, brushing crumbs from her jeans. "Let's go back," she said. "He's probably watching. But this time, I don't care." Nico smiled, rising beside her. "Let him blink first." They walked across the field, four shadows stretched by the sun, eyes forward, no one looking back.

Ella had always been good at noticing the little things. Not the loud things, like who yelled or who cried. But the tiny cracks that showed up right before someone pretended everything was fine. She noticed it the first time when Leo got called out in gym class for switching teams mid-game. He tugged at his sleeves, like the fabric could hide his embarrassment. He rubbed the back of his neck twice before answering. At the time, she thought nothing of it. But the second time, and the third, it started to look more like a pattern than a coincidence.

It was during a reading circle when the habit made itself known again. Leo had been asked about a library book that went missing. He said he hadn't seen it, but his fingers found the collar of his shirt and began fiddling. Ella didn't speak, didn't blink. She just observed. The lie wasn't in his words—it was in the hands that moved without reason, in the way his shoulders tightened when silence fell. She leaned over slightly to Ty and whispered, "He's doing it again."

Ty's eyes didn't follow Leo. He didn't have to. "Sleeve tug or neck rub?" he asked flatly. "Both," Ella replied. Ty smirked, not because it was funny, but because it proved what his father had taught him. "His body's a better truth-teller than his mouth," he muttered. "Classic nervous grooming."

Nico had joined them by the bookshelf during indoor recess. "What's grooming?" he asked. Ty explained in the clearest way he could. "It's stuff you do with your hands when your brain is scrambling. Touching your face, fixing your shirt, rubbing your neck. It's not always lying, but when it happens every time someone asks a question... it adds up." Nico nodded slowly. "So it's like his hands panic even when his face pretends not to?"

"Exactly," Ty said. "His mouth lies. His body tattles."

Jasmin joined them with a folded piece of paper—Leo's old worksheet with suspiciously familiar answers. "He copied again. From Sophie this time," she said, slipping it between the pages of a book for safekeeping. Ella pointed across the room where Leo now stood by the coat hooks, chatting casually with a younger student. "Watch his left hand," she said. "Every time the other kid says something, he rubs his thumb over his palm. Like he's trying to stay in control."

Nico frowned. "Is that normal?" Ty shrugged. "For most kids? Probably just habit. But for Leo, it happens every time he's trying to get someone on his side. It's like his skin knows the truth's about to bend." Jasmin whispered, "Maybe that's why he always wore long sleeves. Hides the signals better." Ella didn't laugh, but her lips twitched. "Too bad his body didn't get the memo."

Mr. Clarke passed them, giving the group a curious look but said nothing. Ty folded his arms. "My dad says that people always leave clues. Not just in what they say, but in what they can't help doing." Nico scratched his head. "So... if Leo's body keeps giving away the lie, why doesn't anyone else notice?"

"Because most people listen with their ears," Jasmin said. "Not their eyes." That line stuck. It hovered between them like chalk dust, weightless but lingering. Ella's gaze wandered back to Leo, who now leaned against the windowsill, laughing at something too hard, too forced.

"There it is," she said. "Laugh too loud, sleeve tug, fake smile, shoulder roll." Ty clicked his tongue. "That's a full set of tells in under ten seconds. If this were poker, he'd be broke." Nico tilted his head. "What happens if we call it out in front of everyone?"

Ty shook his head. "He'd deny. Say it's just habit. Say we're being creepy for watching him. That's what manipulators do—they make you feel weird for noticing their weirdness." Jasmin crossed her arms. "So then what's the point of knowing if we can't do anything about it?"

"You can do something," Ty said firmly. "You trust what you see. That's the first step. Don't let him convince you that your eyes lied." Ella added, "And you look for it in other people. Because now you know how to see it. That's how we stop the cycle."

The bell rang. Everyone stood. As they filed into the hallway, Leo brushed past them. His eyes lingered on Ella just long enough to feel like pressure, not acknowledgment. His hands, once again, crept to the back of his neck. And this time, she didn't flinch. She simply looked at him, straight and even, then turned back to Ty.

"That's how you know," she said quietly. "You watch the part of them they can't control." Ty gave a single nod. "Shadow work," he said. "Truth in motion." They walked into class. Leo sat near the front. Alone. His shirt sleeves were rolled up now, and his neck was red from the rubbing. But no one asked why. Because they already knew.

The sound came from the far end of the hallway—too loud, too sharp, and too quick for the kind of joke that had just been told. Jasmin didn't even need to look to know it was Leo. She'd heard enough real laughs to know what a hollow one sounded like. It rang like a bell someone didn't want to ring but had to, echoing in empty space and demanding attention it hadn't earned. The teacher beside him offered a small, polite smile, but it didn't reach her eyes. Nico caught it too. He didn't laugh. Neither did Ty. The noise had shape, but no heart.

Jasmin stepped closer to the lockers, resting her shoulder against the cold metal. "That wasn't for her," she said quietly. "That laugh was for us." Ty leaned in. "Too loud. Too late. He's trying to cover nerves." Jasmin nodded. "He wanted the hallway to know he's still here. Still confident. Still untouchable." But what she saw was someone trying not to drown. Leo's laugh had no ease to it. No wrinkle in the eyes. No breath behind it. Just performance.

Across the hall, Leo turned and spoke to a group of students a year younger. They didn't say much back. A few gave tight-lipped grins, the kind you give when you're not sure whether to leave or wait to be dismissed. When one of them turned and walked away mid-sentence, Leo gave another loud chuckle—this one even sharper than before. It cracked at the end like a snapped pencil. Jasmin flinched. Ty didn't blink. "He's spiralling," he said, voice low. "The louder he laughs, the less control he has."

It wasn't always this way. There was a time when Leo's laugh used to pull people in. It used to light up corners of the room that even sunlight missed. But that was before people noticed the strings. Before they started seeing who he left behind once the punchlines faded. Now, his laugh didn't feel like inclusion—it felt like deflection. Nico crossed his arms and whispered, "He's laughing to build a wall." Jasmin added, "And no one's trying to climb it."

Sophie passed by him, head down, walking quickly. Leo made no move to speak to her. Not this time. The last time he tried, she said nothing. Just walked away. It was the quietest rebellion they'd ever seen, and the loudest message Sophie had ever delivered. Jasmin remembered how Sophie had once smiled at everything. Now, her face was a blank page Leo had no words for. His laughter couldn't reach her anymore.

Leo ran a hand through his hair as the hallway cleared. The classroom doors were opening. Bell soon. Still, he stayed in the middle of the hall like he was waiting for a stage to rise beneath him. "If he laughs one more time," Ty murmured, "I think the floor might swallow him whole." Jasmin didn't smile. "Or maybe he hopes it will." There was something haunting in watching someone realize their act had worn thin.

They entered the classroom together, eyes fixed forward, voices low. Leo followed seconds later. Another laugh came—this one aimed at something on his phone. No one asked what was funny. No one cared. Even Mr. Clarke didn't look up. That silence was more punishing than any scolding could be. It stretched across the room and settled in the air like dust.

Ella slid into the seat next to Jasmin, opening her notebook with slow, deliberate movements. "He laughed again," she said, not looking up. "Was it real?" Jasmin shook her head. "No. It was hollow. Like a balloon filled with smoke." Ella nodded. "That's how it feels when he talks now. Like you're supposed to clap, even if you don't know why." Nico added softly, "That's not a joke. That's theatre."

Mr. Clarke asked for quiet. The room obeyed. Leo raised his hand to speak, but Clarke called on someone else. For the first time, Leo didn't insist. He dropped his hand slowly, pretending to scratch his temple, as if the rejection hadn't stung. But Ty saw it. "That's the second time he didn't push back," he whispered. "He's shrinking." Jasmin's eyes didn't leave the front of the room. "Or maybe he knows it's not working anymore."

The lesson started. Words filled the board, pages turned, pens scratched. But no one laughed. Not for the rest of the hour. Not even Leo. And when he finally did smile, it was small. Private. Like he was the only one in on the joke—and the joke wasn't funny.

Outside, the wind pushed against the windows. Inside, Leo sat still. Every move he made felt like it wanted to be noticed but hoped not to be questioned. He drummed his fingers once, looked around, then stopped. There were no mirrors in the room. No reflections to correct. No one to convince.

At recess, the younger grades played with their usual noise and chaos. Leo wandered near the sandbox where the Grade 2s were digging with plastic shovels. He stood for a moment, then turned and walked away. Not one child called his name. Jasmin and Ella watched from the benches. "Even the little ones," Ella whispered. "They know." Jasmin nodded slowly. "They just don't have the words for it yet."

Leo tried to laugh again near the bike rack. It fizzled. No audience. No echo. Just air. He rubbed the back of his neck and walked the long way around the school. Nico watched him disappear around the corner. "He's looking for someone to believe him," he said. Ty stood beside him. "But he's the only one who still does."

They didn't celebrate. There was no joy in watching someone fall apart. But there was relief. A quiet, unspoken relief that the truth had finally outrun the noise. Jasmin sighed, steady and slow. "Fake laughs are loud," she said. "But they never last."

It happened between periods, just as the bell rang and the students rose from their desks in one slow ripple. Mr. Clarke had stepped in to collect some attendance sheets, speaking with quiet formality to the teacher near the board. The students barely noticed, but Ty did. Ty always did. His eyes tracked motion differently—like a soldier trained to spot the flicker of a lie in the dark. And what he saw in that moment wasn't big. It wasn't loud. But it was enough.

Leo had flinched. Not dramatically. Not enough to draw stares. But it was real. A faint tightening of the shoulders. A quick downward glance. A second where his body seemed to curl in, just slightly, like he was shrinking from something that hadn't even touched him. Mr. Clarke hadn't raised his voice. Hadn't even looked directly at Leo. But the presence alone had pulled something involuntary from him. A tell.

Ty leaned closer to Jasmin without breaking his line of sight. "Did you see that?" She shook her head. Ty didn't elaborate, not yet. Nico caught the whisper and looked over. He saw Leo brushing imaginary lint from his sleeve, adjusting nothing, pretending nothing had happened. But he moved like someone trying to erase a feeling from his own skin. It was subtle. But it was not nothing.

Once the sheets were collected, Mr. Clarke exited with his usual quiet pace. He nodded once at the class, neither smiling nor frowning. But even after he left, Leo stayed tense. His eyes flicked to the door, then back to his desk, then to no one at all. Ty folded his arms. "His body knows," he whispered. "Even if his mouth hasn't caught up." Jasmin turned. "Knows what?" Ty's voice was soft. "That he's running out of time."

There's a kind of silence that lives between a question and a confession. Leo wore it now. It clung to him like cold air. Even as the class moved around him, he sat unusually still. He reached for a pencil, paused, then set it down again. His breath came in slow pulls, as though he were rationing it. No one else spoke to him. He didn't speak to them either.

Ella entered late from the nurse's office and paused near the back. Her eyes met Ty's, and he gave the smallest nod. She looked at Leo, then back at Ty. No one needed to explain what they saw. Ella sat beside Jasmin and whispered, "What happened?" Jasmin murmured, "His mask slipped." That's what it felt like. For just a second, the armour cracked. Not from a hit—but from the shadow of one.

Leo scratched his neck again. A motion repeated, not because of itch, but of habit. His hand moved without purpose. His foot tapped too quickly. His eyes scanned too much. Nico jotted something in his notebook without taking his eyes off Leo. A single line. He flinched like a liar waiting to be believed.

Mr. Arnett stepped into the doorway, said something to the teacher, then left. Another adult voice. Another dart in Leo's direction. Another twitch in his shoulders. Ty didn't smile. "He's on edge," he said. "His body thinks he's being hunted. That's why he keeps blinking like that." Jasmin frowned. "But no one said anything." Ty turned. "Exactly."

When guilt lives long enough without being spoken, it begins to live in the limbs. The nervous tics, the rushed answers, the long blinks, the awkward laughs. It hides in skin and bone when the tongue refuses to carry the weight. Leo's body was telling a story he hadn't written permission for. His silence was not peace—it was panic.

Sophie walked by, her head down. She did not flinch. She didn't even turn to acknowledge Leo's presence. That quiet distance was louder than a scream. Leo's eyes followed her, but his mouth stayed shut. He bit his bottom lip. The pressure of everything unsaid seemed to be pressing against the walls of his throat. Still, nothing came out.

Recess came and went. Leo walked the perimeter of the yard alone. Once or twice he stopped and turned, like someone who thought he heard his name but hadn't. The other students didn't follow. They didn't mock him. But they didn't reach for him either. And in that vacuum, something began to tighten in Leo's chest. A presence he couldn't shake. It moved with him. It watched him.

By the end of the day, he was quieter than usual. Not polite. Not humble. Just quieter. As if volume was a risk he couldn't afford anymore. He packed his bag in slow motion. Jasmin and Nico didn't speak. Ty only observed. Watching the micro-movements. The tension in the jaw. The unblinking stare at the floor tiles. The foot that shifted too much, then not at all.

Backpacks zipped. Chairs scraped. The bell rang. Mr. Clarke stood outside the door, leaning against the wall. Leo walked out and didn't make eye contact. Mr. Clarke didn't stop him. He didn't need to. His presence was enough. As Leo passed, Ty whispered, "He did it again." Jasmin nodded. "Same shiver?" Ty said, "Exactly the same."

They stood there a little longer, letting the moment settle like dust after a collapse. There was no joy in watching someone unravel. Only clarity. The truth doesn't always shout. Sometimes, it whispers from a nervous shoulder or a tightened breath. Sometimes, it flinches. In the notebook he carried everywhere, Nico wrote five words before they walked home: His mouth lied. His body didn't. Then he closed it, tucked it away, and joined the others without a word.

It started with a sentence. One Nico made up on the spot, just strange enough to sound real if you didn't know better. "The prefrontal lobe stops growing once a person turns eleven," he said to Leo by the lockers. He said it casually, like it was something he read in an article. Like it was just another fact floating in the sea of school hallway chatter. Leo blinked. Nodded slowly. Said nothing at first. That was fine. Nico wasn't expecting an immediate reaction. He was planting something. A trap with no teeth—just truth's absence.

Later that day, in Mr. Clarke's reading group, the moment arrived. Leo, half-smiling, raised his hand while Mr. Clarke discussed how the brain processes language. "Actually," Leo said with theatrical calm, "the prefrontal lobe stops growing at eleven." His voice lifted with that artificial confidence that always came when he was trying to sound clever. Nico looked up from his notes and caught Ty's eye. The trap had snapped.

Ty didn't grin. He didn't need to. He simply leaned his elbow into the desk and gave Nico a soft nod, the kind they had learned to exchange when words weren't safe. Jasmin didn't react either. But her pencil stilled on the page. She was listening now. Mr. Clarke raised a brow. "Where'd you hear that?" Leo paused. "I just… I read it somewhere." His lie was dry. Too smooth. Nico knew the taste of effort.

After the session, Ty and Nico walked together down the long back hall where sunlight always struck the lockers like gold through glass. "He took the bait," Nico whispered. Ty nodded once. "Because he always does." There wasn't smugness in their tone—just confirmation. This wasn't about catching Leo for the sake of it. It was about understanding what kind of truth could be trusted around him, and which truths he would pretend to own.

Jasmin caught up with them before they reached the stairs. "Did you say that on purpose?" she asked. Nico shrugged. "I wanted to know if he'd echo it. He did." She didn't ask why—she already knew. That's what Leo did. He borrowed intelligence like a coat he could drape over his shoulders. But it never fit. The sleeves were always too long, the cut always off. He didn't think in layers. He copied the surface.

Ty folded his arms as they stepped outside into the afternoon air. "He's smart," he said flatly. "But he chooses to be fake." Jasmin looked up. "Is that worse?" Ty nodded. "Yeah. Because when you're pretending to be what you already are, it means you've got something to hide." The wind rustled Ella's loose hair as she joined them by the bike racks. She didn't ask what they were talking about. But she knew from the tone.

Leo lingered by the school fence that day, trying to look unbothered. But every time a teacher passed, he straightened his back too quickly. Every time a student laughed, his head turned too sharply. He was always listening. Not for conversation—but for credit. Nico watched him from the bench. "He doesn't want to be included. He wants to be admired," he murmured. Ty sat beside him. "And that's why he steals other people's lines."

The test hadn't been cruel. It hadn't even been complicated. But it proved what they'd already suspected. Leo didn't listen to understand. He listened to reuse. He scanned for smart-sounding things he could repeat later, reshaped into compliments or arguments, whichever worked better at the time. Nico scratched a sentence into his notebook: Not every echo is honest. Some just bounce off empty walls.

Mr. Clarke passed by as they packed up. "Heading out?" he asked. Nico nodded. "Yeah." He hesitated. "Can I ask something?" Mr. Clarke paused. "Of course." Nico said, "If someone copies your ideas, how do you make sure they don't use them to hurt people?" Mr. Clarke tilted his head. "By making sure your truth is tied to who you are. Not just what you say." He tapped the side of Nico's notebook gently. "That's where it lives."

Jasmin lingered near the edge of the parking lot, watching the younger students play a game of four square. She wasn't smiling. She was thinking. She turned to Ty and said, "You ever wonder if Leo believes himself?" Ty's jaw tightened. "Sometimes I think he believes the lie before it even comes out. Like it's easier than telling the truth." That stayed with all of them.

Back home, Nico sat at his desk and looked at the sentence again. Not every echo is honest. He thought about how many times Leo had borrowed his words, how many conversations had ended with Leo repeating something brilliant only minutes after he'd heard it. Nico didn't want credit. He wanted truth to mean something. He wanted people to mean what they said, not use it as decoration.

That night, they talked in the group chat. Ty shared a story from his dad's files—one about a criminal who had told six different versions of the same night, hoping one would stick. "He thought if he told the lie enough times, it'd get tired of being questioned." Jasmin typed, That's Leo. Ella responded with just three dots. Then finally: Why does he want to sound smart instead of being kind?

Nico didn't have an answer for that. None of them did. But he knew something else now. Knowing someone's lying is one thing. Watching them build a character out of other people's words is another. It's not just dishonest. It's hollow. And hollowness can echo too.

By the time Nico closed his notebook, he felt steadier. The test had worked. But more than that, it had taught him this: liars aren't always loud. Sometimes, they speak in borrowed brilliance. And sometimes, the sharpest truth is the one you say softly—and only once.

Leo tilted his head when Ty repeated the question. "What?" he asked, as though nothing had been said before. "I never said that." But the way his eyes narrowed just a second too fast made Jasmin clench her jaw. It wasn't confusion. It was cover. A clean sweep of denial like erasing chalk off the board, even though the dust still lingered in the air. "You said it last week," Ty replied plainly. "Outside the gym. About Ella. I wrote it down." Leo blinked once. Then shrugged. "Guess I forgot."

Ty didn't raise his voice. He didn't shift in his seat. He pulled a page from his pocket, the corner folded, his handwriting firm in blue ink. "Here." The group stood quietly, the library air warm with waiting. Leo didn't take the paper. He didn't have to. His silence said enough. Nico watched the breath hitch in Leo's chest, the smallest ripple of panic masked as boredom. "Whatever," Leo muttered. "It wasn't a big deal." But it was. Because lies don't disappear. They stain.

"Liars count on forgetfulness," Ty said, folding the paper back into his palm. "But I don't forget." He said it not as a threat, but as a statement of self. Nico nodded slowly, the weight of the moment settling like sand in a jar. "That's how he gets away with things," Jasmin murmured. "He acts like it never happened, and if we hesitate, it's like it didn't." Ella didn't speak. But her hand brushed Jasmin's wrist. Just once. She remembered too.

Ty sat down near the edge of the fiction shelves, resting his notebook across his lap. "Most people forget things that don't matter," he said. "Like what colour socks they wore on Tuesday. Or if they closed their locker twice." He glanced up. "But people don't forget things that hurt. Not really. We just pretend to, because sometimes that's easier than saying it out loud again." Jasmin nodded. "Or because no one believed us the first time."

Leo was already at the door. His hands in his pockets, the smugness faded. He didn't look angry. He looked caught. But in the kind of net that doesn't pull tight until the fish stops thrashing. "You're making a big deal out of nothing," he said, half to the room, half to himself. "You wrote it wrong." Ty didn't answer. He didn't need to. His memory didn't wobble. And Leo knew that now.

Mr. Clarke walked past the open door, glanced in, and paused for half a second. "Everything alright?" he asked. Nico answered for all of them. "We're sorting out what was said." Clarke gave the smallest nod. "Let me know if anyone needs help remembering." And then he continued on, the message clear in its simplicity: adults weren't all blind.

After Leo left, Jasmin sat on the floor beside Ty. "Did you really write it down the same day?" He nodded. "Yeah. I've been writing down a lot of things. Patterns. Things he says that change." Ella looked up. "How do you know what matters and what doesn't?" Ty replied, "If it makes someone flinch, it matters."

Nico pulled his own journal from his bag. "I think we've all been keeping things," he said. "In our heads, in our hands, in our stomachs. I used to think it was just me." Jasmin gave a soft laugh that didn't quite reach her eyes. "That's what he wants. To make you feel like it's just you. So when he forgets, you feel like you have to too."

Ella finally spoke. "But I didn't forget. I just… thought it didn't count." The words were quiet, but every one of them landed. Ty's gaze didn't waver. "It counted. It all counted. That's why he wants us to forget it. Because remembering is how you stop him." The room fell into hush again, the kind of hush that holds truth in its arms like a newborn.

They began listing moments—not aloud, not in any grand confrontation, but with ink and lined paper. They wrote them down: things Leo said, faces he made, how he changed stories in front of different people. "He edits reality," Nico whispered. "Like a bad writer rewriting the ending after the book's already printed."

Sophie added a line to Ty's paper. "I wasn't even supposed to matter," she wrote. "But I do." She didn't say it. She just slid the paper across the carpet. Jasmin read it and passed it back, then traced a smiley face beside it—not because it was funny, but because it was right.

They left the library in twos. Nothing loud. Nothing dramatic. Just kids who remembered things they weren't supposed to. Ty held the notebook to his chest like it was armour. Jasmin carried her silence like it was a sword. Nico walked behind them both, wondering how many lies had vanished into the noise of their days, never questioned. Not anymore.

Leo sat alone near the gym doors, hunched over his phone. But no one texted back. No one sat beside him. The hallway buzzed with quiet revenge—not through yelling, not through gossip—but through memory. And that was enough. Jasmin looked back once. Then didn't again. Because remembering wasn't just an act of defence. It was an act of recovery. And every kid in that group had just reclaimed a part of the story Leo tried to erase.

Mr. Rafferty rested one hand on the windowsill, eyes half-lidded as though he were trying to see the good in every student at once. "Leo's just misunderstood," he said with the calm certainty of someone who'd never truly been hurt by words he couldn't prove. Jasmin didn't answer him right away. She twisted her pencil around her fingers, then tapped it against the edge of the desk. "Maybe," she finally said. "But only if you believe the part he wants you to see." Her voice was gentle, but the words weren't soft. They landed like pebbles on glass.

Nico didn't even pretend to be polite. "They only see what he shows them," he muttered to Jasmin. "We see what he hides." Across the table, Ty's jaw tightened. His binder creaked under his arm as he stood, not to be rude, but because he couldn't sit still another second. "It's not fair," he said, not yelling, but steady. "It's not fair that adults get to decide the story when they're not even in the room when it happens."

Mr. Rafferty looked startled, as if a bird had flown into the classroom. "Ty, I think you're being a little dramatic—" But Ty cut him off with a single raised hand. Not loud. Not rude. Just firm. "My dad teaches RCMP cadets how to detect deception. That's what he does. He trains people to know when someone's lying. I've been learning it since I was six. Do you think maybe I'd know what I'm talking about by now?"

The room shifted. The air changed. Even Rafferty paused, and in that pause, Nico saw the tiniest flicker of something—maybe respect, maybe guilt. Either way, it was enough. Ty turned on his heel and walked straight to the office, his boots quiet but deliberate against the tile floor. Mr. Arnett was at his desk, flipping through a faculty calendar. He looked up and saw Ty before Ty even knocked. "Something wrong, son?"

Ty didn't hesitate. "I want to bring my dad in," he said. "To teach the teachers. About spotting lies. Real ones. The ones that hurt people." Arnett blinked, then leaned forward. "You want your dad to run a session?" Ty nodded. Arnett raised a brow. "Why not you?" Ty's eyebrows shot up. "Me?" Arnett folded his hands. "You see it better than most adults I've met. Why not you?"

It wasn't a joke. That was the part that stunned Ty the most. Arnett meant it. There was no smirk, no sarcasm, no humour in the corners of his eyes. Just belief. The hallway outside the office had gone still. Ty swallowed hard and said, "Okay. I'll start with the Grade Fours." Arnett leaned back in his chair. "Bring your dad too. You'll both be the teachers. We'll make it a rotation."

By the time Ty returned to class, Nico and Jasmin had already heard. Word travelled fast when the truth was in it. "You're gonna teach the teachers?" Jasmin whispered as they crossed paths in the hall. Ty shrugged, but there was pride in it. "And the kids. Some of them already see it. They just need words for what they're seeing." Ella caught up beside them, eyes wide. "You're gonna teach us how to spot lies?" He nodded again. "All of you. Everyone who wants to learn."

That afternoon, Ty wrote out lesson plans. Not childish ones. Real ones. With diagrams and body language notes. Microexpression drawings. Examples of voice cadence. He used coloured pens and lined charts. "If I do this," he told Mr. Clarke, "I want to do it right." Clarke grinned. "You're already doing it better than most." Then handed Ty a set of fresh markers from the teacher drawer. "Go change some minds."

The first session was after lunch the next day. Grades Three and Four sat in a wide circle in the library. Jasmin took attendance. Nico set up chairs. Ty stood by the whiteboard, palms sweating just slightly, heart calm anyway. "This isn't about calling people liars," he began. "It's about knowing what the truth looks like so you don't fall for anything less." The room listened.

He showed them how liars repeat questions. How their bodies twitch, how their eyes sometimes stare too long or dart away too fast. He played a recording of his dad's training session on microexpressions—anger, contempt, fear—all within half a second of footage. "You don't have to memorise this," he told them. "You just have to pay attention."

Mr. Arnett watched from the doorway. He didn't take over. He didn't correct. He just nodded. Like someone finally saw the blueprint of something too many adults had ignored. Ella sat cross-legged in the corner, taking notes like she was in university already. "This," she whispered, "feels like armour." Nico grinned. "It is."

Later that week, the older kids took part. Leo didn't sign up. But he watched from the stairwell. Watched kids nod, watched them practice spotting mismatches and inconsistencies. Watched them talk in truths he couldn't fake. And for the first time, Leo looked unsure—not of them, but of himself.

Ty's lessons spread. By the next month, Mr. Clarke invited him to teach part of Health Class. Miss Kara signed her name on the attendance sheet for a Monday session. Even Mr. Rafferty showed up—sat in the back and didn't say a word, but his eyes didn't leave the page.

"He's learning," Nico said after. "They all are." Jasmin pulled Ty aside one day before class. "You know what the difference is now?" Ty shook his head. "We're not just surviving the lies," she said. "We're stopping them. With truth. And memory. And each other." Ty nodded. "And that," he said, "is how we win."

Ty stood in front of the whiteboard with the marker in his hand, his fingers steady but his mind sharp as a blade. The room was full—not just of kids anymore, but teachers, staff, even the custodian leaned against the wall with his mop paused mid-air. Miss Kara sat with a clipboard on her knees. Mr. Rafferty had crossed his arms but was still taking notes. Mr. Clarke leaned on the corner shelf beside the globe. And Leo, though pretending to browse the nearby bookshelf, kept glancing up. Ty clicked the marker open and drew a face, not cartoonish, but clean—two eyes, a mouth, and lines radiating outward like clock hands.

"Your face," Ty said, "betrays you in less than a second. Microexpressions. That's what they're called. They're not big. They're not loud. They're fast." He underlined the word "fast" three times and turned back to the room. "A fake smile moves from the mouth. A real one reaches the eyes. That's how you tell. Real smiles crinkle here," he tapped the corners of his own eyes. "Fake ones stay flat."

Jasmin raised her hand even though she didn't have to. "But what if the person smiling is really good at pretending?" Ty nodded. "Then you look at what comes before the smile. Microtruths happen before the lie. The tiniest twitch at the mouth. A breath that stalls. Eyes that narrow just a hair too much. You catch the truth not when it's loud—but when it's still afraid of being seen."

Mr. Clarke stepped forward. "Like the half-second before someone says they're fine, but they're not?" Ty nodded again. "Exactly. That flinch? That hesitation? That's the truth bleeding through." He circled the mouth he'd drawn and added a faint line near the temple. "Watch the corners. They always move before the rest of the face catches up."

Leo said nothing from behind the bookshelf, but his eyes narrowed. He knew what this lesson was about. Ty didn't look at him directly. He didn't need to. He was teaching truth, not naming names. "Microexpressions aren't proof in court," Ty went on. "But they're patterns. If someone's face and words don't match—believe the face. It's way harder to control."

Miss Kara furrowed her brow. "But kids lie all the time. How can we know which ones are real?" Ty let the silence land before answering. "Kids lie when they're scared. But when someone lies to control, they don't flinch when they're caught. They double down. They act like the truth is a personal attack. That's when you know you're dealing with manipulation, not just fear."

He showed a video clip next, just ten seconds long—a speaker in a mock interview, caught in a lie. The man smiled mid-sentence, but his eyes narrowed instead of widening. "That's called contempt," Ty explained. "That little smirk on only one side of the mouth? That's not joy. That's superiority. That's someone who thinks they're smarter than you."

Jasmin scribbled it all down, line by line, almost like prayer. Nico leaned forward with his chin in his hand, watching Ty's eyes, not the board. He knew Ty wasn't just saying words—he was remembering. Remembering moments Leo smirked while denying what he did. Remembering when Ella cried and Leo claimed he hadn't said anything wrong. These weren't theories. They were evidence.

Ella quietly raised her hand. "What if the lie feels true because you want it to be?" Ty turned to her with an expression even older than he was. "Then you're not looking for truth," he said gently. "You're looking for comfort. They're not the same. One heals. The other just hides the wound for a while." She nodded slowly, her hands folded in her lap, her mouth tight like a question she'd already answered herself.

Leo leaned on the windowsill now, trying to act casual, but his shoulders gave him away. They tensed during every example. They released when Ty changed subjects. He rubbed his neck twice. Pulled his sleeves. Avoided looking at his reflection in the window glass. Mr. Clarke noticed. So did Mr. Arnett, who'd entered halfway through and taken a seat beside Miss Kara, arms folded but eyes locked on Leo.

Ty passed out laminated cards. On one side: a microexpression. On the back: what it meant. "Disgust. Contempt. Sadness. Anger. Fear. Joy. Surprise." He handed each card like a sword to a knight. "These are truths the body doesn't know how to fake. Study them. Memorise them. You might not always be sure, but you'll be ready to notice."

Mr. Arnett asked, "Why isn't this taught in teacher training?" Ty didn't hesitate. "Because most adults don't want to believe kids see through lies." That silenced the room again, but it wasn't awkward. It was sobering. Even Rafferty lowered his pen and rubbed his chin. "And," Ty added, "they don't want to admit kids are lied to... all the time."

At the end of the session, Mr. Clarke stood beside Ty and faced the class. "If you remember nothing else," he said, "remember this: the truth doesn't always shout. Sometimes it just twitches." Ty smiled then—just slightly. It reached his eyes. Jasmin caught it and smiled back.

Ella stayed behind afterward and took an extra card. "The one with contempt," she whispered. "That's the one I see the most." Ty didn't answer. He just nodded. Nico put a hand on her shoulder and said, "You're not alone now. That's the difference."

As the room emptied, Leo brushed past them, not meeting anyone's eyes. His shoes squeaked too loudly on the floor. His backpack bounced too much, like it was empty. His footsteps didn't match his expression. And Ty, notebook in hand, turned to Nico and whispered, "Even his lies have tells."

Ella didn't raise her hand when Leo spoke. She didn't correct him when he twisted the story. She didn't blink when he claimed he was just trying to help the new girl. She simply folded her arms, kept her breath quiet, and stared at the truth behind his face. She didn't need a teacher's approval or a friend's nod. The voice inside her, the one she used to silence, now whispered clearly: You already know. And that was enough.

The new girl, Mila, had only been there three days. She was small, bright-eyed, polite in that uncertain way new students often are. Leo found her fast, like he always did. He gave her a tour. Showed her the best water fountain. Told her who to sit with. Gave her a pencil with her name scratched into it. And then, on Thursday morning, he told her she owed him her spot at the lunch table. "That's how it works here," he said. But Mila looked confused, not grateful.

Ella saw the moment it shifted. The moment Mila's head tilted, her eyes narrowing just slightly. It wasn't fear—but suspicion. Ella remembered what that moment felt like: being unsure, being polite, and thinking maybe it was her fault. But Mila didn't fold. She said, "No thanks," and went to sit beside Jasmin instead. That, for Ella, was the moment the spell broke—for someone else. And she didn't even need to intervene. The lie exposed itself.

Leo turned back to his usual charm, a smile too bright, a joke too practiced. But his tone sharpened when he thought no one was listening. Ty heard it. Nico did too. "Ungrateful," he muttered under his breath as he walked away from the table, but it landed louder than intended. Miss Kara looked up from her clipboard. So did Mr. Clarke, who was shelving picture books near the beanbags.

Ella, arms still crossed, leaned over to Jasmin. "He's trying again." Jasmin nodded once, calm and clear. "But now everyone knows the rules." Leo had been losing ground slowly, but this was different. This wasn't about suspicion anymore. This was about memory. The kids remembered. Every smile that hurt. Every joke that bruised. Every gift that came with strings.

Ty tapped his foot under the table, watching Leo approach a group of Grade 2s. "He thinks new means naïve," he said. Nico shook his head. "He doesn't know we're watching." And they were. Not just the four of them—but others too. Even Mr. Arnett, who stood near the stairwell with his arms folded, pretending to look at the clock.

Later that day, Mila handed Leo back the pencil. "I don't want it," she said. Leo laughed and said, "Wow. Touchy." But it didn't land. It didn't bounce. It dropped between them like a pebble in dry sand. Sophie, sitting two desks away, wrote something in the corner of her notebook. It wasn't loud. It wasn't revenge. It was record-keeping.

Mr. Clarke had a phrase for it—"collecting the pattern." Ella remembered when he taught them that last month in the library. "One moment isn't always the proof," he'd said. "But many moments make a pattern. And patterns are hard to deny." That phrase echoed now as Ella watched Leo turn his charm back on, this time for a teacher. It worked less every day.

At recess, Leo tried to get a soccer game going. No one joined. Not even the ones who used to. He shouted across the pavement, "Fine! I'll play myself!" and kicked the ball into the fence. It bounced back harder than expected. He muttered something, but no one laughed. The silence was louder than any crowd.

Jasmin, Nico, and Ty didn't gloat. They didn't celebrate. They just watched quietly. "It's not fun seeing him alone," Nico said. "Even if he earned it." Ty nodded. "But that's not our job anymore. Our job is to see the truth. Not to carry his consequences." Ella listened and didn't speak. She didn't need to. Her silence was no longer fear. It was knowing.

Mr. Arnett called Leo into the office after lunch. No one knew exactly why. But when Leo came out, his smile was gone. His pace was slower. His face didn't say angry—it said cornered. He looked toward the classroom windows and caught Ella's eye. She didn't flinch. She didn't smile either. She just looked. And he turned away.

Mila joined them at their table in the library later. She sat between Ella and Jasmin without asking. "Thanks," she said. "For not letting him treat me like... like property." Jasmin laughed softly. "We've all been there." Nico added, "You noticed sooner than we did. That means you're already ahead." Mila shrugged. "I don't like when people act like kings. Especially the ones who say they're helping."

Ty gave her a laminated card. "It's not a test," he said. "Just... tools. You'll know what they mean soon." Mila smiled for real, and for the first time all week, she looked like she belonged. Sophie passed a note to Ella. One sentence. You were right before anyone believed you. Ella folded it carefully and tucked it into her pencil case like a secret worth keeping.

At dismissal, Mr. Clarke waved them over. "You all did something grown-ups forget to do," he said. "You believed your own eyes. That's how the truth gets protected." Nico answered, "Just because they don't see it doesn't mean it's not real." Mr. Clarke's mouth curved into something close to pride. "Exactly."

And as they walked down the hallway, past the lockers and the echoes and the stories half-told, Ella felt the weight lift—not because Leo had stopped, but because she had stopped needing proof. She had her memories. Her instincts. Her voice. And they were louder now than any lie he could tell. She turned the corner, her footsteps steady, and whispered aloud—not to anyone, just to herself—"I believe me." That was the beginning of everything changing.

CHAPTER 8: THE SHADOW WARRIOR'S WAY

Jasmin sat beside Ty on the edge of the jungle gym, where the rusted bolts creaked just enough to sound like a whisper no one else heard. The late sun smeared gold across the pavement, and their shadows stretched long, thin, and sharp across the hopscotch court. Ty hadn't said anything for a while. Not about Leo. Not about Ella. Not about anything. He just sat there, tracing the same chalk line with the toe of his sneaker like he was drawing a map that only he could follow. Jasmin didn't ask right away. She didn't want to break the quiet. But silence had a weight to it now. Not heavy like before. Not cold. But careful.

"You always know," she said finally, not looking at him. "Before anything happens. Like… you see it coming." Ty tilted his head. "It's not magic," he said. "It's training." He picked up a pebble and flicked it with his thumb, watching it bounce once, then roll to a stop by her shoe. "I never told you what my dad does, did I?"

Jasmin shook her head slowly. "You said he travels a lot." "He does," Ty replied. "But not for work like most parents. He's with the RCMP. Special Investigations. Mostly undercover." He paused, like even saying it felt like lifting something heavy. "He doesn't wear a uniform. He doesn't wave a badge. He listens. Watches. Gets inside people's stories without them even knowing he's there." Jasmin's eyes widened. "That's… actually kind of amazing."

"It is," Ty said, but his voice was a little flatter now. "But it's also lonely. I learned early not to get used to routines. Dad taught me how to notice patterns instead. Not what people say, but how they say it. When their voice goes up. When their shoulders drop. He taught me to read the pauses." Jasmin blinked. "The pauses?"

"Yeah," Ty said. "Most people only listen to words. But the space between words? That's where the truth hides." She leaned forward a bit, letting his words sink in. "That's how you knew Leo was lying?" Ty nodded. "It wasn't just what he said. It was what he didn't say. The way he'd answer too quickly. Or too smoothly. No thinking pause. No real hesitation. Just a script." "And the compliments?" Jasmin asked.

Ty snorted softly. "Those were weapons. Disguised as candy. You ever see someone compliment three people in under a minute, then get angry when no one says thank you fast enough?" Jasmin sighed. "Leo." "Exactly," Ty said. "That's not kindness. That's bait." The wind picked up then, not hard, but enough to rustle the leaves in the trees above the yard and kick a few around their feet like little paper secrets. Jasmin brushed one from her knee. "So you learned all this from your dad?" "Mostly," Ty said. "And from watching. My dad calls it 'the shadow way.'"

Jasmin tilted her head. "Like ninjas?" Ty smiled for the first time that afternoon. "Sort of. He told me real shadow warriors don't fight for attention. They don't need applause. They guard people from the dark by stepping into it first. Quietly." Jasmin bit her lip. "That's kind of beautiful." Ty shrugged. "It's also kind of dangerous. You can't flinch. You can't ask for credit. And you definitely can't react too fast. If you do, you lose the thread." "What thread?"

"The one that leads to the lie," Ty said, and his eyes flicked toward the school, where Leo had just walked by the window of the library. "People like Leo? They change the rules depending on the day. That's what makes them hard to stop. You need to wait. Watch. Catch the pattern when it loops back around." Jasmin looked at him carefully. "You think he knows what he's doing?"

Ty didn't answer right away. He just reached into his pocket and pulled out a folded piece of paper. It was small and worn, the edges frayed like it had been read too many times. He handed it to her. On it was a list. Just words, but arranged like puzzle pieces: mirror lies, second-guess spiral, residue, static. "This is what my dad taught me to look for," Ty said. "He used to give this to new recruits. I just copied it down for myself."

Jasmin scanned the list. "These are real?" Ty nodded. "They don't sound real. But when you feel them, you know. You've felt most of them already. That's why you don't laugh when he jokes. That's why you started writing things down. You're keeping track." Jasmin held the paper like it might vanish. "And you?"

"I don't write," Ty said. "I remember. Every detail. Every word he flips. Every name he drops. Every look he throws when teachers aren't watching. I don't need to fight Leo. I just need to see him clearly." Jasmin sat with that for a long moment. "So… what now?" "Now," Ty said, eyes narrowing just slightly, "we teach you how to see, too."

"Like a ninja, right?" Jasmin said, half-grinning, half-serious, as she walked beside Ty across the blacktop where the games had ended but the echoes of arguments still floated. "Shadow warrior sounds like something from cartoons. Like sneaking through shadows with swords and smoke bombs."

Ty stopped short and turned to face her. Not mad. Not even annoyed. Just steady. "That's what most people think," he said. "But it's wrong. Real shadow warriors don't look like anything." Jasmin tilted her head. "So… what do they look like?" Ty knelt to tie his shoe, not because it was loose, but because he needed the second to think. When he stood again, he dusted off his palms like someone preparing for a conversation that mattered. "They look like anybody. You've probably seen five today. You just didn't know it."

Jasmin's brow creased. "What do they do then? If they're not fighting?" "They're still fighting," Ty said. "But the battlefield's different. They fight for truth. Not with punches. Not with swords. They fight by noticing. By remembering. By choosing silence when noise would make things worse. And they don't need anyone to clap for them." Jasmin's face fell just a bit. "That's not what the movies say."

"Movies lie," Ty replied flatly. "A real shadow warrior doesn't pose. Doesn't brag. Doesn't post videos saying how good they are. They walk through halls like they're part of the wall. And they only speak when the words will actually help." Jasmin crossed her arms. "Then how do you know who's one?" "You don't," Ty said. "That's kind of the point. You'll never see a true one unless they want you to. And even then, only when you've earned it."

She took a breath and looked down at her shoes, watching the laces twitch in the breeze. "So… could I be one?" Ty's answer came without hesitation. "You already are. You just haven't finished training." Jasmin blinked. "What kind of training?" "Observation," Ty said, walking again. She followed. "Learning how to spot patterns in people. Noticing which smiles are real and which ones are loaded. Listening not just to what someone says—but to what they avoid."

"But that's just being smart," Jasmin offered, a little unsure now. Ty shook his head. "No. That's the surface. Being smart means you can solve puzzles. Being a shadow warrior means you can solve people. Or at least, avoid being fooled by them." Jasmin bit the inside of her cheek. "So that's why you always knew what Leo was doing." Ty didn't nod. He didn't smile either. "I didn't guess. I saw. He changes too quickly. Adapts. Echoes. But not because he's learning. Because he's trying to get close to something he can use."

They reached the bike racks. The metal bars were cold even in sunlight. Jasmin leaned against one and looked at him again. "So then what's the job of a shadow warrior?" "To protect," Ty answered. "But not loudly. Not like heroes in books who throw themselves in front of everything. A shadow warrior protects the truth. Guards the people who can't see yet. Helps others wake up without waking up the danger." "That sounds hard," she whispered.

Ty nodded. "It is. That's why most people never try. Or they try once, and stop when it gets lonely." She blinked up at him. "Is it lonely?" "Sometimes," Ty said. "But it's lonelier pretending you don't see what's happening when you do." That line settled between them like dust on glass. You could wipe it away, sure—but the fingerprint always stayed. "So," Jasmin said after a while, quieter now. "If I see something… like Leo doing something again… what do I do?"

Ty crouched again, pretending to fix the strap on his backpack. His eyes flicked up to meet hers. "You stay calm. You take a mental note. You don't run to a teacher yet. You wait. You gather. And when the pattern's clear—you call it. But never when you're alone." Jasmin frowned. "Why?" "Because real shadow warriors don't walk alone," he said. "They move in threes. Or fours. That's how truth survives."

She nodded slowly. "Then I want to be one. I mean, really be one. Like… trained." Ty extended a hand. Not for a handshake. Just a silent offer of trust. She placed her fingers in his, and he closed them gently around hers. "Then welcome," he said. "But be ready. The next lesson isn't about seeing Leo." "What's it about?" Ty's voice dropped just a little. "Seeing yourself."

Ella hadn't said much all morning. Not because she was shy, but because she was listening. Ty had taught her that silence was a kind of language. It wasn't just an empty space between words—it was where the real meanings waited. She sat closer to the edge of the group now. Not to disappear, but to notice more. She could see the way Leo scanned the room with his chin slightly raised, the way he laughed a little too late when others joked, always one beat behind like he was waiting to echo. And she saw Ty, steady, unreadable, but not unkind. Like someone who had already mapped the room five steps ahead.

Ty didn't sit in the centre of attention. He never raised his hand unless the question deserved an answer. He didn't fidget, didn't draw lines on his desk, didn't adjust his hoodie every five seconds like most of the other boys. He was still. Not frozen—but deliberate. Like every breath he took had already been rehearsed. It was the way he moved that made Ella realize what power looked like when it wasn't loud.

She leaned over during lunch and asked, "How come you never sit with the popular group?" Ty looked up from his sandwich, the one he always packed himself, even though his dad worked long shifts. "Because I don't need to be seen to know who I am," he said simply, and went back to eating. Ella blinked. No speech. No lecture. Just that. And for some reason, it made more sense than any teacher's essay on confidence.

After they finished lunch, the bell hadn't rung yet, so the kids wandered around the courtyard. Sophie, who'd been quiet for weeks, hovered near the edge of the garden, sketchbook tucked under her arm. She walked up to Ty, tapping her pencil against her wrist. "You're Japanese, right?" she asked softly, but without fear. "Is it your mom's side or your dad's?"

Ty didn't flinch. "Dad," he said. "He was born in Nagoya. Came to Canada for RCMP training." Sophie smiled, a slow, sure one. "That's cool," she said. "You look like him?" "Yeah," Ty answered. "Eyes mostly. And the way we walk." Sophie tilted her head slightly. "Well… you're very handsome." Ty didn't grin. He didn't tease her or look away awkwardly. He simply nodded. "Thank you," he said. "You're very beautiful too."

She looked at him then. Not like she was embarrassed, but like she was seen. Noticed properly. Not as an object, not as a crush, but as someone who mattered. Ella, sitting nearby, watched the whole exchange without a flicker of jealousy. There was something real about it. Quiet, yes—but rooted. Jasmin whispered, "Was that flirting?" Ella shook her head. "No. That was honesty."

Later that day, while everyone was lining up for indoor gym, Ty showed Ella how to shift her stance without words. "Watch," he whispered, nodding toward Leo. "He always stands just a little to the left of whoever he's about to use. So if you move, he has to recalibrate." Ella shifted her foot, subtly, stepping just behind Jasmin. Leo, about to reach for her shoulder, dropped his hand as if he'd thought better of it. He turned away.

"It worked," she murmured. Ty nodded. "Small moves. Big results." Sophie came up beside them during gym. "Ty," she said, "you move like a cat." He tilted his head. "That a compliment or a warning?" Sophie laughed. "Compliment. Definitely compliment." They played dodgeball, but Ty didn't throw hard. He wasn't there to win. He was watching. Calculating. He noticed who aimed for Ella first, who avoided Nico, who whispered about Jasmin when she turned. He didn't say anything. But he noted it all.

After class, Sophie pulled him aside near the lockers. "You always notice stuff before anyone else. How?" "I trained for it," Ty said. "My dad taught me." "He sounds strict." "He's honest," Ty replied. "That's rarer than strict." Sophie smiled again. "I think I'd like to meet him." "Maybe one day," Ty said. "But for now, you already know what he taught me."

She leaned on the locker beside his. "Like what?" "Truth doesn't walk loud," he said. "It walks close to walls. Wears shadows like armour. And never explains itself unless someone's ready to hear it." Sophie lowered her eyes, thoughtful. "That's beautiful." "It's necessary," he said. "Especially when people like Leo make noise to hide what they are."

Ella stood nearby, her head tilted slightly. "Then what do we do?" Ty zipped up his jacket and glanced at each of them. "We move quiet. We watch. And when the time comes, we step forward—not to fight, but to stand." Jasmin's voice floated in from the corner. "Like shadow warriors." He turned, smiled gently. "Exactly."

It happened near the edge of the school field, where Nico had followed Ty out after lunch. The sky was cloudy enough to hold back the heat, and the wind stirred the dandelions along the fence in lazy, thoughtful patterns. Nico had been quiet most of the walk, his mind replaying all the things Leo had said that morning. The sneer. The comments. The smug way he pretended it was all a joke when teachers came around. He kicked at a stone and watched it roll to the base of a pine tree. "How come you never yell at him?" he finally asked.

Ty didn't answer right away. He crouched to tie his shoelace, even though it didn't need tying. When he stood again, he brushed a piece of bark off his knee. "Yelling's loud," he said. "And loud doesn't work on people like him." Nico looked at him, brows pulled down in confusion. "So, what does work?" "Questions," Ty replied, tone even. "They're sharper than punches."

The words sat between them like a chess move. Nico tilted his head, replaying the idea. "You mean like... call him out?" "No," Ty said. "I mean ask things he can't answer without lying. Or exposing himself. A real warrior doesn't throw the first blow. He makes the other person swing wild, then fall into their own mistake." "But what if he keeps getting away with it?" Nico's voice tightened. "What if no one sees it?"

"They will," Ty said. "When they trip over his words." They started walking back toward the doors, just as the wind shifted. It was the kind of moment Nico would remember—not because it was loud, but because it wasn't. Because Ty never tried to sound impressive. Because he meant what he said without trying to win anything by saying it. Inside, the hallway buzzed as kids moved toward their next period. Sophie leaned near her locker, sketchbook clutched close as usual. She looked up as Ty approached. "Hey," she said softly, without her usual filter. "You okay?"

"Yeah," Ty nodded. "Want to come to dinner tomorrow night?" She blinked. "Dinner?" "With my family," he said. "So you can meet my parents." She paused, scanning his face. "Why?" Ty shrugged with one shoulder. "You asked about my dad. This is the easiest way to see who he really is. Who I am too." There was no awkward tension, no blush, no teasing. Just a boy asking plainly. Sophie hesitated only a second. "Okay," she said. "But only if I get to help wash the dishes."

Ty smiled faintly. "Deal." The next afternoon, Sophie arrived right on time. His house was modest—clean, lived in, and full of quiet signals. His mother, an art teacher, wore soft clothes and sharper eyes. His father, unmistakably alert even while setting the table, greeted her with a nod that felt like a measured handshake in word form.

Dinner was chicken teriyaki, miso soup, and steamed rice with pickled vegetables. They talked about books, not grades. Ty's dad asked her what she thought about kids today—not what she wanted to be when she grew up. "Because your opinion now matters more than your title later," he said.

After dinner, Ty's father offered Sophie a glass of barley tea and leaned against the counter. "You asked about my work?" he said. She nodded. "I observe," he said. "People. Motives. Language. When someone speaks too often, I listen to what they avoid saying. When someone's too quiet, I watch how they hold their breath." Sophie tilted her head. "Is that how Ty learned?" Ty's father smiled. "He learned more than I did."

Later, as Ty walked her to the door, she whispered, "Now I get it." He didn't ask what she meant. He knew. She'd seen the map. The next day at school, Ty didn't call attention to anything. But when Leo passed in the hall and muttered something cruel under his breath, Ty turned. "Why do you always do that when no one else is listening?" Leo blinked. "Do what?" Ty said nothing else. Just stared. Leo fumbled, scoffed, walked away too fast. Nico, watching from the side, said, "That was it?" Ty nodded. "You saw him trip." And Nico smiled.

The bell hadn't even stopped echoing when Mr. Arnett's voice crackled over the intercom. "Leo. Please come to the office." It was short. Clipped. Not angry, not stern. But measured, like someone calling in a favour owed. In the hallway, Ty stood already waiting, back straight, arms folded in front of him, not tense but steady. He didn't pace. He didn't speak. When Leo arrived, face unreadable but eyes darting, Ty simply nodded once. It wasn't a greeting. It was more like a signal between scouts in the field.

Inside the office, Mr. Arnett didn't bother with pleasantries. The blinds were tilted just enough to let afternoon light cut across the desk. The principal's voice came quiet. "We're not here to trap you, Leo." He motioned to the empty chair beside Ty. "We're here to ask why." Leo hesitated before sitting, shoulders already arched defensively, as though preparing to be punished, not understood. He looked from Ty to the desk, then back again. Ty didn't smile. He just breathed slow and stayed still.

Mr. Arnett leaned forward, elbows gently set on the desk like he was lowering his weapons first. "You're a clever boy. You know how to read people. But lately, the reading feels more like a rehearsal. Like you've learned what to say, not what to feel." Leo's jaw shifted, eyes narrowing. "I don't know what you mean." But the tone missed the mark—it landed too fast, too prepared. Ty recognized it instantly. It was the same tone he'd used with his mother the first time she found the bruises on his wrist and asked why he kept locking the bathroom door.

"I think you do," Ty said softly. The words carried no challenge. Just air. "I think you know exactly what we mean. And I don't think you want to be like this." Leo looked at him then, really looked—like seeing Ty not as a classmate, but as a mirror that didn't lie. His hands curled around the edge of his chair, trying not to shake.

Mr. Arnett didn't fill the silence. He let it stretch, let it hover like mist in the corners of the room. Ty filled it instead—not with accusation, but with memory. "There's someone in your life who treats you like this, isn't there? Someone who flips the rules. Who praises you, then punishes you. Who makes you feel strong one day and invisible the next." Leo didn't respond, but his mouth tightened. His eyes flickered to the floor like something there might offer escape.

"It's not about blaming them," Ty continued. "But it's about seeing the pattern. And deciding if you want to pass it on—or stop it." The boy across from him looked smaller than usual, his bravado worn thin around the edges. No interruptions. No protests. Only the hum of the office fan and the steady rhythm of Ty's words.

Mr. Arnett leaned back, folding his hands slowly, voice calm but direct. "We've been watching, Leo. Not just the behaviour—but the confusion it causes. The control. You're not in trouble. But you are at a crossroads." He paused, then added, "And Ty volunteered to sit with you. Not to accuse you. But because he believes something can change."

Leo blinked hard, once. His fingers tensed, then relaxed. "Why would he do that?" His voice cracked on the word why, too honest to be staged. Ty met his gaze without flinching. "Because someone did it for me once. They saw past the damage. And because I think, under everything, you're not the villain in this story. You're just stuck playing a role someone else taught you."

The words landed like bricks in soft earth. Not harsh. But heavy. Grounded. Leo swallowed. "He's not—" He stopped. Started again. "My dad's not like people think." Ty nodded. "Most aren't. Not when they're in public. But it's not about shaming them, Leo. It's about deciding if their pain becomes your weapon." That made Leo flinch. He didn't cry. But something inside his defences tilted sideways.

Mr. Arnett reached for a folder and set it down without opening it. "I don't need files to know something hurts, Leo. But I need your help to understand where the hurt goes next. You can talk to me. You can talk to our counsellor. Or, if none of that feels right, you can keep talking to Ty." The offer wasn't a command. It wasn't even a request. It was a doorway being opened, quietly, without a key.

"I don't want people to hate me," Leo said suddenly. His voice wasn't loud, but it cut through the air. "I just want to matter." Ty's reply came without pause. "Then stop using power to feel safe. Start using truth." Leo looked down. His foot tapped once against the carpet. The room felt warm and still, like the world outside had paused to give this moment space.

Mr. Arnett nodded slowly, voice softer now. "Being loved doesn't mean being obeyed. You're allowed to be seen without being feared." Leo didn't answer, but for the first time, he didn't argue either. Ty reached over, not with a handshake, but with an open palm that rested gently on the edge of the desk—close, but not forcing contact.

The invisible observer in the room—who had seen generations of boys and girls come through that office—watched the silence settle like dust. A boy trying to undo what had been done. Another refusing to give up on him. And a man in authority choosing empathy over enforcement.

Ty stood first. Not as a victor. But as someone who knew when to walk away with the truth, not the credit. Leo remained seated, quieter now, eyes still shadowed but no longer hostile. Mr. Arnett let them leave without final words. Because not every truth needs a closing sentence. Some truths just need to be heard.

Leo didn't sit in the chair Mr. Arnett pointed to. He stood beside it instead, arms folded like a fence that dared anyone to climb over. His eyes darted to Ty, then the floor, then back again. Ty didn't say a word at first. He just sat down slowly, crossing one leg over the other the way his father always did in long interviews. Mr. Arnett rested both palms on his desk, elbows locked, the expression on his face quiet but unreadable. The room was still. Only the sound of the hallway clock behind the window ticked forward, as if measuring patience.

Ty didn't blink when he asked it. "Does someone talk to you the way you talk to other kids?" His voice wasn't accusing. It wasn't soft either. It was even, like it had been practised. Leo's face didn't move at first. His arms stayed crossed, chin high. But the room changed. The air got heavier. He didn't answer, not even with a shrug. That silence was louder than a scream. Ty waited, and Mr. Arnett didn't move an inch. They gave Leo room to speak without demanding it. That alone felt new.

"I mean," Ty said again, more gently this time, "does someone treat you like you're wrong all the time? Like you always mess up? Like no matter what you do, it's never enough?" He wasn't listing random things. He was describing something, someone. Leo's eyes flinched, just slightly, and Ty saw it. "Because if that's what's happening," Ty continued, "it makes sense why you'd try to feel powerful somewhere else. I'm not saying it's right. I'm saying I get it." Still, no reply. But Leo's jaw wasn't clenched anymore.

Mr. Arnett finally spoke. "Leo," he said, voice slow, steady, "this isn't about blaming you. It's about helping you see what's happening—inside and out. And Ty's here because he sees more than most." Leo shifted his weight, one foot behind the other now. The posture of someone wanting to bolt but unsure where the door even led. Ty leaned forward a bit. "You don't have to tell us anything if you're not ready. But I promise—on everything—I will always tell you the truth. Even when it hurts."

"And," Ty added, pressing a palm to his chest, "because I love you, I'll call out the lies. When you tell one, I'll call it out. Not in front of everyone. Not loud. But I will. Because I want you to stop lying to yourself too." He looked directly at Leo then. No pity. Just raw steadiness. "And when you're ready to tell the truth—your truth—I'll listen. I won't interrupt. I won't fix it. I'll just hear it. And that's a promise." That word, promise, sat between them like a gift waiting to be unwrapped.

Leo's hands had dropped by his sides now. His fists, once curled, had flattened into loose fingers that trembled just slightly. He opened his mouth, closed it, and tried again. Still no words. But his lip twitched. The first sign of collapse. Mr. Arnett didn't speak. He just nodded once, slowly, as if affirming something sacred without needing it to be spoken aloud. Ty stood up and walked over, slow enough not to alarm him. He waited until Leo's breathing changed—shorter, sharper, uneven.

"Is someone hurting you?" Ty asked again, this time softer than before. Still no answer. But Leo blinked hard, and the first tear dropped. Then another. And another. Until he wasn't standing anymore but leaning forward—falling into Ty's arms. The way a child falls into sleep when the day's been too long. The way someone finally lets go. Ty caught him without hesitation, arms tight and sure. He didn't pat him. He didn't shush him. He just held him like he meant it.

Leo's whole body shook as the tears poured out. Big, ugly, silent ones. The kind no one sees unless they're looking closely. Ty didn't say anything else. He didn't need to. That hug said everything: I see you. I know it hurts. You don't have to be alone anymore. Mr. Arnett quietly got up and stepped out of the office without a word. He understood that this was not a moment for staff. It was a moment for brotherhood. And it was sacred.

Time passed, maybe minutes, maybe more. The clock kept ticking, but no one noticed. When Leo finally pulled back, his face was red, soaked, eyes swollen. But there was something new in them too. A sliver of softness. A tiny thread of trust. Ty wiped Leo's cheek with his sleeve, careful and respectful. Then he sat him down in the chair he hadn't wanted before. This time, Leo didn't resist.

"You're not the only one who's been through this," Ty said. "But you might be the only one who thinks you have to hide it forever. You don't. Not with me. Not here." Leo sniffed, eyes still fixed on the floor. But he nodded. Just once. Enough to mean something. Ty didn't smile. He just nodded back. That was the pact.

Mr. Arnett returned only when the silence had settled. He sat, not behind the desk, but beside it. Closer to them. "You both showed something rare in here," he said quietly. "Leo, you let someone see you. That takes more strength than most adults ever show. Ty, you stood beside truth and didn't demand it. You waited. That's leadership." He didn't clap. He didn't praise. He just acknowledged. And that was enough.

Leo's voice finally came out, small but clear. "I don't know how to fix it." Ty shook his head gently. "You don't have to fix it. You just have to stop pretending it's not broken." Leo looked at him, then at Mr. Arnett, and nodded again. Two nods in one day. A miracle, really. Ty let out a breath he didn't know he was holding. The work had just begun—but the silence had spoken. And the warrior's first mission had been won.

Ty didn't explain anything when they stepped out of Mr. Arnett's office, and Nico didn't ask. They just walked in step, not talking, not rushing, like boys who had seen something they shouldn't have but knew it mattered. There was something in the way Ty carried his shoulders that day—a slight tilt, not defeat, but weight. Nico noticed. Jasmin caught it too. Ella glanced, then looked down. The hallway felt different. Not because anything had changed on the walls, but because they had seen something raw behind one of them. And it was still echoing.

Jasmin passed Ty a folded note before they reached their lockers. It wasn't long. Just three words written in pencil. You okay, Ty? Ty opened it without hiding it. He nodded without smiling. "Yeah," he said, quietly enough that only Nico and Jasmin could hear. "He cried." And they didn't ask who. Because they already knew.

There were stories at lunch. A few whispers, the kind that ripple like a pebble in still water. Leo had been called in. Ty was in there too. Some of the younger kids said it was about a fight. Others said Leo had yelled at Mr. Arnett. One Grade Seven boy claimed Leo punched a desk and made it crack. But none of it was true. The truth wasn't loud. The truth was quiet. It came in tears, not tantrums. And the only ones who saw it were the ones who stayed silent long enough to listen.

Ella waited by the monkey bars, arms folded, not playing. Sophie stood beside her. "You told them?" Ella asked Ty when he joined them. "No," Ty said. "He did. Not with words. But... yeah. He did." His voice didn't rise. He just looked down at his hands like they had touched something fragile and couldn't shake the feeling. "Sometimes people learn how to hurt from the people who are supposed to love them."

Nico was the first to speak after that. "You think someone's doing it to him?" Ty nodded slowly. "I think he lives with somebody who uses silence like a sword. One of those people who says one nice thing in the morning and something cruel at night—and then acts like it's normal." Jasmin's eyes narrowed. "That sounds exactly like what he does." Ty met her eyes and said, "Because it's probably where he learned it."

They didn't pity Leo. That wasn't what this was about. No one said "poor Leo" or made excuses. They didn't excuse the way he twisted words or pulled people close just to drop them. But something had shifted in how they looked at him. The heat was gone. In its place was a strange kind of ache, not for Leo's cruelty—but for the boy beneath it. The one who had never known what real safety looked like. And now didn't know how to give it.

After school, Nico walked with Ty past the parking lot instead of taking his usual bus. "So what now?" he asked. Ty didn't answer right away. He waited until they were at the fence near the bicycle racks, away from the others. Then he said, "I'm going to find out what's going on in his house." Nico blinked. "How?" Ty didn't answer with a plan. Just a promise. "By watching. Listening. Quietly." His voice didn't harden, but it didn't waver either.

"You think someone hurts him?" Nico asked again, a little slower this time. Ty exhaled. "Not the kind that leaves bruises. But the kind that rewires your brain. The kind that makes you think love is something you have to earn by staying quiet, by being useful, by never saying no." Nico swallowed. That kind of hurt didn't show up in attendance records. It didn't trigger alarms or school suspensions. It just sat behind smiles and waited to be copied.

Later that week, Nico sat with Jasmin and Ella on the steps near the back of the school, peeling an orange. "Do you think he knows he's doing it?" he asked. Jasmin thought for a long moment. "I think... maybe not all of it. But I think when he gets scared, he controls things. Because control feels safer than getting hurt again." Ella added, "Or maybe he's scared all the time and just pretends he's not." None of them said more. The orange passed between them, and the peelings fell like paper curls on the pavement.

Ty didn't tell anyone what Leo had said in the office. He didn't need to. It wasn't about betrayal. It was about respect. About honour. The kind of unspoken code real Shadow Warriors follow. The kind where truth is protected by silence, and silence is not weakness—it's armour. That's what Ty meant when he said, "It was necessary." That's all he told the others when they asked. Not because they didn't deserve to know. But because some truths have to be carried, not shared.

That night, Nico couldn't sleep. He kept replaying Ty's voice in his head. "People learn how to hurt from the people who are supposed to love them." That stuck. It stung. He thought of his own family. Of things said in passing. Of the times he had heard sharpness tucked into compliments. He thought about how quickly people defend the ones who hurt them. "They're just tired." "It's my fault." "They had a hard day." All the lines kids learn to say when adults twist kindness into confusion.

The next day, Leo walked down the hall without swagger. No insults. No smirk. Just silence. He didn't look at anyone. Didn't push past. Didn't reach out either. He just moved like someone carrying invisible bags too heavy for a boy his size. Nico watched. Jasmin watched. Ty didn't watch—he observed. And then he nodded, just once, like a signal only he knew how to send. And in that single motion, Nico understood: the signal had been passed.

Not everyone gets to see that kind of moment. Not every student notices when someone drops the armour and doesn't know how to pick it back up. But the ones who do? The ones who stay still long enough to catch it—they carry it differently. Like Ty. Like Jasmin. Like Nico now. They had seen the shadow. And instead of running, they stayed.

Ty still hadn't said what he'd do next. But Nico knew it wasn't over. Not even close. Leo hadn't asked for help. But sometimes help doesn't come with permission. Sometimes it comes quietly, like a hand beneath yours that steadies without grabbing. Like a light that doesn't shine too bright, just enough to show the floor. That's what Ty was becoming. A guide in the dark. A listener in the silence. A truth keeper.

By the end of the week, the others had stopped whispering. The hallway calmed. But something deeper had changed. Not in Leo. Not yet. But in the kids who had chosen to see him differently. Not just as the boy who hurt—but as the boy who was hurting. And for the first time, that was enough to begin something else. Not forgiveness. Not forgetfulness. But a shift. A real one. Because now they knew. The shadow that follows home doesn't have to win.

Jasmin sat on the edge of the bench outside the library, elbows on knees, palms pressed together like she was trying to keep her thoughts from spilling over. Her eyes weren't red, but her voice was quieter than usual. "I feel bad for him," she said. "But that doesn't mean he gets to wreck people." Nico sat across from her, picking at the frayed hem of his hoodie sleeve. "Yeah," he muttered. "Feeling bad isn't the same as letting it happen." Jasmin nodded, then said the part that settled it. "Blame isn't the same as truth."

Ty didn't argue. He leaned against the brick wall beside them, arms crossed, not defensive, just still. "I don't think Leo knows the difference," he said. "Between what he's allowed to feel and what he's allowed to do because of it." He glanced down the hallway, toward the guidance office where Leo had been sent again, not as punishment this time, but because something had cracked, and no one knew how to hold the pieces yet.

The bell rang, but none of them moved. Ella slid beside Jasmin, and Mila joined Nico. No one spoke. The kind of quiet that filled the air wasn't uncomfortable—it was thick with something else. Waiting. Feeling. And a kind of knowing that only happens after you've seen someone completely fall apart. Not in anger, but in truth.

When the door opened at the end of the hall, Leo didn't come out stomping or smirking. He didn't look around to see who was watching. He didn't try to make eye contact or wave it off like he usually did. He just stood there, a half-step behind Ty, like he didn't know where his body was supposed to go next. Then, without a sound, he reached out, and Ty pulled him in.

It wasn't a hug that asked for attention. It wasn't loud. It wasn't staged. It was a collapse. Leo leaned into Ty like a boy who hadn't been held in years, like his body had never been given permission to drop its weight before. His hands gripped Ty's shirt like he didn't trust the ground to stay still beneath him. The sobbing didn't come in bursts—it poured, full and heavy and without pause.

Ty didn't shush him. Didn't pat his back or offer fake reassurances. He just wrapped his arms around Leo's shaking frame and stood there, holding the weight without asking questions. His eyes didn't move from the wall ahead. He wasn't ashamed of the crying, and he wasn't trying to shield it. He just let it happen, like it needed to happen, like the truth had finally broken through the noise.

Jasmin's eyes blurred. She wiped them quickly, but it didn't stop the next ones. Ella sniffed beside her, turning her head slightly so no one would see the wet shimmer on her cheeks. Nico swallowed hard and blinked too many times in a row. Mila's hand reached out, resting gently on Jasmin's shoulder. None of them said a word. None of them had to.

They weren't crying because Leo deserved it. They weren't crying because everything was suddenly fixed. They were crying because something real had broken open, and even if it hurt, it was honest. And honesty deserved to be honoured.

Mr. Arnett stood behind them in the hallway, watching from a respectful distance. He didn't interfere. He didn't speak. He just nodded to himself, slowly, like someone who understood that some lessons don't need chalkboards or checklists—they just need to be witnessed.

Eventually, Leo pulled back, just a little, enough to breathe. His face was blotched red, his lashes stuck together, his lips trembling. But his voice—when it came—was not loud, not clear, and not proud. It was barely there. "I don't know why I'm like this," he said. "I don't want to be." Ty shook his head gently. "It's not about what you've been. It's about what you decide next."

Leo nodded. Once. Then twice. And then buried his face back in Ty's shoulder, the way a child does when they finally trust someone won't let go. It wasn't about weakness. It wasn't about drama. It was about being seen—truly seen—for maybe the first time.

Jasmin whispered, "He's trying." Ella added, "He's scared." Nico said nothing. He just kept his eyes open, kept watching, kept witnessing the moment because sometimes that's the only job that matters. Mila took Ella's hand and held it, no words needed. The signal had passed again, this time not through nods or notes, but through quiet hearts that beat the same rhythm.

No one was pretending anymore. No one was making excuses. And that was the difference. They could care for him without agreeing with him. They could love him without letting him hurt them again. Compassion didn't mean permission. Forgiveness didn't mean forgetting. And blame could never replace truth.

Later, as the group walked out together in silence, Nico looked up at the clouds that had gathered. The sky felt lower than usual, like the world had bent just a little closer. "We don't have to hate him," he said softly. "But we don't have to follow him either." Ty smiled just slightly. "Exactly." That night, Jasmin wrote one line in her journal before bed. Just one sentence. Blame is what they gave him. Truth is what he's trying to find. She underlined it twice. And for the first time since the school year began, her hands didn't shake while she wrote.

Ty waited until the hallway emptied after final bell before sliding the paper under Leo's elbow. It wasn't a message, not in the way kids passed notes or scribbled jokes. It was a folded square, black ink on lined paper, no name, no greeting. Just a single line in Ty's even handwriting: Protect the truth. Never use it to hurt. Always move with purpose. Leo blinked, his fingers slow to touch it, like it might sting. "What's this?" he asked. Ty didn't answer. He simply nodded once, not smiling, not judging. Nico leaned against the doorway, watching like someone who already knew the ending but couldn't tell you the middle yet.

There was no need for drama, not anymore. Ty didn't ask Leo to read it aloud. He didn't explain what it meant. If Leo needed to understand, he would. If he wasn't ready, the paper would wait. Leo held it in his lap and stared like it came from another planet. Ty knelt beside him—not towering over him like Mr. Arnett or glaring like Mr. Clarke. Just level. Just present. "I'm not teaching you how to fight," Ty said finally. "I'm showing you how to stop." Leo opened his mouth to speak, but the words never arrived.

Jasmin had drawn the blinds earlier in the day. The office was warm, quiet, the kind of quiet that feels intentional, not forgotten. "What kind of code is this?" Leo asked, his voice breaking in two places. Ty pointed to the line about purpose. "You've been moving without one," he said. "That's why you hurt people. You hit whatever's close, whatever's easy." Leo dropped his head, and Ty didn't stop him. He let it hang there, like a weight that needed to be noticed before it could be lifted.

Outside the door, Ella sat cross-legged, her fingers folded in her lap. She didn't lean in. She didn't eavesdrop. But she stayed close. Mila did too, quieter than usual, hugging a hoodie against her ribs. They weren't spying. They were guarding. Shadow Warriors, every one of them, and not a ninja costume in sight. "You don't know what it's like at home," Leo whispered finally, and this time, his voice didn't crack—it flattened. Emotionless. As if saying the truth without caring would hurt less than caring too much.

"I don't need to know yet," Ty replied. "But you do." That silenced Leo harder than any scolding ever had. Ty didn't need to shout, didn't need to accuse. He was the mirror and the hand reaching out all at once. "Someone's taught you that power means being loud. Being right. Being the one who talks last." Ty paused. "That's not power. That's panic." Leo wiped his nose on his sleeve, ashamed and too tired to fake otherwise. Nico didn't move. Jasmin didn't flinch. Ella pulled her sleeves over her hands but didn't hide.

"Who taught you this?" Ty asked softly, and Leo looked at the folded paper again. "Nobody," he said too quickly. Then, quieter: "Somebody." That was enough. Ty didn't pry. He didn't need names. He saw the bruises you couldn't photograph, the ones in speech patterns and silence, the ones that lived in the pause before you answered a kind question. "This code isn't about being a hero," Ty said. "It's about not becoming the villain someone else made you."

Leo closed his eyes and leaned back. "I don't want to be like him." The word him lingered, unexplained but obvious. Ty didn't press for more. He gave Leo space to breathe without apology. "You're not," Ty answered. "Not yet. But you could be. Unless you stop now." Leo's fists were still clenched, but they weren't angry. They were scared. Holding on to nothing, trying not to fall.

"I see you," Ty added. "Even when you try to hide behind noise." Leo stared at him, unsure if that was praise or warning. Maybe both. Nico stepped inside and set a bottle of water on the desk without saying a word. Jasmin stood behind him, a single nod exchanged between them. No one raised their voice. No one demanded anything. "You gonna tell everyone I cried?" Leo asked. Ty shook his head. "No," he said. "But they'll know anyway. Not because of me. Because you're going to stop hiding."

For the first time, Leo didn't deflect. He didn't joke. He didn't accuse. He sat still and let the silence hold him. It wasn't kind. It wasn't cruel. It was real. And that was more than he'd had in a long time. "Shadow Warriors don't fight to win," Ty said. "They fight to protect." Leo blinked. "Protect who?" Ty stood. "The part of you that still tells the truth, even if no one listens yet."

Ella stood outside the door, waiting. She didn't ask what had happened. She didn't need to. She saw Ty's face and Leo's slumped shoulders, and that was enough. Jasmin rested a hand on Leo's back for a second. No words. No pity. Just presence. The kind that doesn't cost anything but means everything. "You still have a choice," Ty said as he left the office. "The code's not about your past. It's about your next step."

Leo sat there a long time after they left, staring at the piece of paper in his hand. No instructions. No signature. Just a truth that felt heavier the longer he held it. And in that weight, he found something he hadn't felt in years. Not safety. Not yet. But the beginning of it. The room stayed quiet long after he left it. Quiet, like a promise that hadn't been broken yet. Quiet, like a warrior moving through the shadows, no longer needing to hide. Because truth doesn't hide. It waits. And so do they.

No one left the room in a hurry. The door was open, but the moment wasn't done. Ty sat still on the edge of the office couch, knees bent close, arms settled like they'd been waiting for something other than answers. Leo didn't speak. He didn't smirk, fidget, or flash a sharp grin like he was playing another round in his never-ending game. Instead, he leaned sideways—not fast, not awkward—just enough to touch Ty's shoulder with the weight of his head. He didn't ask for permission. He didn't need to. Ty let him lean there. A stillness held them like a tight-woven thread—fragile, invisible, unbreakable.

Jasmin stayed in the hallway doorway, one foot slightly turned like she might step out, but her arms folded across her middle like she couldn't quite let go. The light in the office was warm. Not the kind that buzzed or flickered. It hummed low, softening the edges of the room, making everything feel quieter than it was. Mr. Arnett stood by his desk, head bowed slightly as though in prayer, but no one spoke of that. He wasn't watching to intrude. He was standing still to let it happen—this small collapse of armour between boys who knew too much.

Leo didn't cry this time. He had cried already—gut-punched sobs that made him shake when no one knew what to do but let it happen. Now he didn't shake. He didn't speak. He didn't even blink much. He sat there against Ty, still as stone, eyes half open, breathing through his nose with that strange glassy wetness still tucked behind his lashes. And then, just barely, just loud enough to hear without needing to repeat it, he said it. "I love you." No stutter. No joke. No preface. Just three syllables wrapped in raw velvet.

Ty didn't answer right away. He didn't pat Leo on the back or grin or even turn to face him. He just tilted his head closer so their temples met, and in that small motion, the reply was already given. His breath was steady. His body stayed soft, unmoving. When he did speak, it was low, almost childlike in its gentleness. "I know." That was all. Not a promise, not a strategy. Just truth. Plain, not dressed up for a courtroom.

Outside, Nico had returned. He didn't knock. He just stepped through the open frame and stood beside Jasmin. His hands were in his pockets, and he didn't fidget. Ella was there too. She kept close to the lockers, eyes set just past the glass pane in the office wall, watching the boys like she might miss something important if she blinked. Sophie arrived last, her backpack slipping off one shoulder. No one told her what happened. She simply came. She knew.

No one had ever seen Leo like this. Not Ella, not Jasmin, not even Nico who had known him long enough to remember when Leo's jokes made the whole room laugh. Something had cracked—not shattered, but opened. The soundlessness of it all was louder than any scolding, deeper than any speech. It was a truth that didn't need to explain itself, and somehow that made it safer. Stronger. Ty let it stay that way.

Jasmin tilted her head just slightly, her eyes narrowing not in suspicion but in comprehension. Her mouth didn't move. She didn't speak, didn't ask what the words meant. But inside, something clicked. She wasn't sure if Leo meant those three words the way people use them at recess or in birthday cards. Maybe he didn't even know what kind of love he meant. But it was real. The kind that leaks through when there's nothing left to defend.

There had been no apology. No confession. No punishment. Just that one phrase, said like it was pulled from a drawer Leo didn't know he had, and then tucked into Ty's shoulder like a letter too hard to read out loud. It wasn't forgiveness, but it was something that sat close to it, breathing slow and deep and hurting in a way that finally felt like healing.

Ella's hand reached gently for Jasmin's, their fingers linking in silence. Not to comfort. To anchor. They were bearing witness, and they knew it. Ty wasn't showing off. Leo wasn't performing. This was not a classroom moment or a hallway theatre. This was a private signal, accidentally public. A flare without fire.

Sophie stepped forward then, quiet as snowfall, and sat on the floor just inside the doorway, knees to her chest. She didn't speak. She didn't need to. She looked at Leo, really looked. Not with pity. Not with fear. With recognition. She'd seen it before—in someone else, or maybe in herself. And like Ty, she understood that truth doesn't always show itself through words. Sometimes it just shows up and sits still.

Mr. Arnett stepped away to give space. He didn't exit the room. He leaned against the wall beside the window, folding his arms in thought, watching without pressing. His role wasn't to fix. His presence was the net that kept everything from breaking. He saw what the others saw— a shift, a turning, a moment no adult could manufacture but every good one should hold open.

Leo breathed out slowly, his chest finally moving like the tension had let go. He didn't speak again. But he stayed beside Ty, leaning without shame. And for once, he didn't scan the room for reactions. He didn't calculate his next move. He didn't try to be impressive or pitiful or loud. He was just… there. And maybe that was the real start of him.

Ty placed a single hand over Leo's and left it. No words. No plan. Just warmth. It was an answer not to the pain but to the boy himself—an answer that said: I see you. You don't have to perform. You're not invisible. You're not unforgivable. You're just tired, and I'm here.

Jasmin, Nico, Ella, and Sophie stood together now, their formation more instinctive than planned. It wasn't a line of defence. It wasn't a circle of protection. It was something else entirely—maybe a beginning. Maybe a gathering. Maybe, just maybe, the first time Leo had ever been part of something real. Outside, the bell hadn't rung yet. But something had ended. And something else, quieter and stronger, had just begun.

Ella sat with her knees drawn up beneath the library table, arms folded quietly as the group spread out around her. Her fingers traced the spine of a closed book, though her eyes never moved to read the title. It was Jasmin who first noticed the shift—how Ella had grown quieter not just in words but in presence, as if her light was dimming itself so no one would see the flicker. Across from her, Ty watched carefully, the way his father had taught him, not for the loud signs but the quiet ones—the trembling of a hand, the stillness of someone who was once curious, the way silence could be armour and a scream all at once.

"I'm tired of being the quiet one," Ella said finally, her voice softer than paper sliding across wood. It wasn't a complaint, not really, more like a confession released from deep inside. "Everyone thinks I'm weak. Like I don't notice anything." Her hands tightened into fists against the tabletop, then relaxed, then tightened again. She didn't look up when she spoke, afraid the words would scatter if she saw anyone listening too closely.

Ty nodded slowly. He didn't speak for a while. He let the air hold her words, let her bravery stay suspended and real without rushing to wrap it up or make it easier. That's something his father had told him—truth doesn't need an echo. It only needs space. Finally, he leaned in, his elbows resting gently on the table's edge, and spoke just loud enough for her to hear. "Being quiet isn't the same as being weak. It means you hear everything." His voice wasn't proud or performative. It was certain, like a rope lowered into a well to pull someone up who thought no one was coming.

Ella blinked. She did not smile at first, but her breathing shifted in a way Ty noticed. A little lighter. A little less clenched. Jasmin looked over from where she'd been sketching something in her notebook and gave Ella a tiny nod, like a pebble tossed gently into a still pond. Nico, sitting on the floor with his back against the bookcase, offered a thumb's up that wasn't a joke this time. Ella noticed all of it. She always had. She just never believed they meant it.

"I always hear when Leo's about to turn," Ella whispered, more to herself than the group. "Before anyone else sees it. The way his voice changes. Or how he tilts his head." She trailed off, eyes flickering toward the window where rain had begun to lace the glass in soft, twisting ribbons. Ty followed her gaze, then turned back to her face.

"That's your strength," Ty said. "You read the weather before the thunder starts. That's why you'll always be ready. That's why Leo can't fool you anymore." There was no arrogance in his tone, only quiet assurance. He wasn't flattering her. He was naming a truth she'd never dared claim for herself.

Jasmin scooted closer along the bench and brushed her shoulder against Ella's. "Leo needs us," she said softly. "But he especially needs someone who can sit with him when he says nothing. Because that's when the real part of him shows." Ella frowned gently, confused. "But why me?" she asked. "Why would he want me around when he doesn't even like me?"

Nico answered from the floor. "Because you never tried to change him. And now, after everything, maybe he wants to change himself. That means he'll look for people who were steady while he was spinning." Ella tilted her head, uncertain. The idea felt too big to hold, but not too heavy to try. In that moment, she started to see herself not as a quiet shadow in the corner, but as the constant point in a spinning room. Maybe silence wasn't hiding. Maybe it was anchoring.

Ty glanced toward the hallway. Leo had not returned to class that morning. He'd stayed back in Mr. Arnett's office for what seemed like hours. Ty had been there earlier, watched Leo crumble in real pain, not performance. He'd felt Leo's weight in his arms—deadweight, not for drama but from exhaustion. "He's been told his whole life that the loudest person wins," Ty said quietly. "So he never learned how to trust the ones who don't yell."

Ella nodded, understanding slowly. "So... you're saying I could help?" Her voice carried a slight rise in hope, though she quickly looked down again, afraid it might be foolish to believe. Ty leaned forward, his tone unwavering. "I'm saying you already are." She looked up this time. Just briefly. But long enough for everyone to see the difference. Her eyes weren't wide with fear anymore. They were narrowed in thought. And when she looked at Jasmin, then Nico, and finally Ty, she did smile. Not the kind that asks for approval. The kind that plants itself in the soil and grows regardless of the weather.

"He doesn't need speeches," Ella said quietly. "He needs truth. And someone who won't let him lie to himself when it counts." Her words hung there, surprising even her. But no one argued. They didn't need to. They understood. Ty nodded once, then reached into his pocket and placed something small on the table. A folded piece of paper. Ella looked puzzled, and Ty explained. "It's the code," he said. "Of the Quiet Ones." She opened it. Four lines written in pencil:

Protect the truth.
Move without anger.
Speak only when it builds.
Never leave someone in the dark.

Ella folded it slowly. She placed it in her backpack without a word. Not because she didn't know what to say. But because some truths are better sealed with silence.

Just then, the bell rang. The library emptied slowly, with whispers of chairs being pushed in and pages turning back to where they belonged. Ella stood, adjusting the strap on her bag. She walked beside Ty, quiet but no longer hidden. Jasmin trailed behind, thoughtful, while Nico pretended not to notice how Ella's chin was now a little higher than before.

None of them spoke as they walked past Mr. Arnett's office. The light was still on. The door was still closed. But the air had changed. Ella paused at the corner, turned back to Ty, and asked, "Is silence always stronger?" Ty smiled—not big, not wide. Just enough. "Only when it's true."

There were ways of knowing things without asking. Jasmin learned that from Ty, not because he taught it with words, but because he lived it with his eyes. He noticed things no one else did. He sat at angles that let him see more than anyone thought he was watching. He smiled at the right time to soften suspicion. He listened not just to voices, but to pauses between them. And slowly, Jasmin realized, he wasn't just paying attention—he was reading. Reading people like books with no covers, no summaries, just tension tucked into every line. And now, she wanted to learn how to read the same way.

Ty never called it spying. Spying was for secrets you wanted to steal. But reading—that was for truths people were too tired to say out loud. "You don't need to catch them lying," he told her in the quiet between classes. "You just need to catch the moment they stop telling the truth." Jasmin tucked that sentence into the back of her mind like a bookmark. And when she watched Leo walk into the hallway the next morning, she didn't stare. She didn't follow. She simply noticed.

Leo was no longer loud. That was new. He kept his head down just enough to look busy, but not guilty. He moved like someone who didn't know what part of himself to carry first. Hands? Shoulders? Eyes? Everything seemed unsure. He didn't glance at her, not directly, but when Sophie waved from her locker, Jasmin caught something strange: Leo smiled. It was tiny. It didn't stretch his face. But it reached his eyes for half a second, before flickering out like a match hit by wind.

She didn't trust the smile. But she trusted what was behind it—fear, maybe. Longing. A hunger for something that didn't come from praise or control. It came from somewhere soft and lost. She'd seen it before. In herself, once. When she didn't have words for sadness yet. When the best she could do was pretend she was fine until someone noticed her being too quiet. Leo wasn't pretending to be fine anymore. He was pretending not to be noticed.

Ty nudged her that day near the drinking fountain. "You see it now, don't you?" he asked gently. "It's not just how he moves—it's what he's trying to hide." Jasmin nodded without needing to explain. She had watched Leo for weeks. She had seen him shift from swagger to shadow. She had felt the silence he left behind when he wasn't around to fill rooms with jokes that turned sharp. But this—this Leo—was quieter than any absence. He was present and silent. That was more honest than anything he'd said all month.

Ella didn't say much, but Jasmin caught her glancing too. The others hadn't spoken about Leo since the meeting in the office. The crying. The hug. The truth no one could fully name. But something had shifted. Jasmin didn't need an announcement to know it. Leo hadn't snapped at anyone in three days. He hadn't complimented anyone either. He just floated between people, trailing the kind of stillness that made you want to whisper around him.

At recess, Jasmin sat on the wooden bench facing the yard. She could see Leo playing wall-ball with Ty, not close, but not distant either. His throws were careful. His smiles were quick. When he lost a point, he didn't yell. He just nodded and let Ty serve again. Jasmin didn't know what to make of it. But she knew this: Leo wasn't performing. He was existing. And sometimes, that was the loudest change of all.

The real shift wasn't in Leo's words or tone. It was in his eyes. Jasmin saw it clearest when Ty said something kind and Leo flinched—like kindness was a stone too smooth to trust. But then Leo would look down, steady his hands, and glance back at Ty with something close to belief. Jasmin studied that look. It was raw. Not defensive. It wasn't the look of someone who wanted control. It was the look of someone who wanted shelter.

Ty called it "emotional reading." He said some people shout, and some people leak. Leo was leaking now—drops of fear, glimmers of hope, cracks in armour that had been shiny for too long. Jasmin didn't pity him. That wasn't the point. Pity was useless. But she did recognize the child under the storm. And when he sat beside Ty during group work and didn't try to take over, she saw it as the clearest paragraph of all.

Later, at the coat hooks, Leo brushed past her lightly. No words. No grin. But Jasmin saw his hand hesitate before grabbing his backpack. It was a moment. Maybe meaningless. Maybe massive. Either way, she read it. And when she turned to Nico, he nodded like he had seen it too. "We're watching," he said quietly. "Not waiting. Watching." Jasmin felt the truth of that settle somewhere between her ribs.

Watching was different from judging. That was Ty's first lesson. Judging snapped like a verdict. Watching stretched like patience. Jasmin hadn't understood that at first. But now she did. Leo didn't need applause. He needed witnesses. He needed someone to see the slow shift of his soul, and still stay beside him. Not because he deserved it, but because someone once stayed beside her too.

At lunch, Jasmin sat across from Sophie, who was watching Ty. Not with crush-eyes, but with admiration. She had learned something too. That silence could build bridges. That not asking questions was sometimes the kindest way to say you cared. Leo said nothing during the whole meal. But when Jasmin stood up to throw away her tray, he whispered something only she could hear. "Thanks." Just that. A single word. No performance. No play.

It wasn't for a compliment. It wasn't bait for more. It was a brick laid in the foundation of something else—maybe the start of truth. Jasmin walked away without replying. She didn't want to scare the moment off. But when she looked over her shoulder, Leo was still sitting with Ty. Still tucked in. Still quiet. And that, she realized, was the message: he was letting himself be seen.

That night, Jasmin wrote in her notebook the things she had learned without anyone teaching her. She wrote: "Silence says more when you know how to hear it." Then she added: "Shadow Warriors don't interrupt. They observe. They defend without needing to strike. They love without needing credit." She underlined that line twice, then closed the book.

She had no cape. No code name. No weapon. But for the first time since all of this started, she felt like she had power. The quiet kind. The kind you earn by watching what others miss. By catching the truth without catching attention. And she smiled—not for anyone to see, but for herself. Because in the silence, she was starting to see the shape of the truth. And in Leo's eyes, she saw something she never expected: the outline of someone who wanted to heal.

Ty didn't pass out worksheets or raise his voice. There was no speech, no click of a pen, not even a chalk mark on the board. Just a quiet glance around the table in the library, where the five of them sat—Jasmin flipping pages in her sketchbook, Ella cupping her hands around her thermos, Nico tilting back in his chair, and Leo staring at the carpet like it might blink first. Ty set his pencil down and said, "Your assignment is to notice things." No one asked him what he meant. They already knew better.

"Noticing isn't spying," he continued, voice low, like it was just for them. "It's not tattling. You don't report. You just learn who talks over people. Who always has to win. Who gives too much too fast. And who never asks for anything, even when they need it most." His eyes flicked to Ella, but only for a second. "You don't change anything yet. You just notice."

Jasmin understood it before the rest of them did. She started keeping notes in the margins of her planner—not about homework, but about hallway patterns. The way one girl always had her hair yanked by another when teachers weren't watching. The boy who only spoke kindly when people were listening. The friend who borrowed things and never gave them back, but always smiled while doing it. "It's weird," she said to Ty. "I feel like I'm reading the room better. Like it's a book."

Leo didn't write anything down. He didn't need to. The truth was already mapped across his memory like a city grid—where he used to stand, who he used to push, the laughs he used to fake. And now, when someone else did it—especially the eighth graders—he spotted it instantly. The way they picked favourites. The way they gave praise that felt sticky. The way they locked eyes with someone just long enough to pin them there. "That one," Leo muttered to Ty one afternoon in the cafeteria. "He's doing the thing I used to do." Ty didn't need to ask which thing. He already knew.

At recess, Leo walked past a small group of younger students gathered by the back fence. One boy flinched when the tallest kid clapped him on the shoulder. The laughter that followed didn't reach the boy's eyes. Leo slowed, not enough to be noticed, but enough to confirm. "Fake friendliness," he whispered to himself. "Pressure hug. Classic."

Back in the library, Nico said, "I saw someone get called a genius just because they helped another kid finish a test. Same words Leo used to use on Jasmin. Praise with a hook." Jasmin nodded. "That's a compliment that turns into a chain," she said. "Ties you up and makes you feel special and trapped at the same time."

"Exactly," said Ty. "Now you're seeing it."

Ella had been quieter during the assignment, but she watched everyone. She started to see which smiles were real and which ones came with conditions. One day, she told Jasmin, "I think I used to smile like that. To get people to like me. Not to tell the truth." Jasmin didn't answer right away, but she touched Ella's hand and said, "We all did."

The next day, Leo hugged Ty in the middle of the hallway. Not for show. Not as an act. Just because the weight got heavy again, and Ty didn't hesitate. He wrapped his arms around Leo like a brother would. It wasn't even a question. And later, when Nico asked if Leo was okay, Ty only said, "He will be. He's learning."

When Mr. Clarke walked by and caught the hug, he didn't interrupt. He just nodded to himself, the way someone does when they've seen this before and wish they hadn't, but they're glad it's finally being undone.

Later that week, Leo asked Ty, "What if I get it wrong again? What if I start acting like... me again?" Ty looked him straight in the eye and answered, "Then I'll call you out. I'll remind you. And I'll hug you again, right after." Leo didn't smile, but he didn't frown either. That was enough.

Ty stood in front of the group again and said, "Truth isn't loud. It's patient. It waits until someone's ready to see it." He passed around strips of paper with a single word written on each: watch, listen, notice, remember. He didn't explain them. They didn't need him to.

That afternoon, Jasmin caught a student watching her too closely. Not in a friendly way. In a copying way. She saw her own hand gestures mirrored five seconds too late. "He's echoing me," she whispered to Ella. Ella frowned. "Like Leo used to do." Jasmin's stomach flipped.

Leo began to understand that showing what he used to be—by pointing it out in others—wasn't betrayal. It was a kind of confession. And each time he did it, it hurt less. He wasn't reporting to be cruel. He was revealing to be kind.

Ty explained that this wasn't about war. "We don't attack people. That's not what Shadow Warriors do. We don't expose them for revenge. We expose patterns to protect people." Nico added, "Sometimes you learn the most by just staying quiet long enough to see who can't stay silent."

By the end of the week, the group had collected thirty small observations. Not judgments. Just patterns. They didn't write names. They wrote truths. Ty folded the notes into a shoebox labelled Training and locked it in his desk. "We don't need weapons," he said. "We have awareness."

Leo lingered behind after the others left. "I want to keep going," he said. "Even if I mess up sometimes." Ty looked at him and said, "You will. That's part of the training too." Then Leo did something he hadn't done in months. He smiled—not the smile he used to use. A different one. One that didn't demand anything back.

Leo didn't expect to be caught. He didn't think Nico would notice, or if he did, that he'd keep it quiet. But Nico had learned by now. You didn't have to shout a lie to call it out. You didn't have to win the room to win the truth. He simply looked at Leo and tilted his head. That was it. No punishment. No judgment. Just truth, pointed out like a thread snagged in a sweater. Leo looked down, embarrassed, and Ty gently stepped between them with calm.

"You want to fix it?" Ty asked him quietly, so only Leo could hear. Leo nodded once. No defence. No denial. Just the weight of what he had said still hanging behind his teeth. It wasn't even a big lie—just one of those twisty kinds, a half-truth meant to make someone else look a bit smaller. But it still counted. In the code Ty was teaching them, even a twist was a tear.

Leo turned and found the girl he'd lied to—Mira, a Grade Six student who was quiet but sharp. He had told someone she cheated on a test, just to make his own answer look smarter. Mira hadn't heard it at the time. But now she watched him approach with a tension in her shoulders that only loosened when she saw Ty trailing behind him like a silent guard. Leo spoke softly, words almost too careful, like he was afraid they'd slip sideways again.

"I lied," he told her. "You didn't cheat. I was just... I don't know why I said it. I'm sorry." Mira blinked. Then nodded. She didn't say it was okay. But she didn't turn away either. That meant something.

When Leo turned back to Ty, his shoulders didn't sink—they straightened. And before either of them could speak, he reached out and hugged Ty. Not a quick hug, not one of those loud, back-slapping kinds boys sometimes give to avoid being honest. This one was silent, solid. The kind that says thank you without needing the word.

Jasmin saw the whole thing from the lockers and leaned toward Nico. "He didn't even fight it," she whispered. "He just… owned it."

"Yeah," Nico said. "Because no one was trying to beat him."

Ty later explained it over lunch. "When you protect someone," he said, "you don't do it to prove you're right. You do it because they matter more than your ego. Real warriors don't show off—they show up."

Ella raised her hand like they were in class. "What if they mess up again?"

Ty shrugged. "Then we protect again. Not forever. But long enough for them to find their truth."

Mila, who usually didn't say much, finally added, "So… we're not trying to catch people. We're just… cleaning the mirror?"

Ty smiled. "Exactly. Sometimes the truth's still there. It's just smudged."

That afternoon, Leo stayed close. Not in a clingy way, but in that quiet orbit kids have when they're trying not to mess up again. He held the door open. He didn't talk over anyone. When another boy made a snide comment, Leo didn't pile on. He just raised one eyebrow, then walked away. That kind of silence landed louder than any defence ever could.

Later, Jasmin asked Nico, "Do you think Leo's really changing?" Nico took a moment. "He's listening. That's how it starts."

Jasmin thought about that as Leo joined them at the edge of the field. He didn't ask to play. He just waited. Not for permission—but for space. They made it without a word. Shadow Warriors, Ty had said, don't chase attention. They protect it. They don't perform for praise. They act because it's right. And right didn't need to announce itself.

Even when Leo dropped the ball and Ella caught it mid-air, he didn't argue. He just smiled. A small one. The kind that didn't ask for anything back. Jasmin smiled too. And didn't say "I told you so." Because real truth? It doesn't need a banner. Just a place to stand.

The door cracked open like a warning. Leo didn't slam it. He didn't even push it hard. But the way his hand gripped the handle—the way his knuckles stayed white against the wood— said everything louder than a yell ever could. The teacher froze for half a second, then kept reading from the book, pretending not to notice. But Nico noticed. Jasmin noticed. And Ty, without even turning his head, already knew.

Leo stood in the doorway, back straight, lips pressed tight. The class had just laughed at something—not at him, not about him—but the laughter scratched something under his skin. He'd been doing better. Weeks now without snapping, without twisting anyone's words. He'd even apologized on his own once. But something today had tipped him. Something small. That's how it always starts.

Ty slid his eyes across the room and stood. "Washroom," he said to the teacher, who barely nodded. His steps were even, unhurried, like this was routine. Maybe it was.

Down the hallway, Leo leaned against the lockers with both fists clenched. The mask was slipping, and he knew it. Not because someone saw through it—but because he couldn't hold it in place any longer. Ty said nothing at first. He didn't stand close. He didn't ask questions. He just walked up slowly and waited. The sound of the hallway lights buzzing above was the only thing between them for a full minute.

Then, quietly, "You left your backpack," Ty said. Leo didn't look at him. "Don't care." Ty nodded once. "Okay." The silence didn't scare Ty. He'd learned long ago that silence is just noise waiting to be understood. So he waited, not for words, but for breath. When Leo finally inhaled, shaky and broken, Ty stepped closer.

"You almost said it," he said. Leo's head tilted, eyes red at the edges. "Said what?" "The truth." That one word made Leo flinch like a slap. Ty saw it and didn't back away. He opened his arms without drama, without force, and waited again. Leo didn't move at first. Then something snapped—not the kind of snap that explodes. The kind that breaks open. A dam that gives up.

Leo stepped forward into Ty's chest. The hug didn't feel earned. It felt necessary. "I hate it," Leo whispered. Ty didn't ask what. He just rubbed his back once, slowly, with that calm rhythm only someone older than their years could know. "I hate that I keep… trying," Leo choked, "and then something—just something—makes me feel like I'm six again and nothing's real and no one's safe." Ty's chin rested lightly on Leo's hair. "You are safe." "No I'm not." "You are. Right now." Leo shook his head. "You don't get it." Ty's voice lowered. "Someone make you feel like this at home?"

There it was. The mask cracked. The air behind Leo's eyes went from storm to surrender. He didn't nod. He didn't speak. But his body answered. His hands unclenched. His shoulders fell. His breath hitched again. "Who?" Ty asked. "I can't." "Okay." Ty didn't press. "But I can help. I don't need to know everything yet."

Leo gripped the sides of Ty's shirt. "You'll hate me." "I already love you." The words hung between them. No echo. No hesitation. Just truth, soft and solid. Leo crumbled. Not like a villain breaking down. Like a boy who had run too far for too long. He cried—not the kind of tears that beg attention, but the kind that release weight. The kind that only fall when the heart decides it can't lie anymore.

Ty held him like a brother would. Not just tight—but steady. Protective. Without question. Without asking Leo to be anything but what he was in that moment: broken, honest, real. When the bell rang, neither of them moved. Back in the classroom, Nico looked at Jasmin. "He almost told the truth," he said. Jasmin looked toward the door. "Maybe he did. Just not to us."

It was the way they walked. That's what made people look twice—not because they were loud, or dressed the same, or even talking much. It was the silence that moved between them, calm and unbothered. Jasmin on the left, Nico beside her. Then Ella, then Ty. No leader. No follower. Just four kids walking side by side like they'd decided something bigger than words. That was the code. That was the sign. Shadow Warriors never announce themselves. They don't need to.

Jasmin had her sleeves rolled up, backpack hanging half-open with a corner of a notebook poking out. She didn't fix it. She didn't care. She felt taller somehow—like every truth she'd faced with Ty and Nico had added an inch to her soul, not her body. Ella walked lightly, but not nervously. She had started holding her chin higher without knowing it, and it showed in how others looked at her. Not like she was fragile, but like she was thinking three steps ahead.

Nico had that stubborn squint in his eyes again—the kind he wore when he was working something out but didn't want help. He'd learned that quiet observation wasn't weakness. That noticing was its own kind of defence. Ty, of course, walked like he always did—like the world was a slow secret waiting to be solved. Calm spine. Long stride. Shoulders not slouched, not stiff. Just ready.

They spotted Leo alone near the back gate. He wasn't waiting for them. He was facing the fence, one hand in his hoodie pocket, the other dragging a stick slowly across the asphalt. His head turned just slightly when he heard them coming.

Ty stepped forward before the others. He didn't run. He didn't call out. He just approached like gravity pulled him there. "Want some company on the way home?" Ty asked, hands in his jacket now. Leo didn't answer at first. He glanced sideways, then down at his shoes, then back at Ty. "Why?" Ty shrugged. "Because I don't want you walking alone today."

Leo's mouth twisted a little, like the answer stung more than he expected. "I'm warning you," he said, voice low. "My dad… he's ten times worse than me." Ty didn't blink. "Okay." Leo narrowed his eyes. "You're not scared of that?" "No," Ty said. "I've seen worse. And I'm not walking in to fight him. I'm walking beside you. That's different."

Leo didn't respond right away. The stick dropped from his fingers, bounced once, then rolled beneath the fence. He looked at Ty again, and something broke—not painfully, but quietly. A wall lowered, just a little. Enough to breathe through. "You really don't hate me?" Leo asked. Ty stepped closer. "Not even close."

There was a moment of stillness. Not dramatic. Not drawn out. Just enough space for a choice. Leo made it. He stepped forward and hugged Ty—not roughly, not awkwardly, but with full weight, like he meant every inch of it. He buried his face into Ty's jacket and held on longer than most boys his age would dare to.

"Thanks," Leo whispered, words thick. "For the truth. For not making me lie. And for treating me like a brother… even after all of it." Ty closed his eyes and held him back, hand at the centre of Leo's back, right where all the fear sat. "You are my brother," Ty said. "Not because you're perfect. But because you let me stand beside you anyway."

Behind them, the others waited. Jasmin didn't speak. Nico didn't smirk. Ella didn't flinch. They knew what was happening. Some moments don't need witnesses. They need respect. When Leo and Ty turned to walk, they didn't take the path through the parking lot. They went the long way—through the trees behind the playground, where the light moved gently and the sidewalk narrowed into two careful steps.

When they left, Jasmin exhaled. "He's not there yet," she said. "No," Nico agreed. "But he's starting." Ella nodded once. "And we're still walking with him." The bell never rang. No one dismissed them. But school was done for the day. And the lesson—that deep, rare one—had settled into them like a stone in a river. It wouldn't leave. It wouldn't fade. Because once you've walked beside someone who almost couldn't be loved—and loved them anyway—you don't forget how that feels. Not ever. And that, Jasmin thought, is the way of the warrior.

CHAPTER 9: THE DAY I LEARNED TO SAY NO

They said it happened in the middle of the night. Quietly. No yelling. No front porch scene like in movies. Just the knock, the badge, and a voice that spoke Leo's full name as if reading the truth from a sealed envelope. Ty didn't flinch when the door opened. He stood still. Not with fists raised—but his eyes did the work. His father stepped forward with the same calm strength Ty carried in his shoulders, and Leo's father, so used to being the mountain in every room, folded. It didn't end in a brawl. It ended in silence. The kind that closes doors and opens windows all in the same breath. Leo didn't say a word as they led his father away, but he reached for Ty's hand before the cruiser disappeared.

Leo moved in that same night. There wasn't a suitcase. Just a backpack, some books, and clothes that didn't match. Mrs. Takashi didn't ask him what he'd been through. She just hugged him with both arms, kissed the top of his head, and said, "You're home now." Mr. Takashi brought down a folded blanket from the closet and set up the cot in Ty's room like it had always been waiting. No questions. No speeches. Just warmth. Leo didn't cry until the lights were off. Then the sobbing came—long, gasping waves that didn't ask permission. Ty rolled over, didn't say a word, and just held him. Not as a soldier. Not as a warrior. But as a brother who meant it.

The next morning, everything at school was the same—and different. Nico noticed first. The way Leo walked beside Ty without the edge. Jasmin saw how Leo looked people in the eye now, not like a dare, but like a boy who wanted to be seen. Ella caught him holding a door open, not for credit, not for control. Just because. But whatever peace they thought they'd found didn't last past first period. That's when Alex walked in.

The new kid was tall, built like someone who always won footraces, and his smile had a point to it. He called the teacher "boss" and dropped a wink like he'd already been here forever. His shoes were clean. His sleeves were rolled. His bag was branded. And when he turned his head to look at the class, you could feel the air shift. Not fear—but something colder. Calculating. Jasmin nudged Nico's foot under the desk. Nico didn't need to look. He already knew.

At recess, Alex found his perch—top step, centre of the courtyard, like a prince surveying a kingdom he hadn't asked permission to rule. His compliments were strange. "Nice shoes, dude—lookin' real Salvation Army." "Cool hair, Jasmin. Kinda retro. Like, 1980s librarian vibes." Nobody knew whether to say thank you or run. That's when Leo saw it.

He'd seen this before. The way someone walks into a space and bends it, just enough that everyone leans without noticing. The way words are wrapped in bows and thrown like darts. Leo didn't speak at first. He just watched. Eyes narrowed. Mouth closed. Ty stood beside him, arms crossed, measuring Alex with the same silent math he used for reading lies.

Later, in the library, Leo hugged Ty again. It wasn't the kind of hug that asks for something. It was the kind that says something. "Thank you," he whispered. "For everything. For that night. For not letting me be like him." Ty didn't reply. He just nodded once and tightened the hug. It was a promise kept, and another one forming.

When Alex passed them in the hallway, he didn't smirk. He smiled. Wide. And held Leo's eyes for just a second too long. "He knows," Leo whispered to Ty. "He knows how to do it. He's like... what I used to be. But slicker." Ty didn't disagree. "Then you already know how to stop him," he said. "You speak his language. But you don't use it."

That afternoon, Nico gathered the group behind the gym. Jasmin. Ella. Sophie. Mila. Leo. And Ty. "He's going to test us," Nico said. "He's going to try to break us apart." Jasmin nodded. "He already did the compliment-backhand thing to me in art. Said I 'had potential' if I stopped trying so hard." Sophie shook her head. "He told my friend Rachel she should smile more. It made her flinch."

Ty knelt in the grass. Picked up a twig. Drew a circle. "This is us. And this—" he marked an arrow into the centre "—is him trying to break the circle. But we hold. Quietly. Without giving him the show." Leo watched the circle closely. He traced his finger over the edge. "We protect it. Even if he tries to be my shadow. I won't let it happen again."

At home that night, Leo helped set the table. He even asked to help cook. Mrs. Takashi smiled gently and handed him a wooden spoon. "Stir slow," she said. "Everything burns if you rush it." Leo held that spoon like it was something sacred. Like a truth he could finally handle without flinching.

By bedtime, Leo looked over at Ty in the dark. "He's not my dad. But he's something. And I think... I think I know how to stop him. With your help." Ty didn't answer. He just reached across the cot, held Leo's hand, and said the words that sealed the night. "Then let's do it. Together. This time, we fight with love." And in the stillness, Leo whispered one last thank you—not to Ty, but to the quiet voice in his heart that finally told him he was safe enough to say it out loud.

It was during second recess when Leo saw it. Alex stood in the middle of the basketball court like it was his personal stage. His audience was a ring of fourth and fifth graders, some with lunchboxes still open, others clutching juice boxes like shields. Alex had a story in motion—something about how real confidence means saying what you want, how you want, to whoever you want. His voice rolled smooth. His grin cut corners. His jokes had teeth. Leo didn't laugh. He just stopped moving.

From where Jasmin sat on the edge of the sandbox with Nico, she saw the shift. Leo's arms folded, but not like he was cold. Like he was guarding something. His chin tucked slightly, and his brows tightened, not in anger, but in memory. She nudged Nico once. "Look at his face," she whispered. Nico followed her gaze, then held it there. "That's not the face of someone amused," he said quietly. "That's the face of someone haunted."

Alex pointed at a boy wearing a shirt with a faded superhero on it. "Nice tee," he said. "Did you win that in a cereal box draw?" The smaller kids laughed, unsure of what the rules were, only knowing they'd rather be beside Alex than under him. The boy shrugged, and his ears flushed red. Leo flinched. Not visibly. Just enough that Jasmin caught it. Just enough that Ty, a few feet away leaning against the tetherball pole, took a single step closer without saying a word.

Leo's hands dropped to his sides. They were clenched. Jasmin stood, walked over, stood beside him like she'd been planning to all morning. "That used to be you," she said, softly. Leo didn't deny it. He didn't blink. "He knows exactly how far to go," Leo murmured. "He stops just short of real trouble. Just like I used to." Jasmin didn't speak. She didn't have to. The silence around them was enough to fill the space between pain and change.

Ty joined them without a word. He placed a hand gently on Leo's shoulder. "You can spot it faster now," he said. "That's how I knew you were turning." Leo looked down at the playground gravel, then up again at Alex. "He's wearing it like armour," Leo said. "But I know what's underneath. That need to win. That need to hurt before getting hurt." His voice cracked near the end, but he caught it before it fell.

Nico approached from behind, dropping down to tie his shoelace like he needed an excuse to be there. "What would you have done back then?" he asked. "Back when you were him." Leo's eyes narrowed. "I would've dared someone to stop me," he said. "I would've dared someone to care enough to notice." Nico nodded. "Then maybe it's our turn to notice."

Alex shifted his performance. He started praising one kid loudly for being "smarter than the rest," while glaring at another who tried to correct him on a math fact. "Man, maybe you should just listen instead of trying to be right all the time," Alex sneered. The air thickened. The kids didn't laugh this time. They just looked at their feet. Power had tilted, but not in Alex's favour anymore. Not with the quiet ones watching.

Leo took a step forward, just one. Not toward Alex—but away from his old self. "He's not just picking on them," Leo said. "He's training them. Like I did. Making them afraid to question him. Making them feel lucky for not being his target. I remember every move because I invented most of them." Jasmin reached for his hand and held it tightly.

Ty looked over at the smaller group, then back at Leo. "You've got a choice now," he said. "You can keep walking forward, or you can go back and drag them with you." Leo didn't answer right away. He watched Alex nudge a kid's backpack off the bench with his foot, then laugh when the boy scrambled to catch it. Jasmin squeezed his hand again. "You're not him anymore," she said. "But you know how he works. That makes you stronger than him."

Sophie arrived at the edge of the court, having seen enough. "He tried to compliment me earlier," she said. "Told me I looked 'interesting.'" Her tone was flat. Tired. Ella joined her. "He told Ty he looked like he practiced smiling in the mirror. I think he was testing the water." Ty only smiled faintly. "He's about to drown in it," he said.

Leo's face hardened again, but it wasn't cruel. This time, it was carved in decision. "I can't punch him. I won't prank him. That's what I would've done before." Ty nodded. "And that's exactly why you won't do it now." Leo stepped backward, closer to his friends. "He doesn't get to win by being louder. Not this time."

At lunch, the group sat together at the back corner table. Leo placed his tray down slowly, eyes still on the door. "He'll come for me first," he said. "He'll test me." Nico looked up from his sandwich. "Let him. You're not who he thinks you are." Jasmin leaned in. "We've got your back." Ella, Sophie, even Mila all nodded.

Leo took a deep breath. "He's not me," he said. "He's a version of what I escaped. And this time, I'm not running." Across the cafeteria, Alex scanned the room. His eyes landed on Leo. He smirked. Then he turned back to his own group of kids, not knowing that his next performance would be watched not by fans—but by warriors. And the difference would be everything.

Leo hadn't touched his sandwich. His elbows were on the lunch table, palms clasped, eyes trained on Alex across the room. Ty sat beside him, tray untouched as well, their silence thick like syrup left in the cold. It wasn't the loudness of Alex's voice that froze Leo still—it was the rhythm. The way he dipped his head when he complimented a girl's shoes, only to smirk and whisper something different to the boy next to him. The way his laughter rose too fast and ended too flat. Leo didn't blink. He just stared, like he was watching something ancient claw itself out of the mirror.

Ty didn't speak, not yet. He knew the look on Leo's face. It was the one he wore the day they walked past his old apartment for the last time. It was the expression of memory trying not to return, and failing. Jasmin slid into the seat across from them, careful not to jostle the table. Ella followed, her tray already picked over. The noise of the lunchroom swelled around them like static, but their table sat inside a hush that belonged only to those who've seen too much and were still trying to see it all anyway.

"I know those moves," Leo finally said. His voice was low, but sharp, like gravel underfoot in the dark. "He mirrors people. Echoes them. Then flips it." He kept watching Alex, who now had his arm slung around the shoulder of a kid in Grade 4, laughing too loud at something that wasn't funny. "I invented some of them," Leo added. This time, he turned away. The words sat in his mouth like rusted coins.

Ty didn't flinch. He folded his arms on the table, keeping his tone calm. "Then you're the one who'll see it before anyone else." That wasn't flattery. It was assignment. It was trust passed like a blade, not tossed like praise. Jasmin leaned forward, expression serious, but gentle. She didn't look at Alex. She looked at Leo. Not accusing. Just listening. "When did you notice it?" she asked.

"Yesterday," Leo admitted. "In the hallway. He copied the way Sophie talks. Same pitch. Same laugh. But he was faking it. Just like I used to." He didn't say it with pride. He said it with the weight of someone naming a ghost by its first name. His fingers trembled slightly against the plastic tray. Ty reached under the table and gave Leo's knee a short squeeze. It steadied him more than words.

"I remember," Ella said slowly, "when you did that with me." Her voice wasn't cruel. She was offering the truth like a bandage, not a blade. Leo nodded, tight-lipped. "I know," he replied. "I didn't understand what I was doing back then. I just knew it worked. People liked me... for a while." The air around the table dropped in temperature. They weren't looking to blame. They were drawing maps.

Alex tossed a crumpled napkin at a kid's head across the room. When the teacher turned, Alex's face turned innocent so fast it looked rehearsed. Nico had just joined the table and caught that exact moment. He sat down without a word and shook his head once. "I saw that," he muttered. Leo didn't look back. He didn't have to. He remembered the steps. The dance didn't change.

Ty said nothing for a moment, then spoke like a blade through fog. "Leo, you're not that anymore." Leo's eyes flicked to him. "But you remember how it works. That's why you're the one who's going to stop it before it spreads." Jasmin nodded once. "You know the mask. You wore it." Leo didn't argue. He knew they weren't asking—they were calling. He could feel it in his chest.

"I don't want to be that person again," Leo whispered. "But I know what he's doing. I can feel it. It's like... watching someone write the same lie you once believed." The words cracked near the end, but Ty didn't let them fall. "Then you don't have to stop being you to stop him. You just have to remember the code." Leo gave a nod so small it almost didn't count. But it did. And everyone at the table felt it.

Ella reached out slowly and placed her hand over Leo's. "You're not alone this time," she said. "That's what's different." He looked down at their hands, then at the others. Jasmin. Ty. Nico. Even Sophie, sitting nearby, watching without interrupting. This wasn't a trial. It was a calling. The silence between them held no guilt—only readiness.

"I know where he's headed," Leo said quietly. "I know what he's going to try next. He's going to split people. Pair them off. Turn one against the other." Jasmin's jaw tightened. "Then we don't let him." Ty said, "We move first." And that, for them, was the plan.

Alex passed by the table then, glancing down at them as though testing for weakness. Leo looked straight up at him, didn't blink. Said nothing. But in that silence was a warning. Not from fear. But from someone who had returned from the fire and now guarded it from burning others. When Alex was gone, Leo breathed out through his nose and turned back. "That used to be me," he said again, but this time there was no shame. There was purpose. There was weight. And maybe for the first time, there was power.

It happened so fast that no one registered the danger until it had already arrived. Sophie had been reaching for a book just inside the library's open doorway, her backpack still slung over one shoulder, one strap hanging loose like a ribbon. The light from the hallway pooled behind her, a soft glow, which made what came next feel like a shadow slipping out from underneath the doorframe. Alex stepped forward with that grin—the one that never quite reached his eyes. Too much teeth, too much tilt to the head. Kindness painted on too thick, like an old wall that's been covered up too many times and still peels underneath.

"You're new here, right?" Alex said, voice dipped in syrup. "I was hoping you'd be smart. Chinese girls usually are." The words didn't land like praise. They landed like bait. His body blocked the doorway now, arm stretched above her head like he was being casual, but his eyes gave him away. Sophie didn't speak. Not because she was afraid. Because she didn't want to waste words on something she already knew wasn't real.

Before anyone else moved, Leo did.

He came from the hallway like a line drawn through sand. There was no yelling. No threats. Just movement. Direct. Measured. Sharp. His steps made no sound, but something about the way he carried himself carved silence around him. Alex barely turned before Leo was standing between them, not close enough to touch, but near enough that Sophie could exhale without fear. Leo's eyes didn't blink. They locked. He didn't look up at Alex. He stared straight through him.

"Back up," Leo said. Not loud. Not threatening. But with enough weight that the floor seemed to absorb it. It wasn't a suggestion. It wasn't even a warning. It was the truth spoken out loud by someone who had once stood in that same spot, playing the same game, and now held no mercy for it. Alex's smirk twitched, then froze. His posture faltered, just slightly. It was the first crack in his glass.

Sophie didn't step away. She didn't run. She stood perfectly still behind Leo, not because she was hiding—but because she was watching. And what she saw wasn't a rescue. It was a reckoning. Leo hadn't said her name. He hadn't looked back to check if she was okay. He didn't need to. His body said everything. The message was loud in silence: You do not touch what is not yours to twist.

Alex's lips curled, but his voice stumbled. "Hey man, I was just being nice." Leo didn't blink. "No, you weren't," he said. "You were trying to trap her in a compliment she didn't ask for, so that if she didn't smile, you could say she was rude." He tilted his head, just enough to make his point without making it personal. "That's not kindness. That's bait. And I've used it before."

The hallway had gone quiet now. Jasmin stood a few feet back, frozen mid-step. Ty was behind her, arms folded but not tense. He'd seen this before. Not Alex. Not Sophie. But this version of Leo. The one who didn't need an audience to do the right thing. The one who used to wound with words and now stood like a shield. It wasn't a performance. It was a vow being lived out loud.

"I don't want trouble," Alex muttered. But his voice had lost its shine. Leo nodded once. "Then walk away." He didn't move. He didn't push. Just stood like a wall someone else had built inside him. Alex glanced at Sophie, tried to recover his charm, but the moment had collapsed. She raised one eyebrow. Just one. And in that small gesture, she returned the power he tried to steal. That was enough to make Alex turn.

As he stepped back into the hallway, Alex tried to laugh, brushing it off like he hadn't just lost control of the scene. But no one laughed with him. The air had changed. Something unspoken had settled in the space between them all, like dust after a collapse. Leo didn't turn until Alex was gone. Then, finally, he looked at Sophie.

"You okay?" he asked. His voice had softened now. No bite. Just warmth, like sunlight on tired shoulders. Sophie nodded, lips parted but no words ready. She didn't need to speak. Her eyes said thank you with a clarity no sentence could match. He nodded back, just once. That was enough.

Ty stepped forward and gently tapped Leo's shoulder. "You didn't hesitate," he said. "Didn't need to." Leo exhaled slowly. "He moved like I used to. I knew what would come next." Jasmin placed her hand on Leo's other shoulder. "And you didn't let it." Leo shrugged, but it didn't hide the flicker in his eyes. He'd never stepped in like that before. Not because he couldn't. Because he hadn't believed he deserved to be the one who did. Now, he did.

They walked back together. Nothing loud. Nothing dramatic. Sophie carried her book with both hands, holding it like something worth keeping. And behind her, Leo walked without speaking. But inside, something had changed. He had used his power—his old tricks, his sharpened sense—not to hurt, but to guard. And that meant everything. The first time Leo intervened wasn't loud. It wasn't bold. It was quiet. Precise. Human. And it was the day the mirror cracked—for good.

Ella didn't raise her voice when she said it. She didn't flinch. She didn't stammer. She simply said the word and let it land in the air between them like a thread cut loose. Alex had asked her twice already, casually, like it was no big deal. "Want to hang out?" he said, leaning against the wall outside the gym as if he didn't care either way. The second time, he added a compliment. "You're the quiet type, I like that." It wasn't praise. It was a hook. And Ella, for the first time in days, had her scissors ready.

"No," she said.

Just that. One syllable. Nothing fancy. No explanation offered. No apology laced into the edges. It didn't echo down the hallway, but it pressed into the space like a beam holding up a roof. Nico, just a few steps away, caught the shift before the others did. He didn't need to hear the rest. He saw Alex's face twitch. That smile that always tried too hard. It stretched, then froze. The laugh came next. Predictable. Too loud. Too quick.

"Okay," Alex chuckled, raising both hands like it didn't matter. "Didn't mean to scare you. Just thought you seemed cool." He turned as if to walk away, but Leo's eyes were already locked on him. It wasn't fear in Leo's face—it was knowledge. He'd heard that laugh before. Used it himself. Not to ease tension, but to punish. To warn. To say: You embarrassed me, and now I'll make you feel it later.

Ella didn't move. She stood there as if planted, spine tall, shoulders relaxed. But her hands were clenched inside her sleeves. Nico stepped closer. Not too close. Just enough to let her know she wasn't alone. He didn't need to speak. She felt him there. And that was when she let out the smallest breath, like a balloon deflating slow so no one would hear it. Leo, still across the hall, didn't blink. He turned, not toward Alex, but toward Ella.

"You did good," Leo said quietly as he reached her side. He didn't speak it to the room. Just to her. "He laughs like that to pretend he won. But he didn't. You said no." Ella looked up at him. "He's not done," she whispered. Leo nodded. "I know. But neither are we."

Ty appeared next, leaning against the lockers as if waiting for nothing in particular. His arms crossed, his gaze calm but ready. "I heard it," he said. "Loudest 'no' I've heard all day." He smiled—not because he was trying to make light of it, but because it deserved recognition. Strength wasn't always thunder. Sometimes it was the absence of apology.

Alex was still within earshot, pretending not to listen. But the stillness behind him gave away the truth—he was. He shifted his weight, muttered something to himself, and disappeared around the corner. The hallway stayed quiet for a moment after, as if holding its breath. Then Jasmin walked up, looping her arm through Ella's.

"You okay?" Jasmin asked gently. Ella didn't answer right away. She looked down at her shoes, then at her own hands, then finally at Nico. "I said no," she repeated. Her voice wasn't louder than before. But something about the way she said it now made Nico want to cheer. Instead, he just nodded. "Yeah. You really did."

The group didn't speak of it much after that. They didn't need to. It became one of those moments that wrote itself into their story without asking for attention. But that afternoon, when they sat on the edge of the field during recess, Leo leaned over to Ella and said something she never forgot. "He's going to try someone else now. That's how people like him work. But we're watching." And Ella smiled—not wide, not for show, but like a candle lit behind her ribs.

Later that day, Sophie passed by Leo and gave him a quiet thumbs-up. She'd seen what happened too. She knew exactly what kind of strength had been summoned in that hallway. And for the first time in weeks, Leo didn't smile back with bravado or snark. He just nodded. Because he knew how hard it was to say no. How risky. How much it cost. And how much it meant.

When the last bell rang, and the crowd spilled out toward the sidewalks and school buses, Ella lagged behind for a moment, tying her shoelace slowly at her locker. Jasmin stayed with her. No one hurried. No one pushed. There was no rush. Just a shared silence between girls who knew that courage sometimes showed up quietly, with a single syllable and a steady hand.

Ty stood by the doors, waiting. He didn't say anything, just raised an eyebrow at Leo as if to ask, "Next move?" Leo shrugged. "Not ours. Hers." And when Ella finally stepped into the sunlight, her shadow stretched beside her like it had grown bigger since that morning. She didn't look behind her. She didn't have to. That was the day "no" echoed louder than any threat. Not because it was shouted. But because it was believed.

They didn't sit at a round table. They didn't pass around plans or maps or notes. They just took their usual spots—on the edge of the playground benches near the field where the autumn wind flicked at their hair and jackets. Ty sat with his elbows on his knees, gaze steady, voice low. Jasmin leaned forward, eyes alert. Ella sat cross-legged on the bench, her arms wrapped around her knees. Nico stood behind them, chewing the end of his sleeve. Sophie and Elia joined last, shoulder to shoulder. And Leo, who once sat at the centre of storm clouds, took the quietest seat—at the edge, watching the wind.

"We're not fighting him," Ty began, "we're outthinking him."

Leo exhaled and sat forward. "He doesn't scream. Doesn't shove. That's what makes him slippery. He flatters people—gives them a nickname or two, tells them they're special. Then, once they trust him, he flips it." His fingers tightened. "Makes them beg to stay on his good side. It's how I used to keep control. Until I didn't want it anymore."

Jasmin nodded. "He told Mila she had 'the best smile in school'—then the next day asked if she'd had dental work done. Like a joke." Elia looked over. "It's not a joke if you mean it to bruise." Leo's gaze darkened, but not from guilt. It was recognition. A ghost he knew, reanimated in another boy's mouth.

"He'll go for whoever looks like they'll flinch," Sophie added. "The ones who say thank you even when they're scared. He clocks that. It's like… he sniffs out self-doubt." Ella didn't speak. She didn't have to. They all knew she'd felt it already.

"So how do we block it?" Nico asked. "How do we cut the wires without setting off the alarm?" Ty smiled at the metaphor. "We don't cut anything. We observe. Step one: pattern recognition." He looked at Leo. "You know his rhythm. Teach us."

Leo took a breath and nodded. "He mirrors people at first. Whatever you like, he likes. He'll copy your jokes. He repeats your words so you think he gets you. Then he tests your loyalty. A small insult, or he 'forgets' something you said. You brush it off. That's the moment he owns you—because now you're too polite to push back."

"Okay," Ty said, nodding. "So we catch that moment. The flip." He stood slowly. "No calling it out. No public scenes. We intercept. One of us watches every time he's alone with someone new. Leo, you're our best observer for him. Ella, you're our conscience. You tell us if it feels wrong, even if it looks okay."

Ella blinked, startled by the assignment. "Me?" Ty nodded without pause. "You see people. You don't jump to conclusions. That's rare." She gave a quiet, nervous smile. Jasmin touched her hand gently, grounding her.

"What if he goes after someone we can't protect?" Elia asked. "Like the kindergartens? He won't stop at our grade." Ty turned to Sophie. "You and I will talk to Ms. Kara and Mr. Clarke. Quietly. No names yet. Just concerns. They trust you." Sophie nodded. "Especially Clarke. He doesn't fall for charm."

The group sat in silence for a moment. Not the fearful kind, but the kind before movement—like wolves reading the wind. "I don't want revenge," Leo finally said. "I just want to break the cycle. Before he turns into what I almost became."

"You didn't become it," Nico said firmly. "You stepped out." Leo didn't smile, but he looked at Nico with quiet gratitude. A brother's look. A look that said, *You saw me change. You know how hard that was.*

Ty stood up fully now. "We don't play his game. We don't mimic his tactics. No whispering campaigns. No fake smiles. Just truth. If someone's being manipulated, we offer them truth. That's our only weapon. And it's sharper than anything he has."

They all stood, slowly, one by one. No oath spoken. No ceremony. But something bound them just the same. The field around them swayed in the breeze, and the bench where they'd gathered held a little more weight than before. A bench now marked by quiet resolve. As they walked back toward the building, Leo lingered for just a moment. He looked over his shoulder to the corner where he'd once schemed, once ruled. And now, all he could think about was how to protect it—from the next version of who he used to be.

Jasmin stood with her arms folded across her chest, back pressed against the brick wall by the bike racks, eyes narrowed like she was watching a puzzle fall into place one calculated move at a time. The others were quiet, waiting. Even Ty didn't interrupt her thoughts. Across the pavement, Alex was holding court again—his voice louder than necessary, his laugh arriving a full second ahead of the joke. Three Grade 5s clung to his every word like it might buy them protection. Jasmin exhaled. "He doesn't actually like people," she finally said. "He likes the reaction they give him."

Sophie tilted her head, curious. "You mean like... attention?" Jasmin nodded, keeping her voice low. "Not just attention. Applause. Validation. He performs. Always. But if there's no audience, he's suddenly bored. Or irritated. I watched him try to compliment Nico yesterday in the hallway, but no one was around. He gave up halfway through his sentence and walked off." She pointed a finger at nothing. "That's how you spot it."

Ty leaned forward slightly, nodding. "Performers always need a stage. No stage, no act." He glanced at Leo. "Sound familiar?" Leo's jaw tensed, not with guilt this time, but with the weight of recognition. "Too familiar," he muttered. "I used to time my jokes to when the hallway was busiest. If no one laughed, I rewrote the script."

Nico frowned. "So what happens if no one claps?" Ella responded without looking up. "He finds someone to blame for the silence." The words came out softer than usual, but sharp nonetheless. She tightened the strap on her backpack like she was securing armour. Jasmin nodded. "Exactly. He needs the cheer. When he doesn't get it, he starts picking people apart, just loud enough for the next laugh."

Leo shifted his weight from one foot to the other. "It's not just about being funny. It's about needing to be in control of how people feel." He looked at the others. "He says something clever, you smile. Then he owns the moment. And if you don't smile, he makes sure you're the one who looks 'too serious' or 'no fun.' It's a trap." Sophie crossed her arms and kicked at a pebble near her foot. "It's exhausting, isn't it?" No one disagreed.

Ty pulled a small black notebook from his back pocket and jotted something quickly. "Observation log," he explained. "If we track the moments he ramps up and when he turns cold, we'll learn his cues." Elia glanced sideways. "That sounds a little... spy-like." "Shadow Warrior training," Ty corrected, not joking. "We learn by seeing. We protect by understanding."

Jasmin looked around the group. "So we don't challenge him directly. Not yet. We just take away the crowd. We don't reward the show. When he flatters someone, we stay neutral. When he mocks someone, we don't laugh." Nico scratched his head. "What if someone does laugh?" Ty answered without hesitation. "We check on the person who got mocked. That's our job. Not the one who delivered the line."

There was a silence that followed, not awkward, but respectful. They were standing inside the pause where courage is measured—not in noise, but in clarity. Leo looked at Jasmin with something close to awe. "You saw through him before I did," he admitted. Jasmin smiled, just barely. "It's easier when you've already seen it once."

Sophie tucked her hair behind her ear and looked down the hallway where Alex had gone. "He's good, though. He reads people. Fast." Ty nodded. "So we have to move slower. Not react. Just observe." Leo added, "And act only when it counts. No flinching."

Jasmin's gaze never left the far corner of the schoolyard. "He's hunting approval. But approval fades. Applause fades. Truth doesn't." Her tone carried the same finality as the closing of a well-worn book. Nico grinned. "We've got truth." Ella added quietly, "And each other."

The bell rang, echoing off the cement and steel around them. Students began to trickle back toward the building in clumps and clusters. Alex's voice was still audible, louder than the rest, arms gesturing like a stage magician mid-act. He didn't even glance their way. But Jasmin didn't need him to.

She turned to Ty. "He doesn't know we're watching, does he?" Ty shook his head. "Not yet." Jasmin smiled. "Good. Let's keep it that way." Leo gave a single nod. "No audience means no act."

As they walked back toward the doors, there were no dramatic speeches. No drawn swords. No great proclamations. Just the quiet march of six students who now knew that a narcissist's greatest weakness wasn't exposure. It was silence. Not the fearful kind. But the kind that refuses to cheer. The kind that watches—and never claps.

There was a hollow kind of hum in the cafeteria that morning, the kind that echoed more off stainless steel than human voices. It wasn't loud, but it was charged, the way the air feels before lightning breaks across a sky already bruised. Leo sat with his tray untouched. His fingers toyed with a fork, rolling it against his thumb and letting it fall back against the table's edge.

Ty had taken a seat beside him without a word, simply present. The others—Jasmin, Nico, Sophie, Ella—were close, but not clustered. No one smothered. No one stared. And then, like a dart across a silk sheet, Alex's voice cut through.

"Hey Leo," he called, too casually, like he already assumed he'd be followed. "Did you see how Elia ran out of gym? Total disaster. Might as well have taped pillows to her arms." A few nearby students chuckled automatically. Not sincerely. It was the kind of laugh people gave to avoid being the next target. Leo didn't move. He just stared at the tray in front of him as if it were holding a verdict.

Ty didn't flinch. He didn't coach him. He didn't even look at him. It was Leo's decision. Not a team tactic. Not a plan. A moment. That rare hinge in time where character steps out from shadow and tests its own weight. Leo didn't raise his voice. He didn't look theatrical. He just blinked, turned slightly toward Alex and said, evenly, "Not this time."

The cafeteria didn't fall silent instantly. But it paused. A few of the younger kids glanced up, uncertain whether a line had just been crossed or drawn. Alex cocked his head, lips twisted in a smirk. "Just joking, man." He reached for his water bottle with that same shrug he gave to every rejection. But his eyes narrowed. He'd felt it. The shift. And so had everyone else.

Leo returned to his tray. Still didn't eat. But his shoulders, once so often drawn up like a shield, eased by a fraction. That alone was louder than any comeback. Ty's hand found his shoulder and stayed there, a firm squeeze. It wasn't approval. It wasn't correction. It was presence. It was a hug, dressed as brotherhood, offered in public with no fear of what it might say to anyone watching.

Nico sat across from them, lips slightly parted, unsure if he'd just witnessed a crack in Leo's old armour—or the first stone of something sturdier. Jasmin glanced at Ella, and for once, Ella didn't look confused. She looked proud. Quietly proud, like someone who'd waited for a truth too long and was now watching it walk on two feet.

"I didn't think he'd do it," Sophie whispered, voice barely audible. Not in doubt. Just awe. Ty looked up and caught her eye. "He did," he said. "And it mattered." There was no speech that followed. No congratulations. Just a ripple of silence that washed through the table like fresh air breaking into a sealed room.

Alex didn't press. He went back to his story, but his sentences stuttered. The energy had shifted. One domino had refused to fall, and suddenly the chain reaction was off. He tried to bait another student with a different joke, but the laughter was weaker this time. Performed. Tired. Leo hadn't given him what he wanted—and everyone knew it.

Later that afternoon, during lunch recess, Leo and Ty leaned against the same tree they always stood near. The breeze pulled lightly at their jackets. Leo leaned his head back, eyes closed for a moment, like he was breathing out something he'd carried for years. Ty didn't ask what it was. He didn't need to. He just reached over and pulled Leo into a hug, the kind you give without ceremony. The kind that says, You chose differently, and I saw it.

Leo didn't cry. He didn't smile either. But he let the hug last. He rested his forehead against Ty's shoulder and exhaled. For a long second, the world just slowed. The boys didn't speak. They didn't need to. Somewhere behind them, kids were shouting over four-square rules and someone had dropped a juice box that leaked sticky red across the pavement. But none of it reached here.

"Was it enough?" Leo finally asked. His voice wasn't hopeful. It was cautious, as though he hadn't yet decided whether this new path had ground beneath it. Ty nodded once. "It was more than enough," he said. "It was the beginning." Leo's hands dropped to his sides. No fists. No tension. Just a boy who had once learned cruelty as protection, now choosing silence as strength.

The others joined them eventually. Jasmin didn't say anything, but her eyes met Leo's and held for a second longer than usual. Ella walked over and stood beside them, a full arm's length away—close enough to say I'm here, far enough to say I trust you. Nico clapped Leo lightly on the shoulder. "Not bad," he muttered. Leo didn't answer. But he didn't need to.

Later, back in class, Ty passed Leo a folded note. No dramatic spy signals. No flair. Just neat handwriting that read: First 'no' was to your dad. Second was to yourself. Keep going. Leo tucked it into the front pocket of his hoodie without unfolding it again. He didn't need to reread it. He already knew what it said.

And for the first time in months, maybe longer, Leo sat through the rest of the school day without looking for applause. He didn't check faces. He didn't play angles. He just... listened. And the silence? It didn't hurt. It held him.

It happened during science. The lesson was on ecosystems and balance, and Mr. Rafferty had barely finished outlining the food chain before Alex decided to chime in. His voice filled the classroom like always, confident and easy, threading humour through half-truths so smoothly that a few kids started nodding before even thinking. "If all the bugs died," Alex said with a smirk, "we'd be fine. Good riddance, right?" A couple kids chuckled. Sophie looked up from her notes and blinked slowly. Her pencil stopped mid-word.

Mr. Rafferty paused, halfway through sketching a diagram on the board, and turned around. He didn't correct the statement, didn't affirm it either. He just said, "Anyone have a different view?" The silence that followed felt long, but not empty. It was waiting for something. Or someone. Sophie felt it too. That quiet, magnetic pull, like truth asking her if she'd like to stand now—or wait for another day.

She raised her hand. Not halfway. All the way. Fingers pointed upright like a promise she was finally ready to make. Ty noticed first. Then Jasmin. Then Leo. Alex rolled his eyes so hard it looked like he was checking for approval in the ceiling. "Here we go," he muttered under his breath. Sophie ignored him.

"I think that's not true," she said softly, but clearly. "If insects disappeared, ecosystems would collapse. Pollination would stop. Soil would fail. Life would unbalance." Her voice didn't rise. It didn't waver. It didn't shrink either. She just said it, the way someone opens a door and refuses to close it again.

Mr. Rafferty nodded, eyebrows lifted. "You're absolutely right, Sophie. Excellent correction." He smiled at her, and she didn't flinch. Her cheeks burned slightly, but she didn't drop her eyes. Not this time. Not for him. Not for anyone. The room went quiet—not in tension, but in recalibration. The axis had shifted by half a degree.

Alex leaned back in his chair, arms folded. "Well, bugs are still gross," he mumbled, his tone half-dismissive. He didn't push harder. He didn't need to. The moment had already slipped from him. Leo, two rows away, watched carefully. He wasn't looking at Alex. He was watching Sophie. A small smile tugged at the corner of his mouth—not amusement, but understanding.

Sophie didn't say anything more for the rest of the class. She didn't need to. One moment was enough. One correction. One truth said out loud. It hadn't been clever or loud or performative. It had been steady. Rooted. And she'd meant every word. The silence that followed it wasn't absence. It was space. A space she had carved for herself with nothing but calm and fact.

At recess, the others didn't rush her. No cheering. No fuss. Jasmin gave her a quiet nod, which Sophie returned. Ty passed her a folded piece of paper with a small drawing—three dots inside a circle. The symbol from their earlier "shadow warrior" training. She smiled down at it. No words, just warmth.

Leo joined her under the climbing bars, where the bark chips stuck to your shoes and the sunlight came through the fence like filtered lines of gold. "You didn't flinch," he said. It wasn't praise. It was recognition. She looked at him, eyes steady. "Neither did you yesterday." They didn't talk after that. They just stood there, both quiet. But neither of them felt small.

Back in the classroom, Alex seemed restless. He bounced his knee under his desk, cracking jokes that didn't land. The teacher wasn't watching. The students weren't laughing. Not in the way he wanted. Not the way he was used to. Something had changed, and he couldn't trace it to its source. It wasn't one big rebellion. It was smaller. Like erosion. Like roots breaking through stone.

Later that day, Sophie found herself alone in the library. She wasn't hiding. She just wanted space to think. She didn't expect Leo to walk in, let alone sit beside her. "I used to call people out like that," he said, tracing his finger along the edge of the table. "Except I made fun of them instead." Sophie closed her book gently and looked at him.

"You were trying to survive," she said. "I was trying to disappear." They sat together in that soft, dusty light for a while. No guilt. No explanations. Just shared history, even if it wasn't shared directly. He nodded. "Maybe we're both learning to show up." Before the bell rang, Ty peeked into the library and grinned. "You coming?" Sophie stood and nodded. "Yeah," she said. "But I'm walking next to you. Not behind." Ty smiled wider, and they walked out together.

That evening, at home, Sophie pulled out her science notebook and added something new to the corner of the last page: "Bugs keep the world in balance. So do words." She underlined it once. Then closed the book, knowing it wasn't the lesson from class she'd remember—but the one she'd written for herself.

Ty had a way of saying things that made everything slow down just enough to land. No music behind his voice, no spotlight when he spoke, but still, people listened. "Bullies don't win by being clever," he told them that morning before recess. "They win because other people follow the rules they make up. If we stop playing the game, the game ends." It was Nico who first asked what game he meant, and Ty didn't hesitate. "The one where you're afraid of not being liked, so you let someone else change who you are." No one argued. Because they'd all played it before.

Elia was the first to act, though it didn't seem like action at all. That lunch hour, when Alex launched into one of his twisted compliments—praising one kid too loudly while glancing sideways at another—Elia didn't laugh. She didn't frown either. She just didn't react. It was nothing on the surface. But it was everything beneath it. Her silence echoed. The air in the cafeteria shifted just enough for others to notice, and for Alex to blink.

Leo saw it first. "That," he whispered to Nico, "is how it starts." And he wasn't talking about Alex's behaviour. He was talking about resistance. That first step away from being controlled. That subtle break in the pattern that sends ripples into the deep. Leo had once relied on applause like oxygen, but now, seeing Elia deny it to Alex, something inside him stilled. Not satisfied. Just... settled.

Later that day, Ty and Leo walked home together the same way they always did—side by side, not speaking much. But the quiet between them wasn't cold. It was waiting. The kind of silence that knew something important was coming. When they reached the porch, Ty's father was already outside, arms folded not in frustration, but something softer. Expectation, maybe. Hope, definitely. Leo's steps slowed.

"I've got something to ask you, Leo," Ty's father said as they stepped into the house. His voice didn't demand. It invited. He waited for Leo to sit down before he spoke again. "We've seen how far you've come. Not just surviving things, but learning. Choosing better. Loving better. We see you, Leo. And we love you back. That's why… if you want it, we'd like you to stay. Not just as a guest. Not just as a friend. But as family. For good."

Leo didn't respond right away. He couldn't. His breath caught somewhere halfway between shock and release. Ty put a hand on his shoulder—not urging, just present. That was all it took. The tears came like they'd been waiting weeks for permission. Leo didn't sob loudly. He didn't fall apart. He folded gently into Ty's arms, forehead resting against his chest like a younger brother who finally knew where home was.

"You don't have to say anything yet," Ty's dad said kindly. But Leo shook his head. He stood up—face wet, chest trembling—and looked both Ty's parents in the eye. "I want this," he said. "I really do." Then his voice cracked, but he didn't turn away. "Thank you for seeing me. For real."

Ty's mom stepped forward and pulled him into her arms like he'd always belonged there. She didn't say much, just whispered, "Welcome home," into his hair. Leo held her tight. Not out of desperation. Out of relief. Out of truth. The kind of truth that doesn't need decoration. It just stands.

Ty stood beside them, silent and proud. He didn't make it about him. He didn't need to. But Leo turned anyway. Hugged him again—different this time. Deeper. Firmer. The way brothers hug when words can't hold what needs to be said. "You gave me my whole life back," Leo murmured. "You really did."

That night, Leo unpacked slowly in the room that used to be just Ty's guest room. Now it was his. Every drawer he opened felt like proof. Every folded shirt, every extra toothbrush in the bathroom, every spare sock in the corner drawer—evidence that he wasn't temporary anymore. That he was wanted, not tolerated. Not managed. Not shaped. Just wanted.

The next morning, his eyes were tired but bright. At school, Alex tried the usual. A whisper here. A smug comment there. But things didn't land the same. Not with Elia, not with Sophie, not even with Nico. The group didn't fight back with words. They didn't play his game. They just stood together—shoulders aligned, backs straight, eyes unafraid.

Alex noticed. His smirk slipped just a little. And Leo, standing beside Ty, met his glance. No scowl. No challenge. Just a quiet nod that said: We see you. We know this script. And we're not in your play anymore.

Narcissistic behaviour doesn't need a title to be called out. It needs to be outgrown. Leo had once worn that mask. He knew how heavy it was. And now, standing in his own skin, without fear of punishment at home, without the chains of secrecy, Leo was ready to help others take theirs off too. The war wasn't over—but the weapons were changing. Ty leaned over and whispered, "You did good, big guy." And Leo smiled. Not wide. Not flashy. Just enough to mean it. Because some victories don't come with cheering. They come with peace. And that was louder than any applause.

Mr. Clarke didn't flinch. He never did. Not when a student raised their voice, not when a child slammed a locker, and certainly not when Alex leaned in with that slippery grin of his. The moment unfolded at the edge of second recess, just outside the library doors, where Thomas—small, jumpy, and always with his zipper half-undone—was being backed into a verbal trap. "Say you did it," Alex murmured, too quiet for most. "You were the one who dropped the markers." Thomas blinked, confused. "But I—" "It's okay," Alex said, cutting him off gently. "Just admit it, and we can move on." Behind him, Miss Kara watched with curious eyes. Mr. Clarke folded his arms slowly. Not once did he interrupt. Not yet.

Jasmin had seen this before. So had Nico. So had Ella. But the difference now was simple. Now the teachers were watching. And not just watching, but seeing. The shift from disbelief to recognition passed like a shadow behind Mr. Clarke's eyes. His feet moved before his voice did. "Alex," he called in a tone that left no room for performance. "Walk with me. Now." There was no scolding. No raised voice. Just movement. Alex stiffened, but obeyed. Thomas stood frozen. Jasmin reached him first, gently touching his shoulder, the same way Ty had done with Leo weeks ago. It was simple, quiet comfort—no spotlight, no lecture. Just, you're okay now.

Inside the staff room, it was Miss Kara who broke the silence first. "He does it with a smile," she whispered to Mr. Clarke, almost ashamed of how long it took her to see it. "The words are kind. But the push? It's still there." Mr. Clarke didn't look at her. He only nodded. "Ty warned me weeks ago," he said, almost to himself. "I thought I understood. But today…" He exhaled. "Today I felt it." That distinction mattered. Some adults listened with their ears. The ones who made a difference listened with their gut.

Back outside, Ty stood near the basketball post with his hands in his coat pockets. Leo approached slowly, no performance, no act. Just a boy with his heart open. "You said they'd start seeing it," Leo muttered. "You said it wouldn't be just us forever." Ty tilted his head and gave a soft grin. "They don't always get it right away," he replied. "But truth doesn't sleep. It waits. Then it lands." Leo nodded, then scratched the back of his neck like he always did when nerves crept in. "Can I tell you something?" he asked. Ty turned fully to face him. "Anything."

"I… I don't know how to say it," Leo began. "Then don't," Ty said. "I'll say it for you." He placed a hand on Leo's shoulder, firm and sure. "Leo's got a forever home now," he announced loud enough for Ella, Nico, Jasmin, Sophie, and Elia to hear. "With real parents. A real family. And me—a very real brother." Leo didn't laugh. He didn't even smile big. He just leaned forward and wrapped his arms around Ty's middle like a kid trying to find gravity again. His voice cracked, but not from shame. "Thanks for saying it for me."

The others approached, but no one interrupted the hug. Ella placed a hand on Leo's back without words. Nico stood to the side, arms crossed, but his eyes told the truth: relief, pride, something like big brother respect. Jasmin stepped closer with a careful smile. "Does this mean you're stuck with Ty now?" she teased lightly. Leo lifted his head just enough to respond. "I don't mind being stuck. Not if it's real." And that word—real—hung in the air like incense. It made the others quiet. It made Ty nod. It made Mr. Clarke, still watching from the doorway, finally believe this was more than progress. This was healing.

At lunch, the tables were rearranged slightly. Leo didn't sit at the end anymore. He didn't try to be in the centre either. He sat next to Sophie, who still rarely spoke but always noticed. She passed him a napkin without being asked. It had a doodle on it—a small heart inside a house. Leo blinked. "Is this…?" Sophie shrugged. "I didn't know what to draw," she whispered. "So I drew what you are now." Leo folded the napkin carefully and tucked it into his pocket like treasure. He didn't thank her with words. Just a hand squeeze, soft but honest.

That afternoon, Miss Kara approached the group. Her voice was lighter, but her face serious. "I owe you all an apology," she said. "For not seeing things earlier. For brushing off what felt small to you but was big in real life." Nico glanced at Ty. Ty didn't speak. He only tilted his head as if to say, Let her finish. Miss Kara continued. "I've started listening more. Not just to what's said. But what's felt." Ella looked up. "That's what Leo's been learning," she offered. "Feelings don't lie. People do." Leo didn't flinch at that. He nodded.

In the hallway, Alex walked alone. No crowd. No audience. No echo. Elia had stopped laughing at his jokes two days ago. Sophie no longer tilted her head when he spoke. Nico didn't even look his way. The spell was breaking. And Alex, whether he admitted it or not, felt the silence press back. Ty watched from a distance and murmured to Leo, "You see? That's what happens when the game ends." Leo replied, "That's what happens when nobody plays."

Ty's parents arrived near dismissal time. Leo didn't run to them. He walked—calm, sure, different. He hugged Ty's mom first, who held him like he'd always been hers. Then Ty's dad clapped a hand on his shoulder and said simply, "Welcome home, son." That word—son—didn't make Leo cry right away. It took a minute. It hit after Ty leaned into his ear and whispered, "You're safe now. Really." That was when Leo folded forward, face in Ty's shoulder again, no shame, just release. Mr. Clarke and Miss Kara watched from the office window, neither speaking for a long while. "He's changed," she finally whispered. "He is changing," Mr. Clarke corrected. "And so are we."

The hallway after the last bell didn't carry the usual chaos. Maybe it was Friday quiet. Maybe it was something else. Nico lingered by his locker longer than usual, staring into the metal slits like they might offer him clarity. He hadn't spoken much all day—not in class, not at lunch, not even when Jasmin offered him half of her honey sandwich, the kind he usually loved. Leo watched from the corner of the bench near the library door. He didn't approach right away. He waited. Waited the way Ty had once waited for him. Then, when the moment softened, he stood.

Nico noticed him coming. Of course he did. Leo didn't sneak up anymore. He walked on purpose now. No bravado, no swagger. Just truth in his feet. "Hey," he said. No games, no fake smile. Just one word—enough to start. Nico looked at him, guarded but open, the way a person might look at a stranger who knew all their secrets. Leo nodded toward the hallway window seat. "Sit?" Nico didn't respond, but he followed. That was permission enough.

They sat side by side, knees apart, not touching. The silence was heavy, but not hostile. Leo took his time. When he finally spoke, his voice had none of the edges it used to carry. "I used to do what you're doing," he said, steady and low. "Pretend I didn't care. Stay quiet even when I wanted to scream. Apologize just to end the moment." Nico's head turned a little, not fully, just enough to show he was listening. Leo kept going. "I used to shut down when I felt too much. Because feeling stuff made me… weak. Or so I thought."

Nico rubbed his thumb across the hem of his sleeve. Leo watched the movement and softened his voice more. "It's not weakness, Nico. It's a warning light. Something inside you is trying to tell you the truth. That you're scared. Or hurt. Or mad. But when you pretend it's not happening, you start becoming someone else. And I know that feeling too well." Nico's hands stilled. He blinked slowly. "So what do I do instead?" he asked, barely audible.

"You listen to yourself," Leo answered. "Not the fake self. The real one. The one that doesn't need to impress anyone or win a game no one else is playing." He reached into his coat pocket and pulled out a folded piece of lined paper. It was old, maybe from before the suspension. He opened it, and there, scribbled in uneven block letters, were three short sentences: "Say what's true. Don't beg for love. Breathe, then speak." Leo placed it between them. "Ty gave me the first one. I came up with the second. And the third… well, that's yours if you want it."

Nico stared at the page for a long time. He didn't touch it, not yet. His eyes traced each word like they were instructions for a new way to exist. "You think I'm scared?" he asked quietly. Leo didn't flinch. "No," he said. "I know you are. And that's okay. I was too. I still am sometimes. But now I have people who let me say that out loud. And it doesn't cost me anything. No punishment. No teasing. Just space to speak."

The hallway dimmed as the sun shifted through the high windows. Only a few students passed by, and none of them interrupted. Jasmin peeked around the corner once, then faded back without saying a word. She knew this was one of those moments. Nico finally reached for the paper, folding it neatly again, pressing the creases like something sacred. "Can I keep it?" he asked. Leo nodded. "It's yours now. But only if you say one true thing before you leave."

Nico breathed in slowly. He looked at the lockers. Then at the floor. Then at Leo. "I don't want to feel invisible anymore," he said. His voice shook, but didn't crack. Leo didn't smile. He just gave him a nod that felt heavier than a hug. "Then don't," Leo whispered. "You don't have to disappear to survive. You just have to be real." He stood to leave, but Nico grabbed his wrist—not hard, just enough to hold. "Thanks," he said. "For not saying it like a teacher."

Leo tilted his head. "That's because I'm not one," he said. "I'm just someone who got tired of lying to himself." Nico let go. He stood too. And for once, when he walked away, his steps didn't echo like someone trying not to be heard. They sounded like someone trying to be.

Ty stood outside near the bike rack, arms crossed, jacket open to the chill. He saw the two boys exit the building separately but watched their shoulders—less hunched, more square. He didn't say anything when Leo walked past, just gave him a slow nod. Leo returned it. "He'll be okay," Leo said. Ty nodded. "Because you told the truth," he replied. "And truth always leaves a light on." Later that night, Nico would open the paper again and write his own sentence beneath the first three. Just four words. "Real friends let you stay." He didn't show it to anyone. Not yet. But he kept it folded under his pillow. Safe. Waiting.

Alex's voice cracked across the hallway like a cue line in a play that had worn out its script. "You're kind of bossy, aren't you?" he said, eyebrows cocked, eyes darting to his followers. They were mostly boys from Grade 7 who didn't have the nerve to laugh but didn't walk away either. Jasmin didn't flinch. She looked at him—squarely, evenly—and then simply turned. Her backpack bounced against her spine as her boots struck the linoleum floor in a rhythm that didn't need to explain itself. She walked away without a word, and somehow, that hollow silence hurt more than anything she could've said aloud.

Alex blinked once. Then again. His grin sagged. Whatever comeback he had ready never left his throat. The other students didn't say anything. There was no slow clap, no cheer. Just the reality of someone calling out power with dignity, and denying it oxygen. The hallway never echoed before like this—not with noise, but with permission. Permission to not play along.

From the opposite side of the corridor, Nico caught Leo's eye and nodded toward the exit. Leo had seen it too. The quiet power, the stand that didn't shout, the line that didn't bend. Jasmin's refusal hadn't needed backup or applause. She had drawn her boundary without a single weapon. Leo breathed in, slow and deep, and for a moment, his ribs felt taller than his shoulders.

By the time the bell rang, Alex had moved on to another room, but the dent remained. People had watched. People had seen. They weren't cheering Jasmin like a hero from a movie—they were adjusting their compasses. Quietly, inwardly, and in a way that stuck. She didn't do it for them. She did it for herself. That's what made it stick.

That afternoon, Ty walked home with Leo as usual, their bags slung low, their hoods pulled up against the biting wind. They didn't speak until they reached the mailbox at the corner of the street—Ty's street. Ty's house. Leo's house, now, too. That's where they saw her—Ty's mom—waiting on the porch in her coat, holding an envelope. She wasn't crying. She was smiling. It was a small smile, but it was made of something stronger than joy. Relief. Security. A kind of sacred right.

She held the envelope out and said nothing. Ty took it. Leo looked at the seal. It was opened. Not secret. Not hidden. She had already read it and wanted him to know. "He signed," she said gently. "Your father. It's done. You're ours now. Forever." There were no theatrical pauses, no dramatic flair. Just truth.

Leo's knees gave out before the tears did. Ty caught him before he hit the porch. Leo buried his face in Ty's chest and sobbed—not with fear or shame, but with the ache of something finally safe. Ty held him like a brother does—not gripping, not squeezing, just a solid hold of someone who knows the whole story and chooses to stay. Leo didn't say thank you. He didn't have to. The tears were the words.

Ty's father came out slowly and stepped beside them. He didn't reach down or lift Leo up. He waited. Leo looked up, finally, and stood on his own feet—not perfectly, not straight, but upright. Then he walked forward and wrapped his arms around the man's middle. Not a shoulder hug. Not a half-hug. A full-bodied, twenty-minute embrace that neither of them rushed. The sky changed colours while they stood there.

No one interrupted. Ty's mom leaned against the post and wiped one tear, only one. Ty sat on the steps and kept watch, silent and calm. He knew what this was. It wasn't drama. It wasn't performance. It was the breaking of a curse. A generational one. A man who broke another man with fear had finally been stripped of power, and the boy left behind had been claimed—not by paper, but by love. Permanently.

When Leo let go, he stayed close. "Thank you," he said, not to the air, but to both of them. "For being my real parents. Not perfect ones. Just real." The woman touched his cheek. The man nodded, silent again, but strong as granite. Ty gave Leo a nod too, and Leo smiled, for real this time.

Later that evening, when the lights in the kitchen glowed soft and golden, Leo took off his shoes and folded his jacket by the door. Not because anyone told him to. But because this was home now, and he wanted to treat it right. He helped Ty set the table. He passed plates. He didn't make jokes. He didn't pretend. He just sat and listened while Ty's mom asked about everyone's day.

When Jasmin's name came up, Leo straightened. "She said no to Alex today," he said, pride in his voice that wasn't self-serving. "Didn't even explain herself." Ty nodded. "Strongest one in the hallway." Leo chuckled, but it didn't cut. It just echoed what was true.

After dinner, Leo wrote his name on the inside of a new book Ty gave him. He didn't write his old last name. He wrote the one on the adoption form. His new one. Then he closed the book softly and pressed it against his chest for a moment. Not for anyone else to see. Just for him.

In his new room, on clean sheets, under a real roof with love that stayed, Leo whispered a word to himself he never used before. Safe. And then, as if sleep had been waiting its whole life to visit him, he finally let go. Ty, from the next room, heard the silence. He smiled. And he slept, too.

The sky hung low that afternoon, its grey weight pressing down like it knew something would shift. The bell had long since rung, and most of the students had cleared the courtyard, their chatter dissolving into the neighbourhood streets. But Ty remained by the bike racks, his hands tucked into his sleeves, his breath steady despite the wind. He wasn't waiting to ambush. He was waiting to speak. The difference was everything.

Alex arrived late, as if he always made the world wait on him. His hoodie was sharp red, the kind that wanted to be seen, and his stride was loose with arrogance. But Ty didn't move. He let Alex see him first. Let the space close slow. When Alex reached the racks and noticed there was no bike there for Ty, he stopped. "What, you waiting to fight or something?" he said, voice too casual, too calculated.

Ty didn't blink. "No," he said, his voice even. "Just needed to ask one thing." That disarmed Alex more than a swing would have. He adjusted his backpack and squinted like Ty had skipped a line in the script. "What's that supposed to mean?" he asked. Ty nodded once. "Who talks to you like that at home?" And the world—briefly—went still.

For a breathless second, Alex didn't say a thing. The wind blew through the chain-link fence behind them, making it hum. He shifted from one foot to the other. His jaw tensed, like something inside had locked its doors. "That's none of your business," he finally said, but it wasn't sharp. It wasn't angry. It was defensive. Quiet. And laced with something too close to truth.

Ty didn't follow up. He didn't push. He didn't try to explain himself or repeat the question. He just looked at Alex, not with judgement, but with awareness. "It wasn't a trap," Ty said, soft enough for only one person to hear. "Just thought someone should ask." That broke something. Not a sob, not a confession. But Alex's stare faltered, and for the first time all week, he didn't grin.

The weight of it settled differently now. Ty had seen the signs before—shoulders too high, humour too sharp, flattery used like currency. He recognized the echo. Because he had just walked his brother out of the same shadow. The difference now was that Leo had said yes to being loved. Alex wasn't there yet. But something shifted behind his eyes, and Ty caught it.

"I don't need your pity," Alex said, but his voice cracked slightly on the last word. Ty shrugged. "Didn't offer any." It was the exact right reply. No softness to make it condescending. No aggression to make it a power move. Just truth standing upright. Alex looked down at the gravel and kicked a stone, then glanced back up like he might say more—but didn't. Ty waited. Then slowly turned and began to walk away.

Alex didn't follow. But he didn't leave right away, either. He stood there longer than he meant to, staring at the place where Ty had been. Something stuck in his throat. Not anger. Not confusion. Just something raw and heavy and old. Like someone had just put a mirror in front of him and walked off without smashing it.

That night, Ty didn't mention the conversation to anyone. Not because it was secret, but because he respected it. Silence had power when it was used the right way. Over dinner, he let Leo talk about his new blanket, about how he picked the softest one in the store. Their mom beamed. Their dad raised his glass in a quiet toast to peace. Leo's peace. Ty's calm was part of that now.

Meanwhile, across town, Alex lay awake in a room that didn't echo laughter. The walls were thin, and the voices behind them even thinner. At one point, he turned off the lights and looked at the ceiling. He didn't know why that boy's voice stayed with him. He didn't know why it made his chest tight. But it did. And for once, Alex didn't blame anyone for how he felt.

The next day at school, he didn't joke in the hallway. He didn't poke fun at the Grade 5s. He just walked straight to his locker and unpacked in silence. Jasmin noticed. So did Nico. Leo saw it, too—and didn't smile. He just nodded once. The signal had been sent. Whether it would be answered or not, time would tell. But in that moment, by the bike rack, something had been asked that couldn't be unasked. And whether Alex liked it or not, the answer had started to rise.

Alex thought the joke would land. His voice cut through the hallway just before lunch, pitching the words like bait into a crowd that had once flinched for his approval. It had the rhythm of cruelty—sharp timing, mockery tucked under a thin layer of irony. He aimed it toward a younger student with a speech delay, weaving the insult into a pun. But this time, it dropped like a brick into a well. No laughs. No echo. Just stillness.

Ella blinked. Nico shifted on his feet. Jasmin locked her arms across her chest and stared at the floor. Sophie didn't even react—she had already turned away before the sentence ended. Ty kept his head slightly tilted, as if watching a cloud pass too slowly. And Leo, now standing slightly in front of the group, didn't say a word. He just breathed out, slow and deep, then glanced at the younger student and gave him a nod. That nod said everything.

Alex stood frozen for a moment, his expression caught somewhere between confusion and disbelief. "What?" he asked, voice pitching upward. "You all got soft or something?" His laugh was short and hollow. Still, nothing came back. Not even a smirk. He looked to Elia, who used to chuckle at anything if it meant keeping peace, but Elia didn't meet his gaze. He was already walking toward the water fountain, pretending he hadn't heard.

That silence wasn't an accident. It was a decision. The kind of decision you only make once it's safe to make it. And Leo had helped build that safety with every moment he hadn't taken the bait, every hug he'd allowed himself to give and receive, every time he'd said no to the shadows he used to dance with. Alex had no idea, but he'd just stepped into a space where the rules were different now. Where kindness didn't bend anymore.

It was in that moment, as Alex opened his mouth again and then closed it, that the front doors of the school opened with a hydraulic whisper. The cold air swept in, followed by measured footsteps. Mr. Clarke looked up from his conversation in the office doorway. Miss Kara adjusted her clipboard. Even Principal Arnett turned toward the entrance, eyebrows raised in curiosity.

Zenji Takashi entered with the calm of someone who didn't need introduction. He didn't walk fast. He didn't demand attention. But the moment he stepped in, the building shifted. His suit was pressed, his shoes clean, his posture deliberate. The students near the lockers parted, instinctively clearing a path without being asked. Some whispered, others stared. But most, especially those who'd felt real fear before, simply watched.

Ty met him halfway, his hands in his jacket pockets, eyes bright with quiet pride. Leo followed close behind, not clinging, not hiding—just present. His steps were lighter than they'd ever been inside these walls. "Dad," Ty said softly. "This is the one I told you about." His eyes flicked toward Alex, who hadn't moved from his spot near the trophy case. Leo stood beside Ty, and for the first time, introduced someone with reverence.

"This is my dad now," Leo said. Not a whisper. Not a shout. Just firm and real. "Zenji Takashi."

Mr. Takashi offered a small bow, more with his eyes than his body. "Thank you for taking care of my boys," he said to Mr. Clarke, who straightened as if standing inspection. Miss Kara gave a gentle nod. "It's our privilege," she said, more sincerely than she'd ever spoken in that hallway. Principal Arnett, too, smiled with something near relief. For once, everyone could see the family Leo had always needed—but never had.

Alex shrank back a little, just enough for Ty to notice. But Ty didn't gloat. He simply said, "He's not here to scare anyone." Then he looked Alex in the eye. "But you needed to see what a real father looks like."

No one clapped. No one gasped. But the moment burned into the hallway walls. Because strength didn't always roar. Sometimes it walked in wearing polished shoes, offering peace where fear once lived. And in that moment, Alex felt something crack—not because of Zenji's presence, but because of everything that stood behind it. Love. Safety. Truth. The kind of family you don't lie to.

Leo stepped forward. Not to gloat. Not to win. Just to be seen. "You don't get to call me broken anymore," he said to no one in particular. And then he turned to his new dad, who rested a hand lightly on his shoulder. Ty clapped Leo on the back once, and together, they walked toward the staff room to sign one last form—the official update to Leo's student record: new legal guardians. Zenji and Naomi Takashi.

And back in the hallway, Alex remained still. He looked at the crowd that had once mirrored his cruelty. Not one of them made eye contact. They had learned. And he hadn't. Not yet. But maybe now he would. That silence was louder than anything Leo had ever said when he was angry. It was the sound of people refusing to play a rigged game. It was a classroom without shadows.

The playground was quieter than usual that afternoon. The chill in the air kept most kids near the edges of the field or huddled under the canopy beside the gym doors. But Leo stood near the climbing bars, still and watchful. He had learned how to observe, not just react. It wasn't fear anymore that made him quiet—it was awareness. It was what Ty had taught him, what Jasmin had confirmed, and what his new family had shown him in silence: that stillness wasn't weakness.

Alex had been circling like usual. He wore that smile that didn't touch his eyes, the one that moved like bait through shallow water. He moved toward a Grade 4 student this time, a boy sitting alone with cracked glasses and a bruised backpack. Alex crouched beside him, not yelling, not mocking—just whispering things no one else could hear. But Leo didn't need to hear. He had said them before. He knew every word that might be coming.

Leo didn't run. He didn't stomp. He walked. A steady pace. A deliberate line across the schoolyard. Ty, standing under the basketball net, saw the shift and stepped back—not out of fear, but out of trust. He knew Leo didn't need backup this time. He needed space to speak the truth on his own terms.

The boy with the glasses looked up when Leo approached. Alex turned his head, expecting a challenge, maybe a shove, something he could weaponize. But Leo didn't flinch. He just stood in front of the younger boy and said it plainly.

"You're not invisible," he said to Alex, voice firm but low. "We see you. And we're not scared."

Alex blinked. There was no audience this time. No one clapped. No one gasped. Even the Grade 4 boy seemed unsure what had just happened. But Leo didn't need anyone to understand it—not right away. He had spoken it for himself. For the boy behind him. For the version of himself he used to be.

Alex stood up straight, taller than Leo by a head, but somehow smaller in presence. His mouth opened, closed. Whatever words he had lined up fell flat before they could launch. And then, without saying anything, he stepped backward, then sideways, and walked away across the pavement. Not defeated. Not reformed. But interrupted. And that interruption mattered.

No one chased after him. The group didn't gather in a circle. There was no celebration, no slogans, no pat on the back. Just a quiet understanding, passed from glance to glance: Leo had chosen. And it was final. The kind of final that doesn't need to be spoken again.

Recess ended. The bell echoed once across the field. Children shuffled back inside in pairs and threes, some still talking, others dragging their feet. But Leo stayed behind for a moment. He looked at the boy with the glasses and offered him a fist bump. The boy hesitated, then bumped it back. That was all.

When school let out, Leo and Ty walked together down the snowy path toward home. They didn't talk much. They didn't need to. The silence was comfortable, full of things already said. Their boots crunched in rhythm across the salted sidewalk. The sun hung low and golden behind the bare trees.

When they got home, the door opened with that same soft creak Leo had come to know in the last few weeks. The smell of supper drifted from the kitchen—soy sauce, garlic, rice warming on the stove. Naomi Takashi turned from the counter, wiping her hands on a towel, her smile patient and real. Zenji stepped out from his study, not in uniform today, just in a sweater and socks. His eyes met Leo's with calm curiosity.

Leo dropped his bag beside the door and looked at them—really looked. "I love you," he said to Naomi first, then to Zenji. His voice didn't crack. His eyes did.

Naomi stepped forward and wrapped him in her arms. "We love you too," she whispered into his hair, holding him like he belonged there. Zenji followed a moment later, resting one hand on Leo's back, steady and strong. And then Ty joined them, arms tight around his brother. "I love you, Leo," Ty said, soft but certain.

Leo didn't answer—not with words. He just nodded against Ty's shoulder and let the warmth fill him, down to the marrow. It didn't feel borrowed. It didn't feel temporary. It felt earned. It felt real. And it was. That night, there were no nightmares. Just quiet dreams, and the knowledge that when you say no for the right reasons, it doesn't end something—it begins something. Something worth defending.

CHAPTER 10: WHAT IF THEY SAY IT'S YOUR FAULT?

It was the kind of morning Nico had waited for without knowing it. The air felt softer somehow, and the usual grind of boots on the playground pavement didn't sound like marching. The front doors opened at precisely 8:05, and instead of Leo storming in, face half-hidden beneath a scowl and hair fallen like a curtain over his eyes, there he was—smiling. Not big. Not loud. But real. Ty walked beside him, not in front, not behind, just shoulder to shoulder, a rhythm they'd fallen into without trying. A few Grade 5s whispered near the lockers, their eyes flicking toward the boy who used to throw words like weapons. But Leo didn't flinch. He gave a nod, the kind that said, I know, and I'm still here.

Jeremy was already standing in line outside the classroom, lips tight, hands fidgeting with the strap of his lunch bag. He didn't look up when Leo passed, but something shifted. Leo didn't say anything at first. He just slowed his steps, crouched next to him without fuss, and whispered, "I get nervous too." Jeremy blinked, his fingers twitching, then nodded with jerky insistence. Leo smiled again, small and steady, like holding a candle out of the wind. "Can I walk with you?" he asked gently, and Jeremy, still silent, nodded again. Nico watched the whole thing from the stairwell, unseen, and his throat tightened. Not because Leo had changed—but because Leo had chosen to.

By second period, whispers had stopped. The kindergarteners, who always waved at Ty, started waving at Leo too. One little girl, wearing a fuzzy pink hoodie, ran up to him in the hall and tugged his sleeve. "You look like a good brother," she said plainly, and ran off without waiting for an answer. Leo turned to Ty, stunned. "Did she just—?" But Ty only nodded. "That's how they see you now." No high-five followed. No bravado. Just quiet walking down the corridor, like they had a job to do.

Alex leaned against the wall outside the resource room, arms folded, grin curled like a fishing hook. "So what now?" he asked Leo. "You're the teacher's pet?" The words were dipped in bait. Leo didn't bite. "No," he said, adjusting his backpack. "I just stopped being what you still are." He didn't raise his voice, didn't perform. He walked away. Ty followed without needing to say a word. In that moment, Alex wasn't in control. And the hallway belonged to someone else.

Inside the office, Mr. Arnett watched from the small security monitor. He turned the volume down on the intercom and smiled to himself. Leo hadn't needed pushing that day. The boy had stepped up first, without warning, without applause. "Good," the principal whispered under his breath, sipping his tea. "Very good." Even the secretary noticed. She leaned in and whispered, "That boy's different now." Arnett simply nodded. "He's becoming who he was meant to be."

Back in class, Jeremy stumbled over his own name when doing roll call. The word came out stuck: "Juh… Juh… Juh…" His face reddened, eyes cast down, breath caught in his chest. Before anyone could laugh or sigh or glance sideways, Leo said calmly, "Jeremy." The teacher looked up. "Thank you, Leo." Jeremy didn't speak again for the rest of the lesson. He just wrote, slowly, carefully. But he sat up straighter. That was enough for now.

At lunch, Ty leaned against the edge of the bench and handed Leo half his sandwich without asking. Leo accepted it. "You know," he muttered between bites, "I thought this would feel weird." Ty shrugged. "Being decent?" Leo smirked. "Being watched while I'm decent." The joke didn't land loud, but it landed gently. Across the room, Jasmin raised her brow at Nico. "Is he actually… okay?" Nico shrugged. "Not okay. But trying. For real this time."

The fourth graders passed the pair in the hall, Jeremy now tucked quietly beside Leo like a shadow that had learned to walk in step. Ty bent low to tie his shoe, and Jeremy whispered something none of them heard. Leo answered with a thumbs-up. It didn't matter what was said. The posture said everything. Safety had a shape. And Leo had become part of it.

There was still a kind of caution in the air, like everyone was waiting for Leo to snap back to his old self. But by recess, no eruption had come. Instead, Leo found a piece of sidewalk chalk and drew a wide ring around a corner of the playground. "Safe zone," he said. "No yelling allowed." A few younger kids followed, uncertain. One little boy asked if it was real. "If you believe it is," Leo said. "Then it is."

Ty sat near the fence, notebook open, pretending to sketch trees while actually watching the interaction. He didn't need to monitor Leo—but he wanted to witness the transformation. There was pride in his eyes, but not ownership. Ty wasn't Leo's master. He was his brother. One forged in silence and fire. And fire remembered its shape even when it stopped burning.

At the end of the day, Jeremy tried again during goodbye. "Th—thank… yuh…" The rest didn't come. He looked away. Leo didn't push. He just smiled and said, "You're welcome." That night, Jeremy's mother called the school. She left a message. "My son said thank you today," her voice cracked. "To a boy named Leo. I just wanted you to know… he's never said that word before. Not once."

Mr. Arnett listened twice. Then he played it for Miss Kara. She cried. "We almost gave up on him," she whispered. "Not Jeremy. Leo." Arnett folded his arms and shook his head. "Never. He just needed to be seen."

As the doors closed behind them, Ty and Leo walked side by side. The street was noisy, full of horns and bikes and laughter. But Leo looked calm. Like he had nothing to prove anymore. "I didn't know it could feel like this," he said suddenly. Ty tilted his head. "Like what?" Leo blinked once. "Like I belong." Ty didn't respond right away. Instead, he held out his fist. Leo bumped it. "You always did," Ty said. "You just didn't know it yet."

At the corner, Leo turned to wave goodbye to Jeremy, who peered out of his car window and grinned. His mouth opened wide, and the word came out clear as daylight: "Bye!" Leo waved back. "That was perfect," he whispered. And he meant it. Inside him, something old crumbled. And something new stood in its place. And it didn't need to be loud to be true.

It happened near the back of the classroom, between coats and backpacks that smelled like recess. A quiet boy named Arjun stood frozen beside his desk, his face pale, shoulders hunched, one hand still gripping the zipper of his lunch bag. The room had not yet settled from the lunch bell, and already the blame had been dropped like a trapdoor beneath him. "He took it," said a Grade 6 girl with long braids and a voice sharpened to cut. "My pencil case's gone. I saw him near my desk." It wasn't a shout. It didn't need to be. It was loud in the way that shame is loud.

Leo heard it from his seat. Heard it, but more than that—he recognized it. The timing, the tone, the tilt of the head and the way her friends had already begun to circle in with little nods of manufactured agreement. It was an act. Practised. Rehearsed. The lie wasn't in the words. It was in the theatre of the accusation. He'd done it himself, more times than he cared to admit. Blaming felt like power once. Now, it felt like poison on his tongue. And he wasn't going to let Arjun drink it.

He stood slowly, but with purpose. Not to be noticed, not to be dramatic. Just enough to matter. Ty saw him move and said nothing. Nico locked eyes with him and gave a single nod. Ella, three desks over, froze with her pencil mid-air, sensing the shift before understanding the reason. Leo crossed the room without looking at the teacher. He didn't need permission. Some things you do because they're right, not because you're told.

"Let me see your bag," Leo said to the girl—not loud, not angry, just steady. She blinked, startled, then clutched it closer. "Why?" Her voice cracked slightly. "Because you're pointing fingers," Leo said, "and I know what that usually means." She tried to laugh, a bitter, fake sound. "What are you, the blame police now?" Leo didn't move. "No. Just someone who used to lie exactly like that." The room quieted. Even the teacher, halfway through a sentence, stopped to watch.

Ty stood up next, but didn't walk forward. He leaned on his desk and folded his arms. His presence was the signal. Jasmin turned in her seat and waited. Arjun looked up, his eyes wide, a mixture of fear and disbelief clouding his face. "I didn't take it," he whispered, voice cracking like a branch underfoot. "I know," Leo said without turning. "I saw your hands the whole time. You didn't go near her desk."

The girl hesitated, then scoffed and dumped her bag onto her desk. Her books tumbled out, along with a crumpled napkin, a broken mechanical pencil, and finally, her own pencil case—half-zipped and stained with marker ink. It had been there all along. "Oops," she muttered, barely audible. "Guess I was wrong." Leo didn't flinch. "No," he said. "You guessed I wouldn't call you out. That's different."

The teacher stepped forward then, clearing his throat with awkward tension. "Thank you, Leo," he said carefully. "That was handled with… maturity." Leo didn't smile. "I'm not trying to impress anyone," he said. "Just trying to fix what I used to break."

He turned to Arjun then, finally, and crouched slightly to meet his eye level. "You're safe. You don't owe anyone an apology." Arjun nodded slowly, his eyes wet but not blinking. "Th-thank you," he whispered. "You're the first one who… believed me."

Later that afternoon, Leo found himself back near the stairwell, this time not hiding or lurking, but waiting. Ty joined him with a juice box and a knowing grin. "That was clean," Ty said. "You didn't overdo it." Leo sighed. "I saw the look in her eyes. It was mine. I couldn't let it happen again." Ty bumped shoulders with him. "Now you know how it feels. Protecting instead of performing."

Jasmin arrived moments later, holding her sketchpad like a shield. "You scared her," she said, half-impressed, half-curious. "Good," Leo replied. "Someone should. She uses lies the way I used to." Nico trailed behind, hands in his pockets. "So what happens next?" he asked. "Next time it'll be someone else. Another kid. Another story." Leo looked up. "Then we do it again."

The next day, Arjun passed Leo in the hall and slipped a note into his hand. It read: I wish I had a big brother like you. Leo folded it carefully, placed it in the back of his binder, and didn't tell anyone. But when Ty asked him why he smiled at nothing during math, Leo just shrugged. "Something good happened," he said. "That's all."

At dismissal, the girl with the braids avoided eye contact. She didn't apologise. She didn't need to. Her silence was the closest thing to admission Leo needed. He'd seen that silence in the mirror too many times not to recognize its weight.

Jeremy stood at the gate waiting for his ride, and when Leo passed, he reached out and tapped his elbow. "I s-saw what you did," he said. Leo looked down at him, brow raised. Jeremy nodded, expression serious. "Th-thank you for being good." Leo ruffled his hair. "Thanks for noticing."

In Ty's room that evening, Zenji Takashi watched from the kitchen as Leo and Ty sprawled on the floor with their homework. Naomi brought them juice and fruit, and for a long time, no one said anything heavy. But later, when the lights dimmed and bedtime crept in, Leo whispered to Ty, "That felt better than getting away with stuff ever did." Ty smiled in the dark. "That's because it was real." And for once, Leo didn't feel like he had to explain it. He just let it be true.

Ty didn't raise his voice when he spoke about blame. He didn't pace the room or throw down dramatic statements like some kind of classroom hero. Instead, he leaned on the edge of the desk during their lunch period while Nico, Ella, Jasmin, and Leo gathered quietly around him. Leo sat cross-legged on the floor, elbows on his knees, hands gripping the edges of his sleeves like he was holding back something old and painful. He was. And Ty could tell. "The thing about blame," Ty said, steady as granite, "is that it doesn't have to be true to stick. It just has to feel possible. That's how they win."

Jasmin tilted her head. "What do you mean feel possible?" she asked. Ty gave a small nod, not surprised she picked up on the nuance. "It means if you already feel bad about something—anything—they can take that feeling and attach it to something you didn't even do. The trick is, if they hand you the shame, and you hold it for them, they win." Ella frowned. "Even if it's not your fault?" "Especially if it's not your fault," Ty answered. "Because then you start thinking you're the broken one. And if they can make you doubt yourself… well, they don't even have to yell anymore."

Leo swallowed. "I used to do that." His voice was low, but no one turned away. No one interrupted. "I'd say someone forgot something, or messed up, or made me mad, and I'd find a way to make it sound like it was their fault. Even if I started it. Especially if I started it." Nico didn't nod. He didn't need to. His silence was enough. "And it worked," Leo added. "Because they didn't know how to push it back."

Ty crossed his arms loosely, watching Leo's face, then the floor. "Did you do it because it gave you power?" Leo looked up. "I did it because I didn't want to be the one getting in trouble. And yeah. Power felt… safer." "It's always about safety," Ty said. "Even if it's fake safety. If you can put the weight on someone else, then you don't have to carry your own."

Ella pulled her knees to her chest. "But what if someone blames you and you really don't know how to prove you didn't do it?" "That's the trap," Ty replied. "That's the trick. That's how they control people. Blame works like a gaslight—it fogs your memory and makes your voice shrink. You start apologizing for being confused. You explain things that didn't happen. And suddenly, they've got the power without ever raising their hand."

Nico leaned forward, elbows on his thighs. "So what do we do when it happens?" Ty didn't hesitate. "Don't carry it. That's the only way it breaks. If someone hands you shame and you don't take it—if you say 'no, that's not mine'—they can't use it anymore. They'll try something else. But that one loses power."

Leo exhaled, long and shaky. "That's what I didn't get. When people didn't react, I thought they were weak. But now I think they were strong. They just didn't give me the reaction I wanted." Jasmin reached out and placed her hand over his without saying anything. Leo didn't move it away.

Ty nodded. "That's why it works. Because it's invisible. No one sees blame being passed. It's not like pushing someone in the hallway. It's whispers. Half-truths. Pity traps. And if no one teaches you the signs, you'll carry that weight your whole life without even knowing it was never yours to hold."

Ella blinked. "That sounds like what happened to Sophie." The others looked up. "Alex blamed her for the note he wrote," she said. "And she almost believed it was her fault for being there." Nico's voice darkened. "That's how he works. It's not just lies. It's guilt he wraps around people like rope. And most don't even know they're tied up."

Ty nodded. "That's why we need to call it out. But not loud. Not showy. Just firm. Blame only has power if we accept it. If we don't? It folds." Leo raised his eyes slowly. "And if it doesn't fold?" Ty shrugged. "Then we hold each other up until it does."

The silence that followed was heavy, but not sad. It was the weight of recognition. The kind of silence that comes when truth has been spoken and no one dares interrupt it. Jasmin's pencil scratched quietly across her notebook as she drew a small shield. She didn't say why. But they all knew.

Ty stepped away from the desk and picked up his lunch bag. "You're all stronger than you think," he said over his shoulder. "Just remember—truth doesn't yell. It doesn't need to. It just stands." Leo whispered something under his breath. Nico caught it. "What'd you say?" Leo looked at him, not ashamed anymore. "I said I think I can stand too." And he meant it.

Ty didn't say a word when Allan walked into the room. Not at first. The new boy introduced himself with perfect manners, his backpack slung casually over one shoulder like he belonged there before he even sat down. His voice was calm, confident, polished—not like a kid finding his place, but like someone who already knew which seat held power and which people would give it to him. Mr. Clarke shook his hand with genuine warmth. "Welcome, Allan. We're glad to have you." The others mumbled greetings, some more interested than others. But Ty's eyes narrowed. Just slightly. Just enough. Because he'd seen that smile before. Not just once. In Leo. In Alex. In himself, years ago, when no one was looking and pretending came easier than truth.

Leo spotted it too, almost instantly. He didn't say anything either. He just lowered his pencil and watched Allan choose a seat—strategically two chairs away from Sophie, directly across from Mila, beside a Grade 6 boy who rarely spoke but listened to everything. It was the kind of choice that wasn't random. Not desperate either. Calculated. Performed. Leo remembered making that same kind of entrance last year, when he didn't care who got hurt as long as he wasn't the one being watched too closely. Ty felt it too. Not fear. Not jealousy. A tension. Like something shifting beneath the floorboards.

"Hi," Allan said cheerfully to Ella, who gave him a polite nod but didn't open the door for conversation. "I like your hair." She blinked. "Thanks." It was too fast, too familiar. Jasmin raised her eyebrows at Nico, who didn't respond out loud. Instead, he scribbled two words on the margin of his notebook and angled it toward Ty without lifting his eyes. Too smooth. Ty's mouth didn't move, but the crease between his eyebrows deepened by a fraction.

At recess, Allan wasted no time. He found Alex within minutes—standing beneath the basketball net, bragging about something no one believed. "You're Alex, right?" Allan asked, his smile just shy of charming. "Heard you've got the best shot here." Alex looked him up and down and grinned. "Guess you heard right." The two boys shook hands. Just like that. Two mirrors meeting. Leo watched from the far bench, eyes narrowed, knees bouncing. "He's not just polite," he muttered. "He's studying us."

Ty didn't answer. He didn't need to. Instead, he stood slowly, brushed the gravel from his jeans, and said to Leo, "Come." Not a command. A brother's word. Leo followed without question. They walked toward the back of the schoolyard where no one else was, where even the birds seemed to listen more closely. "You see it, don't you?" Ty asked. "All of it." Leo nodded. "It's like watching the worst parts of yourself walk back into the room after you finally kicked them out."

"You're not that anymore," Ty said, quiet but unshakeable. "But you remember how it worked. You remember what came next." Leo's voice cracked. "They get in by making you feel lucky they noticed you. Then they test how far they can twist things." "And you?" Ty asked. "How did it feel when no one saw through it?" Leo's answer came without hesitation. "Powerful. Until it wasn't. Until someone did. And it broke."

Jasmin joined them a few minutes later. "He asked Mila if she wanted to hang out after school. Said she looked like someone who had good stories." Ty tilted his head. "What'd she say?" Jasmin smiled. "She said, 'Maybe. But I only share stories with people who ask real questions.'" Ty nodded once. "She's learning."

By the time the final bell rang, Allan had charmed three Grade 4s, two teachers, and at least one hall monitor. He'd offered to help clean up markers, carry a box of sports cones, and even complimented the office secretary on her earrings. Nico rolled his eyes. "He's writing a script," he muttered. "But I don't think he knows we're reading the footnotes."

That night, Leo sat on Ty's bed, legs tucked beneath him, a pillow across his lap. "I'm scared," he admitted. "Not of him. Of me. I don't want to turn into that again." Ty shook his head. "You won't. Because you remember. And because you've got a whole circle now that doesn't let masks sit on your face for long." "I can't tell if he's worse than I was," Leo whispered. "Doesn't matter," Ty replied. "The shadow's the same. And now we name it."

Ella called after dinner. "He told Sophie she reminds him of his sister. Sophie said she doesn't have time for strangers telling lies with compliments." Jasmin snorted in the background. "She's already ahead of where we were last year." "Good," Ty said into the receiver. "Keep your eyes open. Just don't let your guard turn into a sword. We observe. We don't cut."

By Thursday, it was clear that Allan wasn't new to the game. He'd already worked his way into one lunch table, half of gym class, and even tried to sit beside Ty in science. Ty didn't stop him—but he didn't open the door either. He simply answered questions with precision, not invitation. Leo, for his part, stayed quieter than usual. But his eyes were never off Allan. Not once.

During afternoon cleanup, Allan told Jeremy he could help him pronounce his name better—said he had a trick. Ty stepped in. "Jeremy doesn't need fixing," he said gently, but with enough edge that Allan blinked twice before nodding. Jeremy looked up at Ty with wide eyes, and Leo ruffled Jeremy's hair as they passed. "Don't let people name you wrong," Leo said softly. "You already have your name. And it's perfect."

That night, Ty lay awake staring at the ceiling. "We need to talk to Dad," he said. Leo didn't ask why. "Yeah," he said. "Because I think Allan's playing a deeper game." Ty nodded. "And we're not going to play back. We're going to expose it. One layer at a time." And for the first time in a long time, Leo didn't feel like the one being watched. He felt like the one doing the watching.

Ella didn't mean to hear it. She wasn't snooping, and she wasn't looking for trouble. She was standing by the cubby area, zipping up her hoodie, when Alex's voice reached her—not loud, not angry, just measured, calculated, soft enough that he thought no one would catch it. "I saw her take the glue," he said to a seventh grader named Logan, nodding toward a sixth-grade girl named Nessa who hadn't spoken once all morning. Ella's eyebrows twitched. She didn't say anything. Not yet. But something in her tightened, like the way a string hums when it's pulled too far and not quite snapped.

She glanced toward Nessa, who didn't defend herself, didn't even look up. Her fingers twisted in her sleeves, and her shoulders hunched—not guilty, but scared. Alex knew exactly how to spot a kid like that. The quiet ones who wouldn't push back. Ella turned to go, slow and calm, but the words Alex had used looped back in her mind. They weren't just accusations. They were designed to stick. To be whispered and remembered. To make others look away from the liar and toward the innocent. That was the first signal. The first whisper. And it sounded far too familiar.

She waited until lunchtime before she wrote it down. Just a few lines in her journal. Nothing loud. Nothing dangerous. Just the truth. Alex accused Nessa of stealing glue. No one checked. She looked scared. He sounded calm. He wasn't telling the truth. Ella closed the notebook softly and tucked it beneath her lunchbox. Her hand hovered over it for a second. Then she pulled it away. She didn't need to do anything else. Not yet. Because observation came first. Always.

Ty passed her at recess and gave a small nod, no words. Just one shared glance. He had taught her that silence could hold more weight than speeches. And she was beginning to feel it in her chest now—not as fear, but as strength. The kind of strength that didn't need to announce itself. The kind that watched. The kind that waited. She caught Leo looking at Jeremy across the field, where a group of older boys were mocking the way Jeremy tripped over his R's and T's when he tried to explain the rules of the game. Leo stood up without hesitation.

He walked toward Jeremy, his steps calm, his eyes steady. One of the older boys laughed and said, "Can't even say his name right." Leo's hand rested gently on Jeremy's shoulder. "He doesn't have to," Leo said plainly. "We already know it." Jeremy blinked at him, half in confusion, half in something close to relief. The other boys looked at each other, unsure of what had just happened. Leo didn't shout. He didn't threaten. He didn't demand. He just stood there, beside Jeremy, like a wall they couldn't get through.

After they walked away, Jeremy looked up at him and said, "They think I'm d-d-dumb." Leo shook his head. "They're the dumb ones. You're just someone whose mouth takes a little longer to catch up with your thoughts. That's not weakness, Jeremy. That's just a different rhythm." Jeremy didn't answer, but he smiled. That kind of smile—the real kind—was all Leo needed.

Later that afternoon, Ty sat with Ella under the tree near the soccer field. "You saw something," he said. It wasn't a question. Ella nodded. "Alex blamed someone. I don't think anyone else noticed. He made it sound small, but it wasn't." Ty leaned back against the bark. "It never is. The first lie is always soft. That's how they get you to stop listening to your instincts." Ella looked away. "So why do they get away with it?" Ty shrugged. "Because most people are trained to doubt the quiet ones. But not us. Not anymore."

That night, Leo sat at the kitchen table with Zenji and Naomi, eating slow, chewing every bite like it was worth tasting. He still wasn't used to calling them Mom and Dad aloud, but he thought it sometimes. Quietly. Reverently. "Jeremy's got guts," he said between bites. "He still talks even when it's hard. Even when they laugh." Zenji nodded. "That's courage. The silent kind." Naomi reached for his hand and squeezed it once. "You used to fake strength. Now you give the real kind to others."

Ty leaned on the kitchen doorframe, arms folded. "Ella saw something today. Something Alex thought he hid." Leo's eyes sharpened. "Who?" "Nessa," Ty said. "He blamed her for something he did. Ella wrote it down. First step." Leo exhaled slowly. "Then it starts again." Ty shook his head. "Not this time. This time, we're the line they don't cross."

The next morning, Jeremy ran up to Leo before the bell rang. "I d-d-drew you something." He handed him a folded piece of lined paper. Inside was a drawing of two stick figures, one labeled "Me," the other labeled "You," both standing on a hill with capes behind them. "You're a superhero now," Jeremy whispered. "But with no mask." Leo's throat tightened. "Thanks," he said. "I'll keep it in my desk." And he did.

Ella sat beside Jasmin in the library and whispered, "Why do you think people like Alex lie like that?" Jasmin considered. "Because the truth scares them. Because control feels safer than honesty." Ella nodded. "Then we make honesty feel safer. Bit by bit." Jasmin smiled. "That's the warrior way."

When dismissal came, Leo waited at the bottom of the stairs for Jeremy, just like always. And when Jeremy dropped his bag and his pencils scattered, Leo helped him pick them up—without saying a word. Just a look. A nod. A moment that said, "You matter." And Jeremy understood. Alex walked past, smirking. He nodded at Leo, but Leo didn't nod back. He didn't frown either. He just watched. And Alex kept walking. Because he felt it now—the kind of eyes that saw through masks. And the silence that waited behind them.

The library was quiet, not because it was the rule, but because every student felt something sacred was about to happen. Naomi Takashi stood at the front of the room, not behind a podium, not holding papers, but with her hands gently folded, palms open. The moment she smiled, the air changed. It wasn't the kind of smile that asked for applause. It was the kind that said, You're already enough. Her eyes scanned the room without judgement. She saw them all—not as misbehaving kids or quiet ones with secrets, but as people.

She didn't start with her title. She didn't say, "I'm here to talk about wellness." Instead, she walked forward and said, "There is nothing wrong with you." A hush fell deeper than silence. It was the kind of quiet that made the smallest breath feel like thunder. Leo's fingers, which had been locked together under the table, loosened just a little. Jeremy sat straighter in his seat. Ty leaned his chin into his hand, watching his mother speak with the calm strength of someone who had already been through fire.

"When a child breaks something, they often say it wasn't their fault," Naomi continued. "But sometimes, when a child breaks inside, they blame themselves before anyone else has a chance to speak." She didn't raise her voice. She didn't walk the room. She simply stood there, her voice steady. "I want to speak to the ones who have been told they're too sensitive. Too dramatic. Too quiet. Too angry. Too anything. You weren't too much. You were just around people who didn't know how to handle love with that much power."

Leo's heart beat so loudly in his ears he could barely hear the rest. But he caught the next words. They landed like sunlight. "You were never the problem. You were the proof that someone else didn't know how to love." He blinked. Hard. His throat felt thick. His hands trembled, and not from fear—but from release. From something unclenching. From something buried finding air.

Naomi looked directly at Leo without naming him. She didn't need to. "If someone made you feel like you had to earn being loved, they were wrong," she said gently. "Real love doesn't keep score. It doesn't manipulate. It doesn't hide behind gifts or smiles that feel cold underneath. Real love says, 'Even now. Especially now. I see you.'" Leo dropped his gaze. His chest ached—not in panic, but in relief. She had said the words he didn't even know he was waiting to hear.

Jeremy reached for Leo's hand under the table. He didn't say anything. But Leo felt it—the way Jeremy's fingers wrapped his with full trust. Full belief. A kind of love that didn't require Leo to perform or prove anything. And when Naomi finished speaking, she stepped down from the front like nothing extraordinary had happened. But the room stayed still. Not a rustle. Not a whisper. Just hearts beating. One after another, one beside another.

Mr. Arnett stepped forward and thanked her, but his voice was hoarse. His eyes glassed. He had never heard emotional truth delivered like that to children. Not in his years as a teacher. Not from any workshop or textbook. Naomi had given language to something the children already knew—but had never been allowed to say. Ty gave his mother a soft nod as she passed him. She smiled back, but didn't stop. She had no need to be admired. She had only come to deliver the message.

As the bell rang for the next period, students moved slowly, like their feet didn't quite want to leave that space. Leo stayed seated. So did Jeremy. And when Jeremy stood, he turned to Leo, reached up with both arms, and hugged him with the full weight of his tiny fourth-grade body. He didn't say thank you. He didn't say anything. But Leo felt it. In that hug, he was not the villain from before. He was the protector. The safe place. The big brother.

The Principal walked by at just that moment and paused at the sight. For the first time, his face softened in a way Leo had never seen. "That," the Principal said quietly, "is something I'll remember." He didn't ask questions. He didn't hand out praise like a gold sticker. He simply nodded and walked on, letting the truth stand where it was—visible, grounded, alive.

Ty caught up with Leo by the lockers. "You good?" he asked. Leo shrugged. "I don't know. I think so. That thing your mom said... about not being the problem?" Ty nodded. "It's true." Leo looked at him. "Even if I did bad things before?" Ty reached over and flicked Leo's ear. "Especially then. You didn't know how to ask for love. Now you do." Leo didn't argue. For once, he didn't feel the need to.

Later that evening, at dinner, Leo said it out loud. "I'm really glad I live here." Zenji didn't say anything. He just leaned across the table and ruffled Leo's hair. Naomi smiled, still quiet. Ty reached over and stole a carrot from Leo's plate. Leo didn't even scowl. He just laughed. A full sound. A warm sound. The kind you don't fake.

When bedtime came, Leo lingered a moment outside Naomi's room. She noticed. "Want to talk?" she asked. Leo shook his head. "I just wanted to say... thanks. For the thing you said today." Naomi stood and walked over. "I meant every word." Leo nodded. "I know. That's why it hurt. But in the good way." She hugged him. Not because he needed it. But because she did. As he crawled into bed that night, Leo looked out the window. The sky wasn't fully dark yet. One star blinked from behind a cloud. He didn't make a wish. He didn't need to. What he had now wasn't magic. It was real. It was truth. And it had finally found its voice.

The note was folded so small it looked like a candy wrapper. Sophie didn't want to open it. She'd seen how the class passed things like that—like secrets, like traps. But the corner had her name on it in a swirl she didn't recognize. She waited until lunch was almost over to unfold it. When she read the words inside, her stomach dropped. It was cruel. Mean in a way that was soft-edged, but sharp enough to cut. And it had Nico's name signed at the bottom in looping letters that didn't look like Nico at all.

She didn't tell anyone at first. Not even Jasmin. Not even Ella. But Ty saw it. He had been watching the way Sophie's shoulders curled inward, the way her hands clenched the note like it was a piece of garbage she couldn't let go of. He walked over without saying anything, held out his hand, and waited. When Sophie passed him the note, his face didn't change—but his eyes did. He tilted the paper, looked at the signature, then at Nico, and shook his head once. "This isn't his handwriting," he said softly. "Not even close."

Nico looked stunned. "What—what's not mine?" he asked. Ty handed him the note, and Nico read it silently, the colour draining from his face. "I never wrote this," he said, looking around. "I swear." But before anyone could question him, Leo stepped forward, calm, steady, changed. "It was Alex," Leo said. His voice didn't rise. He didn't accuse. He didn't flinch. "I've seen that exact loop on his lowercase 'e'. He thinks people don't notice, but I do."

Ty backed him up. "Same slant. Same spacing between letters. Same habit of switching between capital and lowercase in the same word." Mr. Clarke, who had been walking past, stopped when he heard the word "note." Ty turned to him. "Mr. Clarke, there's been a forgery. Someone tried to make it look like Nico wrote something he didn't. Sophie got hurt because of it." Sophie didn't speak, but she didn't need to. She nodded once, tears prickling at her eyes but refusing to fall.

Mr. Clarke read the note, frowned, and walked straight toward the main office. "Come with me," he said to Ty and Leo. "We'll handle this now." Nico started to follow, but Ty shook his head. "Stay with Sophie," he said. "That's what matters right now." And Nico did. He sat beside her, both of them staring at the empty lunch bag between them like it held something heavy. He didn't ask if she believed him. She didn't ask if it hurt. They both already knew the answers.

Down the hallway, Leo walked beside Ty like they were on a mission—but not the old kind. Not the kind that ended in destruction or bragging. This one was about honour. When they reached the Principal's office, Mr. Arnett met them at the door. He already knew. Ty explained the handwriting. Leo backed him up with examples he'd remembered from group assignments. Mr. Arnett called Alex in with the vice-principal present. Alex denied it, of course. But the note sat between them like a trap he set for himself.

"I'd like to compare this to your previous handwriting samples," Mr. Arnett said without a trace of anger. Just quiet authority. Alex paled. The meeting didn't end with a punishment that day, but the warning was clear. The truth was in motion, and Alex couldn't lie his way out of it forever. Back in the hallway, Jeremy had waited for Leo. He stood just outside the office, his small hands gripping the straps of his backpack. He didn't say anything. He just leaned into Leo's side when he appeared.

Leo smiled softly. "You alright, little man?" Jeremy nodded. "You're my brother," he whispered. Leo blinked but didn't look away. He held out his hand, and Jeremy took it. They walked back to class like that, side by side, the older one guarding the younger without needing to be told how. Mr. Arnett followed behind them slowly. He watched the pair, then stepped quietly beside Leo once they reached the classroom door.

"Leo," Mr. Arnett said gently, "I notice Jeremy sticks to you like glue lately. Is everything alright?" Leo nodded. "Yeah," he said. "He just trusts me. I think… I think he feels safe. I don't mind it." He paused. "Is it okay? I mean, with school stuff?" Mr. Arnett placed a hand on Leo's shoulder. "It's more than okay. It's what this school is supposed to be for." Leo looked up, surprised. "Then I'm glad," he said. "Because I'm not letting him go."

Inside the room, the class watched as Leo walked in with Jeremy still beside him. No one made a joke. No one whispered. They just watched. Something in Leo had changed permanently. He wasn't a boy trying to prove he wasn't bad anymore. He was a boy who had nothing to prove—because he'd already become what he was meant to be. Ty gave him a quick nod across the room, a silent signal passed between brothers.

Jasmin and Ella moved to make space for Jeremy at their group table without being asked. Nico turned toward Leo and mouthed, Thank you. Leo gave a half-smile, the kind that didn't need to be big to be real. Later that day, Jeremy left a sticky note on Leo's desk. It read, in shaky printing, U R My Hero. Leo folded it up slowly and tucked it into his pocket like a sacred scroll.

Ty watched the whole thing from his seat. He didn't say anything until after school. When they were walking home, he bumped Leo's shoulder. "That's twice today you did something I didn't even see coming." Leo grinned. "What can I say? I had a good teacher." Ty laughed. "Nah, bro. You had the courage. That's all you." And somewhere, a page turned—not in a notebook, but in the kind of story that's written in people. In the kind of book you don't read with your eyes, but your life.

It happened fast. Too fast. A hallway whisper turned to a classroom rumour, and then Mr. Arnett was standing in the doorway with his clipboard. His eyes swept the room, and for a moment, it felt like the air paused. "Nico," he said. "Can I see you in my office, please?" Chairs scraped back. Heads turned. Nico blinked, confused. He hadn't said a word all morning. Not one. Jasmin's eyebrows pulled in. Ty straightened. Leo sat still, but something shifted in his chest like an old door unlocking.

Nico walked past Leo on his way out, and Leo could see it—the tiny flinch in his friend's shoulder, the tight line of his jaw. Nico didn't look back. He didn't argue. He just followed the Principal down the hallway like he was used to it. Like blame was a coat that had always fit too well. But Leo knew the truth. He knew exactly who planted this one. Alex had sat too quiet today. Too clean. Too smug. Leo's hands curled under his desk.

Ty was already halfway out of his chair when Leo stood. "Wait," Leo said. "I've got this." Ty nodded once. "We'll be behind you," he replied. Leo didn't wait for permission. He walked out of the classroom like someone finally done with the game. By the time he reached the office, Nico was already inside, seated awkwardly in one of the too-low chairs across from Mr. Arnett. The Principal was flipping through a manila folder, trying to match handwriting samples again. Again.

"This incident," Mr. Arnett began, "has your name on it. It's not severe, but it's inappropriate, and—" He didn't get to finish. Leo opened the door without knocking. "It wasn't him," Leo said, clear and unshaken. "I know it wasn't." Mr. Arnett looked up. "Leo, this is private—" "No, sir," Leo cut in, polite but unbending. "It's not private if the truth isn't invited. I know who wrote that message. Nico didn't. I'll tell you who did. But you called the wrong name."

Mr. Arnett held his gaze for a moment, measuring. Then he slowly set down the folder. "Go on," he said. Leo took a breath. "It's Alex. The tone, the phrasing, even the joke buried inside the insult—it's the same style as before. He's doing it to get attention, to stir things up, to see how far he can go. I used to do it. I know the pattern." Nico watched silently, his fingers curled around the edge of the chair like he might fall off if he let go.

There was a long silence. Mr. Arnett tapped his pen against the side of his desk, then leaned back. "You're certain?" he asked. "More than certain," Leo said. "And you're not saying this to protect your friend?" Leo shook his head. "I'm saying this because I used to be the one who needed protecting—from myself. But now I protect the ones who don't speak loud enough. Nico didn't do this. And Alex is counting on you believing he did." That hit harder than Leo expected. But Mr. Arnett didn't deny it.

Instead, Mr. Arnett turned to Nico. "Did you write anything like this?" "No, sir," Nico replied, his voice low but steady. "I swear on my name." Mr. Arnett folded his hands. "Alright," he said. "I'll re-open this." He looked back at Leo. "Thank you. That took courage." Leo shrugged. "It took clarity," he said. "That's what you gave me here. Clarity. So I'm giving it back." Then, almost as an afterthought, Leo smiled. Not the crooked, performative grin of old, but a soft, still one. "Also, I wanted to tell you something," he added.

Mr. Arnett tilted his head. "Yes?" Leo's voice quieted. "I called my parents 'Mom' and 'Dad' today. For real." Mr. Arnett's eyes warmed, just a little. "And how did that feel?" "Like I finally lived up to what they already believed about me," Leo said. "That I'm worth it. That I'm real now." Nico exhaled slowly, some knot inside him finally letting go. "You didn't just protect me," he said, eyes shining. "You taught me how to stay whole while waiting to be believed."

Ty was waiting outside the office when they came out. "Fixed it?" he asked. Leo nodded. "For now." Ty clapped a hand on his shoulder. "Good. You know how the game works. You just broke it." Leo smiled again, this time with his whole face. "Yeah," he said. "And it's about time somebody did." Nico slipped between them like a shadow at peace, the three of them walking down the corridor as if they'd always known how.

Later that night, Leo curled into the couch at home, the television murmuring in the background. Naomi brought him tea he didn't ask for. Zenji set a hand on his shoulder without needing a reason. And Leo looked up, let his defences down just enough, and said, "Thanks, Dad." Zenji froze for just a breath, then smiled the way only someone who's waited years for that word could. Naomi leaned in, her arm around Leo's back. "And thanks, Mom," Leo added, softer this time. He didn't cry. He didn't tremble. He just breathed like the truth had finally landed. And that night, under the blanket of ordinary warmth, Leo didn't dream of control or chaos or hiding. He dreamed of safety—and woke up still inside it.

They were standing near the cubby benches when it happened. The usual end-of-day rush was slowing to a hush, the noise thinning like mist on a warm window. Sophie stood by the coat hooks, holding her backpack with both hands, and her voice came not as a shout but as a thread of stillness. "Leo used to scare me," she said. Her words dropped into the space like a pin into a well. No one moved. Not even Jeremy. Not even Ty. "He doesn't anymore," Sophie added. "But Alex does."

The quiet that followed wasn't the stunned kind. It wasn't shocked or uncomfortable. It was sacred. The kind of quiet that listens. Jasmin turned to look at her, her eyes wide but not alarmed. Sophie didn't shrink or glance down. She said it plainly, like truth that had waited too long in the back of her throat. Her fingers twitched slightly around the zipper pull of her backpack, but her stance remained firm. Ty gave her one slow nod—not to reward her, but to respect her.

Leo stood just behind the far door, having overheard every word. He didn't come forward. He didn't interrupt. He leaned his back against the hallway wall and let it wash over him. The truth, clear and clean, even when it hurt. Especially when it hurt. He didn't cry. Not yet. But his breathing shifted. He didn't feel shame. He felt release. And when Sophie glanced toward him— knowing exactly where he stood—she gave him a look that said, thank you for changing.

That afternoon, Leo walked Jeremy to the gate, where Jeremy's parents were waiting. They had kind eyes, the kind that scanned without suspicion. Jeremy grinned up at Leo like a brother and clung to his side without needing permission. "Are you the Leo we've been hearing about?" asked his father. "The one who listens better than some grown men?" Leo laughed softly. "That's probably him," he replied. "But yeah. I'm Leo." Jeremy's mother stepped forward and wrapped him in a hug before asking.

"Thank you," she said, her voice trembling. "Thank you for being his friend." Leo didn't answer at first. He just returned the hug and kept his eyes open, blinking slow. "He's not hard to be friends with," Leo whispered. "He's one of the bravest people I know. I'm honoured to know him. Truly." The parents looked at each other, then back at Leo, with something deep and quiet in their expressions—trust, perhaps. Relief. Or maybe the gratitude of people who knew their child was safe.

They hesitated for a beat, then asked gently if Leo might be willing to watch Jeremy for a couple hours one weekend evening so they could have a night out. "We'd pay you for your time, of course," Jeremy's father added quickly. "We want to honour your help." Leo shook his head almost immediately. "No need," he said. "I'd do it because I want to. You don't have to pay me to care about him." His words were soft but rooted, spoken with the kind of steadiness that can't be faked.

They didn't argue. They just nodded with a different kind of respect, the kind that doesn't get handed out easily. Jeremy's mother knelt beside her son and whispered something in his ear. Jeremy nodded excitedly and turned to Leo. "You're my best friend," he said, the words a little shaky on the consonants but full of meaning. "The best one I got." Leo knelt down too, eye level now, and smiled in a way that stretched every part of him. "I'll always be that," he promised. "Always."

Later that evening, Leo told Naomi and Zenji about the day, about Sophie's truth, about the invitation from Jeremy's parents. Naomi sat beside him on the couch, listening as if every word were a thread in a tapestry. Zenji didn't speak much. He just placed a warm hand on Leo's shoulder and left it there. Leo looked between them, then softly said, "I think people are starting to believe me. Not just about what happened. But who I am now."

"You make it easy to believe," Naomi said, her eyes full. "Because you've done the hard work of becoming someone different—someone who protects." Leo looked down, then back at them. "I think I needed to be believed before I could believe in myself." Zenji nodded. "Then let us keep believing. Not just in what you were, but in what you are becoming."

That night, Leo sat on his bed with his journal open. He wrote down Sophie's words. He used to scare me. He doesn't anymore. He stared at them for a long time. Then underneath, he wrote his reply: I used to run from who I was. Now I walk toward who I'm becoming. He closed the journal slowly, like sealing a letter he knew the world would one day read.

Outside, the wind moved through the trees the way truth moves through a crowded room— quiet, invisible, but undeniable. Leo didn't feel like a boy who had failed. He felt like a boy who had been found. And somewhere deep inside, without needing to speak it aloud, he knew that being believed was the beginning of being free.

Ty sat across from Nico at the end of lunch, one knee pulled up, arms resting casually as if the topic weren't about the oldest, cruelest trick in the book. "The game," he said, not loudly, but with that quiet edge that made everyone lean in without realizing. "It only works if you play. That's how people like Alex win. They bait. You bite. That's the trick." Nico was listening with his arms folded tight, his lunch untouched. He'd seen it again—Alex twisting things, bending moments until someone else got blamed for his mess. He wasn't falling for it again.

The group had started spotting the signs faster now. Noticing who Alex praised, and who he punished, all within the same breath. Elia had been one of the first to catch on. She had been friendly with Alex in the beginning, laughing at his jokes, echoing his moods. But lately, she had started sitting farther from him. Not in protest. Not with drama. Just... a shift. The way a flower turns from shadow without needing to explain why. She stopped answering his texts during school. She stopped covering his silence with chatter. It was quiet, but it was power.

Leo noticed too. He hadn't said much, and didn't need to. The way he watched Alex now was different. Not fearful. Not angry. Just alert. Measured. Once, when Alex bumped into a third grader and made the child apologize, Leo stepped in gently but directly. "It's okay," he told the smaller boy, touching his shoulder with care. "You don't owe him an apology. It's not your fault." Alex muttered something about minding business, but Leo didn't answer. He didn't need to. The silence had already peeled back the curtain.

Ella kept track in her notebook. Not to tattle. To learn. To build her awareness like armor. "He only calls people 'buddy' when he's about to accuse them," she wrote, underlining it twice. "And when he smiles with his mouth closed, it's fake." Jasmin nodded when she read it. "I saw him do that to Milo last week. Made him say sorry for pushing, even though it was Alex who tripped him." No one needed to yell. No one needed a megaphone. The patterns spoke for themselves.

Ty pulled the others into a quiet corner near the staff kitchen after recess. "We're not making enemies," he said. "We're making distance." Nico raised an eyebrow. "Same thing." Ty shook his head. "No. Enemies need fuel. Distance doesn't feed the fire." Leo spoke next, his voice lower than usual. "It's like... he keeps throwing rope, and we used to grab it. But what if we just... stop?" Ty smiled. "Exactly. You don't get pulled into a trap if you don't step toward it."

By Thursday, even Mr. Arnett had begun to notice. Elia had started volunteering in the kindie yard. She didn't explain why. She just liked it there. The air was gentler. The smiles more real. When Alex passed her in the hallway, she didn't flinch. She didn't grin either. She offered nothing. He looked at her, confused by the absence of reaction. He needed engagement. He needed performance. Without it, his script didn't work. The scene had no stage.

At lunch, Jeremy sat with Leo under the big tree behind the gym. The little boy was learning how to build a tower from sticks and leaves, not to play but to practice patience. "If it falls," Jeremy said, "we start again?" Leo smiled. "That's what real friends do. We build back." The moment held weight. Not because of the tower, but because of the trust. Jeremy had never trusted anyone the way he trusted Leo. And Leo knew that. He knew how fragile that gift was. He guarded it like a promise.

Inside the school, Ty sat with Jasmin and Ella reviewing a checklist they had started weeks ago. "Who flatters too often. Who interrupts truth. Who rewrites stories." They were ready now. Ready not to confront, but to disengage. There was nothing dramatic about it. Just decisions. Who they gave their energy to. Who they didn't. Alex noticed. Of course he did. Manipulators always notice when the room gets colder without explanation. It unsettled him. His usual rhythm broke. He started making more mistakes.

By the end of the week, Alex made three attempts to stir drama. He failed all three times. No one replied. No one rose to his bait. When he accused Ty of cheating at dodgeball, Ty just blinked at him and said, "I'm not playing that game." When he tried to whisper something cruel about Sophie to Nico, Nico said, "Not interested," and walked away. And when he tripped Jeremy and tried to frame it as an accident, Leo was there, blocking him with his body, no words necessary. Alex walked away angry. But it didn't land. Not this time.

That night, Ty told Naomi over dinner, "I think it's working." She looked up from the pot she was stirring. "What is?" He smiled faintly. "The quiet work. The distance. The kids are noticing. They're choosing not to play." Naomi placed a spoon on the counter and turned to face him. "You planted truth in them," she said. "You taught them how to tell the difference between real and false. And now they're using it."

Ty didn't reply right away. He just nodded and thought of the way Elia had looked when she walked away from Alex that day—calm, strong, and done. Not angry. Not hurt. Just done. He thought of Jeremy laughing beside Leo. Of Jasmin's quiet notetaking. Of Ella watching patterns instead of reacting. Of Nico listening more and doubting less. And of Leo himself. Not chasing approval. Not needing applause. Just being. "The game only works," Ty said finally, "if you play."

For weeks, they had been watching, listening, waiting. Mr. Clarke and Miss Kara were not blind, not anymore. They'd heard the hallway rumours, the odd silences, and the changing tone when Alex entered a room. But it wasn't until Tuesday's lunch period that everything sharpened into focus. The gym echoed with the shuffle of sneakers and the thud of basketballs, but off to the side, near the green mats, a quiet conversation turned into a whisper war. Leo had already caught the look—Alex twisting the corners of his smile like it was a weapon. It wasn't what he said this time. It was what he made someone else say.

The boy apologizing—Matthew, a quiet sixth grader with freckles and an anxious laugh—looked like he'd been cornered by a shadow. He mumbled something about dropping a book he hadn't touched. Alex just nodded slowly, lips pursed in smug agreement. Miss Kara had seen the end of it, and Mr. Clarke had walked in just as Matthew's apology landed. Leo didn't move. He stood beside Ty, hands clenched in the hem of his sweater, ready but still. Miss Kara leaned toward Mr. Clarke and murmured, "Did you see that?" Mr. Clarke's jaw tensed. "Oh, I've seen it before. Not from this kid. But I've seen it."

What happened next didn't explode. It peeled open. Mr. Clarke stepped forward, voice calm, clear, and oddly kind. "Matthew," he said, "what are you apologizing for?" The boy hesitated, darting a glance at Alex, whose eyes sharpened just for a moment. "I… I don't know, sir. I think—I think I dropped the book." Mr. Clarke picked up the hardcover from the floor. It was too clean, too neatly placed to have just been dropped. "This one?" Matthew nodded. "You saw him drop it?" Clarke asked Alex, who smiled politely and said, "Not exactly. But he was closest to it."

Ty shifted just enough to block Jeremy's view. Jeremy, sitting cross-legged on the edge of the mats, looked confused and slightly scared. Leo leaned down and whispered, "It's okay. Watch how the truth stands up." Mr. Clarke placed the book gently into Matthew's hands. "Next time, don't say sorry for something you didn't do. Not unless you want to carry a weight that isn't yours." Matthew's eyes welled with confusion and something like relief. Miss Kara knelt beside him. "You did nothing wrong. It's okay to say that out loud." She looked at Alex but said nothing. Alex blinked slowly, unreadable.

That moment passed, but it marked the beginning of something else. Staff began watching differently—not for noise, but for quiet shifts. For the tone behind compliments. For the pauses after flattery. They started to see the small patterns, the ones Ty and Leo had long learned to track. Teachers who had once brushed off gossip as kid drama began asking questions with gentler voices. They stopped rushing to the loudest story. They started staying for the second version. The change wasn't instant, but it was there. Leo noticed it. Ty noticed it. And so did Jeremy.

Jeremy's world had changed too. At lunch, he sat beside Leo as usual, knees swinging gently from the edge of the bench. His fingers curled into the hem of his sleeves when he got nervous. But today, he didn't need to say much. He just looked up at Leo with big, blinking eyes and said, softly, "I love you." Leo froze, not in discomfort, but in awe. No one moved. Jeremy hadn't whispered it. He said it as plainly as someone might ask for a pencil. And Leo, not hesitating for even a second, placed his hand gently on Jeremy's back and said, "I love you too, little brother."

Ty heard it and smiled into his juice box. Jasmin blinked twice and turned her head slightly so no one would see her tears. Ella didn't hide it. She leaned her head against Jasmin's shoulder and whispered, "He really is different now." Sophie, who sat diagonally across the table, didn't speak but gave Leo a quiet nod. It wasn't just about Leo anymore. It was about what Leo stood for now. Jeremy, the boy with the stumbling speech and hesitant voice, had found someone who didn't flinch or flee. Someone who understood.

Mr. Clarke passed by the table a few minutes later. He didn't stop. But he gave Leo a brief nod—firm, certain, respectful. A nod between men. Leo nodded back, just once, with the full weight of what had been earned. Miss Kara circled the cafeteria, her eyes scanning the tables with new precision. She noticed Alex sitting quietly, eyes darting from person to person, waiting to latch onto someone's weakness. She said nothing but walked just a little slower past his table. A new kind of surveillance had begun.

After lunch, Jeremy asked Leo if he could walk beside him to class. Leo gave him a piggyback ride instead. The halls watched. Some kids smiled. Some stayed quiet. But no one mocked him. No one dared. Ty followed close behind, laughing gently, saying, "You're gonna spoil him." "Good," Leo replied. "He deserves it." It wasn't about being perfect. It was about being present. And Leo was finally present in his own life.

That afternoon, Mr. Clarke met with the staff. They discussed Alex—not in accusation, but in curiosity. How had he gotten so good at disappearing in plain sight? What role had silence played in his tricks? The teachers didn't have all the answers. But they had started to ask better questions. And that was enough for now. Leo had started something, not just for himself, but for every child who needed truth more than applause.

Back in the hallway, Ty bumped Leo's shoulder and said, "You're doing good." Leo shook his head, not to deny the words, but to deflect the praise. "He told me he loved me," he said quietly. "And I believed him." "Then that's all that matters," Ty replied. "That's how we win." Leo looked at Jeremy down the hall and said, "That's how we never lose again."

The hallway was nearly empty when Alex stepped too close. The bell had already rung, but he lingered just long enough to shove his shoulder into Ty's. It wasn't enough to draw attention—just enough to remind the room who he thought he was. Ty didn't flinch. He didn't even shift his weight. He only looked at him, calmly, and said, "You can't bully your way into innocence." The words didn't explode. They didn't echo. But somehow, they felt louder than any yelling ever could.

Alex blinked. He hadn't expected calm. He wanted a scene, something he could spin, something he could blame. But Ty wasn't giving him that. Ty stood his ground, expression unreadable, posture relaxed but deliberate. Leo stood just behind him, arms folded, back straight, eyes quiet. He didn't speak. He didn't glare. He only nodded once, a signal of agreement, a warning not to try anything further. The message was clear: this time, you're not up against someone alone.

Mr. Arnett passed through at that moment, caught the tension, and paused. He didn't interrupt. He only watched. Ty turned to Alex one last time and said, "You don't get to twist truth anymore. Not here." Then he walked away. Leo followed, his steps slow, deliberate, matched in stride. Alex didn't follow. He stood still, caught in his own silence, unsure whether he'd just lost something or exposed it. Either way, no one came to his defence.

Saturday morning came with clear skies and a nervous Jeremy gripping the handle of his backpack like it might float away. Leo met him at the corner near the school. Jeremy smiled when he saw him and took three quick steps forward before stopping. "Hi," he said, and Leo ruffled his hair. "Ready?" Jeremy nodded. "I brought two sandwiches," he added. "One for you and one for me." Leo laughed. "I made two, too. So we're going to have four sandwiches." Jeremy's eyes lit up like it was the greatest math he'd ever heard.

They didn't do anything expensive. No fancy outing, no structured schedule. Just a walk through the park, a sit under the old tree near the baseball diamond, and two hours at the school's jungle gym when no one else was around. They played tag. They told made-up stories. Jeremy tried to climb the monkey bars but fell halfway and landed with a soft thud. Leo didn't laugh. He just offered his hand and said, "You almost had it." Jeremy grinned and tried again. He made it to the top this time.

Lunch was quiet. Sandwiches were swapped. Crusts were debated. Jeremy had strawberry juice, and Leo had apple. They agreed both were the best, but different kinds of best. "Like us," Jeremy said, wiping his mouth with his sleeve. "You're quiet sometimes, and I talk a lot, but we still match." Leo smiled. "Yeah. We do." Then Jeremy looked at him with a seriousness too deep for a Saturday. "I know why you protect me," he said. "It's because somebody didn't protect you." Leo froze. Then nodded. "Yeah," he said. "But I'm glad I can now."

They didn't talk about sadness after that. They played a game where every word had to start with the letter "S." It got ridiculous fast. "Silly sausages slide sideways," Jeremy shouted while falling backward into the grass. Leo laughed so hard his sides hurt. For a few hours, there were no echoes of the past. No ghosts of narcissism. Just two kids, one older, one younger, being loud and being alive. Jeremy never once stumbled on Leo's name.

When it was time to go home, Jeremy's parents were waiting at the curb. He didn't run to them right away. He turned to Leo, arms suddenly shy. Then, without warning, he stepped forward and wrapped both arms around Leo's middle, burying his face in Leo's jacket. "I love you," he whispered. Leo didn't hesitate. He bent down, arms surrounding him like armour, and whispered, "I love you too, buddy." Jeremy pulled back, nodded, and walked to his parents without looking back. He didn't need to.

Leo stood there for a moment after they left. He felt taller somehow, not in height, but in soul. He wasn't just a boy who used to hurt others. He was someone's safe place now. He walked home slowly, thinking about that. He didn't text Ty. He didn't need to. When he arrived, Ty already had hot chocolate made and two mugs ready on the table. "How'd it go?" he asked without looking up. "Perfect," Leo answered, and meant it.

That night, Leo lay awake for a long time. He replayed the moment Jeremy said "I love you" over and over in his head. Not because he didn't believe it, but because it felt like proof. Not just that Jeremy meant it—but that Leo could be that kind of person. The kind someone loved without fear. The kind someone trusted. The kind who didn't have to yell to be heard.

He remembered Ty's calm voice in the hallway. The way it cut through everything. The way it made Alex look small without making Leo look cruel. That was power. Not volume. Not threat. But truth. Spoken without apology. Leo whispered into the dark, "I'll never yell to prove I'm right. I'll speak like Ty." Somewhere, he heard the floor creak, as if Ty had heard it from the hallway. Maybe he had.

By morning, the whisper of change had settled into something stronger. Leo didn't just want to be like Ty. He wanted to become someone new entirely. Someone honest. Someone calm. Someone whose words carried weight not because they were loud—but because they were true. And someone, someday, a little kid like Jeremy might grow up to be.

Alex waited near the water fountain with that too-polite posture of his, eyes alert, lips resting in that half-smile that never touched the soul. Jasmin wasn't expecting him there. She hesitated, but only for a breath. He stepped in front of her, arms loosely crossed, and tilted his head like someone pretending curiosity. "You know," he began, his tone soft like syrup, "some people think you're choosing the wrong side." Jasmin didn't answer right away. She let the silence stretch, testing his patience before she spoke.

"Wrong side of what?" she asked. Her voice wasn't defensive. It wasn't afraid either. Just clear. Measured. Honest. Alex smiled wider, but the grin had teeth. "You know how people talk. You've got a good heart, Jasmin. But sometimes people like Ty and Leo—well—they bring a lot of chaos." He leaned closer, dropping his voice. "And someone's going to get hurt." His words hovered like fog. He expected her to flinch. To take the bait. To lean into worry. He didn't expect what came next.

"No," she said.

It wasn't shouted. It wasn't theatrical. It wasn't even angry. It just was. And it landed like truth always does—heavy, undeniable, final. Alex blinked. Something about that one syllable knocked the wind out of his posture. Jasmin stepped past him without hurrying. She didn't add anything. Didn't explain herself. She left the rest of the sentence behind her, and Alex stood alone in the hallway with nothing to twist. For the first time, he had no script to lean on.

By the lockers, Ty had seen the tail end of it. He didn't say anything either. He just offered Jasmin a nod that meant everything. Leo, too, caught the echo in the hall and smiled softly to himself. Not smugly. Not triumphantly. Just in recognition. That was how a Shadow Warrior said no. Not with a punch, but with purpose. Jasmin didn't need to raise her voice. She didn't need an audience. The truth in her step was enough.

Later, outside near the bike racks, Jeremy stood next to Leo with his backpack clutched to his chest. He'd watched Jasmin too—from a distance—and didn't say anything for a long time. Finally, as Leo locked his bike, Jeremy tugged on the hem of Leo's jacket. Leo turned, crouched slightly to meet his eyes, and waited. Jeremy took a breath, stuttered, started again, and then managed to get it out: "Could you be my brother?"

Leo didn't answer right away. He blinked, not from confusion, but from something closer to awe. Jeremy's eyes weren't pleading. They were wide open with belief. With hope. With that deep-rooted child trust that comes when someone's love feels real. Leo felt something shift in his chest, a kind of grounding he hadn't known he needed. He didn't say yes. Not with words. He just pulled Jeremy into a hug so gentle and so certain it became its own answer.

Jeremy rested there, his small hands gripping the back of Leo's jacket. "Not pretend," he whispered. "Real brother." Leo nodded slowly. "Real," he whispered back. "As real as it gets." Jeremy smiled against his shoulder and held on for a while longer. Ty watched from the steps, arms folded, leaning back slightly, expression soft. He didn't interrupt. He didn't say a word. But he mouthed something that looked like, "Good."

When they returned to class, no one said anything. But something had shifted. People looked at Leo with different eyes now. Not suspicious. Not cautious. But curious. Respectful. Like maybe he was more than just a story someone else used to tell about him. He noticed it but didn't react. That was part of the lesson. Strength didn't need validation. It just needed consistency.

Jasmin sat beside Ella, who whispered, "You really just said no?" Jasmin smiled. "Yup." Ella smiled too, but her eyes were bright. "I want to learn how to do that." Jasmin nodded. "You will." Across the room, Alex was quiet. That was new. His gaze slid over the desks but didn't land anywhere. He looked smaller somehow. Not because anyone had humiliated him—but because someone hadn't played his game.

Mr. Arnett passed by Jeremy's desk and noticed the boy beaming. "Good weekend, Jeremy?" he asked. Jeremy nodded with so much energy he nearly bounced. "Leo's my brother now," he announced. Mr. Arnett paused, then looked at Leo. Leo didn't clarify. He didn't need to. Arnett just smiled. "Glad to hear it," he said. And kept walking. Some truths didn't need a formal declaration. They just needed to be lived.

At lunch, Leo sat with Jeremy on the bench outside. It was cold enough to see their breath, but warm enough not to care. "You think people can really change?" Jeremy asked between bites of his sandwich. Leo nodded. "Yeah," he said. "But only when someone lets them." Jeremy smiled and kicked his feet under the bench. "I'm glad you changed." Leo looked up at the sky. "Me too," he whispered.

That evening, Leo sat at the kitchen table with Ty, helping Naomi prep vegetables for dinner. "Jeremy asked me to be his brother today," he said. Ty glanced up, then back at the carrot he was chopping. "Did you say yes?" Leo smiled. "I didn't have to." Naomi placed a bowl of washed lettuce in front of them and kissed Leo's hair. "Then I guess it's official," she said. "The family's grown again." And it had.

Ty caught the way Alex picked up Elia's books that morning before she could even bend down. He did it with flourish, his back straight, chin slightly lifted, a look of mild nobility painted across his face. "Let me help," he said, not because she asked, not because she needed it, but because he wanted eyes to notice. He placed the books on her desk with a soft smile, then glanced around to see who had watched. A few students murmured polite thanks. Elia smiled back, unsure whether she was grateful or simply avoiding awkwardness. Ty watched it all in silence.

Leo leaned toward him as they exited the classroom for recess. "You saw it too?" he asked quietly, not pointing, not naming. Ty didn't blink. "He carries someone's books just to say he's the hero," he said flatly. "That's not help. That's theatre." Leo nodded, jaw tight. He knew that play too well. Knew the shape of it from the inside. He used to act like that. Holding the door wide open, but only for praise. Asking if someone was okay, but only loud enough for a teacher to hear.

They stood near the fence as Jeremy and the younger kids scrambled across the field. "What's the difference," Leo asked, "between being helpful and using it like a mask?" Ty looked toward the sky a moment before answering. "Real help is quiet," he said. "You don't tell everyone. You just do it, and walk away." Leo stared out past the chain link, eyes tracking Jeremy as he knelt beside a kindergartener who had tripped on their own scarf. No fanfare. Just care. "So," Leo said slowly, "Alex is faking it?" Ty shook his head. "Not always. But mostly."

Inside, Elia sat beside Jasmin and quietly whispered, "Do you think he likes me?" Jasmin looked over at Alex, who was now wiping down a whiteboard that didn't need cleaning. "He likes being liked," Jasmin said carefully. "That's not the same thing." Elia frowned, thinking it through. "But he's so nice lately." Jasmin didn't reply. Instead, she jotted a note in the margin of her notebook: Watch what's quiet, not what's loud.

Leo and Ty returned just in time to see Alex offering Miss Kara a fresh box of markers from the supply closet. "I figured you'd run out," he said with that smile again—practiced, not warm. Miss Kara nodded, appreciative but not moved. She had worked long enough in education to know that some students offer help as currency. Leo paused by the doorframe, arms folded. Ty stood beside him, mirroring the posture without thinking. They were beginning to recognize the signal before the broadcast.

After class, Alex passed Leo in the hallway. "Heard you're taking care of that little kid—Jeremy?" His tone was casual, almost friendly. Leo tilted his head. "Yeah. He's my brother." The look in Alex's eyes flickered just for a moment, that tight moment of envy disguised as curiosity. "Cute," Alex said. "Kids always follow the nice ones." Leo let the silence answer for him. He was done playing polite. Ty later said that kind of silence is sharper than any comeback. It tells the truth without wasting energy.

At lunch, Leo gave Jeremy the bigger half of his sandwich and said nothing about it. Jeremy beamed, swinging his legs under the bench. "You're the best," he mumbled with a full mouth. Leo just nodded, mouth full of water. No one was watching. That was the point. Ty nudged him gently. "See?" he whispered. "That's the real thing. No mask." Leo felt it, deep and still. He hadn't realized how loud his old life had been until now.

In gym class, Alex complimented three different kids within the first five minutes. All three looked at him strangely, uncertain why someone who had once insulted them suddenly wanted to praise their sneakers or their hair or their ability to climb ropes. One even asked, "Are you okay?" But Alex kept smiling. Politeness can be a shield when someone's hiding behind it. And Leo wasn't fooled anymore.

Later that week, Leo walked Sophie back from the office after she had delivered forms. "He helped me yesterday," she said about Alex. "But it felt weird." Leo didn't press. He let her explain on her own terms. "Like... it wasn't for me. It was for him." Leo nodded. "That's how it feels when someone's kindness is a mirror. They only reflect it when they want to see themselves in it."

Ty sat with Miss Kara after class, handing her the feedback folders from the day. "What do you do," he asked, "when a kid is nice for the wrong reason?" Miss Kara sighed. "You watch. You don't accuse. But you don't ignore it either. Sometimes kindness is a rehearsal for power." Ty thought about that all night. He told Leo the next morning. Leo just said, "Then I guess it's our job to keep watching."

By Thursday, even Mr. Clarke had started noticing. "Interesting week," he muttered, mostly to himself, as Alex offered to help put away thirty unassigned math duotangs. "Has he ever been this... enthusiastic before?" Ty smirked. "Maybe he found Jesus." Mr. Clarke raised an eyebrow. "Or maybe he found someone watching." It was all said quietly. No accusations. Just observation. And that was enough.

Jeremy didn't talk much about Alex, but one day he clung to Leo's hand just a little tighter in the hallway after Alex had passed them. "I don't like his eyes," Jeremy said softly. Leo knelt. "Then you listen to your stomach, not his smile." Jeremy nodded seriously. "Okay." Ty overheard and later told Leo, "You've got it now. You're not just protecting. You're teaching. Shadow Warriors raise the next ones."

That night at dinner, Naomi asked, "Anything happen at school today?" Leo paused, then said, "Yeah. Someone carried a bunch of books." Zenji looked up. "And?" Leo shrugged. "Just... felt heavy for the wrong reason." Naomi nodded slowly. "Then you know what to watch for."

In the end, helpfulness is only good if it doesn't hide harm. And the kids were learning, in whispers and glances, how to see past the shine. No cape. No drama. Just truth. Leo saw the mask slipping. And this time, he didn't rip it off. He waited. Because sometimes, the liar unmasks himself when no one claps for the show.

The comment wasn't loud, but Sophie heard it anyway. A girl near the water fountain whispered just loud enough, just clear enough: "She's weak for forgiving him." The other girls nodded like they were experts in justice, like forgiveness made Sophie smaller. But she didn't flinch. She turned her head, met the voice, and said without a tremor, "I didn't forget what he did. I just believe who he is now." The sentence didn't rise in volume, but it landed like stone in water—ripples spreading, hitting everyone in earshot. One of the girls turned away. Another bit her lip. No one answered.

Leo wasn't there to hear it. But the truth of her words followed him, like a quiet echo that warmed the hallway without needing permission. By the time he reached the class doors, Jeremy had already run up to him for his morning hug. His arms barely made it halfway around Leo's ribs, but that never stopped him from squeezing as tight as he could. Leo knelt to receive it every time. Not rushed. Not half-hearted. Jeremy's hugs weren't just affection—they were evidence. That someone small trusted someone who used to be feared.

Sophie stood at the lockers, adjusting her binder, eyes steady. She watched Leo smile at Jeremy and tousle his hair. She watched Ty nod from across the hall, a silent greeting that meant, "You're doing it right." And she felt no shame standing near Leo. Not anymore. There had been a time—weeks ago—that just being in the same room as him made her uneasy. But something had broken open in him. Not shattered. Split. And what came out was something honest. Not perfect. But honest.

At lunch, she sat beside him, not across. Their trays nearly touched. They didn't talk much, but that didn't matter. She watched Jeremy climb up beside Leo with his sandwich and spill mustard onto Leo's sleeve. Leo didn't scowl. Didn't sigh. He just wiped it with a napkin, smiled, and said, "I'll wash it after school." Jeremy looked up like he'd just been handed a medal. Sophie saw it then—the change wasn't performative. It wasn't forced. Leo wasn't playing a part. He was living in one.

Ty leaned back in his chair beside them. "Three hugs a day," he muttered with a small grin. "Pretty good schedule." Leo didn't even try to deny it. "One in the morning, one at lunch, one after school," he recited like scripture. "I don't know what to do with my arms anymore when they're not full of Jeremy." They all chuckled, but beneath the laugh sat something truer than they could name. Sophie saw that too. The hug was routine now, but never meaningless. It was a ritual. A sealing of trust three times daily.

That afternoon, while organizing reading time, Miss Kara gently motioned Sophie over. "You okay sitting beside Leo?" she asked, voice calm, respectful. Sophie nodded. "He's not who he was," she said. "Not to me." Miss Kara gave a small smile, then nodded once and marked something in her attendance folder. Sophie sat beside Leo again, and not a single child in the circle moved away. No one shifted or glared. They'd seen too much by now. The proof was in the silence. The real kind.

Later, walking out with her backpack slung too low, Sophie overheard a different whisper. This one from a younger boy, maybe fourth grade: "Is that Leo's sister?" His friend shrugged. "No, I think she's just always with him." Sophie turned the corner before they noticed she'd heard. She didn't correct them. She didn't have to. The truth was bigger than titles. Bigger than what other people thought they understood.

After school, Jeremy came running again. The final hug of the day. Arms wrapped around Leo's middle, little chin digging into his jacket. "Love you, Leo," he said, almost like a prayer. Leo replied without blinking. "I love you too, Jeremy." Sophie heard it and kept walking, but her steps slowed just a bit. Because some truths deserved space. Deserved silence. Deserved not to be interrupted by analysis.

Ty caught up to her by the gate. "You heard what they said this morning?" he asked casually. "Yeah," Sophie said. "I answered." Ty smiled sideways. "I figured." He paused, then added, "They think forgiveness makes you soft." Sophie looked up at him. "It doesn't." Ty nodded. "No. It makes you unbreakable." Then they both kept walking. No ceremony. No announcement. Just steps moving forward.

Leo hadn't told Sophie thank you for defending him. Not because he forgot, but because he knew she didn't want thanks. She wanted consistency. And he'd given her that now. Not once. Every day. Jeremy started calling her "Miss Sophie" like she was part of the family. Leo didn't correct him. Neither did she.

At bedtime, Leo told Naomi about the comment Sophie answered in the hallway. Naomi listened, hands folded over her lap. "And how did that make you feel?" she asked. Leo didn't rush the answer. "Like I don't have to prove anything anymore." Naomi smiled. "Good. That's called grace, Leo. Not everyone will understand it, but it's real." Leo nodded, pressing the blanket under his chin. "I think she understands it."

Zenji passed the door a moment later and paused to listen. He said nothing. But in the quiet after, Leo's heart beat slower. He wasn't watching his back anymore. He was watching the future.

Sophie brushed her hair that night and stared into the mirror without blinking. "I'm not weak," she whispered to herself, not for reassurance, but as reminder. And then she smiled—not big, not forced. Just enough. Because she knew what others didn't: forgiveness is a choice made by those strong enough to remember and still choose peace. The next morning, Jeremy ran to Leo again, arms wide. Hug number one. Sophie walked in beside them, hand on Jeremy's shoulder. That was the signal. The past had been acknowledged. But it no longer owned them.

It happened during the last ten minutes of the day. The room was humming with the buzz of zippers, backpacks, and half-finished goodbyes when the accusation floated in. A small boy—Felix, Grade 2, with too-long sleeves and shy hands—stood near the window, pale and frozen. Another child was pointing at him, voice smug: "He took it. He was the only one over there." No evidence. No proof. Just certainty wrapped in volume. The teacher's eyes narrowed. But Leo and Ty had already moved.

Without a word, they walked across the room and sat on either side of Felix, folding their arms—not against him, but beside him. They didn't argue. They didn't plead. They just sat, letting their presence say what their mouths didn't need to. Felix's chin trembled, and for a second, he looked like he might cry. But then Ty leaned just close enough to whisper, "We're not leaving." Leo nodded once. "Not till the truth gets its turn."

The teacher noticed. She paused her response mid-sentence and turned back toward the small triangle now formed near the window. The child who accused Felix shrank a little, suddenly less confident. "Well… I'm pretty sure I saw him," he mumbled, retreating toward his chair. The teacher approached, crouched down to Felix's level, and asked gently, "Did you take it?" Felix shook his head, eyes wide. "No, miss. I was watching the cars go by."

Ty didn't speak over anyone. He waited. The moment opened on its own. Another student in the back of the room raised her hand and confessed, "I moved it by accident. I put it in my desk." And just like that, the lie evaporated. Not because it had been fought. Because it had been endured. Exposed. Not with rage, but with presence.

As the others gathered their things again, the teacher gave Felix a soft pat on the shoulder. "Thank you for staying calm." Felix glanced at Ty, then Leo, as if to ask permission to believe her words. Ty nodded. "You did everything right." Leo leaned closer. "And the truth didn't have to shout."

They walked him to the front entrance as the last bell rang. Felix said barely anything, but he looked up at both of them as he left, and his eyes held something new. Not trust. Not yet. But the beginning of it. The seed. Leo knew what that look meant. He used to wear it, years ago—or was it just months?

Outside, the sun had already dipped behind the main building, casting long shadows across the pavement. Kids spilled out in waves, calling goodbyes to friends and waving to parents. Jeremy was already waiting, backpack bouncing as he ran straight for Leo. Hug number three, always on schedule. But this one was different.

He launched into Leo's arms like a rocket, wrapped him tight, and then did something new. He pulled back just far enough, kissed Leo on the cheek, and said with perfect clarity, "I love you. Have a great night." The words weren't rehearsed. Weren't forced through his stutter. They came out clear. Crisp. Meant. Leo couldn't speak right away. His throat closed, and a lump caught him off guard. He blinked twice, willing the moment not to fall apart.

Then he saw Jeremy's parents walking up—quiet, graceful, steady. They didn't say anything grand. They just hugged him. Again. Like he was theirs. Because he was. Not by blood. Not by name. By truth. The kind of truth that doesn't demand anything. It just stays.

Ty stood nearby, arms folded across his chest, watching it all. When Leo finally turned toward him, Ty gave the smallest nod, barely visible. It said everything. You did it. You stayed. You chose the truth over noise. You became what you were always meant to be.

Sophie watched from a few paces back. She didn't wave. She didn't need to. Leo caught her eye and gave the faintest grin. Just enough. Because he knew she'd seen it all. The arc. The turn. The one who was feared had become the one kids ran to. The one who twisted truth was now its shield.

Felix passed by them again on the sidewalk. This time, he lifted one hand in a tiny wave. It wasn't much. But Ty caught it, returned the gesture, and said, "Told you. Truth just needs to stay." Leo placed a hand on Ty's shoulder and said, softly, "Let's keep it safe."

As the last of the buses roared to life, the street emptied. But something fuller lingered behind. A stillness that wasn't silence. A peace that had been earned. Ty turned to Leo and smiled. "Come on, big brother. Let's go home." And with Jeremy's small hand curled into Leo's and the quiet strength of truth holding them steady, they walked toward a night that would not twist anything. Not anymore.

CHAPTER 11: THE ONE WHO ALWAYS HAD TO WIN

Allen had once been the shadow cast behind every cruel whisper, the echo after every staged kindness. He lingered in group photos like he'd earned his place there, smiling too big and offering help that never came without strings. But now, nobody was laughing at his jokes. No one invited him into their circles anymore, not even the ones who used to giggle when he mocked the quiet kids. He had stopped raising his hand in class, stopped leaning too far into conversations he wasn't part of. Allen didn't transfer schools. He didn't get in trouble. He just faded—like a smudge on a mirror that someone finally wiped clean.

Leo noticed it first. Allen wasn't mean anymore, but he wasn't anything. He was quiet. He sat still. He didn't glare at people, and he didn't roll his eyes when someone stuttered. He just blended. Not like a shadow warrior blends, not like Ty taught them. Allen blended like someone who had been seen and didn't like what people saw. Leo knew that look. It was the same one he'd worn months ago before the world tilted and caught him. Before Ty sat beside him and let him cry without questions. Before Jeremy wrapped his arms around his waist and called him "brother" for the first time.

There was no announcement. No moment of reckoning. Just a silence that felt different than the others. Allen didn't need to be pushed out; he walked. During recess, he lingered near the fence line. At lunch, he sat where no one needed to ask him to move. Nobody teased him, and nobody praised him either. He wasn't invisible. He was just… unstuck. And that kind of disappearance didn't come from punishment. It came from truth. The kind that burns quietly until the mask slides off on its own.

Ty saw it too, but didn't mention it right away. He only nodded once when Leo caught Allen pausing at the water fountain, hands twitching like he wanted to speak but didn't know how. "Let him," Ty said simply. "Let him figure it out like you did." Leo didn't argue. He understood. You can't force someone into the truth. You just have to live it loud enough that they start to hear it echo in themselves. Allen's silence wasn't cowardice. It was the first page of a story he hadn't learned how to tell yet.

Ella asked once where Allen had gone, and Jasmin replied, "He's still here. He's just quiet now." Nobody laughed. That was the strange part. Nobody made a joke or offered some dramatic explanation. Because they all knew what it meant to be quiet in a world that only listened to noise. They all knew what it meant to retreat from yourself, not because you were ashamed, but because you were scared to see what you might find.

Leo wasn't angry at Allen. Not anymore. Maybe because he saw himself too clearly in him. Or maybe because he finally understood what Ty meant by love being the kind that stays even when you don't deserve it. Leo didn't need Allen to change. He needed him to want to. That was the difference. That was the line between who Leo had been and who he was now. He didn't want to win anymore. He wanted to walk alongside someone and not be afraid of falling behind.

Jeremy once asked Leo if Allen was bad. Leo knelt and said, "No, just hurt. And sometimes hurt makes people hide in the loudest ways." Jeremy didn't fully get it, but he nodded anyway. He was good at that. He had a heart big enough to hold questions without needing answers right away. And Leo realized then that healing didn't always come with fireworks. Sometimes, it came with a chair no longer filled, a table no longer crowded with lies.

Mr. Clarke saw Allen's shift too. During group work, he didn't assign Allen a partner. He let him pick. Allen chose the quietest kid in the room and didn't speak for most of the project. But he listened. And when the other student stumbled on their words, Allen didn't flinch. He waited. Then offered help—not to be praised, not to be seen, but just because it was the right thing to do. Mr. Clarke nodded, but didn't smile. Some growth is too sacred to spotlight.

Later that week, Ty asked Leo, "Do you miss who he used to be?" Leo shook his head. "I never liked him. But now, I don't think I hate him either." That was progress. That was the kind of forgiveness that didn't forget—but didn't hold chains. Ty said nothing in reply. He didn't need to. He just rested his hand on Leo's shoulder, the same way Leo now did for Jeremy every morning without even realizing it.

By Friday, Allen had found a new pattern. He showed up to class early and left late. He held doors but didn't expect a thank-you. He started doing his own assignments instead of copying someone else's. He wasn't perfect. But he was quiet. And that was enough. Because some kids don't need punishment. They need proof that there's another way to exist. That truth doesn't have to shout to be heard. That love doesn't require applause.

In the lunchroom, Allen sat alone. Not because he was shunned. But because he didn't want to fake his way into friendship anymore. Leo noticed. He walked by. Paused. And said, "You good?" Allen looked up and nodded once. Leo didn't sit down. He didn't invite him over. He just nodded back and kept walking. That was the olive branch. That was the moment Allen knew he wasn't being chased. But the door hadn't closed either.

Ella wrote in her journal that night, "Some people disappear before they get found. Some get found because they disappeared." It wasn't poetic. It was just true. Allen was learning how to be small in the right way. And the others? They were learning how to see without judging, how to forgive without forgetting, how to love without losing themselves. Leo no longer feared kids like Allen. Because he wasn't one anymore.

Alex didn't shout. He didn't throw things or stomp down the hall. His ways were smarter than that. Sharper. Smoother. He interrupted with a laugh, not a glare. He made a joke out of truth so it couldn't stand up anymore. He twisted the facts like a magician twisting balloons—smiling while he did it, always ending with something that looked almost real. But not quite. Ty had seen this pattern before. So had Jasmin. And Ella was starting to write things down. Not to tell. Not to tattle. But to track.

Ty didn't tell them to fight back. He told them to notice. "Watch what he changes," he said. "Not just what he says—but when he says it. Who he says it in front of. What he tries to hide behind." That was the first rule of tracking deception: know the pattern. Alex's pattern wasn't chaos. It was rhythm. Always making sure he had someone on his side, someone to doubt themselves, and someone else to blame. Never alone. Never still. Always ahead of the story.

Leo watched from a distance. He didn't need to write things down. He knew the playbook by heart. Because he'd written parts of it once. He remembered the satisfaction of twisting someone's words just enough to make them second-guess. He remembered flipping stories until even the teacher wasn't sure who had started it. He knew Alex's grin. It wasn't confidence. It was control. And it worked—until someone stopped playing.

That's what Ty taught them. "He can only win if you accept the version he hands you. Don't take it. Don't argue with it either. Just write down what really happened. Date. Time. Words." Jasmin kept her notes folded in her sock. Ella used a small pink notebook with a sticker that said Kindness Isn't Weak. Ty kept his in code. He used symbols for body language, underlines for lies, and tiny stars for when someone's tone didn't match their words.

Alex didn't know he was being watched. That was the beauty of the quiet ones. They didn't glare. They didn't huff. They just listened better than anyone else. Ella wrote about how Alex blamed Mila for breaking the pencil sharpener, even though Mila had been across the room. Jasmin noted that Alex always tried to interrupt Ty when he was helping someone younger. Ty didn't flinch. He just paused. Let Alex speak. Then returned to helping without reacting.

That drove Alex mad. Not the silence—but the refusal to feed the game. One afternoon, he tried to flip the story again. Said Leo had pushed Jeremy near the lockers. But Jeremy—soft-spoken, honest Jeremy—spoke up. "He didn't push me. He caught me. I tripped." Ty nodded. Jasmin wrote it down. Alex smiled too wide and shrugged. "Just saying what I saw," he muttered, but no one believed him.

Leo could have stepped in with fire. He could've told Alex off. But he didn't. He just sat beside Jeremy, rested a hand on his shoulder, and said, "You okay?" That was it. Nothing more. Because sometimes love speaks louder than blame ever could. And sometimes, not reacting is the strongest reaction of all.

Ella noted that Alex always used someone else's name when telling stories. "Mila said…" or "Jeremy told me…" He never stood on his own words. He leaned on other people's uncertainty. But the group wasn't uncertain anymore. They weren't afraid of the twist. They had notes. They had each other. And they had Ty.

Ty showed them how to spot the pause. The shift in breathing when someone's lying. The slight turn of the foot when they're ready to run. "It's not about catching them," he said. "It's about understanding what they're protecting. Most liars aren't trying to hurt—they're trying to hide." That didn't make it okay. But it made it make sense.

Leo shared his past in pieces. Not to excuse it, but to help them see the roots. "I twisted stories to stay in control," he admitted once during lunch. "Because if I controlled the version, I didn't have to feel the truth." Jeremy sat beside him quietly, munching on crackers, then slipped his small hand into Leo's. Leo smiled. "Now I don't need to win. I just want peace."

Ty saw Alex watching from across the room. Watching Jeremy. Watching Leo. Watching the space that used to belong to him—the power he once held. But power earned through fear never lasts. Love lasts. Truth lasts. And Alex? He was running out of versions to hand out.

Jasmin shared her notes with Ty. "Is this what you meant by pattern?" she asked. Ty smiled. "Exactly. When you write down the truth, you don't have to argue. You just hold it. And wait." That waiting wasn't weakness. It was strength in stillness. A lesson the whole group was beginning to live out loud.

Leo started to track the patterns too. Not on paper, but in posture. He noticed when Alex leaned too far into a compliment. When he offered help before it was needed. When he turned every story into a performance. Leo used to do that too. And every time he saw it now, he felt a chill—not from fear, but from memory. He never wanted to go back.

Mr. Clarke caught on slowly. He began to observe, silently, the way Alex always had a version. But he didn't act yet. Not until there was more. That's what the notes were for. Not to accuse. But to prepare. Ty made sure of that. "We don't expose unless the truth demands it," he said. "Not to shame—but to stop the harm."

Ella said one afternoon, "It's like Alex lives in a mirror world. Everything's backwards, but it still looks right if you don't pay attention." Ty nodded. "That's why we pay attention." Jasmin added, "And write it down." They were building something together. A map of truth. A record of light. And Alex? He kept smiling. Kept twisting. But the world around him had changed. Nobody was laughing. Nobody was cheering. They were watching. And writing. And waiting. Quiet warriors with pens instead of swords, notebooks instead of noise.

Jeremy sat between Leo and Ty with wide eyes and chocolate milk on his upper lip, listening closer than he breathed. "Why does Alex always want to win?" he asked, voice half-muffled by sandwich crust. Leo didn't laugh at the question. He nodded. "Because winning is how he knows he's real. If he doesn't win, he feels like nothing." The words sat heavily on the table, but Jeremy didn't flinch. He wiped his lip, kept listening. Ty folded his arms across his tray, his voice calm as water. "That's what real narcissists do, Jeremy. They don't just want to win. They need to. Even if no one else is playing."

Jasmin leaned in from the edge of the bench. "So... it's not about being mean?" Ty shook his head. "Not always. It's about control. If they control the story, the spotlight, or the feeling in the room, then they feel safe.

If they don't—then someone else is in charge. And that's terrifying to them." Leo glanced toward the eighth-grade table where Alex sat spinning a pen between his fingers, eyes scanning the cafeteria like a watchman. "He's not bored," Leo said quietly. "He's looking for his next move."

"You used to do that?" Jeremy asked. He wasn't judging. He was just trying to understand. Leo met his little brother's gaze and nodded. "I did. I always had to win. Even when it didn't make sense. Even when it hurt people. I didn't care about the game. I cared about not losing. I didn't even know what I was trying to win half the time. I just didn't want to feel small." Ty touched Leo's shoulder gently. "Because back then, being small meant being hurt. Now, it just means being loved by someone taller."

Jeremy grinned at that. "I'm small." Leo smiled. "Exactly." Jeremy puffed his chest anyway, but stayed pressed to Leo's side like ivy growing into brick. Ty pointed at Alex across the room. "See the way he leans forward? He's looking for someone slipping up. He watches like a predator—but not to pounce. To twist. If you say something clumsy, he'll use it to make you look bad. Not because he's smarter—but because he's scared of being nothing."

Ella spoke next. "I noticed he only helps people when someone's watching. He carried my books once—but looked around first." Jasmin added, "He raised his hand for every question in class today. Even ones he didn't know." Ty nodded. "That's the mask of always-winning. It's polished, it's loud, and it cracks when no one's watching." Leo leaned down toward Jeremy. "If someone only helps when it's loud... that's not love. That's a show."

Jeremy took that in slowly, nodding little by little. "But what happens if they lose?" he whispered. Ty sighed. "They panic. They lash out. They rewrite the story. If someone else starts getting love or respect, a narcissist sees it as robbery. As if love is a trophy and there's only one to hand out." Leo added, "But real love doesn't run out. That's what Alex never learned. And that's what nearly broke me."

Ty watched Alex now with the eyes of someone who had studied war from the inside. "When a narcissist starts losing power, they either find a new audience... or they try to destroy the one who took the spotlight." Jasmin shifted in her seat. "So if we keep protecting kids like Jeremy, he'll try to hurt us?" Leo shook his head. "He'll try to make us doubt ourselves first. It's not always big. Sometimes it's whispers. Or fake kindness. Or blaming you for the thing he did."

"That's what happened yesterday," Jeremy said softly. "When he said I lost the math paper, but I saw him throw it out." Ty looked straight into his little brother's face. "You saw right. And you told the truth. That's what counts." Jeremy smiled but stayed close, like the truth still needed Leo's shoulder to lean on.

Ella wrote something in her notebook. "So what do we do if he tries to twist it again?" Ty answered, "You don't react fast. You stay steady. You hold your version without shouting it. Narcissists feed off your panic. If you stay calm, they run out of energy." Jasmin whispered, "Like turning off the light in a play." Leo nodded. "Exactly. No audience, no act."

Jeremy tilted his head. "Is it okay if I still feel scared?" Leo put a hand to his little brother's heart. "That just means you're brave. Fear's part of it. But truth doesn't need to be louder than fear. It just has to stand still."

Ty said nothing more. He just watched Alex try again that afternoon—blaming Elia for knocking over a juice box. But this time, Elia didn't shout. She didn't run to a teacher. She just looked Alex in the eye and said, "No." Then turned and walked away. No applause. No fanfare. Just the sound of a game losing its grip. Leo watched it all with a strange peace in his chest. Not the peace of winning. The peace of not needing to anymore. And that, for the first time, made him feel like he could finally breathe.

The desks were pushed into a wide circle. Mr. Clarke stood near the whiteboard but didn't speak much. It was Wellness Hour, a new idea started by Naomi Takashi after her last visit, and this time, the topic was "change." Students shifted uncomfortably, unsure what to share or how deep to go. Jeremy sat closest to Leo, his small hand lightly touching Leo's arm. The contact was gentle, like he was reminding Leo he didn't have to speak if he wasn't ready. But Leo cleared his throat, rose from his chair, and stood at the centre of the circle.

"I want to talk about the old me," he said, voice steady, not rehearsed. "Because... he's not me anymore."

A few students leaned forward. Ty stayed still, calm, letting Leo have the air. Jasmin crossed her arms gently, her gaze steady and kind. Ella gave a single nod. Leo took a breath that seemed to travel all the way to his shoes, then spoke again, slower this time.

"I used to lie. Not just little lies. Big ones. I made people doubt their own memories. I'd say they imagined things I actually did. I'd twist stories. Turn people against each other. Make them fight just so I wouldn't have to explain what I did." He looked down at the carpeted floor, but not out of shame. He was remembering, and it showed. "I made people feel like they were the problem. And then I'd comfort them after. Just to stay in control."

No one laughed. No one whispered. The room held stillness like reverence. "I did it because... I didn't want anyone to look too closely at me," Leo said, lifting his eyes now. "I thought if they saw who I really was, they'd leave. So I wore masks. And every lie I told made the mask thicker."

Jeremy stood slowly, as if asking permission with his body. Leo reached a hand toward him without looking, and Jeremy stepped into his side. His little brother. His anchor. His truth. Leo wrapped an arm around him, kept going.

"But then I met Ty. And he didn't flinch. He didn't yell. He just looked at me like I was already telling the truth, even when I wasn't. And I hated it. Because part of me wanted to lie again. Wanted to run. But he didn't let me."

Ty didn't smile. He just kept watching, honouring the silence with strength. Leo exhaled. "He asked me, 'Does someone talk to you the way you talk to others?' And it broke me. Because the answer was yes."

A few students blinked slowly. Mr. Clarke adjusted his glasses but said nothing. "I started crying in the office," Leo admitted, "not because I got caught. But because someone finally saw me. And didn't walk away."

Jeremy hugged his waist tighter. Leo rested his hand on his brother's head. "Jeremy hugged me every single day after that. Morning. Lunch. After school. Sometimes for no reason. Sometimes for every reason. He never asked for anything back. He just loved me. And that started to change me."

He turned to Ty now. "You told me the truth. Even when I didn't want to hear it. You didn't protect me from myself. You stood beside me while I faced it."

Ty nodded once. Leo's voice dropped to a whisper, but everyone still heard it. "That's how I changed my life. Not with punishment. Not with detention or yelling. But with love. Real love. The kind that tells you the truth—and stays."

He returned to his seat slowly. Jeremy didn't let go. The rest of the circle sat with a different weight now. Not heavy, not sad—just fuller. Honest. Mr. Clarke finally spoke. "Thank you, Leo. That's the kind of bravery that helps others find their way, too."

Jasmin added gently, "I knew something had changed. But I didn't know how much." Ella gave a small nod, "It's all in your eyes now. No more masks." Leo didn't cry, not this time. He didn't need to. Because the truth had finally spoken louder than his old self ever could. Ty gave him a single pat on the shoulder. Jeremy, another hug. The bell hadn't rung yet, but something else had ended. The lie had.

Naomi Takashi didn't stand behind a podium. She never did. She sat in a student's chair, legs crossed, eyes at their level, as if to remind every child in the room that truth doesn't speak down to people. Mr. Clarke had invited her again after Leo's last talk—no special forms, no speech prepared. Just her, because the students listened when she spoke. Today, she began quietly, gently tapping her fingers against her mug. "Let's talk about something confusing," she said. "The difference between control and care."

Jeremy shifted in his seat, adjusting his glasses. Ty gave him a small nod, encouraging. Leo leaned back against the wall near the window, arms folded but face soft. Naomi glanced at him only briefly, then turned back to the class. "Sometimes, people say they're helping you... but it doesn't feel like help, does it?" Several kids nodded. "They say things like, 'I'm only doing this because I care,' or, 'I know what's best for you.' But then, you feel smaller. Less free. Afraid to get it wrong."

Ella raised a hand slightly. "Like when someone does your whole project, but tells the teacher you weren't trying?"

"Exactly," Naomi said. "Control wears a mask that looks like care. It gives you no choice, but says it's love." Her voice never rose. She didn't pace. She just stayed still—like the truth, waiting. "Real care doesn't make you feel smaller. It makes you feel seen. Stronger. Even when it's correcting you, it gives you room to choose."

Leo stood. "Can I give an example?" Naomi nodded. "When I was... when I used to be the other version of me, I'd do things for people—then say they owed me. I'd say I was helping, but really, I was setting traps. I wanted them to need me, not thank me. That wasn't care. That was control." He exhaled slowly. "I was taught that control meant love. But it wasn't."

Jasmin frowned thoughtfully. "So... someone can do something nice but still be hurting you?"

"Yes," Naomi said. "And that's what makes emotional abuse so hard to spot. It's not always yelling. Sometimes it's smiling while stealing your choices." Ty glanced toward Leo with quiet pride. Leo met his gaze and nodded. The silence between them said everything.

Jeremy raised his hand, slowly. "Can... I talk?" Naomi's eyes warmed. "Always." He stood up, legs stiff, but voice clear. "When... when someone blames me... my st-stutter gets worse." He took a breath. "I c-c-can't... talk... if I think I'm... bad." The room held its breath. Leo knelt beside him without a word. Jeremy put a hand on his shoulder. "But when Leo says it's okay, I don't st-st-stutter... as much."

Naomi smiled softly. "Because safety gives the brain space to breathe. That's why care matters. Not fake kindness. Not helpfulness with strings. But honest love that listens, even when nothing's said."

Mr. Clarke wrote two words on the board: Control and Care. "We'll leave those up all week," he said. "And every time we think someone's helping, we'll ask: Which one is it, really?"

Ella muttered, "That explains Alex..." Nico leaned closer to her. "He carries people's books and then brags about it later. That's not help." Ty said nothing, but handed her a folded piece of paper.

On it, a question: Did you feel stronger or smaller after they helped you? Naomi stood, slow and steady. "You all have voices. But sometimes, the world teaches you to whisper them. That's not care either. That's training." Leo's brow furrowed. "I used to do that to people." She touched his arm. "You don't anymore."

After class, Jeremy tugged Naomi's sleeve. "You c-care like my mom does." Naomi crouched to meet him. "That's because I see you the same way she does." He grinned, wide and unfiltered, then turned to Leo. "I love you," he said. Leo smiled, not shy anymore. "I love you too."

Alex stood at the front of the classroom, arms folded, face composed. "I'm sorry," he said, staring straight at Sophie, "if you felt like I was being mean. I was just trying to joke around." The room held still for a moment, but it wasn't the stillness of healing—it was the hush of uncertainty. Sophie looked down at her shoes. The apology didn't land. It hovered like a balloon without a string—empty, inflated, and drifting.

Ty didn't speak right away. He never did when something wasn't real. He simply closed his notebook, slid it into his bag, and stood beside Sophie. "That's not an apology," he said softly, not even looking at Alex. "That's a deflection wrapped in sugar." Several students glanced at one another. Alex blinked. "What do you mean? I said I was sorry."

"No," Leo said, stepping forward, "you said if she felt hurt. That's not taking responsibility. That's handing it back to her." He looked at the others. "A real apology doesn't have a but. It doesn't try to explain the reason. It doesn't need to defend what you did. It just admits it and makes it right." Ty folded his arms quietly, letting Leo speak. This was his turn.

"When I used to mess up," Leo continued, "I'd say things like 'I didn't mean to,' or 'You're too sensitive,' or 'I didn't think it would hurt you.' That's not truth. That's manipulation. I wasn't sorry—I was scared of getting in trouble. I didn't want to feel guilt, so I pushed it onto someone else." Sophie lifted her head slightly. She was listening.

Ty added, "A real apology is a gift. Not a negotiation. It doesn't ask for anything in return. It says: I hurt you. I own it. And I'll do better. That's all." He didn't raise his voice. He never needed to. His calm was sharper than shouting.

Alex opened his mouth as if to speak, then closed it. He looked around and saw that the faces he once controlled weren't on his side anymore. Jasmin crossed her arms. Nico watched with careful eyes. Ella took Sophie's hand beneath the desk. Jeremy blinked up at Leo, then whispered, "That's why I l-l-like you now."

Leo crouched beside Jeremy. "That's because I learned the truth, little brother. And truth is what changes people, not lies pretending to be apologies." Mr. Clarke stepped in at that moment, not with punishment, but affirmation.

"I hope we're all learning what real accountability looks like," he said. "What Leo just did? That was real." Alex stayed quiet. No protest. No defense. Just the subtle flicker of someone who had lost his grip. Perhaps, for the first time, he was beginning to see that charm doesn't erase damage.

After class, Ty found Leo at the lockers. "That was brave," he said. "No, it was necessary," Leo replied. "She deserved the truth." Ty nodded. "Truth is always a gift, even when it hurts." Sophie walked by on her way out and paused. "Thank you," she said to Leo. He smiled gently. "You don't owe me that," he said. "But I'll keep earning it anyway." Jeremy tugged on Leo's sleeve. "W-was that a real a-ap-apology you gave m-m-me... l-last year?" Leo smiled, full-hearted. "The first ones weren't. But the one where I cried? That was." Ty wrapped an arm around both of them. "And that's the one we remember."

Ella didn't speak much during the first half of the day, but she didn't miss a thing. Her eyes flicked from person to person like a shadow tracing light. She saw how Alex acted whenever Ty walked past—shoulders stiffened, smile grew too quick, eyes darted down. She noticed how he never made jokes around Jasmin anymore, not since she stopped laughing. But it was with Leo that the change felt loudest. Alex didn't even look at him unless he had to.

Ty had said it once before and said it again as they stood outside the library during recess. "They don't fear yelling. They fear people who stay calm. People who see through it." Ella turned toward him slowly. "You mean like... not reacting?" Ty nodded. "Exactly. Narcissists feed on attention—good or bad. But when they know you see them and won't play, that's what really scares them."

Leo came out holding Jeremy's backpack. "You should've seen Alex's face when Jeremy asked me if I wanted to play superheroes later. It was like he swallowed a lemon." Ty gave a short smile. "He's losing power. And he knows it." Jeremy, just a few paces behind, was humming a song about dragons and snacks. Ella leaned against the wall. "So... what's the thing they're most afraid of?" Ty thought for a second, then answered plainly. "Being seen without their tricks. No spotlight. No audience. Just... seen."

Leo dropped down to one knee so Jeremy could climb on his back. "So being honest is like shining a flashlight on them?" "Yes," Ty said. "But the flashlight doesn't need to be big. Just steady." Jasmin came out of the side doors and caught that last part. "What about the people they trick? The ones who still believe them?" "They'll come around," Leo said. "Or they won't. But the truth doesn't disappear just because someone doesn't believe it."

Inside the school, Alex sat with Elia. She used to laugh at all his jokes. Now she just blinked slowly and gave small nods without emotion. His voice pitched higher, trying harder. Ella watched from the corner of the hallway window. "He's afraid," she said to no one. "Not of being alone. Of being seen."

Mr. Clarke passed by and gave a gentle nod. "When kids like that lose the mirror, they panic. They don't know who they are without the reflection they control." Ty folded his arms. "Then we give them something better. Stillness. Truth. No performance."

At lunch, Alex made a show of helping someone clean up a spilled tray. He smiled, spoke kindly, even patted the kid's shoulder. But no one clapped. No one complimented him. Jeremy leaned in close to Leo. "W-w-why is he s-s-s-so nice all of a s-sudden?" Leo patted his back. "Because no one's watching him anymore. And that scares him."

In the afternoon, Ty assigned a "quiet mission" to their little group. "Pay attention to who he avoids. That's who holds the power now." Ella wrote it down. Jasmin observed. Nico listened. Jeremy nodded and took Leo's hand.

Later that evening, as they walked home under trees shaking loose their leaves, Leo whispered, "I used to hate people like that. The calm ones. I thought they were boring." Ty laughed once. "Because they made you feel seen?" Leo nodded. "Exactly. And being seen... hurt." "But now?" Ty asked. "Now," Leo said, "it helps me heal." Jeremy held both their hands. "I l-l-like being seen," he said. "By people who love me." Leo squeezed his shoulder. "That's the only kind of being seen that matters."

It was after the last bell, when most kids had rushed home or to after-school sports, that Leo waited by the quiet reading room beside the library. The sun slid low across the tiled floors, and the noise of the school dulled into a calm silence broken only by the soft tick of the clock overhead. Jeremy arrived carrying a folder tucked under his arm and a cautious smile on his face. He didn't speak right away—not because he didn't want to, but because he was still figuring out how. Leo didn't rush him.

They sat cross-legged on the carpet, the smell of paper and pencil shavings thick in the air. Leo pulled a small mirror from his backpack and handed it to Jeremy gently. "Today we're gonna try that thing Ty showed me. Breathing first. Words second. Deal?" Jeremy nodded, eyes wide and serious. He looked in the mirror, then at Leo, then back again. "M-m-m... mirror," he tried. Leo smiled. "Yes. And now breathe."

He guided Jeremy through slow counts—one, two, three in... hold... one, two out. They did it again. And again. Each time Jeremy tried a word, Leo wasn't listening for perfection. He was listening for courage. "Buh-buh... book," Jeremy said, the corners of his mouth tight with focus. "Perfect," Leo said. "Say it like you mean it now." Jeremy repeated the word louder, and this time, it didn't stumble.

They spent twenty minutes with sounds and syllables. Leo never corrected. He demonstrated. If Jeremy stumbled, Leo showed him that it didn't matter. "I used to trip over lies," Leo said once. "You're just learning how to walk through truth." That made Jeremy giggle, and the sound of it echoed sweetly down the empty hallway.

Midway through the lesson, Jeremy looked at Leo with bright eyes and asked, "D-d-d…do I have to t-t-talk like anyone else?" Leo leaned back and shook his head. "Nope. You talk like you. You just learn to walk it out with strength." Jeremy grinned and whispered the word "strength" under his breath three times.

Leo remembered what it felt like to be unsure of your voice—not your speech, but your truth. He remembered being afraid that someone might actually hear the real him and leave. But now, every time Jeremy found his word, Leo felt something steady grow in his chest. A kind of protective pride he couldn't explain, only feel. It was the way Ty looked at him, once. That warmth. That belief.

They practiced greetings next. "H-hi… my name is… J-J-Jeremy." Leo gave him a nod. "Again, like it's your superhero name." Jeremy puffed his chest. "My name… is Jeremy." "There you go," Leo whispered. "And that's how you take space."

When Naomi arrived to pick them up, she peeked through the glass and paused. She didn't open the door right away. She watched her sons—both of them now. One teaching, one learning, and neither ashamed of what they were. Just there for each other. When she stepped inside, Jeremy ran to her and said, "Naomi! I d-did it!" She bent to hug him close. "I saw, sweetheart. I saw everything."

Leo stood beside them and rubbed the back of his neck. "He's been working hard." Naomi turned to him. "So have you, Leo. Don't think I don't notice." Leo blushed and looked at the floor. Jeremy grabbed his hand and held on.

They walked together to the car, with Jeremy humming again, this time confidently. At the curb, he stopped and tugged on Leo's sleeve. "C-c-c…can I do this a-again tomorrow?" Leo looked down and said, "As long as you want. We're not rushing this. It's not about being perfect. It's about being you."

That night, at dinner, Jeremy told his parents that Leo helped him learn his name in superhero voice. They laughed. They cried a little too. Jeremy kissed Leo's cheek before bed and whispered, "You g-g-gave me my voice." Leo closed his eyes and hugged him tight. "No, Jeremy. You always had it. I just helped you find it."

The room wasn't much—just the back corner of the library, where the walls felt padded by books instead of judgment. The old beanbag chairs sagged in quiet acceptance, and the clock on the wall ticked slow like it knew not to rush this kind of thing. Leo sat cross-legged across from Jeremy, holding a small laminated card between them. On it were three words: breathe, slow, speak. Jeremy stared at them like they were a test, but Leo leaned in and said gently, "It's not a race. We're just talking. That's all."

Jeremy blinked and gave a small nod, his chest rising in a steady breath. "Muh…my… na-na-name… is…" His lips tensed, the syllable catching in his throat. Leo didn't flinch. He just breathed with him. "Try it again. Don't force it. Let it ride the breath." Jeremy closed his eyes. "My… name is… Jer… Jer-Jeremy." He winced, but Leo smiled. "There it is," he whispered. "Say it again. That was gold."

They'd been doing this after school for two weeks. Not every day, but often enough that Jeremy started looking forward to it. It wasn't just about talking. It was about feeling safe while he tried. No one laughed. No one rushed him. Leo never finished his sentences. He waited, like a big brother should. And Jeremy bloomed a little more each time because of it.

One afternoon, Leo had brought a mirror. "Not so you can see your face," he explained. "But your strength. Watch how your mouth moves when you breathe first." Jeremy stared at himself. "Do… I… look… okay?" Leo nodded. "You look like someone learning to roar. That's better than okay." The boy chuckled—a short, surprised sound—but it wasn't shaky. It was proud.

When Jeremy's parents came to pick him up, they stayed longer each time. They sat at the back of the library and watched from behind the bookshelves. His mother clutched a tissue but didn't cry. His father just kept whispering, "That's my boy." After a session where Jeremy introduced himself to the librarian without stuttering, they both hugged Leo. Tight. Long. With the kind of gratitude that didn't need words.

"You're his brother," Jeremy's mother had said softly, hands on Leo's shoulders. "We know you're not by blood. But that doesn't matter to us. You're his brother." Leo swallowed hard. "He's mine too," he answered. "I'll always be here for him." Ty watched from a few feet away, his arms folded and his face unreadable—but his eyes were shining. Later, walking home, he nudged Leo. "You're doing real work. That's more than some grownups know how to do." Leo smirked. "He helps me too, you know." Ty tilted his head. "How?" Leo looked up at the sky. "He reminds me I've got something to give."

Back in the library the next week, Leo changed up the session. "Let's try saying what you love," he told Jeremy. "Start with food." Jeremy grinned. "I… I… l-luh-love… m-muh… macaroni!" Leo clapped quietly, then leaned in. "What about people?" Jeremy blushed. "I luh-love… yuh-you." Leo blinked. "I love you too, Jeremy." From that day, Jeremy didn't just try to speak. He wanted to. And the stutters, while still there, didn't scare him anymore. He knew Leo would wait. He knew Leo understood. They were brothers now—by choice, not chance. And sometimes that meant more than blood ever could.

They made up silly phrases to help with breath: "Pancake penguins," "Slinky sunset," "Dragon's doughnut." Jeremy loved the dragon ones best. Leo even brought paper one day and let Jeremy draw himself as a fire-breathing dragon in a superhero cape, with Leo beside him, arms crossed like a protector. "That's you," Jeremy said. "That's us," Leo replied.

One Friday, before Jeremy left, he turned around at the library door and said clearly—no stutter at all—"Thank you, Leo. For teaching me to b-b-believe I c-c-c-could." Leo knelt and hugged him, holding him close. "You did it," he whispered. "You did it, little brother." And Jeremy beamed.

There are words that cling like burrs, sharp and quiet. Not shouted in hallways, not carved into bathroom stalls—but spoken when no one's looking. Jasmin remembered them. So did Leo. It was in the way people used to say his name like it meant nothing. The way teachers looked past him after sending him out of class. The way other kids would share a smirk, a glance, as if he didn't deserve to hear the truth. Not because he was invisible, but because he wasn't expected to understand.

Jasmin sat beside Leo on the front steps of the school, their backpacks crumpled between them like forgotten burdens. It was after drama club, the sun warm but falling fast behind the brick walls. She didn't look at him when she spoke. "You know," she said, her fingers playing with the strap on her shoe, "you were loud. But I don't think you ever wanted to be seen like that." Leo glanced at her, his jaw tightening. "What do you mean?" he asked, but he already knew.

"You used to walk into a room and fill it up with noise. Jokes. Teasing. Even yelling sometimes." She paused. "But I always thought maybe… that was just so no one would notice how small you felt inside." Leo didn't answer right away. His eyes scanned the schoolyard—the empty swings, the chalk-smeared pavement, the spot under the big oak tree where he once pushed a kid just for looking at him funny. That kid never looked him in the eye again.

"They made me small," he finally said, voice low. "Every day. Before I ever knew what I was doing." Jasmin nodded. "I know. I saw it. You weren't born mean. You just didn't want to disappear." For a second, Leo looked as if he might laugh, but he didn't. Instead, he picked up a pebble and rolled it between his fingers. "I thought being loud would make them respect me. But all it did was make me alone. I didn't even realize how empty I was until Ty called me out. And then Jeremy… that kid sees me like I'm magic." He swallowed. "I never had that." "You do now," Jasmin said. "And you earned it."

He looked at her sideways. "Even after all I did?" Jasmin shrugged. "It's not about forgetting. It's about seeing the person who chooses better. I know what strength looks like. And love? Real love? It's loud in a different way." Leo nodded. "Jeremy tells me he loves me three times a day. I count. I didn't ask him to. He just does it." "That's what healing sounds like," Jasmin said. "Not shouting. Not pretending. Just… consistency."

He leaned back against the steps and stared up at the clouds. "You think people ever stop trying to make others small?" he asked. Jasmin followed his gaze. "No. But now we know how to stay tall. And how to lift others too."

There was a pause, heavy and warm. Leo reached down and picked at the fraying edge of his shoelace. "You were always brave," he said. "Even when I wasn't." Jasmin smiled. "I wasn't brave. I was just tired of lies. You're the brave one now, Leo. You stood in front of the same people who used to laugh at you, and you told the truth."

He didn't say thank you. He didn't need to. Jasmin wasn't looking for a reply. She just wanted to name what had been unspoken for too long. The bell tower above them clicked into the hour. It was almost time to go home. Jeremy's parents would be waiting by the fence, and Leo would carry his little brother's backpack just because he wanted to. But before they got up, Leo looked at her one more time. "They don't get to make me small anymore," he said. "I won't let them." Jasmin gave a nod. "Because now you know who you are."

Leo stood first. Held out a hand to help her up. She took it. Side by side, they walked down the front path. Jeremy spotted Leo from across the lot and ran toward him like a comet, arms wide. "Luh-leeo!" he shouted. Leo bent low to catch him. "Hey, little brother," he said, lifting him off the ground in a hug that said everything. Jeremy looked over Leo's shoulder and whispered, "You're big." Leo laughed. "Yeah. I finally am."

Some storms are made of silence, not thunder. Ty knew the difference. He'd seen it in the tilt of Alex's grin, the deliberate way he'd sharpen his tone just enough to cut skin but not draw blood. That day, it was Leo he wanted to bait, but Leo didn't react. Not anymore. So Alex turned to Ty, testing waters he didn't understand.

"You must think you're perfect," Alex said in front of the lockers, eyes narrowed. "Acting like you're the peacekeeper. Like you've never made anyone feel small." Ty blinked, but he didn't flinch. He didn't puff up. Didn't reply right away. He just shifted his weight, calm as stone, and looked at Alex—not with fire, but with depth. "Everyone's made mistakes," he said. "But some of us learn from them."

Alex scoffed, tried again. "You think you're better than me?" Ty leaned forward a fraction, voice soft enough that only Leo, who stood close behind him, could really hear. "When someone's always picking fights," he said, "it's not about who's right. It's the only way they feel alive." Alex blinked. That wasn't the script he'd expected. His mouth opened—then shut. He looked at Leo, hoping for a reaction. Leo gave none. The new Leo didn't need to win.

After Alex had walked off in a huff, Ty turned to Leo with a half-smile. "It's a trick," he said. "They need chaos like some people need sleep. But love's quieter. It doesn't need proof." Leo let out a breath he didn't know he'd been holding. "How do you do that?" he asked. "How do you stay so calm?" Ty shrugged. "Because you're behind me now. And because I remember what it was like to be the angry one."

They walked through the corridor together. A few younger students watched them pass, heads turning—not out of fear, but awe. They weren't the same boys who used to command attention through volume. They moved with steadiness, gravity. Leo paused by the water fountain, bent down for a sip, then wiped his mouth. "Do you really think Alex can change?" "I don't know," Ty answered honestly. "But I know we did."

That landed like truth does. No theatrics. Just weight. In class, Leo caught Jeremy's eye across the room. The younger boy gave a discreet thumbs-up, his own tiny way of saying I see you. Leo smiled back, proud. Later, at recess, Leo sat on the back steps while Ty helped Mr. Clarke with boxes for the library. Jeremy plopped down beside him, kicking his feet. "Do you think I'll be brave like you?" he asked, eyes wide.

Leo didn't answer right away. He looked out across the schoolyard, the games of tag, the skipped ropes. He remembered the boy he used to be—the boy who'd pushed others to feel tall. And then he looked at Jeremy. "You already are," he said. Jeremy leaned his head against Leo's shoulder.

After school, Ty handed Leo a small folded note. "Read it later," he said. "It's not from me. It's from Mom." Leo waited until he was alone to open it. The handwriting was neat, floral, unmistakably Naomi's. You are not your past. You are what you choose to protect. Thank you for choosing my son. And for becoming mine. He folded it gently, pressed it to his chest, and closed his eyes. In the evening, when Ty and Leo were setting the table for dinner, Leo suddenly said, "Thanks for not flinching today." Ty grinned. "I don't flinch for family." Leo grabbed a fork, then added, "I love you, Ty."

Ty didn't miss a beat. "I love you too." That night, when Jeremy called from the phone just to say goodnight, Leo answered, "Sweet dreams, little brother." Jeremy giggled on the other end. "You too, big brother." And in the quiet that followed, Leo knew something deep in his bones: he was home.

The hallway light flickered once, then steadied again, catching on the worn patches of floor just outside the staff room where Leo waited for Jeremy. It was their usual meeting spot, just after cleanup and before the first bell. Jeremy shuffled down the hall with his backpack swaying like a loose tooth, eyes forward, lips moving silently as if practising something before he arrived. He stopped in front of Leo and held out a drawing—crayons pressed hard into paper, a blue sky, two stick figures, and above them in shaky letters: Leo and Me, Best Friends. Jeremy didn't say a word. He just handed it over like it was sacred.

Leo took the paper without speaking. His throat clenched around a word that didn't make it out. Jeremy looked up, eyes wide and hopeful, then whispered, "I used to think you were scary." He paused, watching Leo's face. "But now... now you're my favourite person. Even more than my toys." That last part came out rushed, almost embarrassed, as if it cost him something to say. But he meant it. And Leo knew he meant it.

The hallway was still, just the faint hum of morning routines behind the classroom doors. Leo crouched down to Jeremy's height, and the boy stepped into his arms like it was the most natural thing in the world. Leo wrapped him close, not loosely, not politely, but like someone holding a fragile truth he never thought he'd earn. The weight of those little arms around his neck undid something inside him that hadn't been touched by kindness in years. Leo closed his eyes. He didn't need to speak. The tears came anyway.

Jeremy pulled back just enough to press his cheek to Leo's and whisper, "You're my brother. Not just pretend." His voice cracked slightly. "Like, really. You're my best friend, and my brother." Leo nodded, forehead against Jeremy's temple, not trusting his voice. He had spoken a thousand lies in his life, but this one truth was too big for words.

Leo walked him to the classroom and didn't let go of his hand. Not this time. Inside, a few kids glanced over but didn't say anything. Leo could feel the shift in the air—how his presence no longer carried weight like a threat, but weight like a promise. He helped Jeremy with his chair, placed his bag on the hook, and gave him one more squeeze on the shoulder. Jeremy beamed. A real, open-mouth, no-reservations kind of smile that made Leo feel like he'd won something important. Something nobody could ever take from him.

Back in the hall, Ty leaned against the wall, arms crossed, having watched the whole thing. He didn't say anything until Leo got closer. Then, without any sarcasm or jokes, he said, "That's what a real big brother looks like." Leo didn't deflect. He didn't roll his eyes or shrug it off. He just nodded once and smiled. Quiet, but solid.

Later that day, Jeremy told his teacher that Leo helped him practise words after school. "He makes it feel like it's okay if I stutter," Jeremy explained. "He waits. That's all." The teacher noted it in her planner and smiled softly at Leo during dismissal. Not everything had to be said to be understood. The silence told its own kind of truth.

During lunch, Jeremy asked Leo if he could sit on the edge of the bench, just so he could be closer to him. "I feel braver near you," he whispered. Leo didn't answer with words. He scooted over, patted the space beside him, and let Jeremy lean in as much as he needed. Jasmin saw them from across the yard and gave Leo a small nod, not of approval, but of recognition. She saw what it meant.

When it came time to line up after recess, Jeremy stood beside Leo like a soldier with his commander. Not out of fear, not to hide, but because it was where he belonged. Leo didn't look down at him or ruffle his hair or joke. He just stood beside him, tall and calm, his posture enough to say, "I've got you."

In art class, Jeremy drew another picture. This time, the figures had names. One said Jeremy and the other said Leo. Above it, in blocky print: My Real Big Brother. He didn't show it to Leo yet. He folded it carefully and slid it into his backpack, planning to take it home and show his parents. "They already love you," Jeremy said earlier. "But now they'll really know why."

That night, at pickup, Jeremy's parents smiled wide when Leo came out holding his hand. His mother knelt and hugged Leo first. "Thank you for today," she said quietly. "For everything." His father placed a hand on Leo's shoulder and added, "He talks about you every night. Not like a hero. Like a brother. You're part of our family, you know that?"

Leo felt the lump rise in his throat again. He gave a short nod and blinked hard. Jeremy threw his arms around Leo's waist and said it again, out loud, in front of his parents. "I love you, Leo. You're my brother. Forever." He kissed Leo's shirt where his heart would be, then waved goodbye and ran off, not looking back. He didn't have to.

That night, Leo stood in the hallway of his home, staring at the fridge where Naomi had pinned a new drawing. It was Jeremy's. The one with the names. My Real Big Brother. Ty came up behind him and said, "He means every word of that." Leo didn't answer. He just kept looking at the page, his fingers brushing the edge of the magnet, holding it in place. For the first time in his life, Leo didn't feel like a boy who had to prove anything. He didn't feel like a project, or a problem, or a former villain trying to be good. He felt like a big brother. And that was enough.

The morning air in the hallway held the kind of silence that meant something was wrong. Not loud wrong. Not slammed-door, shouted-words wrong. But that quiet, hovering kind—the sort that wraps itself around the lockers and makes even laughter seem fake. Ty felt it first, and so did Jasmin. Leo walked ahead of them, and though his shoulders stayed square, he knew. It was coming again. Another game. Another twist.

Outside Room 206, Mr. Clarke stood beside a younger boy from Grade 3, arms crossed, face tense. A girl stood nearby, blinking too fast. She kept saying, "I didn't mean to get anyone in trouble. I just told the truth." And there was Alex, arms folded like a prince in exile, calm and collected. "He said it was his pencil case. But it wasn't," Alex stated, voice smooth as ever. "I was just trying to help."

Ty narrowed his eyes. Jasmin nudged Leo's arm. It was all there—the same script, same pauses, same false innocence. Alex stood in the perfect angle to the teacher's line of sight, as if staged. He always positioned himself just right, where the lie could catch the light like a polished stone. The younger boy looked down at his shoes, nodding slowly, already believing he was to blame. Until Mr. Clarke did something different.

He didn't nod. He didn't accept the narrative. Instead, he turned his gaze to Alex and then to the girl. "Why did you say that he said it was his pencil case?" the teacher asked gently. "Did he really say those words, or are you repeating what someone else said he said?" The girl bit her lip. "I... I heard it from Alex."

That changed the air entirely. The blame, that usual shapeshifter, hovered for a moment and then lost its form. Mr. Clarke turned back to Alex, but there was no lecture. No accusation. Just a pause. And then, a single question. "Why did you involve yourself?" It wasn't angry. It wasn't even disappointed. But it was the kind of question that can't be dodged with a compliment or a smile.

Alex didn't answer. He shrugged. That universal shield. But the shrug didn't land this time. It bounced off the space between them and clattered to the floor like something dropped and forgotten. Mr. Clarke glanced down the hallway, where Leo had stopped, arms at his sides. Their eyes met for only a second. A flicker. But it was enough.

He called Leo over. Quietly. Not in front of the others. Just a nod toward the storage room nearby. Leo followed. Ty waited outside with Jasmin and Ella, watching as if guarding something sacred. Inside the room, it was just the two of them. No accusations. No speeches. Just a chair, a clipboard, and the kind of silence that means something's about to change.

Mr. Clarke closed the door, leaned against the shelf, and folded his arms. "I don't know what's different," he began, "but I know it's happening." Leo didn't speak. He didn't need to. Mr. Clarke went on. "I've been a teacher for twenty years. I know when a child's being coached. This isn't that. This is... transformation." He paused again. "Whatever you're doing—it's changing things here."

Leo didn't cry. But he felt it—something rise up in his throat and lodge there, soft and heavy. He thought about Ty, about Jasmin, Ella, Sophie. About Jeremy's wide smile when he stuttered through the word sandwich yesterday and Leo gave him the biggest high five. He thought about the way Jeremy still called him "Buh-Buh-Leo," and how he'd never correct him, because it was perfect.

"Thank you," Leo said, voice steady, barely above a whisper. "I just don't want anyone else to feel like I did." Mr. Clarke nodded slowly, like he understood more than he was letting on. He didn't ask what that meant. He didn't need to. The room was quiet, but not empty. It was full of what mattered.

When Leo stepped back into the hallway, Ty didn't ask what was said. He simply stood beside him and walked beside him down the corridor. Jasmin slipped into step on the other side. Ella stayed close. There were no words, but the air around them shifted again. A line had been crossed, but it wasn't the kind of line that leads to punishment. It was the kind that leads to growth.

Back in the classroom, Alex sat stiff in his seat, arms tight across his chest. The girl who'd repeated his words didn't sit near him. The boy who'd been blamed got his pencil case back. And Mr. Clarke didn't need to explain anything. The truth had stood up for itself this time— and that, more than anything, was the change.

At lunch, Jeremy sat beside Leo as always, peeling the wrapper off his sandwich slowly. "Buh-Buh-Leo?" he said quietly. Leo turned. "Yeah, buddy?" Jeremy smiled with crumbs on his cheek. "You're, like... the boss of truth." Leo snorted, then laughed. He shook his head. "Nah. Truth doesn't need a boss. It just needs people who don't leave it alone." Jeremy thought about that, then nodded. "Then I'll stay with it, too." And he did. They all did. Because the blame may come back around—but this time, it had nowhere left to land.

The sun hit the floor tiles in slanted stripes that morning, warm and patient as always. Leo stood by the window with Jeremy tugging lightly at his sleeve, pointing to a pigeon outside trying to eat a whole crust of bread in one bite. Ty was watching too, one hand in his pocket, the other curled loosely around his water bottle. Jasmin sat near the cubbies, sketching something she wouldn't let anyone see. But even she glanced up when Alex walked by—eyes forward, smile glued in place, voice just loud enough to sound helpful.

Ty didn't move. He just observed. His posture didn't change, but Leo knew what was happening. He could feel it. Alex glanced toward Ty, and something flickered in his eyes. Not annoyance, not anger, not even jealousy. It was something deeper. Something quiet. A twitch behind the gaze. A freeze too fast to be noticed by most. But Leo caught it. He'd worn that look himself once, when the wrong person saw through the right lie.

"They don't like mirrors," Ty murmured, more to the air than to anyone in particular. Leo turned slightly. "What?" Ty's voice was calm. Not a whisper, but not needing volume either. "People like him," Ty said, nodding toward Alex. "They panic when someone calm sees them clearly. Because it reflects everything they pretend to be."

Leo folded his arms and watched. Alex was helping another student zip their coat—smiling too wide, making sure Mr. Arnett could see. When the zip caught and the kid winced, Alex rolled his eyes like the child was being difficult. But then, as Mr. Arnett turned away, Alex's expression vanished into something colder. Then just as quickly, back to warm. It was seamless, practiced. But not invisible anymore.

Jasmin walked up beside them, tapping her pencil against her palm. "He knows we see it," she said flatly. "And he doesn't know what to do with that." Ty nodded. "Because when someone only feels safe by controlling the story, and you stop letting them write it for you... they panic. They either explode, or vanish." Leo tilted his head. "Or both."

They didn't laugh. Not because it wasn't funny. But because it was too close to the truth to be treated like a joke. Ella joined them quietly, carrying Jeremy's lunchbox. "He told me my silence makes people uncomfortable," she said. "I said that wasn't my problem." Ty smiled at that, and even Leo chuckled. "Spoken like a Shadow Warrior," he said.

Later that afternoon, Alex tried to offer help again—carrying chairs during class cleanup. But this time, no one thanked him. Not rudely. Just not performatively. Jasmin nodded once. Ty said nothing. Leo kept packing his bag without even looking up. That silence spoke louder than praise. It unsettled Alex, and they saw it. The way he fidgeted. The way his hand twitched to grab another chair before realizing no one was watching anymore.

"They mirror who they wish they were," Ty said quietly. "Until someone shows them who they actually are." Jeremy asked what that meant, and Leo crouched to his level. "It means sometimes people act kind just so they don't get caught being mean," he said. "But when someone strong sees it, and doesn't flinch, it makes them scared."

Jeremy considered that, blinking behind his glasses. "So... being nice isn't always true?" Leo shook his head gently. "No. Not always. But being calm, and honest, and kind? That's different. That's not acting. That's being." Jeremy nodded. He liked that answer. He didn't say much more—but his hand found Leo's, and that was enough.

In the staff room that evening, Mr. Clarke spoke to Miss Kara in a voice just low enough that only the doorframe heard it. "Have you noticed the shift?" he asked. "Since Leo changed, and Ty started guiding them?" She smiled faintly. "It's like a light turned on," she said. "And now the shadows are uncomfortable."

By Friday, Alex had stopped offering to help. He started avoiding the main group altogether. He didn't sit near Leo, or try to charm the teachers with compliments. And yet, somehow, his presence became louder in the quiet. Ty said that's how some people react when their false power stops working—they withdraw, hoping the world will chase them. But the world didn't. Not this time.

Leo still sat with Jeremy every day at lunch. Jasmin still watched patterns like a quiet scientist. Ella still observed with her strength tucked beneath her stillness. And Ty, he just kept leading with silence that felt like truth. They weren't fighting Alex. They were simply not feeding the illusion anymore. That's what scared Alex the most. It wasn't punishment. It wasn't confrontation. It was the mirror. And the refusal to break it.

The cafeteria hummed with trays, zippers, and half-laughed jokes, the usual din of midday routine. Kids jostled for juice boxes, argued over the last seat at the end of the table, and tore open pudding lids like tiny warriors in a lunchtime war. But at the third table from the window, something different was happening—something too quiet to be missed. Jeremy had taken his seat beside Leo as usual, lunch bag in hand, his fingers pressing the zipper open with slow, concentrated effort. His sandwich looked slightly crushed, but he didn't care. His eyes were focused on someone further down the table—Alex.

Alex leaned over another boy's tray, pointing at a half-eaten muffin. "Weird how your snacks go missing when he's around," he said, nodding toward Jeremy without saying his name. It was quiet, but not quiet enough. The boy blinked, confused, but didn't argue. Others glanced over, and Alex waited for the seed to land. He tilted his head, watching to see if it would grow.

Jeremy's hands shook slightly as he folded the bag back up. His voice came in short bursts now. He started to breathe faster, eyes darting to Leo, but Leo didn't move. He didn't jump in. Not yet. Jeremy licked his lips, took a breath, and then stood. "I—I didn't d-do—" He stopped himself, clenched both fists, and closed his eyes. Then opened them again. "I didn't d-do it. Leo w-was with me." His voice wasn't loud. But it reached every corner of that table like it was made of thunder.

Leo blinked. He hadn't told Jeremy to do that. Hadn't rehearsed or planned. But Jeremy did it anyway—defended not just himself, but Leo too. The stutter made the words tremble, but the truth behind them stood still. A ripple passed down the table. Heads turned. Ty's fork paused halfway to his mouth. Jasmin closed her sketchbook slowly. Ella blinked once and then narrowed her eyes toward Alex.

Alex scoffed, leaning back like he didn't care. "Touchy," he muttered. But no one laughed. No one followed. No one even nodded. His comment dropped like a pebble into a well and vanished. Leo turned to Jeremy, his throat thick, his chest suddenly full. He didn't speak. He couldn't. Instead, he pulled Jeremy into his arms like someone hugging a piece of sky— something too valuable for words.

Jeremy's little arms wrapped tight around Leo's neck. It wasn't awkward. It wasn't shy. It was fierce, like he'd been waiting for that moment his whole life. He pressed a kiss to Leo's cheek with all the gentle power a child can carry, then whispered something only Leo heard. Leo's face went still, eyes blinking fast, mouth fighting a wobble. Then he buried his face in Jeremy's shoulder and held him tighter.

Across the room, Alex stood frozen. His smile twitched. Something in his posture cracked just enough for those watching to see what he'd tried to hide. The lie didn't land. The attention didn't return. And the boy he tried to embarrass had just become the centre of the most powerful thing in the room—love that didn't need to prove itself.

Ty leaned over to Jasmin. "That's what makes them panic," he said quietly. "Not shouting. Not punishment. That." Jasmin tilted her head, watching Alex slink toward the trash bin like a shadow trying to outrun the sun. "Because love can't be faked," she replied. "And he knows it."

Mr. Clarke had witnessed the whole exchange from the doorway, arms folded, leaning against the frame like he'd been listening without meaning to. He didn't step in. Didn't interfere. But his expression softened in a way that said he'd seen something true—something worth remembering. Later, he would tell Miss Kara, "That little one? Jeremy? He's got more strength in him than most grown men I know."

Leo didn't let go right away. He stayed knelt beside Jeremy's chair, one hand resting protectively on the boy's back, the other still holding the kiss Jeremy had left on his cheek like it was sacred. "You're amazing," he finally whispered. "You know that?" Jeremy smiled, pink creeping up his ears. "Y-you're my brother," he said. "Even if we don't match."

"I don't need to match," Leo said. "I just need to love you right." The words came so naturally, so clean and simple, that it startled Leo how easy they felt. Like they'd been hiding in him, waiting for Jeremy's voice to call them out. And that's what Jeremy had done. He'd called out love. Real love. Out loud.

Back at their usual spot on the playground, Jeremy found Ty and climbed up beside him on the climbing frame. "Do you think I was brave?" he asked. Ty didn't look down. He just reached out and mussed Jeremy's hair gently. "You weren't brave," he said. "You were a warrior." And Jeremy grinned so wide it looked like it might crack the sky.

That night, Leo walked through the front door of his new home and was immediately pulled into a hug by his mom, Naomi. "How was school?" she asked, not expecting the lump in his throat or the shimmer in his eyes. "He defended me," Leo whispered. "Like I mattered. Like I'm worth loving." Naomi smiled and pressed a kiss to his forehead. "That's because you are," she said. "Always have been."

And in his room, when Jeremy called to say goodnight, Leo held the phone close and listened to every stuttered syllable like it was gold. Because Jeremy didn't need to be perfect to be powerful. And Leo didn't need to yell to be heard. Love had already said everything for him.

Leo sat at his desk with the room quiet around him, the pencil in his hand warmer than it should have been. The lined paper had already soaked in a few eraser marks, but this time, he didn't plan to erase anything. He wasn't writing for a teacher. He wasn't writing for Jeremy or Ty or even his mom or dad. He was writing to someone who no longer existed—but who used to live inside his skin. The old Leo. The one who thought hurting people was a way to protect himself. The one who used lies like bricks to build a wall no one could get through.

He didn't start with "Dear." That felt too formal. Too gentle. He just wrote the words that came to him first: You don't live here anymore. The pencil scratched softly. He told that old self everything. That he'd made people cry. That he used to like the way power felt in his chest, even when it came at someone else's expense. That he confused control with love. And that Ty had broken that illusion. That Jeremy had burned it to the ground. That Naomi and Zenji had wrapped him in warmth so wide, so permanent, he forgot what cold even was.

He wrote about how he used to wake up angry for no reason, how it felt normal to ruin a day before it had even started. He told that old self that apology wasn't the end of a sentence—it was the start of a new one.

That saying sorry wasn't weak. It was the strongest thing he ever learned to do. He explained how Ty never gave up on him. How Jeremy hugged him every single day like he mattered. How every stuttered "I love you" stitched another thread back into his soul.

Then he stopped writing. He stared at the page. Folded it slowly, evenly, like it was something sacred. He didn't tear it up. He didn't hide it. He placed it inside the bottom drawer of his desk, beside a photo of him and Ty with chocolate ice cream smeared across their chins, and closed it softly. It wasn't a goodbye. Not really. More like a burial. That old version of him didn't need to be remembered. It had served its time. It had been replaced by someone new—someone who no longer flinched when love walked into the room.

Leo stood up and walked to his window. A gentle breeze moved through the screen, and he could smell barbecue from a neighbour's backyard. It was nearly spring break. He smiled, thinking about tomorrow. Jeremy had invited him over again. Just a short walk. Just a few blocks away. That little guy—his little brother, even if their last names didn't match—had asked if Leo could come help build a Lego castle. Jeremy said, "It'll be stronger if we build it together."

Leo had promised something recently. He hadn't said it loud, but he meant every word. He told Jeremy that no matter what, he'd never go back to who he used to be. That Jeremy would never have to be afraid of him. That he would protect him, listen to him, and love him—even on hard days. Especially on hard days. "You're stuck with me now," Leo had said, and Jeremy grinned like someone who didn't mind one bit.

Ty watched all of it happen quietly. The way Leo transformed—not with thunder, but with rain. Gentle, steady, necessary. They weren't born brothers. But some bonds didn't care about blood. Some bonds were built out of shared scars and stitched laughter, out of late-night whispered truths and front porch promises that didn't break in the morning. Leo called Ty's parents Mom and Dad now. It felt right. It didn't feel borrowed. It felt like home.

Even when Leo wasn't at home, he never felt far from it. Jeremy's house was small, yellow, and smelled like cinnamon on Saturdays. His mom always waved from the window. His dad called Leo "Champ" and made jokes about snack taxes. They treated Leo like he belonged—and he did. He wasn't there all the time. He didn't need to be. Because he knew that if he ever knocked, they'd open the door. No questions asked.

At eleven years old, Leo had lived two different lives. One of pain, and one of peace. And he chose peace every single day. Not because it was easier—but because it was real. He had earned it. He had fought for it. Not with fists, but with truth. He had been seen. He had been forgiven. And he had been loved into someone better.

Back at his desk, Leo glanced at the drawer again. He didn't need to read the letter. He didn't need to remember the words. They had done their job. They had closed the chapter. Across town, Jeremy was probably brushing his teeth with that dinosaur-shaped toothbrush he insisted wasn't babyish. He'd be thinking about Lego bricks and whether Leo would arrive before or after lunch. Leo chuckled quietly. "After lunch," he whispered. "But I'll bring snacks."

Before bed, Leo pulled out his phone and sent Jeremy a voice message. Just one line: "Hey, Little Brother. I'm proud of you. See you tomorrow." He pressed send and set the phone down. A few seconds later, a reply came through—Jeremy's soft voice stammering but sure: "L-Love you too, B-Big Brother." Leo closed his eyes and exhaled. The past no longer had a key to this house. The door had been shut. And inside—finally—was warmth.

The classroom windows stayed open most days now, letting in warm breezes that made paper corners flutter and pencil shavings skitter across desks like tiny leaves. You could feel it. In the way the teachers smiled more easily, in how the chairs creaked with a kind of farewell weight. Summer was near. Leo didn't mark the calendar with red ink or countdowns anymore. He marked it with promises—ones he actually planned to keep. This time, it wasn't about escape. It was about expansion. Jeremy was already planning their days with the precision of a general. He had drawn a schedule in marker, complete with smiley faces and a suspicious number of snack breaks.

Leo hadn't just survived the school year—he had earned it. His name no longer lingered in teachers' mouths like a warning. It came with a nod, a look of respect. He wasn't the loudest or the fastest or the star student, but he had become something better: the one others looked to when the room turned cold. The one who stood up before others even noticed someone had been pushed down. The quiet shield. The steady arm. The boy who proved change wasn't just possible—it was powerful.

Jeremy had finished strong. His stutter hadn't disappeared, but it had softened. He had learned to pause, breathe, smile, and start again. And no one rolled their eyes anymore. That was Leo's doing. Jeremy had told his whole class during circle time that Leo was his big brother—even though they didn't live in the same house. No one laughed. Not one person. Sophie even nodded and said, "Yeah, we kind of all see it." And Jeremy had glowed for the rest of the day.

Leo had never planned on spending the entire summer with a little nine-year-old boy who still named his socks and brought action figures to lunch. But now, he couldn't imagine it any other way. Jeremy's parents had asked him, gently but with clear hope, if he'd be open to it—camping, walks, weekend overnights, long afternoons of just being present. "You're good for him," Jeremy's mother had said, eyes shining with something more than relief. "You make him feel safe. That's not small."

Camping was first on the list. Jeremy wanted to build a tent from scratch, fish even if they didn't catch anything, roast marshmallows until they melted off the stick. Leo promised to teach him how to light a fire safely and how to read the sky for weather. Ty said he'd join them for a few days but wanted the brothers to have their own rhythm. "You've earned this time," Ty told Leo. "He chose you. And you chose him."

As for Alex—he still showed up. Still tried to provoke, flatter, manipulate. But the game didn't work anymore. No one passed his notes. No one covered for him when he twisted words or dodged accountability. He sat at lunch alone more days than not, his eyes flicking toward the group of younger students huddled around Leo and Jeremy, as if trying to understand why it no longer worked. He never figured it out. Because he never stopped playing. And they had all quietly quit the game.

Mr. Clarke had pulled Leo aside the last day of school, his voice low and proud. "You don't just walk through the halls anymore," he said. "You hold space here. That matters." Miss Kara gave him a small notebook and told him to keep writing, even if it was just for himself. Leo nodded and promised. He meant it. The old Leo had filled notebooks with half-truths and imagined revenge. The new Leo filled them with Jeremy's quotes, silly doodles, and small victories that no one else would think to record—but he did.

On the final bell of the year, Jeremy ran straight to him, arms wide and voice cracked with joy. "Summer, Leo! We made it!" Leo lifted him easily, spinning him once before setting him down. "We did," he said. "And now we start the real adventure." Jeremy insisted on walking Leo home, even though it was out of the way. They held hands most of the way there, passing kids playing with sidewalk chalk, neighbours tending to front lawns, and the soft sound of sprinklers whirring like sleepy applause.

That night, Leo packed his small overnight bag and added two things at the very end—a flashlight and a laminated speech exercise sheet. Jeremy loved practicing, especially when it didn't feel like school. Leo would make sure to build every day of summer around laughter, comfort, and clarity. "You're not broken," he had told Jeremy once. "Your voice just takes a different road. And I'll walk it with you." Jeremy never forgot that. Neither did Leo.

At dinner, Ty toasted with orange soda. "To my little brother," he said. "And to his little brother. May this summer be full of peace and potato chips." Everyone laughed. Naomi kissed Leo's hair as she cleared the table. Zenji ruffled his son's hair and Leo's too. The family that had once been a dream was now real—and not going anywhere.

Later, after the sun had dipped low and the house quieted, Leo opened the window and leaned out. The air was heavy with summer promise. A dog barked two blocks over. Somewhere, a sprinkler hissed its final breath. Leo whispered to the night, "I am not who I was." And the wind answered back in warm silence. The next morning, he would be at Jeremy's house by ten. They'd play, build, talk, walk, laugh. And Leo would keep his promise. He'd protect without shouting. Teach without boasting. Love without limit. Because truth didn't need a spotlight. It just needed to stay.

CHAPTER 12: SUMMER TIME FUN & LESSONS

The gravel cracked under the tires as the van pulled into Leamington Pines. A few crows scattered from the trees above, flapping lazy black wings against the crisp blue sky. Jeremy pressed his nose to the window. His mouth opened with a soft gasp that never made a sound, and his eyes grew wide as the treetops dipped into sunlight. "We're here?" he whispered, like asking might break it. Leo nodded, watching him. He didn't say anything yet, but he smiled to himself. This wasn't just a camping trip. It was a promise—a silent one he made back in spring. A promise to make this summer different.

They parked near a clearing marked Cedar Hollow A4, just shy of the lake trail. Two tents were already laid out in the trunk—forest green and sun-faded blue. Nothing fancy. Just zippers, mesh, and nylon walls that breathed in the wind. Jeremy's mom, Mrs. Firth, slid the cooler out from the back with a grunt and nudged Leo with her elbow. "You boys pick your tent," she said, half teasing. "But no ghost stories the first night." Mr. Firth laughed and pointed to the campsite map pinned to a wooden board nearby. "Pool's open. Lake's a two-minute walk. Bathrooms are decent enough." Leo took one glance and decided this would do just fine. Better than fine.

Jeremy clung to his side like velcro. "I want to sleep in yours," he said, not even asking. "Of course you do," Leo said with a grin. "But I snore like a dragon." Jeremy shrugged. "I don't care. I'm a dragon, too." That settled it. The green tent became theirs. It leaned slightly to the left once set up, but Leo told Jeremy that just made it look like a pirate ship. That earned a proud nod from the nine-year-old, who immediately climbed in to claim his sleeping bag like it was treasure.

The morning breeze smelled like pine, hot plastic from the sun, and faint campfire smoke curling from distant pits. Leo stood still and took a breath. Then another. Nobody was yelling. Nobody was pretending. The trees were real. The tents were real. And for the first time in a long time, Leo didn't feel like a liar. "This summer's about you," he told Jeremy, his voice quiet. "Not about me. I already know I'm loved." Jeremy didn't reply. He just zipped up the tent flap behind them and smiled like he'd won something.

Leo's adoptive parents would be arriving in a few days. Ty would come with them, likely wearing the exact same hoodie he always did, with the drawstrings chewed and lopsided. Leo missed him already, but he was glad for these first few days alone with Jeremy. They needed this. Brothers by choice, not by blood. Love didn't need DNA. Not when it ran this deep.

They unpacked in slow rhythm—Leo setting out the camping stove with Mr. Firth while Jeremy wandered off to study a cluster of ants dragging breadcrumbs across a tree root. "Leo?" Jeremy called without turning. "Do ants ever get tired?" Leo chuckled. "Probably. But they still keep going." "Like us?" Jeremy asked, this time turning around. Leo didn't answer. He just nodded once, hands buried in the cooler's ice.

Lunch was cold chicken sandwiches and cut-up apples. No screens, no homework, no noise. Just birdsong, lake wind, and the hum of wasps hovering near the juice boxes. Jeremy talked nonstop. About school, about frogs, about a YouTube video he wasn't supposed to watch but did anyway. Leo let him. Every word was a thread weaving this new memory into place.

By midafternoon, they made it to the pool. It shimmered like glass, surrounded by white plastic chairs and a lifeguard chewing gum and flipping through a paperback. Leo didn't swim much, not since that one time last summer when his body had felt too sharp, too awkward. But Jeremy begged, and Leo gave in. The water was cold. Their laughter was louder than they meant it to be.

That night, after hot dogs and toasted marshmallows, Jeremy crawled into the green tent and waited. Leo zipped the flap shut behind him, then turned off the flashlight with a snap. Darkness wrapped around them like velvet. "Can I tell you something?" Jeremy asked. "Always," Leo said. "You're my best brother," Jeremy whispered. "Even if you weren't picked to be mine. I picked you." Leo's throat closed tight. He reached over and tapped Jeremy's hand once. No words. Just a tap. Outside, the stars came out one by one. Quiet. Real. Honest. Just two tents and the sky. And for Leo, it was enough.

The fire from last night had died to a bed of quiet ash. Morning smelled like burnt marshmallow and dew clinging to canvas. Jeremy rolled in his sleeping bag and thudded his head gently against Leo's side. "You awake?" he mumbled. Leo cracked one eye open. "I am now." They both smiled, no teasing, just warmth. Leo reached over and ruffled Jeremy's hair, then pulled the zipper down and peeked outside. The trees rustled gently. The campsite was still. A soft mist rolled along the lake path. It was going to be a good day.

They didn't rush. The best mornings didn't need to. Leo boiled water on the small camping stove while Jeremy brushed his teeth using the water jug perched on a log. Mr. and Mrs. Firth were still asleep in their tent. The quiet let Leo think. His mind drifted to last summer. The one where he didn't smile much. The one where every laugh felt fake and every compliment had an edge. He hadn't meant to be cruel—but he was. He saw it now. Clear as glass. And it stung, not because he regretted being caught, but because he remembered how it felt to carry that much anger alone.

Jeremy skipped over and sat on the log beside him. His pyjama pants were too short at the ankles. His face still held sleep in the corners of his eyes. "What were you like before you met me?" he asked. Leo stirred the cocoa powder into the hot water. "Not like this," he said. "I wasn't kind. Not really." Jeremy tilted his head. "But you're the kindest person I know." Leo handed him the mug. "Now, maybe. But not always. I used to be angry all the time. I didn't even know why."

Jeremy took a sip, grimaced, then smiled. "Too much powder," he muttered, licking his lips. Leo chuckled. "That's how I like it." They sat for a while in the stillness of the clearing. "I used to say mean things," Leo said suddenly, voice lower now. "I used to lie. I used to twist the truth just to stay in control. I didn't even realize I was doing it." Jeremy didn't answer right away. He leaned his shoulder into Leo's. "Why'd you stop?" Leo shrugged. "Because someone loved me anyway. And they didn't let me keep lying. They told me the truth. Then they stayed."

The silence between them wasn't heavy. It was thoughtful. Like watching ripples in a lake spread slowly outward. "Was it Ty?" Jeremy asked. "Yeah," Leo said. "Ty saw everything I tried to hide. He didn't run away. He told me I was wrong. And then he hugged me. Every time." Jeremy smiled. "I would've hugged you too." Leo nodded. "You do. All the time."

They went hiking after breakfast. Just a simple trail that looped behind the campground and led to a shallow stream. Jeremy found a stick he called "The Truth Sword." Leo laughed so hard he almost tripped over a root. "You have to use it to fight lies," Jeremy declared. "But only quiet ones. Not loud ones. Those are easy." Leo gave a low whistle. "That's smarter than most adults I know." Jeremy beamed. "I know."

They crossed the stream by hopping stone to stone. Jeremy almost fell in once but didn't. Leo didn't reach to catch him. He wanted Jeremy to know he could do it on his own. "You don't have to be like I was," Leo said, once they were back on solid ground. "You don't ever have to pretend to be mean so people will listen. You don't have to scare anyone to be strong." Jeremy looked down at his stick. "But people who scare others always win." Leo bent down so their eyes met. "Not forever. They just think they do. Then one day, no one believes them anymore. That day hurts. But it's the start of something better."

Jeremy looked up. "Like what?" "Like becoming someone who tells the truth even when it's hard. Someone who protects instead of punishes. Someone who knows that love is louder than lies." Jeremy blinked. Then hugged him, tight and wordless. "You're not a bully," Jeremy whispered. "You're my big brother." Leo held onto him like the words were fragile. "And you're mine. Even if we picked each other."

They sat by the stream until the wind picked up and the bugs returned. Back at the campsite, Mr. Firth grilled pancakes on the campfire grate while Mrs. Firth cleaned out the cooler. Jeremy told them about the Truth Sword and how he used it to fight invisible lies. Leo didn't correct him. He let the story stretch. Let the magic of childhood do what it does best—turn pain into protection, fear into strength.

Later that evening, Ty arrived with a backpack, a grin, and a story about missing three buses and walking the last mile. Jeremy jumped on him like a puppy. Leo followed close behind. No masks. No games. Just brothers—real and chosen. They stayed up late, all three, trading flashlight shadows on the ceiling of the green tent. Leo watched them laugh and knew, finally, that the boy he used to be wouldn't come back. Not when love stood guard at the door. Not when Jeremy believed him. Not when he finally believed in himself.

The fire popped softly, each crack a tiny voice in the quiet. Flames licked the maple logs with slow patience. Stars began peeking out over the trees, and the lake beyond the trail turned to liquid silver. Jeremy sat cross-legged by the fire, clutching a stick he'd been roasting marshmallows with all week. Its tip had burned off hours ago, but he liked the feel of it in his hand. Leo was beside him, carving gentle lines into the dirt with another stick, listening to the night and to his little brother's breathing. Mr. and Mrs. Firth sat a little further back, sipping cocoa, speaking quietly to one another with the soft rhythm of parents at ease.

Jeremy's voice broke the stillness. "Leo… can I tell you something?" Leo stopped drawing. His head turned but he didn't rush the boy. "Always." Jeremy shifted a bit, pressing his knees closer to his chest. He wasn't smiling. "It's not my secret. But it's heavy." Leo nodded. "You can still share it. Especially if it's heavy." Jeremy looked down. "My friend Sophie… not our Sophie, a different one. She told me her uncle yells at her all the time. Loud yelling. And when she cries, he says it's her fault." He swallowed. "She told me not to tell. That it'd ruin everything."

Leo sat up straighter, the fire catching his expression in small orange flashes. "And you carried that for her?" Jeremy nodded. "For a month." Leo's hand reached out and rested on his shoulder. "That was kind. But also dangerous." Jeremy's eyes flickered. "I didn't know what to do." "You just did the right thing," Leo said softly. "Telling someone you trust isn't betrayal. It's protection. And you are someone I trust."

Jeremy's face softened. "But she said I had to promise. That I'd ruin her family if I told." Leo's eyes met his, gentle and unblinking. "Real secrets protect people. Fake secrets protect pain. When someone tells you to hide something that hurts, they're asking you to help keep the hurt going." Jeremy didn't answer right away. He just leaned forward and rested his head on Leo's chest. The older boy wrapped both arms around him. The fire cracked again, like it agreed.

"I want to tell Sophie's mom," Jeremy whispered. "But I don't know how." Leo nodded into the top of his head. "We can talk about it. Maybe even tell her together, or find someone who can help." Jeremy looked up. "You'd come with me?" "Of course," Leo said. "You're my brother." Jeremy hugged him tighter.

After a few moments, Jeremy let go and sat back down, but closer now. "I always feel better after I talk to you," he said. Leo smiled. "That's what brothers do. They hold the heavy stuff with you. Even the stuff you're scared to name." Jeremy sniffed. "Is that why you told Ty everything?" "Exactly," Leo said. "I was scared to say it all. But once I did… it didn't win anymore."

The firelight danced across their faces. Mr. Firth stood quietly and brought over two more blankets. "Getting chilly," he said, draping one over Jeremy's shoulders and offering the other to Leo. He didn't ask what they were talking about. He didn't need to. Sometimes silence means trust.

Jeremy's small hand crept over and took Leo's. "You're the best brother I ever picked," he said. Leo chuckled. "You only picked one." "Still the best," Jeremy answered. He leaned in and kissed Leo on the cheek. A quiet, pure gesture that made Leo blink once, deeply. "Thanks, Jer," he said. "That means more than you know."

They sat by the fire until the flames shrank low and the night grew full. Then they climbed into their tent, zipped up the door, and laid side by side in their sleeping bags. Jeremy fell asleep first. Leo stayed awake a little longer, listening to the crickets outside and the slow, even breaths of the little boy beside him. He was more than a brother. He was becoming the kind of protector he'd always needed. And now, someone else had him. Someone who would never ask him to carry hurt alone. Someone who would teach him that the truth should never stay hidden.

The next morning came slow and golden, sunlight slipping through the canvas like whispers on purpose. Birds called back and forth like kids on opposite ends of the schoolyard. Leo had already unzipped the tent and set out a plate of peanut butter toast for Jeremy when he stirred. The younger boy sat up, rubbing his face, hair a sleepy crown of curls. "You get up too early," he mumbled. "You snore too loud," Leo teased, tossing him a sock. Jeremy laughed, but the sound didn't quite stretch into his eyes. Leo noticed.

They sat outside together, feet tucked under their chairs, toast in hand. Jeremy didn't eat his. He kept peeling at the crust, quiet again. The silence between them wasn't heavy yet, but it was getting there. "Still thinking about Sophie?" Leo asked gently. Jeremy nodded. "And something else."

Leo gave him time. Jeremy watched a red squirrel hop across the dirt path and disappear into the brush before he spoke again. "One time," he said, "I told my old friend from the neighbourhood that I wanted to tell someone what her cousin did. She got really mad. She said, 'You'd ruin everything if you told.'" His voice dropped to almost nothing. "So I didn't."

Leo didn't speak right away. He looked straight ahead, then down at his hands. "That sentence," he said finally, "is a trap." Jeremy blinked. "It is?" "Yup," Leo said, his voice low and even. "It makes you think you're the one causing the problem, just by saying the truth. But guess what?" Jeremy looked at him. "You're not. The person who says that? They already know what's wrong. They're trying to stop you from being the one who fixes it."

Jeremy swallowed. "But what if she was right? What if I did ruin everything?" Leo turned to face him. "Then 'everything' wasn't built right in the first place." The breeze caught the edge of the tent, flapping it like a flag. Jeremy looked down at his toast. "I just didn't want anyone to hate me." "Real love doesn't come with a gag order," Leo said softly.

There was a pause. "What's a gag order?" "When someone tries to make you stay quiet. Like you're not allowed to speak. Some people do it with fear, or guilt, or even hugs that feel like traps." Jeremy looked startled. "Hugs can be traps?" "Fake ones, yeah. Not the ones you give me." Jeremy smiled, a little. "Good."

They stayed there for a while, the squirrels returning and the sun rising higher, baking the pine needles into a warm, earthy perfume. Finally, Jeremy said, "I think she said that to protect herself. Not me." Leo nodded. "You're getting it."

Jeremy leaned over, resting his head against Leo's shoulder. "Thanks for not saying I was dumb." "You're not dumb," Leo said. "You're brave. And the bravest kids are the ones who say the hard stuff out loud—even when people say not to." Jeremy thought on that for a while. Then, softly, "Even if it ruins something?" "If it ruins a lie, that's not a loss. That's a rescue."

Mr. Firth called from the truck, saying it was time to hike. Jeremy stood slowly, brushing crumbs off his lap. Leo watched him go ahead, shoes kicking up little puffs of dust. "Hey Jeremy?" he called. Jeremy turned. "If someone ever says that to you again—'You'll ruin everything'—just say, 'Maybe that everything needed to be ruined.'" Jeremy gave a little salute and nodded. They headed off into the trees, sunlight skipping between branches. Jeremy's step was lighter now, his silence a little less afraid. He had just learned something people twice his age still struggle to grasp. The truth doesn't ruin everything. The truth ruins lies. And that's exactly what it's meant to do.

The sun had tipped past the pines, dropping long shadows across the campsite by the time Ty's truck pulled up. The familiar crunch of tires over gravel made Jeremy leap to his feet with a grin so wide it could've cracked sky. He ran to meet Ty before the engine even cut off, arms thrown around his waist. Ty lifted him easily, swinging him once, then set him down with a marshmallow bag rustling in his hand. "Thought you guys might be low on these," Ty said, tossing the bag to Leo.

Leo caught it and smirked. "We rationed. Barely." Jeremy danced in a circle. "Campfire night!" Mr. Firth chuckled as he set a second lawn chair by the pit. Mrs. Firth handed Ty a mug of cider and nodded toward the tent. "We doubled your sleeping bag. Nights get chilly." Ty thanked her and sank into the chair beside Leo, nodding quietly.

The fire was already cracking by dusk. Sticks were found, marshmallows speared, and the smell of sugar and smoke folded itself into the warm hum of the night. Jeremy sat squished between Leo and Ty, asking a million questions in one breath. "Do you think raccoons ever steal marshmallows? Have you ever caught a firefly? Can you really tell if someone's lying just by watching their eyes?"

Ty blinked. "That last one's my favourite." Leo leaned back, curious. "You're actually going to show him?" "Only if he asks smart." Jeremy sat straighter. "How can you tell if someone's lying?" Ty poked at the fire. "Well," he said slowly, "first, you listen to what they say. Then, you listen to what they don't say." Jeremy blinked. "You can hear what someone doesn't say?"

Leo answered for him. "Sometimes silence screams louder than words." Jeremy looked between them, chewing on that. "But what if the person says it's a secret? What if they say you're being mean for telling?" Ty stirred the coals gently. "Then they're scared of the truth. Because truth doesn't hurt good guys. It only hurts liars."

The sentence settled over them like ash. Jeremy looked down at his shoes. "So if I tell the truth, and someone gets mad... that doesn't mean I'm bad?" "Nope," Ty said firmly. "It means they're hiding something. And you're shining light on it." Leo nodded, watching Jeremy. "Telling the truth is like opening a window. Liars hate fresh air."

The flames danced between them. Jeremy leaned against Leo's arm, quiet for a while. Then, in a voice no louder than the fire's crackle, he said, "I think you saved me, Leo. From stuff I didn't even know I needed saving from." Leo didn't laugh. Didn't deflect. Didn't shrug. Instead, for the first time, he kissed Jeremy gently on the cheek. "And you saved me right back," he whispered. Jeremy's face turned red, but he smiled. "Boys don't usually do that." "Real brothers do," Leo said.

Ty smiled but didn't interrupt. He just looked up at the stars beginning to poke through the sky like pinholes in a curtain. "The truth," he said softly, "isn't supposed to feel like thunder. It's supposed to feel like air—fresh and honest. If someone says you'll wreck things by telling it, maybe the thing needs to be wrecked." Jeremy closed his eyes and let the words settle. They were heavy, but good. Like a blanket on a cool night. The fire burned down to glowing coals. And somewhere inside Jeremy, something solid began to build—a quiet sense that truth didn't make you bad. It made you brave.

Leo crouched in front of the cooler and pulled out two water bottles, tossing one to Jeremy who nearly missed it in his excitement. The sun had climbed to its highest perch, soaking the campsite in golden heat. Birds rustled somewhere in the trees, and every now and then a breeze slipped through the pines, cool as lake water. Jeremy took a long sip and wiped his mouth with the back of his arm. "What are we doing now?"

Leo grinned. "Lie detection training." Jeremy's face lit up. "Really?" Leo tapped two fingers against his own temple. "Real Shadow Warriors know how to spot dishonesty with nothing but their eyes and ears. Ty taught me. Now I'm teaching you." Jeremy bounced on the spot like a coil spring. "Okay! What do I do first?"

They sat on a patch of flat grass near the fire pit. Leo looked serious now. "First rule: listen to how fast they talk. Liars rush." Jeremy nodded. "Second?" "Second rule: look for nervous laughs. People who lie often smile weirdly, or laugh where it doesn't make sense." Jeremy's eyes widened. "Like at the wrong part of a story?" "Exactly."

Leo leaned back on one elbow. "Now, watch my face. I'm gonna tell two things. One's real, one's fake. Ready?" Jeremy nodded so hard his curls bounced. Leo cleared his throat. "Okay. Number one: I once ate a spider on a dare. Number two: I fell off my bunk bed and blamed it on the dog." Jeremy squinted, then grinned. "The second one is real!"

Leo raised an eyebrow. "How'd you know?" "You blinked after the first one. And your mouth twitched funny." Leo laughed. "You're a natural." Jeremy clapped his hands. "Again!"

They went for five more rounds. Each time, Jeremy studied Leo's voice, his blinking, the way his shoulders moved. "You blink faster when you lie," Jeremy noted. "And your 'uh' is longer." Leo gave him a slow clap. "That's better than most adults catch."

They moved into sillier rounds. "I'm secretly a squirrel." "I live on the moon." "I brushed my teeth with ketchup once." Jeremy burst out laughing at the last one. "That one's real!" Leo laughed too. "Fine. I did. By accident."

Once they settled, Jeremy wiped a tear from his cheek, still giggling. "This is the best day ever." Leo looked at him warmly. "I want you to always know how to spot a lie, Jeremy. Not just for fun, but for safety." Jeremy looked thoughtful. "Like if someone tries to trick me?" "Exactly. If someone makes you feel weird inside, or like something's off, trust that."

Jeremy nodded slowly. "Okay. So if someone says, 'I didn't mean to,' but their eyes look mean, that's a lie?" "Sometimes, yeah. Especially if they say it over and over but keep doing the same thing."

Jeremy picked up a stick and began tracing circles in the dirt. "What if someone says I'm lying, but I'm not?" Leo reached over and gently stopped his hand. "That's the hardest one. But you hold your truth anyway. Even if they roll their eyes. Even if they laugh. Even if they walk away."

Jeremy looked up. "Even if it's someone big?" Leo's voice was soft. "Especially then." A crow called from deep in the trees, sharp and sudden. Jeremy looked up, then back at Leo. "Can we make a game out of it tomorrow? Lie Detector Tag?" Leo smiled. "Absolutely. But you'll win. Every time."

Jeremy beamed. "Good. I want to be the kind of person who knows things. Like you." Leo gave his shoulder a squeeze. "You already are. You just don't know how good you are at it yet." They sat together for a while, two brothers in sunlight, listening to the quiet honesty of summer.

The fire had gone quiet, just a soft bed of red coals now, like the heartbeat of the earth under their feet. Leo leaned back against the trunk of a crooked pine, legs stretched out and crossed at the ankles. Jeremy sat beside him, hugging his knees, his marshmallow stick forgotten in the grass. Crickets had taken over the air, their song steady and restless. The wind had stopped playing. Everything waited. "Leo," Jeremy said, voice almost too small to hear, "why would someone lie to me?"

Leo turned his head slowly, not surprised, not startled—just ready. He didn't smile. He didn't rush. He let the silence breathe, as if the question deserved its own space in the air before anything answered it. "Because sometimes," he said quietly, "the lie helps them do something they couldn't do if you knew the truth." Jeremy looked down at his sneakers. "Like what?"

"Like trick you. Or make you do something you wouldn't do if you knew what was really going on." Leo picked up a twig and broke it clean in two. "Some people lie to keep control. Some lie to avoid getting caught. And some lie just to see if they can get away with it."

Jeremy's eyes stayed on the coals. "That's mean." "Yeah," Leo said. "It is." Jeremy's mouth turned down, not in a pout, but in that slow, sinking way that showed thinking—real thinking—was happening. "But I'm just a kid. Why lie to a kid?"

Leo turned to face him. "Because you believe fast. Because you want to trust. Because you think people mean what they say." Jeremy blinked. "Is that bad?" "No," Leo said firmly. "That's beautiful. That's what they're afraid of. That's why they lie. So they can twist that beauty and use it."

Jeremy sniffled once but didn't cry. "Did someone lie to you like that?" Leo stared straight ahead. "Yeah. More than once." He looked down at his hands. "I used to lie too, Jeremy. Not always on purpose. Sometimes because I didn't know what truth felt like anymore." Jeremy looked over. "Do you now?" Leo nodded. "I'm learning. Every day."

Jeremy touched his own chest with one small hand. "How do you know what the truth feels like?" "It feels quiet inside," Leo said. "Like your heart isn't racing. Like you don't have to double-check what you said. Like your stomach doesn't twist." Jeremy nodded. "When I tell the truth, I feel calm. Like breathing." Leo smiled, just a little. "Exactly."

They sat like that for a while. No need to fill the air with more than was needed. Then Jeremy whispered, "So it's not my fault?" Leo reached over and placed a hand on the back of Jeremy's neck. "No. It's not your fault when someone lies to you. It's not because you're dumb. It's because they want something you wouldn't give if you knew."

Jeremy's voice wavered. "So if someone says something like, 'You better not tell,' it's a lie, right?" "It's a trap," Leo said. "Real love doesn't need secrets. And it never needs silence to stay safe." Jeremy blinked hard. "You're the best big brother ever." Leo chuckled. "Well... I'm trying to be." Jeremy leaned his head against Leo's arm. "You already are."

The fire dimmed even more. The moon lifted like a shy guest peeking through the trees. Somewhere deeper in the woods, a loon cried out and then fell silent again. Jeremy pulled his knees up again, curled tighter, his voice soft as leaves. "If someone lies to me again... I think I'll know." Leo nodded. "You will." Jeremy smiled, eyes heavy with sleep. "Because I've got you." And that, Leo knew, was the only truth that would never be broken.

The fire cracked louder now, snapping like a mischievous friend interrupting their thoughts. Leo dropped another stick in and watched the sparks shoot skyward like tiny promises. Jeremy's cheeks were flushed from laughing too hard. He'd been giggling since sunset, but it wasn't nervous laughter—it was real, round-bellied, unshaped by fear. Leo hadn't seen joy like that on him in days, maybe longer. He nudged Jeremy with his elbow. "Wanna play a game?"

Jeremy tilted his head. "What game?" "Truth or Trick," Leo said, eyes glinting in the orange firelight. "One of us tells two stories. One's true. One's not. You guess which one's the trick." Jeremy's face lit up like someone had handed him keys to a secret kingdom. "Okay! You go first!"

Leo cleared his throat dramatically, trying to look serious. "Alright. First story: When I was five, I thought pickles were frog tails and cried for two hours when someone put them in my sandwich. Second story: I once jumped off a moving swing, did a full somersault, and landed on my feet like a superhero." Jeremy's eyebrows scrunched. He squinted into Leo's face like a detective. "The pickle one's real," he said. "You're scared of weird food." Leo clutched his chest in fake agony. "You caught me." He handed over an invisible point. "Your turn."

Jeremy rubbed his hands together like an evil genius. "Okay. One: I once sleepwalked into the hallway and woke up with my face in the laundry basket. Two: I once ate ten marshmallows in one minute without chewing." eo tilted his head, pretending to ponder. "You're not a marshmallow swallower. The sleepwalking story's true." Yup!" Jeremy beamed, clapping once. "That was too easy."

They went back and forth like that, story after story. Ty even joined for a round, tossing in a tale about pretending to be a spy in Japan and accidentally stealing his cousin's shoes. Jeremy guessed his lie in under ten seconds. "Too specific," he declared. "You always make up details when you're fibbing."

By round three, Jeremy had yet to miss a single guess. He was bouncing on his toes now, wrapped in a too-big hoodie that made him look like a walking campfire spark. Leo held up his hands in surrender. "Alright, alright. I get it. You've got the radar now."

Jeremy's smile slowed as he walked over, arms wide. "That's 'cause you taught me." He threw himself into Leo's chest, knocking Leo back with a half-gasp and a full laugh. Leo hugged him hard, arms wrapping around that little body like he never wanted to let go. Jeremy looked up and whispered, "I love you, Leo. Like, real deep love."

Leo swallowed, not the kind of swallow you do when your throat's dry, but the kind you do when something warm burns through your heart and doesn't stop. "I love you too, little guy. Always." They stayed like that, firelight dancing across their faces, stars just beginning to crack the black above them. The adults were a hundred feet away, sipping tea and letting the kids have their world. In that circle of light, that echo of trust, no lie could live.

Jeremy pulled back just far enough to look Leo in the eye. "You never trick me. Not even once." Leo ruffled his hair. "That's 'cause I don't have to." The fire popped again, louder this time, like applause. Jeremy settled back on the log, arms folded behind his head. "Tomorrow, let's do it again. But I'm gonna make it harder." Leo leaned back beside him. "Bring it on, Sherlock."

The game wasn't just a game anymore. It was armour. And Leo knew now—he hadn't just given Jeremy a trick detector. He'd given him something bigger. The kind of strength that doesn't leave bruises but never bends. Jeremy closed his eyes. "This was the best day of my whole life." Leo looked up at the sky. "Mine too."

The morning was still soft when Leo opened his eyes, and sunlight hadn't fully settled into the tent. There was a quiet, almost sacred stillness in the space, and the only sound was the gentle rhythm of breath from Jeremy, curled like a small bird against his chest. Leo hadn't moved in over an hour. He could feel the steady thump of his own heartbeat against Jeremy's ear, and realized, with quiet awe, that the boy was listening—not just to the rhythm, but to the safety behind it. Jeremy's small hand clutched the hem of Leo's T-shirt as though sleep had taken him mid-hug. Leo didn't move. Not even a shift. Not even a breath out of sync. He knew better than to disturb that kind of trust.

By the time Jeremy stirred, the light had changed to golden, brushing gently across the seams of the tent fabric like a whisper of welcome. Leo placed one arm around Jeremy's back and drew him in with the kind of hug that didn't need to be explained. It was real. No conditions. No strings. Just warmth that reached the bones. Jeremy yawned into Leo's neck and mumbled something that sounded like, "Morning, Leo," before pressing a soft, sleepy kiss to his cheek. Leo smiled and kissed his temple in return, whispering, "Let's go see if there's bacon." Jeremy's smile grew from his heart outward, and he clung to Leo for one last second before stretching with a tiny squeak.

Breakfast was already on the camp stove by the time the boys stumbled out of their tent, rubbing eyes and grinning at the smell of toast and maple sausage. Ty was already there, crouched near the fire pit with a stick in one hand and a marshmallow in the other, pretending he didn't notice the smoky trail running up his sleeve. Jeremy's parents sat together sipping their coffee like it was a holiday of peace. It was. For all of them. Leo took his usual spot beside Ty while Jeremy plopped into his lap like a lazy cat, holding onto his wrist as if afraid he'd float away in the wind.

After breakfast, the three boys wandered toward the clearing beyond the campsite. Ty had brought along a foldable chair and placed it like a throne in the shade. Leo sat cross-legged in the grass. Jeremy pressed himself into Leo's side, and the conversation turned quiet—heavier than usual for a morning with pancakes. Jeremy fidgeted with the hem of his shirt, then finally asked, "What if someone tells you not to tell? Like really mean it?" The question floated out like a stone dropped into a pond. It made ripples no one could ignore.

Leo's shoulders didn't stiffen, and his eyes didn't widen. Instead, he nodded once—slow, like he'd been waiting for that question all summer. He gently took Jeremy's hand and said, "If someone tells you 'don't tell,' and it makes your stomach hurt? They're not trying to protect you. They're protecting themselves." Jeremy blinked and looked down at their hands. His thumb moved over Leo's knuckle like he was tracing the words into his skin so he wouldn't forget.

Ty nodded from the chair and added, "When someone needs you to stay silent so badly that they scare you, or guilt you, or make you think something bad will happen if you speak up? That's already a sign something's wrong." He leaned forward and spoke with steady eyes. "If it feels wrong, it probably is." The air didn't feel heavy now—it felt solid. Like truth had stepped into the circle and wasn't planning to leave.

Jeremy stayed quiet for a moment, then looked at Leo with wide, brown eyes. "But what if they said I'd ruin everything? What if something bad really does happen because I said something?" His voice didn't tremble, but his words held the weight of children who've seen too much and been told too little. Leo reached out, cradled the back of Jeremy's head, and pulled him gently to his chest. "Then it's not your fault," he said into the boy's hair. "You didn't ruin anything. They did. You just told the truth."

The wind picked up in the trees like it was applauding quietly. Jeremy nestled in closer, and Ty looked toward the lake in silence. Then he spoke—not with anger, but with clarity. "A lie is like a shadow, Jeremy. It moves when people move. It twists with the light. But truth? Truth doesn't need to hide. Truth stands still. Even when you're scared. Even when no one else believes you yet." Jeremy looked up with a seriousness that didn't belong on a nine-year-old's face, but Leo met it with the heart of a twelve-year-old who knew exactly what pain looked like—and how healing could happen.

"Even if someone says you're bad for telling," Leo said, "that doesn't make it true. Bad people like to call brave people the enemy. That's how they try to win." Jeremy's lips tightened, and then he nodded once—fierce, like he wanted to prove something to Leo. Maybe to himself.

They didn't move from that spot for a long time. Birds called overhead. A squirrel barked from somewhere in the branches. But the campfire logs remained empty, the marshmallows untouched. This was a different kind of feast. Truth was being passed around like food.

Ty got up slowly, dusted his knees, and said, "You know, when I was little, someone told me not to tell either." Leo raised an eyebrow, surprised. "It wasn't anything big. Just a lie someone made up about me. But they told me if I said anything, everyone would think I was weak." He paused. "I didn't say anything. And guess what? They kept lying." Jeremy turned to him sharply. "So what did you do?" Ty smiled. "Eventually? I told. And when I did, the lie stopped following me around."

That was when Jeremy stood up, brushed his hands on his shorts, and said, "Then I'm gonna tell too." No dramatic speech. No music swelling in the background. Just a child who had learned something true—and believed in it enough to speak it back to the world. Leo stood too, placed a hand on his little brother's shoulder, and nodded. "That's what big brothers are for," he said. "To help you tell the truth, even when it's hard."

Jeremy grinned and whispered, "I love you, Leo." Then without warning, he hugged him so tightly it pushed the air from Leo's lungs. Leo hugged him back, harder. No words now. Just breath and heartbeat and trust in the open air. Ty watched with the kind of expression that meant nothing needed to be said—because this, this was enough. And far beyond the trees, the sunlight poured into the lake like gold being spilled on glass. It stayed that way for a long time.

They had finished washing the breakfast plates by the water tap when Leo stood quietly by the lake, staring across its stillness like it held answers he hadn't asked for in a long time. Jeremy was chasing dragonflies near the reeds, his laughter blending with the rustling of the birch leaves. Ty was teaching Jeremy's dad how to tie a perfect square knot for the firewood bundle. Jeremy's mom had gone to the car to grab sunscreen, leaving Leo alone with his thoughts for just long enough for them to sting. The lake didn't judge. It simply reflected the truth, however murky.

When Jeremy came skipping back, cheeks flushed and knees speckled with dust, he grabbed Leo's hand without asking and tugged him toward the fallen log they'd turned into a seat the day before. "Tell me something real," Jeremy said suddenly, and Leo blinked. "What do you mean?" he asked. Jeremy kicked his feet against the dirt. "Something nobody else knows. Something true." The demand didn't feel childish. It felt sacred. And Leo, no longer a boy who dodged questions, nodded slowly.

"There was a time," Leo began, "when I didn't know who to be. So I told a lie that stuck to me like glue." Jeremy leaned into his side, waiting. Leo didn't rush. "It was back in third grade. Everyone liked this one kid—kind, funny, smart. I wanted people to like me like that, too. So I started acting like him. I even told someone that I helped a lost dog find its way home, just like he had. But I hadn't. I made it up. And for a while, people looked at me like I was special." He stopped and ran a hand through his hair. "But it wasn't real. I was pretending to be someone who already existed, and worse—I was lying to myself. I didn't know how to be just… Leo."

Jeremy didn't interrupt. He just hugged Leo's arm and said, "You're the best brother now." No doubt in his voice. No hesitation. Just belief. Leo smiled at that, but then Jeremy added, "Do you think pretending makes people bad?" Leo shook his head. "No. I think staying fake on purpose makes people afraid. And that fear turns into anger. That's what happened to me. I was angry for a long time. Because I thought the lie made me stronger. It didn't. It made me smaller."

There was a long silence between them after that. But Jeremy had another question, the kind that doesn't come out unless a child feels completely safe. "Why do some grown-ups say it's bad to kiss your brother?" His voice was tiny, but his eyes were serious. "I kissed you last night, and Ty kissed his dad on the cheek, but my cousin said that's not allowed in their church." The words floated like ash—not heavy, but left a trace on everything they touched.

Leo didn't flinch. He looked his brother straight in the eyes and said, "Because some people don't understand love unless it fits their rules. And if something doesn't match those rules, they call it bad." Jeremy frowned. "But we love each other. And I kiss Mom and Dad. And you. Sometimes even Ty. That's not bad." His voice cracked a little. "That's just love, right?"

"It is love," Leo said, squeezing Jeremy's hand. "And I don't care what anyone else says. Love isn't dirty. Love doesn't need to hide. And when someone tells you it's bad to love your family in kind, safe ways? They're not protecting love. They're controlling it." Jeremy blinked hard. "Why would they do that?" Leo didn't soften the answer. "Control, little brother. Just like the kids who say, 'don't tell,' some adults say, 'don't feel,' or 'don't touch,' or 'don't cry,' because they're scared of what might happen if people feel too free."

Jeremy's face shifted in that quiet way when a child is processing something far bigger than their size, but not bigger than their heart. He nodded slowly. "So love is good. And truth is safe. But lies… they're for power?" Leo hugged him close and whispered, "Exactly." He placed a hand on the back of Jeremy's neck and said softly, "The people who told you not to hug your dad or kiss your brother on the cheek? They were taught fear, not truth. And if you want to be a warrior like Ty and me, you learn to spot fear in other people's lies. Then you love harder."

Ty, who had just wandered into earshot with a bundle of dry pine branches, paused behind the log, listening. He didn't interrupt. He just watched the way Leo was handling the weight with quiet grace. Jeremy noticed him and waved him over. "Ty, is it okay to kiss your family on the cheek?" Ty nodded without missing a beat. "Every time I hug my dad, I do. And every time I see my mom, I kiss her hand. It's called honour. Don't let fear teach you shame."

Jeremy leaned his head against Leo's shoulder and whispered, "Good. Then I'm doing it forever." Leo laughed under his breath, the kind that shakes loose the last pieces of guilt. "I hope you do." He paused. "You saved me, you know." Jeremy looked up. "I did?" Leo nodded. "Every hug. Every truth. You helped me remember who I really am. And now I want to help you keep that truth safe inside you—so nobody ever lies it out of you."

The fire crackled nearby. Birds called again in the trees. And the world didn't change. But Leo had. And Jeremy would never forget the moment his brother made it clear: love that's real doesn't follow rules made by fear. It follows the rhythm of truth. And that rhythm? That's what they were dancing to now.

The shadows stretched long across the campsite by late afternoon. A quiet wind had picked up from the lake, carrying the smell of damp wood and last night's fire into the trees. Jeremy had wandered to the picnic table with a pad of paper, scribbling cartoon faces with exaggerated noses and large eyes. Leo leaned nearby on the arm of the bench, watching his little brother draw without speaking. The moment hung between them like a hammock, full of comfort, full of sway.

Jeremy didn't look up when he asked it. "What if the one lying is an adult?" The question floated out, soft and serious. His pencil paused mid-curve. Leo didn't rush to answer. He knew the weight of that kind of question. It doesn't come from nowhere. It lives under the skin, waiting for a day when it feels safe to rise.

Leo sat down slowly, folding his arms across the table, gaze locked on the sketch of a smiling bear Jeremy had half-finished. He took a breath that didn't sound too deep or too slow. "Then you go to another adult," he said, steady and clear. "One who listens. One who cares." Jeremy nodded, but Leo kept going. "And if that adult doesn't believe you, you go to another one. And another. And you keep going until someone does."

Jeremy's shoulders sank with a quiet relief. He didn't say anything yet, but Leo saw the way his hand started drawing again—faster, more relaxed. "Some people think grown-ups always tell the truth just because they're older," Leo continued. "But that's not true. Some adults lie even more than kids do. Because they know how to cover it better."

Jeremy looked up then. "Have you met one?" Leo didn't flinch. "Yes. More than one." The silence that followed wasn't heavy. It was honest. "They smiled in public. Said the right words. But behind closed doors, they twisted things. Told kids to stay quiet. Made them feel small. That's how I knew they were lying. Real truth doesn't need to scare you into silence."

"But what if the other adult doesn't believe you either?" Jeremy asked again, the worry pulling at the edges of his mouth. Leo leaned in closer, lowering his voice to a whisper meant only for warriors. "Then you come find me. Or Ty. Or Mom. Or Dad. Or someone like Mr. Clarke. Someone who watches with their ears, not just their eyes. Someone who hears things other people miss."

Jeremy chewed his bottom lip. "What if the lie is really big? Like the kind that could break everything?" Leo nodded slowly. "That's the kind of lie that needs truth the most. Because if it's big enough to break things, that means it's already doing damage. You're not breaking anything by telling the truth. You're just turning the light on."

Jeremy blinked, then scribbled something on the corner of his page. It wasn't a drawing this time—it was a sentence: Truth saves. He didn't say it out loud, but Leo saw it. And Leo smiled. "I used to think keeping secrets made me strong," he said softly. "But now I know that sharing them, when they're hurting someone, is what makes you brave."

A sudden gust of wind scattered Jeremy's paper across the table, and Leo reached out to pin them down. One page flew into the fire pit, where only ashes lived now. Jeremy didn't panic. He just shrugged. "That one was a lie anyway," he said. Leo chuckled and ruffled his hair. "Good riddance."

They sat there a little longer. Jeremy's parents were still hiking back from the dock with Ty, who had gone to check on the rental canoe. The camp was peaceful. Not perfect, but peaceful—the kind that settles in your chest when the truth's been spoken out loud.

"Leo?" Jeremy asked again. "How do you know if an adult is the kind that listens?" Leo paused. "They don't interrupt. They look you in the eye. And they never make you feel silly for speaking." Jeremy nodded slowly. "Okay. Then I think Mr. Clarke's one. And so's Dad. And Mom. And you. And Ty."

Leo smiled. "Then you've already got a whole army." Jeremy grinned. "A truth army." He lifted his pencil like a sword. "I'm the youngest knight." Leo nodded proudly. "And you've already passed your first quest."

The sun glinted off the lake in sharp, golden slivers. Leo reached into the cooler beside the table and tossed Jeremy a juice box. "For bravery," he said. Jeremy popped the straw through the top and toasted the sky. "To the truth. No matter who's lying." Leo raised his water bottle and tapped it against Jeremy's. "To the ones who don't stay silent." And in that small corner of the world—two brothers, one truth army, and no lies allowed—summer felt like the safest place it had ever been.

The fire crackled low as the stars began to appear, scattered like whispered promises across the dusk-washed sky. Leo sat cross-legged by the pit, poking at the glowing wood with a long stick, while Jeremy sprawled belly-down on the blanket beside him, chin in his hands, still buzzing from roasted marshmallows and one too many riddles. Ty crouched nearby, quietly watching the way the flames shifted, bending like reeds under the weight of the night wind. Then, without turning, he said something that caught both boys still.

"Your gut knows before your brain does."

Jeremy blinked. "Huh?"

Ty looked over his shoulder, voice calm. "When something's wrong. When a person's lying. Or when a situation doesn't feel right. Your body knows. It tightens. Your heartbeat changes. Your breath slows down or speeds up. That's your gut talking to you." He tapped his chest lightly with two fingers. "Right here. It always speaks first."

Leo nodded slowly, as though Ty had confirmed something he'd known but never put words to. Jeremy sat up a little straighter. "So it's not just my imagination?" he asked. "That weird, swirly feeling in my stomach sometimes?" Ty shook his head. "Nope. That's your early warning system. Shadow Warriors rely on it."

They were quiet for a moment, letting the idea settle like sand in a glass jar. Leo tossed another stick into the fire. "Sometimes I didn't listen," he said quietly. "When I was younger. I'd feel something off, but I'd brush it off. Tell myself I was being dramatic. But every time I ignored that feeling—something bad followed."

Jeremy chewed on the string of his hoodie, staring into the flames. "But what if you can't say anything? Like, if someone's watching. Or if it's not safe to talk?" Ty smiled softly, reaching into his backpack. He pulled out a small black notebook, flipping to a page filled with scribbles and symbols. "That's when you use code words," he said. "Every good team has them."

Leo grinned. "You brought the code book?" Ty shrugged. "I always bring the code book."

He passed it to Jeremy, who stared at it like it held ancient spells. "Pick one," Ty said. "Pick a word you can say that means 'I'm not okay'—without actually saying it. Something you could whisper, or text, or say in a sentence that sounds normal." Jeremy's eyes scanned the list. He landed on one and smiled. "Lighthouse," he said. "If I say lighthouse, that means… I need someone. I need help."

Ty nodded. "Lighthouse it is."

Leo leaned in. "Mine's fog." Ty raised an eyebrow. "Still fog?" Leo nodded. "If I ever say it out of nowhere, it means I feel lost. Like something's not right. You'll know." Ty gave a half-smile. "Still poetic." Leo grinned.

They gave Jeremy time to think. He stared at the stars, then back at the fire. "Lighthouse," he whispered again, as though testing how it tasted on his tongue. "It's like… when I feel scared but don't want to say 'I'm scared' in front of people." Leo nodded. "Exactly. It lets you speak without being cornered."

They practiced a few more words. If Jeremy ever texted "red sweater," that meant he wanted to leave. "Rain boots" meant someone nearby made him uncomfortable. And "empty backpack" meant he had something he wanted to share, but not in public. Each phrase was coded in plain sight—ordinary to others, but clear to their circle.

"Why not just say the real thing?" Jeremy asked after a while. Ty put the notebook away. "Sometimes you can't. Not because you're not brave. But because timing matters. And because staying safe isn't weakness. It's wisdom."

Leo reached out and ruffled Jeremy's hair. "You're learning fast, little knight." Jeremy smiled, cheeks pink from the fire. "That's 'cause I've got the best teachers."

Their mom called from the camper to remind them it was bedtime soon. Jeremy yawned, but he didn't get up. He leaned against Leo's side, feeling the quiet thrum of his brother's heartbeat. "My stomach feels calm now," he said sleepily. "Like my gut's saying thank you."

Leo whispered, "That's because you listened." Ty gathered the remaining snack wrappers and packed the marshmallow sticks. "You're not just learning how to spot lies," he said. "You're learning how to trust yourself. That's even more important."

The fire dimmed into soft orange coals, glowing like truth under a layer of ash. The night pressed in like a soft blanket, full of dreams not yet dreamed. And the three of them—one older brother reborn, one little brother just beginning, and one guide watching from the shadows— stood together under the stars with hearts that now knew how to listen. Their words were quiet. But their code was strong.

The sun had begun its slow descent, turning the edges of the lake into gold-laced ripples. Jeremy and Leo were stretched out under the awning of the camper trailer, each with a popsicle slowly melting between their fingers. The fire pit crackled with last night's ash, and the wind played with the edges of their picnic blanket. It had been a slow day—no heavy lessons, just the sort of wandering chatter brothers share when the world feels gentle. Jeremy's head was resting against Leo's ribs, and the silence between them wasn't awkward. It was understood. "Leo," Jeremy asked, not lifting his head, "are all secrets bad?"

Leo blinked toward the treetops and gave the question the full weight of a moment before answering. "No. Some secrets are kind. Like surprise birthday parties. Or not telling Mom you made her a thank-you card. That's a good secret. One that protects happiness." Jeremy nodded slowly, turning his popsicle stick in his hand. "But what about secrets that make your stomach twist?"

Leo shifted, sitting up slightly so he could see Jeremy's face. "Those are the ones that don't belong to you. They're the kind someone makes you hold to keep them safe, not you." Jeremy frowned, lips pursed in thought. "Like if someone says... 'Don't tell, or I'll get in trouble'?" Leo nodded. "Exactly. If a secret feels heavy, like it's squishing your heart, that's a clue it's not yours to carry."

Ty joined them a moment later, sitting cross-legged and offering a water bottle. "What're we talking about?" he asked. Jeremy glanced up at Leo. "Good secrets and bad secrets," he said. "Leo said if it feels twisty in your belly, it's probably not a good one." Ty gave a short nod of approval. "That's right. Secrets that protect joy feel light. Ones that protect someone's bad choices? They weigh you down."

Jeremy squinted. "How do you know the difference?" Ty leaned forward. "Ask yourself: is this secret hiding something fun—or something unfair? If it's hiding something unfair, then it's a secret meant to keep someone in control. And that's not okay." Jeremy leaned his shoulder into Leo again, thinking hard.

Leo ran a gentle hand through Jeremy's curls. "When I was younger," he began, voice slow and steady, "I kept bad secrets. I was told not to tell anyone when I felt scared. I was told I'd get in trouble if I said what was really happening. And the more I kept quiet, the more I felt like I was doing something wrong." Jeremy's eyes widened. "But you weren't," he whispered. "You were just a kid." Leo smiled softly. "Exactly. But I didn't know that then."

The sun hit the treeline, turning the whole campsite into a shadowed golden dome. Jeremy's parents stepped out from the camper, holding plates of sandwiches and laughing at something one of them had said. They paused when they saw Leo's face, open and honest, calm in a way that took years to earn. Jeremy looked up and, without saying anything, pointed at Leo. "He's the reason I don't keep bad secrets anymore," he said proudly.

Jeremy's mother walked over first. She knelt beside Leo, cupped his cheek in both hands, and kissed him gently—not on the forehead, but fully, deliberately, with the same kind of love one offers a son who has earned his place without needing to beg for it. She said nothing. Jeremy's father followed, placed one steady hand on Leo's shoulder, and did the same.

Leo blinked back emotion, but his eyes betrayed the shimmer. This wasn't a moment made for big words. It was made for truth, the kind that didn't need to hide behind metaphors or explanations. "You loved him like a brother," Jeremy's mom whispered. "You gave him safety." Leo managed a quiet smile. "He gave it back to me." Ty nodded solemnly. "That's how it works," he said. "When secrets get replaced by trust, something new begins. Something clean."

Jeremy leaned forward suddenly, wrapping both arms around Leo's waist. "You're my favourite secret," he whispered. "Except you're not a secret anymore." They all laughed, the sound breaking the heaviness like sunlight breaking through cloud cover. But it wasn't nervous laughter. It was honest. That was the difference Leo now understood: truth makes laughter easier. Lies make laughter brittle.

That night, as the stars crawled overhead and the fire faded into memory, Jeremy crawled into his sleeping bag beside Leo. "I think... I think if someone ever tells me to keep a secret that hurts," he murmured, "I'll say no." Leo reached out and held Jeremy's small hand. "I know you will." The wind whispered through the branches like applause, and the dark didn't feel as big anymore. Because the truth—when shared—shrinks shadows and makes brothers out of boys.

Jeremy sat on the mossy stump near the firepit, legs swinging like he hadn't a care in the world. But his shoulders were drawn back, straighter than usual. Leo noticed it first. Ty was tying down the cooler lid behind them when Jeremy looked up and said something they weren't expecting.

"Back at school, before summer," he said slowly, "this kid named Jacob told me I could trust him. Said he was gonna help me with my drawings." He reached down for a stick and began to dig in the dirt with it. "But then he took one of my drawings and passed it around like it was his." The stick broke. He tossed the piece aside without looking at it. "He smiled the whole time."

Leo's breath caught, and he sat beside Jeremy without a word. He didn't interrupt. He didn't jump in with advice. He waited. Jeremy didn't need saving—he needed to be heard. After a long pause, Jeremy kept going. "He told me not to tell the teacher, said it'd make things worse. But I remembered what you said—about how people who tell you to keep quiet usually already know they're doing something wrong." His voice didn't shake. It didn't rise. It held still, steady, like a line drawn in sand. "So I told."

Ty turned then, leaned against the cooler with arms folded and a proud but silent grin. Leo's chest filled with something that almost hurt. Pride and sorrow and something older than both. He reached over and nudged Jeremy with his shoulder. "And what happened?" he asked gently.

Jeremy smiled, just a bit. "She believed me. The teacher. She said it took guts." He picked up another stick, lighter and smoother this time. "Jacob got in trouble. He tried to say it was a joke. But I didn't laugh. I just walked away." He looked at Leo then, eyes so sure they could've been carved from truth itself. "And I wasn't scared. Not even a little."

Leo didn't blink. He nodded once. "You knew it was a lie," he said, voice low. "And you knew what to do." Jeremy grinned. "Because you taught me," he said. "You and Ty both. But mostly you, Leo." The name didn't sound casual. It was reverent, a word blessed by trust. And without waiting for permission or checking for approval, Jeremy leaned in and gave Leo a firm kiss on the lips.

Leo didn't flinch. He didn't pull away. He didn't look around to see who was watching. He just smiled, and placed a hand behind Jeremy's head. "That's how I know you'll never turn into who I used to be," he said. "Because you speak up."

The fire cracked. A soft wind rustled the tarp above the tent. The world felt quiet, but it wasn't the kind of quiet that hides things. It was the quiet that says everything's safe. Ty finally moved closer and crouched beside them. "You just passed the hardest test of all," he told Jeremy. "You spoke the truth when it would've been easier to say nothing."

Jeremy shrugged. "It didn't feel scary once I started." He looked at Leo again. "Why does religion say kissing your brother's bad? Even when it's just love?" He wasn't asking with rebellion. He wasn't trying to pick a fight. He was seeking understanding. And Leo, for once, didn't fumble for a soft answer.

"As I explained once before buddy, It's about control," Leo said simply. "You see Jeremy, some people think love has to follow specific rules. And if it doesn't, they get scared, and when they can't control that love, they get scared that they no longer have control over you." He rubbed the back of his neck. "But truth doesn't live in fear. And if love is kind, and real, and doesn't hurt anybody... then the rule is wrong. Not the love." Ty nodded behind them. "That's what shadow warriors know," he said. "Real love doesn't need approval. It just needs to be true." Jeremy leaned into Leo's side again. "Then I'm not hiding it. Not ever." "Good," Leo said. "Because you don't need to."

The fire popped again. The air smelled like pine and smoke and warm earth. Jeremy's feet kicked out into the dirt, one bare toe tracing a circle. "I wanna teach someone else too," he said after a while. "Like another kid who's scared. Like I was." Leo's voice dropped even lower. "You already are." Jeremy smiled into Leo's shirt. "Then I guess I'm a teacher now." "Better than me at your age," Leo whispered, placing a quick kiss on the top of his brother's head. "Way better."

Ty cleared his throat softly. "And wiser." "Not wiser than you," Jeremy teased. Ty shrugged with mock humility. "It's close." Jeremy looked up. "Can I tell Mom and Dad this story?" Leo squeezed his shoulder. "You better." Ty reached for the marshmallow bag. "And while you do, I'll make the s'mores. Wisdom should always be rewarded." The day slipped on, soft as a secret kept for all the right reasons. And this one, at last, was the kind you were allowed to tell.

Jeremy's bare feet pattered across the dewy grass as the morning sun cracked through the trees. The tent flap swayed in the breeze, and somewhere behind him, Leo's voice called out, half-laughing, half-commanding. "Don't start folding it without me!" Jeremy giggled so hard his arms flailed as he dove into the sleeping bag to steal the last pillow before Leo could get to it. Their breathless grins matched, twin sunbursts lighting up the soft blue morning. A crow called from the trees, and behind the boys, Jeremy's dad yawned his way out of the screen tent with a travel mug in hand. He didn't say anything. He just smiled. This was what happy looked like.

Leo bent down beside the tent's corner flap and gave it a tug, the nylon rustling as it collapsed inwards. "You're folding it backwards," he teased. Jeremy shrugged and tried again, following Leo's instructions a little too excitedly. Ty wandered over from the gravel path just in time to catch a lopsided corner before it flopped onto Leo's foot. "Tag me in, boys," Ty said with a smirk, high-fiving them both. Jeremy beamed like the sun itself had cheered for him. He stood a little taller beside his older brothers. Not by blood—but by something deeper. By truth.

As the flap collapsed for real this time, Leo watched Jeremy's fingers tighten on the nylon. He was smaller than Leo remembered from the start of the summer, though he hadn't changed at all in height. It wasn't that Jeremy had shrunk—it was that Leo had grown. Not in inches. But in weight. In heart. In presence. He hadn't meant to change this much. He hadn't planned to. But Jeremy's love had made it unavoidable. There was no going back. The boy who used to control people with lies now protected the truth with all the strength he had.

Jeremy looked up at him mid-fold. "Leo," he said in a whisper only loud enough for Leo's heart to hear, "Do you think next summer will be like this too?" Leo paused, not because he didn't know the answer, but because the answer mattered more than anything. "I hope it's even better," he said, resting a hand on Jeremy's shoulder. "But this one? I think we're gonna remember this one forever." Jeremy nodded. He didn't say anything, just folded the flap one more time, perfectly in half, then smiled. It wasn't the kind of smile that asks for praise. It was the kind that says, I know you love me.

Behind them, Jeremy's mom zipped the cooler closed and began sorting the breakfast dishes into the blue storage bin. Ty offered to carry the camp stove back to the van, but not before watching the boys as if checking something silently. A pulse of peace passed between them all, like a sigh from the trees above. Jeremy's dad reached over and squeezed Leo's shoulder once, brief but real. It didn't need a speech. That single touch said, You belong here now. And Leo believed it.

The final pegs came out of the ground with a snap. Jeremy counted each one like it was treasure, tucking them into the little green bag with exaggerated care. "Mission complete," he declared. "Operation Tent Tidy: Success." Leo saluted him with a grin and gave him a gentle bump with his shoulder. Jeremy bumped him back twice as hard. "You're getting strong," Leo said, ruffling his hair. "I've been working out," Jeremy said seriously, flexing one noodle-thin arm. "Lifting truth all summer long." Leo laughed out loud. The kind of laugh that doesn't carry guilt. The kind that has nowhere to hide because it doesn't need to.

Once the tent was tucked away in its sack, Leo sat cross-legged near the firepit's remains, watching the smoke drift lazily into the trees. Jeremy flopped down beside him, head bumping his brother's arm. "You smell like marshmallows and lake water," Leo teased. "So do you," Jeremy said without missing a beat. The kind of back-and-forth that didn't need winners. Just rhythm. Just love. They stared at the coals for a while, neither needing to talk. The silence was thick, but not heavy. Just honest.

Ty crouched behind them with two water bottles and handed one to Leo. "Thanks," Leo said. Ty didn't nod. He just looked at Leo a second longer than usual, then turned back to help with the van. Leo knew what that look meant. It meant I'm proud of you, but Ty didn't say it with words. Shadow Warriors rarely did. Leo's chest filled with something solid and calm. Not pride. Not yet. But peace.

Jeremy looked up. "Do you think I could help someone else now?" he asked. The question didn't come from a place of ego. It came from somewhere deeper. Somewhere Leo recognized. "You already have," Leo said. "You helped me. More than you know." Jeremy blinked, then smiled again. That same soft smile from earlier, the one that didn't need permission. "Okay," he said. "Then I'll help more people too." And Leo nodded, because he believed him.

As the van door slammed shut on the last packed tote, Jeremy climbed into the back seat and stuck his head out the window like a puppy. Leo laughed and reached over to buckle him in, even though Jeremy could do it himself. "Safety first," Leo said. "Love first," Jeremy corrected, grinning. Leo rolled his eyes and kissed the top of his head. "Fine. Both first."

The gravel crunched beneath the van as it rolled out of the site. Trees zipped by in flickers of green. Leo watched them blur, one after the other, until the campground faded in the rear-view. He didn't feel sad. Not really. It wasn't the end. It was the kind of ending that opens a new chapter. One where he didn't have to prove he was worth loving. One where he didn't have to win. He just had to be.

In the front seat, Jeremy's parents talked quietly about the drive and the weather. Ty leaned his head against the glass and dozed. Leo glanced once more at Jeremy beside him, fast asleep with his cheek pressed against the window and one hand still clutching the edge of Leo's shirt. He hadn't let go the entire ride. Leo smiled. Not the kind of smile that demands attention. The kind that says, This is enough. Because it was. This was what love looked like.

The last bit of gear was unpacked and stored. The laundry machine hummed behind Jeremy's house, working through a mountain of smoke-scented clothes. But the summer wasn't done. Not even close. Camping might've ended, but Leo had no intention of leaving Jeremy's side. He'd promised—out loud, and more than once—that this summer belonged to his little brother. Not just the games and marshmallows. The lessons too. The ones people always forgot to teach children. Especially the ones who stuttered.

Jeremy sat on the porch, holding his comic book upside down—not because he couldn't read, but because his thoughts were bouncing too fast to focus. Leo sat beside him, his knee nudging Jeremy's. "You want to talk today?" he asked. Jeremy shook his head, then nodded. Then shrugged. Leo didn't press him. He just said, "We don't have to talk. We can listen." That's when Jeremy looked up, wide-eyed. "L-listen to w-what?" Leo smiled. "To you. Even when it's quiet."

Later that afternoon, they sat at the kitchen table with slices of watermelon and half-finished drawings. Leo leaned on one elbow, watching Jeremy talk about a game they might design one day. There it was again. That familiar hitch. The soft stammer. The hesitation like a hand clutched at Jeremy's throat, even when the words weren't scary. "You know," Leo said gently, "you don't stutter like that when we're at the lake." Jeremy froze. His eyes flickered down. "I… d-d-don't?" Leo shook his head. "Not even once."

That stuck with Jeremy. For the next hour, he tried to recall what had felt different. "I g-guess…" he began, stopping himself. "I-I didn't th-think about messing up." Leo nodded. "Because no one was watching for mistakes. We were just… together." Jeremy nodded, slowly, the realization seeping in. "It's school," Leo said. "That place makes you feel like you're not allowed to breathe wrong." He didn't say it to be cruel. He said it because it was true.

The next day, Leo brought a notebook out onto the porch. He'd written out phrases—simple ones at first. "I like red." "My name is Jeremy." "You are my brother." Each line had a little star beside it. "What are these f-f-for?" Jeremy asked. Leo tapped the stars. "One for each time you say it like you mean it. Not perfect. Just like you mean it." Jeremy's face lit up. Not from pride. From permission.

They did it again the next day. And the next. Some days were easier. Other days, Jeremy threw the notebook and cried into Leo's hoodie, frustrated with himself for something he couldn't control. "You're not broken," Leo would say, every time. "And you're not a problem. You're a person." It wasn't a speech. It was truth. The kind of truth Leo wished someone had said to him a year ago.

One evening, as the sky turned that honey-soft gold, Leo explained something new. "When you feel like the words are jammed, it's not always your mouth. Sometimes, it's your chest. Fear lives there." Jeremy stared at him like he'd unlocked a secret vault. "S-s-scared?" Leo nodded. "Yeah. Like… afraid someone's gonna laugh. Or ignore you. Or… pretend they didn't hear." Jeremy's lip trembled. "T-that happens a l-l-lot." Leo didn't pretend to be surprised. He just said, "That's their problem. Not yours."

Jeremy blinked hard. "So… so I c-can say stuff even if it's… messy?" Leo scooted closer. "Especially if it's messy." Then he added, "Messy is honest." That night, Jeremy spoke to his dad at dinner without mumbling or trailing off. He still stuttered—but he didn't hide. And when his voice cracked over a big word, Leo gave a thumbs-up from across the table. Jeremy grinned and powered through.

The next morning, Leo caught Jeremy rehearsing in the mirror. "I c-c-can do this. I c-c-c-can say this." Leo didn't interrupt. He just waited outside the door until Jeremy emerged. "Want to try something else?" Leo asked. Jeremy nodded instantly. "Okay. You tell me a hard truth, and I'll do the same. No rules. Just say it." Jeremy thought for a moment, then looked Leo square in the eye. "Sometimes I… wish I was like you. C-c-calm." Leo blinked, caught off guard. "Jeremy… I'm only calm because I was angry for too long."

Jeremy didn't understand at first. But Leo explained. "I was always trying to be what people wanted. So I controlled people. I lied. I bullied. You don't do that. You just try to be kind—even when it's hard. That's real courage." Jeremy looked down, then slowly leaned forward, resting his head on Leo's chest. "Your h-heart's going fast," he whispered. "Yeah," Leo whispered back. "'Cause I mean what I said."

That afternoon, they practiced new phrases. Not short ones. Honest ones. "I'm allowed to be scared." "I'm allowed to take my time." "I'm not broken." Jeremy stuttered through each one, then grinned like he'd just crossed a finish line. Leo clapped once and said, "Again." And Jeremy did. And again. And again. Until the notebook was full of stars.

On the last Friday of July, they sat beneath the trees with popsicles in hand. Jeremy said, "I th-th-think I like m-m-me." Leo nearly dropped his popsicle. "Say that again?" Jeremy laughed. "I like m-m-me." Leo pulled him into a hug so fast the popsicle stuck to his shirt. Neither of them cared. Jeremy buried his head into Leo's neck and whispered, "You're the r-r-reason."

Leo didn't correct him. He didn't say, No, it was you. He just hugged him tighter. Because he knew that sometimes, love sounds like stutters. Sometimes, healing looks like a notebook full of crooked stars. And sometimes, being a brother means making space for someone's broken rhythm—until it becomes music. Summer wasn't over. Not even close. And the lessons? They'd just begun.

CHAPTER 13: WHAT JEREMY LEARNED THAT SUMMER

Behind the tall grass that ran wild along the edge of the yard, where the morning birds had not quite finished their songs, Leo and Jeremy sat quietly on the old bench Jeremy's dad had built last spring. The sun was low but rising fast, warming the wooden slats under their legs, while the shadows of the porch stretched long across the lawn. No one spoke. Not because they had nothing to say—but because this was the kind of quiet you didn't interrupt. The kind that didn't feel empty anymore. Jeremy's shoulders weren't up near his ears. His hands were still. His breathing didn't hitch or race or catch on invisible wires like it used to. For the first time in months—maybe ever—he wasn't trying to fill the silence. He was letting it hold him.

Leo looked down at his knees and gave them a light tap, not impatiently, just a small rhythm to match the pace of the wind. "You okay?" he asked, not too loud. Jeremy nodded but didn't answer. That was fine. Leo didn't need him to. There was something about being back from the woods, back from the firelight and marshmallows and loons calling over the lake, that made the stillness feel different now. Less lonely. More like home. Jeremy finally whispered, "It used to feel scary." Leo tilted his head. Jeremy stared straight ahead. "Quiet. I thought it meant someone was mad. Or like something was about to happen."

Leo didn't flinch. "Me too," he said. "I used to fill every space with words. Even if they weren't true." That made Jeremy glance sideways, his eyes soft. "Now I kinda like it," he said, his voice small but certain. "It's like... my ears get to rest." Leo smiled. "Your heart too." They didn't need to explain further. Both boys knew what it meant. They'd both come from houses where quiet wasn't safe. Where silence screamed and footsteps cracked like thunder. Where yelling was always hiding behind the wall.

Jeremy rested his head on Leo's shoulder, just for a minute. Just long enough to say thank you without saying anything. Leo didn't move away. He let it happen. The breeze played with the leaves above them, and for a moment, the world forgot to rush. Jeremy pointed at the clouds. "That one looks like a bear." Leo squinted. "More like a squished jellybean." Jeremy laughed—not a sharp one, but the kind that rolls out slow, as if it forgot it was hiding.

They'd been home for about an hour. His parents were inside making breakfast, the smell of cinnamon toast drifting through the open window. Jeremy hadn't run to his room or turned on the TV. He didn't hide. He sat out back because that's where he felt strongest now. Leo didn't suggest it. Jeremy just did it. That was new. It used to take coaxing, reminders, reassurances. Now it just took Leo being near. Jeremy felt like he could breathe wider around him.

"Do you remember the first night in the tent?" Jeremy asked suddenly. Leo chuckled. "You mean when you screamed because a pinecone dropped on the tarp?" Jeremy grinned. "I thought it was a bear." "It was a pinecone." "I know that now." The teasing didn't sting. It never did with Leo. Not anymore. Because Leo didn't use laughter as a leash. He used it to lift. "I kept stuttering so bad that first day," Jeremy said. "Even saying hi was hard." Leo nodded, thoughtful. "But not by the end."

Jeremy shifted, letting his legs dangle off the side of the bench. "Do you think... it was because I was scared?" "Probably," Leo said honestly. "But scared doesn't mean broken." Jeremy didn't reply. Not right away. He looked down at his hands, tracing his thumb over the small scab near his knuckle from climbing a tree that week. "I don't want to be scared at school anymore." Leo leaned in a little. "Then don't go alone. I'll be there." Jeremy nodded. "You're like a big brother." "I am your big brother," Leo said, softly but without hesitation.

A robin landed on the fence post nearby. It chirped once, tilted its head, and fluttered off. Neither boy moved. "It's weird," Jeremy said. "I used to think talking made me safer. Like if I filled the space, people wouldn't yell." "And now?" Leo asked. "Now I like the space," Jeremy said. "It's mine." That made Leo smile. A real one. Not the fake kind that stretches but doesn't warm. This one held something proud inside it.

There was a time Leo wouldn't have been able to sit this long in one spot. He'd fidget, twist, bounce his leg, interrupt. Always needing attention. Always needing someone else to tell him who he was. But with Jeremy, there was no game. Just truth. And that truth didn't need to shout to be strong. "My mom said I seem taller," Jeremy said out of nowhere. Leo laughed. "You do. That's what happens when you stop curling into yourself." Jeremy made a face. "I do not curl." "You did," Leo teased. "But not anymore."

Jeremy's parents stepped onto the porch, voices low and loving. They didn't interrupt either. They saw the bench, the boys, the moment. And they let it be. That was the kind of parenting Leo wasn't used to. But it was the kind Jeremy deserved. "Breakfast's ready," Jeremy's dad called. "Five minutes," Jeremy said, and for once, he didn't ask permission with his eyes. He just said it. Leo gave him a slow nod. "That was brave," he whispered. "What?" "Answering like that."

Jeremy stood up and stretched. "The air even smells different," he said. "You're just not afraid of it anymore," Leo answered. They headed inside together, shoulder to shoulder, not rushing. The summer had shifted something in both of them, not just in ways you could see, but in the way they carried silence—like it was something sacred now, not something to survive. Jeremy wasn't trying to be louder. He was learning that quiet could still hold his power. And that maybe... it always had.

The quilt sagged slightly over their heads, pinned in place by books, couch cushions, and a hockey stick that Leo had carefully wedged against the side table. Flashlights glowed upward against the roof of the blanket fort, casting soft shapes and bending shadows that danced like quiet memories in the space between them. Jeremy had added a pillow from his bed and two juice boxes—one for each of them, grape and apple. It wasn't fancy, but it was safe. The kind of safe that made you want to ask questions you'd never ask in daylight. And Jeremy had one that had been floating in his chest since the day Leo moved into their home.

"Leo?" he said, squinting at the older boy from across the fort. Leo was lying on his side, head propped on one arm, the other hand tapping a soft rhythm on the floor as if keeping time with the shadows. "Yeah?" Jeremy shifted. "Why did you lie before? Like, when you first got to school. You were really different. People listened to you. But it didn't feel... right. Not all the time." He paused, watching Leo's face. "Why did you become that way?"

Leo didn't pretend to misunderstand. He didn't laugh it off. He didn't toss a pillow to change the subject. He just stopped tapping and looked at Jeremy, flashlight angled toward the wall now, not between them. "Because sometimes," he said, slowly, "the truth would've made me lose control of everything." He didn't blink when he said it. He didn't soften the edges. Jeremy didn't speak yet. He could feel something big behind Leo's eyes, and he wanted to let it come out without stepping on it.

"When I was living with... with him," Leo said, not naming the man who shared his blood but none of his heart, "I had to read moods like weather. You could tell how the day was going to go by the way he closed the door. Loud meant get out of the way. Quiet meant something worse." Leo picked at a thread on the blanket beside him, not because he was nervous, but because some stories need movement to survive the telling. "So, I started lying. Just little things at first. Like saying I'd eaten when I hadn't. Saying I wasn't scared when I was shaking. Saying it didn't hurt when it did."

Jeremy's eyes didn't leave his. "Did it help?" Leo gave a small shrug. "Not really. But it made me feel like I had some kind of armour." The air inside the fort felt warmer now. Not hot. Just filled with something heavier than silence. "When I got to school," Leo went on, "I didn't know how to stop. People liked it when I was funny or confident or made them feel special. So I used that. I used compliments like tools. Like I could trade praise for safety. Make friends before they could hate me."

Jeremy nodded slowly. "But it wasn't real?" "No," Leo said. "Not really. I didn't even know who I was back then." He turned his flashlight down toward the floor and twisted it in his fingers. "Ty knew though. Even when I tried to push him away. He saw through everything. That was annoying at first." Jeremy gave a small laugh, and Leo smiled too, but it faded quick. "Then Ty's dad stepped in. Saw the bruises. The fear. And they didn't just ask questions—they did something. And that... changed everything."

For a long moment, Jeremy didn't speak. Then he whispered, "I didn't know you were hurt like that." Leo nodded. "A lot of people didn't. Because I hid it well. I smiled just right. I knew how to mirror kindness. But I didn't know how to feel it until I got here." He touched his hand to his chest. "Truth felt dangerous back then. Now it feels like... breathing right." Jeremy stared at him with eyes wide and bright. "I'm glad you're here now."

Leo looked at him, truly looked. "I'm glad you're here too." He gave Jeremy's knee a gentle bump with his own. "And you never have to lie around me. Not ever." Jeremy nodded again, slower this time. "Sometimes I feel like if I mess up, people won't like me anymore." Leo raised an eyebrow. "Jeremy, you could spill juice on my math homework, call my drawing of a horse a dog, and snore all night—and I'd still be your brother."

Jeremy laughed into his juice box, a real laugh, one that echoed slightly in the small space. "I only snored once!" Leo chuckled. "It shook the tent." The tension broke, but not the meaning. The truth had landed. And neither of them would pretend it didn't matter. Jeremy reached over, nudged Leo's arm, then leaned against him, just a little. "You think I'll stop stuttering one day?" Leo didn't hesitate. "I think you already are."

Jeremy blinked. "Really?" "Yup," Leo said. "You don't stumble when you talk to me. You don't second-guess. You just talk." Jeremy tilted his head. "But what if I still do sometimes?" "Then I'll wait for you," Leo said. "And if anybody laughs, I'll make sure they hear from me." Jeremy's eyes lit with something new—safety that didn't come with rules or performance. Just love.

Outside the blanket fort, voices stirred. His parents were in the kitchen, probably setting plates. The day was just beginning. But this moment—the space between flashlights and truth—was the one Jeremy would remember. Not because it was dramatic. But because someone had answered a hard question without flinching. Because a lie had been replaced with a truth. And because the one who used to manipulate... was now the one who taught him how to be free.

The sky was painted in soft navy when Mr. Firth leaned out the back door and called the boys inside for dinner. The barbecue had been cleaned, the frisbee tucked into the garage, and the cicadas had started to hum a tune only summer could write. Jeremy's cheeks were flushed from laughter, and Leo's arms were scraped just lightly enough from climbing the tree out back that he felt like a kid instead of someone who'd once had to grow up too fast. The table was already set when they entered—corn on the cob, buttered rice, grilled chicken, lemonade in blue plastic cups that felt like home.

Mr. Firth reached to ruffle Jeremy's hair, and Jeremy grinned and ducked. "You two sure kept yourselves busy," he said, grinning at Leo. Leo smiled, not the kind that meant look at me, but the kind that said thank you for letting me be here. "Best day I've had all summer," Leo replied, and meant it. Mrs. Firth, her apron dusted with flour from a morning pie, set the peach cobbler on the stovetop to cool. "Well, good," she said. "Then maybe you'll stay the night?" She glanced toward Jeremy, whose eyes had already widened.

Leo blinked. "Stay over?" Jeremy's voice rose with the kind of hope that doesn't come around often. "Please?" Leo nodded slowly. "If it's really okay." "Of course it is," Mrs. Firth said with a soft clap of her hands.

"You're part of the family now." Leo felt a warmth rush up his neck, something he hadn't felt often—not just being wanted, but being welcomed without question. "Thank you," he said, standing straighter. He kissed her cheek without thinking, the way Ty's mom had taught him. She smiled and patted his arm. "Sleep wherever you two like. Just no wrestling on the stairs."

The bedtime routine was ordinary—pyjamas, tooth brushing, whispers in the hallway. Leo borrowed a pair of Jeremy's extra pyjamas, the ones with too-long cuffs, and pulled a spare blanket from the hall closet. They settled into Jeremy's bed, twin-sized but big enough for two boys used to sharing space. The lights went out with a click, and for a while, everything was still. Then the rain came—soft, not sharp—and tapped gently against the window. Jeremy listened for a moment, then whispered, "I always think rain sounds like thinking."

Leo smiled into the dark. "Yeah. Or like dreams that want to be heard." It was quiet again, until somewhere after midnight. Jeremy's footsteps were soft on the hardwood, careful as they crossed the short hall to the bathroom. But it wasn't the flush or the faucet that woke Leo—it was the small shuffle of feet returning to the room and stopping just inside the doorway. "Leo?" Jeremy whispered. "Can I—can I sleep with you? I... I still get scared sometimes." Leo didn't say anything at first. He just pulled the blanket back with one hand, and Jeremy climbed in.

They didn't say much. Jeremy lay still for a while, pressed close, his body warm and curled like someone trying to disappear into the quiet. His breathing was shallow at first, like he was waiting to be told no. Leo didn't move. He didn't sigh or shift or ask what scared him. He just laid his arm over Jeremy's shoulder and pulled the blanket higher, tucking it close around them both. "It's okay," he whispered, just once. "You're not alone." And Jeremy melted into the warmth.

An hour passed. Maybe more. Jeremy stirred once, murmured something about a shadow, and Leo smoothed his hair gently with the back of his hand. The boy beside him had trusted him, not just with stories, but with stillness. With vulnerability. With the space that exists between panic and peace. Leo knew that weight. And he carried it carefully. Somewhere before dawn, when the stars were beginning to fade into the soft blue of August morning, Leo whispered into Jeremy's hair, "I love you, Jeremy."

It wasn't loud. It wasn't planned. It just fell out like a truth that had waited its turn. Jeremy didn't reply. Not in words. But he tightened his hold on Leo's sleeve, and his body softened in reply. Leo lay there with eyes wide open, staring into the soft folds of the ceiling above, listening to the breath of the boy beside him. The rain had stopped. But the safety hadn't. And that mattered more than words.

Leo had never called anyone brother before—not out loud. But Jeremy made it easy. He loved without performance. Without masks. Without needing Leo to be anything but there. And that night, something changed. Not because of a big confession or some dramatic rescue, but because Leo stayed when Jeremy needed him most. No pretending. No power. Just presence.

By morning, the sun had crept into the room with soft golden feet. Jeremy was still curled beside him, his hand wrapped gently in the corner of Leo's pyjama top. Leo didn't move. Not yet. Not because he was tired—but because he knew that moments like these don't last forever. And when you've spent most of your life watching for danger, safety feels like a miracle.

When Mrs. Firth came to check on them, she stopped in the doorway and just smiled. She didn't say a word. She just pulled the door a little more closed to block the light and let them sleep a little longer. Leo felt it even without looking. The way she protected them. The way love moved quietly, without needing applause.

That hug—Jeremy's late-night reach for comfort—lasted all night not because of how tightly it held, but because of what it meant. Leo had become more than a protector. He had become a place. A home. And Jeremy? He knew now, with more than words, that love didn't need to be loud to be true.

They sat together on the back porch steps after breakfast, the air still cool enough that the wood felt damp beneath their pyjama pants. A breeze rustled through the trees at the edge of the yard, carrying the scent of cut grass and something warm from the kitchen—maybe leftover waffles, maybe cinnamon. Jeremy had his knees tucked to his chest and Leo sat beside him, one arm resting lazily over the railing, letting the silence stretch as far as it wanted. Jeremy's fingers picked at the thread of his sleeve, not tearing it, just following the line.

"I w-w-wish I didn't t-talk l-like th-this," Jeremy said at last, his voice a small ripple in the morning. He didn't look at Leo when he said it. He didn't have to. "It m-makes me feel s-s-s-stuck. Like I'm b-b-broken or s-some—" He stopped. The word hurt. He didn't want to finish it. Leo didn't jump in. Didn't correct him or rush to fix the pause. He let the air hold it.

"I don't think you're broken," Leo said, slow and steady. "I think your voice is just figuring out how to feel safe." He picked up a stick from beside the step and traced a loose circle in the dirt at their feet. "When something matters to you, your heart holds it close. And sometimes, your mouth can't push it out fast. That doesn't mean you're wrong. It means you care."

Jeremy's shoulders slumped. Not in defeat—just in relief. Like someone had finally seen the whole picture and didn't ask him to shrink it. He pressed his face into his knees for a second, breathing through the tightness that always came with being understood. Leo leaned over and rested his chin on Jeremy's head. "You ever notice," he said gently, "how people who talk the fastest are usually the ones hiding something?"

Jeremy blinked. "R-really?" "Yeah," Leo said. "Like they're trying to outrun what they feel. But you—you stop. You try. You mean every word. That takes guts." For a while, the wind did the talking. The maple tree by the fence waved gently. Jeremy reached over and touched Leo's hand without looking. He didn't squeeze it. He just wanted to make sure it was there. "D-d-does it m-make y-you m-m-mad?" he asked. "W-when I can't say stuff f-fast?"

Leo tilted his head, lips pressing together for a second like he wanted to laugh but didn't. "Nah. Makes me pay more attention. You ever notice how the world talks over people? You're the opposite. You make people stop and actually listen. That's power, not weakness." Jeremy blinked fast. "I-I d-don't feel p-p-powerful." "That's 'cause you're growing into it," Leo said. "Takes time. Like your voice is still building its muscles."

"Muscles?" Jeremy giggled. "Yeah," Leo nodded. "And every time you speak, even with a stutter, you're lifting something. You're lifting truth." That did something. Jeremy's chest lifted with a fuller breath, one that didn't catch in his throat the same way. He rested his cheek against Leo's arm and let his eyes close for just a moment. "M-m-my v-voice is s-s-strong?"

"Stronger than you think," Leo whispered. "Stronger than mine was when I was your age. And way more honest." They sat like that until the sun crept higher and the porch warmed beneath them. Mrs. Firth stepped out briefly, saw the way they sat, and quietly stepped back in without a word. She didn't need to ask. She could see that something important was happening—something only boys like Leo and Jeremy could share in that way.

Leo finally wrapped his arms around Jeremy and pulled him close. "Your voice," he said quietly, "it doesn't need to change for me to love it. I love you exactly the way you are." Jeremy buried his face into Leo's chest, a tiny sob escaping that didn't come from sadness, but from release.

They didn't talk for a while. But they didn't have to. The hug said what words couldn't. That Leo was more than a friend. That he was safety. That Jeremy didn't need to fight his own mouth anymore to be understood. "I'm not b-b-broken?" Jeremy asked again, just to be sure. Leo kissed the top of his head. "Not even close."

When the wind changed, and a bird called out from the trees, Jeremy pulled back just enough to meet Leo's eyes. He didn't stutter that time. "Thank you." And Leo smiled, proud of the silence that followed. Because in that quiet, Jeremy had spoken the loudest he ever had.

Jeremy had always noticed the difference in the way people listened. Some people stared past you, nodding like their heads were on springs, just waiting for you to run out of breath so they could tell their own story. Others leaned forward too eagerly, interrupting like they were helping, when really they were just trying to make your sentence into theirs. But Leo… Leo never rushed. When he listened, it felt like the room slowed down to make space for what you were trying to say, even if your voice tripped over the first few words.

The kitchen smelled like home. Mrs. Firth had a towel draped over one shoulder and a familiar percolator humming near the stove. It clicked and bubbled softly, and even the clock on the wall seemed to keep time more gently here. She turned from the sink and smiled at Leo as if she'd known him for years. "Leo," she asked, "do you drink coffee?" Her voice had no test in it. Just warmth, like it was okay to like something even if you were still figuring yourself out.

Leo answered without the hesitation people expected from kids. "Yes, ma'am. But where I live now, they only drink tea." He didn't seem apologetic about it. He wasn't trying to impress anyone. He just said it, softly, like someone telling the truth in a way that didn't need to be defended. Mrs. Firth nodded, pleased.

"Well, then I think it's time you had something real. Percolated. None of that machine stuff," she said, tapping the lid of the pot with the back of a spoon. "How do you take it?" Leo smiled, just barely. "Two cream. No sugar, please." "I like that. Polite, but clear," she said. "Coming right up."

Jeremy sat at the table watching the exchange unfold like a movie he'd already seen but hadn't understood until now. There was something about the way Leo stood there—hands still, back straight, eyes soft—that made him seem older than he was. Not because he acted like an adult, but because he wasn't trying to be one. He just was himself. Whole, quiet, confident in a way Jeremy hadn't thought possible for a kid not yet twelve.

The mug clinked softly as Mrs. Firth set it in front of him, steam curling above the rim. Leo cupped it in both hands and inhaled gently before taking a sip. His eyes didn't close, but something behind them did. Something opened, too. He looked at her and said with a steady voice, "Thank you. This is the best thing I've tasted all week."

Jeremy blinked. "Y-you didn't th-thank her b-b-before," he whispered. Leo turned to him and nodded. "You're right. I should have." He looked at Mrs. Firth again. "Thank you. I mean it." And that was it. No fuss. No embarrassment. Just a boy owning a moment without shrinking inside it.

Later, after the dishes were done and the day began to lean into its quieter hour, they moved to the living room. Leo sat in the corner of the couch, one leg folded underneath him, the coffee still warm in his hand. Jeremy sat close, sketchbook in lap, but his pencil unmoving. He wasn't drawing. He was watching. Not Leo's hands or his face—but his listening. That stillness. That present-ness that made every word Jeremy hadn't said yet feel welcome.

He started talking. Nothing important. Just words about marshmallows burning at camp, and how Leo was braver than anyone when it came to jumping off the dock. But Leo didn't laugh at the silly parts or interrupt with his own version. He just listened. Fully. Like Jeremy's voice had weight. And meaning. Even when it wavered. Especially when it wavered.

There were pauses. Big ones. And Leo didn't fill them. He didn't finish Jeremy's sentences. He didn't glance at a phone or twitch his leg with boredom. He just sat there, eyes gentle, waiting for the words to catch up with the thoughts behind them. Jeremy hadn't known it could feel like this—to be heard before you'd even found the right syllables.

"W-why d-do y-you l-l-listen like th-that?" Jeremy asked softly, his fingers curled around the spine of his notebook. Leo didn't blink. "Because I know what it feels like when nobody does." Jeremy looked down at his lap. "D-does it ever s-stop hurting?" Leo took another slow sip and set the mug on the table. "Not always. But when someone really hears you, it stops hurting for a while." He looked at Jeremy then, not like a teacher but like a friend who had fallen through the same cracks and was now showing him where they led.

Mrs. Firth passed by with a laundry basket, offering them both a little nod as she disappeared down the hall. Jeremy shifted closer, leaning into Leo's side like he was anchoring himself to something safe. Leo didn't move. He let the boy rest there, steady and silent. Jeremy didn't have to say anything. That was the gift Leo gave. Silence without judgment. Attention without pressure. "I-I wanna l-l-learn how t-to l-l-listen like th-that," Jeremy whispered. Leo wrapped an arm around his shoulders and said, "Then you already are."

They didn't speak after that. They didn't need to. The room held the kind of peace that didn't need music or games to fill it. Just the slow rhythm of breath, the warmth of trust, and the kind of quiet that made even the smallest voice feel heard. And in that moment, Jeremy believed—maybe for the first time—that his voice was enough.

Jeremy had never been in a canoe without gripping both sides like they were the last thing keeping him from drowning. Even on still water, his heart jumped at every ripple, every shift in the breeze. But Leo didn't flinch. He sat with the paddle resting across his lap, his knees steady, bare feet planted like roots on the floor of the boat. Jeremy watched him closely, trying to mimic the calm. They were only twenty feet from shore, the sun painting soft streaks over the surface, but for Jeremy, it felt like the middle of an ocean.

Leo glanced over, noticed the whiteness in Jeremy's knuckles, and didn't say anything right away. He let the silence settle between them like a warm towel. Then, just as the canoe gave its first uncertain sway from a wake sent by a nearby jet ski, Leo chuckled. It wasn't a laugh at Jeremy. It was the kind that wrapped around fear like a blanket and dared it to stay.

"I think the lake's trying to scare us," Leo said. "But it'll lose. Even waves calm down after a while." Jeremy's eyes widened. "Y-you s-s-sure?" Leo tapped the edge of the canoe gently with his paddle. "I'm still here. You're still here. And the canoe? It's still floating. That's all the proof I need."

From the dock, Mr. Firth held up a hand to wave, one foot resting on the faded wooden bench where he and Jeremy often sat to talk about stars and fireflies. Mrs. Firth stood beside him with a towel over one shoulder and a thermos in her hands. She didn't call out, didn't interrupt. She just watched them glide slowly toward the edge of the cove. Leo turned the paddle once and steered them gently left. The wobble returned. Jeremy gasped, then gripped the sides again—but this time, he didn't look afraid. He looked like he was bracing himself to trust.

Back at the house, the Braun percolator hummed with purpose. It had been Mr. Firth's since university, and he still insisted that no other machine brewed a proper cup. Mrs. Firth poured three coffees—one for herself, one for her husband, and one for Leo. The scent alone made the house feel older and warmer. Not like a museum, but like a memory being lived in real time. She handed Leo his mug when he returned from the lake, hair windblown and cheeks rosy from sun and laughter. "Two creams, no sugar," she said, repeating his order without needing to ask.

Leo took the mug carefully, cupped it in both hands, and smiled. "Still the best." Ty and his parents had arrived just before dinner. Mr. and Mrs. Takashi bowed lightly, as they always did, even though Jeremy's parents had gently reminded them that it wasn't necessary in their house. Leo offered a small nod in return. He was respectful, but quieter than usual. Ty noticed, but didn't press. It wasn't discomfort exactly—it was a kind of gentle withdrawal, like Leo was stepping out of a role he played at home and into the one he truly preferred here.

During dessert, Mr. Firth joked about the old canoe being "impossible to flip unless you really try." Leo grinned and told him they'd given it a fair test. Jeremy added that he panicked, but Leo didn't. "He laughed," Jeremy said with pride. "H-he always d-does when I'm scared." Mrs. Takashi smiled and touched her son's shoulder. Ty sat up straighter. "That's because Leo believes fear isn't a stop sign," he said. "It's just a curve in the road."

The conversation turned to school, to new teachers and September nerves. Jeremy barely stuttered through his sentences now. Mrs. Firth leaned close to whisper in Leo's ear. "You've helped him more than any program we tried." Leo looked down at his coffee. "I didn't do much." "You showed up," she said. "And you stayed."

Later that night, after dishes and marshmallows and a quiet walk along the backyard path, Jeremy came up behind Leo without saying a word and hugged him around the waist. Mr. and Mrs. Firth joined a moment later, arms wrapping gently over both boys. It wasn't a ceremony. It wasn't even a goodbye. It was just a long, wordless moment that said: you belong.

Across the room, Mrs. Takashi stood watching. She didn't speak, but her expression was thoughtful. She pulled her husband aside in the hallway a few minutes later. "He's more himself here," she said in Japanese, keeping her voice low. "Not because he doesn't love us. But because this rhythm matches his." Mr. Takashi nodded. "No pressure to bow. No lectures about tradition. No raw fish." "Or miso soup," she added, smiling. "And he finally gets his coffee." Ty, listening from the stairs, spoke up. "He still loves us. He's just... softer here."

No one disagreed. No one felt offended. They understood what it meant to belong in more than one place, to be loved by many, and to feel safe only in some. Mr. Firth brought out one last round of coffee for the adults, offered a hot chocolate for Jeremy, and sat back with a quiet sigh that said more than any toast ever could. Leo sat beside Jeremy on the couch, letting the boy's head rest on his shoulder. The lights were low. The house was full. The canoe hadn't flipped. The waves had calmed. And for now, at least, nothing needed to be fixed.

They were sitting at the breakfast table, toast still warm, the jam dish licked clean at the corners by someone's spoon, when Jeremy stood up without meaning to. He clutched his juice glass like it was a microphone, eyes flicking to Leo, then to his parents, and then back to Leo again. "So... I saw a chipmunk last night," he said, and Leo nodded, waiting. Jeremy didn't seem nervous. He took a breath, eyes bright, and continued. "It came out near the fire pit. Real quiet. But then—it ran right across the log pile, grabbed the marshmallow we dropped, and zipped back into the woods."

Everyone froze. Not because of the chipmunk. But because he hadn't stuttered. Not once. Not on a single word. Jeremy blinked, as if catching up to the room's silence. "Did I say it... all?" Leo stood first. Not with a cheer. Not with a joke. Just a soft clap. Two palms meeting in steady rhythm, warm and proud. He stepped forward and wrapped his arms around Jeremy, pulling him close. "You said it, Jem," he whispered. "You said it all."

Mrs. Firth covered her mouth. Not from shock, but from the sudden rush of tears that came too fast to hide. Mr. Firth set his coffee down slowly, eyes misting. The sunlight caught Jeremy's cheeks as he leaned into Leo, face pressed to his shoulder, and the whole room felt like a bell being rung without a sound.

"I think..." Jeremy said after a moment, voice barely louder than a breath, "I think I wasn't scared that time." Leo held him tighter. "Then that's all that matters." They stood that way for longer than most people would have allowed. But not in this house. Here, hugs didn't expire. Here, warmth wasn't rationed. Mr. Firth got up and began clearing the dishes, whistling a little. Mrs. Firth wiped her eyes, then sat beside Leo and Jeremy and rested her hand lightly on both boys' backs.

"You proud of him?" she asked. Leo smiled without needing to answer. That evening, while Jeremy was drawing on the back patio, Leo sat inside with Mr. and Mrs. Firth. They were folding laundry—ordinary things like socks and pillowcases—but the mood was tender, like someone had placed velvet around the moment. Mrs. Firth looked up, her tone gentle. "Leo, can I ask you something personal?"

He didn't hesitate. "Of course." "Are you happy where you live now? With Ty and his family?" Leo set down the towel he'd been folding and leaned back in the chair. "I love them very much," he said slowly. "They're beautiful people. They gave me a second chance. They listen. They care. Ty's like my real brother." He paused, thoughtful. "But sometimes... I don't feel quite at home." Mr. Firth raised a brow. "What makes you feel that way?"

Leo fiddled with the edge of the towel. "It's little things. Things you wouldn't think matter. Like... the food. There's no coffee in the house. They drink only tea. I miss the smell of coffee in the morning. And they eat a lot of fish, but it's raw, and I just... I can't get used to that." Mrs. Firth smiled kindly. "It's okay not to love everything about a place."

"I love them," Leo said again, firmer now. "It's just... not easy to feel comfortable all the time." Mr. Firth nodded, picking up a pair of folded jeans. "Comfort's funny. It's not about what people do for you. It's about where your body stops bracing." Leo looked up. "That's what you are here," Mr. Firth continued. "You're not bracing."

Outside, Jeremy laughed—high and real, not nervous. Leo stood to join him, leaving the rest of the laundry half-folded. Mrs. Firth didn't stop him. He opened the patio door, letting the breeze inside. Jeremy was crouched by a flowerpot, pointing at something in the dirt. "Leo! Look! Ants!" he shouted. "They're carrying the whole chip bag crumb I dropped!"

Leo came closer. "Think they'll share?" Jeremy giggled. "Not a chance." They both knelt, knees in the dirt, shoulders touching. And again, Jeremy said it all—without a stutter, without a blink, without fear. Not because he was cured. But because love had silenced the panic before it could speak.

The lake didn't move much that day. It just sat, flat and silver, like a mirror turned sideways. The breeze was faint, barely enough to stir the grass along the shore, and even the birds seemed reluctant to interrupt the hush that had settled over everything. Jeremy had come looking for Leo only because the house felt emptier without him. It wasn't that Leo had disappeared—he wasn't the vanishing kind anymore. But something had drawn him down to the dock, to the water's edge, where old feelings sometimes rose like fog from the surface. Jeremy spotted him near the second bench, facing the lake, his back hunched just slightly. One hand held his wrist, the other hung at his side. His head was down.

Jeremy didn't call his name. He walked instead—barefoot, slow—down the path, each step careful, as if the quiet might break if pressed too hard. When he was close enough to see Leo's shoulders rise and fall in uneven rhythm, he paused. There was no mistaking the redness around Leo's eyes, the streaks on his cheeks that hadn't quite dried. His fists were clenched, white-knuckled, knotted in that silent way boys sometimes carry pain when they haven't yet found where to put it.

"You okay?" Jeremy asked, barely above a whisper. Leo didn't turn. "Not really." Jeremy sat down beside him, legs crossed, facing the same direction. The lake didn't blink. Neither did the sky. "Wanna talk about it?" Leo inhaled sharply, his jaw twitching. "I was thinking about the way I used to be." Jeremy tilted his head, waiting.

"The lies," Leo said. "The way I played people. Pretended to be nice so I could get stuff. The way I made others feel small just so I could feel tall. I think about it sometimes and... I hate it." Jeremy reached out slowly and placed his hand on Leo's knee. He didn't grip. Just touched, steady and warm. "You don't do that anymore."

Leo let out a shaky breath that caught halfway up his chest. "But I did. And it wasn't by accident. I knew what I was doing. I didn't just mess up. I chose it." Jeremy looked at him then, eyes round and calm. "But you're choosing something else now." "I don't feel like I deserve all this," Leo whispered. "You. Your parents. Ty. The love. The forgiveness." Jeremy didn't flinch. "But you have it."

Leo's shoulders buckled then, the weight of that truth pressing into him harder than any punishment ever had. He let his fists go. Let the tears come freely. They weren't loud. They weren't sharp. They fell like drops from a cup that had been too full for too long. Jeremy didn't pull away. He leaned in. Wrapped his arms around Leo and rested his chin on his shoulder. "I love you," he said. "You're my brother. Not because of what you did. But because of who you are now."

Leo shook his head. "You shouldn't have to be the one to make me feel okay." Jeremy smiled gently. "I don't have to. I just want to." For a long time, they sat like that—two boys in a world that had once hurt them both, now holding each other in a space it could no longer reach. The lake stayed still. The breeze curled around them like a lullaby. In that sacred quiet, Leo sobbed softly, not for what he had lost, but for what he was finally safe enough to feel.

He had never cried like that before. Not when it mattered. Not when anyone stayed. Jeremy stayed. Mr. Firth came down the path about twenty minutes later, saw the two of them from a distance, and turned around without saying a word. Some moments aren't meant to be witnessed. Only honoured.

When Leo finally lifted his head, his face was streaked and damp, but his eyes were clearer than they had been in weeks. "Thanks," he said. "For what?" "For being here. For saying that. For... not making me explain everything." Jeremy leaned his head against Leo's arm. "You don't have to explain everything to be forgiven." Leo smiled through the wetness. "I want to be better than I was."

"You already are," Jeremy said. "And tomorrow you'll be even better." Leo let the sun hit his face then, eyes closed, body relaxed. The storm had passed—not the kind in the sky, but the kind that lives in memory. And Jeremy, brave little soul that he was, stayed steady. Not as a counsellor. Not as a hero. Just as a friend who knew how much it mattered when someone cries and isn't left alone.

The trail behind the Firths' property curved like a question mark, dipping between two old cedar trees before sloping down toward the riverbank. You wouldn't see the stone unless you were looking for it. Flat, wide, and grey as an old photograph, it sat just where the water met the roots, warmed by sun but worn smooth by rain. Leo spotted it first—said it looked like a skipping stone for giants. But when they crouched beside it, running their fingers along the edge, it was clear this rock wasn't meant to be thrown. It was meant to stay.

Jeremy was the one who suggested they mark it. "Like a flag," he said, "but one that nobody else sees." Leo laughed and said it was more like a secret handshake, only in stone. They brought out a pocketknife from the shed—one of the old kinds Mr. Firth used when carving kindling—and took turns carving their initials into the surface. J.F. and L.T., scratched deep enough to stay through storms.

It wasn't easy. The blade was sharp, but the rock was stubborn. Jeremy's hands trembled a little when he started. Not from fear, but from the newness of doing something that might last longer than his own voice. Leo steadied his wrist without a word. Together, they etched something small that felt enormous.

"There," Jeremy said, brushing off the dust with his sleeve. "Now if you ever forget who you are, or who loves you, you just come back here." Leo looked at him, surprised. "I was about to say the same thing to you." They sat side by side, their legs brushing, the rock between them like a third heart that couldn't beat but still held something alive. The river moved lazily behind them. Not rushing, not loud—just steady. Like breath. Like time when it's kind.

Leo cleared his throat. "If anyone ever hurts you again—makes you feel small, or stupid, or like you don't belong—I want you to come back here. Put your hand on this rock and remember. You're loved. Okay? Always." Jeremy didn't answer right away. He nodded first, slow and sure. Then he whispered, "Same for you."

The sun cast shadows across the grass, and a dragonfly dipped once, twice, then vanished into the trees. Leo picked up a stick and began tracing a circle around the rock. "This is ours," he said. "Even if we move. Even if we grow up and forget half the things we knew when we were kids. This place—this stone—it won't forget."

Jeremy smiled. "Can we name it?" Leo blinked, then chuckled. "Name the rock?" "Yeah." "What would you name a rock?" Jeremy looked serious. "Anchor." Leo nodded slowly. "Yeah. That works."

The name didn't have to be carved. It was felt. Spoken into the dirt and water and branches around them, like the start of a story no one could erase. They stood up, brushing grass from their legs, and looked down once more at what they'd made. It wasn't fancy. Just a couple initials on a forgotten rock by a quiet riverbank. But to them, it was the opposite of forgotten. It was proof. Leo pulled Jeremy into a one-armed hug and said nothing more. He didn't need to. The squeeze said it all. The weight of memory, of protection, of brotherhood without blood.

Later that evening, when the wind picked up and the sky turned a soft kind of gold, Leo returned alone for a moment and pressed his fingers to the stone. His name. Jeremy's name. He said, "I'll come back here if I ever feel like lying again. Or pretending. Or hiding. I'll come here and remember who I promised to be." And in the silence, the rock said nothing back—but Leo swore he heard something settle inside him, like a knot undoing. That rock wasn't just a rock. It was their anchor.

The night in Jeremy's backyard was warm but quiet, the kind of quiet that settles gently on your shoulders instead of pressing down. A few stars blinked through the navy sky, their light gentle enough not to interrupt. The fire pit popped now and then, throwing sparks that danced before falling back to the ground. Jeremy and Leo had set up their tent earlier with Mr. Firth's help, but now it was just the two of them sitting in their camping chairs, knees close, socks warmed by the fire, and eyes heavy with the peace of summer air. They weren't in a forest or a big campsite, but somehow the fence felt like trees and the porch light might as well have been a moon. Leo leaned forward and poked at the fire with a stick, not to do anything to it, just because it felt like the right thing to do in that moment.

Jeremy watched him quietly, his hands wrapped around a tin camping mug filled with hot chocolate, the kind with little marshmallows that refused to melt all the way. The silence between them wasn't awkward. It was safe. It was the kind of silence you only have with someone who doesn't expect you to fill every second with noise. After a while, Leo tilted his head, glanced sideways at Jeremy, and gave a half-smile that said, I think you're ready. He didn't even say it out loud yet. Just nodded once, as if the fire itself had told him it was time. Jeremy didn't speak either, just waited.

"There's rules," Leo said, finally, his voice low like he didn't want the fence to overhear. "But not like the kind grown-ups make. These ones aren't written on paper. They're in the way we act. And once you learn them, you never forget." Jeremy leaned in just a little, resting his elbows on his knees. Leo turned to him and said, "These are the Campfire Rules. Shadow Warrior rules. You ready?" Jeremy nodded once, the same way Leo had.

"Rule One," Leo said, holding up a single finger. "Protect the truth." Jeremy whispered the words, almost reverently. "Protect the truth." "Rule Two," Leo continued, holding up another. "Don't use it to hurt." Jeremy furrowed his brow. "Even if someone lies about you first?" Leo looked straight into the flames. "Especially then. Anyone can throw truth like a knife. It takes real strength to hold it gently."

Jeremy didn't speak. He looked at the fire the same way Leo did. "Rule Three," Leo said, "Don't show off. Just show up." He didn't smile when he said it. He wasn't performing. He just meant it. "Nobody needs to see you do the right thing. You just need to do it. Quietly. That's what real Shadow Warriors do."

Jeremy repeated all three rules under his breath. Protect the truth. Don't use it to hurt. Don't show off. Just show up. Each one landed like a stone in his chest, not heavy—but real. He looked down at the dirt, picked up a small stick, and began drawing each rule carefully, one under the other, like a list that couldn't be erased. Leo watched him, never interrupting.

"They're not always easy," Leo said. "You'll want to yell sometimes. You'll want to fight. You'll want people to see how good you're being, and you'll want them to clap. But the ones who matter already know, and the ones who don't... they never will." Jeremy looked up at him, eyes wide, and Leo nodded gently. "That's part of it too."

A breeze swept the smoke away from them just in time. Jeremy breathed in the warm scent of pine needles and campfire wood and cocoa and safety. He took a long sip, and when he looked up again, Leo was staring at him with an expression Jeremy didn't yet know how to name. Something between pride and memory. Like he'd been Jeremy once. Like he remembered what it felt like to be small and scared and wanting to be brave.

"Can I make a rule?" Jeremy asked. His voice wasn't loud. He didn't have to shout. Leo nodded. "If it's good." Jeremy looked back at his list and added a fourth line in the dirt. "Tell someone when you're scared. Someone who listens." Leo's voice was soft. "That's a good one." Jeremy added another under it. "And... hug your brother if he's sad. Even if he says he's not." Leo closed his eyes for a moment and smiled—not a wide grin, just a real one. "That one's a keeper."

The fire popped again. A marshmallow fell off a stick and hit the dirt with a tiny thump, but no one moved to save it. Leo leaned back in his chair, hands behind his head, legs stretched out. Jeremy leaned over and rested his head lightly on Leo's shoulder. They didn't say anything for a full minute. Then Jeremy whispered, "Do you think I'll be a good one?" Leo didn't look at him. "You already are."

They both watched the smoke drift up, curling around the stars, rising so slowly it almost looked like it wasn't moving at all. And somewhere in the backyard, under a sky that had seen centuries, a new Warrior was named—not because of anything loud, or flashy, or strong. But because he knew when to listen. When to speak. And how to love with quiet arms that held tighter than any noise ever could.

The lawn had been freshly mowed that morning, its lines crisp like quiet sentences across green pages. Mrs. Firth stood at the kitchen window with a tea towel in her hands, but she wasn't drying anything anymore. Her hands were still, holding damp porcelain like it might fall if she let the moment shift too quickly. She watched her son run barefoot across the grass, his arms spread out like wings that didn't flap but still lifted. Leo stood near the edge of the patio, watching Jeremy without needing to follow. Just watching. Not guarding. Not leading. Just standing like a tree nearby—one Jeremy could lean on but didn't need to hold.

Mr. Firth came up behind her with two mugs of coffee, one of them already cooling from distraction. He followed her gaze. "They've been out there for an hour," he said softly. "Not a single stammer." His voice carried something like wonder, but not surprise. More like reverence. Like watching someone learn to walk after thinking they never would. She didn't answer at first. Her lips parted slightly, but there were no words ready. Just the kind of silence that lives in parents when their child suddenly grows in front of them and they don't know how to catch it.

Jeremy wasn't shouting. He wasn't rushing. He was telling Leo a story—something about a raccoon in the composter, a whole comic opera of squeaks and banana peels and heroic broom rescues.

But more than the story, what stood out was the way he told it. His words landed with clarity, one after another like stepping stones. No trips. No stumbles. He didn't pause to restart a sentence three times, or flick his fingers against his thigh. He wasn't blinking fast or looking at the ground. He was present. Solid. Like he belonged in his voice now.

Mrs. Firth finally found her voice and said, "His posture's different. Do you see it?" Mr. Firth nodded without blinking. Jeremy wasn't hunched like he used to be. His shoulders were back, his chin forward just slightly. He looked taller—not by inches, but by something else. By decision. By belief. As though something inside him had stood up straight and pulled the rest of him with it. And Leo, only a step away, looked at Jeremy not like a protector, but like a witness. Like he knew exactly how far Jeremy had come, and how far he still could go.

They watched the boys trade stories, Jeremy laughing now, Leo tossing a handful of grass toward the sky like confetti, letting it fall over both of them. There was no one else in the world in that moment. Just the two of them in a backyard bordered by low fences and tall sunflowers, beneath the lazy orbit of dragonflies and distant lawn mowers. It was August. Late enough to feel like the end of something, but still warm enough to believe in new beginnings.

Later, when the boys came in for water and slices of cantaloupe, Mrs. Firth met Jeremy at the screen door. She knelt slightly—not all the way, just enough to be eye-level. "I heard the raccoon story," she said. "You didn't stutter once." Jeremy shrugged. Not embarrassed. Not proud. Just honest. "I didn't feel like I had to." She nodded slowly. "You never have to. You get to choose." He tilted his head. "Even with words?" she smiled. "Especially with words."

Mr. Firth put a hand on Leo's shoulder as the boys passed through the kitchen. "Whatever you're doing," he said, "keep doing it." Leo didn't reply, just offered a small nod, the kind that held more meaning than whole sentences from other boys. He wasn't trying to be humble. He was simply honest. He didn't see what he was doing as special. He saw it as necessary.

That evening, over grilled vegetables and turkey burgers, Jeremy offered to help set the table without being asked. He moved confidently, not with bravado but with calm. He spoke with clarity when asking for the mustard. He told a new story—this one about a frog in Ty's garden—and again, the stutter didn't come. Leo listened as if it were the only story in the world. He laughed at the right places, nodded in others, but mostly, he let Jeremy be the loudest voice at the table.

Mrs. Firth looked at her son across the table, his hands gesturing, his fork dancing above his plate, and felt a knot inside her loosen. The one that had lived there since preschool. Since the first time Jeremy tried to say his name and couldn't. Since the teacher had gently suggested a therapist. Since the time a boy at a birthday party said "spit it out already" and Jeremy didn't speak for the rest of the week. That knot, tight as a stone, had lived in her every day since. And now it was slowly coming undone.

After dinner, as the sun sank low behind the trees and the crickets began to stir in the grass, Mr. Firth took a photo of the two boys sitting on the porch steps, their arms touching but not clinging. Jeremy leaned slightly into Leo's side, and Leo tilted his head to rest on Jeremy's hair. No smiles. Just stillness. Just real. When the photo clicked, neither boy moved. Mr. Firth didn't need to ask them to pose. He had only captured what was already happening.

Later that night, Mrs. Firth found Leo folding the spare blanket in the guest room. "Did you need anything?" she asked. Leo shook his head. "Just making sure it's neat." She looked at him for a moment longer, then said, "He doesn't just speak better because of practice. He speaks better because he knows he's safe." Leo didn't answer. He just placed the blanket gently over the arm of the chair and walked past her with the soft steps of someone raised by silence.

When she returned to her room, she stood for a long time at the window, watching the two boys through the curtain. They sat under the stars again, just like before. No words this time. Just breathing. Just belonging. And in that hush of night, she said a thank you—not to anyone in particular, just to the sky, to the summer, to whatever force had brought Leo into their world in time to help Jeremy remember that he was never broken. Just waiting.

The living room was dim, lit only by the warm amber glow of a side lamp that flickered slightly when the fridge kicked in. Jeremy sat at the far end of the couch, his legs curled beneath him, the blanket from the guest bed pulled up to his chest like armour he wasn't ready to drop. His father sat in the recliner by the window, newspaper folded neatly beside him, reading glasses perched halfway down his nose. The soft hum of a late summer night came in through the half-open window—crickets, distant traffic, the occasional bark of a dog two streets over.

There had been quiet all evening. Not the awkward kind, not even the thoughtful kind. Just the kind that settles in when everyone's tired and peaceful and not sure whether to start a new conversation or let the day finish with silence. Mr. Firth had offered to put on a documentary about birds. Jeremy had nodded but never pressed play. The remote rested on the arm of the couch, untouched. Leo had already gone upstairs, whispering goodnight with a yawn and a rub of Jeremy's hair as he passed. Only Jeremy and his dad remained. And the quiet had weight to it.

Then Jeremy turned slightly and asked, not in a whisper but not quite in full volume either, "Dad… did I start stuttering after that teacher yelled at me last year?" He didn't look up when he asked. His eyes stayed on the television screen, which hadn't moved, hadn't flickered, hadn't played anything. But the question landed like a bell rung in the middle of a chapel. The words echoed in the stillness. Mr. Firth didn't answer right away. He lowered the glasses down onto the newspaper and rubbed the bridge of his nose with his thumb and forefinger, a gesture that said he was holding back something older than tears.

"I've wondered that too," he said eventually, and his voice came out softer than he'd intended. "Maybe. Maybe it started there. Or maybe that moment just made something already small inside you… shrink a little more." Jeremy looked up now. Just a glance. He wasn't asking for blame. He was asking for understanding. He wanted to know if someone else had noticed the day his voice had started hiding. The day the sounds got tangled up in fear and confusion and grown-up fury that didn't belong in a Grade 3 classroom.

"I remember that day," his father continued. "You came home and didn't speak until bedtime. Your mom and I asked you what happened, and you said, 'Nothing. It's fine.' And then the next morning, your voice caught on your name. And then it caught on your lunch order. And then it kept catching." He swallowed hard. "We thought it would pass. We thought it was nerves. We didn't know it had already sunk its claws in." Jeremy didn't interrupt. He just listened. Because now he was learning that the story had always been shared—even when it wasn't spoken aloud.

"I didn't know she yelled like that," Mr. Firth went on, and now his hands were folded in his lap, unmoving. "We only found out later from another parent. You didn't want to tell us. You said it would get her in trouble. You were trying to protect her." His voice cracked, not with anger but something more painful—parental regret. "You were nine. You were already trying to protect someone who had hurt you." Jeremy blinked slowly. That sounded like something Leo would do. Maybe it's why they understood each other.

"Did I do something wrong that day?" Jeremy asked, not accusatory, just curious. Still holding the blanket. Still waiting. "Was I too loud? Did I mess up the assignment? Did she think I was being rude?" His father shook his head slowly, then leaned forward, elbows on knees, hands clasped together like he was holding a truth he wasn't sure how to release. "You did absolutely nothing wrong," he said, firm now. "You asked a question. That's all. A normal, thoughtful question. And she didn't like that you interrupted her story. She didn't like that you were curious."

Jeremy let out a breath he didn't know he was holding. It came out shaky, like a note in the wrong key. "So it wasn't my fault?" The words hung there like a final test. His father stood up and crossed the room. Sat down next to him. "No," he said again. "It wasn't your fault. Not even a little bit." He placed a hand gently on Jeremy's back, between his shoulder blades, right where Leo would rest his palm when Jeremy was nervous. "I should have said that a year ago. I'm sorry we didn't see it faster."

Jeremy leaned into him without another word. The blanket slipped a little, fell to his lap, but neither of them moved to pick it up. Mr. Firth wrapped an arm around his son's shoulders and held him steady, the way a lighthouse holds a ship in the fog. Jeremy's breathing slowed. Not quite calm, but steadier than it had been when he asked the question. His father didn't say anything more for several minutes. He just let his son lean. Let the moment hold its own shape.

When Jeremy finally spoke again, his voice was barely above the hum of the fridge motor. "She scared me." Mr. Firth nodded once. "She shouldn't have. That wasn't your job to carry." Another pause, long and full. "I don't think I'm scared of her anymore," Jeremy said after a while. "But sometimes I still feel like I'm going to stutter—even when I don't." His father nodded again. "That's okay. Feelings are allowed to stay longer than the things that caused them."

The rest of the night passed quietly. They sat there for a little while longer, until the clock struck ten and the lamp flickered again. Jeremy stood up, stretched, and said goodnight. But before heading upstairs, he paused. "Thanks for not saying it's just a phase," he said. "I know it might get better. But it's not fake." Mr. Firth placed a hand over his heart. "I know, buddy. It's real. And you're real. And your voice matters—even when it needs a few extra seconds to come out." Jeremy smiled, a small, private smile. Then he climbed the stairs without looking back.

The dinner table was quieter than usual, but not in a way that meant anything was wrong. It was a kind of soft, full quiet—the kind that happens when every plate has something warm on it, every face around the table is lit by the gold of a low sun through the patio door, and no one feels the need to talk just to fill space. Leo sat between Jeremy and Mrs. Firth, his shoulders relaxed, his feet tucked under the chair in a way that showed he'd forgotten to stay tense. Jeremy was already on his second helping of mashed potatoes, which made Leo smile. Mr. Firth was pouring water from a sweating pitcher, and Mrs. Firth was watching steam rise from the green beans like it was the most peaceful sight in the world.

Halfway through the meal, the moment arrived—not as a planned event, not even as something intentional. Mrs. Firth reached toward the bowl in front of Leo and said, gently, with no ceremony at all, "Leo, can you pass the potatoes, sweetheart?" The word slid out like butter from a dish, smooth and natural, as though it had always belonged there. Leo didn't flinch. He didn't freeze. He just looked at her hand reaching toward the bowl, and passed it with both hands, like something sacred. His lips parted slightly, but no sound came out. Not yet.

And then came the next piece. Mr. Firth, still chewing a bite of roast chicken, gave a small nod of thanks and said, clear as anything, "Thanks, son." He didn't emphasize it. Didn't look up to see how Leo would react. Didn't say it like a test. He said it like a man who'd just spoken something that had already been true for a long while and was only now being said aloud. Leo didn't speak then either. He simply looked down at his plate, at the half-eaten carrots and the neat triangle of stuffing left beside the drumstick, and blinked twice. His fork stayed still. But something inside him did not.

Jeremy didn't look at Leo right away. He just kept eating, but slower now, like he was waiting for the silence to explain itself. It didn't. Not all at once. Mrs. Firth returned to slicing her food with care. Mr. Firth reached for the gravy boat and offered it to Leo without a word. Leo took it with both hands and nodded. It wasn't that the air had changed—it was that Leo had. Just a little. Like a stone warming in a patch of sun it didn't think it deserved.

Ten minutes later, after the table had thinned of food and Jeremy had started picking peas out of his salad, Mrs. Firth said, as though it had been on her mind for a while, "Leo, we were talking earlier—your third night here, I think. And we just wanted to ask..." She looked to her husband, who nodded once. She looked back at Leo. "Would you want to stay here? Not just sleep over. Not just camp out in the yard. We mean... live here. If that's something you'd want." Mr. Firth added, softly, "That spare bedroom upstairs—it's never been used. But it could be yours."

The silence that followed was not empty. It was full of breath and memory and ache. Leo looked between them, his lips parted again, his eyes wide but not frightened. Just stunned. He searched for Jeremy's face, and found him already looking. Jeremy's fork was down. His fingers curled around the rim of his plate like he was holding in a secret. "You don't have to decide tonight," Mrs. Firth said. "Or ever, really. We just wanted you to know the offer is real. And it doesn't come with rules. Just love."

Leo opened his mouth. Closed it. Tried again. And then finally said, barely loud enough to carry across the table, "I thought I'd already ruined every place I could go." Mr. Firth leaned back gently in his chair and folded his hands. "You didn't ruin anything, son. Not here. You helped us build something." Jeremy pushed his chair back just a little and scooted over, his elbow brushing Leo's. "I want you here," he said plainly. "It doesn't feel right when you're not."

Tears didn't fall all at once. They didn't flood. But they came—slow, steady, and quiet. Leo wiped one from under his chin with the back of his wrist and sniffed. He didn't sob. He didn't shake. He just let himself be still while the truth settled. Mrs. Firth reached out and placed her hand on his, palm soft and sure. Mr. Firth stood up and cleared three of the plates without comment, like routine would help ground the moment.

After dinner, Jeremy took Leo upstairs without a word. They didn't talk while brushing teeth. They didn't talk while changing into pyjamas. But when the lamp by the guest bed flicked off and the room went dim, Jeremy whispered across the pillows, "You're already my brother. I don't care how many bedrooms you sleep in." Leo didn't answer. He reached across the small gap between their beds, grabbed Jeremy's wrist, and gave it a squeeze that said everything.

In the morning, the sun poured in through the curtains like it had been waiting. Leo came downstairs to find a folded sheet of paper on the kitchen table with his name on it. Inside was a drawing Jeremy had made—a house with four stick figures. Two tall. Two short. One had spiky hair and glasses. The other held a marshmallow on a stick. Above it, Jeremy had written in crooked capitals, "HOME." Leo folded the paper slowly, and slid it into his pocket. Then he sat down for breakfast, not as a guest—but as someone who finally had a place where no one needed him to earn the right to stay.

The game started during a walk down the gravel path behind the Firths' garden. Jeremy had kicked a pine cone across the dust and asked, "Can I still play the Shadow Warrior game even if I'm not quiet all the time?" Leo had crouched beside him, picking up the pine cone and rolling it in his hand. "Shadow Warriors don't have to be quiet all the time," he'd said. "They just have to know when silence speaks louder than noise." And from there, a new game was born—one Jeremy called Spot the Lie. It didn't need cards or dice. It only needed memory, patterns, and trust.

They played it while brushing their teeth, while fishing off the dock, even while peeling carrots beside Mrs. Firth. The rules were simple: if someone says something that doesn't line up with what they said before, or if their eyes move too much—or not enough—you pause, you think, and you whisper, "That's a red flag." Jeremy loved the way Leo made the game serious but fun. Leo never made fun of anyone. He just explained things as if the truth was a kind of puzzle you could learn to solve.

"That's one right there," Leo said, pointing to the TV screen during a news interview where a politician blinked seventeen times in half a minute. "Eyes dodge, mouth smiles too wide. That's too much sugar. No protein." Jeremy laughed but nodded, leaning back against Leo's shoulder. "What about when they change the story?" he asked. "Like if they said their dog was brown, but last week they said it was white?" Leo tilted his head and tapped the side of his temple. "That's a classic one. Flip-flop stories are slippery. Narcissists change the facts to match their feelings."

Later that afternoon, while Jeremy was still giggling about how someone on TV claimed they forgot their own birthday, Mr. Allan Firth stepped into the living room with a folded piece of paper in his hand. He looked serious, but not stern. "Leo, Jeremy, can I borrow you both for a moment?" The boys looked up. Leo stood first. Jeremy followed, his hand brushing Leo's as they walked. Mr. Firth led them to the dining room, where the curtains had been drawn just enough to soften the sun without blocking it out.

Mr. Firth didn't sit down. He just stood by the dining table and said, "I've spoken to Mr. and Mrs. Takashi." Leo's shoulders tensed for just a breath, and then released. "They're coming over tomorrow evening. We've all agreed it's time to talk. Not just about visits. About where you feel at home." He glanced at Leo gently. "They love you. That hasn't changed. But they also understand what comfort means, and how family looks different for every child."

Jeremy reached for Leo's sleeve and tugged once. "They're not mad," he whispered. "Right?" Mr. Firth answered before Leo could. "Not at all. In fact, they were the ones who said, 'Leo should live where he breathes easiest.'" Leo looked down. His fingers curled against the edge of the chair, but he nodded. "I do," he said. "Here." It wasn't dramatic. It wasn't loud. It was clear. And it stayed in the air long after he said it.

That night, over grilled cheese sandwiches and tomato soup, Jeremy asked if they could play Spot the Lie again. Leo smiled. "Let's make it trickier. I'll act out a lie, and you tell me what's off." He stood up and said in a cheery voice, "No, I'm not mad you forgot to invite me. I love being left out!" Jeremy cracked up, then leaned forward. "Eyes tight, voice too high, hands in fists. You're pretending not to care, but you do!" Leo bowed. "Well done, Shadow Cadet."

As the laughter settled, Mr. Firth walked over to the table and set down a folder. "This," he said, "is everything we need to apply for guardianship. If that's what you want, Leo. No pressure. Just possibilities." Leo didn't open the folder. He looked up at Mr. Firth and said, "Can I still call them Mom and Dad?" Mr. Firth knelt beside his chair. "You can call us whatever feels right. But yes—if you want that, it's yours."

Jeremy scooted his chair over and pressed his side against Leo's. "Then we can be brothers for real." Leo rested his chin on top of Jeremy's head. "We already are," he said. "This just makes it official." The next morning, Leo found a sticky note on his pillow. In Jeremy's handwriting it said: "No lies. Just love. Signed, Your Brother." Leo folded it and put it in his pocket beside the note from the lake house. Truth folded better than lies.

In the final round of their game that day, Jeremy tried to trick Leo with a story about a talking squirrel who told him he could speak French. Leo didn't blink. "Lie," he said. "Squirrels speak Italian." They both burst out laughing, tumbling into the cushions like two boys who hadn't known each other just a year ago, but now couldn't imagine life apart.

Mr. and Mrs. Firth watched from the doorway, arms around each other. Mrs. Firth said softly, "They found something strong in each other." Mr. Firth replied, "They found home." Outside, the wind shifted in the trees like it was making room for something new. Something honest.

The breeze felt different that morning. It moved slower, like it wasn't in a rush to get anywhere. Jeremy sat on the back steps with his knees tucked against his chest, watching the way the dew clung to the grass longer than usual. Leo stood beside him, sipping from a mug that said Best Big Brother—a gift from Jeremy two days earlier. The air smelled like August. Like everything good was about to change shape but hadn't yet. Neither of them said it out loud, but they both knew: summer was ending.

"I don't want school to ruin this," Jeremy said, not looking up. "What if things go back to how they were? What if I forget how to be brave?" Leo sat beside him and set the mug down between them. He didn't rush his words. "It won't ruin anything," he said. "Because now you know what real feels like. And once you know, you can't un-know it. You're stronger now. And stronger stays." Jeremy leaned his shoulder against Leo's. That was answer enough.

Inside the kitchen, Mr. and Mrs. Firth stood by the phone. The cordless handset sat in its cradle, quiet but heavy. The paperwork for guardianship had been filled out, signed, and was ready for submission. What remained was an agreement from Mr. and Mrs. Takashi. They hadn't refused. But they hadn't replied either. Lisa Firth had called that morning and left a message. Allan had emailed. Still, the answer hadn't come. And the silence was beginning to stretch.

Leo's twelfth birthday was five days away. It would be his first birthday in a house where he felt steady. The Firths were planning something small but meaningful—just the four of them, maybe Ty if his parents allowed, and a cake with chocolate ganache because Leo didn't like icing. "Too sweet," he'd said. "I want something honest." Jeremy had helped Allan secretly carve a plaque that read Leo's Room, which they planned to screw into the door the night before his birthday. Whether or not the adoption came through, he belonged there.

The mailman came at noon. Leo raced Jeremy to the box. There was no letter from the Takashi household, but there was a package—Leo's name written carefully across the top. Inside was a book on photography from Mr. Takashi, and a note written by hand from Mrs. Takashi: Leo, we love you. We'll support whatever brings you joy and peace. We believe this might. There was no mention of guardianship. No objection either. Just love, folded gently.

That evening, after dinner, Jeremy asked if they could camp one last night in the backyard. "One more fire," he said. "One more marshmallow story. One more game of Spot the Lie." Leo smiled and nodded. They built the fire slowly, piece by piece, and sat with blankets around their shoulders as the stars began to punch tiny holes in the darkening sky. "You know," Leo said, tossing a twig into the flames, "some goodbyes don't mean the end. They just mean things get rearranged."

Jeremy watched the flames flicker and nodded. "Like puzzles." Leo turned to him. "Exactly like puzzles. The picture's still there—it just takes a little time to find where everything fits." When the fire died down to embers, Jeremy leaned close. "You're coming back to school with me, right?" Leo answered without hesitation. "Of course I am. I'm not just a summer friend."

Later that night, Jeremy woke briefly and walked into the hallway, still half-asleep. He saw Mr. Firth at the kitchen table, rereading the message from Mrs. Takashi. Leo's school enrollment papers sat on the table beside him, along with the temporary guardianship forms. Jeremy didn't say anything. He just walked over, hugged Mr. Firth around the middle, and went back to bed. Allan didn't move. He just rested a hand gently on Jeremy's head before the boy slipped away again.

Morning came with cool light. Leo packed his summer things into a small duffle, even though he knew he wasn't really leaving. He left the duffle unzipped. Jeremy placed a comic book inside it before they left for town, just in case. At the pharmacy, Leo helped Mrs. Firth choose cough drops, and at the grocery store, Jeremy whispered that he wanted to buy Leo's birthday card himself. They agreed he'd pay with loonies and quarters from his blue piggy bank.

On the ride home, no one spoke much. But it wasn't tense—it was just quiet, like the air itself was holding its breath. When they pulled into the driveway, there was an envelope taped to the front door. Lisa reached for it, heart quickened. The envelope bore elegant penmanship. She opened it carefully. Inside was a formal letter from the Takashi's. It read: Leo is your son now. With our blessing. With our thanks. With our love.

Leo read it once, then twice. He folded it small and placed it in his back pocket. Jeremy didn't wait for permission—he threw his arms around Leo and said, "Happy almost birthday, big brother." Lisa Firth wiped her eyes and walked inside. Allan stayed on the porch with the boys. "You're not a visitor anymore," he said to Leo. "You're home."

In the days leading up to his birthday, Leo helped Jeremy prep his school backpack, label folders, and practice walking down the street like he owned it. "Walk like your voice already works," Leo coached. "Even when it stutters. That's strength, not weakness." Jeremy didn't answer. He just nodded, then whispered, "I love you."

The air cooled that night. August never rushed its ending. Leo stood on the porch alone for a while after the others had gone to bed. He looked up at the stars, then at the sky's edge where summer leaned into September. And for once, goodbye didn't hurt. Not when it had brought him home.

The blue spiral notebook had sat mostly untouched on the top shelf of Jeremy's closet all summer, tucked beside a flashlight and a shoebox of old Pokémon cards. But that morning, the day after Leo's twelfth birthday, Jeremy pulled it down gently and turned to the second blank page—he'd always skipped the first one, too afraid of doing it wrong. He used a mechanical pencil, the kind with the squishy grip and twist-up eraser, and for a long time, he didn't write anything. He just looked at the page like it might tell him how to begin.

When the first sentence came, it wasn't neat. But it was honest. "I don't feel broken anymore." He stared at those words. Then pressed the pencil down harder, wrote them again beneath the first line, like he needed to see them twice. I don't feel broken anymore. He kept writing, not pausing to erase, not stuttering on the page the way he sometimes did in his voice. And by the time the sun had moved across his window, a whole page was full.

"I have a big brother. He's not perfect. But he's real. And he listens. And he doesn't laugh when I can't find the right word. He waits. And I think maybe that's what family means." Jeremy closed the notebook for a moment, set it in his lap, and pressed both palms over the cover like he was locking the truth in with his hands. Outside, he could hear Leo and Mr. Firth talking about planting trees by the fence. Their voices drifted in like sunlight.

"Leo says I'm stronger now. I don't know if I believe it every minute, but I believe it more than I don't. And sometimes that's enough." Jeremy looked out the window. The trees weren't turning yet, but the air had changed. It smelled like sharpened pencils and lunchboxes and sneakers that weren't quite broken in. School was fifteen days away. He counted them with a small sigh. But this time, the ache in his stomach wasn't fear. It was something else. Like excitement. Or maybe readiness.

"I know what truth feels like now. It's quiet. It doesn't shout to be believed. It just sits with you, like a hug that doesn't need arms." Jeremy wrote slower now. His hand was starting to cramp, but he didn't want to stop. He glanced at his calendar—his birthday was in two days. Ten years old. Double digits. And this year, for the first time, he didn't want fewer candles. He wanted every single one, lit bright and held steady. Not because he wanted to be older, but because he finally knew who he was growing into.

Downstairs, Leo called out that the lemonade was ready. Jeremy ignored it for a moment, just long enough to finish his last paragraph. "I like the way I talk now. Even if it's slow. Even if it stutters sometimes. Because it's mine. And it's not scared anymore." He didn't sign his name. He didn't need to. He just tucked the notebook back on the shelf—but not at the top. He left it on the desk, open to that page. Because it wasn't a secret anymore.

That night, as the sun dropped behind the trees and the Firth family sat outside with fleece blankets across their laps, Jeremy rested his head against Leo's shoulder and whispered, "Did you ever think we'd end up here?" Leo didn't answer right away. He just squeezed Jeremy's shoulder and looked at the firepit glowing low. "Not in a million years," he finally said. "But I'm glad we did."

Lisa handed out warm chocolate chip cookies wrapped in napkins, and Allan told a story about Leo helping him fix the shed earlier that week. Jeremy beamed with pride, like it was his own story being told. Leo didn't shrug it off like he used to. He just smiled and said, "We made a good team." It was a quiet moment. But not empty. It was full of belonging.

Inside the house, the spare bedroom had already been painted over in pale blue. The plaque reading Leo's Room was mounted on the door now, not with tape but with tiny gold screws, drilled in gently by Allan and Leo together. Inside, Jeremy had left a birthday card on the pillow. It read: "Happy Birthday to my big brother. You saved me. I'm going to save you too, even if you don't need saving anymore."

Later that night, Leo sat at the edge of Jeremy's bed while he fell asleep. He hadn't meant to, but his hand found the boy's hair and ruffled it lightly, like Mr. Firth often did to him. Jeremy stirred but didn't wake. "Good night, little brother," Leo whispered. "And thanks for writing the truth." Then he kissed Jeremy's forehead and turned off the lamp.

Fifteen days remained before school. And Leo had already made a promise—one he hadn't spoken out loud, but one he kept in every step. He would be there. Not just as a student. But as a shield. A bridge. A witness. A brother. And this time, Jeremy would walk into class not as a stuttering boy trying to hide—but as a child who knew how much he mattered. Because Leo had taught him. And because now, he believed it for himself.

The clock blinked 9:47 p.m. Leo stood in the hallway for a moment, looking at the photos pinned on the cork board—the one Jeremy had filled with paper leaves where every leaf held a kind sentence Leo had said to him over the summer. "You did a good job." "You're funny." "I like how your brain works." Leo smiled. Then turned off the hallway light.

Downstairs, Lisa and Allan sat at the table filling out one last form—final consent to permanent guardianship. Lisa handed the pen to Allan, who signed with a steady hand. "He's ours," she whispered. Allan nodded, holding the papers like they were sacred. "And we're his." Upstairs, Leo curled into bed and pulled the quilt over his chest. The house was silent—but not the kind of silent that hurts. It was the kind that meant rest. The kind that let you breathe. And in that silence, Leo knew with every beat of his heart—he was home.

CHAPTER 14: WHEN KINDNESS IS A WEAPON

The bell hadn't rung yet, and the hallways stood still in that moment of hush before the doors opened wide. But even before the sound, even before the stampede of runners and the first-late yawns of teachers, two figures moved through the school gate like they'd already earned their place. Leo held Jeremy's hand—not like a brother who needed to be strong, but like someone who simply remembered what it felt like to be small. His grip wasn't tight. It was sure. Like he wasn't pulling Jeremy along or dragging him through. He was walking with him, exactly side by side, in pace, in rhythm, and in heart.

Jeremy's shoes weren't the newest, and his backpack had a scrape on one side, but that didn't matter. What mattered was the way he walked: head up, no quick glances behind, no shoulders hunched into that nervous turtle shape he used to wear in Grade Four. His new homeroom was upstairs this year—Grade Five now—but he didn't mind the climb. Not today. Not with Leo's hand in his. His thumb brushed against Leo's every so often, like a safety switch he didn't know he still needed. And Leo, without words, would give the faintest squeeze back, no more than a breath. Just enough to say, I'm still here.

The name on Leo's record now read "Leo Mason Takashi-Firth," printed neatly on his student file and etched even more permanently in Jeremy's mind. Leo had told him it felt weird at first, having all those syllables. Like carrying two full stories instead of one. But he liked how it sounded—like two houses shaking hands and promising to build something better together. Jeremy thought it sounded strong. Like someone who had survived the dark and still chose light. Like someone who could carry more than one name because he carried more than one truth.

No one teased them that morning. No one dared. Not because Leo had become aggressive again—he hadn't. He didn't snarl or shove or raise his voice. He just walked differently now. Not like he owned the hallway, but like he wasn't afraid of it anymore. He met eyes if people stared. He smiled if they nodded. He kept his chin level, and that was enough. Some kids parted when they saw them coming—not out of fear, but out of respect, or maybe confusion. Because Leo used to come alone, and now he didn't. Now he came with Jeremy, and it was clear they belonged to each other.

Jeremy still stuttered sometimes. But he didn't today. When they passed Miss Penner at the front entrance, Jeremy said, "Good morning," and the words came out like smooth marbles, round and full and not dropped halfway through. Miss Penner, still new enough not to know what that meant, smiled politely and moved aside. But Leo noticed. He glanced down at Jeremy with a quiet grin, the kind that said, I saw that. I'm proud of you. And Jeremy, catching the look, nodded back. No words. Just breath shared in triumph.

The lockers buzzed with the usual chatter, the clatter of combinations spinning wrong twice before clicking right. Jasmin spotted them first and waved with both arms. Ty appeared beside her like he'd been waiting. Nico nudged Ella, who tugged Sophie's sleeve. All of them had returned, changed just enough to carry the summer inside their eyes, but still the same where it counted. The group made space near the second floor stairwell, and Leo led Jeremy over like it had already been arranged. And maybe it had.

They didn't rush. Jeremy's stride had gotten longer over the summer, and Leo matched it like he was measuring each step. Nobody asked why they were still holding hands. Nobody even blinked. If anything, a few younger students glanced up and looked safer just seeing it. A big brother walking with his little brother. No teasing, no pretending. Just presence. Just truth. One of the lunch aides caught the sight through the office window and said nothing. But she smiled, just a little, and turned back to her coffee.

Inside, the classroom walls had changed colours. Posters were new. Chairs had been rearranged. But the air still held that dusty mix of pencil lead and wax crayon, familiar and sharp. Leo let go of Jeremy's hand only once he reached the fifth grade hallway, right at the corner where their paths split. Jeremy turned, and Leo knelt just a little—not a full crouch, but enough to look him in the eye. He whispered something. No one heard what. But Jeremy nodded like it was sacred, and then turned and walked into his new class alone.

Leo didn't follow. He watched until the door closed behind Jeremy and then turned to head toward his own class. His face didn't show nerves. Just a steady quiet, the kind that comes after a storm. He'd been in this school for over a year now, but this was the first time he walked in like he truly belonged. And he did. Every bruise of reputation had faded, replaced by something deeper. He wasn't feared now—he was respected. He wasn't whispered about—he was trusted.

Ty met him at the top of the stairs with a raised brow and a grin. "You ready?" he asked, like the first class of the year was a battlefield, and Leo was walking in with armour made from old scars and new hope. Leo didn't answer with words. He just gave Ty a bump on the shoulder, light but solid. Then he walked into Room 7-2 and took his seat at the far end of the third row, beside Nico and two desks behind Jasmin. Ella was one row over. Sophie waved from near the window.

Jeremy's day was happening elsewhere, but he wasn't far. At recess, they'd meet again. At lunch, they'd sit on the bench near the edge of the field, like they always had. Leo had already packed extra snacks for him—cheese crackers, the kind Jeremy liked, and a juice box with his name scribbled in Sharpie. That's what big brothers did. Not just the ones born into the title, but the ones who chose it. Who earned it in moments and marbles and flashlight stories under blanket forts.

No one said anything when Leo opened his binder and pulled out a pencil he'd sharpened the night before. But Miss Penner, watching from the front of the classroom, made a mental note of the way he sat. Back straight. Eyes clear. No hesitation. She didn't know the story behind him—not yet. But she would. Soon. Because Leo wasn't here just to learn. He was here to teach. And not with chalk or diagrams. With silence. With steadiness. With kindness that had weight behind it.

In another hallway, Jeremy was being asked to introduce himself. "I'm Jeremy," he said. Just that. No tremble. No delay. And one of the kids in the class asked, "Is that your brother who walked you in?" Jeremy nodded. "Yep," he said. "That's Leo." And the way he said it—full of love, full of pride, full of safety—was the beginning of a new kind of year.

Outside, the late-summer wind blew just hard enough to make the flag shift on its pole. Inside, a boy named Leo sat with both his names, both his histories, and both his futures lined up before him like neat rows of notebooks. And for once, there were no battles waiting in the hallway. Only beginnings.

He showed up in the doorway like nothing had happened. Like the past had been neatly swept under the gym mats or folded into forgotten library books. Alex's smile had not changed. It curled the same way, with corners that lifted too quickly and eyes that didn't follow. He walked in with the same swing in his step, the kind that dared people to remember the worst things he'd said while pretending he hadn't said anything at all. But this time, something was different. Not in him. In the air. In the way the others stood still.

Jasmin saw him first and said nothing. Her backpack was already unzipped, binder in her lap, pencil gripped like she was ready to take notes that hadn't yet begun. She didn't blink. Just watched. Like someone watching a fox approach the chicken coop—not scared, just aware. Ella straightened her spine, one hand draped casually over the back of her chair. Her legs didn't swing this time. They planted themselves flat to the floor. Grounded. Nico glanced at Ty. Ty didn't move. He just watched the grin coming through the door and kept his expression unreadable.

Leo didn't turn around immediately. He was already seated, facing forward, chin resting on the palm of his hand like he'd known this moment was coming. And when the voice arrived—"Hey, guys"—it didn't land like a greeting. It landed like a dare. That old sweet tone. That mock-casual pitch. But no one responded. Not the way Alex expected. No polite "hi" from Sophie. No awkward wave from Nico. No half-smile from Ella. Nothing. Just air thick with unspoken memory.

Alex blinked once. It threw him. Not visibly, not enough for a teacher to notice. But enough. His eyes scanned the group like he was recalibrating the game board and realizing someone had moved the pieces while he wasn't looking.

The desk he usually sat in was still empty, but the kids around it weren't. They'd shifted slightly. Made space that didn't include him. Not hostile. Not loud. But undeniable. And Alex, who once thrived in confusion, now stood in the centre of perfect clarity.

Miss Penner, still arranging her files at the front, glanced up and said, "Morning, everyone." She didn't know yet. Not the way Mr. Arnett did. Not the way Mr. Clarke had come to understand. She saw a boy enter with a smile and a bag over one shoulder and assumed things were as they should be. But Ty's eyes didn't leave Alex, and Leo's fingers tapped once against the top of his desk, a quiet rhythm of warning only the group could decode.

There was no greeting from Leo. No invitation. But there was a glance. Just one. Over his shoulder. Leo looked at Alex for three full seconds, then turned back to his notebook. That single glance landed like a verdict. Alex swallowed. Not because he feared Leo. That part had faded. What shook him now was the realization that Leo no longer played his game. He didn't react. He didn't shrink. He didn't rise. He simply dismissed him—without words, without effort. And dismissal, for a narcissist, is the deepest cut.

Sophie fiddled with her water bottle cap. She looked up once, locked eyes with Alex, and tilted her head just slightly. Not in confusion. In defiance. The kind a girl learns when she decides her voice doesn't have to raise to be heard. The kind that says, You don't fool me anymore. Alex broke eye contact first. Jasmin scribbled something in her margin that looked nothing like a school note. It was probably a list. She liked lists when she felt uncertain. She wasn't uncertain now.

Ty eventually moved, but not toward Alex. He stood and crossed to Leo's desk, handed him a folded slip of paper, and said, "It's done." Leo nodded. Ty walked back. Not a glance at Alex. Not a word. That paper wasn't part of any assignment. It was a message. A confirmation. Alex wasn't just walking into a room with bad memories. He was walking into a room that had re-written the rules while he was gone—and nobody told him.

Alex tried again at lunch. He approached the field where Jeremy and Leo sat sharing crackers and stories, and opened with, "Hey Leo, long time no see." Leo looked up, smiled politely, and said, "Not long enough." Jeremy blinked, confused. But Leo patted his brother's back and stood without rushing. "Come on," he said gently, "let's sit under the tree today." They moved without another word. Alex stood there, bag half-unzipped, words stuck between grin and scowl. It didn't land the way he expected. None of it did.

Back inside, Alex tried being charming. He complimented Sophie's shoes. She said, "They're not new." He laughed too loudly and told Ella her hair looked nice. She replied, "It always looks this way." He turned to Nico and asked, "Still playing chess?" Nico answered, "I upgraded to strategy games." Alex's grin frayed at the edges. He'd counted on their silence. He hadn't prepared for their clarity.

When the class ended, Miss Penner stood awkwardly by the door, watching the students pack up. She caught the tail end of Alex's sentence to Leo: "No hard feelings, right?" Leo didn't answer. Ty did. "That depends who you're asking. The old Leo or the real one?" The room went still. Miss Penner didn't know the context, but she noted the tension. She made a note on her clipboard: Watch this dynamic. Ask Mr. Arnett.

Alex's smile cracked slightly then. Not fully gone. Not erased. But no longer seamless. He walked down the hallway alone, and for the first time, no one followed. No one stayed behind to talk. No one offered a second chance. And the sound of his footsteps—unmatched, unmirrored—echoed louder than his words ever had.

Alex waited until the cafeteria buzzed loud enough to drown suspicion. He never struck in silence. His compliments always came when there were ears nearby—enough noise to mask the sting, enough witnesses to make the trap look generous. Sophie was mid-laugh, wiping salad dressing from the rim of her container lid when Alex leaned in with that slow, syrupy voice. "You're actually kinda clever, y'know. For someone who used to hide behind Leo all the time." The word actually hit first. Then used to. The insult was gift-wrapped. Sophie didn't unwrap it.

Jasmin caught it immediately. She'd been watching Alex for that exact move. Compliments meant to shrink. Smiles that cornered. Praise like rope. Sophie didn't react—not the way she used to. She tightened the grip on her spoon but didn't speak. Jasmin angled her head slightly and met Alex's eyes from across the table. There was no confusion in her gaze. Just recognition. She knew exactly what he was doing. And he knew that she knew.

Ella sat beside Sophie, shifting her tray half an inch closer. Not protectively, not with dramatics, but intentionally. Her hand rested on the corner of Sophie's sleeve like an anchor. Leo noticed from the far table. He said nothing. Just raised an eyebrow across the room at Jasmin. She gave a slight nod. Signal received. The group's new language wasn't hand signs or code words—it was posture, timing, and the sharp instincts earned by surviving liars.

Ty leaned closer to Leo. "Did you see it?" he asked. Leo nodded once. "His net just missed." Ty smiled faintly. "He's rusty." And that was true. Since the last confrontation in the hall months ago, Alex had returned with tactics instead of teeth. But poison in a cup still kills slowly. Leo knew the feeling. He used to be that exact boy.

Earlier that morning, Leo had tucked a folded envelope into his pocket—addressed in neat cursive, with Miss Penner's name written across the front. Inside was a letter. A personal one. Not a cry for attention, not a dramatic expose. Just facts. Truth written in quiet ink. It explained how narcissists often smiled in daylight and bruised in shadows. How his biological father—always "Sir" in public—called him names in private no child should ever hear. How Leo had once learned to fake kindness like a language, because it bought him time, because it disguised the fear.

At the start of lunch, Leo handed the envelope to Miss Penner, who was on supervision by the door. She thanked him and tucked it beneath a binder, thinking it was an assignment. She hadn't read it yet. But Leo had placed it in her care like a key. She would know what to do with it—if she was paying attention. She hadn't interfered with Alex so far. But eyes open slowly. And truth often enters on paper.

Back in the cafeteria, Sophie reached for her juice box, paused, and turned to Jasmin. "Was that supposed to be a compliment?" she asked, low but clear. Jasmin smiled, but not warmly. "Only if you like being called a coward in a tuxedo," she replied. Sophie blinked, then laughed. Just once. Enough. Alex's face barely changed, but the air shifted. The net had snapped. And the fish swam free.

Alex glanced at Nico next, testing the waters elsewhere. "You're getting good at math now, huh? Surprising." Nico didn't even look up. "Not really. Just finally learned to subtract bad influences." Ty choked on his milk carton. Sophie laughed again. Jasmin grinned without teeth. Leo stayed quiet. This wasn't his moment. It was theirs.

Miss Penner stood at the edge of the room now, watching more intently. Something in her expression faltered when she heard the exchange. She had known praise as kindness all her life—until now. These compliments didn't land like kindness. They landed like leashes. The letter Leo had given her now felt heavier in her tote.

Ella tapped her spoon against the table twice. It wasn't random. It was one of the group's private cues—Ty had trained them to notice rhythm. Control has rhythm, he once said. Lies repeat themselves. So they made music out of honesty. Tap once for confusion. Tap twice for danger wrapped in sugar. Sophie responded with a light knock of her own. A signal: seen and safe.

Leo rose with his tray, moved through the rows without a word, and stopped beside Miss Penner. He didn't speak at first. Just stood beside her, as if waiting for her to notice what the students already knew. She opened her mouth to ask a question but stopped. Then said, "Thank you for the note." Leo nodded. "It's not everything," he said. "But it's enough to start."

Alex pretended not to notice the quiet rebellion. He munched his sandwich, exaggeratedly loud, like noise would restore his crown. But his eyes flicked too often toward the centre table. He was measuring losses now. Small ones. The kind you don't feel until the silence gets heavier than applause.

At the end of lunch, Sophie stood first. "Let's eat outside tomorrow," she said. No one argued. Jeremy joined them by the door, holding Leo's hand like a flag of peace. Alex tried one last trick: "Hey, Soph—sorry if I sounded weird earlier." Sophie tilted her head and replied, "That's the thing about sounding weird. You usually don't know when you do it." Then she walked away. And with her, the whole table moved. Not quickly. Not in protest. Just in unity. Like a current changing direction. Alex stayed behind, holding a spoon and a smirk, both fading.

Ella didn't ask for help. That's what made it so uncomfortable. She was at her locker, reaching for the math duotang she'd dropped, when Alex swooped in like a superhero no one called. He scooped it up before she bent down, flashed his perfect-toothed grin, and held it out like a trophy. "I got it," he said, voice syrupy-smooth. "You're welcome." She didn't say anything. She just took it and nodded. But something was already wrong.

The favour was cheap. The price came later.

At recess, it showed up like a bill. "Hey, Ella," Alex said, sidling up beside her near the fence. "Think you could tell Miss Penner I helped you today? Might help with, y'know… my image." Ella blinked. "Why?" she asked, not rudely—just directly. "Because I helped you. Like, obviously," he replied, tone firming just slightly under the sweetness. She remembered Leo's words then, from the week before: Real kindness doesn't ask for receipts.

She didn't respond. She didn't need to. Her silence was clear. But Alex kept pushing. "It's not a big deal. Just a sentence. You know she's watching everything." That part was true. Miss Penner had taken Mr. Arnett's advice and was now observing the social web like a detective. She'd already spoken to Sophie and Jasmin. She was learning. Slowly.

Ella crossed her arms. "So you only helped me so I'd say something nice to a teacher?" Alex laughed. "No, no—of course not. I just thought it might help. You know. We all need help sometimes." The fake humility was as loud as the lunch bell. Ella wasn't fooled. She had lived through Leo's worst months. She'd learned the difference between kindness and control disguised as kindness. Between helping and banking.

Ty was nearby, chatting with Nico and kicking at the gravel beneath the portable steps. He glanced over when he heard the tone shift. Alex had a way of slipping just enough threat into his voice to trigger Ty's radar. Leo was already watching. He didn't intervene, though—not yet. Ella had earned her strength. This moment was hers.

"I don't owe you anything," she said. It wasn't loud. It didn't need to be. Alex's face twitched. "I didn't say you did," he replied, that defensive lilt creeping into his tone. She didn't move. "Then why are you keeping score?" He rolled his eyes. "Forget it." But she didn't. And neither did Leo.

Later that afternoon, after second nutrition break, Leo walked up beside her while they waited for math class to begin. "That was good," he said. Ella shrugged. "It felt weird. He made it seem like I owed him because he picked something up for me." Leo nodded. "That's not a favour. That's currency. And you didn't ask to be part of his economy." She grinned at that. "Economy?" "Yeah," Leo said. "Kindness isn't real if it comes with a receipt."

They entered the classroom together. Miss Penner smiled faintly as they passed, her eyes pausing on Ella just a second longer than usual. She was reading something—maybe the rhythm of their steps, maybe the defiance in Ella's shoulders. She jotted a note on her clipboard. Ty would later joke that she was becoming their apprentice.

The math lesson was about balance, equations, value. Funny how it all lined up. When Miss Penner asked for examples of "fair trades," Alex's hand shot up. "Helping someone pick up their stuff," he said, glancing sideways at Ella. "And then maybe they speak up for you later." The room went still. Miss Penner didn't nod. Instead, she asked, "Is that a trade? Or a transaction?"

Nico raised his hand. "It's only a trade if both people know the deal ahead of time." Miss Penner smiled. "Exactly. Consent matters in kindness too." That was the moment Leo knew she had read the letter. Maybe even twice. Ty, from the back, caught Leo's eye and tapped his pencil three times against his desk—an old signal for She's listening now. Leo nodded once in return. The message was clear.

At lunch, the group sat together on the west side of the cafeteria, beside the windows. Ella told Sophie what happened. Sophie just shook her head and muttered, "He's still trying to charm his way out of trouble." Jasmin added, "He doesn't know we've all learned the difference." Jeremy, sitting close to Leo, looked up and asked, "What difference?" Leo ruffled his hair. "Real kindness feels free. It never expects you to pay for it later."

Ella pushed her juice box toward Jeremy. "Want the rest of this?" Jeremy shook his head. "You sure?" "Yeah. But thank you." She smiled. "You said thank you. That means you noticed. That's what makes it different." Ty nodded. "Favour has rules. Kindness doesn't need them." Nico added, "Kindness is what you do when no one's looking. Alex always checks for a spotlight." From the far end of the room, Alex watched the group, his tray untouched. His compliments weren't landing anymore. His smiles felt tired. His help came with fine print—and they were reading it all now, out loud, and together.

Miss Penner noticed the quiet first. Not the loudness of laughter or the clatter of chairs that usually defined the start of a school year, but the way the group of students around Leo Mason Takashi-Firth held their silence like a posture. Not withdrawn, not scared—just alert. They moved like they were listening for something more than instructions. It wasn't fear that kept them quiet. It was readiness. And she didn't know what to make of it yet.

Alex, by contrast, moved like static. He never seemed to stop talking. His hands performed every sentence with small flourishes, palms open when praised, fingers clutched when overlooked. Miss Penner made a note of it during Tuesday's opening bell and again on Wednesday during the group project pairing. He spoke too often, too fast, and always with an eye on someone else's reaction. Most new teachers might've called him confident. But something didn't sit right with her.

It was Mr. Arnett who finally sat her down. Friday morning, fifteen minutes before the first bell, he knocked gently on the side of her open classroom door. "Mind if I step in for a second?" She welcomed him in with a smile, brushing the chalk dust from her palms. "I wanted to ask how you're finding the students," he began. She gave a careful nod. "They're bright. Especially that group—Ty, Jasmin, Leo, Nico, Ella, Sophie… they're close-knit."

He crossed his arms, then lowered his voice. "They're more than close-knit, Penner. They're trained." She blinked. "Trained?" "Not by me," he added quickly. "But by life. And by each other. Especially Ty and Leo." She raised a brow. "In what way?" He tapped the frame of the doorway. "They've lived through manipulation and learned how to recognize it. They spot lies faster than we do, and they know how to protect their own." He paused. "They've dealt with someone named Alex before. You might want to listen when they speak."

She did. That day, she stopped glancing past them and started watching their expressions. During English, when she asked a question about persuasive language, Ty raised his hand and explained, "Sometimes, people say something nice just to make you feel like you owe them later. That's not persuasion. That's a trap." She'd smiled, but the classroom stayed quiet. No laughter. No teasing. They were serious. All of them.

At recess, she stood by the edge of the blacktop, clipboard pressed against her chest. Alex was helping another boy—Sammy—pick up a spilled water bottle. But she caught the tone. "Now you owe me," Alex said, not joking. Not at all. Sammy gave a nervous chuckle and nodded. Miss Penner looked to the far corner where Ty and Leo sat on the ground in the shade, quietly watching. Ty didn't smile. Leo whispered something to him. Neither moved.

In the lunchroom, she circled slowly between tables, noting who laughed too loud and who didn't speak at all. Ella sat beside Sophie, neither eating much, both angled slightly away from Alex's table. Jeremy was with Leo, as always, his tray tidily arranged. When someone bumped Jeremy's elbow and nearly spilled his milk, Leo caught it before it hit the table. Miss Penner saw how calm Leo stayed. How no apology was needed. Just a nod between brothers.

That afternoon, she called on Leo to answer a comprehension question. He stood slowly, responded clearly, and then paused. "Miss Penner," he said carefully, "do you believe kindness is always kind?" She blinked, caught off guard by the question's shape. "I think kindness should be kind," she answered. He nodded once. "Sometimes it isn't." And then he sat back down. The room held its breath for five full seconds before Jasmin exhaled audibly and scribbled something into her notebook.

Miss Penner didn't speak again for another minute. But when she did, her tone was different. She began phrasing her questions with more weight, more respect. It wasn't that the students were smarter than expected—it was that they carried things most students didn't have to. They weren't just survivors. They were guides for each other, and now, possibly, for her.

In the hallway after the final bell, she leaned near Mr. Arnett's office as he stepped out to greet a parent. "You were right," she said softly. "They know." He nodded once. "They always do. Most adults just aren't trained to hear them." She straightened. "I'd like to learn." He offered a half-smile. "Then keep your ears open and don't assume innocence just because someone says something with a smile."

That evening, at home, she took out her own notebook—not the school-issued one, but the kind she kept for personal reflections. She wrote, The ones who speak quietly often carry the loudest truths. Today, I saw the cost of kindness when used as currency. The students are not just learning. They are teaching me. Then she underlined listen first twice and folded the page to mark it. And the next morning, when Leo entered her classroom, she didn't greet him like a teacher would greet any student. She said, "Good morning, Leo. I'm glad you're here." And he nodded—not because he had to—but because he meant it.

Sophie had always been taught to be polite. Not just in words, but in presence. If someone smiled at her, she smiled back. That was the rule, wasn't it? Even if the smile didn't feel right. Even if it made her stomach twist just a little. You smiled, you nodded, you pretended. Because that was safer than whatever happened if you didn't. She had done it for years, even with Leo, back when he made her uneasy. But this time, walking into the first week of Grade 7, something in her resisted.

Alex's smile met her at the classroom door. It wasn't wide, not forced. It was that quiet, subtle grin that curled only one side of his mouth. The kind that said, I see you, and you'd better play along. The kind that tried to make everything that had happened last year vanish behind a set of straight, white teeth. It landed in front of her like a trap hidden in plain view. She had seen it before. She had fallen for it before. But not this time.

She didn't smile. Not even a polite flicker. She looked at him with soft, level eyes, blinked once, and kept walking. Her heart thundered, but her pace did not falter. Alex's grin twitched—just slightly—as if something cracked behind it. She took her seat beside Ella and focused on unpacking her pencil case. Her fingers shook, but her spine held straight. Ella noticed. So did Ty, who sat just behind her. So did Leo, who offered nothing more than a quiet nod.

It was that nod, simple and brief, that told her she had done the right thing. He didn't praise her. Didn't congratulate her. He just looked up, caught her eyes, and nodded once like a brother who knew how hard that moment had been. Leo of all people. The one who used to scare her. The one who used to wear the same smile Alex did now. It struck her suddenly that Leo's face no longer held that shape. He didn't smirk. He didn't perform. He just was.

Later that day, in the cafeteria, she saw Alex try the same grin on Ella. This time it came paired with a compliment about her hair. "It really suits your face," he said smoothly, with just the right volume to sound sincere. Ella's face stayed blank. "Thanks," she said, but she didn't turn. Didn't offer him her full face. Didn't invite more. Sophie felt the quiet current between them like an invisible cord—the way Ella deflected, the way Alex recoiled. The performance was unraveling.

Sophie kept her tray close, sitting beside Nico and across from Jeremy, who was watching Leo intently. She hadn't realized how much quieter Jeremy had become—not shy, but still. Like he was learning the world from the inside out now, not just reacting to it. Leo leaned down and whispered something to him about mashed potatoes, and Jeremy laughed without flinching. That small laugh felt like sunlight. It made her chest ache with something close to pride.

She turned back toward the lunchroom's far table where Alex now sat alone, biting into his sandwich without looking up. She didn't feel sorry for him. Not yet. There had been too many notes, too many stares, too many almost-accidental brushes of his hand against hers in line. She had not imagined them. And the moment she stopped smiling back, they stopped, too. That was what frightened her the most—how easily a predator adjusted to a new boundary.

When the bell rang and trays scraped across the plastic tables, she stood slowly. Ella bumped her shoulder and said, "Nice job today." Sophie pretended not to know what she meant. "For what?" Ella grinned. "You didn't play the game." Sophie shrugged. "I don't think I ever liked the rules." They both laughed—quietly, cautiously. It wasn't quite a victory march, but it was a step. Maybe the first real one.

In afternoon reading group, Miss Penner handed Sophie the copy of The Giver they'd be using for the semester. As she reached to take it, Miss Penner said, low and sincere, "I saw what you did earlier. That takes strength." Sophie blinked. She hadn't expected to be noticed. She certainly hadn't expected it to be named. All she managed was, "Thank you," before turning quickly to hide the heat rising in her cheeks.

She opened the book and stared at the first page. Words swam, unsteady, until she blinked again. Leo shifted in the desk across the room, scribbling something in the margin of his notebook. Ty caught her looking and smiled—not the kind that asked anything of her. Just the kind that said, I saw that too. And somehow, that made it feel more real. More permanent.

Sophie didn't tell her parents that night what had happened. Not because she didn't trust them—but because it was hers. A moment she had claimed. For once, she didn't need someone else to validate it. She brushed her teeth while replaying the hallway. The smirk. The silence. The nod. And for the first time, she looked in the mirror and didn't ask herself, Was I too rude? or Should I have smiled? She asked instead, What will I do next time?

Sophie found the folded note just before the afternoon bell, half-tucked under her workbook like a bad memory that never left quietly. It wasn't in an envelope. Just paper, folded once and creased at the edges, like someone had held it too long before delivering it. She knew that kind of fold. The kind that meant hesitation. The kind that meant it was never meant to be kind. She opened it slowly, eyes narrowing as the words revealed themselves in short, sharp strokes. It wasn't long. Just one sentence: Still think anyone really loves you? Ask Leo. Signed—L.

The capital L hooked in a way she recognized immediately. Leo never curled his letters. His penmanship had changed since summer, but even at his worst, he had never written like this. The loops were too wide, the lowercase e too shallow, the slant forced. This wasn't Leo's hand. She stared at the page and felt her stomach drop, not from the words, but from the cruelty of recycling an old lie. The trick wasn't even new. Alex had done this before, and apparently, he thought she'd still fall for it.

She stood up without asking and walked directly to Ty. No whispering. No coded glances. Just one step, then another, until she stood before his desk and held out the note. "Check this," she said, her voice low but steady. Ty took it with both hands, studied the loops, the pressure, the flow. He didn't say anything right away. He reached for his own pencil case and pulled out a sheet of lined paper—Leo's spelling test from the morning. Different pen, same hand. Ty nodded once and said, "This isn't him."

"Alex?" she asked plainly. Ty nodded again.

They didn't run to Mr. Arnett. They didn't file a report. Leo walked past at that very moment, and Ty held up the note in one hand. Leo took it without asking, scanned the words, then clenched it into a tight, angry ball. His jaw locked. He turned, eyes scanning the hallway like a soldier checking for the source of fire. And then he saw him—Alex, standing at his locker, pretending to look for a pencil that wasn't missing.

Leo didn't run. He walked. Each step deliberate. The hallway cleared like water parting around a rock. The moment was silent, the tension louder than any bell. Leo reached Alex, didn't ask a thing, didn't speak a word. He simply stared until Alex turned to meet his eyes, startled. "What?" Alex scoffed, playing innocent. "Did you get your feelings hurt?" The smirk came back, and that was when Leo's fist landed square on the bridge of Alex's nose.

There was a short, sharp sound—skin on skin, bone shifting under pressure—and then a gasp from someone near the lockers. Alex stumbled backward, hands flying to his face, blood already beginning to leak between his fingers. "He hit me!" Alex cried, voice shrill. "He just—he hit me!" But Leo stood still, arms at his side, unmoved. Ty stepped forward. Jasmin. Ella. Sophie. All of them there. None of them flinched.

Mr. Arnett had come down the hallway at the first cry. He had seen the tail end of the punch and the immediate aftermath. The group braced for what they assumed was coming—detention, suspension, at least a lecture. But the Principal didn't call Leo into his office. He didn't raise his voice. He didn't even look surprised. He stared at Alex, then looked Leo in the eye and said flatly, "Good. He deserved it." Then turned and walked away.

The hallway was stunned. Even some of the teachers paused, blinking like someone had spoken in a new language. Alex stood frozen, holding his nose with one hand, pointing wildly with the other. "He assaulted me! That's violence! That's—" But nobody moved to defend him. No crowd gathered. No justice came on his behalf. He looked around and saw only silence, only students who had seen too much already to fall for another lie.

Leo walked back toward the group, unshaken. Sophie met his gaze and nodded once. "Thanks," she whispered. Leo didn't answer. He didn't need to. His silence was a full sentence. Ty placed a hand on Leo's shoulder and said quietly, "That's one." Leo looked confused for half a second, and Ty clarified: "That's the first time you hit someone for the right reason."

Ella said nothing at all. She handed Leo a tissue from her pocket. Not to coddle. Not to baby. Just because his knuckles had split slightly on the punch, and blood didn't suit him. Jasmin gave Alex one final look, then walked the other direction. Sophie followed, the note still clutched in her palm, now more important as evidence of something ugly that refused to change. Alex wasn't dangerous because he was loud. He was dangerous because he smiled while lying.

After school, Leo sat quietly on the front steps. Jeremy had heard the story already—news travelled fast. He brought Leo a bandage, wrapped it around his brother's hand, and didn't say a word. That was the best part. He didn't ask what happened. He just knew it had to be done. Leo looked up at the sky and let out a breath. "I didn't like doing that," he said at last. "But I'm glad I did." Ty, leaning against the railing nearby, said, "You didn't lose control. You made a choice. That's the difference."

Leo didn't respond. He stared at his bandaged knuckle and thought about how much smaller the lie had become once it was dragged into daylight. She liked that question better. And on the next day, when Alex held the door open with that same grin and said, "Morning," to nobody in particular—Sophie walked past him again. Quiet. Steady. Free.

Sophie found the folded note just before the afternoon bell, half-tucked under her workbook like a bad memory that never left quietly. It wasn't in an envelope. Just paper, folded once and creased at the edges, like someone had held it too long before delivering it. She knew that kind of fold. The kind that meant hesitation. The kind that meant it was never meant to be kind. She opened it slowly, eyes narrowing as the words revealed themselves in short, sharp strokes. It wasn't long. Just one sentence: Still think anyone really loves you? Ask Leo. Signed—L.

The capital L hooked in a way she recognized immediately. Leo never curled his letters. His penmanship had changed since summer, but even at his worst, he had never written like this. The loops were too wide, the lowercase e too shallow, the slant forced. This wasn't Leo's hand. She stared at the page and felt her stomach drop, not from the words, but from the cruelty of recycling an old lie. The trick wasn't even new. Alex had done this before, and apparently, he thought she'd still fall for it.

She stood up without asking and walked directly to Ty. No whispering. No coded glances. Just one step, then another, until she stood before his desk and held out the note. "Check this," she said, her voice low but steady. Ty took it with both hands, studied the loops, the pressure, the flow. He didn't say anything right away. He reached for his own pencil case and pulled out a sheet of lined paper—Leo's spelling test from the morning. Different pen, same hand. Ty nodded once and said, "This isn't him."

"Alex?" she asked plainly. Ty nodded again.

They didn't run to Mr. Arnett. They didn't file a report. Leo walked past at that very moment, and Ty held up the note in one hand. Leo took it without asking, scanned the words, then clenched it into a tight, angry ball. His jaw locked. He turned, eyes scanning the hallway like a soldier checking for the source of fire. And then he saw him—Alex, standing at his locker, pretending to look for a pencil that wasn't missing.

Leo didn't run. He walked. Each step deliberate. The hallway cleared like water parting around a rock. The moment was silent, the tension louder than any bell. Leo reached Alex, didn't ask a thing, didn't speak a word. He simply stared until Alex turned to meet his eyes, startled. "What?" Alex scoffed, playing innocent. "Did you get your feelings hurt?" The smirk came back, and that was when Leo's fist landed square on the bridge of Alex's nose.

There was a short, sharp sound—skin on skin, bone shifting under pressure—and then a gasp from someone near the lockers. Alex stumbled backward, hands flying to his face, blood already beginning to leak between his fingers. "He hit me!" Alex cried, voice shrill. "He just—he hit me!" But Leo stood still, arms at his side, unmoved. Ty stepped forward. Jasmin. Ella. Sophie. All of them there. None of them flinched.

Mr. Arnett had come down the hallway at the first cry. He had seen the tail end of the punch and the immediate aftermath. The group braced for what they assumed was coming—detention, suspension, at least a lecture. But the Principal didn't call Leo into his office. He didn't raise his voice. He didn't even look surprised. He stared at Alex, then looked Leo in the eye and said flatly, "Good. He deserved it." Then turned and walked away.

The hallway was stunned. Even some of the teachers paused, blinking like someone had spoken in a new language. Alex stood frozen, holding his nose with one hand, pointing wildly with the other. "He assaulted me! That's violence! That's—" But nobody moved to defend him. No crowd gathered. No justice came on his behalf. He looked around and saw only silence, only students who had seen too much already to fall for another lie.

Leo walked back toward the group, unshaken. Sophie met his gaze and nodded once. "Thanks," she whispered. Leo didn't answer. He didn't need to. His silence was a full sentence. Ty placed a hand on Leo's shoulder and said quietly, "That's one." Leo looked confused for half a second, and Ty clarified: "That's the first time you hit someone for the right reason."

Ella said nothing at all. She handed Leo a tissue from her pocket. Not to coddle. Not to baby. Just because his knuckles had split slightly on the punch, and blood didn't suit him. Jasmin gave Alex one final look, then walked the other direction. Sophie followed, the note still clutched in her palm, now more important as evidence of something ugly that refused to change. Alex wasn't dangerous because he was loud. He was dangerous because he smiled while lying.

After school, Leo sat quietly on the front steps. Jeremy had heard the story already—news travelled fast. He brought Leo a bandage, wrapped it around his brother's hand, and didn't say a word. That was the best part. He didn't ask what happened. He just knew it had to be done.

Leo looked up at the sky and let out a breath. "I didn't like doing that," he said at last. "But I'm glad I did." Ty, leaning against the railing nearby, said, "You didn't lose control. You made a choice. That's the difference." Leo didn't respond. He stared at his bandaged knuckle and thought about how much smaller the lie had become once it was dragged into daylight.

The hallway was unusually quiet after recess, the kind of quiet that follows tension, not peace. Ella stood by her cubby, adjusting the strap of her backpack while talking softly to Jasmin about homework. Nothing loud. Nothing boastful. Just a shared list of what was due and which assignments needed group work. The rest of the class filtered in slowly, but Alex lingered in the doorway, one shoulder pressed to the frame like a sentry who didn't belong in any kingdom but insisted on standing guard.

He hadn't said much since the note incident. The bruising around his nose had faded, but the puffed ego hadn't. He'd gone back to smiling—smiling in that way that made people question themselves after. Smiling with too many teeth, too much ease, too little soul. Miss Penner had kept an eye on him, but Alex was cleverer now. He didn't insult. He praised. And like all good manipulators, he learned that compliments cut deeper when laced with intent.

"That colour looks amazing on you," Alex said loudly, loud enough for everyone to hear, pointing at Ella's deep maroon hoodie. "Honestly, you're probably the best-dressed in the whole class. Always have been."

Ella turned slightly, not out of flattery but out of caution. There was nothing wrong with the words—at least not on paper. But something about the way they were delivered made her pause. His eyes weren't soft. They were fixed, calculating. The compliment was too public, too performative, like he wanted everyone to hear what he said. She forced a smile out of social habit, but her shoulders stayed stiff.

Jasmin felt it too. She narrowed her eyes, not at Ella but at Alex, then stepped slightly in front of her friend, like a breeze bracing before it became a storm. "Thanks," Ella said plainly, voice stripped of warmth, and turned back to her cubby without a word of encouragement. That should've ended it. But Alex wasn't finished.

"You should let me sit beside you for the group project," he added, grinning again. "I mean, it makes sense. You're smart and stylish, kind of the full package."

This time, it wasn't just Ella who heard it. Sophie had been nearby, grabbing her pencil case from the shelf, and she froze. Not physically. Just in expression. Her eyes locked on Alex, then flicked to Ella, then to Jasmin. She leaned in, quietly but clearly, and whispered to Ella without hesitation. "He does that when he wants something."

Ella blinked slowly. The weight of the compliment hit her differently now. She suddenly felt like a fish who hadn't seen the hook. Sophie didn't wait for a reply. She just walked back to her seat and opened her notebook like nothing had happened.

Miss Penner had seen the exchange. She watched from her desk without interrupting, but her fingers hovered over her own notepad. Her pen was already uncapped.

Leo, across the room, caught the look on Ella's face and then looked at Alex, who now pretended to be engaged in unpacking his supplies. He didn't say anything. He didn't need to. His expression was a full page of understanding. The kind that doesn't judge—it just sees.

Ella sat down, opened her math folder, and said, loud enough for no one and everyone, "Compliments don't mean much when they come with a bill." Her voice didn't rise. It landed. A quiet truth that echoed far more than any shout. Ty tilted his head in agreement, eyes not on her but on Alex, who now looked decidedly less smug.

For the rest of the lesson, Alex said nothing. He didn't even raise his hand. The room had turned on him, not with hatred but with knowledge. They were watching him now—not like prey, but like students observing a specimen they had already classified.

Sophie scribbled a note to herself in the margin of her notebook. Don't trust the words. Trust the pattern. She'd heard Ty say it once. Now it made perfect sense.

Miss Penner stood and began the lesson. But before she turned to the whiteboard, she paused, looked directly at Ella, and said gently, "Well said." Nothing more. Just that.

Ella nodded. Not with pride, but with certainty. She wasn't confused anymore.

At lunch, the group sat together like they always did—quiet, steady, present. No one repeated what had happened. It didn't need to be discussed. They had learned that not all harm came in harshness. Some of it came in sugar-coated control. And they weren't eating it anymore. Alex sat two tables away, chewing his sandwich slower than usual, trying to listen, trying to figure out where he had lost the thread. He still smiled. But nobody smiled back.

Miss Penner had only been teaching for three weeks, but already the silence spoke louder than the school bell. It wasn't the usual hush of tired students or kids zoning out after recess. This silence had structure. She saw it in the way Jasmin's eyes narrowed just before Alex opened his mouth, in the way Ella tapped her pencil once when he entered the room, and in the quick glance Ty gave Leo whenever Alex complimented someone too loudly. It was choreography, but not one she'd taught. And Ty—well, Ty never moved without intention.

She'd always believed she was a good observer. Her university professors had praised her classroom management. But nothing in her training had prepared her for kindness used as a weapon. Miss Penner had read books about bullying, seen documentaries, even taken workshops about conflict resolution, but nothing prepared her for the way Alex's words unsettled a room without raising his voice.

The turning point had come the day Ty asked to speak after class. He hadn't asked for help. He hadn't even said Alex's name. He had simply stood at her desk when the final bell rang and said, "There's more than one way to control people. Sometimes, being nice is one of them." She hadn't known how to respond. She'd nodded, written it down in her planner, and told herself she'd think about it later. But the moment had lodged itself in her spine like a splinter.

Since then, she watched differently. Not just for volume or language, but tone. Timing. Who looked down. Who looked around. Who never looked up. She noticed that every time Alex gave a compliment, he looked directly at the person—but only long enough to make them uncomfortable. His smile didn't warm a face; it cornered it. His phrasing was always just vague enough to be taken as friendly, just loud enough to be overheard. "You look better today." "You're finally on top of things." "Didn't think you'd get it right, but good for you." Words that seemed kind—until you felt them.

She also noticed how the others didn't react with praise or acknowledgment. They went still, like prey scenting danger. Ella didn't argue. Jasmin didn't confront. They simply watched. And Leo—Leo had become something else entirely. A mirror, perhaps. He didn't call Alex out in public anymore. He let the weight of the silence speak for itself. His eyes didn't blink when Alex spoke. That unnerved her most.

The shift in her vision didn't come all at once. It came in details: the way Sophie folded her arms tighter when Alex sat near her, the way Elia subtly moved her lunch tray to the other end of the table after a compliment, and the way Jeremy seemed to stiffen even when Alex wasn't speaking to him. These weren't coincidences. These were survival responses.

She jotted notes in her margin. Praise can be pressure. Compliments can be control. Watch body language—not just words. Ty's advice had been to observe before reacting. That's what she was doing now—just watching. But her pen didn't stop moving.

It unsettled her, the realization that she had almost missed all of it. Her instinct had been to protect Alex—the well-spoken boy with tidy handwriting and a pleasant tone. The one who said "thank you" and "excuse me." But politeness is not character. And charm is not kindness.

During reading period, Alex leaned across the aisle and whispered to Jasmin, "I like your new haircut. Makes your face look less round." She didn't respond. But Miss Penner saw the pause, saw the flicker of doubt in Jasmin's shoulders. That was the cost. Not the words—but the second-guessing they triggered. That single moment of wondering whether the compliment was a weapon or a gift.

She called for quiet, but her voice was softer now, not out of weakness, but deliberation. She was choosing her presence differently. Mr. Arnett had warned her weeks ago that this group wasn't average. "They'll teach you more than you'll teach them," he'd said. She hadn't understood then. She did now.

At lunch, she didn't sit in the staff room. She walked the perimeter of the cafeteria with her clipboard, not making announcements, not watching for spilt juice or missing cutlery—but scanning the spaces between words. She saw Alex offer his pudding to Sophie. She declined. He smiled, too wide. Sophie looked at Leo. Leo didn't speak. Just nodded once.

Later that day, she asked Ty to stay behind again. "What do I look for?" she asked. No preamble. Just honesty. Ty didn't hesitate. "When someone gives praise that makes someone smaller, not stronger. That's how you know." And that was the clearest line she'd been given.

Back in her apartment that evening, she opened a fresh notebook. On the first page, she wrote in bold ink: Kindness is not control. Learn the difference. Teach it when you do. She underlined it twice. She went to sleep watching faces in her mind—faces of the students who smiled without fear, and the one who always smiled like he knew he was being watched.

There was no announcement, no whispered plan, no tap on the shoulder to say stand here. Yet when the bell rang and the halls thickened with the shuffle of shoes and slamming lockers, they moved as one. Ty stood first, by the glass trophy case. Leo walked forward without a word and took his place beside him. Then Jasmin, eyes calm but watchful, planted herself to Ty's left. Nico adjusted his backpack and leaned casually on the railing. Ella, Sophie, and Elia didn't speak. They just arrived. No one needed to ask why.

It wasn't a blockade. It wasn't a protest. It was presence. Their backs didn't lean. Their arms didn't cross. They didn't stare anyone down. They simply stood. Seven students in a straight line against the cinderblock wall, forming a silent boundary between everything they had built—and everything they would not let back in. It wasn't about Alex. Not entirely. It was about truth. The kind that didn't flinch. The kind that didn't play along to keep things smooth.

Alex came around the corner like he always did, walking too slow, smile already fixed in place, head tilted as if he were amused before anything happened. He wore his backpack on one shoulder and his shirt collar slightly open, like he wanted to look relaxed. But his eyes faltered the moment he saw them. He slowed. Not much. But enough.

The hallway was wide. There was plenty of space to pass. No one blocked his way. Not physically. But Alex didn't approach. He stopped four lockers away. Then shifted. A flicker of confusion crossed his face, then indignation, then something resembling caution. He glanced toward the classroom door. He looked at Ty, then at Leo. And then, without a word, he turned. Took the longer route down the next corridor. Not a single one of them moved.

Miss Penner had stepped out of the classroom just as the moment unfolded. She didn't speak either. She simply leaned against the doorframe and watched. Her arms folded gently, not in judgment, but in attention. She saw how the line never tensed. They weren't a wall of threat. They were a message. They weren't confronting—they were reminding. That the old games wouldn't work here anymore.

Jeremy peeked out from the adjacent classroom and caught sight of his brother standing so still, so sure. His chest lifted. It was the kind of moment that lodged itself into a child's memory, the kind you revisit when you're older and trying to remember what bravery looked like when it wore a school sweater and a bookbag. It didn't yell. It didn't boast. It just stood.

Later, when Sophie sat beside Leo in the cafeteria, she asked, "Did you plan that?" Leo shook his head. "Didn't have to." That was all he said. Jasmin told Miss Penner quietly during indoor recess, "Sometimes, standing still is louder than shouting." The teacher nodded. She was learning the difference too.

Mr. Arnett heard about it within the hour. One of the Grade 6 students described it to him in great detail—how Alex walked the other way without a single word being said. The Principal smiled, tapped the desk, and said, "Good. They know how to protect without pushing." He didn't send for any of them.

It was Ty who later explained it best to Miss Penner. "We're not trying to scare him. We just don't owe him our comfort anymore." She wrote that down. She'd never heard it phrased like that. But she'd felt it before, in staff rooms, in old friendships, in places she used to shrink to stay safe.

That day, for the first time in months, Alex didn't talk much. He didn't hand out compliments. He didn't make jokes loud enough to be overheard. He sat alone at lunch. Leo never looked his way. He just sat with Jeremy and told him stories about chipmunks and summer fires.

Miss Penner kept watching. Not Alex, this time. But Leo. Ty. Jasmin. She watched how peace moved through them—not forced, not brittle, but alive. They were teaching her a language without speaking it. A kind of grammar of justice that didn't need capitals or punctuation. Just presence. By the time the dismissal bell rang, Alex had already left the building. No goodbyes. No fake smiles. Just an early exit and the shadow of something he couldn't bend anymore. And still, no one had said a word.

The door closed quietly behind the last student. Miss Penner didn't say anything at first. She walked to her desk, then stopped, turned around, and leaned against its edge, arms crossed not with judgment, but with a kind of caution that asked for truth without demanding it. "I'd like to ask you all something," she said. "But only if you want to share." Her tone wasn't the usual kind—the one teachers use when they're trying to sound soft but already have the answers. This one felt... real.

Leo looked at Ty first. Ty gave the faintest nod, the kind of signal they'd used many times before when deciding whether someone was safe enough to hold what they knew. Jasmin folded her arms and leaned forward slightly. Nico stayed quiet but attentive. Ella kept her hands in her lap. Sophie sat cross-legged on the floor without a word. Elia leaned back in the chair nearest the bookshelf, her eyes locked on Miss Penner's every move. No one moved to leave. That was answer enough.

"It's about Alex, isn't it?" Miss Penner asked. She didn't pretend to be surprised. She didn't pretend to know. "I've noticed some... patterns. But I'm not sure what I'm seeing yet."

Ty didn't smile. He didn't frown either. He just sat forward, elbows on knees, voice level. "Kindness isn't always kind. That's the part most adults miss." He glanced at Leo. "Sometimes it's used like a rope. To tie you up. Or to pull you in close just so they can control how far you go."

Leo didn't speak for a moment. He was remembering. Then he looked right at her and said, "People like Alex don't always yell. They compliment you, then they trap you. They say something nice in front of other people so you feel too polite to walk away." Miss Penner's eyes didn't leave his. She didn't interrupt. She didn't shift. She simply nodded once, like she was adjusting an inner lens that had been out of focus for far too long. "And this has happened to all of you?"

"Different ways," Jasmin said. "But yeah. He used to say things that made me feel important, but only when I agreed with him. If I didn't, he'd ignore me for a week." Ella added, "He helped me once with a project. Then kept bringing it up every time he wanted something from me."

Nico spoke softly. "He said I was the smartest in the class. Then asked me to lie to the principal for him." Miss Penner's posture shifted just slightly, like a crack had formed in her assumptions. Not large enough to break her, but wide enough to change what came next.

Ty continued, "We're not saying people can't change. But if no one says anything, people like that just learn how to smile better." Leo leaned forward now, too. "The trick is that their kindness always costs you something. Your silence. Your loyalty. Your guilt." He glanced down, then added, "That's how I used to be. Before I got called out."

Sophie looked up. "He used to scare me. Now he just makes me tired. I don't trust any sentence that starts with 'You're so—' anymore. Not from him." Elia nodded. "It's not about him being mean. It's about him being fake. Everything feels sticky when he's too nice."

Miss Penner was writing now, not to distract herself, but to capture it. Her pen moved quickly, pausing only when the words hit too close to something she'd once lived through herself. She didn't tell them that part. She just kept listening. "Is that why you all stood in the hallway?" she asked. Jasmin answered. "We weren't blocking him. We were just reminding him—he doesn't get to walk through us anymore."

Miss Penner placed her notebook down and stood fully upright. "I want to do better. I want to see it when it happens. I want to stop brushing it off as personality or charm." Her voice had steadied. "Will you keep teaching me?"

The group didn't answer with words. Ty offered her the same quiet nod he once gave Leo when they first met. Jasmin smiled. Ella stood and began pushing the chairs back in place. Sophie helped without being asked. Nico straightened the papers on the desk. Leo gave a short, quiet, "We already have."

The hallway was buzzing again. First week of school, and the walls already knew everything. Who got taller. Who cut their hair. Who cried over the summer. Who came back braver. And who hadn't changed at all. It echoed in the way kids looked at each other, the way they leaned into lockers or walked past someone too quickly. It didn't take long for Alex to start working the crowd. His smile was polished, as always. His eyes sharp. His voice smoother than most grownups could manage when they were lying.

Ella stood near the drinking fountain, twisting the cap back on her water bottle slowly. She was alone for a moment, sorting through her thoughts in the same way she always did: quietly, with care, like folding laundry and stacking each shirt just right. She didn't notice Alex until his voice landed next to her shoulder, too close, too sudden.

"You know," he said, "you're the prettiest one here this year."

She turned her head slowly, not surprised. Not startled. Just done. She looked him in the eye with the kind of patience you learn after being tricked enough times not to flinch. Around them, other students paused—but not in admiration. In anticipation. Everyone had heard Alex use that same phrase last year, with different names, different angles, but the same trap door underneath.

Ella didn't smile. She didn't say thank you. She didn't ask what he meant. She didn't offer him the performance he wanted—the bashful pause, the lifted chin, the sudden blush. Instead, she let the silence stretch just long enough to cut through the charm like a wire through glass. Then, she said it flatly, not with anger, not with sass, but with truth.

"That's not a compliment," she said. "Not when you want something from me."

Her voice didn't raise. Her feet didn't shift. Her shoulders didn't drop. She spoke the words as if she were reciting her own address—nothing to argue with, just fact. And once they were out, she stepped past him, her water bottle tucked against her chest, and moved into the classroom without looking back.

For a second, no one said a word. Then Sophie grinned. Jasmin let out a slow exhale through her nose. Nico mouthed, "Whoa." Ty, watching from the lockers, gave the smallest nod and turned away, not needing to say a thing. Alex stood there, caught. Not insulted. Not attacked. But revealed. His compliment, like a balloon with no string, just drifted into the air and vanished.

He turned, hoping to find someone who'd laugh with him, play it off, make it a joke. But the crowd had already moved. No one met his eyes. No one picked up the line. It lay there, limp and empty on the floor, and no one wanted to be seen touching it.

In the classroom, Ella took her seat near the window. She didn't feel proud. She felt steady. That was better. The kind of steadiness that doesn't shake when someone tries to decorate a chain and call it jewellery. Miss Penner, already seated at her desk, glanced up just long enough to catch Ella's eye. No words passed between them, but the teacher's gaze lingered, thoughtful.

Later that day, during lunch, Leo passed Ella in the hallway. He didn't make a show of it. Just offered her the same thing Ty once offered him: a small nod, full of respect. Not for what she said, but for the choice not to let flattery own her. Ella smiled softly and kept walking.

At the lunch table, the group settled into their usual quiet rhythm. No one mentioned what had happened. No one needed to. That's the thing about truth—it echoes without needing to shout. Alex sat alone at a far table, stirring his pudding like it owed him something. The weight of being seen with no mask left him quieter than usual.

Ella didn't gloat. She didn't whisper about it to the others. She didn't even write about it in her notebook later. She just sipped her juice box, opened her sandwich, and let the moment live where it belonged—in the past.

She had learned something important, something her grandmother once told her on a swing set in her backyard: that sometimes, people wrap control in compliments because it's easier to get close when you pretend you're giving. And when you unwrap it, if all that's left is silence, then it wasn't a gift. It was bait. That afternoon, Miss Penner added a line to her notes. She had begun keeping a small journal behind her attendance binder. Today's entry read: "Ella taught me that not all compliments are meant to uplift. Some are hooks. And saying no isn't rudeness. It's protection."

Miss Penner closed the door behind her softly, more like someone entering a chapel than a classroom. She stood with the kind of posture teachers use when they're still deciding whether to speak or listen first. The desks were cleared of books. The lights dimmed just enough by the clouds pressing at the windows. Jasmin sat cross-legged on top of one of the desks, arms folded lightly over her lap, eyes watching the floor, not out of fear, but precision. Ty leaned against the counter near the pencil sharpener, silent. Leo stayed near the back, saying nothing. This moment wasn't his to lead.

"I wanted to ask you something," Miss Penner said, voice low enough to show she was serious. "Not as your teacher. Just as a person."

Jasmin lifted her eyes but didn't speak yet. It was the pause that made the words worth waiting for. There was a confidence to her silence that Miss Penner hadn't seen in students before—certainly not in seventh grade. Jasmin finally gave a small nod, not offering permission, exactly, but inviting the moment to unfold.

"I'm trying to understand the difference," Miss Penner continued, "between what kindness looks like, and what it feels like when it's not real. When it's used to... control. I don't want to miss it. Not anymore."

Jasmin didn't nod again. Instead, she reached into her backpack and pulled out her sketchbook—not for the art inside, but because of what was tucked into the front flap. A small piece of folded paper. She handed it over without explanation. Miss Penner unfolded it slowly. It was a list. Six sentences. Scribbled in red pen, each beginning with the words You should be grateful...

You should be grateful I let you sit at my table.
You should be grateful I said you looked pretty.
You should be grateful I didn't tell everyone what you said.
You should be grateful I even talk to you.
You should be grateful I invited you, even if it was a joke.
You should be grateful I picked you at all.

Jasmin said nothing while Miss Penner read. The teacher's face didn't move. Not a twitch. Just a stillness that held sorrow and realization in the same breath. She folded the paper back and handed it to Jasmin without a word. "That's what fake kindness feels like," Jasmin said, her voice steady now. "It feels like being chosen, but only so someone can remind you that they could've chosen someone else. It feels like a gift that you're not allowed to unwrap unless you agree to feel small."

Miss Penner sat in one of the front-row chairs, legs crossed, hands folded neatly, as if trying to shrink herself without leaving the room. "How long did it take you to name it?" "I didn't," Jasmin replied. "Ty did. Then Leo did. Then Sophie said it. But I felt it a long time before I could say it out loud." "Where did you feel it?" Miss Penner asked gently, almost whispering.

"In my gut," Jasmin said. "That's where it always starts. When something feels wrong, even when the words sound nice. It twists. Like someone's moving your spine around. You want to believe them. But your stomach won't let you." Miss Penner nodded slowly. "I think I've felt that too. As an adult." "Everyone does," Jasmin said. "But kids get told to ignore it more. To be polite. To be grateful. To smile even when it hurts. But the truth is—real kindness never makes you afraid."

Leo looked over from the windowsill. Not a word passed from him. Not even a nod. Just the look of someone seeing truth told clean. Ty added, "She's right. We all used to think it was just our fault for not saying thank you loud enough. But it's not gratitude if you're scared to say no."

The rain started outside, not heavy, just enough to wrap the windows in soft grey. It made the classroom feel separate from the world, as if this conversation existed in its own weather. Miss Penner sat back in her chair, eyes flicking from one face to the next, knowing that she wasn't just learning how to teach differently—she was learning how to see.

Jasmin stood and walked toward the whiteboard. She picked up a marker and wrote three words: Kindness doesn't trap. She set the marker down, returned to her desk, and sat. Not like she needed to be applauded. Not like it had been a performance. Just a truth said out loud, finally. Miss Penner opened her binder and wrote down the words exactly as they were, word for word. Her fingers paused just a second longer than normal. Then she underlined them. Outside, the bell rang—but no one moved. Not yet.

Dismissal always brought noise. Zippers, shrieks, lunch bags thudding back into backpacks with the graceless speed of children on the edge of freedom. The hallway churned with bodies half-running, half-listening, while teachers hovered like gentle border guards trying to maintain a line they no longer owned. Leo stood by the doors, shoulders relaxed, arms crossed loosely, not in defiance, but calm. His eyes scanned the room as if none of it surprised him anymore. Nothing jarred him. Not even Alex.

Mr. Firth's grey SUV pulled up slowly to the school's looped pick-up zone. A familiar vehicle now. Reliable. Jeremy burst out of the Grade 5 exit with a bounce in his stride, cheeks pink with laughter. He ran to Leo with both arms open, no hesitation. "Big Brother!" he called, already halfway into the hug. "I love you, Leo!"

Leo crouched low as Jeremy collided into him with the full force of ten-year-old joy. He didn't say anything at first. He just hugged him back, letting the words settle deep, not as surprise, but as home. Then Leo stood, hand resting on Jeremy's shoulder like he'd been doing it for years.

The driver's door opened. Mr. Firth stepped out, smoothing his tie with one hand, the other already raised in welcome. He didn't shout. He didn't even raise his voice. He simply smiled and said, "Ready to go, son?" That word—son—didn't hang in the air. It didn't ripple like some bomb dropped in front of an audience. It landed softly, gently, as though it had always been there. Like a coat Leo was finally allowed to wear without asking first. Leo didn't cry. He didn't grin either. He just nodded, slow and sure, his voice steady as he replied, "Yeah. I'm ready."

Alex had been standing near the water fountain with his lunch bag still half-zipped. His gaze flicked from Leo to Mr. Firth to Jeremy, then back again, trying to arrange a new story in his head. One that made sense. One where Leo was still the outsider. Still the angry boy with too much shadow and not enough home. But that story no longer fit. It collapsed on itself before Alex could even sell it to his own thoughts.

Leo turned toward the doors, one hand gripping Jeremy's backpack strap lightly to keep him close, not out of control, but care. As they stepped into the sun, the light caught the soft outline of the boy he used to be—but didn't follow him down the steps. Mr. Firth opened the passenger door for Jeremy, then the rear one for Leo. "We've got spaghetti and garlic bread waiting," he said, like it was nothing, like it was everything.

Jeremy grinned and climbed in, kicking his shoes off without being told. Leo took a moment before getting in. He looked back once. Not long. Just long enough to notice Alex still watching. Alex stood completely still. Not angry. Not smug. Just confused. Like the rules had changed again and no one had given him the memo. He wasn't scared, but he wasn't sure either. That uncertainty clung to him like static.

Leo shut the door behind him, clicked his seatbelt, and leaned slightly toward the front. "Thank you for the ride," he said. Mr. Firth glanced at him through the mirror. "Any time, son," he said again. As if there had never been another title to use. The car pulled away from the school. The building behind them grew smaller, but the feeling in Leo's chest didn't. If anything, it expanded. It didn't hurt. It didn't tighten. It spread out like something earned, not owed. And in the silence that followed, Jeremy reached across the seat and rested his head on Leo's arm.

Leo didn't speak. He didn't need to. He just tilted his head against Jeremy's lightly and closed his eyes. The world didn't have to cheer. No music swelled. But something invisible snapped into place, quiet and real. Leo had been called many things before. Now, he was called son.

Lunch didn't start loud. It hadn't for a while. Not since Alex lost his audience. The cafeteria echoed with the usual clatter—plastic trays sliding, forks tapping, milk cartons folded and flattened like origami by bored hands. But at Table Seven, where Leo and Jeremy sat with their group, the noise came differently. Not in volume, but in closeness. No one raised their voice to be heard. No one needed to.

Leo pulled out Jeremy's chair before he sat in his own. It wasn't for show. No one noticed except Jeremy, and that was the point. Jeremy sat down with his sandwich, unzipping his lunch bag with a calmness he hadn't shown last year. His hands didn't tremble. His breathing stayed even. He took the first bite without checking if anyone was watching.

Across from them, Ty peeled the sticker off his apple. Jasmin passed a napkin across the table when Nico's juice box leaked. Ella offered a piece of her banana muffin to Sophie, who accepted it with a nod. Small kindnesses passed back and forth, like breathing. They didn't explain them. They just gave them.

Alex sat two tables away. Alone again. His lunch unopened. He still wore that same grin when he walked in—flickering with ease and pretend comfort—but now it had nowhere to land. No one mirrored it back. And that left it exposed. An awkward smile with no scaffolding beneath it.

Leo opened his thermos and dipped a piece of garlic bread into the spaghetti inside. Mr. Firth had packed it that morning. Lisa added a note in the lid that said, "Proud of you. Eat it all, okay?" Jeremy saw the note too and grinned so wide his sandwich tilted sideways. "You got a note?" he whispered. "That's awesome." Leo slid the note across to him and said, "You can keep it." Jeremy tucked it gently into the front pocket of his hoodie like a treasure. He didn't look around. He didn't wonder who was watching. He was too busy feeling safe.

Then Leo did something unexpected. He reached across the table, hooked an arm around Jeremy's shoulder, and pulled him into a side-hug. Not for comfort. Not for show. Just because it was real. "I love you, Jeremy," he said aloud, not whispered, not hidden behind hands. His voice was warm, steady, and full.

Nobody laughed. Not even close. No one rolled their eyes. No one called them weird. Ty looked up and smiled softly. Jasmin grinned with her whole face. Ella winked. Sophie clasped her hands together under the table, proud. Even Nico, who didn't do hugs much, nodded with respect. Jeremy didn't say "I love you" back in that moment. He didn't have to. His whole body leaned into the hug like an answer already spoken. His feet swung under the bench with a kind of ease he hadn't known in Grade Four.

Across the room, Alex sat straighter. Then slouched. Then glanced over. Then away. His face didn't break—but it did crack a little at the edges. There was no spotlight for him here. No scattered laughter to draw in. Just one group of kids who had decided that real power didn't come from volume.

Miss Penner stood near the garbage bins, eyes skimming across tables. When she reached Table Seven, she stopped. Watched. Made a note in her mind, and didn't move for another few seconds. Noticed how calm can look like leadership. How silence can roar.

Ty leaned over his tray and said, "This is the strongest table in the school." "Because we're loud?" Nico asked. "No," Ty answered. "Because we don't have to be." Sophie broke her muffin in two and passed half to Jeremy. "No lunch trades," she teased gently. Jeremy beamed. "Except for muffins."

Their laughter was soft. Not performative. Not for anyone else. And Leo, still with one arm loosely around Jeremy, closed his eyes for just a second—not to escape, but to anchor. He didn't need applause. He didn't need permission. He had his brother beside him, his group intact, and nothing left to prove. They all ate slowly. Purposefully. Without fear.

Miss Penner waited until the hallway emptied and the last zipper had been pulled shut. Only the hum of the overhead lights and the creak of her teacher's chair filled the room now. The windows were still cracked from recess, letting in the tail end of late September warmth. She sat alone at her desk with her planner open, the cover now folded beneath her wrist to make it lie flat. It was never the lesson plans that mattered most, she was beginning to realize. Not anymore.

She took out a fresh page from the back of her planner, flipped it sideways, and wrote across the top: Observation Notes. Below it, with a fine-point black pen, she wrote: "Kindness without sincerity is just another kind of lie. The students taught me that." She stared at the sentence for a long moment, her own words surprising her. She hadn't known she would write that until it appeared. But it was true. Completely true.

That morning, she had watched Ella walk away from a compliment like it was a trick door. She had seen Sophie choose silence instead of smiling back. She had seen Leo hug his brother in a cafeteria full of students and not once check to see who was watching. None of these things were in the curriculum. But they carried more weight than anything printed in the government's weekly learning objectives.

She picked up her red pen next—not to correct, but to underline. Just another kind of lie. She drew a slow, careful line beneath the phrase. Her pen paused again at the bottom of the page. Then she wrote: "The ones who know the truth don't shout it. They live it. Every day. Quietly." There had been a shift in her this week, and she knew it. It hadn't come from the staff room or any professional development seminar. It had come from twelve-year-olds who spoke like elders when the world pretended not to see.

She turned back to her attendance log from that morning. Every name there—but now, each one felt different. Leo Mason Takashi-Firth. That was a name she would not forget. Nor would she forget the calm with which he held his brother's hand as they walked in. Or the steadiness in his voice when he answered questions others would've dodged. Or the stillness of his eyes when Alex tried again to spin the room in his direction.

Miss Penner never liked getting involved in student drama. That had been her posture since teacher's college: stay neutral, stay professional, stay objective. But watching Ty speak about deception like it was a code he'd memorized, and then watching the others nod—not performatively, but with shared memory—she knew neutrality wouldn't cut it. Not with this group. Not with this year.

In the bottom corner of the page, she started a new list: Patterns to Watch For. She numbered it. 1) Compliments followed by requests. 2) Public praise, private pressure. 3) Rewritten stories—same plot, different names. 4) Smiles that don't reach the eyes. 5) Forced gratitude. She paused, added one more: 6) Silence used as a shield, not as cruelty.

She tapped the pen twice against her chin and looked out the window. Across the yard, Leo and Jeremy were walking toward the gate. Jeremy was swinging his lunch bag in wide, happy arcs. Leo held it steady when it got too close to the fence. Nothing dramatic. Just instinct. Just protection. Miss Penner smiled to herself and added: 7) Brothers who protect, even when no one asks them to.

The bell rang for the last time that day—a long, drawn-out buzz. Her fingers lingered on the desk edge. She knew now that she had to be more than a teacher. She had to become a student again. The right kind of student. The kind who lets children teach her what no degree ever could.

She flipped to a clean sheet in the notebook and titled it: The Difference Between Kind and Nice. She drew a line down the middle. On the left, she wrote: Kind – for the other person. On the right: Nice – for yourself. Then she added a final note beneath: Kindness doesn't chase approval. It just shows up and stays. There was a knock on the classroom door. Mr. Arnett stepped in with a clipboard and raised his eyebrows. "You look deep in thought."

Miss Penner closed her notebook slowly, careful not to smudge the ink. "Just learning," she said. "From the ones who already figured it out." He nodded, didn't press further, and left with a quiet respect she hadn't expected. She opened her notebook again the moment the door clicked shut. At the bottom of the page, in bold capital letters, she wrote: I TRUST THEM. And she meant it. Every word.

CHAPTER 15: WHAT I WOULD TELL MY YOUNGER SELF

If Leo could have stepped backwards in time, even just for a minute, he wouldn't have brought a lecture. He wouldn't have yelled. He wouldn't have carried a flashlight to shine in his old self's face. He would've just sat beside the boy on that empty bench behind the school—sat quietly, maybe placed one sneaker next to the old scuffed-up pair, maybe leaned in without touching, without asking, just waiting until the silence between them felt like trust and not punishment. If he could've, he would've said only one thing: "You were scared. Not bad." And maybe that would've been enough.

Back then, he wouldn't have recognized himself now. Not with the softness in his voice or the careful way he walks past kids who used to flinch when he came near. The old Leo didn't know what gentleness looked like. He thought it was weakness. He thought quiet kids were easy to break and that loud ones won. That's the lie he was raised on, whispered in angry voices, sharpened like a stick, always pointed at someone else. He didn't know kindness could build walls thicker than meanness ever could.

So he sat on the back step of the school now, alone, writing in a notebook he used to draw monsters in. This time, no fangs. No shadows. No claws. Just words. The kind that spill out when no one's looking. The kind he needed last year but no one had said out loud. Jeremy was still inside with Jasmin and Nico, finishing a group project. Leo asked for five minutes alone, and they gave it to him without asking why. That was new. That was love.

He stared at the spot on the step where he used to throw rocks at ants just to feel something snap under his thumb. Not because he liked hurting anything. He just didn't know how else to feel in control. He remembered how his backpack straps used to be twisted up from gripping them too tight, how he'd wait for the bell to ring just so he could cut through the crowd like a blade and nobody would notice he was bleeding on the inside.

The version of him from then would've laughed at the idea of writing letters to himself. He would've mocked it. Called it weak. Called it dumb. But the version now didn't feel like mocking anything. He felt like offering a seat to the boy who used to cry when no one was watching, the boy who shouted not because he was angry—but because nobody was listening. And in his own voice, finally calm, Leo whispered the words no one gave him back then: "You were scared. Not bad."

If that boy had looked up and asked what that meant, Leo would've explained it like this. He would've said: "Being scared doesn't make you cruel. But no one helped you unlearn it. You thought pushing made you strong. You thought controlling made you safe. But you weren't safe, were you? You were always afraid of someone bigger doing it to you first." And maybe that boy, the one he used to be, would nod. Maybe his fists would loosen. Maybe he'd believe it.

Sometimes, Leo wondered how much of his old self was still curled up inside him, like a shadow hiding behind his ribs. But days like this told him something truer: that shadow had shape, yes—but not roots. It didn't grow. It didn't belong. And it didn't get to speak anymore. Not now. Not with Jeremy calling him "big brother" and not with Ty calling him "honourable" and not with Jasmin letting him sit beside her again. That shadow wasn't his voice. It was just an echo that finally stopped bouncing off the walls.

The thing that used to scare Leo the most wasn't being mean. It was being known. It was the idea that someone might see how much he hated himself back then and think he deserved it. That was the secret fear. That the pain inside him made him rotten, made him broken. But now, Leo looked at Jeremy, who loved him with open eyes. And he realized—being seen isn't dangerous. Not anymore. It's proof that you matter. Even when you're still healing.

He imagined turning to that younger Leo and saying, "You survive this." Not just that, but more. "You get better. You laugh again. You make friends who call you out when you lie. You learn how to listen without needing to win. You find a house that doesn't slam doors. You find a mom who tucks you in. You find a dad who calls you 'son.' And you find a little brother who makes you want to stay soft forever."

Jeremy came outside, slow and barefoot on the hot pavement. He sat beside Leo, not saying anything, just leaning. "You writing again?" he asked without peeking at the notebook. Leo nodded. "To myself," he said. Jeremy tilted his head. "You miss you?" Leo smiled. "Nah. I just wanted to say something to him. Something I wish someone had said to me before I became someone I hated."

The bell rang and birds scattered like paper scraps off the fence. Leo closed the notebook without snapping the cover. He didn't write a sign-off. Didn't need one. The words were already living inside him now. He'd memorized them in his bones. And if that old version of him ever came back, even just in a nightmare or an echo, Leo knew what he'd say. "I see you. I don't hate you. But I'm not you anymore." And maybe that would be enough.

Jeremy didn't look up when he asked. He just kept drawing circles in the dust with the side of his shoe, like maybe the question was something he wasn't supposed to say out loud. "What did it feel like?" he said finally. "When you were mean to people. On purpose." The way he said on purpose was soft, but it landed like a drop of ink in a glass of water—slow, spreading, impossible to ignore. Leo didn't flinch. He just took a breath through his nose and answered without blinking: "Empty. But safe. And fake."

He didn't expect to say it that way. Not in those words. But once they were out, he felt his shoulders shift, like truth had weight but also made things lighter. Jeremy nodded like he understood. Then he added, "Safe how?" Leo blinked at the gravel, unsure if his throat wanted to close or open. "Like… like if I was the one hurting people, nobody could hurt me first. I thought if I kept winning, I'd never get hurt. But really, I just didn't let anyone close enough to matter."

Jeremy chewed the inside of his cheek like he was trying to eat the thought before it swallowed him. Then he said, "So it wasn't really safe. Just fake safe." Leo nodded. "Yeah. Exactly." They sat there a moment longer, just the wind brushing past like it was listening too. Jeremy said, "You don't do that anymore." And Leo felt the heat rise behind his eyes. He didn't cry. Not yet. But the feeling was there—stronger than fear. It was something heavier. Something real.

"I know," Leo whispered. "You're the reason." Jeremy looked at him, puzzled. "Me?" Leo didn't hesitate. "You made me want to protect someone more than I wanted to protect myself. That's real. That's scary. But it's real." Jeremy reached into his pocket, pulled out a piece of gum, and handed it over without looking. "Real's better," he said. "Even if it's scary." Leo took it. Not because he needed gum. But because a brother's offering shouldn't be left hanging.

They sat together on the old wooden bench near the bike racks, legs dangling like younger boys who'd never had to lie to survive. Leo didn't try to explain more. He just let the words hang there, like clothes drying in the wind—wrinkled, maybe, but clean. Jeremy broke the silence again. "Do you ever miss it? Like… being in charge? Feeling like the scariest one?" Leo tilted his head. "Not once," he said. "But sometimes I still hear that voice in my head. The old one. Telling me I'm gonna mess up. That I'm gonna slip back."

"And then?" Jeremy asked. Leo turned to him, eyes steady. "Then I remember who I am now. Who you think I am. And that voice shuts up." Jeremy smiled, a real one. No hooks, no strings, just the simple lift of corners that came from being seen and knowing it was okay. "I think I'd punch that old voice," Jeremy said. "If I could." Leo laughed, for real. "You already did. With every hug you gave me even when I didn't deserve it."

It didn't feel like a lesson. It felt like sunlight. Like two boys sharing the same sky and realizing it could stretch bigger than what they came from. Leo reached into his backpack and pulled out an old pencil case—the one Jeremy had doodled on with permanent marker. "You remember this?" he asked. Jeremy squinted. "Yeah. I wrote your name wrong." Leo turned it over. "You spelled it 'Leow.'" Jeremy shrugged. "It still sounds like a superhero name."

Maybe that's what this was. Not redemption. Not recovery. But recognition. Leo didn't have to earn his place anymore. He just had to stay real. Stay kind. Stay soft where it counted. Jeremy didn't want a perfect brother. He wanted the kind who told the truth. Even when it stung. Even when it was scary. Even when the truth sounded like "I used to be mean. But I'm not anymore."

They watched a butterfly circle the yard. Jeremy whispered, "Real brothers don't scare each other." Leo nodded. "Real brothers don't lie to each other either." And just like that, the scar between who he was and who he'd become didn't hurt anymore. It was just there. A reminder. A mark, not a wound. And the boy beside him? That was family. The real kind.

He stood up and held out a hand. Jeremy grabbed it without hesitation. "Where we going?" Jeremy asked. Leo smiled. "Inside. Time to finish our math." Jeremy groaned. "I liked the feelings talk better." "Me too," Leo said. And they went in, shoulder to shoulder, the past behind them—and no fear of slipping back.

It wasn't a loud moment. Not one of those crashing, movie-scene realizations where the world spins and time slows down. It was worse. Quieter. Like a whisper in a library you're not supposed to hear. Leo remembered it clearly—not just the date, but the air, the colour of the carpet, the hum of the hallway lights just outside the library doors. It had been late spring, still cool enough for sweaters, but warm enough that the windows were cracked open. He had walked in expecting silence and found his own reflection—only it wasn't in a mirror. It was in someone else's behaviour.

A younger student—probably Grade 5—was cornered near the shelves, holding his binder against his chest like it could stop the words being flung at him. The boy doing the talking? Smooth. Smiling. Even kind-sounding on the surface. "It's okay," the boy said, patting the younger one's shoulder. "But seriously, you should've done better. Now I have to fix it for you again. And it's kinda making me look bad." That was the sentence. The exact words Leo had used months earlier on Nico. Like a script had been passed between them.

He froze. Not just in place—but inside. His bones stayed still, but something in him shattered. It was like watching himself, but through a mirror that had cracked—so the smile twisted, the words echoed wrong, and the boy on the other side of it wasn't him anymore. He wanted to look away. He wanted to run. But instead, his feet carried him forward. Straight to the kid who looked like he might cry. Leo knelt. Not beside the boy who was doing the talking, but beside the one being talked down to. "You don't have to fix anything," he whispered. "You didn't mess it up."

The other kid blinked. Leo didn't wait for thanks. He stood and looked the mirror-boy in the eye. "Don't say that again," he said. The boy scoffed. "Say what?" Leo didn't flinch. "Any of it. Just stop." And then he turned and walked straight to Ty—who had been shelving books on the far wall and saw everything. Leo didn't make it more than five steps before the weight crushed him. Not physically. Emotionally. The truth had collapsed on his chest like a shelf full of every lie he'd ever told.

He dropped to his knees right in front of Ty. Didn't even pretend to be fine. The sob broke before he could catch it. Ty knelt, wrapped both arms around him, and whispered, "Let it out. Don't hold anything." And Leo did. For the first time in his life, he cried like a boy who had stopped lying to himself. No words. No excuses. Just tears. And not the kind that beg for sympathy—but the kind that say, I see what I was. And I don't want to be that anymore.

Ty never let go. Not once. Not when the bell rang. Not when other students peeked in. Not even when Leo's nose ran and his words became hiccups. He just held him like a real brother would. Quiet. Solid. Present. And when Leo finally pulled back, red-eyed and puffy, Ty didn't say "It's okay." He said, "Now we build something better." Leo nodded. And from that moment forward, they were brothers—not just in the way they sat at lunch or shared inside jokes. But in the way real loyalty is formed—in fire.

That moment became a cornerstone. A day not written in ink, but in the echo of change. Now, months later, with summer behind them and a chill creeping back into the air, Leo remembered it with reverence. It wasn't a memory. It was a turning point. A time he chose to stop being the cracked reflection and become the kind of boy he could face in the mirror. Jeremy didn't know that story yet. But someday, he would.

Leo often thought back to that day when he felt scared he might slip. Not into old habits—but into silence. Into pretending things didn't hurt when they did. And each time, he pictured Ty's arms around him, not letting go. He didn't just cry that day. He changed. And the change held. Because love held him there. Truth held him there. And a brother's quiet, unshaken embrace told him he didn't have to go back.

Now, on September 15th, sitting with Jeremy in the schoolyard, Leo could finally say it out loud. "I saw myself once," he said. "In someone else. And I hated it. But that's how I knew I had to change. Not for them. For me." Jeremy, wide-eyed, whispered, "Did it work?" Leo smiled—not big, not showy. Just enough. "Yeah," he said. "Because someone saw me break. And stayed."

Leo didn't say it right away. Not even to Ty. Not even to Mr. and Mrs. Firth. Because the truth felt too raw—like skin that had healed over a wound but still hurt when pressed. He remembered sitting by the window once, as a younger version of himself, watching snow fall and wondering if anyone would miss him if he disappeared under it. Not because he was dramatic. Not because he was sad. But because it had never been said. Not plainly. Not cleanly. Not honestly. He had never once been told, "I love you," just because he existed.

It was always wrapped in something else—performance, obedience, results. His father only showed something close to affection when Leo did exactly what was expected. And even then, it came in the form of pride, not love. "That's my boy," only followed test scores or perfect table manners. Never a scraped knee. Never a panic attack. Never silence. Leo learned early that praise had a price, and affection came with conditions. He never stopped trying to pay it.

He thought back to the moments he had faked it. The smiles. The jokes. The loud bravado that filled rooms but never made him feel fuller. It was all a script. The "I'm fine" lines. The charm. The laugh that sounded right but felt wrong. No one had noticed the gap between what he said and what he meant. Or worse, they noticed and looked away. The grownups in his life didn't ask. The kids followed his lead. And he started to believe that love was earned. And if he wasn't earning it, he was invisible.

But everything changed when he met Jeremy. Jeremy didn't ask for proof. He didn't wait for Leo to perform. He just liked him. Sat next to him on purpose. Hugged him like it was normal. Said "I missed you" on Mondays like it wasn't strange. At first, Leo thought Jeremy was just soft-hearted. Then he realized Jeremy was teaching him something. That maybe love didn't need to be earned. Maybe it just was. Not loud. Not showy. Just there.

He remembered the first time Mrs. Firth hugged him after he'd spilled spaghetti all over the floor. He had braced for yelling. Instead, she knelt beside him, laughed softly, and said, "We'll clean it together. No big deal." Then she kissed the side of his head. No achievement. No performance. Just presence. That moment stayed in his chest like a warm ember.

He hadn't realized how badly he needed that kind of love until he saw what it looked like without strings. And now, he thought about Alex. The new boy. The one who smiled like he needed something. The one who cornered kids with compliments that made them owe him. Leo watched him and didn't feel hate. He felt something worse—recognition. The same sharp smiles. The same shifting tones. The same game of "be useful or be ignored." And he knew exactly what it meant: Alex hadn't heard it either.

Leo didn't excuse Alex's behaviour. He couldn't. But he understood it. The way Alex puffed up his chest to feel important. The way he punished silence with isolation. The way he held favours like weapons. It was all a cover for the same empty space Leo had once carried in his own chest. The space where "I love you" should have gone. The space where safety should have lived.

And Leo made a quiet decision. Not to fix Alex. But to never let another kid wonder what he had wondered. To never let someone feel like they had to earn kindness or chase approval. He couldn't go back in time and hold his younger self. But he could sit beside Jeremy, tell him he was loved every single day, and prove it with actions too. That was the letter he'd write backwards—one stitched in behaviour, not just words.

When he looked at Jeremy now, laughing over a joke that made no sense, Leo felt it. Not pity. Not guilt. Just clarity. "You never have to fake it for me," he said softly. Jeremy blinked, mid-chew. "Fake what?" "Anything," Leo said. "You're already enough." Jeremy grinned. "I know." And somehow, those two words wrapped around Leo's heart like a bandage. Because that's all he had needed to hear, once. Long ago. Before the pretending. Before the twisting. Before the mask. Love, Leo now understood, wasn't something to be begged for. It wasn't a goal. It wasn't a prize. It was a home. And now that he had one, he was going to build more. One word, one hug, one truth at a time.

Leo hadn't noticed it at first. Jeremy was always looking at him—wide-eyed, curious, bright—but this time was different. It was a Thursday afternoon, the light slanting just enough through the classroom window to draw lazy rectangles across the floor. Leo had just handed Jeremy the pencil case he'd dropped. Nothing heroic. Nothing big. But Jeremy looked at him like he'd just been handed the world. And not because of the pencil case. That wasn't it. Leo knew the look. It wasn't gratitude. It was something deeper. Something truer.

There was no flinch. No calculation. No weighing of what Leo might want in return. Jeremy just looked. Calm. Settled. Steady. Like Leo had always been this version of himself, not the one who once used kindness as currency or smiles as traps. That gaze held no history, only presence. And that's when it landed—really landed—that Leo had changed. Not just on the outside. Not just for show. But deeply, silently, completely.

He looked down at his own hands, remembering what they used to do—how they used to clench in his pockets when he was scheming, how they used to shove when words failed, how they used to manipulate the angles of a hallway to make someone feel boxed in. Those same hands now brushed crumbs off Jeremy's hoodie and fixed the strap on his backpack. Without effort. Without needing thanks. Leo didn't recognize his old self anymore—and that was good.

There was a time when Leo needed people to see him a certain way. Cool. In control. Untouchable. He built that mask with precision, using whatever he could: fake compliments, fake apologies, fake laughs. But Jeremy didn't need any of that. He didn't know that Leo. He only knew this one—the one who walked beside him, not ahead or behind. The one who listened more than he talked. The one who didn't need to win every conversation just to feel real.

Jeremy's eyes held him there. Not with pressure. With peace. And that kind of peace made Leo feel seen without being judged, and safe without being shielded. "You're not waiting for me to mess up," Leo whispered under his breath, as if Jeremy could hear his thoughts. Jeremy blinked and smiled. "Why would I do that?" he said aloud. Just like that. As if love was the easiest thing in the world to give.

Leo swallowed back the sting in his throat. Because it shouldn't have been a big deal. But it was. It was everything. That one moment told him more than any mirror ever could. Because even when he'd started acting better, he didn't know if he really was better. What if it was just another performance? What if he slipped? What if underneath it all, the old Leo was still crouching, waiting for a chance to come back?

But Jeremy didn't look like he saw a monster in hiding. He looked like he saw a brother. A safe person. A true one. And in Jeremy's eyes, Leo found something he hadn't expected—permission to believe it. Permission to stop bracing. Permission to live like this new version wasn't temporary or fake. It was permanent. Chosen. Real.

That afternoon, Leo walked slower than usual. On purpose. Letting Jeremy set the pace. He didn't feel the need to explain anything or perform for anyone. Ty gave him a quiet nod from across the yard—the kind that said, "Yeah, I saw that." Jasmin looked up from her book and smiled, no sarcasm. Ella waved. Sophie mouthed "Hi" like they were in on some small secret. And Leo waved back without shrinking, without puffing up. Just… being.

Later, as they sat at the kitchen table eating apple slices, Jeremy tapped Leo's arm. "You okay?" Leo nodded. "Yeah." He hesitated. Then added, "I just noticed something." Jeremy waited. Leo smiled, small but true. "You look at me like I'm already the person I want to be." Jeremy shrugged, crunching into an apple. "You are," he said through a mouthful. Leo looked down at his plate, heart steady. No panic. No lies. No noise. Just the echo of truth that had finally caught up with him: he didn't have to be afraid of who he used to be anymore. Because Jeremy wasn't afraid. And neither was he.

Leo ran his finger along the kitchen counter slowly, tracing circles in the crumbs from toast they'd eaten hours ago. Jeremy was still finishing his milk, legs swinging from the stool, humming softly to a song only he seemed to hear. Leo looked at him, then away. He felt the words building, rising up his throat like steam in a kettle. He hadn't said it out loud before—not this part, not this trick.

"You know what I used to do?" he asked, his voice low but clear. Jeremy looked up mid-hum, nodding with those wide, patient eyes. "I'd say something nice to someone—like, 'Hey, cool shoes' or 'You're really smart'—just to get them to say something back to me." Leo shrugged. "It worked most of the time. People love feeling seen. So they'd see me back." Jeremy blinked, brows scrunching slightly. "That's not a trick," he said slowly. "That's a trap." He didn't say it to be mean. He didn't even frown. He just looked… disappointed. Like someone who found out a favourite story was built on a lie.

Leo winced, not at the words, but at the truth they carried. A trap. That was exactly what it had been. A little kindness, wrapped in ribbon, delivered with a grin—and wired with expectations. If they didn't say something back, if they didn't return the praise, Leo would feel ripped off. Like they broke the deal he never told them they were making. He'd call them rude. Distant. Maybe even fake. But all along, it had been him setting the bait.

"I didn't even know I was doing it at first," Leo admitted. "It just felt like… survival. Like if people didn't think I was awesome, I'd disappear. Or worse—be ignored." He tapped his fingers. "It wasn't really about liking them. It was about needing them to like me." Jeremy's legs stopped swinging. He stared at his glass, then back at Leo. "But you like me," he said softly, almost as if he needed to double-check. "You don't say nice stuff just so I say it back, right?"

Leo shook his head. "No. Not with you. Never with you." And it was true. Something about Jeremy made all those old moves fall away. Leo didn't feel like he was performing around him. He didn't have to choreograph every smile or measure every word. Jeremy liked him without needing a script. That felt rare. Sacred, even.

"But how do I know?" Jeremy asked. "How does anyone know if someone's being real?" Leo thought about that. Really thought. "I guess it's when they say something kind... and then walk away. Like they don't need to hear anything back. They're okay if it ends with you feeling good." Jeremy nodded slowly. "That makes sense." Leo reached across the counter and tousled his brother's hair. "I didn't used to know that." He paused. "But now I do. And I'm not going back to that trap thing. Ever."

Jeremy grinned, milk moustache and all. "Good. Because your compliments are actually really good now." Leo chuckled. "Thanks. That one I'll take." They sat in silence for a bit, comfortable and full. Leo leaned back in his chair, staring at the ceiling. He used to watch every move someone made after he gave them a compliment. Did they blush? Did they smile? Did they return the favour? If they didn't, he'd feel robbed. That was the part no one ever told him about manipulation—it doesn't always feel like bullying. Sometimes it feels like desperation dressed up as charm.

"I remember this one time," Leo said suddenly, "I told a girl she had a nice voice. But I only said it because I wanted her to say I was funny. She didn't. So I started ignoring her. I thought I was punishing her. But really, I was punishing myself. Because I missed out on a good friend." Jeremy's face fell. "That's sad." "Yeah," Leo said. "It was."

He didn't need to do that anymore. Not with Jeremy. Not with Ty. Not with Jasmin or Ella or Sophie. The compliments he gave now weren't bait. They were gifts. With no receipts and no return policies. And for the first time, that felt more powerful than any trick he ever pulled.

The hugs Leo remembered were quiet bargains. You get one if you earn it. If you do well. If you don't make a fuss. They were short—quick enough to check the box but not long enough to mean it. They ended just when he needed them most, as if love had a timer. As if warmth had to be deserved first. No one ever said that out loud, but he felt it in the grip that never lingered and in the arms that vanished as soon as his usefulness did.

But Jeremy's hugs—those were a different species entirely. They arrived unannounced and refused to follow the rules. Leo didn't have to ace a test, win a game, or fake a smile to earn one. He could come home tired, upset, or not say a word, and Jeremy would wrap his little arms around him like he was holding a treasure, not a person. He squeezed tight—not too tight—and didn't let go until the pain leaked out through Leo's skin in a way words never could.

That day, Leo had walked home with his shoulders hunched. It wasn't anything dramatic—just one of those days when the air felt heavier than it should. Something about watching Alex mimic the way Leo used to manipulate others had curled a cold rope in his stomach. He hadn't spoken on the walk home. Jeremy noticed. Of course he did.

When they reached the porch, Jeremy slipped his backpack off and tilted his head. "You okay?" he asked, already knowing the answer. Leo gave a half-shrug, half-nod. "Just tired." Jeremy didn't ask more. He stepped forward and hugged him. Just like that. No instructions. No conditions. No waiting to be invited.

And as he squeezed, he said it. "I love you, Leo." Three words. Not loud, not whispered. Just steady. Real. Like bricks in a foundation Leo didn't know was being laid under his feet. Leo hadn't answered. Not at first. He'd just stood there, letting the hug happen. Letting it work. Jeremy didn't pull away, didn't glance at a clock, didn't let the moment expire like all the ones from the past had. The hug didn't ask him to smile, perform, or promise. It just held.

And Leo cracked. Not all the way. Not into pieces. But enough for a little of that tightness to melt. He bent slightly, his arms finally folding around Jeremy, his chin resting gently on his brother's crown. He closed his eyes. He didn't have to explain. He didn't have to ask. He was loved. And it didn't run out.

He wondered what life would've been like if he'd had that sooner—hugs that stayed. Words that didn't vanish. Love that didn't have a return policy. Maybe he wouldn't have needed to build walls. Maybe he wouldn't have hurt people just to make them stay. Jeremy tugged at his shirt a little. "I mean it," he said. "Even when you're grumpy." Leo smiled into his hair. "Even when I'm grumpy?"

"Especially then," Jeremy said. "That's when you need it more." Leo breathed in deep. "I love you too." Jeremy nodded against his chest. "I know." That was the part that really undid Leo—not the words themselves, but the fact that Jeremy knew. He didn't doubt it. He didn't need proof or performance. He just knew. And Leo, for once, didn't feel the need to convince anyone of anything. He was allowed to exist, exactly as he was, on a tired afternoon in September, and still be held like something precious.

That night, Leo wrote something in his notebook—something he wished he'd heard when he was eight. When he was the kid who chased love like it was always almost his. You are huggable even when you're messy. You are lovable even when you're not impressive. You are not a job interview. You are not a prize. You're a person. And someone will love you just for being real.

The cards were old and soft at the edges, bent from a thousand tiny fingers and maybe two thousand mistakes. Leo held them like glass, careful not to bend them more, even though he used to throw cards when the game didn't go his way. Jeremy sat across from him with a grin stretched wide enough to touch both ears, holding his cards with both hands like a magician about to pull off something amazing. Leo already knew the hand Jeremy had—he'd seen him clumsily peek, half-showing the Ace like a secret no one was supposed to know but everyone saw. And even though Leo held a straight flush, something cold and unbeatable, he folded without blinking. Not because he wanted to be kind. Because, for the first time, he just didn't need to win.

There was a time when losing made him feel like shrinking. When the silence after a loss echoed louder than any praise he'd ever gotten. Back then, he needed to be the smartest, the fastest, the loudest. He had to win because if he didn't, maybe he wouldn't matter anymore. It was like his entire self was built on a scoreboard, and every lost point chipped away a little more of who he was supposed to be. When he was younger, no one told him he was worth anything just for being. He had to do something—be useful, be funny, be impressive. If he wasn't first, then he may as well be invisible. That's what it felt like.

So he won. He made sure of it. He twisted rules without ever saying it out loud, made people laugh just before he struck with something sharper, and kept the spotlight like it was oxygen. And if someone else tried to shine, he dimmed them. He saw it now—not just as a kid who was once cruel, but as a kid who was scared to be unseen. A boy who thought being on top was the only way to not fall apart. Now, looking at Jeremy across the table, he saw something else. Not competition. Not threat. Not someone to beat. Just a brother. A light. A reason.

Jeremy slammed down his winning hand with a cheer so big it startled the family dog off the couch. "Yes! I win!" he said, throwing both fists in the air like a champion in a stadium. Leo smiled. Not the kind of smile that hides poison. A real one. The kind that lives behind your eyes. "You sure did," he said, voice calm, even proud. And he meant it. Every word. Every bit of it. He didn't want to take the win. He wanted to give it.

They played again, and again after that. Leo let Jeremy win every time, not because he thought Jeremy needed to win, but because it didn't matter to Leo anymore. He wasn't keeping score. He wasn't adding it to some secret tally in his head to prove he was better. He didn't need the win. The win was watching Jeremy glow. The win was hearing his laugh crack like a beam of sunlight through the ceiling. The win was quiet now. Gentle. A hug in a game of kings and jokers.

Once, Leo remembered teasing a girl for losing. Ella, maybe. Or Jasmin. He didn't remember the game, but he remembered the way they looked down after. The silence. The shame. He didn't call it bullying. He called it "just playing around." But it wasn't play. Not really. It was control. He could feel it now. He had shaped moments like a sculptor, carving other people down until he stood taller. That wasn't a win. That was fear wearing a crown.

Jeremy looked up after another win, this time squinting suspiciously. "Are you letting me win?" he asked, one eyebrow raised like an old detective in a kid's movie. Leo chuckled. "Maybe. But not because I think you can't. Because your smile is better than any trophy." Jeremy blinked twice and turned pink from the ears down. Then he grinned again and shouted, "Best outta five!" and dealt the cards with flair.

Leo watched him. He didn't need to say anything else. That moment didn't ask for more words. It was clean. Uncluttered. Like a floor swept after company leaves. He realised he used to live like every interaction was a game, and the other kids were pieces. Now they were people. Now he saw them. Not as threats. As mirrors. As sparks. As songs.

There were kids like Alex now—the ones who needed to win, no matter the cost. Leo understood them in a way he wished he didn't. He could see it from a hundred feet away. The hunger behind the grin. The way a hand stayed just a second too long on someone's shoulder, or the way "great job" was said like a sentence with an invisible string tied to it. Leo knew those tricks because they used to be his. But he didn't miss them.

He thought of what he'd say to himself a year ago, if he could send a whisper back through time. Maybe something like: "You don't need to be the best to be loved." Or maybe even better: "You're not playing against anyone. You never were." He wondered what his younger self would say back. Maybe laugh. Maybe roll his eyes. Maybe listen.

Jeremy flicked a card across the table, and it landed upside-down on Leo's lap. "Oops," he said with a giggle. Leo picked it up and turned it over—Queen of Hearts. He stared at it for a second longer than needed, then placed it down gently, like it meant something sacred. Maybe it did. That night, when they packed up the deck, Jeremy said, "Thanks for playing with me." Leo nodded. "Thanks for beating me." Jeremy paused, smiled slyly, and added, "I didn't just beat you. I crushed you." Leo laughed out loud, and it didn't sting. It warmed.

He used to think control was strength. That power was winning. That love had to be earned. But now he knew better. Love didn't demand a scoreboard. It didn't punish second place. And it didn't need tricks. Just time. Just truth. Just someone to sit across the table and let the game be the game—not a war, not a trap, not a mask. And the day Leo didn't want to win anymore was the day he realised he already had.

The cupboard snapped shut with the force of a windstorm, the sound cracking through the kitchen like a branch breaking in the woods. For a moment, the world held its breath. But Leo didn't. His shoulders stayed where they were, soft and low. His eyes didn't widen. His jaw didn't lock. His fists stayed loose at his sides. There was no storm rising behind his ribs. Just breath. Smooth and quiet. He blinked once and turned his head, watching Jeremy fumble with the cereal box and mutter, "Sorry, that was loud." Leo only nodded and whispered to himself, "That's how I know I've changed."

There was a time—not that long ago—when every sudden sound was a loaded question. When a slammed cupboard meant danger. When a shoe dropping upstairs could mean shouting, or worse. When the volume of a voice was a weapon and silence was a punishment. Back then, Leo flinched at everything. Not always on the outside, but deep inside where nobody could see. It was a kind of invisible jump, a twitch behind the ribs, a drop in the gut like a roller coaster that never stopped. And it came from knowing that loudness meant control.

He'd once spilled a cup in the kitchen. Just water. But the sound of it falling had echoed like thunder. His father had turned with eyes like drills and a voice sharp enough to split wood. Leo had said sorry before he'd even taken a breath. That's how trained he was—how automatic the fear became. It wasn't the cupboard or the glass or the water. It was the reaction. It was always the reaction. That's what taught him to flinch. That's what taught him to brace.

He remembered Jasmin once whispering that she hated loud noises, too. That they reminded her of things she couldn't quite name. And Nico, who always turned his head just a little when a locker slammed shut. These weren't weaknesses. These were memories that stuck to the skin like burrs in a field. And they stayed until something—someone—taught you how to take them off without bleeding.

But now, this day, this moment in the kitchen, Leo didn't flinch. Not because he forced himself not to. Not because he was being brave or pretending. He just didn't. His body didn't fire the alarm. His mind didn't light up with warnings. The fear had uncurled, like a leaf finally trusting the sun. And it was because of one thing. One person. Jeremy.

Jeremy didn't raise his voice when frustrated. He didn't stomp when upset. He didn't make noise to feel big. If he slammed a cupboard, it was truly by accident, not performance. And more importantly, when he made a mistake, he didn't hide behind laughter or pretend it was someone else's fault. He just looked Leo in the eye and said sorry. Not to make Leo feel bad. Not to draw attention. Just because he meant it.

Leo found himself watching Jeremy's back as he poured cereal, the sleeves of his hoodie pushed up, a streak of milk already drying on the counter. It was so ordinary. So quiet. So... safe. And that, more than any apology or therapy or apology book or behaviour plan, was what changed Leo's reflexes. Safety did that. Time did that. Love did that.

He had a moment—a flash memory—of slamming his own locker last year, just to make someone jump. He'd laughed. He'd called it a joke. But it wasn't. It was control. It was dominance through sound. He hated that memory now. It made his stomach knot. But he didn't push it away. He just let it pass, like a wave he no longer needed to surf.

Jeremy looked up then, eyes curious. "You okay?" he asked. Leo nodded. "Yeah. I didn't jump." Jeremy squinted, not understanding. "At the cupboard," Leo clarified. "I didn't flinch." Jeremy smiled small, like it meant something sacred. Maybe it did. Maybe it was a bigger win than any card game or basketball score or essay grade. Maybe peace was measured in seconds of stillness.

Leo walked over and helped put the cereal box back in the cupboard. Slowly. Quietly. No slams. No fear. Just the click of the latch closing like a whisper. Jeremy grabbed a spoon and said, "You wanna sit with me?" And Leo said yes without thinking, because that's who he was now—someone who sat, not stormed. Someone who breathed, not broke.

He thought of what he'd say to his younger self again. Maybe just this: "It won't always feel this loud inside." Maybe that would be enough. Maybe that younger version of himself would hear it and believe him. Maybe not. But it would've been a start.

As they sat together, Leo let his hand rest on the table, palm open, not clenched. And when Jeremy laughed with cereal in his mouth, it didn't make Leo jump. It made him laugh, too. And that, more than anything, told him who he was becoming. He didn't flinch anymore. And that meant he was finally safe—even inside himself.

Jeremy sat on the bottom step, fiddling with the frayed edge of his sock, while Leo leaned against the wall across from him, arms loosely crossed, the light from the hallway spilling gold across both their knees. The house was quiet in the best kind of way—safe, settled, with no shouts hiding around corners. Jeremy tilted his head, curious but gentle, and asked, "What was the hardest word for you?" Leo didn't answer right away. He knew the answer. Had known it for months. But saying it aloud made it real. And real had once meant danger.

He let the quiet stretch between them, like the pause before jumping into a cold pool. Finally, he said, "Sorry." He didn't whisper it. Didn't choke on it. Just said it, plain and solid. But still, the word landed with a weight that pressed on his ribs. Jeremy blinked, confused for half a second, then nodded. "Because you didn't mean it?" he asked. Leo shook his head. "No. Because I did." And that was the first time he'd ever admitted it out loud—not just to someone else, but to himself.

It hadn't been that Leo didn't want to say sorry. It was that sorry meant stepping out from the armour. Meant standing there without the shield of a joke or the smirk of a fake win. It meant being seen, completely, without defence. And when you grew up in a house where being seen got you punished, sorry wasn't a word—it was a target. It was a confession that might be twisted. Or used. Or ignored. So he'd learned not to say it. Not really. He'd fake it when needed, sure. He'd toss out a "my bad" or a "whatever" if it got him what he wanted. But a real sorry? That was rare. Almost extinct.

He could remember the first time he truly wanted to say it. It was the day he made Nico cry in the hallway. Called him clingy. Loud enough for others to hear. It had been easy to brush off in the moment, to walk away like nothing mattered. But later that night, in his room, Leo had felt it like a bruise on his heart. He'd opened his mouth to whisper, "I'm sorry," just to the air. But the words caught like thorns in his throat. His tongue had frozen. His chest tightened. The room had stayed silent.

And now, sitting across from a little brother who had never once made him feel unsafe, Leo could finally say the word without bracing for the strike that never came. "It made me feel naked," he added. "Back then, if I said sorry, I thought it'd make me weak." Jeremy's brows knotted, thoughtful in the way only he could be. "But now it makes you strong?" he asked. Leo shrugged, but there was something steady in the way he lifted his head. "Now it makes me real."

Jeremy kicked his feet out in front of him, tapping the stair with his heel. "I say sorry a lot," he said, not sad, not proud. Just a truth. "Sometimes even when I didn't do anything wrong." Leo's chest ached. "I used to make people do that," he said, voice rough. "Make them feel like everything was their fault. That's how I kept control." And there it was again—the truth. Heavy, but cleaner than a lie. It didn't stink like guilt anymore. It just sat beside him, quiet and honest.

Leo tilted his head back and looked at the ceiling. "I think I was afraid that if I said sorry, people would see the cracks. And then they'd leave." He paused. "But you didn't." Jeremy stood, walked over, and sat beside Leo on the floor, leaning against him like a cat curling into its warmest spot. "You didn't leave either," Jeremy whispered. "Even when you saw my cracks." Leo's hand found the back of Jeremy's head, fingers settling in the softness of his hair.

He thought back to the day he'd first said sorry and meant it—to Jasmin, after telling a lie about her to the others. She hadn't smiled when he said it. She'd just nodded, tight-lipped, like she wasn't ready to believe it yet. But he'd meant it. Every syllable. And it had taken everything in him not to crumble under the shame of it. But afterward, something inside him had settled. Like a bone finally clicking back into place.

"Sorry isn't just a word," Leo said now, more to himself than to Jeremy. "It's a bridge. And I used to burn every one." Jeremy reached for Leo's hand and squeezed it. "You build them now," he said. "Even little ones. Every day." Leo smiled. Not a smug one. Not a fake one. Just real. And it felt like breathing after a long swim.

The hallway light hummed, the kind of quiet that only homes with love inside ever earn. Jeremy stood again, tugging Leo's hand. "Let's go make popcorn," he said. "But if I burn it again, I'm not saying sorry this time." Leo laughed. "Deal," he replied, standing up with him, knees cracking. "But if I drop the bowl, I will." And he meant it.

He followed Jeremy into the kitchen, watching the way the younger boy moved—confident in the way only kids who feel safe can be. And Leo knew, deep in his chest, that he would never again use silence as a weapon. Never again make someone afraid of a simple word. Because now he had one more tool in his heart. One more truth in his hands. And he would say it. Freely. Truthfully. Whenever it mattered. Sorry. Because now, it wasn't a weakness. It was a beginning.

Leo stood in front of the bathroom mirror, not to fix his hair or straighten his shirt, but to look. Really look. Not at his face, but at the eyes staring back—eyes that used to flicker with calculation, with the scramble to be liked or feared or both. Now, they looked steadier. Not softer, not colder. Just real. And real was new. "I'll never do it again," he said quietly, not to the reflection, but to the person he used to be. "Not ever again." The words weren't dramatic. They were just true.

He used to confuse cruelty with cleverness. If someone cried, it meant he had control. If someone apologized first, it meant he'd won. But now, just thinking about it made his stomach turn. He pressed his palms flat on the counter, leaned in, and whispered, "I used to think being kind made you weak. I used to think scared people were pathetic." He didn't blink. "That was a lie. And I was the one telling it."

It had taken months—months of watching Jeremy, of listening to Ty, of seeing Jasmin hold her ground without ever raising her voice—to understand what real strength looked like. It didn't shove. It didn't corner. It didn't gaslight someone until they forgot their own name. Real strength stood still, even when it shook. Real strength said, "That hurt me," without hurting back. Real strength never needed to prove itself.

Leo walked down the hall, bare feet quiet on the hardwood, and found Jeremy curled in the blanket fort they'd made two days ago and never quite took down. Jeremy looked up with a half-smile. "You thinking again?" he asked. Leo grinned. "Always." He knelt beside the blanket doorway and pushed a cushion aside. "Can I come in?" Jeremy nodded and scooted over.

They sat in the soft hush of the fort—pillows around them, flashlight casting shadows on the fabric roof. "Wanna know something I'll never do again?" Leo asked. Jeremy raised his eyebrows. "Eat your vegetables?" Leo chuckled. "Well, probably that too. But something bigger." Jeremy tilted his head, curious. "I'll never call someone weak for being kind," Leo said. "Not ever."

Jeremy's eyes narrowed, not in judgment, but in thought. "Why did you used to?" he asked. Leo sighed. "Because I was scared. Scared that if someone was kind and still strong, I wouldn't know who I was anymore." He picked at the edge of a thread in the blanket. "So I'd say they were soft. Or scared. Or fake. Just to make myself feel like I wasn't the weak one."

Jeremy nodded slowly. "That's kind of like gaslighting, isn't it?" Leo blinked. Jeremy knew the word. Knew it well. "Yeah," Leo admitted. "Exactly like it. I'd make people doubt what they felt, so they'd look to me for the truth. It was the ugliest trick I ever learned." He didn't try to dress it up. Not with Jeremy. Not anymore.

The flashlight flickered slightly, and Leo leaned over to twist the cap, tightening it. "You know what else I'll never do again?" he asked, not waiting for Jeremy to guess. "I'll never make someone feel small just to feel bigger." He let the words hang there, solid as bricks. "Because when I did that, I wasn't strong. I was empty."

Jeremy shifted closer and leaned his head against Leo's arm. "I'm glad you stopped." Just like that. No lecture. No sermon. Just the truth. Leo felt it like a warm patch on a wound he didn't know was still healing. "Me too," he whispered.

They sat in silence for a while, the good kind, the kind that didn't need to be filled. Then Jeremy asked, "Do you think Alex will stop?" Leo exhaled slowly. "I hope so. But I don't know. Not everyone gets a second chance the way I did." He reached over and nudged Jeremy's knee. "But if he ever asks, I'll be honest. I'll tell him what I used to do. And I'll tell him what I'll never do again."

Jeremy smiled, quiet and proud. "That's like being a Shadow Warrior, right? Saying the truth even if it's hard?" Leo nodded. "Exactly. And protecting people by being better—not louder." They bumped shoulders. It felt like a handshake between hearts.

Later that night, when the fort was empty and the stars stretched quietly across the sky, Leo wrote the words down in his notebook. Not to forget them, but to promise them. I'll never call kindness weak. I'll never gaslight again. I'll never hide my hurt behind someone else's. I'll be strong the right way. He folded the page and tucked it into the spine of the book—his own truth, pressed into paper, held there by the boy he used to be and the brother who'd taught him better.

Leo remembered how loud his voice used to get when he felt small inside. It wasn't just yelling. It was the way he filled space on purpose—cutting people off mid-sentence, interrupting with facts, shouting over someone else's emotions just so he didn't have to listen to his own. In those moments, his voice felt like a shield, thick and unbreakable. But what he never admitted, not even to himself, was that it was also a mask. The louder he got, the more frightened he really was.

Back then, silence terrified him. It gave too much space to be questioned. If someone paused, they might see him for what he truly was: unsure, angry, and aching for approval. So he filled every second with sound. Words layered over words, jokes twisted into jabs, facts stacked like bricks—anything to sound like he was winning. It took him a long time to see the difference between noise and strength. Even longer to realise the loudest person wasn't always the one telling the truth.

He remembered one day in class—before everything changed—when Ella tried to explain how Leo's words hurt her. She spoke quietly, almost nervously, but with so much honesty that it made the room feel warmer. And Leo had laughed. Not because it was funny. But because laughter had always drowned out shame. The memory made him sick now. Not because she'd called him out. But because he'd made her feel small for being brave enough to whisper what he should've been shouting all along: I'm hurting.

Now, sitting on the porch with Jeremy nestled under his arm, Leo stayed quiet. Not because he didn't have something to say, but because Jeremy was talking. And listening, really listening, was harder than it used to be. Harder, but better. "When I get nervous," Jeremy said, kicking his feet, "sometimes I talk really fast so no one sees it." Leo smiled and nodded. "I used to do that too. But I did it louder." He looked out at the yard, sunlit and honest. "I thought if I sounded sure, I wouldn't feel scared."

Jeremy turned toward him. "But that didn't work?" Leo shook his head. "Not even once." He ran a hand through his hair. "You can shout a lie a hundred times, but it still won't make it true. And the people who really love you? They hear what's underneath anyway." Jeremy looked thoughtful, like he was folding Leo's words into a pocket he'd keep them in for later. That made Leo proud in a way he couldn't explain.

At school, he saw it happen again. Alex—sharp, smug, always one sentence away from a fight—was shouting at Ty about something small. A game. A pencil. Something that didn't even matter. But Ty didn't shout back. He stood still, calm as stone. Then, in a voice so soft it made everyone lean in, Ty said, "I'm not here to fight with you, Alex. I'm just here to learn." The silence that followed hit harder than anything Leo had ever thrown. Alex blinked. The moment cracked. And Leo knew—Ty had won.

That's when Leo wrote it in his journal. Quiet doesn't mean weak. It means measured. Loud doesn't mean strong. It just means scared. And he meant every word. Because now he saw it clearly: his loudest days were his most frightened ones. The times he yelled were the moments he was drowning. The louder he was, the less he was being heard. It was like trying to play music with a hammer. You'd make noise. But not meaning.

He shared that with Jeremy one night, curled up on the couch beneath a blanket. "Being loud felt like power," he said, "but it wasn't. It was panic with a microphone." Jeremy looked up. "So what's power really feel like?" Leo paused, then said, "Like this. Sitting still. Letting you speak. And not needing to win." Jeremy nodded, and Leo noticed something in his eyes—trust that had nothing to do with volume and everything to do with presence.

Leo started practising it on purpose. When a classmate interrupted him, he let the silence fill the space before speaking again. When someone else made a point he disagreed with, he didn't jump in right away. He waited. And in the waiting, he saw things more clearly. Heard more honestly. And he felt… calmer. Not in control like before. Just whole. And that was a kind of power he didn't know he could have.

He watched others cling to noise like it was armour. He recognised it now—not as strength, but as a desperate plea. He could almost feel their fear hidden beneath every loud denial, every over-the-top boast. And instead of mocking it like he used to, he felt something surprising: compassion. "I used to be that loud," he would think. "I know that echo. I know how hollow it is."

At home, when Jeremy slammed a door by mistake, Leo didn't bark a command to be careful. He didn't shout. He didn't even sigh. He just walked over, helped him with the groceries he'd dropped, and whispered, "You okay?" Jeremy nodded, and that was that. No storm. No performance. Just two brothers in a kitchen, trusting each other not to make things worse.

He used to think people who whispered didn't matter. That they were background noise in a world run by shouting. But now he knew—it's the quiet voices you have to listen hardest for. Because they're the ones telling the truth. They're the ones carrying it like a candle through a hurricane. And that takes more strength than yelling ever could.

He wrote a letter to his younger self that night. You don't need to be the loudest. You just need to be honest. That's where real power lives. Not in shouting—but in standing still, and meaning every word. He folded it gently and placed it in the same journal he always used, the one with the frayed edge and the truth tucked into every page. And as he turned out the light, Leo didn't fear being misunderstood anymore. He didn't fear being ignored. Because he finally understood that when the truth is real, it doesn't need to be shouted. It just needs to be lived.

Leo used to count how many people laughed at his jokes. He could list names by heart—those who smiled when he passed, those who waved first, those who texted back fast. He thought it mattered. That being liked was the same as being safe. The more attention he got, the more real he felt. But underneath that craving was a silence he could never outrun. The silence that asked, What happens when they stop liking you?

Every morning back then, he'd plan who to charm, who to tease just enough, who to compliment in a way that sounded natural but wasn't. It was a game. But it cost more than it paid. If someone didn't laugh, he'd feel it like a bruise. If someone ignored him, he'd obsess for hours. A single shrug from a classmate could ruin his day. Because back then, being liked meant he was winning. And being disliked meant something inside him was broken.

The truth broke open slowly. It started the day Jeremy handed him a drawing—a messy, colourful, crooked drawing of the two of them. Leo looked at it and asked, "Why'd you draw this?" Jeremy shrugged. "Just 'cause. I like you." No performance. No trade. Just a statement that settled into Leo's bones like something sacred. It was the first time he felt what it meant to be loved for real. Not for doing. Just for being.

That night, Leo stared at the drawing. It didn't matter that the eyes were too big, or that he had three fingers instead of five. It mattered that it came from truth. That Jeremy wasn't trying to earn anything. That he had simply wanted to give. It was the first time Leo felt chosen without trying. The hunger for attention didn't vanish all at once—but it started to starve. And that silence in his chest became a little softer.

He began to see it all differently. At school, he watched kids bend themselves backwards to stay in the good books of whoever was loudest. He saw compliments traded like currency. Secrets passed to stay in circles. He knew the dance. He had choreographed half of it. But now it looked different. Now it looked exhausting. And fake. He wanted no part in it anymore.

Jeremy asked him once, while they were building a puzzle at home, "Do you want everyone to like you?" Leo paused. Then answered carefully. "I used to. I thought if everyone liked me, then maybe I'd like me too." Jeremy blinked. "That's not how it works." And somehow, in that moment, Leo knew he was right. He laughed—not to be liked, but because the truth felt light for once.

He used to take surveys in his head. Did she laugh? Did he text back? Did they talk about me? Did I matter today? It was constant. He shaped himself into what he thought others wanted. Smarter, funnier, tougher, louder. Whatever got him another smile. But all it did was bury him deeper. Until there was nothing left but the shell of a boy who couldn't rest unless someone else approved first.

He told Nico one day, during a lunch break under the oak tree, "I think I was addicted to being liked." Nico didn't laugh. Didn't tease. He just nodded and said, "Yeah. That's how they trap us." Leo looked puzzled. "Who?" Nico tapped his chest. "The people who smile with rules behind their teeth. The ones who only like you when you act a certain way." Leo swallowed. That used to be him.

Now, he liked quiet rooms. Ones where he didn't have to perform. Where he could just be. Like the living room at home, when Jeremy's reading beside him. Or the walk to school, when no one's talking but everything's being said. Or Ty's backyard, where sometimes they just kick a ball and breathe. These were the places where truth lived. Places where being liked didn't matter. Because being loved already happened.

He saw it again when Alex made a joke in class that turned mean. Everyone laughed but Jeremy. Jeremy didn't even blink. He just said, "That wasn't kind," and kept colouring. Alex tried to recover. Tried to rope him in with a smirk. But Jeremy didn't budge. Leo watched, stunned. That kind of courage—saying no to someone loud—it was power. And it came from knowing you didn't need to be liked by people who weren't kind.

Leo thought about the kids who still chased that feeling. Who twisted themselves into smaller shapes to fit into bigger crowds. He wanted to tell them what he learned the hard way. That being liked is like standing in sunlight that someone else controls. The second you stop dancing, they flip the switch. But being loved? That's like carrying the sun in your chest. And no one can take it from you.

He shared that with Jeremy one evening as they brushed their teeth. "You don't need everyone to like you," he said, spitting out foam. "You just need a few to love you the real way." Jeremy wiped his chin. "I know. I already got you." Leo smiled. The real kind. The kind that didn't need applause. The kind that lived behind his ribs and didn't ask for more.

Later that night, Leo wrote another letter in his journal. Dear younger me: You thought you needed to be liked to survive. But what you really needed was to be loved—by people who saw you when you weren't performing. Who stayed even when you were quiet. Who forgave when you were clumsy. Who hugged you long enough to remember. He underlined that last word. Remember.

And then he tucked the drawing Jeremy made into the back of his notebook. Not because he needed proof. But because it reminded him how far he'd come. From a boy who begged for attention to a young man who knew his worth. Not because he was liked. But because he was loved.

Leo used to lie still with his eyes closed, pretending. Not because he was tired. Not because he was ready for dreams. But because it was the only way to disappear. At home, sleep wasn't safety. It was survival. The quieter he was, the longer he might go unnoticed. The slower he breathed, the fewer questions he'd be asked. There were nights when the shouting downstairs twisted into footsteps upstairs, and every creak in the floorboards meant, Be still. Be nothing. Don't be seen. He learned to mimic peace long before he ever felt it.

He remembered clenching his hands under the pillow. Not from cold. From fear. There were times he wasn't sure what he'd done wrong—only that a wrongness hung in the air, waiting to catch him with its claws. Being in bed meant bracing for it. He used to fold himself small, as though shrinking might make him harder to yell at. His heart would race even as his face stayed blank. "Just act asleep," he'd whisper inside his mind. "Just act."

In those days, pillows weren't soft. They were shields. Blankets weren't warm. They were camouflage. The bedroom light meant danger, because if it flicked on, it meant he was about to be seen, and being seen was never safe. He mastered stillness before he ever learned rest. Real sleep, the kind that melts you, the kind that forgives your body for being tired—it wasn't something he knew existed. Not until the Firth house.

The first night with them, he tried the old habit. Lay still. Waited for footsteps. Measured the silence. But all he heard was Jeremy breathing in the room next door. That and the soft hum of wind against the windowpane. He counted the seconds. Five minutes. Ten. Twenty. No shouting. No doors slamming. No dread sneaking up his spine. Just the low tick of the hallway clock. And something else—his own breath slowing.

He didn't sleep that night. But he didn't pretend either. It was something in between. A limbo of waiting. Waiting to see if this was a trick. If this family's warmth was only on the outside. But morning came. No one slammed open his door. No one interrogated him. No one asked why he didn't say goodnight loud enough. There was just sunlight. And the smell of toast. And Jeremy peeking in with bedhead and a smile.

It wasn't until the third night that Leo drifted. For real. He didn't plan it. Didn't even notice it happening. One minute he was staring at the ceiling, the next he was waking up with a blanket tucked around him, and his arm around a stuffed bear that wasn't even his. He blinked, confused. Did I fall asleep? Did I… feel safe? The answer hung in the warmth of his chest. Not loud. Just steady.

He told no one for days. Not because it wasn't important. But because he didn't have words for it yet. How do you explain to someone that sleep used to feel like danger? That silence used to mean a storm was coming? But Jeremy noticed. Of course he did. One night, he climbed into Leo's bed with a book and said, "You don't curl up anymore." Leo looked at him, confused. Jeremy clarified, "You sleep stretched out now. That's how I know you feel safe."

Leo didn't answer. But his throat tightened in a way that said more than words. It was strange—this feeling of not needing to hide in his own skin. He started doing little things: leaving his door cracked open, asking for another pillow, laughing before bed. These weren't just habits. They were declarations. Of healing. Of reclaiming space. Of saying, I belong here. I can rest here.

He began dreaming again. Real dreams. Not nightmares wrapped in shouting. Dreams of the schoolyard. Of puzzles on the kitchen table. Of Jeremy chasing him through the grass while their new dad grilled burgers. Leo would wake up smiling, not startled. And when he told Jeremy about the dreams, the little brother would grin and say, "Told you this house was magic." Leo didn't correct him. Maybe it was.

One afternoon, Ty came over and asked how Leo was doing. Just casually, over a game of chess. Leo looked at him and said, "I sleep now." Ty tilted his head. "Like nap-nap sleep?" Leo nodded. "No pretending. No flinching. Just sleep." Ty didn't need more explanation. He leaned back and smiled like someone who'd just seen something sacred happen. Because it had.

The biggest shift came the night Leo fell asleep without even realizing he'd gotten into bed. He'd helped Jeremy with homework, folded some laundry, then sat on his mattress with a book. Next thing he knew, the sun was back. The clock read 6:03. And he was still in yesterday's clothes. No teeth brushed. No final thoughts spiralling. Just sleep. Deep. Forgiving. Real.

That was the morning he looked in the mirror and said it out loud: "I'm safe here." No one had to say it to him first. No one had to prove it with bribes or gifts or smiles that weren't real. He just knew. And knowing changed everything. Even the way he walked into school. Even the way he blinked when someone called his name.

He used to carry sleep deprivation like a badge of honour. Now he carried rest like a quiet weapon. Not to hurt. To protect. Because when you're rested, your heart has time to tell the truth. When you're safe, your muscles stop bracing. And when you're home, even sleep becomes a kind of prayer. Not one you say out loud. Just one your body answers when the world finally stops spinning.

Leo told Jeremy a few weeks later, as they lay side by side in a tent in the backyard, "I used to fake sleep every night. Thought if I pretended hard enough, no one would hurt me." Jeremy stared up at the stars and said, "You don't have to pretend anymore." Leo reached for his hand and squeezed it once. "I know." And that night, with crickets humming and grass beneath them, Leo closed his eyes—not because he had to. But because he could.

Leo sat with his knees pulled to his chest, a pencil shaking between his fingers and a blank page staring back at him like it wanted to know everything at once. He didn't start with "Dear me." That felt fake. Like talking to a ghost he hadn't forgiven yet. Instead, he just started writing. His hand moved before he gave it permission. His first sentence read, You're not bad. It landed on the page like a whisper he'd waited years to hear. He looked at it for a long time before the next words came.

You're not broken. You're scared. And that's not your fault. The kid he used to be would never have believed those words. That kid would've laughed, sneered, maybe even torn the letter in half and claimed it didn't matter. But it would have mattered. It would have mattered so much it would've hurt. And that's why Leo kept writing.

You survive. He pressed hard into the pencil at that point. The lead scratched louder. His teeth clenched. He remembered the walls of his old bedroom, the yelling, the nights he faked sleep with one ear open. And it gets good. He paused there, afraid to even believe his own sentence. Then something inside him shifted. Something that once stayed hidden under sarcasm and smirks and half-truths finally breathed.

Leo thought about what changed him. Not just time. Not just growing up. But people. Names. Faces. Ty. Nico. Jasmin. Ella. Sophie. Even Mr. Clarke, who always knew when something wasn't right. And Jeremy. Especially Jeremy. That boy's love was like water in the desert. It didn't demand. It didn't shrink. It just existed, every single day.

He kept writing. One day you'll cry in front of them. All of them. And they won't laugh. They won't roll their eyes. They won't ask you to explain. They'll listen. Then they'll hold you. And you'll know, for the first time, that you're not disgusting. That your tears are human, not weak. Leo stopped again. Not from fear. From gratitude.

He remembered the day. It was just before the second week of September ended. The afternoon light spilled through the classroom like melted gold, and Nico had made a joke that cracked him open without warning. He laughed too hard. Then the laughter turned into tears. Real ones. No script. No performance. Just everything falling loose at once.

Jasmin had leaned across the desk, her arms circling him fast. Ty rubbed his shoulder like brothers do. Ella whispered, "It's okay, Leo. You're okay." And Nico, who never usually said the heavy things, said it this time: "We love you, man. For real." Leo sobbed harder. Not because he felt alone. Because he didn't. And that feeling was bigger than anything he'd ever handled before.

He didn't think. He just said it. "I love you all. So much." It came out cracked. Wet. Honest. Like something pure breaking free after years in a box. And they believed him. They didn't doubt or pause or joke it off. They knew. And he saw it in their eyes that they'd always known. They were just waiting for him to be ready to say it.

The letter trembled in his lap. He wasn't writing anymore. He was holding the pencil and staring out the window where Jeremy was helping rake leaves into a pile almost as tall as him. He felt the lump rise in his throat again. Not the old lump. Not the one from guilt or fear or the need to control. This one was soft. Clean. Like truth.

He went back to the letter. You'll stop pretending someday. You'll stop twisting words. You'll stop chasing the next win. And in its place, you'll find a quiet you never thought existed. You'll sleep through the night. You'll let yourself lose. You'll mean it when you say sorry. And when someone hugs you, you'll believe they mean it too.

Leo signed it without thinking. Just his name. No flourish. No initials. Just "Leo," like a boy finally learning to live in the skin of his own name. He folded the paper once, then twice, then slipped it into the small memory box his new mom had given him for personal things. It felt right there. Not hidden. Not displayed. Just kept.

Later that night, he told Jeremy he'd written something important. Jeremy didn't ask to read it. He just asked, "Was it to someone you love?" Leo smiled. "Kind of. It was to someone I've learned to love." Jeremy blinked with his too-big eyes and said, "I'm glad you love you now. I always did." Leo felt the tears coming again, but this time, they didn't need to be explained.

He didn't cry like before. It wasn't breaking anymore. It was mending. He cried with his whole heart this time—because it was whole. He told Jeremy thank you. And Jeremy said, "You're welcome. But you did the work." Leo said, "You made it possible." And neither of them was wrong.

The next day, Leo walked into school with his letter in his pocket. He didn't plan on sharing it. But knowing it was there mattered. A map from who he was to who he is. A bridge. A mirror. A promise. He bumped into Nico at the lockers. Nico raised a brow and said, "What's that look on your face?" Leo replied, "Peace." Nico nodded. "Good look." And that was the end of it. Or the beginning.

Jeremy found it by accident. Or maybe not. It was folded neatly and left on his pillow, not hidden, not left out carelessly. There were no names on the outside. No stickers. Just a fold that said someone meant for it to be found—not by the world, but by one person. And today, that person was Jeremy. He picked it up gently, turning it over once in his hand. The hallway was quiet. Leo's door was cracked open, but he wasn't in bed. Jeremy cleared his throat, perched on the side of his mattress, and began to read.

To the kid I used to be,

You're not bad. I know you think you are. I know you feel like the mess no one wants to clean up. But that's not true. You're just scared. You were made scared. Not by choice. You were pushed into fear like a shirt too tight for your own skin. And no one helped you breathe.

You are not the things you did to survive. You are not the words you used to stay in control. You are not the silence you forced on other people just so you wouldn't feel smaller than them. You did those things because you thought power would make the fear go away. But fear doesn't listen to loud. Fear listens to love.

You wanted someone to choose you without testing you. To love you without making you earn it. You didn't need a perfect version of yourself to be loved. You needed someone to see the mess and stay anyway. And guess what? They did. They showed up. They stayed.

You survived nights when you didn't sleep because the house felt full of eyes. You survived mornings where you were already sorry before you opened your mouth. You survived words that hit harder than fists. You survived pretending it didn't hurt. That's enough. You don't owe anyone more proof.

You tried to control people because you didn't believe anyone would stay if you didn't. You lied because you thought honesty was dangerous. You gaslighted because you were scared to admit you were wrong. I see it now. And I forgive you. That doesn't mean it was okay. It means I'm healing.

One day, you'll find people who don't flinch when you're honest. Who don't run when you cry. Who don't make you choose between being loved and being real. They'll just love you. Even when you're quiet. Even when you mess up. Especially then.

You'll have a brother who doesn't keep score. You'll have friends who remember your smile and not your worst day. You'll wake up in a house where you're not scared of your own name. You'll stop walking like you're in someone else's shadow.

You'll say 'sorry' and mean it. You'll hear 'I love you' and believe it. You'll lose arguments and still feel whole. You'll stop needing to be the loudest in the room to feel like you belong there. And someday, you'll write a letter like this, not because someone asked you to—but because someone out there still needs it.

And maybe that someone is you. Still. Even now. That's okay too.

So let me say this again, and this time, try to believe it:

You're not bad. You're not broken. You're not unlovable. You're healing.

And healing doesn't look perfect. It looks like crying when someone hugs you and not pulling away. It looks like choosing kindness when you're mad. It looks like asking for help without choking on shame. It looks like love. Real love. The kind that stays.

I'm proud of you. I'm proud of us. We made it.

Love,
Leo.

Jeremy blinked slowly. He didn't read it like a whisper. He didn't rush the lines or fumble the sentences. He gave every word weight. When he reached the end, he didn't fold the letter right away. He held it against his chest and breathed. In and out. Once. Then again. The hallway behind him stayed still.

Leo stood there, frozen by the weight of his own heart. His arms were crossed like he wasn't sure whether to step in or walk away. But Jeremy looked up, right on cue, and smiled like he'd been waiting to meet that letter his whole life. "I didn't know paper could cry," he said. "But I think this one did."

Leo chuckled through a breath that didn't quite finish. "It's been crying a long time," he said, finally stepping into the room. "It just needed someone kind to read it." Jeremy patted the bed beside him, and Leo sat without hesitation. They didn't hug right away. They didn't need to. They just sat.

Jeremy looked at him sideways. "Do you still hear the kid in your head sometimes?" Leo nodded. "Yeah. But now I talk back." Jeremy smiled. "Tell him I like him." Leo reached over and ruffled Jeremy's hair. "He likes you too." No more words were needed. The letter stayed unfolded on the pillow, like a bridge between what was and what is. Leo didn't reach for it. He let it rest. Just like himself.

CHAPTER 16: TRUE HAPPINESS VS. FALSE HAPPINESS

The balloons were blue and silver, bobbing in little clusters over every table. Kids wore paper crowns and rubbed icing on their faces while shouting over the music. Jeremy clung to his cupcake, licking the icing first, then slowly picking the bottom apart. Leo stood behind him most of the time, watching from the wall like a shadow that didn't quite belong in all the spinning lights. At ten years old, Jeremy hadn't asked for the party. It was for someone else in his class—a boy named Caleb who only liked Leo when others were watching. Leo whispered that truth once under his breath, when no one could hear. "He's nice when it's loud," he'd said. "That's not the same as being real."

Jeremy laughed a few times during the party. He played a round of musical chairs and won, then lost, then didn't care. Someone handed him a bag of candy and a toy whistle. The noise hurt his ears, so he held the whistle instead of blowing it. When the cake came out, Jeremy didn't make a wish. Leo noticed. "You didn't wish," he said. Jeremy shrugged. "Didn't need to. It's not my birthday." But something in his voice wilted, like a flower that had been stepped on by accident. Leo leaned in closer but didn't ask again.

They walked home together while the sky changed colours. Jeremy still held the whistle. He hadn't said much. His steps dragged behind Leo's. At the corner of the park, Leo finally asked, "Was it fun?" Jeremy looked up, blinking. "I guess," he said. "I liked the cake. And I liked the lights." He paused. "But I feel tired. Not sleep tired. Just… all empty inside." Leo didn't answer right away. He took Jeremy's hand and squeezed it gently. "That's called too much at once," he said. "Sometimes fun stuff isn't joy. It just keeps your brain too busy to notice."

Jeremy didn't argue. He trusted Leo like a door trusts its hinge. At home, they tossed their party favours on the kitchen table and went upstairs. The room smelled like pine and paper. Leo had a shelf full of small wooden boxes, one for each truth he wanted to keep. He picked up one and handed it to Jeremy. "Here," he said. "Let's put today in this one." Jeremy blinked. "Why?" Leo's voice was soft. "So we can look at it later and figure out what kind of fun doesn't feel empty."

That night, Jeremy crawled into bed without asking for screen time. He stared at the ceiling, then turned to Leo, who was reading a book about mountains. "Leo," he said, "why does real happy feel so quiet?" Leo smiled without looking up. "Because it doesn't need to be loud. That's how you know it's strong." Jeremy thought about that. He pictured a big bear sleeping under the snow, strong even in silence. He nodded slowly, then closed his eyes.

In the morning, Jeremy woke up earlier than usual. He didn't reach for his tablet. Instead, he sat up and watched Leo sleep for a minute. He thought about Caleb's party, about the music and noise and flashing lights. He thought about the laughter that felt like a firecracker—loud, bright, and gone too fast. He remembered the part where he sat alone, holding the whistle, not knowing if he was allowed to be quiet. He didn't want that kind of fun again.

Over breakfast, Jeremy asked Leo, "Do you think I'm boring?" Leo looked confused. "Why?" Jeremy shrugged. "Because I didn't like the party." Leo put his spoon down. "Not liking loud doesn't make you boring. It means you like things that last." He leaned forward. "Boring people copy fun. You look for the real kind." Jeremy grinned, a small grin that didn't try too hard. That made Leo smile too.

At school, Jeremy walked slower through the halls. He didn't chase after the noisy crowd. He waved politely at Caleb, but he didn't sit next to him. Instead, he sat beside a quiet kid named Aiden who always drew trees on his math sheets. They didn't talk much, but Jeremy liked the silence. It didn't scratch. It sat there, warm and folded.

Later, during recess, Leo watched from the fence as Jeremy offered Aiden a piece of his granola bar. They didn't laugh or wrestle or yell. But their shoulders leaned just enough toward each other to say something stronger than noise. Leo felt his chest expand a little, not from pride but from relief. Jeremy was starting to tell the difference. That mattered.

After school, Miss Penner pulled Leo aside. "Your brother was very calm today," she said. "He seems... content." Leo nodded. "He's learning what happiness really is." Miss Penner smiled. "Most adults haven't figured that out." Leo didn't reply. He just tucked his books under his arm and walked home.

That night, they didn't talk about the party. They didn't talk about anything flashy. Leo taught Jeremy how to fold a paper crane. Jeremy messed up four times. Then he laughed and got it right on the fifth. "This is better than cake," he whispered. Leo didn't argue. By bedtime, there were no fireworks in their memory of the day. Just a crane on the windowsill, a quiet room, and a calm heart that didn't need loud music to know it was full.

Ty sat cross-legged at the back of the classroom, cutting shapes from thick red paper for the school kindness project. The rest of the group had gone to lunch early, but he stayed behind to finish. His hands moved slow, careful, exact. Leo and Jeremy entered just as the scissors clicked the last corner off. Ty looked up and smiled—not the quick grin people give when they want you to like them, but the slow kind that stays even when nobody's watching. He didn't speak right away. He held the heart-shaped paper between his fingers, as if it mattered.

Leo dropped his backpack and leaned on the desk. "You could've done that later," he said. Ty shook his head. "I said I'd finish it today." Jeremy sat beside him. "It's just a paper heart," he said, gently. Ty turned the heart over, showing the back. It had a message in tiny letters: You matter, even when no one says it. Ty passed it to Jeremy. "That's not just paper," he said. "That's going on someone's locker. Could be the only kind thing they read all week."

There was something in Ty's voice that made Leo sit straighter. Not loud. Not proud. But strong. The kind of strong you don't see right away. "You feel good?" Leo asked. Ty nodded once. "Yeah. Not jump-up-and-down good. But the kind that lingers. It stays after the noise is gone." Jeremy looked confused. "Like what kind?" Ty paused. "Like when you help someone and you don't tell anyone. Or when someone trusts you with something big. It's quiet. But it's real."

That afternoon, Ty helped Ella carry her projects to the art room. She didn't ask. He just noticed the way her arms shook and walked over. "I've got the heavy one," he said. She looked surprised, then smiled—barely. No teachers saw. No one clapped. But Ella held her head higher after. Jasmin saw it too. "You're like a secret helper," she said. Ty shrugged. "It's not a secret. I just don't need credit."

After school, the sky clouded over with soft grey. Ty walked home alone for once. He didn't have music playing. He didn't check his phone. He just walked slow, breathing in the kind of air that makes you think. He passed a mailbox and tucked a note inside for a classmate whose dog had passed away. No one saw him write it. He didn't sign his name. But he smiled again—that same kind of smile as before.

Later that evening, Leo and Jeremy sat across from Ty in his living room. Ty was helping Jeremy build a puzzle. "Do you remember that time I taught you to tie your shoes?" Ty asked. Jeremy nodded. "You didn't tell anyone I couldn't." Ty smirked. "That's what made it stick. I didn't need to." Jeremy looked down at his hands, now knotting string like it was second nature. "That kinda happy stayed a long time," he whispered.

Leo leaned back in his chair. "It's weird," he said. "The happiest moments I remember… weren't when I got something. They were when I gave something. Or told the truth. Or stopped being scared." Ty looked at him carefully. "That's because your real self came out. And it liked what it saw." Leo blinked. He hadn't thought of it that way.

Jeremy pulled another puzzle piece into place. "So… happy isn't loud?" Ty shook his head. "Not always. Real happy is like roots. You don't see them. But they're the reason the tree stays up." Leo nodded slowly. "And fake happy's like fireworks. Big flash. Then gone." Ty added, "And sometimes it leaves smoke."

The puzzle was almost done now. Just one piece missing. Jeremy frowned. "We lost one." Ty smiled. "No, we just haven't found it yet." He reached under the edge of the couch and pulled out the last piece. Jeremy cheered quietly, fitting it in with a soft click. "Perfect," he whispered.

The puzzle showed a fox sitting in a field of wildflowers, quiet and still, but full of life. Jeremy stared at it for a long moment. "This feels like happy." Leo leaned closer. "Because you made it. You stayed. You didn't quit. And now it's yours." Ty added, "That's the kind that lingers." Jeremy placed his hand over the fox. "I wanna feel this more. The quiet kind." Leo smiled. "You will. Just don't chase it. Let it grow." They turned off the lights. No music. No flashing screens. Just the fox puzzle and the feeling that stayed.

Jasmin stood near the corner of the hallway where a group of kids had gathered, shoulders huddled, necks bent toward a phone screen. A boy from Grade 7 had pulled up a clip—some prank video involving a fake spider, a teacher's yelp, and loud, glitchy music. The hallway filled with howls. Even Ty chuckled faintly. But Jasmin didn't get it. She tilted her head, blinked twice, and gave a laugh just soft enough not to be noticed as fake. It felt like tossing a balloon into a tornado—light, pointless, and quickly lost.

The laughter spiraled upward, louder and faster, until one of the kids repeated a joke from the video. Something about a teacher's voice being "like a duck in a blender." Jasmin smiled because everyone else did, but inside she didn't move. It wasn't that she didn't understand the joke. It was that it didn't reach her. Like knocking on the outside of a house with all the windows sealed shut. She had nothing against the others. She just didn't feel what they felt. And for a moment, she wondered if something was wrong with her.

Later that afternoon, in the library's quiet back room, she dropped her books too hard on the table. Nico looked up from his sketchbook. "Bad day?" he asked. She shrugged, sliding into the chair beside him. "I laughed at something I didn't think was funny." He paused, then nodded. "So did I. Earlier. The pencil-drop game in math. Didn't make sense, but everyone cracked up. I smiled just so no one would ask what was wrong."

They sat in the stillness for a moment, surrounded by shelves and the smell of paper. Jasmin rubbed her wrist where her bracelet usually sat. She had taken it off that morning and forgotten it in her locker. It felt like forgetting part of her voice. "I keep wondering," she said quietly, "if maybe I'm too serious." Nico shook his head. "No. I think maybe you're just paying attention."

Jasmin's eyes flicked toward him. "To what?" He set his pencil down. "To what feels real. And what doesn't." His fingers drummed once on the table. "Real laughs… they kind of rise out of you before you know they're there. Like a bubble. You don't have to grab them. They find you." Jasmin leaned back. "Then why do I keep forcing it?" Nico gave a soft smile. "Because everyone else is. And you don't want to be the one sitting out."

There was something deeply uncomfortable about that truth. Jasmin wrapped her arms around herself. "But when I laugh like that, it feels like I'm erasing me." Nico nodded again. "That's because you are. A little. Every time you pretend, you're giving away a piece of something that's only yours." She sat with that thought a while. It wasn't dramatic. It was just true.

Outside the window, a flock of birds scattered into the grey sky. Nico traced one with his finger. "You know what I remember laughing at for real?" he said. Jasmin tilted her head. "What?" "The time Jeremy sneezed during the assembly and his whole row of chairs fell over like dominoes." Jasmin snorted. "I remember that! It was so loud!" "Yeah," Nico said. "And it wasn't supposed to be funny. It just… was. Because it was real."

Jasmin smiled without trying. "Okay, that one's still funny." "Exactly," Nico said. "We didn't have to decide to laugh. We just did. Like our hearts beat first and our brains caught up later." Jasmin let out a long breath. "That kind of happy feels better. Not all buzzy and fake." Nico opened his sketchbook again and began outlining a bird mid-flight. "You're not wrong for not laughing, Jasmin. You're just honest."

The next day, someone passed around another clip during recess. Same boy, same jokes. Jasmin watched from across the bench but didn't join. Instead, she sat with Jeremy and helped him learn how to fold a paper star. "Does this look right?" he asked. She gently bent one corner back. "Close. Let's fix this wing." Jeremy laughed when it flopped over. Jasmin laughed too. This time, she meant it. As the bell rang, she stood taller. The kind of tall that has nothing to do with height. Nico walked past and gave her a nod. Just that. No joke. No performance. But enough to say he saw her. She nodded back. It was all she needed.

Jeremy's fingers hovered over the final square of the board. He looked up once more, his face pinched with calculation and disbelief. He had two spaces to move. The spinner stopped at three. Everyone stared—then Nico gasped. "Wait… that means you win!" Jeremy blinked, checked the board again, then again, then blinked harder. He moved his piece forward anyway, landing on the final castle square with a small clack. For a moment, the world went silent in his head.

Leo clapped first. Nico followed. Jasmin gave a proud little cheer, and even Ty smiled behind folded arms. Jeremy looked down at the board as if it were about to change its mind. Then, slowly, he raised his fists in the air and yelled, "Yes! I finally won!" He stood up on his chair and danced in place, his socks slipping slightly against the plastic seat. "I never win this game! Never!" His voice echoed through the classroom nook, joy flooding every inch of him.

But five minutes later, when the board was packed up and his hands were clean, Jeremy sat quietly by the reading mat. His back rested against the wall, and he hugged his knees. Leo approached carefully, crouched beside him. "Hey," Leo said. "You beat us all. That was amazing." Jeremy nodded, but his smile had folded in on itself. "Yeah," he said flatly. "It was."

Leo didn't sit yet. He stayed low, eye level. "Something feels off?" Jeremy nodded, shrugging at the same time. "I thought I'd feel better." "You don't?" Leo asked. Jeremy looked toward the window. "I mean… I do. Kind of. But it's like I felt big, and now I feel small again. Like the happy fell off me." Leo sat down beside him. "It's weird, isn't it?" he said softly. "Sometimes we think winning will fix everything. But it only fixes the game."

Jeremy turned to him, confused. Leo offered a small smile. "You wanted to win because you always lose, right?" "Yeah." "And it felt great—for like five minutes?" "Four," Jeremy muttered. Leo laughed. "Okay, four. But then… nothing changed?" Jeremy nodded again. Leo glanced at the others, still resetting a different game nearby. "I used to feel that way too. Every time I won something, I thought it would make me feel better. But the better didn't last."

Jeremy leaned his head against the wall. "So what does last?" Leo thought for a long second. "Growing," he said. "Getting better at something. Not just winning. But understanding why you lost last time. Or helping someone else win next time." Jeremy squinted at him. "Helping someone else win?" "Yeah. Like, when I teach someone how to play and they get better because of me—that makes me feel something deeper than just beating them."

Jeremy turned the idea over. "So… real happy isn't just about beating people?" "Nope," Leo said. "It's about beating the part of you that thought you weren't good enough." Jeremy blinked. "That's deep." Leo smiled. "Ty says stuff like that all the time. I just steal it."

A small laugh slipped from Jeremy's mouth. "It still counts if you mean it." Leo looked thoughtful. "I guess it does." Then he added, "You know, there's nothing wrong with winning. It's fun. But if it's the only way you feel good about yourself, that happy will keep slipping away." Jeremy looked at his shoes. "So what should I feel proud about?" Leo nudged his arm. "You played fair. You didn't cheat. You stayed focused. You even helped Nico with the rulebook when he got confused. That stuff matters."

Jeremy's mouth tugged sideways. "Even more than the win?" "Especially more," Leo said. "Because that's the part of you that stays." They sat there, letting the hum of the class fill the silence. Eventually, Jeremy sat up straighter. "Maybe next time I'll try a new game. Something harder." "That's how you grow," Leo said. "Not just by winning. But by learning." Jeremy nodded, not for Leo's sake but for his own. Something had landed—not on the game board, but in his heart. And this time, it wasn't slipping away.

Ella didn't show it to anyone. Not right away. She kept the drawing tucked under her math notebook like a secret waiting for no one. It was a picture of a tree—not the kind you learn in class, with careful roots and boring symmetry, but one she'd made up in her head. It was curved and bent sideways, like it had grown through storms. Its branches were full of colours that didn't belong to leaves. The trunk had gold lines like scars. There was no sun in the sky, but the tree still glowed. And for the first time, Ella liked something she made without waiting to be told it was good.

She had drawn it during morning bellwork, when most kids were half asleep and no one cared what anyone else was doing. Jasmin was flipping through her planner. Leo had his head on the desk. Nico was scribbling jokes in the margin of his worksheet. Ella's pencil moved like it had its own mind. No one noticed. And she liked it that way.

Usually, she'd ask, "Do you like it?" before she was even done. She'd turn it so someone could see. Even Leo, once. Especially Leo. Because back then, a nod from him made her feel like she mattered. Like her work had worth. But now? Now it felt different. This drawing wasn't for that. It was for her. And she didn't care if anyone clapped.

At recess, she tucked it into her backpack without showing a soul. Not because she was hiding it—but because it didn't need applause to be real. She sat on the swing and watched the clouds. Her hands were covered in pencil smudges. She didn't wipe them off.

Ty sat beside her without asking. His hands held nothing. "You seem lighter today," he said gently. Ella looked at him. "How do you know that?" "Because you're not looking around for someone to notice you," he said. "You're just being." She didn't argue. She didn't pretend. She let the truth rest between them like a third swing.

Back inside, Miss Penner asked for volunteers to show something they made during free time. A few kids raised their hands. Ella didn't. She kept her drawing in her bag. Not because she was shy—but because she was satisfied. There was a difference. Leo had looked at her once, during class. Like he was waiting for her to flash something his way, hold it up and say, "Look at this!" But she didn't. She didn't need his eyes to make it valuable.

During art period, Jasmin leaned over. "Did you draw something today?" Ella nodded. "Yeah." "Can I see?" Ella paused. "Maybe later," she said. Jasmin nodded. She didn't push. And that meant even more.

At home that night, Ella taped the drawing to her bedroom wall. Not the fridge. Not her phone. Not online. Just her own wall, beside her window. Where the light touched it in the morning. Where it was hers.

Real joy doesn't shout. It doesn't beg for compliments. It's not a parade with music and clapping. Sometimes it's just a pencil, a page, and a feeling that you made something worth keeping. Not because someone said so—but because it feels like a piece of you. And that's enough. When Jeremy saw it two days later, he said, "Whoa, that's cool." Ella smiled. "Thanks." But she didn't beam. She didn't glow like she used to. Not because she wasn't happy—but because she already had been, before he even saw it.

Nico had filmed it during lunch. Just a quick clip of Jeremy stacking four apples on top of each other like wobbly bowling pins and pretending he was the "Lunch Table King." Everyone laughed. Even Ty cracked a grin. It was harmless, silly, the kind of thing that made school feel like a place to breathe. Nico posted it later with a funny caption and a crown emoji. Within twenty minutes, it had over fifty likes.

By that evening, it crossed a hundred. Nico refreshed the screen like it was homework. One hundred thirty-one. One hundred thirty-seven. Hearts flew up in red dots. Some kids from other grades commented with laugh-cry faces. One person reposted it. For a moment—just one glowing, buzzing moment—Nico felt famous.

But two hours later, he checked again. One hundred thirty-nine. No new notifications. No new hearts. He stared at the number as if it owed him more. His chest felt tight in a way that wasn't exciting anymore. He scrolled through old posts. Some had fifty likes. Some had twelve. One had four. He frowned. "Was this my best one?" he whispered to himself.

The next morning, he walked into class expecting someone to mention the video. Maybe clap him on the back. Ask how he got Jeremy to balance all those apples. But no one said anything. They were talking about a new meme, someone else's post, a dog in a raincoat. The spotlight had already moved.

Jeremy didn't bring it up either. He just smiled and offered Nico half a banana muffin. "You okay?" he asked, without needing a reason. Nico nodded too fast. "Yeah. Just tired." But the tired wasn't in his body—it was in the quiet.

At recess, Nico found Ty sitting against the wall near the dodgeball shed, flipping through a graphic novel. "You ever post something and then feel... empty after?" Nico asked. Ty didn't even look up. "Yup." "Even when people liked it?" "Especially then."

That stopped Nico. "Why especially?" Ty finally looked at him. "Because if the likes are the best part, what happens when they stop coming?" Nico didn't answer. He just sat down beside him and hugged his knees.

Ty tapped the book closed. "Real happiness isn't hungry. It doesn't need more and more to feel okay." "So what does it need?" Nico asked. "A reason that's not about getting seen," Ty said. "Like when we helped Jeremy with reading. Nobody clapped. But didn't it still feel good?"

Nico thought back. He remembered the way Jeremy had whispered the words out loud without stuttering for the first time, and the look on his face when no one laughed. That had felt better than a hundred hearts on a screen. He hadn't needed a notification. He had just known.

"I guess I forgot," Nico muttered. "Everyone does," Ty said, "because screens make forgetting easy." They sat there in the sun, not posting it, not filming it, just letting the quiet settle like something worth keeping. That night, Nico didn't check the post again. He turned off notifications and printed a photo from the day they built Jeremy's paper fort in art class instead. He taped it to his bedroom wall. No comments. No hearts. Just one memory he didn't need to share to keep.

Jeremy didn't ask permission. That was the first part. He waited until the lunchroom buzzed with trays and chairs and chatter, and then slipped three wrapped candies from Leo's backpack. Leo had brought them for later, but Jeremy thought one or two would go unnoticed. He stuffed them in his hoodie pocket and waited until recess.

Behind the portable, shielded from view, Jeremy ripped the foil open like he was unwrapping treasure. Sweet. Sticky. Gone too fast. The second one vanished before the guilt could register. By the third, his fingers were trembling, but he didn't stop. It wasn't hunger. It was the thrill of it. Doing something sneaky. Getting away with it. The sugar buzzed through his chest like a drumline.

For five minutes, he felt unbeatable. His feet moved faster in the soccer game. His laughs were louder. The world turned shinier. But then the shaking started. Not on the outside—but inside. His head felt light. His stomach turned sour. The wind felt colder than it had a moment ago. He sat down hard by the fence and wrapped his arms around his knees.

Leo noticed. Of course he noticed. He jogged over and crouched beside him, one eyebrow raised. "What happened?" Jeremy shrugged. "I don't feel good." Leo didn't scold. He didn't guess. He just waited. And eventually, Jeremy whispered, "I took your candy." His voice cracked. "All of it."

Leo blinked, surprised, but not angry. "You could've just asked." "I thought it'd make me feel better." Leo nodded slowly. "Did it?" Jeremy wiped his nose on his sleeve and shook his head. "Not really. It felt fun at first. Then... not."

Leo sat beside him and rested his arms on his knees. "That's how fake happy feels," he said. "It jumps in fast. Feels loud. But then it crashes, and you're stuck under it." Jeremy looked up. "Like a sugar storm?" Leo smirked. "Exactly like that."

They sat in silence. The kind of silence that didn't need to punish, just to teach. Leo reached into his pocket and pulled out one last candy he'd hidden. He handed it to Jeremy. "This one's not a secret. If you want it, you can have it. But I think you should wait till you feel okay again."

Jeremy looked at the wrapper. He didn't open it. Just held it, like it was a choice he got to make for real this time. "What if I still want it later?" "Then it'll still be here," Leo said. "And it won't be hiding." By the time the bell rang, the spinning had stopped. Jeremy stood up a little slower, steadier, the candy still in his hand. He didn't feel full. But he didn't feel hollow either. And maybe that was the first real piece of happy he'd earned all day.

The joke wasn't even that funny. Not really. But Alex told it loud, with a crooked grin and a sharp tone that made the younger kids near the monkey bars pause mid-swing. Leo laughed out of habit, not out of heart. It was a reflex—the kind you build when someone powerful wants an audience. His laugh came out louder than it needed to, and too fast, like he was racing to stay in Alex's good books.

But the second the echo of it landed, Leo saw Ella's shoulders twitch. She hadn't looked up when Alex made the comment. But now her eyes were fixed on the ground, and her lips pressed into a line so tight it seemed painful to keep closed. The joke had been about someone "always being in the way," and Alex's head had turned ever so slightly in Ella's direction when he said it.

Leo's face froze mid-laugh. He blinked, then replayed the sound in his mind. Not just the joke, but his own voice, his own laugh, his own part in it. Ella wasn't looking at him. She wasn't crying either. But her entire body had shifted—smaller, tighter, like she wanted to disappear inside her coat. It was like watching a balloon shrink without popping.

Ty stood nearby, silent as ever, eyes scanning the group like a weather reader sensing the turn of wind. He didn't say anything, but his expression held Leo in place like a mirror that didn't lie. Leo's hands dropped to his sides, the laughter gone from his stomach, replaced with a knot.

"Hey," Leo said softly, but Ella didn't respond. She stepped away toward the corner of the playground and sat on the lowest rung of the climbing frame, her arms folded. That's when Leo felt it. Not guilt. Not exactly. It was something heavier than that. He had laughed, and it had caused someone else to fold in on herself. That wasn't happy. That was harm with a smile. He sat beside Ty, not expecting comfort. Just not wanting to be alone with the feeling. "I laughed," he said quietly. "Yeah," Ty answered. "I saw." Leo swallowed hard. "She thinks I think it's funny." Ty nodded. "You know it wasn't."

Leo pressed his palms against his knees. "I think I've done that before. Before I changed." Ty didn't argue. He didn't have to. The truth already sat between them like an invisible rope, pulling at Leo's chest. "You didn't mean it," Ty said eventually, "but you still joined in." Leo's shoulders slumped. "I didn't protect her." "You still can," Ty said. "Next time." Leo stood and walked slowly toward Ella. She didn't look up, but she didn't move away either. He didn't sit too close. Just enough to show he saw her. "That joke wasn't funny," he said. "Not to me. Not really. I'm sorry I laughed."

Ella didn't speak right away. But when she finally looked at him, her eyes weren't angry. Just tired. "Okay," she said softly. And then, "Thank you." Leo nodded, then walked away without waiting for more. It wasn't about being forgiven. It was about seeing the bruise that joy should never leave.

Jeremy didn't say much when the teacher praised him for his group work. He just nodded, tapped his pencil twice, and kept his eyes on the desk. But Leo saw it. The quiet pride. The smile that didn't need anyone else's approval to matter. That was the third time this week Jeremy hadn't stuttered when he spoke aloud. And it had been nearly a full month since Leo had heard his voice tremble with panic. It hadn't been a miracle or magic trick. It had been moments. Gentle, steady ones. Like Ty said—real joy doesn't always make noise.

Ty had explained it a few days ago while they sat under the big willow near the back field. "My dad told me once," he said, picking at the grass, "that real happy whispers. Like the feeling when someone trusts you enough to sleep near you. Or when you don't have to explain yourself and you're still loved." Leo had nodded slowly then. Now he felt it settle in his bones.

After school, Jeremy and Leo walked home together. No talking. Just footsteps on the pavement, bookbags thudding softly against their backs. At the corner before their street, Leo stopped him. "Hey," he said. Jeremy turned. "You know you haven't stuttered once this month, right?"

Jeremy blinked. "Really?" "Yeah," Leo said. "I noticed. I'm proud of you." Jeremy didn't answer. He just dropped his bag, flung his arms around Leo's middle, and hugged him. Not a quick pat-hug like kids do when they feel awkward. This was full-body. Real. Tight. The kind that said everything words didn't. Leo didn't move for a moment, surprised. Then he hugged back. Not because he felt obligated. But because he meant it.

They got home just as the sun dipped low, and Mrs. Firth opened the front door with a smile that stretched across her whole face. "Boys!" she called. "Dinner's almost ready." Mr. Firth followed behind, setting his phone aside and walking straight up to the two of them. "You both look like something good happened."

Leo shrugged, but Jeremy stepped forward and said, clearly and without pause, "Leo told me he was proud of me." His eyes shimmered. "For not stuttering." Mr. Firth knelt, both arms wide, and Jeremy fell into him. Mrs. Firth reached them too, and suddenly it wasn't just a hallway—it was a hug. Four people. Two grown-ups. Two kids. One big silence. Except it wasn't silent. It was full. Whole. Complete.

"I'm proud of you too," Mr. Firth said into Jeremy's hair. "And you," he added, squeezing Leo's shoulder. "You've become a man who lifts others." Leo didn't cry. Not because he wasn't close, but because it wasn't a sad moment. It was peace. Safety. And those don't ask for tears. They just hold you and tell you it's okay to be exactly who you are.

Later that night, after dishes and pajamas and brushing teeth, Jeremy sat on the edge of his bed. "That was happy," he whispered. "I think that's what happy really is." Leo sat beside him, ruffling his hair. "Yeah," he said. "It's not loud. But it stays." They didn't need music, or parties, or trophies. They had each other. They had truth. And that was more than enough.

Miss Penner didn't say much when she hung the picture. Just used two pins, smoothed the paper flat against the corkboard, and smiled a little. "Lovely use of space, Ella," she said. Then she turned back to her clipboard and moved on. No fuss. No big announcement. Just a quiet moment that passed like a leaf falling gently to the ground. But for Ella, it stayed. The picture—her picture—had made it onto the wall.

It was a drawing of a field with sunlight coming through clouds. Two girls sat on the hill, back to back. They didn't smile. They weren't waving. They were just still. It wasn't fancy or colourful, but it was true. And every time Ella walked past the board on her way to math or science, she slowed down. Just a little. Just long enough to see it was still there.

No one else really noticed. Not like with Leo's comic strips or Nico's science fair display. No one clapped. No one asked, "Did you draw that?" It wasn't a spotlight moment. But it didn't have to be. It was hers. And it stayed. And that made something settle inside her like warm soup after a cold walk home.

Jasmin passed her in the hallway once, glanced at the board, and nodded. "That's yours, right?" she whispered. Ella smiled and nodded back. That was enough. She didn't need more. She didn't need applause or stickers or ten compliments. Just the knowing that something she made—something true—was seen and allowed to remain.

Jeremy had asked once why people wanted to win things. "So others know they're good?" he guessed. But Leo said sometimes the best parts of you don't come with prizes. They just live quietly on walls, or in hugs, or in the space between someone trusting you enough to tell the truth.

Ella had drawn the picture during a lunch break, just after Ty explained the difference between false kindness and real love. She didn't have the words for it then. But her pencil did. The girls on the hill didn't need to talk. They were enough just sitting near each other. And that's what she wanted to remember.

All week, the picture stayed. On Wednesday, someone bumped into the board and a corner curled. Miss Penner smoothed it again. Didn't say anything. Just cared for it like it mattered. That made Ella smile the deepest. Because the care was quiet. Real things usually are.

She never said, "That's my art." Never pointed. Never bragged. But every time she saw it, she felt it. Not like sugar. Not like a compliment that fades after ten minutes. But like sunlight warming her shoulder without asking for attention.

On Friday afternoon, she passed by it one last time before the weekend. The hall was empty. No one saw her pause. No one saw her fingers brush the edge of the board. But she felt it. She felt proud. And that kind of proud didn't need witnesses.

When she got home, her mother asked how school was. Ella said, "Good." That was it. She didn't mention the drawing. But later that night, she sketched again. This time, a quiet scene of a boy and a younger boy planting something in a garden. She smiled to herself. Maybe she'd give it to Jeremy. Because now she knew: happiness wasn't loud. It didn't vanish when people stopped looking. It didn't need to be performed or praised. It just had to be true.

Jasmin didn't stand up to speak. She didn't raise her hand fast or loud. She just sat still, fingers locked together under the desk, and let the words come out the way leaves drop when they're ready—not forced, not planned, but natural and slow. "I didn't feel safe when Allen kept talking over me in the group project," she said. Her voice didn't shake, but her stomach did.

Miss Penner paused, marker still pressed against the whiteboard. It was a moment that felt too quiet to be safe—but it wasn't dangerous. Just… holding. Then the teacher turned around fully, looked at Jasmin directly, and said, "Thank you for telling me. That matters."

Jasmin's lungs filled like she hadn't been breathing the whole week. Not because she needed applause. Not because she wanted Allen in trouble. But because something real had finally made it past her throat, and the world didn't fall apart when it landed. Someone had heard her and believed her.

The class didn't cheer. No one clapped. In fact, some kids looked away, embarrassed. But Ty didn't. Nico didn't. Ella turned her head, just slightly, just enough. Those three glances were more comforting than all the stickers in the world.

It wasn't a big accusation. Jasmin didn't want it to be. She didn't name everything Allen had done. She didn't list the times he'd taken credit for her ideas or teased her "jumpy" reactions in the hallway. She just named one moment. One truth. And waited to see if it would be crushed or caught.

Miss Penner didn't push further. She just nodded once, wrote group feedback check-in on Monday's to-do list, and went back to the lesson. But everything had changed. Because someone who had power had decided not to look away.

Jasmin didn't smile right away. It took about seven minutes. It came when she leaned over her math book and saw the corner of her eraser poking from the pencil case—chewed and bent, exactly the way she'd left it. Nothing was wrong. And that was the smile: the world hadn't punished her for telling the truth.

Ty met her eyes after class. He didn't say anything. Just gave her the Shadow Warrior nod. Nico bumped her shoulder gently in the hall. Ella handed her a crumpled note that said only, "Thank you for saying it." Jasmin folded it three times and tucked it in her pocket, not her binder.

At recess, Allen didn't say anything either. He stayed with Alex, laughing louder than usual. His eyes didn't meet hers. But his silence wasn't heavy—it was just noise in the background now. Jasmin realized she didn't need to decode his mood today. She didn't need to manage how he felt. Not anymore.

Back at home, she didn't tell her parents what happened. Not because it didn't matter, but because it was hers. This wasn't a story to hand off. This was a moment stitched into her spine—quiet, invisible, but holding her taller.

When she brushed her teeth that night, she caught a glimpse of herself in the mirror. Not the usual glance. This time she stared. She didn't see a brave warrior or a wounded girl. She just saw Jasmin. And for the first time in a long time, that was enough.

The smile that finally crept across her face wasn't wide. It wasn't gleeful. It was the kind of smile that folds into your bones, slow and soft. The kind that doesn't scream, "Look at me!" but instead whispers, "I made it." Because relief is happiness too. The real kind. The kind that doesn't spike and crash. The kind that doesn't need likes, gifts, or praise to live. Just truth. And someone who says, "I believe you."

It started with the battery dying. Nico didn't plan for it, didn't charge it overnight like he usually did. His tablet blinked red, then black, and for a few seconds he just stared at the blank screen like it had betrayed him. There was no game to finish. No video to tap next. Just the kind of silence that usually made him twitchy.

Outside the kitchen window, old Mr. Bell was hunched over the side garden again. Bent knees. Dirt-stained gloves. That little patch of earth beside the driveway had looked like nothing but mud for weeks. But something had changed. Tiny green shoots peeked up in lines, like shy soldiers just arriving on the field. Nico blinked again. Then opened the back door.

Mr. Bell looked up when he heard the door creak. He didn't speak first. He never did. Nico liked that about him. He just nodded once and kept digging. There were six tomato plants, a row of beans, and a circle that looked like it might be herbs but could've been weeds. Nico stepped closer. No buzzing, no music, no screen glow. Just air.

"Want to help?" Mr. Bell said at last, nodding toward a small trowel in the dirt.

Nico hesitated. Then crouched down and picked it up. The handle was rough and splintered, like it had been used a thousand summers before this one. He dug beside the man's shadow, not asking where, just watching until he understood. It was all rhythm. Lift, press, turn. Drop the roots in. Cover. Pat.

An hour passed. Then two. Nico didn't notice the time at first—only the light changing. Shadows moved across the fence. A breeze tugged his sleeves. He wiped sweat from his forehead with the back of his hand and looked around. The garden was fuller now. Not finished, but changed. "Funny how some things grow slower," Mr. Bell murmured. "But they stay longer, too."

Nico nodded. He didn't need it explained. Not really. His chest felt different than when he won in a game, or beat a level, or got three hundred likes on a dance post. This was quieter. But it hummed. It was warm in the middle of his ribs, and it didn't leave when he blinked.

Back inside, he washed dirt from under his nails. His fingers smelled like mint and soil. That night, he didn't even look for the charger. The tablet stayed on the shelf. He lay in bed and thought about the green shoots, the neat lines they made, the way roots held tight to the earth even before they showed above it.

At school the next day, Jasmin asked what video he watched over the weekend. Nico shrugged. "Didn't watch one. Dug a garden instead." She blinked. Then smiled. Not surprised. Not teasing. Just pleased. He didn't tell her about the ache in his shoulders or the dirt he'd found in his ears. He didn't need to. That was part of it too. Real joy didn't need a post. It didn't need applause. It didn't even need words sometimes. It just needed time. And attention. And truth.

During recess, Leo pulled out his phone and laughed at a meme. Jeremy leaned in. Nico didn't. He looked at the tree line behind the portables instead and thought about which plants might grow best in shade. That evening, when his mum offered screen time, he asked to go back next door instead. Mr. Bell just nodded again and handed him a rake. The work was slower this time. But Nico smiled. The screen could wait. Because some joys don't blink. They bloom.

Jeremy sat with his knees pulled up on the bench by the gym doors, his backpack still on like he didn't know whether he was leaving or staying. The Grade 5 hallway echoed faintly with the sound of older kids laughing about something a teacher said, but Jeremy wasn't listening. He stared at the floor like it had said something mean to him and he hadn't figured out how to reply yet. His shoelaces were uneven—again—and one loop kept slipping loose like it didn't want to hold anything together anymore. Leo didn't say hi at first. He just sat down beside him slowly, the way you do when you know someone's silence isn't an accident.

Jeremy sniffed once, wiped his nose with his sleeve even though there was a tissue poking out the side pocket of his backpack. His face didn't look tear-streaked, but it didn't look alright either. Leo leaned back against the wall, tilted his head to the side, and just waited. The silence between them wasn't empty. It was thick with that quiet kind of noise that only people who've been through something understand. It didn't take a lot of words to recognize that kind of weight. You just had to know what it felt like when the air between your ribs didn't want to move.

When Jeremy finally looked up, his voice was small but not cracked. "They were laughing… but not at the joke." He didn't say who 'they' were, and Leo didn't ask. He didn't need to. The ache in Jeremy's voice said enough. It was one of those days where being in the room felt like being invisible and exposed all at once. Where you laugh along so nobody sees the hurt, even though it's sitting right behind your teeth.

Leo turned toward him and gave the smallest nod. Not a big brother nod. Not a I-know-how-to-fix-this nod. Just the kind that said, I see it too. Then he did something Jeremy didn't expect. He opened his arms—not fast, not with a smile, not like it was for show. Just quietly, slowly, like an old promise being kept. Jeremy hesitated for less than a second before scooting into the space Leo made. And when Leo wrapped his arms around him, Jeremy's shoulders dropped a little, like he'd been holding them up too long.

There was no music. No bell rang. No crowd watching or clapping. Just two boys sitting on the floor of a quiet hallway, one holding the other because sometimes that's the only thing that makes sense. Leo didn't talk. He didn't offer advice or solutions or questions. He just held on, like the hug itself was the answer. And maybe it was.

Jeremy's arms wrapped around Leo's middle tight—not desperate, not loose, but real. His chin found a place just under Leo's shoulder. He didn't cry. Not out loud. But his breath hitched once, and Leo felt it. Felt it the way people feel thunder in their chest before it cracks the sky. Leo pressed his cheek against the top of Jeremy's head and let him stay there as long as he needed. Not until a certain number of seconds passed. Not until someone told them to move. Just long enough for Jeremy to feel like he wasn't alone anymore.

That hug, for all its silence, was louder than every joke told that day. Louder than the teasing laughs, the sarcastic grins, the fake compliments thrown like coins into a wishing well. It didn't ask for anything. Didn't demand a smile or a thank you. It just was. Solid. Present. Kind. And in a world full of people trying to be funny or cool or loud, that quiet act of love stood out like a lighthouse.

After a while, Jeremy pulled back, not because he was finished hurting, but because he knew he didn't have to carry it alone anymore. His eyes didn't sparkle, but they didn't sink either. He looked at Leo like someone who just got handed back a piece of themselves they thought was lost. "Thanks," he said. One word. That was all. But it landed in Leo's chest like an oath.

Leo gave him a gentle squeeze on the shoulder before standing up. He didn't say you're welcome, because this wasn't a favour. This was family now. Chosen, tested, and real. He helped Jeremy to his feet and they started walking back to class, not talking much, not needing to. They weren't just going back to finish a worksheet or hand in homework. They were walking back as brothers who'd figured something out: some moments don't need applause. They need presence.

That hug wasn't flashy. It didn't go viral. No teacher mentioned it, and no student asked about it. But it stayed. In Jeremy's bones. In Leo's memory. In the way they glanced at each other in the lunchroom and knew they'd always have a place to sit. In the way Jeremy started listening closer to other kids who looked like they might be holding in a storm. It was a moment that didn't fade, because it was made from truth, not noise.

Later that night, Leo mentioned it to his dad in the kitchen. "We hugged today. It was the only thing I could think to do." His dad smiled, ruffled his hair, and said, "You did more than most people ever learn how to." Leo didn't need the praise. But something about hearing it from someone who meant it made the hug feel even heavier—in the good way.

Jeremy didn't talk about it with anyone else. But that night, when his mom asked how his day was, he just nodded and said, "Better." Then he wrapped his arms around her tight and held on for one whole minute longer than usual. She didn't ask why. But she smiled like she knew. Because hugs, the real ones, say things that words can't.

In the days that followed, Jeremy walked a little taller. Not because he was suddenly fearless, but because he knew someone would catch him if he fell. That made all the difference. And Leo? He didn't start hugging everyone. But he looked for the moments when someone needed it. And when those moments came, he stepped in. Quiet. Solid. Unshaken. They'd both remember that day—not for what was said, or even what was felt—but for the fact that in a world that rushes and laughs and forgets, someone stopped. Someone stayed. And someone held on.

Alex had a habit of arriving five minutes late and pretending it was fashion. He walked into the classroom that morning with something scribbled in purple marker across the front of his T-shirt: #ChalkChallenge. Nico blinked, confused. It wasn't a thing. Not yet. But Alex acted like it had already taken over the world. He held up a piece of white chalk, winked dramatically, and tossed it over his shoulder like he was on stage. A few kids laughed. One clapped. The others just watched him the way people watch a street performer they didn't pay for.

At recess, he spun the story further. "It's going viral," he told two fourth graders, tossing chalk dust in the air. "Started in Vancouver, now it's here. You throw a piece of chalk and say something bold. Everyone's doing it." He didn't look at Ty, or Nico, or Jasmin. He aimed the whole act at kids who didn't know him well. Fresh audience. New followers. That was the goal. Jeremy, holding Leo's hand like he always did during first break, looked confused. "Why throw chalk?" he asked. "Because it's fun," Alex shot back, too fast. "Because it gets likes."

Ty didn't laugh. He just watched. Alex wasn't smiling for joy. He was grinning like someone who just discovered a new trick and needed it to work. Desperately. Nico stood beside the basketball court and said nothing. He'd seen this before. Last time it was Push-Up Tag. Before that, it was Glue Stick Dodge. Nothing ever lasted. It wasn't about fun. It was about being the one who made noise, even if it echoed empty.

Ella stood near the back, not playing. She leaned on the fence, arms folded, eyes narrowed—not mean, just thoughtful. When Alex tossed another piece of chalk and shouted something about being "the future," she tilted her head like she was watching a puppet repeat its routine for the fourth time. She didn't look impressed. She looked tired.

Later, in the hallway near the library, Alex crouched to pull more chalk from his backpack—this time coloured sticks. "Limited edition," he told Elia. "Only the best influencers have these." She nodded politely, but her eyebrows didn't move. He lined them up on the floor like they were trophies. Then, as if expecting applause, he whispered loud enough for the room to hear, "Watch how fast this trend catches on."

No one filmed it. No one shared it. No one said the words out loud, but the silence was clear: it was over before it started. Alex stood up, scanned the room, and shrugged. "I guess the vibe's wrong today." Even his voice lacked the usual spark. The edges of his performance were wearing thin. Leo passed him without speaking, just holding a folder under one arm like he had a place to be. The hallway didn't feel big enough for Alex anymore.

Back inside, Ty and Ella sat near the back table during library time. Ella leaned closer and whispered, "That's not happy. That's hungry." Ty glanced sideways at her. There was no smirk in her voice. Just something deeply sad and quietly right. The kind of sentence people don't always know they're saying until it lands. Ty nodded. "Yeah. Hungry's a good word." Then he opened his sketchbook and drew an empty plate.

Alex walked past them ten minutes later, slower now, the chalk long gone from his hands. He peeked toward the librarian like maybe she'd ask about his shirt. She didn't. She asked Leo to carry some books instead. He watched, puzzled, then kept walking. You could feel it—his storm had passed without thunder.

Nico whispered to Jasmin, "Why does he keep doing that?" Jasmin didn't answer at first. She looked down at her desk and fiddled with a pencil. Then she said, softly, "Because for one minute, he feels seen." The pencil snapped mid-spin. She didn't pick it up. Nico didn't press further. Some truths didn't need echoing. They just needed space.

By the end of the day, no one mentioned the Chalk Challenge. No one followed it. No one even remembered it. Not even Alex. He'd already moved on to something else—whistling loudly between lockers and pretending someone famous had replied to his post. No one asked for proof. They knew better now. Noise wasn't the same as happiness.

That night, Alex posted a photo of his chalk-smeared shirt with the caption: "New trend alert. Who's in?" It got four likes. Two from burner accounts. One from someone in B.C. he didn't know. One from an old classmate who thought it was a joke. The post didn't trend. He deleted it by midnight. No one noticed.

Meanwhile, Jeremy fell asleep in his top bunk with Leo reading beside him. They hadn't said much after dinner. Just sat, just breathed, just rested. No performance. No audience. Just real peace. Jeremy mumbled, "Leo? That stuff Alex does... is it happy?" Leo closed the book and whispered, "No. It's just noise pretending to be joy." Jeremy didn't answer. He was already dreaming.

Ella, at home, drew a picture of a boy standing on stage holding up chalk. The audience seats were empty. She folded it in half and slipped it in her desk drawer. She didn't show anyone. Not yet. Maybe not ever. But she knew what it meant. That smile Alex wore today—it had teeth. And those teeth bit into him most of all.

Ty asked his dad that night, "Can you ever be full if you're always hungry for attention?" His father looked up from the sink, drying a plate. "No," he said quietly. "Hunger grows when you feed it the wrong things." Ty wrote that down in the back of his notebook under a title he'd just made up: Real Joy Doesn't Beg.

By the next morning, someone had copied Alex's shirt. But they'd drawn a smiley face over the hashtag and written, "Don't need trends to be awesome." It wasn't clear who did it. But Alex didn't comment. He looked at it once in the hallway, nodded slightly, and kept walking. No performance. Just a pause. And for once, no spotlight followed.

The sun wasn't loud that day. It didn't blaze or burn or draw attention. It simply settled—quietly, warmly—across the schoolyard where six children sat beneath the broad arms of the old maple tree by the fence. Its roots had risen slightly through the soil, just enough to feel like a seat if you knew where to lean. Jasmin found her spot first, her back against the bark, knees tucked to her chest. Nico sat beside her, one leg stretched out, the other bent like he was preparing to think about something but not say it yet. Ty didn't sit right away. He crouched, observed the shape of the moment, then folded himself cross-legged beside Jeremy, who was already mid-hug against Leo's side.

No one said they planned to meet there. No one called it a gathering. It wasn't a meeting. It wasn't a mission. It wasn't even recess, not officially. It was one of those rare stolen spaces in the day where no one had to be anything. And that was the joy of it. Ella arrived last, her notebook tucked under her arm, hair slightly tangled from the wind. She didn't ask what they were doing. She just looked once at Jasmin, then at the open patch of grass beside Ty, and sat down without asking permission. That alone felt sacred.

No one spoke for the first two minutes. Jeremy leaned his head back and looked up through the canopy of green above them, blinking at the spaces between the leaves. "It smells like the ground is smiling," he whispered to Leo, who let out a soft laugh through his nose. "Yeah," Leo said. "That's a weirdly true thing." Nico plucked a small stick from the soil and began dragging lines in the dirt without a plan. Jasmin watched him, then closed her eyes for just a moment. Just a second of silence to breathe without defending herself from the world.

There was no game. No phone. No music. Just the breeze and the occasional squeal of younger kids in the distance. The sound didn't reach them fully. It filtered through the leaves like a radio turned low in the next room. That distance made it sweeter somehow. Ty shifted his weight and crossed his arms loosely. "You know," he said quietly, "this is what it feels like." Nico looked up. "Feels like what?" Ty didn't answer immediately. He let the quiet hang. Then he said, "This. This is joy. It's not loud. It's not bright. It's just… here."

Jasmin nodded slowly, eyes still closed. "It doesn't ask for anything," she murmured. "It just lets us be." Jeremy rolled onto his side and looked at each of them, one by one, with his eyes wide and blinking slowly like he was trying to memorize the moment. "It's like... it's like when you stop thinking," he said. "Like your brain's not trying to win anymore." Leo reached over and ruffled Jeremy's hair once. Not enough to mess it up. Just enough to answer.

Ella opened her notebook but didn't write anything. She just held it on her lap and ran her finger down the spine. "Maybe this is what grown-ups mean when they say peace," she said, almost to herself. "Except we didn't need a cottage or a lake or anything. Just this." Ty looked sideways at her, then at the others, and finally at the space between them all. "Maybe that's why most people miss it. Because they're too busy building something to sit under a tree."

The wind shifted slightly. A few leaves danced. None of the children moved. The sun warmed their knees, their shoulders, the tops of their heads. No one reached for it. It just touched them. Nico finally spoke again. "You ever notice how fake happy always wants something back? Like a trade?" He didn't look at anyone in particular, just kept drawing lines in the dirt. "This doesn't. This just is." Jasmin opened her eyes slowly and whispered, "Maybe that's what truth feels like too."

Leo leaned his head back against the bark and closed his eyes. "It's like we're invisible," he said. "But not in a bad way. Not like ignored. More like... nobody's watching us, and we're still okay." Jeremy tucked his arm into Leo's and said, "That's how I feel with you." It wasn't a declaration. It wasn't a confession. It was a truth that only needed saying once. Ty gave a small nod that barely counted as movement, but it was full of weight.

For nearly ten minutes, no one moved from that space. Not out of obligation. Not because anyone told them to. But because something inside them had rooted—deep, quiet, and sacred. No one needed applause. No one needed a picture. No one needed proof that they were together. Their presence was enough. Their stillness wasn't a void; it was full.

Then, gently, Jasmin stood. Not rushed. Not awkward. She just stood because her legs told her they were ready. Nico followed a moment later, brushing dirt from his palms. Jeremy lingered a little longer beside Leo, then finally let go. "Can we do this again?" he asked, voice not desperate, just hopeful. Leo answered with a nod and a soft, "Anytime you need."

Ella didn't close her notebook. She walked with it open, like maybe she'd write it down later. Or maybe she wouldn't. Some truths, she was learning, belonged to the body more than the page. Ty picked up a small acorn and turned it over in his hand. "This moment," he whispered to himself, "isn't for sharing. It's for growing." No one heard him. No one needed to. And though no one clapped or laughed or cheered, something inside each of them whispered a quiet yes. This was what real joy felt like. Not stolen. Not bought. Not staged. Just found. And like the shade of the tree, it needed nothing from them but stillness.

The room was darker than usual, not because the lights were off—they always were by this time—but because the day itself had ended softly. No thunder of laughter, no last-minute scramble to check a screen or grab forgotten homework. Just the quiet way joy sometimes lands without needing to be noticed. The glow of the nightlight, shaped like a lighthouse, spilled amber light across the edges of Jeremy's blanket. It lit the books stacked near the foot of the bed, the same ones Leo had started reading aloud, one chapter per night, even if Jeremy was already half-asleep.

Leo sat upright on the edge of his brother's mattress, back against the wall, feet pulled up. He wasn't in a rush. There was no phone in his hand. No backpack beside him. Just the stillness of evening and the knowledge that no part of this moment needed fixing. Jeremy blinked slowly under the quilt, the weight of the blanket and the day both helping him settle. He had asked for the window to stay open a crack, and the air that floated in was just cool enough to make the covers feel like comfort, not burden.

After a few minutes of quiet, Jeremy turned his head slightly toward Leo, his voice barely louder than a breath. "Today felt good," he said, pausing like he needed to check his words before releasing them. "Even the quiet parts." Leo looked down at him, smiled gently, and gave a single nod. "That's how you know it's the real kind," he said. "It doesn't need to be big to stay with you."

Jeremy's mouth curved into a soft grin. He didn't open his eyes fully. He just spoke again, this time not hesitating. "You are the best brother in the world," he whispered. "I love you, Leo. I always will." And there was no ceremony to it. No overthinking. No audience. Just the kind of love that only children can say without guarding it first.

Leo didn't cry, but something behind his eyes softened in a way only real love can unlock. He reached down and slid under the covers beside Jeremy without making a sound. It was a small bed, not built for two, but they made space the way people do when love is stronger than comfort. Leo gently pulled Jeremy into his arms, one hand on the small of his back, the other tucking the quilt around them both. Jeremy's head fit just beneath Leo's chin, as if the world had carved him a place there.

They didn't speak after that. The wind outside played gently with the leaves. A car passed in the distance, too far to matter. And in the centre of it all—this quiet room, this shared bed, this invisible circle of safety—two brothers rested in a stillness that held no fear. Leo's eyes closed slowly. He didn't sleep right away. He just listened to Jeremy's breathing shift, soften, and settle into the steady rhythm of trust.

There had been loud days before. Ones filled with chaos, confusion, even cruelty. Leo had once believed that kind of noise was what life needed to feel full. He had chased laughs that didn't last. Jokes that left bruises. He had tried on smiles that belonged to other people. But tonight was different. Tonight, nothing had to be said twice. Nothing had to be earned. It had simply arrived—and stayed.

Jeremy's hand curled around the fabric of Leo's shirt, small fingers folding gently as if anchoring himself without even realizing it. Leo didn't shift away. He let it be. Some kinds of peace are learned only when you stop pulling away. And Leo, finally, had stopped pulling.

Outside the door, the house had gone quiet too. Mr. and Mrs. Firth had passed by earlier, seen the boys together, and said nothing. They knew. Real joy didn't need to announce itself. It didn't call attention. It settled like dusk—slow, earned, and kind. The hallway light clicked off. The only sound was the soft hum of the refrigerator down the hall and the distant creak of old floors exhaling.

In the stillness, Leo finally let his mind quiet. Not silence forced by fear or anger—but a kind of rest that arrived when nothing had to be proved. He breathed in, not sharply, but with the kind of ease that meant his body had finally learned what safety felt like. That it was here now. That it wasn't going away.

Jeremy, already asleep, had a faint smile on his lips, the kind you see on children who have been hugged long enough to believe the world might not break them. His arm stayed wrapped around Leo's side, and Leo knew without question that this night, this feeling, would root deep. It was the kind of moment memory builds homes around.

As the moon shifted across the sky and painted silver lines across the windowpane, Leo whispered one thing, just once, barely more than air. "I'll always protect you." Not because anyone asked him to. Not because he had to make up for anything. But because he wanted to. Because this was who he was now. And joy—real joy—was knowing you didn't need to be anyone else to be loved. No thunder. No climax. Just warmth. Two boys wrapped in a night that asked for nothing. A lighthouse glow on the wall. A quilt that held more than heat. And a kind of peace that didn't end when the lights went out.

CHAPTER 17: WHEN THE VILLAIN WAS ONCE THE VICTIM

Leo stood up slowly. He hadn't asked permission, and no one told him to speak. Mr. Clarke had only given a soft nod, which was strange, because it wasn't the kind of day for presentations. There were no cue cards in Leo's hands. No posters. No books. Just that look—the kind that stretches behind the eyes when something important needs to come out. He didn't stand tall, but he didn't slouch either. His fingers twitched against the desk for a moment. Then he looked at the class and said it. "Once, I was the villain." His voice didn't rise. It didn't break. It just landed.

No one moved. Not even Alex, who usually made some kind of face. Nico kept his hands flat on the desk. Jasmin's lips parted, but she didn't breathe in. Jeremy leaned forward, elbows tucked tight to his ribs like he might miss the rest if he so much as blinked. Even Ella—who had once looked at Leo with eyes full of fog—was clear now. She watched him like she wanted to believe the next sentence before it was even said. Leo glanced toward Ty. That glance meant: Are you still with me? Ty gave the smallest nod, the kind only brothers understand. Leo took a breath.

"I cried in his arms," Leo said, and he didn't bother to pretend it was embarrassing. "Not once. Three times." He looked at the class like they needed to hear the number. "The first time was after I tried to act like it was all a joke. I said I didn't care. But he knew. Ty knew. I collapsed into him, right there in the hallway." Leo's voice didn't wobble, but something behind it thinned, like a thread being pulled through cloth. "The second time was after I got called into the office and they asked me questions I didn't want to answer. But I still said yes. Because someone had to stop him."

The room tilted. Not literally—but emotionally. Everyone felt it. Ty didn't look away. He stayed still, his chin raised just slightly, like a quiet sentinel. Leo's voice lowered. "My dad's in jail now. Not Ty's dad. Mine. Ty's dad is the one who arrested him." He paused. "Because of what he did to me." Someone near the back of the room shifted, but made no sound. It was a shift of understanding, not of discomfort. "That was the third time I cried in Ty's arms. After it was over. After he was gone. I didn't know what to feel. I didn't know if I was still me. Or if I was just some leftover piece of him."

There was no noise. No foot tapping, no backpack rustle, not even a cough. It was as if the classroom itself had paused its breathing. "I used to be mean because I didn't know how to be anything else," Leo said. "I used to laugh when people were scared, because that was the only time I didn't feel small. I lied. I tricked. I blamed other people for everything I did, because I didn't want to admit where I came from." He scratched the back of his hand. "But Ty didn't let me keep lying. Jasmin didn't either. And Nico? He just kept showing up anyway. That made it harder to stay the villain."

Jeremy blinked slowly. He was holding a pencil that had stopped moving five minutes ago. Leo looked toward him for only a second before facing the class again. "Some of you were scared of me," Leo said, and he didn't say it with shame, but with honesty. "Some of you hated me. I get it. I really do. I earned it. I made people cry, and then I told them they were too sensitive. I called them names when I didn't want them to look too close. I used people. I used Ella. I used Nico. I used all of you." There was no apology in his voice yet—just a declaration. The apology would come later.

Jasmin's foot tapped once, then stopped. It wasn't impatience. It was memory. Her arms folded across her chest the way they did when she didn't want to feel too much. Nico looked at the back of his hand, the same one Leo had slapped in the hallway once during a fake high-five. Ella didn't cry, but her fingers pressed hard against her pencil case. Everyone was holding something. Even Mr. Clarke.

"I'm telling this story," Leo said, "not because I want anyone to forgive me. I'm not owed that. I'm telling it because there might be someone in this room who's standing where I used to stand. Who's pretending, every day, to be tougher than they are. Who's saying mean things so they don't have to remember what it felt like to be small." His eyes landed on Alex. It wasn't an accusation. It wasn't even sharp. It was a reflection.

Alex didn't move, but something in his neck twitched. His shoulders had been too still for too long. His jaw looked like it wanted to open and shut all at once. His foot tapped once. Then twice. Then stilled. Leo's voice grew quieter. "I thought I had to be that person forever. I thought once you start acting like that, you never get to stop. That it becomes who you are. But the truth is—it doesn't. It's a choice. And someone has to show you how to make a different one."

Someone exhaled sharply. It might have been Ty. It might have been the air itself. "I'm not perfect now," Leo said. "I still mess up. Sometimes I still feel that old itch—the one that tells me to laugh too loud or roll my eyes or say something cutting. But now I know what it is. I know where it came from. And I don't let it talk for me anymore."

The silence that followed wasn't hollow. It was full—of weight, of reckoning, of memory. Leo looked down for the first time. Then back up. "I was the villain," he said again. "But not anymore." Alex's chair squeaked softly. Not a big movement. Just enough to say something had shifted inside him, too. No one spoke. No one needed to. Leo had started with a story. But he'd ended with a mirror. And it had reflected more than just him.

Ty didn't stand up. He didn't move to the front of the class or ask anyone to listen. He stayed exactly where he was—hands on his desk, elbows steady, eyes soft but sharp, like someone who could see the broken piece behind the glass but knew better than to tap it too hard. "What made you hurt people, Leo?" he asked, and his voice wasn't loud. It didn't need to be. It curved around the room like a thread pulled through each heart. Leo turned his head, not away—but toward it, like he'd been waiting for someone to ask the right question and not let him dodge it.

Leo didn't answer at first. He glanced around the room again, like maybe now the silence felt heavier than before. "You want the truth?" he asked, but it wasn't a real question. It was his own warning. His voice wasn't angry. It wasn't scared either. It was just tired of circling the long way around the pain. "Okay," he said, more to himself than to Ty. "Okay, I'll tell you." He didn't blink as he stared forward. "It started the day my mom died. I was five. She went into the hospital and didn't come back. I remember sitting on the edge of the bed waiting for her. She never came home."

Someone inhaled sharply. Leo didn't flinch. "My dad... he didn't cry. He didn't explain anything. He just looked at me and said, 'What are you looking at? She's gone. Get used to it.' And I think... that was the first time I felt like I was less than a person." He said it plainly. It wasn't a story. It was a memory sealed tight and sharp. "After that, it wasn't about what I wanted or what I needed. It was about what I did wrong. Every day, I was wrong. Even when I wasn't. Especially when I wasn't. That's when it really hurt."

Ty didn't interrupt. He just waited. The others didn't speak. The room felt like a place between two worlds—before Leo's truth, and after it. "My dad was a narcissist," Leo said, trying the word like it still tasted unfamiliar. "I didn't know what that meant until Ty told me. A person who thinks they're always right. Who only feels big when they make you feel small. Who blames you for their mess. And if you cry, they call you weak. If you fight back, they call you disrespectful. If you freeze up, they call you useless." His hands gripped the edge of his desk. "You never win. You just stop trying."

Ty didn't nod. He let the silence ask its own question. Leo answered it. "He'd tell me I imagined things. That I was too sensitive. That Mom wouldn't have spoiled me like this. He made it sound like remembering her was a kind of betrayal. And every time I got upset, he told me I was ungrateful. That I should be lucky he was still raising me." Leo looked down at his hands like they belonged to someone else. "But he wasn't raising me. He was hollowing me out. He made me apologize for things I didn't do. He'd say I broke something even when I wasn't in the room. I started saying sorry before I even knew why."

Nico blinked. He'd done that before. He'd said sorry after tripping when someone else shoved him. He'd said sorry for being late when he was the one who got locked out. The word sorry had been twisted in Leo's mouth until it didn't mean responsibility. It meant survival.

"There was this one night," Leo continued, "I tried to hide in the laundry room because I got a math question wrong. Just one. He said I was stupid. Said Mom would've been ashamed of me. I didn't even cry. I just sat there with the dryer on, listening to it spin, because the sound helped me pretend I was somewhere else." His voice didn't crack. It stayed even. But no one missed the way the words hit the floor like stones.

Ty leaned in, just slightly. "And when did you start doing what he did?"

Leo didn't answer right away. Then: "Grade Three. I remember because it was the first time I made someone else cry on purpose." He looked up. "And I felt powerful for three seconds. Just three. And then empty for the rest of the day. But I did it again anyway. Because I didn't want to be the one crying anymore. I didn't want to be the soft one. I didn't want to be the target." He sighed. "So I became the attacker."

Ty nodded once. "He trained you to be him."

"Yeah," Leo whispered. "He did." His voice came back a little stronger after that. "But you trained me different. You made me see it. You didn't just forgive me. You asked me why. You asked me to tell it with my own mouth." He looked around the room again. "That's harder than pretending it never happened. It's harder than hiding behind a joke. But it sticks." He met Ty's eyes. "You made me stop echoing him. You made me speak for me."

Jeremy shifted in his seat. It wasn't nervous. It was quiet awe. Jasmin's eyes glistened, but she didn't wipe them. Nico looked down, then up again—fierce and soft, all at once.

"I didn't turn into him by accident," Leo said. "But I don't have to keep being him on purpose. I get to choose now." Ty leaned back slightly, letting that truth settle into the centre of the room. "And what would you tell someone who's just starting to turn mean?" Leo didn't hesitate. "I'd tell them they're not broken. They're scared. But scared doesn't have to mean cruel. And if someone made you feel small your whole life... it doesn't mean you only get to feel big by shrinking someone else."

Alex shifted. This time it was not subtle. He blinked hard. Then looked at the floor, like something inside him was trying to come up. Ty's voice was soft. "And would you say all villains used to be victims?" Leo thought for a second. "Not all. Some people just like hurting others. But the ones who were hurt first—they need someone to show them how to stop." His voice tightened, but didn't break. "I got that. I got you. Now I want to be that for someone else." The air changed. It felt... cleaner. But heavy still. Like truth had done its work and left behind silence to let the healing begin. Leo had answered the question. Not with excuses. Not with blame. But with truth—and that's what made it real.

Leo's hands stayed clenched at his sides, but the room was listening. Not with their ears—those had been trained for noise. This was a kind of listening that lived behind the eyes. He looked at no one, not even Ty, and began speaking like someone cracking open a door they'd nailed shut years ago. "At my old house," Leo said, "you only got told you were good if you didn't cry. Or ask questions. Or even look like you had your own thoughts." The class didn't move. Not even Alex.

He said it slowly, like his mouth was sore from memory. "If I did something perfect, I'd get a nod. Maybe a pat. But only if no one else was watching. He said hugs made kids weak." His voice didn't break. But his fingers curled tighter. "He told me, 'If people see you being soft, they'll eat you alive.' So, I stopped being soft." The word hung in the air like it didn't belong in a school.

Ty sat perfectly still. He wasn't reacting—not with his mouth, not even with his eyebrows. He just let Leo speak. Let the words float like puzzle pieces across the floor, knowing everyone else would start putting them together in their heads. Leo continued, "Smiles in my house meant you passed a test. They weren't for fun. They weren't for love. They were for getting it right."

Some of the kids shifted. A few blinked slowly, the way you do when something hits you in the chest and you don't want anyone to notice. Jasmin placed her hand gently on her knee, anchoring herself. Nico looked at the floor, where the shadows stretched long beneath Leo's sneakers.

"I used to think," Leo said carefully, "that love meant proving you weren't a problem. That if someone praised you, it was so they could use you next. Praise was the butter before the knife." One girl near the window softly gasped, then covered her mouth. Leo didn't look. He just spoke.

He took a shallow breath and went on. "When my mom was alive, she hugged me even when I was loud. She smiled even when I spilled things. But after she died, he said she babied me. Said I'd never survive the real world if I didn't toughen up. That's when the rules changed." There was no bitterness in Leo's voice, only a worn-out kind of truth. The kind that doesn't shout because it already knows how loud it echoed in his head.

"My dad told me love was for babies. So I turned myself into something else. Something not soft. Something not breakable. Something mean." Leo didn't shake when he said that. He stood taller, as though naming it made it less powerful.

Ty finally blinked. "Do you still believe that now?" he asked, not softly but respectfully. Like he knew the answer and just wanted Leo to hear himself say it. Leo didn't answer right away. He took two full breaths, the second one deeper than the first.

"No," he said at last. "Not anymore. But it's hard to unlearn when your body still flinches at hugs. When you still think silence is safer than speaking up. When you hear someone say something nice and your first thought is, What do they want?" That line didn't make anyone laugh. It didn't make anyone nod. It just settled over them like fog.

Alex shifted in his seat, not fidgeting—just moving enough to look uncomfortable. He was watching Leo now, not like an enemy, but like someone who had seen their own reflection in a window they thought was just glass. A reflection they didn't recognize.

Leo stepped forward one inch. "If you grow up in a trap, even freedom feels fake at first. I didn't know I could be loved without a leash. Not until Ty." His voice dropped, but the silence around him amplified every word. "Ty's family didn't praise me to use me. They didn't smile just to make me obey. They loved me when I was still messed up."

A murmur passed through the room, low and unsure. One boy near the back rubbed his eyes. A girl near the corner tightened her ponytail but didn't speak. No one interrupted. No one dared to.

"Love shouldn't feel like pressure," Leo said, "or like something you can lose if you say the wrong thing. That's not love. That's control." He looked at Ty. "I thought I had to earn every kind word. But Ty gave them away like they weren't rare. And they stuck."

Ty's eyes didn't blink this time. He nodded slowly, like a soldier returning a salute. "And now?" he asked. "What do you think love is now?" Leo exhaled. "It's not about being useful," he said. "It's about being seen, even when you're not perfect. Maybe especially then." Nico looked up. Jasmin looked over. Alex looked down. And for a second—a brief, unmeasured second—the villain didn't look like a villain at all.

The whiteboard marker squeaked like a whisper as Ty drew the letters across the board. He didn't rush. He didn't speak. Each word landed like a brick laid carefully into a wall that hadn't stood upright in years. "What do you believe about yourself?" he wrote in firm, slow lines. Then he capped the marker and turned around. No lecture. No speech. Just a quiet moment with a sentence staring back at twenty-eight faces who weren't ready for it—but needed it.

Jasmin was the first to blink. Not because she didn't understand it, but because she did. The sentence had a way of reaching straight past the shell you wore to school and tapping the part of you no one asked about. She stared at it like it was a mirror she'd never looked into properly before. Not the kind that told you how your hair looked, but the kind that told you what you'd been taught to think of your own reflection.

Ty didn't move from where he stood. He just raised a hand slightly, like a conductor before the first note. "Before you answer that," he said, "I want you to know something. That sentence didn't start with you. It came from somewhere. Someone." He let the silence stretch. "Most of us didn't write the first thing we ever believed about ourselves. We just copied it."

Leo closed his eyes slowly, his breath deepening. Nico glanced toward Jasmin, who hadn't moved her gaze from the board. She was holding her pencil, not to write, but as though it anchored her to the moment. Ty walked slowly between the desks. "Think back," he said, "to the first time someone called you lazy. Or stupid. Or dramatic. Or annoying. Maybe they didn't even say it. Maybe they just looked at you like it was already true."

One of the younger boys near the back lowered his head. A girl near the windows squinted, like memory stung her eyes. Ty continued, "You took that sentence. You didn't want to, but you did. You folded it up like a note you didn't write, and you kept it in your pocket. And after a while, you started reading it like it was true."

The room didn't creak, didn't fidget. It just breathed—slow and wary. Jasmin swallowed and whispered, "I always believed I was hard to like." Ty heard her, even though the room wasn't meant to. He nodded. "Who wrote that first?" he asked, but not as a challenge. Just a breadcrumb back to the beginning. Jasmin looked down. "My aunt," she said. "When I was five. I asked her why she never hugged me. She said, 'You make things harder.'"

The room didn't flinch—but something inside each kid did. Leo stared at the ceiling. Nico scribbled a circle on his paper, just to keep his hands from sitting still. Ty didn't fill the silence. He let it sit beside Jasmin, respectful and unafraid. "You've been copying her handwriting in your head," he said, "for years. But it's not your script."

Jasmin looked up, eyes sharp with something that wasn't quite tears. "How do I erase it?" she asked. The sentence on the board hadn't changed. But the meaning of it had. Ty pointed at the words again. "By writing your own. Out loud. And again. And again. Until it sounds more like you and less like them."

Leo leaned forward. "What if you believed something wrong about yourself for so long it feels like truth?" Ty nodded. "Then it's time to test it. Hold it up to real love. Real safety. Real friends. See if it still stands."

Nico raised his hand quietly. "What if no one ever said anything mean, but they just ignored you? Like you were invisible?" Ty stopped walking. He looked right at Nico. "Then the sentence wasn't written in words. It was written in silence. That's the trickiest one to rewrite—but it can be done."

Jasmin finally picked up her pencil and began writing in the corner of her page. She didn't show anyone what it said. But her lips moved once as she whispered the words to herself. Nico watched her and did the same. Leo reached into his notebook and tore a page out completely.

Ty walked back to the front, marker in hand. "Sometimes," he said, "the best thing you can do with a sentence someone else wrote for you—is return it." He scribbled over the board with a long black line and then, beside it, wrote three smaller words: "Try again. Now."

Alex sat completely still. His fingers were curled under the desk, pressing into his palms. His mouth stayed closed, but his heart was making noise only he could hear. A sentence long buried had started whispering again—and he didn't like what it said. Not because it was wrong. But because it was still there.

Leo didn't pace. He didn't hold a paper. He didn't need to. He stood near the front of the classroom, just far enough from Ty's desk to feel like it was his turn to speak. His voice didn't shake, but it didn't pretend to be strong either. It was the kind of voice that had been silenced too long and was now learning how to be steady again. "He used to call me stupid. Every day," Leo said. "Like brushing his teeth. Like it was just part of his routine."

Not a single person shifted. Even Nico, who usually had to move his legs every few seconds, froze in place. Jasmin's hands curled softly over the lip of her desk, not gripping, but holding on. No one whispered. No one cracked a pencil lead by mistake. Even the teacher—Mr. Clarke—stayed still, as though his role in this moment was to listen, not teach.

Leo took a breath, then went on. "Sometimes it was lazy. Or selfish. Or liar. He had this list." He glanced down. "He kept it in his head, but I memorized it too. Because if I didn't, I wouldn't know what mood he was in that day." He blinked slowly. "I got good at figuring out what kind of insult was coming. Based on how he chewed his food. Or if he sat down too fast."

A girl in the second row dropped her gaze to her desk. Not because she wasn't listening, but because she didn't want him to see her eyes filling. Across the room, a boy with short brown curls took his hood off for the first time that day. Ty stood quietly beside the whiteboard, watching Leo with the patience of someone who already knew what this cost.

"He used to tell me I was the reason she died," Leo said. His breath caught, not like a sob but like a choke. "My mom." The room didn't blink. Not a shuffle. Not even a breath out of place. "She died when I was five," Leo continued. "And he said it was because I cried too much that night. That I gave her a headache and made it worse."

Jasmin pressed her hand against her chest. Nico looked away, jaw tense, as though the words had climbed down into his stomach and found a place to sit. Mr. Clarke leaned forward just an inch—but he didn't interrupt. This wasn't his story to hold. It was Leo's. And Leo was holding it now with both hands, even if they still trembled.

"He said she would've lived if I'd just been quiet." Leo's voice didn't rise. It didn't ask for pity. It simply laid the memory out like a worn cloth, already faded but not forgotten. "So I learned to be quiet. I learned that if I said less, maybe he'd stop blaming me. But he never did."

One girl whispered something so soft it was inaudible. But her friend touched her arm and shook her head gently. Let him finish. Let it come out all the way. Leo swallowed hard. "He never let me forget it. Not once. Even when I tried to do good things—he'd say, 'Oh, so now you're pretending to be perfect?' He'd call me a fake. A phony. He said I was performing for strangers."

Alex, sitting against the far wall, stared at the side of Leo's face with a strange kind of stillness. His hands were tucked under his legs. His ears had gone pink. His eyes were neither narrow nor wide—but unreadable. Ty noticed. But he didn't react. This moment was for Leo. The rest would come later.

Leo looked down at his shoes. "I tried so hard to be someone else. That's why I copied you," he said quietly to Nico. "And you," he said, glancing at Jasmin. "Because I didn't think being me was safe. Or good. Or even real." Nico blinked once. Jasmin didn't move.

The room stayed quiet—not frozen out of fear, but out of respect. There was a strange holiness to it. Like church, but not the kind with windows and pews. This was something sacred because it was raw. Because it was unguarded. Because no one was pretending anymore.

"I thought being mean meant I was in control," Leo said. "I thought if I hurt first, I couldn't get hurt second." His voice cracked. Just a little. Just enough. "But I still got hurt. Every day. Even when I was the one doing the damage." He rubbed his knuckles with his thumb, as though the story lived under his skin.

Mr. Clarke let out a long breath—but still said nothing. The children didn't whisper. No glances were exchanged. It was as if the entire room had made a pact: this story mattered more than anything else right now. And no one wanted to be the first to look away.

"Now I'm here," Leo finished. "And I'm not pretending anymore." He looked toward Ty, then back to the class. "I don't want to be the villain anymore. I want to be the one who notices the quiet kid before he turns mean." He looked down again, then straightened his shoulders. "Because the villain I was... was just a boy who never got helped." No one blinked.

No one moved right away, not even when Leo finally sat back down. His chair made a tiny creak against the tile, but the room didn't fill in the silence. No one clapped. No one whispered. It wasn't that kind of moment. It was the kind of quiet that follows something real. The kind that holds breath in the spaces between sentences because something sacred just got said. Mr. Clarke glanced at the clock but didn't say a word about time. That day, the bell would wait.

Jeremy was the first to move. He didn't raise his hand. He didn't ask. He didn't check to see if it was okay. He just got up, quietly, chair legs squeaking slightly as he dragged it across the floor. A few kids glanced up, expecting a trip to the garbage or a paper hand-in. But Jeremy didn't go to the front. He moved his chair beside Leo's and sat down.

That's all. He just sat down. Right next to him. Shoulder almost touching. Leo looked up, startled for a second, and then caught his breath when he saw who it was. Jeremy didn't make a show of it. He didn't say anything at first. He didn't look around to check what people thought. He just looked at Leo, and nodded, like he understood something more than words could cover.

Leo gave a tiny nod back. Not the kind you practice in front of a mirror, but the kind that's only ever used once or twice in your life—the kind you give when you're afraid to hope, but hope anyway. Jeremy reached over and gently placed a hand on Leo's wrist, not to stop him, not to hold him back, but just to say, I'm here.

And then, in a voice so warm it melted the space between them, Jeremy said, "I love you, Leo." It wasn't loud. It wasn't embarrassed. It was the sort of sentence that had no shame, no strings, and no fear attached. It just existed, like a blanket laid across shivering shoulders. Leo stared at him, stunned. He didn't say anything right away. He couldn't. He just looked down, and his throat closed up tight.

Jeremy leaned forward and wrapped his arms around Leo, not shy, not performative. Just arms. Just warmth. Just full-hearted, little brother love. And for a long second, Leo didn't move. But then he breathed in and wrapped his arms around Jeremy, too. And the class watched—not like a show, not like entertainment, but like something holy was happening, and they didn't want to miss a frame.

Ty glanced toward Jasmin. She didn't smile. She didn't need to. Her eyes said everything. Nico sat still too, just watching the way Leo held his hands, like they weren't made for hurting anymore. Leo's shoulders shook once. Just once. He didn't cry out loud. But his eyes were glassed over, and he held Jeremy like someone who never thought he'd be held again.

Someone near the window sniffed. Another child cleared their throat, just once, trying to keep it together. But no one teased. No one rolled their eyes. The classroom had learned something this hour that couldn't be written on the board. That pain passed down becomes pain passed forward—unless someone chooses to stop the chain.

Jeremy looked up at the class, still hugging Leo, and said softly, "He's not like that anymore." He looked around, not to accuse, but to make something clear. "He's my big brother now." One of the younger boys in the back sat up straighter. A girl near the front blinked hard and wiped at her eye. Nobody argued.

Leo pulled back, just a little, enough to look Jeremy in the face. He opened his mouth, but words didn't come fast. When they did, they were soft, hoarse, real. "Thanks, Jer." And Jeremy, like he'd been waiting his whole life for this moment, replied with another squeeze. "I knew it was still you."

Mr. Clarke didn't interrupt. He stood with his hand over his heart and nodded once. Not performative. Not a teacher's moment. A human one. Then he walked slowly to his desk and sat down as if the lesson had already been taught—and it didn't come from him.

Ty gave a single nod, the kind he'd given Jasmin once before. The Shadow Warrior's signal. Quiet truth, passed in silence. Jasmin returned it without a blink. Nico glanced toward Alex, who was very, very still. His eyes weren't on Leo. They were locked somewhere inside himself. But for now, no one moved toward Alex. Because the story didn't belong to him yet. It belonged to the one who stopped the chain.

Ty didn't raise his voice when he stepped forward. He didn't rush the moment or speak like he was teaching a class. He simply walked—slow and steady—across the quiet floor of the classroom, his eyes never leaving Leo. The weight of the air hadn't lifted since Jeremy had wrapped his arms around him. It was a sacred silence, and Ty moved inside it with reverence. He reached Leo's side and didn't stand above him. He knelt. One knee down. Level with his friend. And then he said it—clear, sure, and warm. "I love you, Leo. You're still my brother too."

Leo didn't blink. His eyes, rimmed red but brave, locked onto Ty's. The way he'd looked at Jeremy before, he now looked at Ty—as if trying to memorize him, not the outside, but the part you can't point to. Leo pulled Ty close with both arms, tighter than before, not like someone clinging to a raft, but like someone honouring the person who threw it. "Thank you," Leo whispered into Ty's shoulder. "I love you too."

Ty's hand stayed on Leo's back for a moment longer. Then he pulled back gently and nodded once. The whole class watched, not like spectators, but like listeners to something older than all of them. Ty stood again, but this time he didn't return to his desk. He turned toward the room, hands at his sides, face calm. "Anger," he said, "can be taught. Just like a story."

A few heads tilted. No one interrupted. Ty glanced at Mr. Clarke, who gave him a small nod, then leaned back in his chair as if yielding the floor. "It can get passed down," Ty continued. "Like bedtime stories, only it's the kind you never wanted to hear. Someone yells, you learn to yell. Someone hits, you learn to brace. Someone lies, you learn not to speak."

Leo nodded slowly. "Like it gets planted in your bones," he said. "Even if you don't want it there." "Exactly," Ty said. "And you can carry it for years before you even know it's not yours. But it feels like yours. It starts sounding like your own voice." Nico shifted slightly in his chair. Jasmin stared ahead, her fingers gripping her pencil without writing. A few students from the younger grades sat motionless near the back, expressions unreadable but eyes full. Leo stood now, beside Ty, not slouching, not hiding. Just standing.

"I used to think I was angry," Leo said quietly. "But I wasn't. Not at first. I was just scared. But when you get punished for being scared, you learn to show something else. You learn to punch instead of cry." Ty reached over and lightly touched Leo's shoulder. "That's why I said I love you," he murmured again, "because I know what it's like when no one teaches you better. But we're teaching each other now."

Leo turned back to the class. He wasn't stiff, but he wasn't casual either. This wasn't performance. It was testimony. "When I said 'I love you' to Jeremy, it wasn't to make myself look good," he said. "It was because he loved me even when I didn't deserve it. And when I said it to Ty, it was because he pulled me back when I was going full-speed into the kind of man my dad was."

A soft shuffle broke the silence. It came from the corner—Alex, shifting in his seat, blinking more than usual, staring down at the floor like it was full of secrets. No one addressed him. Not yet. The room was still on Leo. "I didn't know what love was," Leo said. "I thought it was what my dad gave. Praise when I followed orders. Smiles when I stayed quiet. But that wasn't love. That was fear dressed up nice." Jeremy reached for Leo's hand again, just gently. Leo smiled, then continued. "Ty showed me the difference. He showed me that love listens. That it pulls you back from the edge, even when you're not ready to admit you're on it."

Ty gave a small bow of the head, nothing showy. Just honour. Jasmin's eyes were misted now. She didn't wipe them. She just looked, and nodded slowly. "Forgiveness," Leo added, "isn't pretending it didn't happen. It's saying, 'I see you're trying now, and I'll give you space to grow.' That's what they gave me. That's what made me change. And that's why I'm not afraid to say I love you anymore."

The room stayed still. Mr. Clarke placed his pen gently on the desk, folded his hands, and watched. Ty stepped aside now, letting Leo stand alone, but not abandoned. Jeremy didn't let go of his hand. Nico finally spoke, his voice low but sure. "That's the difference between a villain and a survivor. One stays angry. The other learns to breathe again." Leo looked at him, and for the first time since the beginning of the chapter, smiled. And it was real.

Ty reached into the drawer at the side of the classroom, the one with loose whiteboard markers and backup tissues. But instead of pulling out a worksheet or some visual aid, he pulled out something smooth, framed, and reflective. A rectangular mirror, small enough to hold in one hand, but large enough to see your own eyes. He held it up to the class and said, "Let's try something."

He didn't explain first. He let the object speak before he did. Most of the class stared, unsure if it was a trick, an art project, or something from the drama closet. Mr. Clarke gave no direction. He trusted Ty now, the same way a gardener trusts good rain. Ty turned the mirror toward himself and looked directly into it. Not for show. For real.

"Say something mean to yourself," Ty said, still looking at his reflection. "Go on. Pick something you've believed for way too long. The kind of sentence that shows up in your head before anyone else even speaks."

He handed the mirror to Jasmin without waiting for someone to volunteer. She looked startled but didn't flinch. She looked into the glass, her lips pressing tight, then parting slightly. Her voice was barely above a whisper. "You're too much," she said. "Too loud. Too bossy."

There was no laughter. No correction. Ty nodded gently, stepped forward, and asked one question: "Who said it first?" Jasmin blinked hard. "My aunt," she answered after a long pause. "Every time I asked questions." Ty nodded again. "Was she right?" "No," Jasmin said, stronger this time. "She just didn't like when I noticed things." Ty took the mirror and handed it next to Nico. Nico's jaw tightened before he even spoke. He knew his turn was coming, and he hadn't decided whether he wanted it or not. But he took the mirror. Stared. And said, "You're not smart enough."

Ty didn't ask this time. Nico answered before being prompted. "My dad," he said. "When I spelled something wrong in Grade 2. He didn't even look at the drawing I made. Just the mistake." Leo was breathing through his nose now, slow and steady, holding back tears like someone balancing water in cupped hands. He hadn't taken the mirror yet. But he knew he would. Ty saw it, didn't force it, just waited. Then gently passed it to Leo with both hands.

Leo took it. Looked down. Looked up. Then down again. He didn't speak right away. But when he did, it didn't sound like his voice anymore. "You were born wrong," he said. The sentence hit the floor like a hammer. "You were born broken." "Who said it first?" Ty asked, even softer than before. "My dad," Leo whispered. "The day after my mom's funeral. I knocked over a vase. He said it while sweeping the pieces."

Jeremy let out a sound that was almost a sob but caught it in his throat. He stood and walked across the room without waiting for permission. "Can I have the mirror?" he asked Ty. Ty gave it to him silently. Jeremy held it up to himself. "You're annoying," he said. Then, "You're just a tag-along." His face trembled, but he didn't look away. "Who said it first?" Ty asked gently.

"Other kids," Jeremy said. "Before Leo." "Do you believe it?" Ty asked. Jeremy shook his head fast. "Not anymore." Ty put the mirror down on the table at the centre of the classroom. "We don't come up with these lies on our own," he said. "Someone teaches them to us. And if we're not careful, we start teaching them to others."

Leo raised his hand—not to answer a question, but to add. "And sometimes, we don't even know we're doing it," he said. "Sometimes we call someone else the same thing we heard, just to not feel alone with it." Jasmin nodded. "But saying it out loud makes it easier to let go." Ty looked at each of them. "Exactly," he said. "It doesn't fix it. But it breaks the mirror just enough that you can see past it."

The classroom stayed quiet. No desks creaked. No feet shuffled. Even Mr. Clarke didn't shift in his chair. For one breathless moment, the entire room sat inside that truth, still and solemn, as if watching a wave pass beneath the surface—too deep to splash, but strong enough to shift the entire tide.

The classroom had gone still again. It wasn't silence like before a test, or the quiet that fell when Mr. Clarke raised his hand. This silence was the kind that grew when something honest was said aloud. The kind that moved through the air like a slow breath. Ella sat with her fingers threaded together, eyes on her knees. She hadn't spoken the entire lesson. But now, she raised her head, just a little, just enough to meet Leo's eyes.

"I thought it was me," she said, the words barely more than a whisper. "When he was mean to me… I thought I was the problem."

Leo didn't look away. He didn't wince or apologize right away, either. He just listened, the way Ty had taught him to. He held her gaze gently, like something fragile but important. Then he stood, slowly, walked across the room, and knelt beside her chair. Everyone else held their breath.

"It wasn't you," Leo said, steady and clear. "It never was."

Ella's face crumpled at the edges. Not from shame, but from something deeper—like her heart had been holding in a sob for months, and now it wasn't afraid to show itself. Leo didn't speak again. He just opened his arms—not wide, not dramatic, just enough to ask without asking.

Ella leaned forward like she was falling into something she hadn't believed existed anymore. She let herself be held. And when she did, her whole body trembled, not like fear, but like relief. Her fists stayed at her sides for a second, then wrapped around his back. She didn't sob. She just breathed. And for that moment, she didn't let go.

It didn't last forever. It didn't need to. Leo didn't squeeze tighter or make it a scene. He let her step back when she was ready. But in that short space of quiet closeness, something shifted. Not just between them, but in the room. The kind of shift that said a page had turned and wouldn't be flipped back.

Leo walked back to his desk, pulled a pen from the inside of his pencil case, and a sheet of loose paper from his binder. His hand shook slightly, but he didn't stop. He wrote slowly, carefully, as if every word deserved breath and weight. When he was done, he folded the paper once, stood again, and handed it to Ella.

She opened it in front of him. There, in clear blue ink, it read: I love you, Ella. I am beyond sorry for everything I said and did to you. Beneath it, he had written his full name—Leo Mason Takashi-Firth. There was no scribble, no scratch-out. Just the truth. Ella didn't cry again. She held the note with both hands, like it was something sacred. Something rare. She looked up at him and nodded once, firmly. "Thank you," she said. Nothing more. Nothing less.

Jasmin exhaled audibly. She'd been holding her breath without realizing it. Ty offered a small, proud smile from across the room. He didn't say anything, but his eyes carried an entire chapter of respect. Leo returned to his seat, not with pride or performance, but with quiet dignity. His hands didn't shake anymore. For the first time in a long time, he sat without folding in on himself. He didn't try to make himself smaller. He didn't hide.

Jeremy leaned over and whispered something that made Leo grin. No one heard what was said, but it didn't need repeating. It was the kind of thing brothers say when words aren't big enough for feelings. Mr. Clarke stood slowly, looked at Leo, then at Ella, and said only, "Thank you. Both of you." He didn't lecture or praise. He simply witnessed. That was enough.

Ella put the note into the front pocket of her backpack, zipped it, and placed a hand over it briefly—like sealing a promise. She looked toward the door, then back at Leo, and gave a smile. Not the performative kind. The kind that comes after a long night and the first true morning. No one clapped. No one said "aww." The class didn't need to. Everyone had seen something bigger than themselves. They didn't need to name it. They just knew.

Jasmin didn't make a sound. Her hands stayed in her lap, fingers curled into each other like they were trying to hold something still. Her face didn't move. Her eyes didn't blink more than usual. But inside, the pressure was sharp. It wasn't the kind of pain that begged to spill out, like Ella's had. It was the kind that sank into bone, silent and stubborn, and stayed there.

She didn't cry when Leo hugged Ella. She didn't cry when Jeremy told Leo he loved him. She didn't even cry when Ty's voice cracked just a little in front of everyone. But her chest had started to ache, and she didn't know why exactly. Not at first. Until she realized that her own silence wasn't strength. It was just where she'd hidden her hurt.

Leo noticed. Maybe because he knew what that kind of stillness looked like. Maybe because he'd worn it himself. He didn't stare. He didn't pressure her. But slowly, quietly, he stood up from his chair again. And he walked toward her—not like someone trying to fix something, but like someone asking permission.

He didn't say her name out loud. He didn't need to. Jasmin's eyes flicked up just once to meet his, and then back down. Leo stopped in front of her and opened his arms—not too wide, not with any expectation. It was a gesture of respect more than a hug. A question, not a demand.

Jasmin hesitated. Her breath caught for a second in her throat. Not because she was afraid of him now. That had passed. She knew Leo's heart was different. It wasn't that. It was the part of her that wasn't used to being seen, even when she was right there in front of everyone. Being invisible can become a habit, especially when people only notice you when you break.

She didn't get up. But she did reach out—just a little. One hand left her lap and rested against Leo's side, like she was testing gravity. Leo didn't move. He just waited. And when Jasmin finally leaned forward, it was slow, like pulling a truth from a very quiet place inside herself.

They hugged. Briefly. Not tightly. But enough. Leo's hand touched her back once, then let go. And that was all it took for Jasmin to breathe again. Not a full exhale. But a release. A loosening of something she hadn't known was clenched.

Ty watched without interrupting. Jeremy gave a small nod. Ella, still holding her note, sat straighter, as if Jasmin's moment gave her permission to stand taller too. Mr. Clarke didn't interfere. He just took a step back and let the silence stretch, unbroken and meaningful.

Jasmin sat down again. Her hands returned to her lap, but this time, they weren't twisted tight. She still didn't cry. But her shoulders softened. And the ache in her chest, while still there, didn't feel quite so alone.

Leo returned to his seat without looking for applause. He wasn't trying to be a hero. He wasn't performing. He just wanted to be what he hadn't been before: safe. For others. For himself. For the girl who never made a scene, but always noticed everyone else's.

Jasmin looked out the window for a moment. The sky was cloudy but not dark. The light came in crooked through the blinds, dust floating in the gold stripes. It reminded her of mornings at her grandmother's house. Of quiet safety. Of small things that lasted longer than noise.

She hadn't said anything. Not yet. But she would. When it was time. When the words inside her stopped feeling like bruises and started feeling like pieces that could be shared. For now, she let the moment hold her without breaking her open. Ty leaned slightly toward her, close enough that only she could hear him. "You don't have to cry," he whispered. "Just don't carry it alone." She didn't answer. She didn't need to. Her hands unfolded slowly. And for the first time that morning, she moved them apart.

The question came not from anger, but from somewhere else—somewhere that sounded like confusion. It wasn't loud, either. Just a soft voice from the third row, behind Nico and beside Ella. A quiet boy named Ethan, who usually didn't speak unless called on, had raised his hand and, after being nodded to, said the words: "Why didn't you stop?"

Leo blinked. He didn't flinch. He didn't dodge it. He stood again, even though the silence afterward made his ears ring. The classroom felt like it had no air. But he stood, anyway. He looked not at Ethan, but around the room. Every face was different now—softer, maybe, or unsure, or still. No one laughed. Not even Alex, who had gone pale long before this part of the morning began. "I didn't stop," Leo said, and his voice was steady but quiet, "because I didn't know how. And no one told me to."

He let the sentence hang there. He didn't rush to explain it. He didn't try to cushion the blow. He just told the truth and let it rest between all of them like a stone dropped into water. The ripples moved outward slowly, quietly, across the faces of kids who had seen what he was like before—but had never asked what made him that way.

"When I was little," he continued, "I thought being strong meant scaring people. That's how I was raised. That's what I saw every day. When I made someone cry, I thought it meant I was winning. But I wasn't. I was just passing on the same pain I'd been given. And I didn't know that until Ty showed me."

Leo turned his head slightly toward Ty, who gave a respectful nod, not trying to steal the moment or soften it. Just honouring it. Leo went on. "I didn't stop," he said again, "because stopping meant admitting I was wrong. And where I came from, being wrong meant being nothing. I didn't want to be nothing."

No one moved. Even Mr. Clarke didn't speak. His hands were folded in front of him, not in judgment, but in thought. Nico had his pencil frozen halfway through a margin doodle. Jasmin's lips were pressed together, not in disapproval but in patience. Ella sat with her arms across her stomach, as though hugging the hurt Leo had once given her—but letting it go one inch at a time.

Leo walked forward two steps. Just enough to be near the centre of the room. "For those of you I've hurt," he said, louder now—not yelling, just reaching farther, "I'm here for you. With open arms. Always."

Jeremy looked up first. No hesitation. No conditions. Just a smile and the smallest nod, like he was already standing inside those open arms. Ella shifted in her seat, watching Leo closely, her lips forming the word okay without sound. Jasmin blinked once and unfolded her arms. And Ethan, the boy who had asked the question, simply said, "Thank you."

Leo stood for another second. He didn't cry. Not because he didn't feel it—but because the moment wasn't about him anymore. He had said the truth. He had owned it. And now it belonged to everyone. Ty stood next. "Truth heals faster than silence," he said. "But only if you share it."

Mr. Clarke stepped forward, his face unreadable. Then, slowly, he walked to the whiteboard and underlined Ty's sentence from earlier: What do you believe about yourself? Then he added a new one underneath: You can rewrite it now. Alex didn't speak. But his shoulders had hunched in closer. His hands fidgeted in his lap. And when Leo sat down again, there was a pause—brief but real—where Alex almost said something. Almost. But not yet.

Alex didn't raise his hand. He didn't clear his throat or ask for the bathroom pass. He didn't even glance toward the door like a kid planning an escape. One second he was in his chair, legs crossed and arms clamped tight across his middle, and the next, his chair scraped back so hard it tipped over, and he was gone. The door slammed before anyone could speak. No words. No sound but the echo.

Ty stood, but didn't follow. Neither did Leo. No one said his name. There wasn't time. By the time the door stopped shaking on its hinges, Alex's footsteps were already fading down the hall, heavy and loud and uneven. A second later came another sound—the unmistakable bang of a washroom door being thrown open, and then silence again.

The class didn't move. Jeremy looked up at Mr. Clarke. Jasmin looked at the empty desk. Ella pressed both her hands against her stomach like she'd felt the motion in her own skin. Nico glanced at Ty, but even Ty just stood still. The weight of it dropped like a stone, and all of them sat in its shadow.

"Don't go after him," Leo said, his voice low. "He's not ready for that yet." Mr. Clarke nodded once. "He's not," he said. "But someone should be ready for him when he comes back." Ty crossed the room and sat beside Leo without speaking. Jasmin looked over her shoulder toward the door. "Do you think he's okay?" she asked, voice quieter than usual. No one answered right away. It wasn't a question with a quick reply.

The hallway buzzed faintly through the windows, and then came the sound. It wasn't just gagging—it was retching. Hard, guttural, awful. It rang through the thin washroom walls and echoed down the corridor. The noise was sharp enough to make Jeremy wince. It went on, then paused, then came again. Kids around the room flinched but didn't laugh. Not one smirk. Because even if they didn't know what Alex was feeling, they could hear what his body was doing—and it wasn't fake.

Nico whispered, "It sounded like he was going to be sick before he even stood up." Ty nodded. "He was holding it in for a long time," he replied. "The body always knows before the mouth does." Ella wrapped her arms around herself and looked at Leo. "Did you ever feel like that?" she asked. Leo didn't blink. "Worse," he said. "But I never let anyone see it."

Jasmin shifted in her seat. "But he let us see it," she said softly. "Even if he didn't mean to." Mr. Clarke picked up the chair Alex had knocked over and set it upright again. He didn't brush the dust from the floor. He didn't make a speech. He just looked at the seat, then out the window, and waited.

From the hall came the sound of a toilet flushing. Then silence again. Then water. Then nothing. "Do we help him?" Jeremy asked. His voice cracked. Leo looked at Ty. Ty didn't answer yet. "You don't catch someone who's still falling," Leo said at last. "You wait at the bottom and hold out your hand." Jasmin nodded slowly. "But what if he never reaches the bottom?" she whispered. Nico answered, almost to himself, "Then we just wait longer."

For several minutes, the classroom said nothing more. Time passed differently after a storm. The desks seemed closer. The air, thinner. The truth sat among them like a shadow they had all agreed to sit with instead of chase away. Then the door opened. It wasn't Alex. It was the school secretary. She stepped inside, looked around the room, and said, "Mr. Clarke, the nurse is with him now. He'll be alright."

Mr. Clarke nodded again. "Thank you." And with that, she left. Leo looked down at his hands. "He heard me," he said quietly. "And his body understood it before his mind did." "Is that what healing looks like?" Jeremy asked. Ty smiled without showing his teeth. "It's what the beginning of it feels like."

The hallway was quieter than it had ever been. Even the light above the library doors flickered without sound, as though the whole building understood what had just happened. From across the corridor, just beyond the wooden door marked "Boys," came the sound no one wanted to acknowledge—violent, guttural, and unmistakably real. Alex was throwing up. Not like someone faking it to leave gym class. Not like someone making noise for sympathy. This was the kind of sick that pulled your whole body forward, made your hands shake and your ribs spasm. The kind of sick that emptied more than your stomach. It emptied whatever you were holding inside.

Leo didn't move at first. His eyes were fixed on the linoleum floor, and his fingers tapped gently against the side of his desk, counting something no one else could see. Ty stood beside him. Not tense. Not waiting. Just… still. Jeremy had both hands wrapped around his pencil case, but his eyes weren't on it. They were on the wall, where the sound came from again—louder this time. A splatter. A gasp. And then silence again. But no one forgot it. Not for a second.

Jasmin's hands were tight in her lap. She didn't flinch, but the grip gave her away. Nico had shifted sideways in his chair, angling himself to see the hallway, though he didn't need to. The sound did all the seeing for him. Ella had gone pale. She didn't cover her ears. She didn't whisper to Jasmin. She just looked ahead, mouth slightly open, like a question had frozen there and didn't know how to ask itself. Miss Penner blinked twice, then sat on the corner of her desk and said nothing. For once, that was the right thing to do.

Leo stood first. It wasn't dramatic. He didn't slam his hands on the desk or shout anyone's name. He just stood, like something had finally clicked in his spine, and he had no more time to sit down. His voice came out low but steady. "We need to help him. Today. Not tomorrow. Not later. Now." Mr. Clarke, leaning against the back wall like he'd been deciding whether to interrupt or disappear, finally stepped forward. "What do you mean help him?" he asked. Not like a challenge—like an invitation.

Leo turned, fully facing the class, then Mr. Clarke. "He's sick," he said. "But not just his stomach. He's breaking open right now. I know what that feels like." His hand trembled slightly as he pointed toward the hallway. "That sound? I've made that sound. I've been there. The thing is, nobody ever stopped to say, 'Maybe he's not evil. Maybe he's just bleeding where no one can see.'" No one interrupted. Ty placed a hand gently on Leo's shoulder, a quiet reminder that he wasn't alone.

"We can't just watch," Leo continued. "This... this is the moment. This is the first sign someone might finally be ready to change. Or at least, to understand what they've been doing. He needs to hear the truth. But not like punishment. Like medicine. That's what saved me. That's what helped me stop being my dad's echo." His voice cracked slightly on the word "dad," but he didn't stop. He steadied himself. "I don't know if he'll hear it today. But it has to start today."

Jeremy finally looked up. His eyes were wet. "Are we gonna go in there?" he asked, not with fear but with that honest child wonder that doesn't hide. Leo shook his head gently. "Not yet. Not while he's still sick. But after? Yes." Mr. Clarke crossed his arms—not to block, but to focus. "What do you plan to say?" he asked. Leo looked at Ty, then back at the teacher. "I want to tell him it's not his fault. And I want to say that from someone who used to be him."

There was a hush after that. No footsteps in the hallway. No pencils scribbling. Just a stillness that wrapped around the moment and pressed gently on everyone's chest. Jasmin finally exhaled, like she'd been waiting for someone else to say those words. Ty spoke next, calm and sure. "It won't work all at once," he said. "It's not a movie scene. But if we speak truth without anger... he might hear it. The real kind. The truth that sticks."

Mr. Clarke nodded. "Alright," he said. "I'm in. But this isn't just a one-time fix. This might take a few days." Leo smiled, tired but ready. "I know," he replied. "I've got time. And so does he." Ella finally spoke. "We're not going to pretend it didn't happen, right?" Leo shook his head. "No. But we're not going to shame him either. He's already drowning. We just hand him the rope. He'll decide what to do with it."

The class didn't break into applause. No one cheered. But one by one, the kids nodded. Even Nico, who never said much. Jeremy whispered, "We save him the way we wish someone saved us." That was enough. Leo walked to the door and placed his hand on the handle. Not to open it—just to let the wall know he was there. The sound had stopped. But the moment had just begun. He turned around and said, "Let's get ready. He's going to need all of us."

Mr. Clarke stepped forward again, no longer a background figure. "Then we start this tomorrow. Early. First thing." Leo nodded. "He'll probably push back," he warned. "He might lie, blame, lash out. I did." Ty grinned slightly. "And we handled you just fine." Leo laughed quietly. "Fair." The class shifted back into motion, slowly. The bell hadn't rung yet, but the moment had finished ringing.

Ty whispered to Nico as they gathered their books, "That sound? That was the sound of the truth coming up. And it's messy, but it's honest." Nico didn't smile, but he nodded. Jasmin slipped a tissue into her pocket, not for herself—but for whoever might need it tomorrow. Ella tied her shoelace tightly, like getting ready for something she couldn't explain yet. Jeremy stayed beside Leo, small but solid. The hallway stayed quiet, but the door behind it? That was where the next part of the story would start. And Leo knew now—he was ready to walk through it. Not as the villain. Not anymore.

Jeremy's voice barely broke the space between them, a whisper so small it might've floated away with the dust. But it didn't. It landed squarely between Ty's ears and heart, sharp in its innocence. "Is he the villain now?" Jeremy asked, not as accusation, but as a child desperate for meaning. His fingers were pressed into the denim at his knees, his body curled slightly toward Ty like the words needed a place to fall. Ty didn't answer right away. He looked up, not toward the hallway where Alex had disappeared, but toward Leo—who was now seated, head low, thoughts turning like gears.

"I don't think so," Ty said finally, his voice as even as a breath on a windowpane. "Maybe he's someone who just got told the truth too fast." The room didn't move, but the atmosphere shifted slightly. Not heavy. Not light. Just different. Jeremy nodded slowly, as if the idea made sense in the bones before it reached the brain. He tucked the question back into his chest like a note folded into a pocket. Leo looked over then, and though he hadn't heard the words, something in his gaze said he understood them anyway.

"I was that kid," Leo said aloud, not dramatically, but like someone placing a stone gently on the ground. "And when I was, people didn't ask if I was the villain. They just assumed I was." The class listened, not frozen but still. Mr. Clarke sat down this time, not standing like an authority figure, but leaning forward like someone trying to see with more than just his eyes. No one interrupted. No one filled the silence. Because the silence was finally doing what it was meant to do—listen.

"He's scared," Leo said. "The kind of scared that makes your stomach flip. The kind that makes you angry instead of honest. That's what I was." Ty nodded, barely moving. "He might still lie," Leo admitted. "He might still hurt. But that's not the whole story. That's just where he is now." The truth was steady in Leo's mouth. Not forced. Not heavy. Just placed, like a stepping stone for someone else to follow when they're ready.

Jasmin leaned against the edge of the bookshelf, arms folded tight but face softening. "I used to think people like him just liked power. But what if they only learned one way to survive?" she asked, mostly to herself. Ella nodded, slowly. "If no one tells you love isn't supposed to hurt, then maybe you think pain is part of love." The air between the students became more than shared—it became sacred. The kind of shared space that only builds when truth lays itself down without needing to win.

Jeremy whispered again, this time louder. "So he's not bad?" Ty shook his head gently. "He's not free yet." That was all. Not a declaration. Not a pardon. Just an understanding. Nico, who hadn't spoken in ten minutes, finally said, "Then he's not done." And everyone knew what that meant. They couldn't label him yet. Because his story was still writing itself.

"Sometimes being told the truth hurts more than the lie ever did," Leo said. "Especially when you've lived the lie so long you started calling it home." Mr. Clarke scribbled something down but didn't read it aloud. His eyes were on Alex's empty seat. "We don't rescue him," he said carefully. "But we don't abandon him either." Ty added, "We invite him back. But not as a liar. Not as a manipulator. As someone trying to start over."

Jeremy bit his bottom lip and finally looked over at Leo. "How do you know when someone's really starting over?" Leo answered without pause. "They stop needing to win. They start needing to understand." Jeremy nodded, small but sure. Jasmin asked the next question. "And if he hurts someone again?" Ty answered. "Then we protect the person who was hurt. But we still believe people can choose to be different tomorrow than they were yesterday."

There was a moment where the idea hung in the room like dust in the light, visible but weightless. The kids didn't clap. They didn't sigh. They just held the moment together, like a group folding a flag slowly, respectfully, understanding what it meant to the person who carried it before. Ella turned to Leo and asked, "Did you know when you changed?" Leo smiled faintly. "No. But Ty did. And then Jeremy did. And then I did."

From outside the classroom, the footsteps of the nurse returned. The door opened gently. "He's lying down now," she said softly. "He's shaken. Not sick anymore. Just quiet." Mr. Clarke nodded. "He'll stay in the nurse's office for a while. He doesn't need a crowd." The kids agreed with silence. No protest. Just understanding. That was new.

Ty turned to Jeremy and placed a hand on his back. "You asked a hard question," he said. "That takes courage." Jeremy shrugged. "I just didn't want to call someone a villain who might just be sad." Leo nodded. "You're already helping him. You just don't know it yet." Ty's hand stayed on Jeremy's shoulder a little longer, until the boy breathed slower. And for the first time that day, no one was trying to fix anyone. They were just seeing each other.

Leo didn't wait for the nurse to speak. He stood up before the hallway footsteps stopped echoing, and walked to the door without being asked, without needing a signal. His body wasn't rigid. It wasn't trembling. He moved like someone who had once needed saving and remembered exactly what it felt like to be forgotten. As the door opened, the light from the hallway poured in at a slant, catching the edge of his sneakers. Alex stood there, shoulders hunched in, eyes barely meeting the room. The nurse gave a nod and stepped back. This moment didn't belong to her.

Without saying anything too loud or too soft, Leo simply lifted his hand and placed it gently on Alex's shoulder. It wasn't a grab. It wasn't even a hold. It was the kind of contact that asks permission even as it offers comfort. "Hey," Leo said, low and kind. "You feeling any better?" His words carried no judgment. Only warmth. The kind that made a sick stomach settle just enough to listen. Alex didn't answer at first. He didn't even nod. But he didn't pull away either.

"I'm not here to embarrass you," Leo said. "I'm not here to fix you either. I'm just here because I know what that hallway feels like." He gave the shoulder a little squeeze before letting it go. "And I know what it's like when you don't even know what you're feeling. But it hits anyway. And it takes your legs right out." Alex shifted slightly. His eyes were red, but his jaw was tight. He hadn't broken yet, but the wall was thin. Leo knew that wall. He helped build his own once.

"What's happening to you," Leo said, slower now, "is not your fault." He waited. Let the words land. "What's happening to you... is not your fault." He said it again, firmer, as though carving it into the air. "It's not your fault." He didn't say it like a teacher. He said it like someone who needed someone to say it to him once and never did. "Whatever voice is in your head, the one that says you're bad, or broken, or doomed—it's not your fault."

Alex blinked fast, then slower. His chest lifted once like a hiccup, then twice. Leo took a small step forward, arms not open, but not crossed either. "If you cry," he said quietly, "that's not weakness. That's proof you're still in there. And that's the part I want to talk to." Alex's eyes brimmed, but the tears didn't fall. Leo didn't press. He simply waited.

After a long silence, Leo opened his arms—not wide, not dramatic, just enough to offer, not demand. "You don't have to take this hug. But I'll stay right here until you're ready." Alex didn't move. His lip twitched once. His fists unclenched slightly. Then clenched again. Still, no words. Still, no collapse. Leo held still. "You don't have to be okay right now. You just have to stay."

Behind them, the classroom was hushed. Ty had moved to the side with Jeremy, who was holding Jasmin's hand now. Even Mr. Clarke stood back, not interfering, not rescuing. Letting Leo lead the way. "You're not alone," Leo whispered. "You never were. Even if it felt like it." Then, without changing tone, he added again: "What's happening to you is not your fault."

Alex finally looked him in the eye. Just for a second. That was enough. Leo took a breath and let it out. "But what you do next?" Leo said. "That's yours. That's the part that's up to you." He stepped back just a little, but not far. Then he said it—the phrase Ty had taught him to hold onto in the hardest moment: "Let him choose." The room felt it. Like the weight had shifted onto new shoulders—but not as a burden. As a chance.

Alex didn't step forward. He didn't walk away either. But something changed in his face. Not a smile. Not a crack. Just something that loosened. Leo nodded gently. "We'll be in here. Not watching. Just waiting. If you want in, come in. If you want to sit in the corner and say nothing, do that. But don't leave yourself behind." Then he turned, walking back into the room, slow but sure, like someone who trusted the echo to follow.

When Leo returned to his seat, Jeremy whispered, "Did it work?" Leo didn't answer right away. "I don't know," he said. "But I meant it. And sometimes that's the only part that matters." Ty gave one nod. Jasmin smiled just barely. Mr. Clarke wrote something in his notebook and underlined it twice. In the hallway, no one moved. But the door remained open.

The bell rang, but no one rushed to their feet. Not even Nico. Backpacks stayed zipped, chairs stayed still. Even the room seemed unsure whether to return to routine. Mr. Clarke stood at the back, near the windows, his hands clasped together in front of him like he was guarding something invisible. No one had to say it aloud, but everyone knew—whatever just happened wasn't over. Not yet.

Leo stayed by the door until Alex moved. And when he did, it wasn't loud. It wasn't dramatic. It was just a few slow steps inward, shoulders bent, eyes lowered, each footstep landing like it was testing whether the ground would hold him. Jeremy slid over slightly without being asked, and Ty looked toward the desk across from his own and tapped it once with his hand. That was enough of a welcome.

Alex didn't sit right away. He looked at Leo instead. And for the first time since the hallway, his mouth opened. "I didn't think anyone would believe me if I ever said it." The sentence cracked as it came out, like glass flexing under too much weight. He gripped the back of a chair but didn't sit down. "I didn't think anyone'd believe me. Because I was already acting like him."

No one interrupted. No one blinked. Even the pencil that rolled off Jasmin's desk made no sound as it hit the floor. Leo nodded slowly, keeping his body low and his voice even. "We'll believe you," he said. "If you want to tell it." Ty gave a quiet nod, too. No pressure. But no pity either. Just space. Space that stayed open long enough for truth to make it across the room.

Alex glanced toward the hallway again. But the door was already shut. Not locked. Just closed. His hands trembled at the wrists, and he let go of the chair and instead knelt down next to the bookshelf near the whiteboard. "My dad," he began, then stopped. Then tried again. "He didn't yell. That would've been better." He swallowed, hard. "He was quiet. He said things in ways that made me feel small. Made me think it was my fault when Mom left."

Ty's head bowed slightly, and Jeremy leaned forward on his desk like he was listening with his whole body. Leo crouched next to Alex now, letting him talk without looking him directly in the eye. "Three months before school started," Alex said. "He died." His fingers curled into the carpet. "No one knew what to say. I didn't even cry. Not at the funeral. Not after. Just… nothing."

It wasn't silence that followed. It was a different kind of sound—a stillness with shape to it. The kind that held weight. The kind that told the truth, even if no one else did. Alex began to shake. It started in his fingers, then his shoulders, then his breath. His back hunched forward, and he leaned against the base of the whiteboard, like his own story had knocked the strength out of him. Leo moved beside him, not fast, but purposeful.

Without asking permission, Leo placed one hand against Alex's spine and the other on his shoulder. The touch wasn't heavy, but it anchored him. "I've been there," Leo whispered. "I've felt that emptiness like a hole in my chest, like you're still standing but you're not really here." Alex's legs gave out from under him. Leo caught him before he hit the floor, gently guiding him to sit. It wasn't a collapse. It was a letting go.

Alex leaned forward, breathing shallow, his hands in fists against his thighs. "I thought if I acted like him, I'd be strong," he whispered, his voice cracking under the weight of what it carried. "I thought hurting people first meant they couldn't hurt me." He didn't cry in sobs. His tears weren't loud. They were the kind that burn slow and steady, the kind that fall without asking. Leo didn't let go.

Leo placed his arms around him—not to rescue, but to stay. To keep company with the grief. "You can let it out," Leo said. "You're not alone here. Not anymore." Alex's breathing slowed, but his whole body trembled. "Just let it go. As much as today will allow. Let it go for now." Ty knelt on the other side. Not to crowd, but to balance. And to bear witness.

Ella and Jasmin stayed quiet, but their eyes never left him. Nico reached into his desk and pulled out the box of tissues, placing it gently near the floor without needing praise. Mr. Clarke watched from behind his desk, his own eyes full of something unsaid. The room had shifted. Not because of noise. But because of what had been named.

"I didn't want to be like him," Alex whispered. "I just didn't know another way." Leo held him a little tighter. Not like a hero. Not like a saint. Just like a brother who had once knelt on the same carpet, feeling the same tremble. "You don't have to be," Leo said. "Not anymore." And finally, Alex's head dropped onto Leo's shoulder—not because he was weak, but because he didn't have to carry it alone anymore.

Ty didn't say much at first. He simply shifted his posture so Alex could see both him and Leo in the same glance. There was something careful about how Ty sat—shoulders relaxed, eyes soft, hands resting open on his knees like he was saying, *You're safe now* without saying anything at all. The room had dropped into a different kind of silence again, one with permission instead of fear. For the first time since school began, Alex didn't look like he was preparing for an attack.

Jeremy inched forward a little, still quiet, still watching. He had always been quiet, even in his boldest moments. But this time, it wasn't fear that kept him quiet—it was reverence. He was watching something sacred. Mr. Clarke stepped closer too, pulling his chair beside them and sitting down low. His knees cracked as he bent, but he didn't wince. He simply placed a hand over his heart for a moment, and nodded once toward Leo. The signal was clear: *Keep going. He needs you.*

Leo adjusted his position so his back was to the rest of the class, sheltering Alex just a bit more from the many eyes that now watched without judgement. He didn't raise his voice. "When my dad said I was worthless," Leo began, "I believed him. Because he said it with a smile. Because he said it after a hug. Because he made me think love and pain were the same thing." Alex's breath hitched like someone had just struck a match in his chest.

"That's what he did too," Alex whispered. "My dad. He'd give me something—like a game, or a new hoodie—and then he'd tell me I owed him. That I had to earn it. That if I said no, it meant I didn't love him. Or that I was ungrateful. I couldn't figure it out. I still can't." His voice cracked, and he blinked hard. Leo didn't answer right away. He just listened. That was part of it too.

Ty took over the next thread of truth. "What they do is trick your brain," he said gently. "They link praise to pressure. They link safety to silence. So when you finally try to speak, it feels like you're betraying the only home you've ever known." Ty didn't raise his voice either. But every word carried the weight of truth. Jasmin's face had gone pale again, but her eyes didn't flinch this time.

Alex buried his face in his hands. "I copied him," he muttered. "I thought that was how you be strong. I thought people only listened when you made them afraid of not listening." Leo leaned a little closer. "You don't have to stay that version," he whispered. "You're allowed to outgrow what you were taught. You're allowed to rewrite the part of the story where you're still the villain."

Jeremy nodded, and for the first time, he found his voice. "Leo used to scare me," he said. "But he doesn't anymore. Because he tells the truth now. He says sorry and he means it. You can do that too." It wasn't a lecture. It wasn't a command. Just a child telling another child that healing was real. Jasmin stood up from her desk and crossed the room with quiet footsteps. She crouched next to Alex and placed one hand on his elbow. "I forgive you," she said softly. "Even if you didn't ask yet."

Alex looked at her, tears falling down both cheeks now. "I'm sorry," he whispered. "I didn't know how else to be. I was just trying to survive." Jasmin nodded once, then sat cross-legged beside him like they were in kindergarten again, sharing toys instead of truths. But maybe it was the same thing.

Leo pulled something from his backpack—a small notepad. He flipped through the pages until he found the one he'd written that morning. He passed it to Alex. You're not your past. You're what you choose to become. In big, looping letters, Leo had signed his name underneath it. "You can keep that," he said. "Write your own under it later, if you want."

Mr. Clarke cleared his throat once, the kind of sound adults make when their own tears sneak up on them. "We'll take the rest of the day off from worksheets," he said, voice steady but eyes shining. "Today's lesson already happened. It was real. It matters more." A few students exhaled, and one near the back clapped quietly before realizing it wasn't that kind of moment. The hands stopped—but the hearts stayed open.

Ty looked around the room, eyes catching each classmate one by one. "This is what happens when someone tells the truth and doesn't get punished for it," he said. "This is what happens when pain doesn't stay buried." He reached toward Alex and tapped the corner of the notepad still in his lap. "Write it out," he said. "Even if it doesn't make sense yet." Alex looked down at the paper. His hands still trembled. But he didn't look away this time.

Alex didn't move at first. His hands stayed clenched in his lap, fists pressed so tight his knuckles paled. The notepad Leo had given him sat like a fragile truth on top of his knees. No one rushed him. Not Ty. Not Leo. Not Jeremy. Not even the clock. The air didn't shift. It held still like it understood something holy was about to happen. When he finally did breathe, it came out like a gust from somewhere ancient—somewhere buried beneath the layers of performance he had worn since the day his father died.

"I hated him," Alex whispered, his voice a paper cut through silence. "But I still wanted him to say he loved me. And when he didn't… I made people feel how I felt. That's what I did. That's what I've been doing." His throat locked. His eyes darted toward the window like he wanted to throw the confession outside, but no one let it fall. Ty stayed beside him, unmoved. Leo sat closer. Jasmin didn't blink. Jeremy's hand reached up and rested gently on Alex's shoulder like a flag declaring you're still one of us.

Alex's breath hitched, and then the tears came. But these weren't the sharp, angry tears that accompanied a bruised ego or a playground scolding. These were body-shaking sobs that dragged themselves up from some locked vault inside his spine. He doubled over, arms crossed tight against his chest, and the cry escaped like thunder—ugly, gasping, holy thunder. Mr. Clarke didn't step in. He sat still, one hand on his desk, the other resting near his wedding ring, nodding to himself like he remembered the sound from long ago in his own childhood.

Leo caught him before he tipped fully forward, steadying him by the back of the neck like a brother would. He didn't speak. He didn't tell him it was okay. He let it be not okay. He held space for the agony. For the admission. For the betrayal Alex had suffered. And for the damage Alex had done. Forgiveness wasn't spoken yet. But the holding was the beginning of it. Ty placed a folded sweatshirt under Alex's knees without a word. Jeremy handed over a box of tissues without being asked. And Jasmin simply sat beside them all and closed her eyes, whispering something only her heart could hear.

Alex's words came back in fragments. "He never hugged me. Not once. Not even when I… even when I…" His shoulders locked. "He told me real men don't cry. He said if I cried again, he'd lock me outside." The room didn't react. Not with gasps. Not with shock. They just listened. Because they understood that silence was the only answer that held honour in this moment. Alex blinked and looked at Leo, face flushed and swollen. "How did you stop hating him?"

Leo breathed in through his nose, slow and deliberate. "I didn't," he said. "Not at first. I hated him so much I became him. Until Ty told me I didn't have to. That I could love myself more than I hated him." His voice didn't waver. It anchored. It led. Ty nodded slowly. "That's the truth," he said. "You don't forgive him to save him. You forgive him so he doesn't own you anymore."

Alex blinked. Something shifted in his jaw, in his spine, in the way his hands loosened. "I don't want to be him anymore," he whispered. "I don't even want to win. I just want to stop." Leo placed his forehead gently against Alex's, no words, just that closeness. A kind of soul-knock. Jeremy reached again. Jasmin took the other side. Ty wrapped one arm around them all. The group held. They didn't fix him. They received him.

Then came the final piece. Alex pulled Leo's notepad to his chest. He opened to the next clean page and wrote the words slow, like every letter cost him a secret. I hurt people because I was hurting. But I'm done now. I want to be someone safe. He signed it with his name. Then looked up, stunned at what his own hand had done.

Mr. Clarke cleared his throat, softly. "I think," he said, "today, the real school day just started." He looked at the clock. "And I think the lesson was worth every minute." No one responded aloud. But every face nodded in some small way. Because today wasn't about books. Or marks. Or behaviour points. It was about the moment the villain laid down his sword and reached out his hand. Alex cried again. But this time, it wasn't from pain. It was from the terrifying freedom of not pretending anymore. And no one—no one—let go.

CHAPTER 18: YOU'RE NOT ALONE ANYMORE

It was the kind of morning that didn't make noise. Grey clouds hovered low like a ceiling that hadn't been raised yet, and the air felt flat, like it didn't want to bother anyone. Alex walked with both hands in his pockets, his backpack strap swinging behind him like it didn't belong to him. He didn't rush. He didn't drag his feet. He just moved like someone who knew no one would ask why he was late. Not because he didn't matter, but because no one had ever noticed he was early.

The sidewalk had small cracks where the roots of old trees had pushed up from beneath. Alex stepped over them like he had memorized each one. One, two, three. Then the garbage bin with the broken lid. Then the fence with the missing slat. He passed them all without looking up. He didn't have a lunch bag. Just a bruised apple in his side pocket and an old sandwich wrapped in a napkin that was already tearing from the corners. He hadn't packed it. It was left on the counter next to a sink full of dishes. He didn't ask whose sink. He just took it.

Halfway down the block, his shoelace came untied. He didn't stop. He just walked slower, dragging the loose string like it might hold him in place. A car passed. He didn't wave. A jogger crossed the street. He didn't nod. No one made eye contact. That was normal. That was safe. You don't get judged if no one knows you're there.

Ty stood behind a tree across the road. He didn't move either. Just watched. Quiet. Careful. Hidden in the way only a real friend knows how to be—when watching is a kind of protection. He didn't want to scare Alex, or make him feel followed. He just needed to be sure. Because something in the way Alex's shoulders stayed crooked, even when his steps were straight, said enough.

At the corner, Alex hesitated. Not because he didn't know the way. But because he wasn't sure if the school wanted him. He knew the teachers said hello. But he also knew they didn't know where he slept. Or why his homework smelled like fabric softener on one side and basement mildew on the other. Or why he always had to return pencils. He never kept the ones he borrowed.

When he reached the schoolyard, kids were already shouting across the pavement, tossing backpacks, trading gum, laughing without worry. Alex didn't look at them. He just crossed straight to the bench near the farthest tree—the one without a name carved into it. The one that didn't belong to any group. He sat. Back straight. Legs still. Like he didn't want to take up too much space on the bench. Or in the world.

Behind the school fence, Ty moved closer. Still quiet. Still watching. He had learned from Leo how to read the things people didn't say. And Alex was saying a thousand things with his silence. His hair was clean but not brushed. His hoodie was zipped to the top even though the air was humid. And his shoes had the kind of wear on the soles that meant no one had bought them since his feet stopped growing.

Inside the classroom, Jasmin was adjusting chairs. Ella was finishing her water bottle. Jeremy was trying to draw a circle without using the stencil. None of them had seen Alex yet. Not today. But they would. And they would notice things they hadn't noticed before. The empty space beside his desk. The way he opened his notebook like it already had a mistake in it. The way he winced every time the intercom made a sound, as though someone might call his name and take something away.

Mr. Clarke passed the doorway holding a folder in one hand and a coffee in the other. He paused. Just long enough to glance out the window and see the outline of a boy on the bench. The same bench. Same spot. He didn't speak. But he lowered the folder to his side and stared a moment longer than usual. Something about today didn't sit right.

Ty finally crossed the field. Not directly. A slow arc. The kind that doesn't alert, just drifts closer until he could sit on the grass near the bench without speaking. He didn't look at Alex. He looked at the clouds. Then the fence. Then his own shoes. "Nice walk?" he said eventually, without weight. No pressure. No spotlight. Just air.

Alex didn't answer. But he didn't move away either. That was the first signal. Ty pulled out a granola bar. Unwrapped it halfway. "Not hungry?" he asked, holding it out like it was nothing. Alex looked at it, then at Ty, then at the ground again. But his hand reached out. Slow. Careful. He took it. Didn't eat. Just held it. Inside the school, the bell rang. Kids shuffled, ran, shoved, shouted. Ty stood up first. Brushed off his jeans. "You coming?" he asked, looking down but not smiling. Alex stood. Slower. But he stood.

When they reached the doors, Alex hesitated again. Ty didn't push. He just waited. Then opened the door, held it, and said, "You first." It wasn't a joke. It wasn't a trick. It was the kind of gesture people don't make unless they mean it. Alex stepped through. And Ty followed close behind.

The first thing Ty noticed was the socks. Not the colour—they were dark grey—but the fact they hadn't changed. Three days in a row now. Same slight fold at the ankle. Same patch of worn threads above the heel. He didn't point it out. Ty was trained better than that. But his eyes stayed there for a moment longer than they should have, long enough to memorize the wrinkle pattern. It wasn't judgment. It was surveillance of the quiet kind.

Leo picked up on something else. The backpack. He'd seen it before—old army green canvas, one zipper tooth missing near the top, a safety pin holding one strap together. But what struck him this time was the way it sagged. Like it wasn't holding much. Or maybe it was holding too much of the wrong kind. The bruises on the bottom corners hadn't changed either. Same scuffs. Same dirt mark like it had been dropped onto gravel more than once. Leo didn't ask. He just kept watching from across the room.

Alex sat with both hands in his lap, elbows tight to his sides. He didn't fidget. He didn't doodle. His pencil lay straight across the desk, parallel to the edge like he'd lined it up with purpose. But his fingers didn't reach for it. His eyes weren't on the board. They weren't anywhere. Just floating somewhere near his knees.

Miss Penner took attendance slowly that morning. She said each name like it might crack. When she called Alex's, he nodded. Didn't speak. Just nodded. Then dropped his head even lower. There were no bags under his eyes, but there was something dull about his expression. Like he'd used up his face already before the day began.

Jasmin noticed the smell—not dirty, not bad, just not fresh. Like someone had gone to sleep without brushing their teeth, then woken up without breakfast. It wasn't enough to draw attention. Just enough to draw concern. She leaned slightly toward Ella and whispered something soft. Ella listened, then blinked once, slow and full. She turned her head just a little, then whispered back.

"I don't think he has a real home," Ella said. The words landed like a pin dropped on a marble floor. Quiet, but sharp. And once heard, they couldn't be unheard. Jasmin didn't respond. She just looked down at her notebook and tapped her pen three times. Tap. Tap. Tap. She'd only ever done that when something scared her.

Ty didn't need the whisper. He already knew. He saw it in the way Alex drank water at recess—three full cups at the fountain like he was storing it. In the way he never opened his lunch until someone else had started eating. And in the way he sat far from radiators even when the classroom was cold. Kids without homes didn't like warmth they couldn't keep.

During silent reading, Alex didn't open his book. He stared at the cover. His thumb rubbed the corner over and over like it might peel away. Ty caught the movement from two desks away. He didn't speak. Just folded a sticky note into a triangle and passed it to Leo. Leo read it without blinking.

Watch the signs. He's not okay.

Leo looked up once, then down. He didn't fold the note. He didn't write back. He just stood up to sharpen his pencil and made sure to walk past Alex's desk. Just close enough to glance without looking. The pencil was already sharp, but he sharpened it anyway.

Mr. Clarke passed by the window, paused, then entered. He didn't speak right away. Just scanned the room. Something about his face said he was looking for something he couldn't name yet. His eyes landed on Alex. Then on Ty. Then on Leo. He nodded slightly, more to himself than to anyone else, and sat at his desk.

When recess was called, Alex didn't move first. He waited. Let the others leave. Let the noise rush out like floodwaters. Then he stood. Shoulders hunched, as if expecting a shove that never came. He walked to the back door, hands deep in his hoodie. No jacket. Still no lunch.

Ty was waiting for him by the stairwell. He didn't say anything. Just walked beside him like it was planned. Leo caught up a moment later, pulling a half-squished granola bar from his hoodie pocket and offering it without a word. Alex took it. Still no eye contact. But he took it.

Outside, the wind was soft. The sky had cleared but not completely. It looked undecided. Alex stood at the edge of the yard near the bike racks. He didn't have a bike. But he stood like someone who used to. Maybe one that wasn't his. Maybe one that got taken back. Ella watched him from across the field. She tugged Jasmin's sleeve. "He walks alone," she said. "Every morning. I think from that side street past the 7-Eleven." Jasmin's heart knocked once. "That's... not near any houses."

Leo walked past, circled back, and stopped beside the girls. "We're watching him now," he said. "The way people watched me, even when I didn't ask." He didn't smile. He just nodded once. "We don't let this go unnoticed. Not again." Ty stood beside Alex. Both boys stared out at nothing for a moment. Then Ty said, "You know... it's okay to say something." Alex didn't answer. But his shoulders moved. Just a little. Enough.

It was the sort of question that came so quietly, it had to be true. Jeremy didn't raise his hand. He didn't ask for the floor. He just looked over at Ty and asked it softly—like a pebble tossed into still water. "Where does Alex go when the bell rings?" He didn't mean recess or lunch. Everyone understood that right away. He meant after the final bell. The one that meant home.

Ty didn't answer right away. His pencil stopped moving, though, and that told Nico more than words could. Ty always wrote with motion, even during class. He was always sketching or scribbling or taking mental notes disguised as margin doodles. But the pencil stopped. Jeremy's words had pinned something.

Jasmin looked up too. Her mouth was slightly open, as if the question had lifted something she hadn't been ready to see. She closed her notebook, slowly. One finger rested on the spine. "I never see him with anyone," she whispered. "No one picks him up." The air around them settled like dust.

Leo leaned forward in his chair. "You ever see him on the bus?" he asked Nico. Nico shook his head. "No. Never." Leo nodded slowly, his brows narrowing. "Then he walks. Alone." There was no drama in his voice. Just fact. Cold, simple, and sharp as glass.

Mr. Clarke was at his desk grading something, or at least pretending to. But the silence made him look up. He studied the circle of faces around Jeremy—faces that had once been guarded, but were now open, focused, changed. "What's this about?" he asked, setting down his pen.

Jeremy turned to him. "Mr. Clarke," he said, "where does Alex go after school?" It was asked with all the innocence in the world, and all the seriousness too. Mr. Clarke blinked once, and that was answer enough. "I'm not sure," he admitted. "But I can find out." His voice was honest. His concern was real.

"No one ever drops him off," Ella added, tugging at her sleeve. "And he doesn't have a lunch bag. He just... watches us eat sometimes." The room didn't fill with noise. It fell deeper into silence. A different kind now. One that listened, because it had to.

Ty stood. Not quickly. Not dramatically. Just stood with purpose, his feet firm. "We should have asked this sooner," he said. "We noticed everything except where he goes when he leaves." His voice wasn't scolding. It was full of grief. The quiet kind. The kind that already knew the answer might not be good.

Leo rested his chin on his folded hands. "I think I know which direction he walks," he said. "South. Towards the apartment blocks past the discount grocery." Jasmin nodded. "The ones with the locked front doors?" Leo nodded back. "Yeah. The buzzer kind. Could be anyone behind those."

"Has anyone been to his place?" Mr. Clarke asked. No hands went up. No voices offered names. "He hasn't invited anyone," Nico said. "Not once." "Doesn't talk about family either," Ty added. "At all." "Or pets," said Ella. "Or favourite dinners," said Jeremy. The pattern began to form in all their minds.

"He doesn't talk about birthdays," said Jasmin, and that one struck the deepest. Mr. Clarke made a note. "All right," he said softly. "I'll speak to the office. If no one's contacted us as a guardian, we may need to find out if Alex is listed under a temporary placement or kinship foster."

"Is that bad?" Jeremy asked. Mr. Clarke's face tightened for a second, but his voice stayed calm. "It's not bad. It just means... someone might not be there the way we expect. It means Alex might be doing more alone than any of us realized."

Ty sat back down but didn't stop watching the doorway. "Then we make sure he's not alone anymore," he said, flat and firm. "Starting today." Leo didn't speak. He just nodded once, and that one nod held everything: agreement, promise, and memory.

"I'll follow from a distance after school," Ty said. "Not close. Not creepy. Just enough to know where he goes. Enough to report back so we can help. I won't talk to him unless I need to." Mr. Clarke hesitated, then gave a slow nod. "Only if you feel safe. Otherwise, I'll make the inquiry."

"I'll come too," Leo said. "Not to follow. Just to wait near the crossing where we saw him walk before. If he needs someone, I'll be there." He looked down at his desk. "Nobody should have to go home alone... if home isn't really home."

There was no bell to end the conversation. No transition music. Just a hush, like the room was bracing for something it couldn't name. Jeremy looked up at the clock. Still fifteen minutes until lunch. But already, things felt different.

Jasmin slipped a sticky note into her sleeve with Alex's name written on it. Not as a label. Not as a warning. But as a reminder. She didn't want to forget to care again. That was the real danger. Not what they didn't know. But what they knew now—and chose to do nothing about.

The classroom emptied in ripples, not waves. Some students lingered near the hooks, tying shoes too slowly or rechecking their bags just to stay a little longer. Mr. Clarke watched them out of the corner of his eye, his hands resting on his desk like anchors. Leo gave him a glance—not asking, just telling. Telling him it was time to act. Mr. Clarke nodded. He waited for the last backpack zipper, the final shuffle of indoor shoes returned to cubbies. Then he turned his chair to face the window and reached for the old beige landline still plugged in beneath his desk.

He didn't call the office. That was too slow. And too filtered. He reached instead for a contact number saved in a small black leather book in the back drawer. He kept it for moments just like this. The number was handwritten in faded ink, barely legible, but he knew it by heart. He'd written it himself ten years ago during a workshop no one else had taken seriously. "Emergency Child Welfare Liaison – North Durham District." It rang twice. Then three times. Then silence.

"Clarke," he said into the receiver. "It's... urgent. I need to ask about a student. First name Alex. I'm afraid I don't have a last name yet. But he's in Grade 7 at St. Peter's Elementary. Yes, that one." The voice on the other end was calm, clipped. Routine. Mr. Clarke hated routine right now. The routine voice asked for details, identifiers. Mr. Clarke described Alex as carefully as he could without sounding clinical. Tall for his age. Quiet. Avoids eye contact. Wears the same socks. No lunch. No pick-ups. No drop-offs.

There was a pause. The pause went on too long. When the voice returned, it was changed. Still professional, but hesitant. "That file's... complicated," the woman said, and Mr. Clarke felt the cold wash over him like a window left cracked in winter. "Can you confirm if there's a current guardian on record?" he asked, barely breathing. The voice hesitated again. "Technically, yes. But there's no immediate kin contact listed. He's listed under transitional observation. Which... to be honest, usually means the system hasn't confirmed where he's staying."

Mr. Clarke's hand tightened on the receiver. "Then where is he staying?" The voice didn't have a clear answer. "Possibly with a family friend. Possibly alone. There's mention of a deceased mother. Father unknown or absent.

He's not flagged for full protection yet. No reports filed. But we haven't had a welfare home check since June. Nothing since school resumed." Mr. Clarke looked toward the hallway. The silence in his room now felt dangerous. "So he's invisible," he said. "That's what you're telling me."

There was no disagreement. Only a sigh. "He's not flagged," the voice repeated. "But you noticed something. That matters. We can assign a social worker. But it'll take at least seventy-two hours." Mr. Clarke shook his head. "He doesn't have seventy-two hours. He might not even have a place to sleep tonight." The woman on the other end didn't argue. She only said, "I'll escalate it. But keep him safe until then, if you can."

He hung up without thanking her. Not out of rudeness, but because gratitude wasn't what he felt. He felt urgency, sorrow, guilt. The kind that clings to the corners of the chest like wet cloth. He rose from his chair and stood by the window, hands behind his back. It was recess now. Children ran in different directions across the field, all of them accounted for, all of them known. Except one.

Alex sat alone on the edge of the pavement, picking at a crack in the concrete. Not pretending to be busy. Not faking a game. Just sitting. His posture was folded in, knees tucked close, elbows resting on them, back curved like a shell. Mr. Clarke watched him for a long time. No one approached. No one waved. Alex didn't even look up.

He thought of all the protocols, the checklists, the endless paperwork that was supposed to catch things like this. None of it had. The boy was seventeen feet away and still invisible. Mr. Clarke had worked this job for over two decades. He had seen bruises and hunger and tears that no child knew how to name. But invisibility—that was the most dangerous of all.

He stepped away from the window and opened his laptop. He began composing a letter—not to the board, not to the district, but to his wife. "There's a boy here," he wrote, "who has no one. We may be the first to notice. I know it's sudden, but I need to ask—would we be willing?" He stopped, erased willing, and wrote ready. Then deleted that too. Finally, he typed: Would we be able to love him, if he needs us?

He didn't hit send yet. He just stared at the blinking cursor. Because this wasn't just about policy anymore. This was personal. This was heart. This was the same feeling he remembered from years ago, when they still hoped for children of their own. A space had always been waiting. They had just never known who it was for.

He rose from his chair again and left the email open. He would speak the words to her instead. He turned off the screen and stepped out into the hallway. The children were returning from recess, laughter echoing off lockers. Except for one. Alex wasn't among them. Mr. Clarke turned toward the playground again.

He didn't need the social worker's permission to walk a child home if that child had nowhere else to go. He didn't need paperwork to care. Not for now. Just presence. Just action. He was already moving when the next bell rang, his heart steady, his steps quiet.

The news came in pieces, not all at once, as if the truth itself was embarrassed to be seen in full daylight. It began when the office secretary whispered something to Mr. Clarke in the hallway. A file folder clutched under her arm like a secret too heavy to hold for long. Then came the quiet moment in the staff lounge when she mouthed the words: "He doesn't have a bedroom." It landed like a stone dropped into a still pond, rippling far beyond the first splash. Mr. Clarke didn't ask again. He simply nodded and went back to class, a little heavier in the chest than when he'd left it.

Leo and Ty sat at the back of the room, eyes trained not on the chalkboard but on Alex's chair. It was empty again, and not because he was sick. The boy had taken an early recess and hadn't returned. Jasmin kept her hand folded tight in her lap, her pencil unmoving. Ella leaned slightly toward her, whispering, "Do you think he's okay?" Jasmin didn't answer. Not because she didn't know, but because she feared the answer more than the question.

By second nutrition break, the class had started to hum with quiet knowing. Kids notice more than teachers admit. The hallway talk shifted, not with meanness, but concern. "I heard he's staying with some cousin," Nico whispered to Jeremy. "But not, like, a real one. Just one of those people you only see at funerals." Jeremy blinked, then said, "But who makes him lunch?" Nico shook his head. "I don't think anyone."

Ty followed Mr. Clarke after dismissal that day. He didn't ask permission. He simply waited beside the classroom door until the hallway cleared, then walked quietly with the man whose face had changed over the last two days. Mr. Clarke didn't pretend not to notice. "You heard something?" Ty asked softly. Mr. Clarke didn't lie. "Yes. A few things." He reached into his folder and passed Ty a small sheet of paper. Not official, just a note jotted down during the call: Lives with second cousin. No bedroom. No known birthday celebrations. No known legal guardianship. No known biological relatives living.

Ty read it once. Then again. He passed it back without saying a word. But in his silence, Mr. Clarke heard everything. That night, Leo found a folded piece of notebook paper left in his locker. Ty had slipped it in without fanfare. It read: We need to find out where he lays his head. A boy can't heal without a pillow to call his own. Leo folded the note and kept it in his shoe.

The next morning, Alex showed up twenty minutes late. His hair wasn't brushed, and the sleeves of his hoodie were damp like they'd been hand-washed in a sink that didn't drain well. No lunch bag. No backpack. Just him. Mr. Clarke didn't mark him late. He marked him present. Because he was. Barely. But present. When Leo offered him a spot beside him at the reading table, Alex hesitated. Then sat.

Later, when the class was asked to write about "what home means to you," Alex's page stayed blank. But he flipped it over and started writing on the back. No one saw what he wrote. Not until Jeremy found the paper stuck to the floor after dismissal. He picked it up and read the words: I sleep on the couch. It's cold and smells like dog food. They let me stay there because they have space, but not because they care. I don't think they remember my name unless I do something wrong. I keep my dad's birth certificate in my shoe so it doesn't get thrown away.

Jeremy brought the paper to Ty. Ty read it twice before folding it into quarters. Then he passed it to Leo. Leo didn't cry. But he stood up from the lunch table and walked straight to Mr. Clarke's office. He knocked once, didn't wait to be invited in. "He needs a room," he said plainly. "Not a couch. Not a floor. A room. And a door he can close. And a pillow he picked out himself. And a drawer for socks. And someone who remembers his birthday without asking."

Mr. Clarke listened. Then he opened his desk drawer and pulled out a folder he hadn't shown anyone yet. "I've already started the paperwork," he said. "He doesn't know it yet, but I called Family and Children's Services again this morning. I also called my wife. We've talked about it before. We'd love to be the ones to offer him that room. If he'll take it."

Leo nodded once. "He will. Just don't call it charity." Mr. Clarke smiled. "We won't."

The next day, Alex's backpack reappeared. A different one. A little newer. Still worn, but it had a zipper that worked. And when he unzipped it during lunch, a peanut butter sandwich sat wrapped in tinfoil beside an apple that hadn't been bruised. The class didn't say a word. But Nico noticed the glint of something else—hope, maybe. It didn't shine, not yet. But it flickered.

When Ty leaned over and whispered, "Do you know your birthday?" Alex shook his head. "I think it's sometime in October. Or maybe late September." Ella scribbled something in her notebook and passed it around. On the last Friday of September, the kids planned a surprise. Not with cake or balloons, but with a gift that mattered more—a keychain. Just one. But it had a name on it. His name. And the words: You have a place. Always. The truth is, couches aren't beds. And spare rooms don't always feel like homes. But sometimes, all it takes is one honest adult and a few brave friends to make a boy believe he deserves more than a space to crash. He deserves a life. And now, he might get one.

It wasn't after class, or even at lunch. It was mid-morning recess when Leo tapped quietly on the corner of Mr. Clarke's desk, waiting not for permission but attention. When the teacher looked up, Leo didn't waste words. "Can we go to Alex's house?" he asked plainly. "Just to see. Just to make sure it's really… okay." Mr. Clarke didn't respond right away. He looked at Leo—not past him, not around him, but at him—as though trying to gauge if this was about curiosity or concern. Then he answered with a teacher's caution and a father's heart. "Only if Alex says yes."

Leo nodded once. That answer made sense. Everything after this would hinge on Alex. Whether he felt safe. Whether he could trust someone enough to open a door that had been closed a very long time. Leo approached Alex during library time. He didn't rush it. He sat beside him with a book neither of them read. After a few minutes, Leo whispered, "I want to see your place. Not because I'm nosy. Because I want to know where you sleep. That's all." Alex didn't speak. He turned the page. Then nodded, almost too small to see. "Okay," he said. "Just don't call it a home. Because it isn't."

Mr. Clarke drove. He'd already spoken to the cousin, a distant woman named Martha who agreed with a tired sigh. "He can come, sure," she'd said. "But don't expect a tour." She left the porch light on when they arrived, though it was still daylight. The house stood low and squat, its roof bowed slightly as if burdened by too many winters. The screen door hung slightly askew. Leo walked up the steps without waiting, turned to Alex, and said gently, "I'll knock. You stand beside me if you want." Alex stood beside him.

The cousin opened the door but didn't step aside. She was thin, drawn like paper, and her eyes darted behind the boys. "Just you three?" she asked. Mr. Clarke nodded. "This won't take long," he said. She moved slowly, letting them pass like she was making an exception she didn't agree with. Inside smelled faintly of cigarette smoke and canned beans. The floors creaked with every shift in weight. There were piles of laundry on the couch. And under the pile, a single pillow and a crumpled fleece blanket. No sheet. No frame. No bed.

"That's where I sleep," Alex said, pointing. "Unless they have guests. Then I go on the floor." Leo said nothing. He didn't flinch. He didn't frown. He just sat down beside the laundry and picked up the pillow. It was flat and cold. No indent. No imprint of a boy who'd grown into it. He held it for a moment, then set it back carefully, like he was returning something sacred. "You deserve better than this," he said. Not loud. Not angry. Just true.

Ty walked to the corner where a backpack hung from a bent nail in the wall. It was the same one Alex used on his first week back—the one with the broken zipper. "Do you keep your stuff in here?" Ty asked. Alex shrugged. "The stuff that's mine, yeah. There's not much." Ty opened it. Inside was a single spiral notebook, a toothbrush in a sandwich bag, and the folded copy of his father's birth certificate. "He kept this on his desk," Alex said. "I think it was the only real thing he left."

Mr. Clarke paced the small living room, taking in the cracked blinds and stained carpet, the empty dog bowl beneath the side table. He didn't take pictures. He didn't ask questions. He just watched. After a while, he asked, "Do you ever feel safe here?" Alex didn't answer immediately. Then he said, "No one talks to me. No one hits me. But no one sees me either. So I don't know."

That was enough. Mr. Clarke didn't push further. Instead, he turned to Martha and asked, "Would you be open to another placement?" She blinked like she didn't hear. "Another what?" Mr. Clarke softened his tone. "Someone else who could give him a room. A space that's his. Permanently." She shrugged. "If it keeps him out of trouble, fine. I never wanted this gig anyway. He just showed up."

That was all Leo needed to hear. He turned to Alex and asked, "Can we leave?" Alex nodded. But he stopped at the door. He walked back to the couch and grabbed the pillow. Just the pillow. He didn't say why. He didn't need to. He carried it under one arm all the way back to the car. When they pulled up to Mr. Clarke's driveway twenty minutes later, Alex looked out the window like he was watching someone else's movie. The lawn was mowed. The porch light was still on. There were shoes on a welcome mat.

"We won't force anything," Mr. Clarke said. "But you have a choice now. Would you like to come inside?" Alex didn't speak. He opened the door and stepped out slowly. Leo stayed behind, waiting, watching. Ty waited too. When Alex turned back and said, "Are you coming?" they both stepped out in silence. Together, they followed him inside.

There was dinner waiting—nothing fancy. Soup, bread, something warm. Mr. Clarke's wife, a soft-eyed woman with gentle hands, greeted Alex like she'd known him for years. She didn't ask questions. She offered seconds. And when Alex excused himself to the washroom, she turned to Mr. Clarke and said, "He's starving. And not just for food." Leo sat at the kitchen table, watching it unfold. He looked down at the pillow still clutched in Alex's arms. It didn't belong in this house—but Alex did. Somehow, that made sense. Somehow, everything did.

They didn't come at night. That would've been cruel. Mr. Clarke arranged it just after four in the afternoon, when school was still close enough in memory that Alex wouldn't feel ambushed. The car ride was mostly silent, save for the shuffle of Leo adjusting the seatbelt and Ty's occasional glance out the window. Mr. Clarke said little, just the address again, and the reminder that they were only there to observe—not to accuse, not to fix, not yet. "Let the house speak," he'd said quietly. "Sometimes it does."

They pulled into a narrow driveway lined with overgrown grass. The home stood behind a skeletal fence with two missing slats and a third dangling like a loose tooth. It was supposed to be a duplex, but the distinction between the two halves had long been blurred by rust and silence. The mailbox hung open. No name. No stickers. Just rust flakes and a spiderweb. Leo stepped out first and stood in front of the door. His knock wasn't loud, but it was firm. Ty stood beside him, and Mr. Clarke stayed by the car, watching.

No one came. They waited thirty seconds, then sixty. Leo knocked again. Still nothing. Ty looked toward a second-floor window, the curtains barely moving. "Someone's home," he whispered. Just then, the door creaked. A teenager, maybe seventeen, opened it with a face full of sleep and a hoodie pulled over half his eyes. He looked at Alex and muttered, "You again?" Alex said nothing. He didn't enter. He didn't nod. He just stepped aside as if afraid of his own front step.

Ty saw it first—the doorframe, warped from years of moisture. Leo touched it without thinking, running his finger along the inside edge. Alex flinched. Not a full-body jerk, but enough. Enough for Ty to look closer. There, beneath the paint, was a ring of black, creeping like a bruise down the wall. Mold. Not new, either. The smell hit next—damp clothes, spoiled wood, something underneath that lingered too long. Leo coughed and stepped back.

Inside, it was worse. No overhead light. Just a dim glow from a kitchen bulb in the next room. The couch had a sheet over it, stained at the corners. There were no pictures on the walls. No welcome. No trace of childhood. The teenager shuffled toward a back room without saying another word. Alex stayed near the door. "He's my cousin," he said quietly. "I think." Mr. Clarke finally entered and stood behind the boys, careful not to step too far in. "This is it?" he asked gently.

Alex nodded. "He doesn't care where I go, as long as I don't make noise." Ty walked to the corner, where a pile of clothes slumped in what looked like a dog bed. "Is this your stuff?" he asked. Alex shrugged. "Some of it. I sleep here sometimes." Leo picked up a towel from the pile. It was still wet. Not damp—wet. The smell made his nose wrinkle. He didn't say anything.

Then they saw the mould again—this time above the baseboards, stretching behind a bookcase that hadn't moved in years. Mr. Clarke pulled out his phone, snapped a single photo. "We don't need more," he said. "This is enough." Ty turned to Alex. "You don't have to stay here. You know that, right?" Alex didn't answer. But his shoulders sank. Not in defeat, but in relief. The kind that breaks bones because it finally lets them stop pretending to be strong.

Leo walked back toward the door and stood in the frame again. "You flinched earlier," he said. "I saw it. I know why. I used to flinch too." Alex met his eyes but didn't speak. Ty added, "You deserve walls that don't smell like fear. You deserve to be noticed." Still, Alex didn't speak. But his hands gripped the edge of his too-small backpack, like he was holding onto something that could carry him out.

Mr. Clarke made one last phone call before they left. This time, it wasn't to a social worker. It was to his wife. "The boys are right," he told her. "He can't stay here." Her voice on the other end was calm. "Bring him home," she said. "We already have soup on."

Alex walked out without saying goodbye to his cousin. No one tried to stop him. No door slammed. No demand followed. The only sound was his own breath, steady for the first time. Leo walked behind him this time, like a shield. Ty walked beside him like a friend. Mr. Clarke brought up the rear, leaving the door behind them to shut on its own. They didn't talk much on the ride home. But at the stoplight near the school, Alex looked up and said, "Thank you for knocking. No one ever has before." Leo replied, "We'll keep knocking. Until you open the right one."

Jeremy didn't plan it like a ceremony. There was no speech, no classroom announcement, no special fold or ribbon. It happened the way most things that matter do—with a moment that could've been missed if you weren't paying attention. They were in the hallway near the resource room, right after recess, the sky still spitting little flakes of early snow that didn't know whether to melt or stay. Jeremy held something under his arm, wrapped but not hidden, and when he spotted Alex standing by the water fountain, he walked over without a single ounce of hesitation.

Alex didn't say anything. He rarely did in moments like that. His eyes darted down the hall like he might still be seen as a joke, or worse, a threat. But Jeremy just stood there, both hands now holding the folded square. It was a blanket, blue and soft, thick enough to feel like a hug even when nobody was there. Jeremy offered it wordlessly at first. Alex didn't move. His hands were in his pockets. But Jeremy didn't withdraw.

Then Jeremy spoke. "My mom makes good soup," he said. "You can come over." The words landed gently, almost too lightly to believe. Alex didn't reply right away. But his eyes went to the blanket. He didn't look at Jeremy. He looked at the thing itself, like it might vanish if he blinked. Jeremy pressed it into his arms without pushing, without demanding. It wasn't a gift that came with rules. Just a soft square of warmth, held out like a key.

Alex's hands took it slowly. Not in a way that said he wanted it. In a way that said he didn't know if he was allowed. His fingers gripped the fabric like it might be taken back. But Jeremy didn't move. He stood beside him, hands now empty, watching like someone who knew how long it took for kindness to land when you'd never trusted it before.

No one else saw it. No teachers. No classmates. Just the water fountain bubbling behind them and the quiet shuffle of snow boots against tile. Alex didn't say thank you. He didn't have to. His knuckles turned white with how tight he held the blanket. It didn't drop to his side, didn't fold under his arm again. He cradled it like something breakable. Something alive.

Jeremy didn't smile big. He gave a little nod and said, "You can sit beside me at lunch if you want. No one's sitting on the other side anyway." And with that, he walked away—just a few steps, not far. Not to vanish. Just to make room for Alex to decide. Whether he followed or not, it was his choice. That was the difference. That was the gift too.

Alex stood in the hallway for another full minute before moving. Not frozen. Just adjusting to the temperature of kindness. Like when you step inside from the cold and your fingers ache before they thaw. That's how it looked, the way his shoulders rose and fell, the way he blinked longer than usual.

When he walked into the classroom, the blanket still in his arms, no one laughed. Nico saw it first and gave a nod like, "Yeah. Good." Ty caught Leo's eye and didn't need to say a thing. It was understood. Leo leaned back in his chair just enough for Alex to pass behind him without flinching. That mattered. It always matters who makes space for your silence.

Miss Penner glanced up from her papers, then back down, but not before her eyes paused on the blanket. She didn't say a word. She just wrote something quick in the corner of her planner and closed it with care, as if deciding something important had just been confirmed.

Jeremy scooted to one side, clearing room without asking. His lunch sat unopened, an extra spoon already set beside the lid. When Alex sat down, Jeremy didn't say anything. He just opened the container and offered it up. The soup was warm. Not hot enough to burn, but just warm enough to remind you someone made it for you on purpose. That feeling stuck longer than the flavour.

Alex took a spoonful and nodded. That was all. But Jeremy beamed like it was Christmas. He didn't cheer or punch the air or brag. He just whispered, "Told you it's good," and kept eating like this was the most normal lunch of his life. And for the first time, it might've been for Alex too.

Ty whispered something to Leo at the back of the room. "That was the realest gift I've ever seen," he said. Leo nodded. "Jeremy doesn't try. He just is. That's why it works." Behind them, Alex took another bite. His back wasn't hunched. His shoulders weren't locked. The blanket stayed folded on his lap like a shield he didn't need to raise anymore.

Jeremy told a joke later, one of his small ones about a squirrel and a stick that made no sense. Alex snorted. Then covered his mouth. Jeremy didn't call it out. He just told the punchline and let it land quietly. That was enough. Some laughter doesn't have to be loud to heal something broken.

And still, Alex didn't let go of the blanket. Even when the bell rang, even when it was time to change for gym, he tucked it in his cubby like it was a passport. Something that proved he belonged somewhere now. Somewhere warm. Somewhere real. He didn't say thank you. But Jeremy didn't need it. The blanket said it louder than words.

The house was quiet. Not the kind of quiet that comes with sleep, but the thoughtful hush that settles in when something important is waiting to be said. Mr. Clarke didn't turn off the bedside lamp, even though he normally did before climbing into bed. Instead, he sat on the edge, still dressed from the day, tie loosened but not yet removed, hands clasped over his knees. His wife was already tucked in, reading glasses perched low on her nose, a biography open beside her pillow. She turned a page slowly, but she wasn't really reading.

He didn't speak right away. He ran a hand through his short-cropped hair and stared at the floor like it held answers. Finally, without shifting his gaze, he said, "I think we were meant to meet him." His voice was low, nearly a whisper, but it carried weight. The kind that lives in your chest, not just your ears.

His wife looked up immediately. There was no confusion in her face, no pause to ask who he meant. She knew. Of course she knew. Her expression softened in a way that only love and understanding can soften a face, and she closed her book without marking the page. She didn't blink. She didn't smile. She just nodded once—slowly, deliberately. That was all.

Mr. Clarke breathed out through his nose. He hadn't realized he'd been holding his breath until then. He looked at her, finally, eyes searching hers for hesitation. There was none. Not a trace. Just that deep, unwavering stillness of someone who's already made the decision in her heart long before he ever spoke it out loud.

"I've never seen a kid like him," he continued, his voice still low. "Not because he's troubled. Not because of what he's done. But because of what he's survived. The boy is... I don't even know what word fits. He's raw. Guarded. But when he laughs—which is rare—it's like hearing a locked door open. You know it shouldn't sound that pure after everything."

His wife reached out and placed her hand over his. It was gentle, but it anchored him. He kept talking. "He's been sleeping on a couch," he said, and his voice caught slightly. "In a house where no one says good morning. Where no one makes soup. Where birthdays come and go without candles. He brought in a blanket today like it was treasure. You should've seen how he held it. Like it proved something. That he mattered. That someone saw him."

Still, she didn't interrupt. She let the silence hold space for him, as she always did. After nearly fifteen years of marriage, they had come to speak best through pauses. Through what wasn't said. She squeezed his hand, and he squeezed back. It was more than enough.

"He's not just a boy who needs a place," Mr. Clarke added after a long pause. "He's a boy who needs to belong. There's a difference." He shook his head and looked down again. "And we've been trying for how long?" His voice cracked then—not from grief, but from memory. From all the empty bedrooms, all the appointments, all the unspoken aches that had stretched between them like wire for years.

His wife touched the side of his face gently and said, "Then let's make sure he knows he's already loved. Even if he doesn't believe it yet." That was her way. Not grand speeches. Not emotional declarations. Just quiet truth, given without hesitation, like a seed pressed into earth. She always knew when to speak and when to simply be.

Mr. Clarke nodded. His eyes were glassy now, but no tears fell. "Tomorrow," he said. "I'll talk to the office. I'll call Children's Aid. I'll do it all right. But tonight, I just needed to know we were both sure."

She gave the faintest smile. "I knew when you said his name."

He looked at her for a long moment. "You're going to be so good for him," he whispered. "And he won't even know why right away. But someday he'll thank you." She shook her head. "I don't need a thank you. I just want him safe. I just want him warm."

They sat in silence again, their hands still together. Outside, the wind pressed gently against the window like a soft knock. Somewhere across town, Alex was curled up with a blanket he hadn't let go of since lunch, and Mr. Clarke knew that tomorrow would be the day that everything began to change. Not loudly. Not all at once. But it would change. He stood, finally, and turned off the lamp. The room fell into darkness—but it wasn't lonely anymore. It was the kind of dark that comes after a long conversation. The kind that holds meaning. The kind that means you're not alone.

The office was quiet in a way that made Alex nervous. Not the sharp quiet of discipline, but the soft kind that comes with carpets and bookshelves and chairs that don't creak when you sit down. He didn't usually look around in here. Most of the time, he kept his eyes low, said only what he had to say, and left without touching anything. But today, something caught him. Just off to the right of Mr. Clarke's desk, near the small stack of notes he always carried in his blazer, was a wooden photo frame. The frame wasn't crooked. It wasn't dusty. It sat upright, proud, like someone had polished it on purpose.

Alex took two steps closer. The word "Someday" was carved into the wood—clean, deep, and careful. It wasn't just printed. Someone had chosen that word. Really chosen it. And behind the glass was a photo of a nursery. Not a baby in it. Just the room. Walls painted soft blue, with a mobile hanging from the ceiling in the shape of stars and moons. A white crib with no blankets yet. An empty bookshelf. A rocking chair by the window. It looked like the beginning of something. Or the middle. Or the end. Alex couldn't tell which.

He reached out, slowly. Not to pick it up, just to rest his fingers against the glass. Something about it felt sacred. Like touching it too quickly might break whatever hope it had been built on. His fingertip landed near the bottom corner, just beside the edge of the rocking chair. He didn't breathe for a moment. Then, quietly, without turning around, he asked, "Still empty?"

Mr. Clarke didn't answer right away. He had been sitting at his desk, writing something in his small spiral notebook. The same kind he carried everywhere. He looked up, pen still in hand, and followed Alex's gaze. He didn't speak immediately, but the expression on his face changed. He closed the notebook. Removed his glasses. Folded his hands in front of him. And finally said, "Yes. It is. But not forever."

Alex didn't nod. He didn't move. His hand stayed on the frame. The room felt heavier somehow, but warmer too. There was something about that answer that filled the silence without ending it. It let the quiet stay meaningful. He turned his head slightly, just enough to look at Mr. Clarke from the corner of his eye. "Was it for someone?" he asked. The words felt awkward in his mouth. Not because he didn't care, but because caring still felt like it came with a price.

Mr. Clarke leaned forward, elbows on the desk. "It was," he said. "Still is. We didn't know who. Just knew we were waiting for someone who needed us."

That word again—needed. Alex had heard it before, but always with a string. You need to earn this. You need to behave. You need to be more. You need to stop being so much. But this time it didn't feel like a demand. It felt like an open door. One that had been unlocked for a long time, just waiting for someone brave enough to push it.

"I'm not a baby," Alex muttered, more to himself than to Mr. Clarke. His hand dropped from the frame. "I don't need…" He didn't finish. His voice trailed off like the end of a sentence that didn't know how to land.

Mr. Clarke stood slowly and walked around the desk. He didn't approach quickly. He didn't kneel. He simply stood beside Alex and looked at the frame with him. They both stared at the photo, saying nothing for a long moment. Then Mr. Clarke said, "That room was built for hope. And hope doesn't come with an age limit."

Alex blinked. Once. Hard. Then looked away. "Do you still want… someone?" he asked. His voice was quieter now, like he wasn't sure if asking meant admitting he hoped the answer might be yes.

"I don't think want is the word anymore," Mr. Clarke said. "I think it's need now. For me. For my wife. For our home. We're ready for that room to be full."

Alex didn't respond. But something shifted in the way he stood. His shoulders didn't quite rise—but they didn't drop as far, either. He looked at the frame one last time, then let his hand fall back to his side. "It's a nice room," he said. "Looks peaceful."

"It will be," Mr. Clarke said. "Whenever it's time." Alex stepped back. Not away—just enough to give the frame its space again. "Do you think the person it was for… would know it was safe?" Mr. Clarke turned to face him. "I think they'd feel it. Not right away. But slowly. Like warmth from a blanket you didn't know you needed."

Alex's face didn't change much. But the corners of his mouth moved in a way that might've been the beginning of something—not a smile, exactly, but not a frown either. He looked down at the floor, then back at the photo. "I never had a room that stayed mine," he said. "I mean, ever." Mr. Clarke nodded. "Then maybe it's time."

Alex didn't answer. But for the first time since he'd stepped inside the office, he sat down in the chair across from the desk—on his own. No one told him to. No one had to. The frame sat where it was, still as ever. But now, for the first time, it was being seen by the person who might just belong in it.

Mr. Clarke didn't rush the question. He said it like someone laying down a clean sheet, folding each corner carefully, smoothing the fabric flat. No tone of urgency. No press of expectation. Just a breath, spoken out loud with respect. "Would you want to live with us?" he said, as if it were the gentlest thing in the world to offer, but also the most sacred. The words didn't hover or demand. They settled quietly in the room like sunlight on wood.

Alex didn't react right away. His face didn't change, but his posture did. He shifted in his chair, not like someone avoiding the question but like someone who wasn't sure their legs belonged under a table like this. The kind of question that had never been asked of him. Not even once. Not in his memory. Not without some kind of catch. He stared down at his shoes. The laces were uneven, one frayed at the end. He picked at it like it held the answer.

Mr. Clarke waited. Not with fidgeting or pacing, but with presence. His body stayed still, his breath unhurried. Sometimes grown-ups fill silence too quickly. They crowd it with reassurance or explanation or softening phrases. Mr. Clarke didn't. He trusted the quiet to do its work. He trusted the question to land where it needed to. Alex noticed that. And that noticing felt like something had cracked.

Alex's hands were clenched, but not like fists. More like he was holding something invisible. Maybe an idea he wasn't sure he was allowed to touch. His lips parted just slightly. Then shut again. Then opened again. Nothing came out. His throat worked once. Then again. He blinked three times in a row, too fast. His body wasn't ready yet. But his eyes—they were starting to say something his mouth hadn't found words for.

"Only if…" he whispered, then stopped. He looked over at the photo frame. The one with "Someday" carved across the top. His voice was barely audible now. "Only if it's real. I can't do pretend."

Mr. Clarke took a step forward, but didn't sit. He placed both hands gently on the edge of his desk, palms down. "Alex," he said, calm and clear, "I don't offer pretend. I don't do charity. I don't do pity. And I don't rescue people. I build family. That's all I know how to do."

That word again—family. Not in the way he'd heard it used before, not as a reason to stay quiet or be grateful or not complain. Not as a threat dressed up as closeness. No, Mr. Clarke said it like something to grow into. Something with depth and soil and roots. Something that didn't care where you started—only where you were willing to go.

Alex leaned back slightly. The chair creaked, but he didn't flinch. He looked up at the ceiling for a moment, not searching for answers, but maybe for permission. His eyes welled before he realized they had. A tear broke the rim of his right eye and fell, silent as breath, down his cheek. He didn't wipe it.

"I don't know how to say yes to something like that," he said. "Not yet." Mr. Clarke nodded, just once. "You don't have to. Not today." The relief in that statement was a kindness Alex hadn't expected. He nodded, too, slow and deliberate. "But I think I need… to stay near it for a while. To see if it's really warm."

"You can," Mr. Clarke said. "Every single day, if you want. Come early. Stay late. Talk or don't. It's your pace. Your choice." Alex pressed his palms against his knees. His legs still didn't know whether to stand or stay seated. But something in his chest had shifted. A click in a lock, maybe. The kind of movement you don't hear—but feel.

"Do I… get to keep my last name?" he asked suddenly, eyes sharpening as the thought overtook him. "I don't want to erase it." Mr. Clarke sat at the corner of the desk, just enough to be at eye level. "No one erases anything," he said. "We build on it. Your name matters. Who you are matters. Nothing will be taken away. Only added."

Alex nodded, this time without hesitation. It wasn't a yes to the question. But it was a yes to him. And that was enough for now. The room stayed silent. Not heavy anymore. Just full. Like something had moved in. Outside, the last bell of the day rang. Students ran past the door, backpacks bouncing, voices high. But inside this room, time moved slower. On purpose. Like healing had its own schedule.

Alex stood up, slowly, and walked to the door. But before he reached the handle, he turned back. His voice cracked a little, but he got the words out. "I think… I want to come back tomorrow." Mr. Clarke smiled—not wide. Just real. "I'll be here." Alex opened the door. Stepped into the hallway. And for the first time, it didn't feel like leaving.

The moment didn't need applause. It didn't need a speech, or a teacher clapping his hands together like something grand had been decided. It needed quiet. The kind of quiet that grows between people who understand each other without words.

Ty stood first, his chair legs whispering against the floor. Then Leo rose beside him, steady, calm, already in motion before the idea became sound. They crossed the room in silence, not a march, not a performance. Just boys who'd learned what real friendship meant, and now offered it the only way that made sense—by being present.

Alex was still near the threshold of the hallway, the door behind him not fully closed, his breath still thin in his chest. He hadn't said yes, not out loud. But the way he'd lingered there, the way he glanced over his shoulder and waited without knowing why—that was its own kind of answer. He didn't know yet what he'd agreed to. But his body had already accepted it. His arms weren't crossed. His shoulders weren't tight. And when Ty placed a hand gently on his back, Alex didn't pull away.

Leo didn't speak either. He didn't need to. He stood just beside Alex, not too close, not too far, and raised one arm, elbow bent like a question. An open invitation, not a demand. A gesture that said, Only if you want to. Only if you're ready. And Alex, without moving his lips, nodded. It was the kind of nod that came from the centre of a person—not from politeness, not from fear, but from the soul.

Ty moved in second, wrapping his other arm around Alex's shoulders so the three of them stood like a single shape, a quiet structure built from trust and forgiveness. They didn't sway. They didn't pat each other's backs. They just stood. The hallway lights were dull above them, buzzing faintly, but something warmer glowed between them—something the eye couldn't trace but the heart could feel.

Alex's face tightened first. His jaw clenched, his eyes narrowed, not in anger, but in resistance. The kind of resistance that comes when a person isn't sure they're allowed to soften. But Leo's hand pressed gently against the small of his back, just once, and something inside Alex cracked open. Not broken. Just no longer sealed shut.

A single tear rolled down from the corner of his eye. He didn't brush it away. Neither did the others. Ty adjusted his stance slightly, making the hold more solid. Alex leaned into it—first with doubt, then with decision. It was like he'd been waiting for this shape his whole life. The exact curve of arms that didn't let go too quickly. The kind of embrace that didn't press for answers, didn't ask for apologies, didn't label him with pity. It was love, but quiet. Real friendship, but reverent.

No one in the hallway spoke. Jeremy had paused at the corner and simply watched, one hand against the wall, wide-eyed but smiling softly. Jasmin stood nearby, her hands folded in front of her like she didn't want to intrude, but knew she'd just witnessed something holy. Ella wiped under her eye with the sleeve of her cardigan, not in sadness, but in awe. Not even Mr. Clarke interrupted. He knew when the air was sacred.

It wasn't a long hug. Not one of those dramatic, stage-kind that lasted too long and turned awkward. It lasted exactly as long as it needed to. When Alex finally pulled back, his hands stayed gripping Leo's arms for a second longer, like anchors. He breathed deeply, once. Twice. And when he let go, his spine stayed straighter.

"I didn't know it could feel like that," Alex whispered. The words barely rose above the hum of the exit sign overhead. But both boys heard it. They heard it like a bell in a silent room. Leo nodded and smiled—not wide, just real. "That's what it's supposed to feel like." Ty didn't add anything. His job wasn't to explain. It was just to be there. To be the part that stays when everyone else leaves. To make sure the quiet didn't become emptiness.

Alex turned to the wall, his hand brushing it like he needed something to touch that wasn't a person. His eyes were still shining, but he wasn't blinking as fast anymore. "I don't know what to do next." "You don't have to," Leo said. "We've got time." Ty added, "We go slow. Together." The bell rang, announcing the start of last period. Kids flooded the halls, voices bouncing off lockers. But the three of them stayed right where they were, letting the moment breathe. Letting Alex breathe. Letting love finish what silence had begun.

Alex didn't mean to sound sharp. The words came out too fast, like they'd been waiting behind his teeth for too long. His voice cracked on the last word, and he swallowed hard to bury it again. "I'm not… some kind of pity project." The phrase landed heavy in the room. It hung there, not like an accusation, but like a wound reopened. He looked down at the rug in Mr. Clarke's office, the faded pattern suddenly too loud. His shoulders curled in, not from anger, but defence. It wasn't defiance—it was fear dressed in armour.

Mr. Clarke didn't blink. He didn't rush forward or offer a correction wrapped in a smile. He just held Alex's eyes with his own, steady as stone but soft at the edges. There was no recoil in his face. Just presence. "No, you're not," he said plainly, the kind of plain that leaves no room for argument. "You're someone's dream."

That sentence didn't feel like words. It felt like a door creaking open inside Alex's chest— one he'd boarded shut years ago. He looked up slowly, his jaw tight, as if waiting for the sentence to be followed by a condition. A catch. A transaction. But none came. Just silence. Just Mr. Clarke, standing there like he wasn't going anywhere.

Alex opened his mouth to speak, but closed it again. He wasn't sure which part confused him more—the fact that he'd been seen, or the fact that someone didn't flinch when he got loud. "You don't even know me," he mumbled. It was half a statement, half a question. The kind of line meant to push people away gently, with just enough force to see if they'd stay.

"We've been trying to have a child for eight years," Mr. Clarke said. He sat down slowly, not across from Alex like a teacher, but beside him. Equal. Grounded. "Doctors, tests, paperwork, waiting lists. We thought maybe it would never happen. But we kept that nursery ready. Just in case." His voice didn't waver, but it bent slightly around the memories. "We kept the door open. We bought a frame that said 'Someday.' We didn't know it would be you. But now we do."

Alex blinked hard. His lip curled in for a second like he was going to scoff. But he didn't. His body refused to commit to disbelief. His spine leaned forward instead. The part of him that wanted to fold in retreated—slowly. "Why me?"

"Because you were always the one," Mr. Clarke said. "We just hadn't met you yet."

The office filled with a kind of stillness that was heavy, but not uncomfortable. It pressed on the skin, not the bones. Outside, the muffled sound of children laughing at recess barely reached them, like the world had stepped aside for this moment. Alex's fingers toyed with a corner of his sleeve. "But what if I mess it up?" he whispered.

Mr. Clarke didn't answer right away. He let the silence do its job. Then he said, "Families aren't perfect. They're not made of rules and checklists. They're made of people who don't leave when it gets hard." He leaned forward, elbows on his knees, looking at Alex the way someone looks at a map they've finally found after being lost. "You're not a project. You're a person. One we already care about."

Alex clenched his jaw again, this time trying to trap a sob instead of a sharp word. "I've never been anyone's dream before," he admitted. It was the kind of confession that sounded like a whisper but echoed like a bell. "I don't even know how to be that."

"You don't have to know how," Mr. Clarke said gently. "You just have to let yourself be loved."

That broke something. Not in a painful way—but in the kind of way ice breaks in a river come spring. Slow, sure, and permanent. Alex's face twisted as he tried to hold the tears back, but the truth had already cracked through. He covered his eyes with his hands, shoulders beginning to shake—not violently, but deeply. Like something old was leaving his body. Something he hadn't had words for until now.

Mr. Clarke didn't touch him. He didn't press. He waited. Just sat there, still, solid, quiet. The way real love waits. Not with pressure. With patience. The clock ticked twice before Alex pulled his hands down again. His cheeks were red. His eyes were rimmed with salt. But there was something cleaner about him now—something newer in the way he sat.

"You mean it?" he asked. Not as a challenge, but as a scared boy trying not to hope too much. "With every part of who I am," Mr. Clarke said. "And so does my wife. You'd never be a chore, Alex. You'd be our child." Alex didn't move. Not yet. But something in his breath changed. He was still trembling. Still unsure. But now he was facing forward. Listening. Not running. And that was enough.

The couch sagged in the middle, like a tired sigh that had been held in for years. The fabric smelled faintly of mildew and teenage cologne, and one armrest had long since lost its padding. Alex didn't pack anything from it. There was nothing to pack. No pillows that felt like his, no blankets that still held warmth from the night before. He stood there for a moment, backpack slung over one shoulder, looking down at the cushion he'd called a bed. He didn't cry. He didn't flinch. He just exhaled and whispered, "Goodbye."

Outside, the school van Mr. Clarke had borrowed hummed in the driveway. The sun was low but warm, setting the trees behind the house aglow. Alex didn't look back again. He climbed into the front seat, not the back, and Mr. Clarke didn't treat him like a passenger. He treated him like a son. They didn't speak much on the drive. They didn't need to. Sometimes healing doesn't come from words. It comes from being allowed to be silent in someone else's peace.

When they pulled into the driveway of Mr. Clarke's modest brick house, Alex stared out the window. The front lawn was just grass and a maple tree, no swing set, no toys, no garden gnome. But it looked safe. It looked real. The porch light was already on, even though it wasn't dark yet. As if someone had left it on just for him. As if someone was waiting. He sat still until Mr. Clarke nodded toward the door and said gently, "It opens for you now."

Mrs. Clarke met them at the door in slippers and a sweatshirt that read "Not All Heroes Wear Capes." Her eyes were soft, not sparkly. Her arms were already opening. She didn't say "Welcome." She said, "You're home." And somehow, that was bigger. Alex let her hug him, not stiffly like before, but all the way this time. His arms came around her back like they'd always belonged there. It felt warm and terrifying. Like being seen without armour.

They didn't give him a tour. They gave him space. "When you're ready," Mr. Clarke said, "you can see your room." Not the room. Your room. Alex stood in the hallway, looking at a closed white door with a paper star taped to it. Written in marker was just his name. No decorations. No slogans. Just truth. He turned the knob slowly. It didn't creak. The hinges had been oiled. Someone had cared.

Inside, the bed was twin-sized, dressed in soft grey sheets and a navy blue blanket. There was a dresser, a reading lamp, a window with the curtain tied open. Nothing too flashy. But it smelled like lemon and something else—lavender, maybe. A nightlight sat unlit on the dresser, just in case. There was one photo on the wall already. Not of Mr. and Mrs. Clarke. Not of Alex. Just an empty frame. Below it, the word New had been written in black pen.

He sat on the edge of the bed, slowly. The mattress didn't groan. It held him like it wanted to. He bounced once, testing the softness, then leaned back on both hands. For the first time, there was no remote control poking his hip, no springs jutting up through his spine. It was his. Not borrowed. Not bargained for. His.

Mr. Clarke stepped into the doorway and watched quietly. "It's okay if it doesn't feel real yet," he said. "Love doesn't always show up how we expect. Sometimes, it wears quiet shoes and carries boxes instead of balloons."

Alex nodded. He didn't speak. But the way his shoulders dropped said everything. He took off his backpack and unzipped it. Out came the only thing he had brought from his old life—a wrinkled copy of his birth certificate and a hand-drawn picture of himself and a woman who looked like his mother. It had been folded too many times, the edges fraying. He placed it carefully on the nightstand and ran one finger over the paper. Then he looked back at Mr. Clarke and said, "Can I put this here?"

Mr. Clarke walked over, picked up the photo frame, and said, "Let's make it the first picture we frame together." And they did. Together.

That night, Alex slept in a bed for the first time in over a year. He didn't have to fight for a blanket. He didn't have to brace himself for footsteps in the hallway. He didn't dream of running. He dreamed of staying. And in the morning, when he came downstairs to the smell of pancakes and Mrs. Clarke humming softly in the kitchen, he didn't feel like a guest. He felt like he belonged. The couch from the old place was never spoken of again. But if he had to name what replaced it, he would have said this: Love in disguise.

The table was already set when Alex came downstairs. There were cloth napkins instead of paper towels, and the cutlery was evenly spaced beside the plates. A glass of water shimmered in front of each seat. At his place, the napkin had been folded into a triangle. It wasn't fancy, but it was intentional. That small gesture alone nearly froze him where he stood. He wasn't used to being expected—let alone prepared for.

Mrs. Clarke wore an apron with a purple sunflower stitched in the middle. She moved like someone who had long imagined feeding more than just two people. As she placed the bowl of roasted potatoes at the centre of the table, she looked up and said softly, "I wasn't sure what you liked, so I made everything I could." Alex didn't know how to respond to that. He sat down instead and tried to quiet the drum in his chest.

Leo was already seated beside him, grinning as he stabbed a carrot. "You'll like the meatloaf," he whispered, as though sharing a sacred school secret. "She puts brown sugar in the ketchup topping. I don't know how it works, but it does." Alex nodded once. Across from him, Ty winked but didn't say a word. He just passed the rolls without waiting to be asked. The bread was warm in Alex's hand.

The sound of plates being filled, forks tapping gently against porcelain, and chairs shifting slightly—it all felt like music he hadn't heard before. Not noise. Not chaos. Just the rhythm of people who weren't pretending. Mr. Clarke sat at the head of the table, calm and soft-spoken, asking no one in particular, "What was the best moment of your day?" There was no pressure to answer. Only space.

When it came around to Alex, he nearly panicked. Words didn't come easily yet. But Jeremy, seated to his right, gave him a little nudge and said, "Mine was seeing you at school again." No teasing. No irony. Just truth. That bought Alex enough courage to mumble, "I liked... the smell of the food." And nobody laughed. Nobody made it weird. They just nodded like it was the perfect answer.

The meatloaf was sweet and tangy, and the mashed potatoes had butter in them—actual butter. The kind you notice. Alex wasn't used to tasting food. He was used to consuming it, fast and quiet. But here, the bites were slow. They filled him without rushing. At first, he wasn't sure how to pace himself. But then he noticed no one was watching him. They were just... eating.

Mrs. Clarke told a story about a time Mr. Clarke got mustard all over his tie on a first date, and Jeremy laughed so hard he spilled his milk. No one scolded him. Ty handed him a towel and said, "Best splash landing of the week." Alex found himself smiling—not a fake one. A surprised one. A real one that caught even him off guard. When he noticed it, he didn't pull it back. He just let it stay.

Near the end of the meal, Mrs. Clarke placed a small bowl of berries in front of him. Strawberries. Blackberries. Raspberries. He stared for a second too long. "You can have more," she said gently. "No one's counting." That sentence sat heavier in his chest than any food ever had. He nodded again. Took one bite. Then another. And still, no one watched him like he was fragile or pitiful. He was just part of it. A boy eating fruit after meatloaf.

The clinking of cutlery slowed as the meal ended. Plates were cleaned naturally, not ordered. Jeremy started gathering them up without being asked, and Leo joined in. Alex stood to help too, unsure of the steps, but willing. Mrs. Clarke gently placed a hand on his shoulder. "You can just sit," she said. "You've done enough today." Alex didn't sit. He kept helping. Because something in him wanted to.

When the kitchen was quiet again, and everyone had moved to the living room, Alex stayed behind for a moment. He looked at the now-empty table. The water glasses, half full. The napkins slightly crumpled. The scent of roasted potatoes still hanging in the air like comfort. It was a meal. A real one. And he had been part of it. That mattered. More than he could explain.

Later, when he joined the others on the couch, Jeremy leaned against him and yawned without permission. Just leaned. Trust without instruction. Alex didn't move. He let the warmth settle in. Ty handed him a pillow for his lap. Leo nudged him with an elbow and said, "Told you about the meatloaf." Alex chuckled softly, and when he did, his chest didn't hurt. Not even a little.

He looked around the room, at the pictures on the walls, the shelves filled with books and not broken things, the light that came from a lamp and not a screen. And he realized something that made his breath catch: he was home. It didn't shout. It didn't sing. It just sat in his bones and let him rest.

They sat in a circle that didn't look rehearsed. It wasn't perfect. The chairs weren't evenly spaced. Jeremy was half-sitting on his knees, Jasmin's leg bounced nervously, and Sophie's hair kept falling in her face. But it was a circle just the same. And in the middle sat Alex—no longer hunched, no longer flinching. Just sitting. Holding the silence with both hands like it might spill if he let go too soon.

Leo was the first to speak, but not with a speech. "We all love you, Alex," he said plainly, like a fact already known. He didn't gesture for applause. He didn't raise his voice. He just said it like someone saying, There's sunshine today. Obvious. True. Alex blinked, but he didn't hide this time. His eyes welled, but they stayed open.

Ty leaned forward on his elbows, voice even. "You have family now. Real family. Not the kind that forgets your birthday or tells you that you're in the way. You have a home where your name is on the wall, not just your backpack." He didn't smile when he said it. He just held Alex's eyes like a lighthouse. Something to return to when the waves came back.

Ella added her piece with a shake in her voice. "And you don't owe us anything for that. You don't have to be perfect or funny or easy to like. You're already enough. Just by sitting there." She tucked her knees to her chest and looked at her lap, but her words floated and stayed.

Nico, who had once been blamed for everything, rubbed his thumb along the seam of his jeans. "You're not the villain anymore. And maybe... maybe you never were. Maybe no one told you the truth fast enough." He wasn't accusing. He was freeing him. Alex looked up, startled at the sound of it.

Jeremy scooted closer without asking. He reached over and touched Alex's knee. "You can always come over. My mom said your spot at dinner is forever now." His voice cracked on forever, but he didn't fix it. He just sat beside him, a younger brother who knew the value of a full plate and a clean fork.

Jasmin didn't speak right away. When she did, her voice had gravel in it. "I forgive you, Alex. Not because someone told me to. But because I can see that you're not who you were. And neither am I." She didn't cry. But her voice did. It curled at the edges and leaned into the room like a note in a familiar song.

Sophie lifted her chin just a little. "You listened when we spoke. That's rare. So many don't. That's why I believe you can be part of this circle for real." Then she handed him a folded piece of paper. On it was a drawing she'd made of the group. Eight small cartoon figures holding hands, with Alex drawn right in the middle. Smiling.

Leo leaned forward now. His voice was softer than it had ever been. "You have your own room now. Your own pillow. Your own door that you can lock and open without fear. That's your room, in your house, with your real parents. Mr. and Mrs. Clarke didn't just take you in. They chose you. You were chosen, Alex."

Alex shook then. Not from fear this time. From the flood of it. All of it. The warmth, the kindness, the safety that didn't feel borrowed. He pressed the heels of his hands to his eyes, but it was too late. The tears came in waves. Not crashing ones. Just steady. Honest. Cleansing.

No one interrupted. No one told him to calm down. They let it happen. They gave him space, but not distance. They stayed close. Quiet. Anchored. And when the sob turned into breathing again, Leo passed him a tissue and said, "That's what we're here for. For this. For all of it."

When Alex could finally speak, he said just four words: "I'm not alone anymore." He didn't shout them. Didn't whisper them. Just said them in the voice of someone who had been underwater for years and finally came up for air. Ty nodded once. "That's right. You're not. Not today. Not tomorrow. Not ever again." He placed his hand on Alex's shoulder, gentle, present, brotherly.

They sat like that for a long time. The circle didn't close. It stayed open. Not because the meeting wasn't over—but because their story wasn't. The chapters would keep writing themselves in laughter, in quiet hallway moments, in dinners and late-night calls and walks home side by side.

At the very end, Leo looked right into the camera. Not for a video. Not for attention. But because he knew someone—somewhere—was reading. "You're not alone anymore," he said again, and this time, it wasn't just for Alex. "Neither is anyone reading this." The room didn't cheer. It just held the weight of truth. And that, more than anything else, was enough.

EPILOGUE – THE TRUTH IS STILL YOURS

No one told the trees when to start turning gold. They just did. No one needed to announce that the hallway felt lighter now, or that the air around the lockers didn't feel as sharp. But it did. Somewhere between the last chapter and now, the school changed shape—not with new paint or rules, but with the quiet bravery of the ones who chose truth over pretending. The ones who said, "That's not okay," and kept saying it. The ones who stayed soft, even after being hurt. That's what made it safer. That's what made it better.

Leo no longer checked over his shoulder when he laughed. Not because the world was perfect, but because he knew whose arms would catch him if it wasn't. Ty still moved like a shadow when he needed to, but more kids followed his steps now. Nico walked taller. Jasmin spoke louder. Ella stopped apologizing for having feelings. Jeremy never stopped hugging. Sophie started writing again—tiny poems folded into books she shared with the younger grades. And Alex? Alex had a bed now. Not a couch. Not a sleeping bag. A bed. And a door that stayed open on purpose.

There were still hard days. That never changed. Some mornings started with silence that felt heavy. Some lockers still slammed harder than they needed to. Some teachers still missed the signs. But the difference now was that the kids noticed for each other. They looked sideways. They paid attention. They remembered. Because once you've been seen, really seen, you never forget how to see someone else. And once you've been lied to, and found your way back, you can usually spot the lies sooner. Even when they wear smiles.

The Shadow Warrior code wasn't written in a notebook or printed on the wall. It was passed quietly, eye to eye. Protect the truth. Never use it to hurt. Move with purpose. Speak when it matters. Listen harder than you speak. And don't wait to be perfect before you show up for someone. Show up messy. Show up unsure. But show up. That's how Leo did it. That's how Ty did it. That's how all of them became protectors instead of repeaters. That's how they broke the cycle.

Sometimes it takes one kid to hold up a mirror and say, "That wasn't me. That was what someone told me I was." Sometimes it takes a second kid to say, "Then let's find out who you really are." And sometimes, it takes a third to say, "I'll come too." What happened in this book wasn't a fantasy. It wasn't magic. It was kids noticing pain and not turning away. It was children becoming safe places for each other. It was truth, spoken out loud—even when it shook.

You, the one holding this book, might still have questions. You might wonder if your truth is too small, too quiet, or too strange to be real. It's not. If you feel something's off—even when everyone else smiles—*you're not imagining it*. If someone's kindness feels like a leash, or a favour feels like a trap, *you're not being rude for noticing*. If someone says, "It was just a joke," but it bruises somewhere inside, *you're allowed to say it wasn't funny*. That's your right. That's your voice. That's your truth.

This book didn't fix everything. It wasn't supposed to. It was supposed to hand you the map—the one someone else had to draw the hard way. The map that says, *you are allowed to leave when the rules keep changing. You are allowed to say no, even if no one else does. You are allowed to trust your gut, even when your head is full of fog.* You are allowed to rest. You are allowed to speak. You are allowed to be seen.

Let's say it clearly, one last time:
You're not weak for crying.
You're not dramatic for noticing.
You're not difficult for saying, "That hurt."
And you're not alone—not anymore.

There are kids like Ty, who learn truth like a language and speak it fluently in silence. There are kids like Leo, who turned the very poison they were given into medicine. There are kids like you, who are reading this and nodding a little, even if no one else sees. You're part of this story too. You always were.

So, when the next person smiles at you but their eyes don't, pay attention. When someone says, "You're too sensitive," remember—that might be your gift. When you feel something isn't right, but can't prove it yet, don't throw that feeling away. Sit with it. Ask it questions. Bring it into the light. Because truth doesn't mind questions. Lies do.

If you ever forget this, read the book again. Not because the answers are here—but because the reminders are. The love is here. The safety is here. The family you choose is here. Leo and Jeremy and Ty and Jasmin and Sophie and Ella and Nico are here. They were written for you. They are you.

So, go on.
Speak softly.
Look bravely.
Choose wisely.
And remember—

You're not alone anymore.

www.ingramcontent.com/pod-product-compliance
Lightning Source LLC
Chambersburg PA
CBHW081145290426
44108CB00018B/2441